Time Out

Rome

timeout.com/rome

Penguin Books

PENGUIN BOOKS

Published by the Penguin Group
Penguin Books Ltd, 80 Strand, London WC2R ORL, England
Penguin Books USA Inc., 375 Hudson Street, New York, New York 10014, USA
Penguin Books Australia Ltd, 250 Camberwell Road, Camberwell, Victoria 3124, Australia
Penguin Books Canada Ltd, 10 Alcorn Avenue, Toronto, Ontario, Canada M4V 3B2
Penguin Books (NZ) Ltd, cnr Rosedale and Airborne Roads, Albany, Auckland, New Zealand

Penguin Books Ltd, Registered Offices: Harmondsworth, Middlesex, England

First published 1994
Second edition 1996
Third edition 1998
Fourth edition 1999
Fifth edition 2001

Sixth edition 2003
10 9 8 7 6 5 4 3 2 1

Copyright © Time Out Group Ltd 1994, 1996, 1998, 1999, 2000, 2001, 2003
All rights reserved

Colour reprographics by Icon, Crowne House, 56-58 Southwark Street, London SE1 1UN
Printed and bound by Cayfosa-Quebecor, Ctra. de Caldes, Km 3 08 130 Sta, Perpètua de Mogoda, Barcelona, Spain

Edited and designed by
Time Out Guides Limited
Universal House
251 Tottenham Court Road
London W1T 7AB
Tel + 44 (0)20 7813 3000
Fax + 44 (0)20 7813 6001
Email guides@timeout.com
www.timeout.com

Editorial

Editor Anne Hanley
Deputy Editor Simon Coppock
Listings Editor Fulvia Angelini
Proofreader Tamsin Shelton
Indexer Cathy Heath

Editorial Director Peter Fiennes
Series Editor Ruth Jarvis
Deputy Series Editor Lesley McCave
Guides Co-ordinator Anna Norman

Design

Group Art Director John Oakey
Art Director Mandy Martin
Art Editor Scott Moore
Senior Designer Tracey Ridgewell
Designers Astrid Kogler, Sam Lands
Digital Imaging Dan Conway
Ad Make-up Charlotte Blythe
Picture Editor Kerri Littlefield
Acting Picture Editor Kit Burnet
Acting Deputy Picture Editor Martha Houghton
Picture Desk Trainee Bella Wood

Advertising

Group Commercial Director Lesley Gill
Sales Director Mark Phillips
International Sales Manager Ross Canadé
Advertising Sales (Rome) MAD & Co. International
Advertising Assistant Sabrina Ancilleri

Administration

Chairman Tony Elliott
Managing Director Mike Hardwick
Group Financial Director Richard Waterlow
Group Marketing Director Christine Cort
Marketing Manager Mandy Martinez
US Publicity & Marketing Associate Rosella Albanese
Group General Manager Nichola Coulthard
Guides Production Director Mark Lamond
Production Controller Samantha Furniss
Accountant Sarah Bostock

Features in this guide were written, updated and researched by:

Introduction Anne Hanley. **History** Anne Hanley (*Hadrian* Julia Crosse). **Rome Today** Sarah Delaney (*Once, not future, kings* Peter Douglas). **Architecture** Simone Marchesi. **Art in Rome** Frederick Ilchman. **Accommodation** Agnes Crawford. **Sightseeing** Julia Crosse, Sylvie Hogg (*True genius, New and newer* Simone Marchesi). **Eating Out** Lee Marshall. **Cafés, Bars & *Gelaterie*** Dana Klitzberg. **Shops & Services** Raffaella Malaguti. **Festivals & Events** Anne Hanley. **Children** Philippa Hitchen. **Film** Lee Marshall. **Galleries** Simone Marchesi. **Gay & Lesbian** Peter Douglas. **Music: Classical & Opera** Linda Bordoni. **Nightlife & Music** Raffaella Malaguti. **Sport & Fitness** Sylvie Hogg. **Theatre & Dance** Linda Bordoni. **Trips Out of Town** Giulia Bernardini, Carol Glatz, Philippa Hitchen, Anne Hanley, Sylvie Hogg. **Directory** Fabrizio Giusto (*Glossary* Anne Hanley).

The Editor would like to thank: Fulvia Angelini for constant support and untiring work, and Elisabetta at Metamorfosi. Special thanks to Lee and Clara Marshall.

MAD & Co. Advertising & Marketing Director: Margherita Tedone. Tel: +39 06 3550 9145 Fax: +39 06 3550 1775
Sales Executives (Rome) Marta Colluccia, Maria Teresa Tedone.

Maps by LS International Cartography, via Sanremo 17, 20133 Milan, Italy.

Photography by Adam Eastland except: pages 21, 33, 35, 134, 271 Corbis Images; 61 Italian Tourist Board; 7, 12, 13, 95, AKG London.

Contents

Introduction

What is it about Rome? You gawp at the Colosseum, gasp at the Pantheon, strain your neck muscles admiring the ceiling of the Sistine Chapel. You stroll through the Roman Forum and saunter across Michelangelo's exercise in urban planning on the Capitoline. You're wowed by ancient wonders in the Capitoline museum and Renaissance marvels in the Galleria Borghese. Yet, after this full immersion in the icons of Western culture, you feel dissatisfied. As you board your plane to return home, you know somehow that you've barely scraped the surface.

The Eternal City's like that. Visit once or ten times – even live there for 20 years – and you'll never feel that you've exhausted its possibilities. After you've trawled through galleries, churches and archaeological sites, there's always something to draw you in. There are the novelties – new attractions, cutting-edge architectural projects – and of course there are the many treasures that lie at the capital's doorstep.

Statistics show that Rome's magnetism is waxing rather than waning, assisted, undoubtedly, by bargain-basement airlines that have transformed the Roman holiday from a once-in-a-lifetime luxury into an occasional, affordable perk. Rome-lovers can and do return, frequently. It is to them that we dedicate our series of 'Then what?' boxes and the extended Trips Out of Town section of this sixth edition of the guide.

Whether you're a returnee or a neophyte, a Rome-lover or a Rome-bearer, there's one attraction that will continue to hold you in its thrall. It's clichéd, of course, to talk of the chaotic workaday life of Rome – fuelled by car fumes, coffee and cellphones – as great theatre. But the drama that is acted out here is endlessly gripping. Buy your ticket, take your seat at the ever-changing tableau of unforgettable images and feel yourself being drawn into it too. Forget throwing three coins into the fountain. It's Rome itself that will beckon you back.

ABOUT THE TIME OUT CITY GUIDES

The *Time Out Rome Guide* is one of an expanding series of Time Out City Guides produced by the people behind London and New York's successful listings magazines. Our guides are all written and updated by resident experts who have striven to provide you with all the most up-to-date information you'll need to explore the city, whether you're a local or first-time visitor.

THE LOWDOWN ON THE LISTINGS

Above all, we've tried to make this book as useful as possible. Addresses, telephone numbers, websites, transport information, opening times, admission prices and credit card details are all included in our listings. And, as far as possible, we've given details of facilities, services and events, all checked and correct at the time we went to press. However, in Rome, opening hours – both of small shops and major tourist attractions – are subject to abrupt changes, the former by personal and the latter by official whim. Before you go out of your way, we would advise you whenever possible to phone and check opening times. While every effort has been made to ensure the accuracy of the information contained here, the publishers cannot accept responsibility for any errors it may contain.

PRICES AND PAYMENT

Prices throughout this guide are given in euros (€). The prices we've supplied should be treated as guidelines, not gospel. If they vary wildly from those we've quoted, please write and let us know. We aim to give the best and most up-to-date advice, so we always want to know if you've been badly treated or overcharged.

We have noted whether venues take credit cards but have only listed the major cards – American Express (**AmEx**), Diners Club (**DC**), MasterCard (**MC**) and Visa (**V**). Many business will also accept other cards, including **JCB**. Some shops, restaurants and attractions take travellers' cheques.

THE LIE OF THE LAND

We have divided the city into areas that correspond to the coloured zones on the street maps on pages 332 to 339. For a map showing the different city areas and how they relate to each other, *see p331*. In those chapters where listings are *not* divided by area, the area name has been added to the end of the address: note that this is there to help you locate the area on the map more easily; it is *not* part of the official address. Map references, indicating page and grid reference, are also given for all venues in areas covered by our maps.

TELEPHONE NUMBERS

You must dial area codes with all numbers, even for local calls. Hence all Rome land-line numbers begin 06, whether you're calling from inside or outside the city. From abroad, you must dial 39 (the international dialling code for Italy) followed by the number given, *including* the zero. Mobile phone numbers begin with 3; until recently they began 03 and you'll still find many written that way: drop the zero. For more information on telephones and codes, *see p314*.

ESSENTIAL INFORMATION

For all the practical information you'll need for visiting the city – including emergency phone numbers, visa and customs information, advice on facilities for the disabled, emergency telephone numbers, a list of useful websites and the full lowdown on the local transport network in and around Rome – turn to the **Directory** chapter. You'll find it at the back of this guide, starting on page 298.

LET US KNOW WHAT YOU THINK

We hope you enjoy the *Time Out Rome Guide*, and we'd like to know what you think of it. We welcome tips for places that you consider we should include in future editions and take notice of your criticism of our choices. There's a reader's reply card at the back of this book – or you can email us at guides@timeout.com.

> There is an online version of this guide, as well as weekly events listings for over 35 international cities, at **www.timeout.com**.

In Context

Features

History

Founded on myth and military might, Rome grew through religion and cultural wealth.

According to ancient Roman historians, Rome was founded by Romulus on 21 April 753 BC, an unusually precise date for the foundation of a city. But in a metropolis where the line between myth and history was blithely blurred in the interests of self-glorification, this precision should come as no surprise. Even today this date is celebrated as the city's official 'birthday' (see p233).

ROMULUS AND REMUS

The twins Romulus and Remus were the fruits of a rape by the god of war, Mars, of a local princess, called Rhea Silvia. Cast adrift as babies on the Tiber and washed into the marshy area below the Palatine hill, the twins were suckled by a she-wolf (see p71 **Canine concern or prostitute's pity?**) until found by a shepherd. Romulus rose to be leader of his tribe, quarrelled with and killed his brother, founded the city and then, deciding that his community was short on females, abducted all the women of the neighbouring Sabine tribe.

Myth aside, ninth-century BC huts have been excavated on the Palatine – proof there was a primitive village there, at least. The first historically documented king of Rome was an Etruscan, Tarquinius Priscus, who reigned from 616 BC. It was probably Etruscans who drained the marshy area between the seven hills to create the Forum, hub of the city's political, economic and religious life.

According to Roman historians, in 509 BC the son of King Tarquinius Superbus raped Lucretia, the wife of Collatinus, a Roman. The next day, before killing herself, she told her husband and his friend Brutus what happened, and in revenge they led a rebellion against the Tarquins. The Etruscan dynasty was expelled and the Roman Republic founded, with Brutus and Collatinus as its first consuls.

This is doubtless a romanticised account of what happened, but in time Etruscan influence over the region did wane and authority passed to Rome's magistrates. Chief among these were the two annually elected consuls, who guided a council of elders called the Senate. Only the few

Hadrian

Best known in the Anglo-Saxon world as the emperor who built a wall across Britain to keep the wild Scots out of civilised (for which read Romanised) Britain, Hadrian – or Adriano as the Italians call him – also left some impressive bricks-and-mortar reminders of himself strewn across the capital from which he reigned from AD 117 to 138.

The emperor was buried, together with his wife Sabina and their adopted son Ceionius Commodus, in a huge mausoleum beside the River Tiber. Surmounted by a shining bronze horse-drawn *quadriga* or chariot – with Hadrian at the reins, naturally – the circular mound of earth was planted with cypress trees and concealed an inner burial chamber approached by an ingenious spiral ramp. If you can't find 'Hadrian's mausoleum' marked on your map, that's because it was encased inside the imposing **Castel Sant'Angelo** (*see p151*) in the Middle Ages.

But the finest surviving building of the ancient world – the **Pantheon** (*see p105*) – is a more appropriate monument to the well-travelled, cultured and bookish emperor. Hadrian's Pantheon, erected in AD 118-25,

was the third such building on the spot: the first temple, dedicated to all the gods, was destroyed by fire; the second was destroyed by lightning. The dedication that can still be made out on its façade was a polite formula honouring the predecessor whose temple had burned down: Marcus Agrippa. It bamboozled archaeologists for centuries.

Being a god himself, Hadrian eventually got a temple dedicated just to him. The **Tempio di Adriano** (Temple of Hadrian, *see p104*) in piazza di Pietra was built in 145 by Antoninus Pius, who was Hadrian's designated heir. A line of 11 lofty Corinthian columns, embedded within a building last used as the city's stock exchange (or Borsa) and now housing temporary exhibitions, hint at the magnificence of the original shrine.

If you have time for only one trip out of Rome, visit Hadrian's sumptuous summer palace at Tivoli (*see p288* **Villa Adriana**). The emperor's travels around his domains inspired building projects on the site, including the circular *teatro marittimo*, where Hadrian liked to withdraw with his books.

ancient families or clans who formed the patrician class could participate in the political life of the Republic; only they could vote, be appointed to the Senate or hold important public and religious offices.

The lower classes, or plebeians, struggled for a greater say in their own affairs. In 494 BC the office of Tribune of the Plebeians was created to represent their interests, and by 367 BC a plebeian could hold the office of consul. The class system, however, was maintained – rich or successful plebeians were simply designated patricians.

All the Romans of the Republic were united by a belief in their right to conquer other tribes. Their superb military organisation, and an agile policy of divide and rule in making alliances, allowed them to pick off the neighbouring peoples of central and southern Italy, and bring the other communities – including the Etruscans – under Roman control. To ensure the spread of Roman power, new cities were established in conquered territories and an extensive infrastructure was created to support the many conquests. The first great Roman road, the via Appia (*see p150* **Appian Way**), was begun in 312 BC. Shortly afterwards work started on the Acqua Appia, the first aqueduct

to bring fresh water to the city. The port of Ostia (*see p276* **Ostia Antica**) – founded at the mouth of the Tiber in 380 BC – expanded rapidly. Barges plied the river, bringing corn, wine, oil and building materials into Rome.

Rome's expansion brought her into conflict with two equally powerful peoples: the Carthaginians of North Africa and Spain, and the Greeks, who had colonised southern Italy and Sicily. The latter were expelled from mainland Italy in 272 BC, but the Punic Wars against the Carthaginians lasted for almost 120 years and Rome was more than once in mortal danger. In 219 BC Hannibal made his historic crossing of the Alps, gaining control of much of Italy, but was too cautious to launch an assault on Rome. Carthage was finally destroyed in 146 BC, leaving Rome in control of the western Mediterranean.

In the early days of the Republic most Romans, rich or poor, had been farmers, tending to their own land or livestock in the surrounding countryside. Wars like those against Carthage, however, required huge standing armies. At the same time, much of the land in Italy had been been laid waste, either by Hannibal or the Roman armies. Wealthy Romans bought huge estates at knock-down prices, while landless peasants flocked to the capital. By the end of the second century BC the Romans were a race of soldiers, engineers, administrators and merchants, supported by tribute in the form of money and goods from defeated enemies and the slave labour of prisoners taken in battle. Keeping the mass of the Roman poor content required the exaction of still more tribute money from the conquered territories. A parasitic relationship was thus established, in which all classes in Rome lived off the rest of the Empire.

The political situation in the first century BC became more and more anarchic. Vast armies were required to fight distant wars on the boundaries of the Empire; soldiers came to owe greater loyalty to their general, who rewarded them with the fruits of conquest, than to the government back in Rome. The result was a succession of civil wars between rival generals.

Julius Caesar and Pompey, the two greatest generals of the first century BC, tried to bury their differences in a triumvirate with Crassus, but in 49 BC Caesar, then governor of Gaul, defied the Senate by bringing his army into Italy ('crossing the Rubicon', the muddy stream that marked the border). All opposition was swept aside and for the last six years of his life Julius Caesar ruled Rome as a dictator. The Republican spirit was not quite dead, though: in 44 BC he was assassinated. His death did not lead to the restoration of the Republic. Instead there was a power struggle between Mark Antony and Caesar's nephew, Octavian, which escalated into a full-blown civil war.

PAX ROMANA

Octavian eventually defeated Mark Antony and Cleopatra at the Battle of Actium in 31 BC. The Empire now stretched from Gaul and Spain in the west to Egypt and Asia Minor in the east. To hold it together a single central power was needed. Octavian felt that the person to embody such authority was himself and took the name Augustus (meaning 'favoured by the gods').

To give greater authority to his assumption of absolute power, Augustus encouraged the cult of his uncle Julius Caesar as a god, building a temple to him in the Forum. The Ara Pacis (*see p97*), decorated with a frieze showing Augustus and his family, was a reminder that it was he who had brought peace to the Roman world. Later in his reign, statues of Augustus sprang up all over the Empire, and he was more than happy to be worshipped as a god himself.

Augustus lived on the Palatine hill (*see p67*) in a relatively modest house. Later emperors indulged their apparently limitless wealth and power to the full, building a series of extravagant palaces. The last member of

Augustus' family to inherit the Empire was the megalomaniac Nero, who built himself the biggest palace Rome had ever seen: the Domus Aurea or 'Golden House' (*see p135*).

When Nero died in AD 68 with no heir, the Empire was up for grabs. Generals converged from across the Empire to claim the throne, and the eventual winner was a bluff soldier called Vespasian, founder of the Flavian dynasty.

ROME AT THE TOP

Over the next 100 years Rome enjoyed an era of unparalleled stability. The Empire reached its greatest extent during the reign of Trajan (98-117). Thereafter it was a matter of protecting the existing boundaries and making sure civil war did not threaten the Empire from within.

Peace throughout the Mediterranean encouraged trade and brought even greater prosperity to Rome. At the same time, however, the power and influence of the capital and its inhabitants declined. Many talented Imperial officials, generals and even emperors were Greeks, North Africans or Spaniards: Trajan and Hadrian were both born in Spain, for example.

To keep an increasingly disparate mass of people content, emperors relied on the policy neatly summed up in the poet Juvenal's phrase 'bread and circuses'. From the first century AD a regular handout of grain was given to the poor, ostensibly to maintain a supply of fit young men for the army, but also to ensure that unrest in the city was kept to a minimum. Such a degree of generosity to the poor of Rome necessitated still further exploitation of the outlying provinces of the Empire: even in years of famine, Spain and Egypt were required to send grain to Rome.

'Imperial Rome was the most populous metropolis the world had ever seen.'

The other means used to keep over a million fairly idle souls quiet and loyal to their emperor was the staging of lavish public entertainments. The most famous venue for such spectacles was the Colosseum (*see p69*), which was built by the emperors Vespasian and Domitian and completed in AD 96.

Imperial Rome was the most populous metropolis the world had ever seen. In Augustus' day its population was about one million. By the reign of Trajan a century later it had risen to 1,500,000. No other city would even approach this size until the 19th century. Rome was superbly equipped too, with eight bridges across the Tiber, magnificent major buildings and 18 large squares.

The golden age of Rome ended with the death of Emperor Marcus Aurelius in AD 180. Defending the eastern provinces and fortifying the borders along the Danube and the Rhine placed a huge strain on the Imperial purse and the manpower of the legions. Moreover, the exploitative relationship between the Roman state and its distant provinces meant that the latter were unable – and at times unwilling – to defend themselves.

The threat from barbarian invaders and civil wars became so serious that in the third century the Emperor Aurelius was obliged to fortify the city of Rome with massive defences. The Aurelian Wall (*see p155* **Walls**), which was later reinforced by medieval popes, still surrounds much of the city. It is a splendid – but misleading – monument to the engineering skills of the ancient Romans. In its heyday, the city needed no defences. Its protection lay in the vastness of its Empire and the guaranteed security of the *Pax romana*.

A NEW RELIGION

The end of the third century AD was a turning point in the history of Rome. Radical decisions taken by two powerful emperors, Diocletian (284-305) and Constantine (306-37), ensured that the city's days as head of a great empire were numbered. Diocletian established new capital cities at Mediolanum (Milan) and Nicomedia (in present-day Turkey). He divided the Empire into four sectors, sharing power with a second 'Augustus' – Maximian – and two 'Caesars', Constantius and Galerius. The priorities of the over-extended Empire were now to defend the Rhine and Danube borders against invading Germanic tribes and the eastern provinces from the Persians. Rome was abandoned to itself.

The reign of Diocletian is also remembered as one of the periods of most intense persecution of Christians in the Empire. Christian communities had been established in Rome very soon after the death of Christ, centred in clandestine meeting houses called *tituli*. Christianity, though, was just one of many mystical cults that had spread from the Middle East through the Roman Empire. Its followers were probably fewer than the devotees of Mithraism, a Persian religion open only to men, but Christianity's promise of personal salvation in the afterlife had great appeal among the oppressed – slaves, freedmen, women. Within two decades of Diocletian's persecutions, Emperor Constantine would first tolerate Christianity and then recognise it as the Empire's official religion.

When Constantius, Constantine's father and commander of the western provinces, died at York in 306, his army acclaimed young Constantine as 'Augustus' in his place. The early part of his reign was taken up with campaigns against rival emperors, the most powerful being Maxentius, who commanded Italy and North Africa.

The decisive battle was fought just to the north of Rome at the Milvian Bridge (Ponte Milvio) in 312. Before the battle a flaming cross is said to have appeared in the sky, bearing the words 'by this sign shall you conquer'. As the legend goes, Constantine's cavalry then swept Maxentius' superior forces into the Tiber. The following year, in the Edict of Milan, Constantine decreed that Christianity be tolerated throughout the Empire. Later in his reign, when he had gained control of the Eastern Empire and started to build his new capital city at Byzantium/Constantinople (now Istanbul), it became the state religion.

Christianity was much stronger in the East than in the West, and its effect on Roman life was at first limited, the new faith simply co-existing with other religions. Constantine's reign saw the building of three great basilicas, but these were situated on the outskirts of the city. St Peter's (*see p145*) and St Paul's Without the Walls (San Paolo fuori le Mura; *see p159*) were built over existing shrines, and the Bishop of Rome was given land to build a basilica beside the Aurelian Wall – San Giovanni in Laterano (*see p132*). To give Rome credibility as a centre of its new religion, fragments of the 'True Cross' were brought from the Holy Land by Constantine's mother, St Helena. Meanwhile, life in fourth-century Rome went on much as before. The departure of part of the Imperial court to Constantinople was a heavy blow to a city accustomed to considering itself *caput mundi*, the capital of the world, but the old pagan holidays were still observed, games were staged and bread was doled out to the poor.

All around, however, the Roman world was falling apart. Constantine learned nothing from the conflicts created by Diocletian's division of power: on his death he left the Empire to be split between his three sons. From this point on, the Western Empire and the Byzantine Empire were two separate entities, united for the last time under Theodosius in the late fourth century. Byzantium would stand for another 1,000 years, while Rome's glorious palaces, temples, aqueducts, statues and fountains were destroyed by waves of Germanic invaders.

The first great shock came in 410, when Alaric's Visigoths marched into Italy and sacked Rome. Even more significant was the conquest of North Africa by the Vandals in 435, which cut Rome off from its main source of grain. In 455 the Vandals, too, sacked Rome, removing everything they could carry. After this the Western Empire survived in name only.

Brits abroad Pope Adrian IV

It's a long way from Abbots Langley, Hertfordshire, to the centre of world power, but charismatic Nicholas Breakspear took the trip in his stride as he passed through ecclesiastical postings in France and Italy to become, in 1154, Pope Adrian IV.

The only Englishman ever to occupy the throne of St Peter, Adrian found himself in the hot seat when the headstrong, power-hungry German, Frederick I Barbarossa, demanded to be crowned Holy Roman Emperor in 1155. With the coveted crown firmly on Frederick's head, it then fell to Adrian to deal with the wrath of the Roman senate – which lost a bloody battle against the German troops in an attempt to maintain the city's traditional privileges – and with Frederick himself: the Holy Roman Emperor felt that he now had *caput mundi* firmly under his thumb. But Adrian was wily enough to handle the intricacies of medieval diplomacy and kept Frederick's influence in check.

In southern Italy Adrian backed rebel Norman barons in their struggle against the Norman King William of Sicily, forging an unlikely alliance with the Eastern Empire in Byzantium – less than a century after the great schism between Eastern and Western Christian churches. The alliance showed Frederick that the pontiff had other imperial friends on whom he could rely; it also helped pope and rebels score early victories. The situation was reversed in 1156, however: the Byzantine forces were routed and Adrian was forced to sign the Treaty of Benevento, which recognised William as ruler of all southern Italy (although it made the Sicilian king a liege man of the pontiff).

Infuriated, Frederick stormed back across the Alps, only to find himself up against stiff resistance from the northern Italian *comuni* united in the Lombard League – a handy buffer zone between the German emperor and the Vatican state – that had sworn a mutual-defence pact when their representatives visited Adrian in 1159. The emperor's attack prompted Adrian to declare, under the terms of the pact, that Frederick had 40 days to withdraw – or face excommunication. Then, in September of that year, the English pope died before he could carry out his threat.

The great aqueducts supplying water to Rome ceased to function, while much of the Italian countryside was laid waste. The emperors in Rome had become nothing more than puppets of the assorted Germanic invaders who controlled the Italian peninsula. The last emperor, Romulus, was given the diminutive nickname Augustulus, since he was such a feeble shadow of the Empire's founder. In 476 he was deposed by the German chieftain Odoacer, who styled himself King of Italy. Odoacer was in turn deposed by Theodoric the Ostrogoth, who invaded Italy with the support of Byzantium and established an urbane court in Ravenna that provided stable government for the next 30 years.

In the sixth century much of Italy was reconquered by the Eastern Empire. Then, in around 567, yet another Germanic tribe swept in. The Lombards overran much of the centre of the peninsula, but when they threatened to besiege Rome they met their match in Pope Gregory the Great (590-604), who bought them off with tribute. Gregory was a tireless organiser, overseeing the running of the estates that had been acquired by the Church throughout Western Europe, encouraging the establishment of new monasteries and sending missionaries as far afield as pagan Britain.

He also did a great deal to build up the prestige of the papacy. Rome had been merely one of the centres of the early Church, the others – Byzantium, Jerusalem, Antioch and Alexandria – all being in the East. Disputes were sometimes referred to the Bishop of Rome, but many Christians, particularly in the Eastern churches, did not accord him overall primacy. Then the collapse of all secular government in the West – and above all in Italy – meant that the papacy emerged almost by default as the sole centre of authority, with the pope a political leader as well as head of the Roman Church.

LIFE AMID THE RUINS

The Dark Ages must have been particularly galling for the inhabitants of Rome, living as they did among the magnificent ruins of a vanished golden age. There was no fresh water, as the aqueducts cut during the invasions of the fifth century had never been repaired. Disease was rife. Formerly built-up areas reverted to grazing land, or were planted with vegetables by land-owning religious orders. Fear of attack meant that the countryside around the city was practically deserted. Having reached over a million at the height of the Empire, Rome's population could be counted in no more than hundreds by the sixth century. Ancient ruins became convenient quarries for builders. Marble and other limestone was burned to make cement, most of which was used to repair fortifications.

For several centuries the city still owed nominal allegiance to the emperor in Byzantium and his representative in Italy, the exarch, whose court was at Ravenna. However, the exarch's troops were normally too busy defending their own cities in north-east Italy to be of much help to Rome. The city did have a military commander – a *dux* – and a *comune* (city council) that met, as the Comune di Roma still does, on the Capitoline hill. But the papacy also had its courts and administration. In the end the power of the Church prevailed; this would lead to a permanent rift with Byzantium and the Eastern Orthodox churches.

A NEW EMPIRE

During the Dark Ages, the Roman nobles who controlled the papacy and the city set out to re-establish something akin to the old empire. When the Lombards seized Ravenna in 751 and threatened to do the same to Rome, Pope Stephen II enlisted Pepin, King of the Franks, as defender of the Church. The papacy's alliance with the Franks grew with the victories of Pepin's son, Charlemagne, over the Lombards and was sealed on Christmas Day 800, when the pope caught Charlemagne unawares in St Peter's and crowned him Holy Roman Emperor.

Rome appeared to have recovered much of its long-lost power and prestige. It had the protection of an emperor and was blessed by the pope, who in return was rewarded by the gift of large areas of land in central Italy. As things turned out, this arrangement caused nothing but trouble for the next 500 years, as popes, emperors and other monarchs vied to determine whose power was greatest. Roman nobles took sides in these disputes, seizing every opportunity to promote members of their own families to the papacy and frequently reducing the city to a state of anarchy. At regular intervals one faction or another would idealistically declare Rome to be a republic once more, to no real effect.

The prestige of the papacy reached a low ebb in the tenth century, when the Frankish Empire collapsed and the papal crown was passed around between a series of dissolute Roman nobles. One of these, John XII (955-64), was obliged to call on the Saxon King Otto for

Brits abroad The Pretenders

James II, Britain's last Catholic monarch, never made it further south than France after being deposed in 1688. But what better place than the HQ of Catholicism for his descendants to hole up and plot their return to power?

James Edward, the Old Pretender (1688-1766), was lured to the Eternal City in 1717. His attempts to regain the family throne in campaigns launched from France had proved fruitless. But staunchly refusing to give up hope of getting one of his own back on to the English throne, Pope Clement XI gave James Edward a palazzo in piazza Santissimi Apostoli and a devout Polish wife – Maria Clementina Sobieski – with whom to produce feisty Catholic offspring. Rome buzzed with British spies and Jacobite sympathisers.

From this marriage made in the Vatican came Charles Edward (1720-88), also known as the Young Pretender or Bonnie Prince Charlie (pictured). Scots in their hundreds – later thousands – rallied to his call after Charles and a handful of friends landed on Scotland's west coast in 1745. But beating the English on Scottish territory was one thing, invading England quite another: Charles's raggle-taggle fighting force disintegrated as it marched south, forcing the Young Pretender to turn tail. He then took a walloping on Culloden Moor in April 1746. So well publicised was the defeated pretender's drunken and debauched progress back to Rome that the pope refused to support his claim to the throne any longer. It must have been with some relief that Church authorities saw this uncomfortable protégé buried by his father in the Vatican Grottos (*see p147*) in 1788.

Sixtus IV had the Vatican frescoed. *See p14.*

assistance and crowned him Holy Roman Emperor, but then immediately thought better of it. He began to plot against Otto, who rushed to Rome and commanded the clergy and people never again to elect a pope without the consent of himself or his successors.

Papal independence was reasserted in the second half of the 11th century by Pope Gregory VII (1073-85), who also established many of the distinctive institutions of the Church. It was Gregory who first made celibacy obligatory for priests; he set up the College of Cardinals, giving it sole authority to elect all future popes. He also insisted that no bishop or abbot could be invested by a lay ruler such as a king or emperor, which led to a cataclysmic struggle for power with the Emperor Henry IV.

When Henry marched on Rome in 1084, bringing with him a new papal candidate, Gregory demanded help from Robert Guiscard, leader of the Normans who had a strong power base in southern Italy. By the time Robert arrived, Rome had already capitulated to Henry's army; in protest, the Normans indulged in a three-day orgy of looting, then set fire to the little that was still standing. From the Palatine to San Giovanni in Laterano nothing remained but the blackened hulks of once-great *palazzi* and the smoking ruins of churches.

Gregory slunk out of his hiding place in Castel Sant'Angelo (*see p151*) and left Rome a broken man; he died the following year.

Despite conflict between rival factions – usually headed by the powerful Colonna and Orsini families – the 12th and 13th centuries were a time of great architectural innovation in Rome. The creative spirit of the Middle Ages is preserved in beautiful cloisters like those of San Giovanni (*see p132*) and in Romanesque churches with graceful brick bell towers and floors of fine mosaic.

Rome's prestige, however, suffered a severe blow in 1309, when the French overruled the College of Cardinals and imposed their own candidate as pope, who promptly decamped to Avignon. A pope returned to Rome in 1378, but the situation became farcical, with three pontiffs laying claim to St Peter's throne. Stability was only restored in 1417, when Oddo Colonna was elected as Pope Martin V at the Council of Constance, marking the end of the Great Schism. He returned to Rome in 1420 to find the city and surrounding Papal States in a ruinous condition.

RENAISSANCE ROME

With the reign of Martin V (1417-31) some semblance of dignity was restored to the office of Christ's Vicar on Earth. It was at this time that the perennial uncertainty as to who ruled the city was solved: henceforth the city councillors would be nominees of the pope. At this time the popes also made the Vatican their principal residence: it offered greater security than their traditional seat in the Lateran Palace.

Successive popes took advantage of this new sense of authority; Rome became an international city once more. Meanwhile, the renewed prestige of the papacy enabled it to draw funds from all over Catholic Europe in the form of tithes and taxes. The papacy also developed the money-spinning idea of the Holy Year, first instituted in 1300 and repeated in 1423, 1450 and 1475. Such measures enabled the Church to finance the lavish artistic patronage of Renaissance Rome.

Nicholas V (1447-55) is remembered as the pope who brought the spirit of the Renaissance to Rome. A lover of philosophy, science and the arts, he founded the Vatican Library and had many ancient Greek texts translated into Latin. He also made plans to rebuild St Peter's, the structure of which was perilously unstable. The Venetian Pope Paul II (1464-71) built the city's first great Renaissance palazzo, the massive Palazzo Venezia (see p65), and his successor Sixtus IV invited leading artists from Tuscany and Umbria – Botticelli, Perugino, Ghirlandaio and Pinturicchio – to fresco the walls of his new Sistine Chapel in the Vatican.

Since the papacy had become such a fat prize, the great families of Italy redoubled their efforts to secure it, ensuring they always had younger sons groomed and ready as potential popes. The French and Spanish kings usually had their own candidates too. Political clout, rather than spirituality, was the prime concern of Renaissance popes. Sixtus IV and his successors Innocent VIII and Alexander VI (the infamous Rodrigo Borgia) devoted far more of

their energies to politics and war than spiritual matters. Papal armies were continually in the field, carving out an ever-increasing area of central Italy for the Church.

The epitome of the worldly Renaissance pope, Julius II (1503-13), made the idea of a strong papal state a reality, at the same time reviving the dream of restoring Rome to its former greatness as the spiritual capital of the world. He began the magnificent collection of classical sculpture that is the nucleus of today's Vatican Museums (see p147) and invited the greatest architects, sculptors and painters of the day to Rome, including Bramante, Michelangelo and Raphael. Julius's rule was not as enlightened as he liked to think, but he did issue a bull forbidding simony (the buying or selling of church offices) in papal elections. In his own financial dealings, he depended on the advice and loans of the fabulously wealthy Sienese banker Agostino Chigi, whose beautiful villa, now known as the Villa Farnesina (see p119), still gives a vivid impression of the luxurious way of life of the papal court.

Julius's successors accomplished far less than he did. Some were simply bon viveurs, like Giovanni de' Medici who, on being made Pope Leo X in 1513, said to his brother, 'God has given us the papacy. Let us enjoy it.' Enjoy it he did. A great patron of the arts, his other passions were hunting, music, theatre and throwing spectacular dinner parties. He plunged the papacy into debt, spending huge sums on French hounds, Icelandic falcons and banquets of nightingale pies, peacock's tongues and lampreys cooked in Cretan wine.

Future popes had to face two great threats to the status quo of Catholic Europe: the protests of Martin Luther against the Catholic Church – and Roman extravagance in particular – and

Brits abroad Tobias Smollett

Novelist, travel writer and polemicist Tobias Smollett visited Rome in 1763. In his *Travels Through France and Italy* he praised much, but criticised still more.

'As for the Tyber, it is, in comparison with the Thames, no more than an inconsiderable stream, foul, deep and rapid.'

'The noble piazza Navona is adorned with three or four fountains, one of which is perhaps the most magnificent in Europe, and all of them discharge vast streams of water: but, notwithstanding this provision,

the piazza is almost as dirty as West Smithfield, where the cattle are sold in London. The corridores, arcades and even staircases of their most elegant palaces, are depositories of nastiness.'

'I was not at all pleased with the famous statue of the dead Christ in his mother's lap, by Michael Angelo. The figure of Christ is as much emaciated, as if he had died of a consumption: besides, there is something indelicate, not to say indecent, in the attitude and design of a man's body, stark naked, lying upon the knees of a woman.'

the growing rivalry between Francis I of France and Spanish king and Holy Roman Emperor Charles V, who were establishing themselves as the dominant powers in Europe.

The year 1523 saw the death of Pope Adrian VI, a Flemish protégé of Charles V and the last non-Italian pope until 1978. He was succeeded by Clement VII, formerly Giulio de' Medici, who rather unwisely backed France against the all-powerful emperor. Charles captured the Duchy of Milan in 1525 and threatened to take over the whole of Italy in retaliation for the pope's disloyalty. In 1527 a large and ill-disciplined Imperial army, many of whom were Germans with Lutheran condemnations of Rome ringing in their ears, sacked the city. Chiefly interested in gold and ready money, the looters also destroyed churches and thousands of houses, burnt or stole countless relics and works of art, looted tombs, and killed indiscriminately. The dead rotted in the streets for months.

Pope Clement held out for seven months in Castel Sant'Angelo, but eventually slunk away in disguise. He returned the following year, crowning Charles as Holy Roman Emperor in Bologna shortly afterwards. In return, Charles grudgingly confirmed Clement VII's sovereignty over the Papal States.

COUNTER-REFORMATION

The Sack of Rome put an abrupt end to the Renaissance popes' dream of making Rome a great political power. The primary concerns now were to rebuild the city and push forward the Counter-Reformation, the Catholic Church's response to Protestantism.

The first great Counter-Reformation pope was Alessandro Farnese, Paul III (1534-49), who had produced four illegitimate children during his riotous youth. He realised that if Catholicism was to hold its own against austere Protestantism, lavish ecclesiastical lifestyles had to be restrained. Paul summoned the Council of Trent to redefine Catholicism and encouraged new religious groups such as the Jesuits – founded by the Spaniard Ignatius of Loyola and approved in 1540 – over older, discredited orders. From their mother church in Rome, the Gesù (see p109), the Jesuits led the fight against heresy and set out to convert the world.

Pope Paul IV (1555-9), the next major reformer, was a firm believer in the Inquisition, burning heretics and homosexuals, and strict censorship. He expelled all Jews from the Papal States, except for those in Rome itself, whom he confined to the Ghetto in 1556 (see p109).

By the end of the 16th century, the authority of the papacy was on the wane outside Rome, and the papal treasury was increasingly dependent on loans. In the following century

popes continued to spend money as if the Vatican's wealth was inexhaustible, commissioning architects of the stature of Bernini and Borromini to design the churches, *palazzi* and fountains that would transform the face of the Eternal City forever (see chapter **Architecture**). Inevitably, the economy of the Papal States became chronically depressed.

'A Europe-wide resurgence of interest in the classical past was under way.'

If two centuries of papal opulence had turned monumental Rome into a spectacular sight, squalor and poverty were still the norm for most of its people: the streets of Trastevere and the Monti district (the Suburra or ancient Rome's great slum) were filthy and dangerous, and the Jewish population lived in even more insanitary conditions in the Ghetto. The city was, however, a more peaceful place to live. The rich no longer shut themselves up in fortress-like *palazzi*, but built delightful villas in landscaped parks, such as Villa Borghese (see p85) and Villa Pamphili (see p161). Notwithstanding the waning prestige of the popes, Rome had many attractions. A Europe-wide resurgence of interest in the classical past was under way, and shortly the city would discover the joys – and earning power – of tourism. Rome was about to be invaded again.

GRAND TOURISTS

By the 18th century a visit to Rome as part of a 'Grand Tour' was near-obligatory for any European gentleman who aspired to be cultured, and Romans responded eagerly to this new influx. The city produced little great art or architecture at this time, due in part to the poor state of papal finances. The two great Roman sights that date from this period, the Spanish Steps (see p93) and the Fontana di Trevi (see p79), are a late flowering of earlier Roman baroque. The few big building projects undertaken were for the benefit of tourists, notably Giuseppe Valadier's splendid park on the Pincio (see p85) and the neo-classical facelift he gave to piazza del Popolo (see p96).

Although on the surface Rome was a cultured city, there were many customs that reeked of medieval superstition. Smollett (see p14 **Brits abroad: Tobias Smollett**), Gibbon and Goethe, forgetting the full brutality of ancient Rome, all remarked on the contrast between the sophistication of vanished civilisation and the barbarism lurking beneath the surface of papal Rome. Some executions were still carried out by means of the *martello*: the condemned man was

Brits abroad Florence Nightingale

Florence Nightingale spent the winter of 1847-8 in Rome.

'I could not sleep for knowing myself in the Eternal City and towards dawn I got up, scoured myself, and cleaned myself from the dust of many days, and as soon as it was daylight, (forgive an old fool who found herself for the first time in her old age in the land of Rome) I went out, and I almost

ran till I came to St Peter's. I would not look to the right or left […] till I came to the Colonnades, and there was the first ray of the rising sun just touching the top of the fountain. […] I stopped, for my mind was out of breath, to recover its strength before I went in. No event in my life, except my death, can ever be greater than that first entrance into St Peter's.'

beaten about the temples with a hammer, before having his throat cut and his stomach ripped open. This humane method remained in use until the 1820s.

Executions were traditionally staged in the piazza del Popolo, and often timed to coincide with the *carnevale*, a period of frantic merrymaking before Lent. For a few days via del Corso was one long masked ball, as bands played and people showered each other with confetti, flour, water and more dangerous missiles. The centrepiece was the race of riderless horses along the Corso. They had heavy balls covered with spikes dangling at their sides, and boiling pitch pumped into their recta to get them moving.

Rome was a city of spectacle for much of the rest of the year as well. In summer, piazza Navona was flooded by blocking the outlets of the fountains, and the nobility sploshed around the piazza in their carriages. The only time the city fell quiet was in late summer, when everyone who could left for their villas in the Alban hills to escape the stifling heat and the threat of malaria.

ROMANTIC REBELLIONS

In 1798 everything changed. French troops under Napoleon occupied the city and Rome became a republic once more. Pope Pius VI, a feeble old man, was exiled from the city and died in France.

Like most attempts to restore the Roman Republic, this one was short-lived. The next pope, Pius VII, elected in Venice, signed a concordat with Napoleon in 1801, which allowed him to return to Rome. The papacy was expelled for a second time when French troops returned in 1808. Napoleon promised the city a modernising, reforming administration, but Romans were not keen to be conscripted into his armies. When the pope finally reclaimed Rome after the fall of Napoleon in 1814, its noble families and many of the people welcomed his return.

The patchwork of duchies, principalities and kingdoms that had existed in Italy before Napoleon's invasions was restored after 1815. The Papal States were handed back to Pius VII. Nevertheless, the brief taste of liberty under the French had helped inspire a movement for unification, modernisation and independence from the domination of foreign rulers.

The Risorgimento was a movement for the unification of the country, but in itself it was very diverse. Its supporters ranged from liberals who believed in unification for economic reasons to conservatives who looked to the papacy itself to unify Italy. Initially, the most prominent members were the idealistic republicans of the Giovine Italia (Young Italy) movement, headed by Giuseppe Mazzini. They were flanked by more extreme groups and secret societies, such as the Carbonari.

Two reactionary popes, Leo XII (1823-9) and Gregory XVI (1831-46), used a network of police spies and censorship to put down any opposition. Most of the unrest in the Papal States, though, was in the north; in Rome life went on much as before. Travellers continued to visit, and Shelley, Dickens and Lord Macaulay all passed through, only to be horrified at the repressive regime.

The election of a new pope in 1846 aroused great optimism. Pius IX came to the throne with a liberal reputation and immediately announced an amnesty for over 400 political prisoners. However, the spate of revolutions that spread through Europe in 1848 radically altered his attitude. In November that year his chief minister was assassinated and Pius fled in panic. In his absence, a popular assembly declared Rome a republic. Seizing the chance to make his dream reality, Mazzini rushed to the city, where he was chosen as one of a triumvirate of rulers. Meanwhile, another idealist arrived in Rome to defend the Republic, at the head of 500 armed followers. He was Giuseppe Garibaldi, a former sailor who had gained military experience fighting in wars of liberation in South America.

Ironically, it was Republican France, with Napoleon I's nephew Louis Napoleon as president, that decided it was duty-bound to restore the pope to Rome. Louis Napoleon's motivation was simple: he wanted to stop Austrian power spreading further within Italy. A French force marched on Rome, but was repelled by the *garibaldini* (followers of Garibaldi) – a ragbag mixture of former papal troops, young volunteers and enthusiastic citizens. The French attacked again in greater numbers, mounting their assault from the gardens of Villa Pamphili. For the whole of June 1849 the defenders fought valiantly from their positions on the Gianicolo, but the end of the Republic was by now inevitable.

For the next 20 years, while the rest of Italy was being united under King Vittorio Emanuele of Piedmont, a garrison of French troops protected Pope Pius from invasion. Garibaldi protested vainly to the politicians of the new state – it was, he said, a question of *Roma o morte* ('Rome or death') – but the Kingdom of Italy, established in 1860, was not prepared to take on Napoleon III's France. Meanwhile, the former liberal Pius IX was becoming more and more reactionary. In 1869 he convened the first Vatican Council in order to set down the Catholic Church's response to the upheavals of the industrial age. It did so with intransigence, making the doctrine of papal infallibility an official dogma of the Church for the first time.

ROME, ITALY

Even though it was still under papal rule, Rome had been chosen as the capital of the newly unified kingdom. In 1870, with the defeat of Napoleon III in the Franco-Prussian War, the French withdrew from Rome and unification

troops occupied the city. Pius IX withdrew into the Vatican, refusing to hand over the keys of the Quirinale, the future residence of the Italian royal family – the troops had to break in.

There followed the most rapid period of change Rome had experienced since the fall of the Empire. The new capital needed government buildings and housing for the civil servants who worked in them. Church properties were confiscated and for a time government officials worked in converted monasteries and convents. Two aristocratic *palazzi* were adapted to house the Italian parliament: Palazzo di Montecitorio (*see p96*) became the Lower House, and Palazzo Madama (*see p103*) the Senate.

> ### 'Mussolini's ambition was to transform the country into a dynamic, aggressive society.'

The city's great building boom lasted for over 30 years (*see chapter* **Architecture**). New avenues appeared: via Nazionale and via Cavour linked the old city with the new Stazione Termini in the east, and corso Vittorio Emanuele was driven through the historic centre. The new ministries were often massive piles quite out of keeping with their surroundings; still more extravagant was the monstrous Vittoriale, the marble monument to Vittorio Emanuele erected in piazza Venezia.

Though Rome was little affected by World War I, social unrest broke out following the war, with the fear of Socialism encouraging the rise of Fascism. Benito Mussolini was a radical journalist who, having become alienated from the far left, shifted to the extreme right. Like so many before him, he turned to ancient Rome to find an emblem to embody his idea of a

Brits abroad George Eliot

In Eliot's *Middlemarch* (1872), heroine Dorothea Brooke realises that marriage – and the Eternal City – aren't all she had expected them to be during her Roman honeymoon.

'The weight of unintelligible Rome might lie easily on bright nymphs to whom it formed a background for the brilliant picnic of Anglo-foreign society; but Dorothea had no such defence against deep impressions. Ruins and basilicas, palaces and colossi, set in the midst of a sordid present, where all that was

living and warm-blooded seemed sunk in the deep degeneracy of a superstition divorced from reverence [...] the long vistas of white forms whose marble eyes seem to hold the monotonous light of an alien world: all this vast wreck of ambitious ideals, sensuous and spiritual, mixed confusedly with the signs of breathing forgetfulness and degradation, at first jarred her as with an electric shock and then urged themselves on her with that ache belonging to a glut of confused ideas which check the flow of emotion.'

Vittorio Emanuele II – united Italy's first monarch. *See p17*.

totalitarian state: *fasces*, bundles of rods tied round an axe, were carried by the Roman *lictors* (marshals) as they walked in front of the city's consuls. In 1922 Mussolini sent his Blackshirt squads on their 'March on Rome', demanding – and winning – full power in government. He had been prepared to back out at the first sign of real resistance by the constitutional parties, and himself made the 'March' by train.

Mussolini's ambition was to transform the country into a dynamic, aggressive society. Among other things, he wanted to put Italians in uniform and stop them eating pasta, which he thought made them lazy and un-warlike. His ideas for changing the face of Rome were equally far-fetched. He planned to rebuild the city in gleaming marble, with fora, obelisks and heroic statues proclaiming *il Duce* ('the Leader') as a modern Augustus at the head of a new Roman Empire. The most prominent surviving monuments to his megalomania are the suburb of EUR (*see p160*), which was planned as the site for an international exhibition of Fascism, and the Foro Italico sports complex (*see p156*).

When put to the test in World War II, Fascist Italy rapidly foundered. Mussolini was ousted from power in 1943 and the citizens of Rome had no difficulty in switching their allegiance. During the period of German occupation that

followed, Italian partisans showed themselves capable of acts of great courage. Rome was declared an open city – the *Roma, città aperta* of Rossellini's great film – meaning that the Germans agreed not to defend it, pitching their defence south of the city around Frascati (*see p292*). While other Italian cities and towns were pounded by bombs, Rome suffered only one serious bombing raid during the whole war.

After the war Italy voted to become a republic and Rome quickly adapted to the new political structures. *Partitocrazia* – government by a group of political parties sharing power and dividing up lucrative government jobs and contracts between them – suited the Roman approach to life well. The political unrest of the 1970s affected Rome less than it did Milan or Turin, with Romans simply swimming with the political tide: they voted in their first Communist mayor in 1976.

The city benefited greatly from Italy's post-war economic boom, spreading radially along its major arterial roads. The problem for the post-war city authorities has been how to preserve the old city yet still encourage development. Rome's main industry is still being itself, whether as capital of Italy or historical relic, and the city continues to thrive, trading as it has done for the last 1,500 years on its unforgettable past.

Key events

= dates based on legend

*753 BC Romulus kills Remus and founds the city of Rome.
*750 BC Rape of the Sabine Women.
*616 BC Tarquin elected king. Forum drained.
*509 BC Tarquins ousted after rape of Lucretia.
*507-6 BC Roman Republic founded. The Latins and Etruscans declare war.
*494 BC Plebeians revolt. Tribunate founded.
*450 BC Roman Law is codified.
434 BC War against the Etruscans.
390 BC Gauls sack Rome.
264-146 BC Punic Wars against Carthage. In 212 Rome conquers Sicily; in 146 Carthage is destroyed.
200-168 BC Rome conquers Greece. Greek gods introduced to Rome.
60-50 BC First triumvirate: Julius Caesar, Pompey, Crassus.
55 BC Caesar invades Britain.
51-49 BC Caesar conquers Gaul and crosses the Rubicon.
48 BC Caesar defeats Pompey and meets Cleopatra.
45 BC Caesar declared emperor.
44 BC Caesar assassinated.
43-32 BC Second triumvirate: Octavian, Mark Antony and Lepidus.

PAX ROMANA
31 BC Antony and Cleopatra defeated at Actium; Octavian (Augustus) becomes sole ruler.
41 Caligula assassinated. Claudius accedes.
64 City slums cleared in great fire; Nero rules.
67 Saints Peter and Paul are martyred.
80 Construction of Colosseum begins.
125 Completion, to Hadrian's designs, of the Pantheon.
164-180 Great Plague throughout the Empire.
284-305 Diocletian splits Empire into East and West.

A NEW RELIGION
313 Constantine's Edict of Milan makes Christianity legal.
382 Severe persecution of pagans.
410 Alaric the Goth sacks Rome.
475-6 Byzantium becomes seat of Empire. Goths rule Rome.
c567 Lombards overrun much of Italy.
778 Charlemagne defeats last Lombard king.

800 Pope crowns Charlemagne Holy Roman Emperor.
1084 Rome sacked, first by Holy Roman Emperor Henry IV then by Normans under Robert Guiscard.
1097 First Crusade begins.
1300 First Holy Year.
1309 Pope Clement V moves papacy to Avignon.
1347 Cola di Rienzo sets up Roman republic.
1417 End of Great Schism in the papacy.
1420 Pope returns definitely to Rome.

RENAISSANCE ROME
1494 Charles VIII of France invades Italy.
1508 Michelangelo begins painting the Sistine chapel ceiling.
1527 Rome sacked by imperial army.
1556 Roman Jews confined to the Ghetto.
1563 Council of Trent launches the Counter-Reformation.
1585 Sixtus V begins to change city's layout.
1626 The new St Peter's is consecrated.
1773 Jesuits expelled from Rome.

TOURISTS & ROMANTICS
1798 French exile pope and declare Rome a republic.
1806 End of Holy Roman Empire.
1808 Rome made a 'free city' in Napoleon's empire.
1821 Death of John Keats in Rome.
1848 Revolutionaries declare Roman Republic; they are put down by French troops, who occupy the city until 1870.

ROME, ITALY
1870 Italian army enters Rome, which becomes capital of a united Italy.
1922 Mussolini marches on Rome.
1929 Lateran Treaty creates the Vatican State.
1944 Rome liberated.
1946 Referendum makes Italy a republic.
1957 Common Market Treaty signed in Rome.
1960 Olympic Games held in Rome.
1962 Second Vatican Council: church reform.
1981 John Paul II shot in St Peter's Square.
1993 Tangentopoli corruption investigations begin: political parties crumble; summer Mafia bombs kill 11 in Rome, Florence, Milan; in December Francesco Rutelli becomes Rome's first Green mayor.
2000 Jubilee Holy Year.
2001 Media magnate Silvio Berlusconi elected prime minister.

POLIDORI®

M E N S W E A R - R O M E

Polidori has a hint of the playful in its meanswear that distinguishes it from the traditional top-line sportswear designers. Yes, there are stacks of cashmere v-necks and racks of tweed jackets in its Via Borgognona store. But they are displayed against blond wood with steel accents and on glass-topped tables. There are glints of chartreuse green in some of their argyle socks, and the leather section includes snazzy jackets in addition to the usual shoes and belts. Custom-made suits and coats are available in addition to fabrics and the ready-to-wear line. The opening of the new store in 2000 was a homecoming for the brand. Fausto Polidori founded the company with a fabric store for women's wear at this same exact location in 1946. It grew rapidly, swept along with Italy's postwar economic boom. Polidori fabrics were requested by the famous designers of the time: Valentino, Lancetti, André Lang and Balestra. The name became one of the must-haves among Italy's film stars, both male and female. Liz Taylor is known to have stocked up on Polidori fabrics during her visits to Rome. Polidori reached an even wider market in the 1970's with a menswear boutique on Via Condotti.

Part of the Polidori boutique is devoted to the Beretta sportswear brand, a classy line of jackets, pants, shoes, knits and leather goods with a self-described "country flavor". Many of their classic pieces integrate the latest wind-and-rainproof materials into cotton and wool. Beretta's history makes Polidori look like a fledgling company. It was founded in 1526, when it specialized in arms production. It is still owned and run by members of the Beretta family.

exclusive shop-in-shop for

Via Borgognona, 4/a - 00187 Roma
tel. 06 678 48 43 fax 06 699 41 170 www.Polidori.it

Rome Today

Romans love their new, spruced-up city – but are happy that some of the old ways remain.

It would be stretching things to talk of a Roman Renaissance, but the changes in look, feel and function that have taken place in Italy's capital over the last decade are nothing short of astonishing. Even five or six years ago, tourists were forced to run the gauntlet of *palazzi* and churches swathed in uniformly dark grey soot, archaeological sites transformed by lack of explanations into senseless heaps of masonry, and museums that had a habit of closing just when they wanted to visit. Rome, of course, was lovely… but oh so culturally backwards.

What a difference ten years have made. From lovely pastel yellow, grey, peach and cream tints on countless historic buildings to major new museums and ambitious contemporary building projects, Rome has wiped off the grime and shaken up the dust after decades of neglect.

Much of the momentum came from former Mayor Francesco Rutelli, who swept to power on a Green ticket in December 1993. Bolstered by central government of the same centre-left persuasion as his own administration and an immense injection of special financing for the 2000 Holy Year, Rutelli threw himself into making the city more presentable to the 30 million expected tourist-pilgrims: extensive digging in the via dei Fori Imperiali (*see p71*) archaeological sites began; funds were allocated for restoring monuments and churches; the

city's inadequate transport was beefed up. The Culture Ministry lent a hand too, opening the Domus Aurea (*see p135*), the Galleria Borghese (*see p85*), the Terme di Diocleziano (*see p140*) and several other major spaces.

The Rutelli administration went beyond restoring the old: in a real break from a past that saw contemporary architecture in the Eternal City as sacrilegious, it initiated major new works that included Zaha Hadid's MAXXI, a convention centre in EUR by Italian architect Massimiliano Fuksas and the controversial new pavilion for the Ara Pacis by American Richard Meier (*for all, see chapter* **Architecture**).

The performing arts took a turn too. Now well established, the Estate Romana festival (*see p234*) continues to bring world-class artists to stunning outdoor venues; in autumn, the RomaEuropa Festival (*see p234*) showcases cutting-edge dance, theatre and music.

Cynics will tell you that this is the perfect window of opportunity to enjoy the Eternal City. After its Holy Year wash-and-brush-up, the city's looking great, but little has been done to reduce the smog-producing traffic that was to blame for much of the decay in the first place. The job of keeping things going falls to Walter Veltroni, Rome's mayor since 2001. A former secretary of the Democratici di sinistra – the former Communist party – the jazz- and

Real Roman shops on via Condotti.

the main law courts and offices of public broadcaster RAI to protest against what they see as media manipulation by the government.

Not only have tourist Rome and Roma *capitale* changed, but so has life in the workaday city of Romans themselves. Many frustrations have evaporated: public phones generally work (a rather useless improvement in one of the world's most cellphone-saturated countries), as do cash machines; outdoor seating in cafés is orderly and limited, no longer forcing pedestrians off the pavement and into the screaming traffic; the bureaucracy that used to make life hell has been (somewhat) streamlined.

But growing affluence and its accompanying desire for international uniformity mean that some Roman characteristics are being squeezed out. The near-monopoly of the charming and dependable neighbourhood trattoria has collapsed, undermined by the advent of more sophisticated eating and drinking places. Traditional *vini e olii* – holes in walls where locals quaffed Castelli wine as the owner threw together something to eat out back – are difficult to find. You won't see a lot of laundry hanging out of windows. Little old ladies no longer bring their dogs to their local trat. Campo de' Fiori (*see p108*) – not so long ago a salt-of-the-earth produce market – is now invaded by hawkers of imitation leather goods by day and becomes a mega-pub by night. Street markets and corner *alimentari* are being forced out by supermarkets. Globalisation has wreaked havoc in the *centro storico*, where long-running family shops and restaurants are being pushed out by international chains.

'Visitors to St Peter's are a source of huge revenues for the Eternal City.'

That said, Rome retains its endearing quality of being a bit more laid-back – more naturally gifted when it comes to leisurely enjoyment – than Milan, though without the apparent indolence of Naples. Romans live comfortably cheek by jowl with extraordinary beauty and cultural wealth; if it looks like they're unaffected by it, it's a front. The immense queues that form outside a newly opened sight or exhibition consist to a large extent of locals. In a poll commissioned recently by city hall, Romans aged 15 to 29 described their city as 'magic', 'unique' and '*bellissima*'; a large majority had no intention of ever leaving.

One decisive bastion against unbridled change and consumerism is – like it or not – the Vatican. Rome's history, urban layout, atmosphere and traditions are all intertwined with the

cinema-loving mayor continues to treat culture as a high priority. But unlike Rutelli, Veltroni has to do business with a centre-right national government, and a president of the Lazio region – Francesco Storace – who hails from the Alleanza nazionale party, heirs to Mussolini's Fascists. (Storace's suggestion that 'biased', 'leftist' history textbooks should be rewritten has been taken up by his cronies in parliament; his suggestion that child support should be granted from the moment of conception rather than birth, and his moves to starve family-planning clinics of funds have made him the bugbear of feminist groups.)

Being the seat of the national government is a double-edged sword for the city, especially since the conservative Casa delle libertà coalition headed by media mogul Silvio Berlusconi came to power in 2001. Once called upon only to host the occasional march by discontented students or unions seeking better pay and conditions, there has recently been a startling revival of flagging civic spirit, with the city becoming the stage for frequent (often bitter) protests against Berlusconi's government. In 2002 anti-government demonstrations drew millions to the Circo Massimo (*see p68*) and the square in front of San Giovanni Laterano (*see p131*). More modest, but growing in strength, the Girotondo ('ring-a-ring o' roses') movement – founded by Italian intellectuals, including film director Nanni Moretti (*see chapter* **Film**) – has built well-publicised human chains around peculiarities, vicissitudes and politics of this tiny walled state and its first citizen, the pope. Likely candidates to replace the aged, ailing pontiff come and go, but John Paul clings on, never ceasing to exert his moral suasion to bring about an odd mixture of conservative policies in Italy and socially progressive and humanitarian objectives abroad. Long, tough civil rights battles were needed before the Vatican veto on birth control, abortion and divorce in Italy was finally overridden in the 1970s. Vatican opposition to Sunday shopping meant that this phenomenon didn't hit Rome until the mid 1990s.

Romans have lived with this powerful, if apparently anachronistic, presence since the fourth century, when Constantine made Christianity the official religion of the Roman Empire. The relationship has often been rocky, even violent, but always symbiotic. It remains so to this day: visitors and pilgrims to St Peter's are a source of huge revenues for the Eternal City; in return, the Holy See benefits from deference and

support – including financial support, as during the preparations for the celebrations in 2000. The closest thing to an institutional crisis came when then-Mayor Rutelli allowed the World Gay Pride parade during the Holy Year. John Paul II was incensed, despite the fact that Rutelli bowed to Vatican pressure and changed the procession's route to avoid passing churches.

It's an odd – not to say unique – mixture: millennia of uninterrupted history, its glories still marvellously and proudly on show; a 21st-century city living in the shadow of a medieval theocracy; a medieval urban fabric struggling to meet the demands of modern citizens; a city that values its heritage but craves the fruits of modern, global consumerism. But the mixture clearly appeals. Some 4.24 million foreigners and 2.5 million non-Roman Italian visitors were attracted to the Eternal City in 2001 alone. Rome's continued popularity – indeed the city's very nature – will depend on its ability to maintain this balance.

Once, not future, kings

Every day tourists line up at the Pantheon (see p105) to add their names to a long list overlooked by a cloaked officer of the Order of Savoy. Few of them realise that this is no guest book: they are, in fact, signing their support for Italy's ex-royal family. For Emperor Hadrian's temple to all the gods is also the personal mausoleum of the Savoy dynasty, though their relatively short stint on the Italian throne meant that only two monarchs – Vittorio Emanuele II and Umberto I – actually ended up there.

A referendum in 1946 brought an end to the 75-year-old monarchy, a slim majority choosing the novelty of a republic over the continuance of a royal house that had rubber-stamped Mussolini's Fascism. To drive the message home, a new constitution forbade male pretenders of the defunct dynasty from setting foot on Italian soil.

Although subsequent royal carry-ons – shady business deals, in-fighting over the family jewels, shooting incidents and murder trials – have further tarnished the Savoia regal image, the latest generation of Italian parliamentarians are a forgiving lot: 2002 saw legislation passed that brings to an end the ban on the ex-princes of the realm.

While the former royals did, somewhat grudgingly, pledge their allegiance to the constitution, government-embarrassing rumours soon followed concerning the

Savoys' alleged desire to be awarded an appropriate des-res in the capital. It would merely be compensation, after all, for losing the Quirinale palace (see p82) to the President of the Republic.

Gun-toting Vittorio Emanuele and son-and-heir Emanuele Filiberto have made Di-like promises to visit the needy of Naples and bring Savoy succour to earthquake victims. However – Emanuele Filiberto's starring role in a TV advertisement for bottled olives aside – their only act during a first lightning visit to Italian soil in December 2002 was to be received by the pope in the Vatican. Then they zoomed back to their Swiss banking business without so much as pausing to shake the hand of the Italian president.

A second, longer visit to Naples in March 2003 was equally devoid of populist gestures. Amid unlikely anachronistic scuffles between supporters of the Savoia dynasty and the Bourbon family that ruled southern Italy until Unification, the ex-royals visited their erstwhile palace and were wined and dined by the cream of the Italian aristocracy.

It was a first, conclusive sign that, with the constitutional ban lifted, the Savoys will inevitably be swept back into their ex-realm's A-to-Z class celebrity maelstrom. Visitors be warned: no chic restaurant or suit-and-tie nightclub will be safe... the paparazzi are already recharging their flashguns.

Architecture

Austere and exuberant, ancient and modern – all have their place in Rome's rich architectural heritage.

Outside many of central Rome's key monuments and buildings there are detailed explanatory panels. Read all of them and you'll have completed an intensive, exhaustive course in the history of Western architecture.

Yet Rome is not a polished, sterile open-air museum: it's a vibrant city where past and present live nonchalantly side by side. Moreover, there are a host of architectural must-sees over and above Rome's classical ruins, Renaissance palaces and baroque churches. Today the city is learning to value its unique 20th-century heritage and, at the same time, it's being transformed by exciting new projects.

THE ANCIENT CITY

The major buildings of ancient Rome were designed to express the glamour, sophistication and clout of the city. But it was a while before the Romans developed much in the way of their own architectural styles. If the Romans had the Etruscans to thank for insights into hydraulics and town planning, it was the Greek system of

orders – sequences of columns of different proportions based on their width – that was followed for important façades. The main Greek orders were Doric (plain and sturdy), Ionic (more slender and ornate) and Corinthian (the most delicate and ornate of all). The **Colosseum** (*see p69*) is a good example of how they were used: hefty Doric at the bottom to support the construction; lighter, more elegant Ionic in the middle; and the decorative Corinthian top layer.

It wasn't only columns that were copied from Greece: whole genres of building were based on Greek models. Temples were colonnaded and either rectangular, like the temples of **Saturn** or **Portunus**, or circular, like the temples of **Vesta** and **Hercules Victor** (for all, *see p75* **Foro Romano**). Theatres were derived from Greek models too.

The Romans did eventually come up with their own ideas: elliptical arenas – known as amphitheatres – designed for blood sports; rectangular meeting houses flanked by columns, known as basilicas; and efficient plumbing and heating systems, complete with hot running water. Perhaps most importantly, the Romans took the arch to unprecedented heights of perfection, giving the world its first large-scale, free-standing masonry.

The commonest stone found around Rome was soft, volcanic tufa. This was not an ideal building material, and as early as the third century BC a form of concrete was developed, made of pozzolana (a volcanic ash), lime and tufa rubble. This was not aesthetically pleasing, so buildings were faced with veneers of coloured marble or travertine (a calcareous limestone).

Without concrete, constructing the **Pantheon** (see p105) would have been impossible. The huge hemispherical dome is the largest cast-concrete construction made before the 20th century. Other feats of cast-concrete engineering include the **Terme di Diocleziano** (see p140) and **Terme di Caracalla** (see p129).

Brick, the other fundamental Roman building material, was used to face buildings, to lend internal support to concrete walls, and as a material in its own right. The most impressive example is the **Mercati di Traiano** (see p72).

EARLY CHRISTIAN ROME

There are traces of the early Christians everywhere in Rome – and they're not confined to dank catacombs or the scant, buried remains of *tituli* (the earliest Christian meeting houses). Scores of early churches survive too; although in many cases the original building is hidden beneath later accretions, the tell-tale signs are there if you know what to look for.

Early Christian basilical churches are the ghosts of ancient Roman basilicas. Churches founded in the fourth and fifth centuries such as **San Paolo fuori le Mura** (see p159), **San Giovanni in Laterano** (see p131), **Santi Quattro Coronati** (see p128), **Santa Maria in Trastevere** (see p118) and **San Pietro in Vincoli** (see p136) are the most tangible connection we have with the interiors of ancient civic Rome: go into any of them and imagine them with no later decoration. The construction is generally simple and stately. Most are rectangular, with a flat roof and a colonnade separating a tall nave from lower aisles. Natural light enters the nave from high windows. Behind the altar, opposite the entrance, is an apse topped by a conch (domed roof). Perhaps the best example of all is **Santa Sabina** (see p122), which was shorn of later additions in a no-holds-barred restoration in the 1930s.

> ▶ See p317 **Glossary** for architectural and artistic terms.

The fortunes of the Catholic Church are well reflected in architecture. When it was poor, as in the fifth century, buildings were plain and functional; when it was rich, in periods such as the eighth and 12th centuries, churches were adorned with brilliant mosaics. The most magnificent to have survived are in **Santa Maria Maggiore** (see p139), **Santa Prassede** (see p134) and **Santa Maria in Trastevere** (see p118). Many churches were decorated with cosmati-work: carved and inlaid pulpits, choirs, candlesticks and floors. Very occasionally, circular churches were built, perhaps inspired by Roman tombs like Hadrian's mausoleum (now **Castel Sant'Angelo**, see p149). The dazzling mosaic-caked **Santa Costanza** (see p158) was probably built in the fourth century as a mausoleum for the daughters of Emperor Constantine; its contemporary, **Santo Stefano Rotondo** (see p128), may have been inspired by the church of the Holy Sepulchre in Jerusalem.

During the Middle Ages, Rome's influential families were engaged in an almost constant battle for power – a fact that was reflected in the civic architecture of the city. Construction was unrestricted and unplanned: the tortuous warren of streets in the Monti district (see chapter **Monti & Esquilino**) is a result. Anyone who could, opted for a fortress-home with lookout towers like **Torre delle Milizie**, behind the Mercati di Traiano (see p72).

The quarrels between the families were to have long-lasting effects: with daggers constantly drawn, they failed to impose a Roman candidate on the throne of St Peter's. France stepped in, had Clement V elected, and helped him shift the papacy to Avignon in 1309, where it remained until 1378. The international funds that used to shore up the spendthrift papacy were diverted to the French city and Rome was left bankrupt. The Gothic passed the city by (the one exception being the church of **Santa Maria sopra Minerva**, see p106). The early Renaissance, too, was lost on the shadow of its former self that Rome had become.

THE RENAISSANCE

In the late 14th century a huge revolution in art, architecture and thought was under way in Tuscany. In crumbling, medieval Rome it was not until the following century that the Renaissance began to gather momentum (the sole exception being the group of artists around genius Pietro Cavallini, see also p32.

In 1445 the Florentine architect Antonio Filarete created one of Rome's first significant Renaissance works: the magnificent central bronze doors of **St Peter's** (see p143).

Pope Nicholas V (1447-55), who knew the architectural theorist Leon Battista Alberti and other key protagonists of the early Renaissance, decided that if Rome was to take on fully its role as focus of Christianity, it had to look the part. After consultations with Alberti, Nicholas commissioned restoration work on St Peter's, which at the time was in imminent danger of collapse. Meanwhile, those with lucrative church connections built fabulous palaces: in 1508 papal banker Agostino Chigi commissioned a lavish villa, now the **Villa Farnesina** (*see p119*), and in 1515 work started on **Palazzo Farnese** (*see p282*) for Cardinal Alessandro Farnese.

Pope Pius II (1458-64), a cultured Tuscan steeped in classical literature, put a stop to the quarrying of ancient buildings for construction materials. Sixtus IV (1471-84) had roads paved and widened, churches such as **Santa Maria della Pace** (*see p100*) and **Santa Maria del Popolo** (*see p96*) rebuilt, and the **Sistine Chapel** (*see p147*) built and decorated by some of the foremost artists of the day.

Rome's Renaissance reached its peak with Julius II (1503-13), who made Donato Bramante his chief architect. Bramante came to Rome from Milan in 1499, and in 1502 built the **Tempietto** (*see p121*) to mark the spot thought to be that of St Peter's execution. A domed cylinder surrounded by a Tuscan Doric colonnade, the Tempietto came closer than any other building to the spirit of antiquity.

Julius also commissioned Michelangelo to sculpt his tomb and fresco the ceiling of the Sistine Chapel, and Raphael to decorate the *stanze* (private apartments) in the Vatican palace. Not satisfied with the restoration of **St Peter's** initiated by his predecessors, Julius decided to scrap the old building and start again. The job was given to Bramante, and in 1506 the foundation stone was laid.

Work began on Bramante's Greek-cross design, but was halted after his death in 1514. In 1547 Michelangelo took over, reverting to the centralised design but increasing the scale tremendously. During the papacy of Sixtus V (1585-90) – an obsessive planner responsible for the layout of much of modern Rome – Giacomo Del Duca erected the dome. The original Greek-cross design was finally scuppered by Paul V (1605-21). In accordance with Counter-Reformation dictates, he commissioned Carlo Maderno to lengthen the nave into a Latin cross.

THE COUNTER-REFORMATION

The second half of the 16th century in Rome was dominated by the austere reforms of the Council of Trent (1545-63), designed to counter the ideas of Luther's Reformation, and by the establishment of heavy-handed new religious orders such as the Jesuits and Oratorians. The earliest churches of the period, such as

the **Chiesa Nuova** (*see p98*), were thus plain and provided with long naves suitable for processions. The **Gesù** (*see p109*), with its wide nave, was deemed ideal for the purposes of the Jesuits, as no architectural obstacles came between the preacher and his flock.

As the Counter-Reformation gathered pace, great cycles of decoration teaching the mysteries of the faith (such as the Cappella Sistina of **Santa Maria Maggiore**) or inspiring the onlooker to identify with the sufferings of martyrs (as in the bloodthirsty frescos of **Santo Stefano Rotondo**, *see p128*) began to appear.

BAROQUE

On their heels came an increasingly exuberant, theatrical style of architecture: the baroque. It is to a great extent the endlessly inventive confections of the baroque that make Rome what it is today. Architects such as Giacomo della Porta and Domenico Fontana (1543-1607) set the scene in which the real shapers of the baroque grew up: Gian Lorenzo Bernini, Francesco Borromini and Pietro da Cortona.

'Bernini said quarrelsome Borromini had "been sent to destroy architecture".'

Bernini virtually made the baroque his own, with his imaginative use of marble, bronze and stucco, his combination of sensuality and mysticism. He was jealously guarded by his Barberini patrons, carrying out much of the decoration of the interior of St Peter's for the Barberini Pope Urban VIII. He so dominated the arts that Borromini, Rome's other great genius of the era, was relatively neglected.

Bernini said that quarrelsome, neurotic Borromini 'had been sent to destroy architecture', and for centuries Borromini was vilified as a wild iconoclast. Today he is recognised as one of the great masters of the period, perhaps greatest of all in the inventive use of ground plan and the creation of spatial effects. The most startling examples of his work are **San Carlino alle Quattro Fontane** (*see p83*) and **Sant'Ivo alla Sapienza** (*see p104*), both of which broke all established rules. Perhaps because of his temperament (he was manic depressive and eventually committed suicide), Borromini never attained Bernini's status, but his lay patrons allowed him a freedom to develop his ideas that he might not have enjoyed had he worked for the popes with their particular agendas.

Like Bernini, Pietro da Cortona created some of his greatest works for the Barberini popes. He was principally a painter; his most significant contribution to architecture was his

Modernism the Roman way

The building boom that followed the 1870s Unification of Italy changed the cityscape irrevocably but ultimately failed to modernise Rome, a failure that Mussolini seized on as an excuse for drawing up ambitious plans to create a metropolis worthy of his glorious Fascist empire. No slouch where propaganda was concerned, Mussolini quickly grasped the need for an architectural style striking enough to convey the spirit of a new era.

Since the early '20s a group of young Italian architects had been developing a new architectural idiom – *razionalismo* – combining European functionalism with the rigour and elegance of the Mediterranean/classical tradition: minimalist, but rejecting an architecture merely based on the aesthetic principles of the machine. Initially, the *razionalisti* saw Fascism as a modernising force and were happy to participate in the state-sponsored building spree of the late '20s and early '30s. Rome revels in some of the finest rationalist architecture: post office buildings in via Marmorata, Testaccio, by **Adalberto Libera** and in piazza Bologna (pictured) by **Mario Ridolfi** , and the Casa della Gioventù in largo Ascianghi, Trastevere, by **Luigi Moretti** (all 1933-5) are true masterpieces not only of *razionalismo* but of the modern movement.

By the '30s the *razionalisti* had realised that they were propaganda pawns. Their faith in Fascism started to wane, but they carried on contributing to some of Mussolini's most ambitious projects: in the Città Universitaria campus (1933-5, *see p158*) – masterplanned by the regime's official architect **Marcello Piacentini** – three beautifully proportioned and original buildings, **Giò Ponti**'s Istituto di Matematica, **Giovanni Michelucci**'s Istituto di Mineralogia and the Istituto di Fisica by **Giuseppe Pagano**, stand out above the monotonously monumental architecture and oversized squares and boulevards. Then in 1938 an attempt to work under Piacentini on the E42 project to build the district now

known as EUR (*see p160*) came to an acrimonious halt. The *razionalisti* could no longer compromise between their design approach and the crude classicism of the Fascist authorities. With the exception of Libera, who completed his outstanding Palazzo dei Congressi, they pulled out of the EUR design team.

World War II brought an abrupt end to Mussolini's grand plans, but not to *razionalismo*, which influenced much of the architecture of the post-war reconstruction. The stunning concourse of Termini station (completed in 1950) is a fine example, as are Luigi Moretti's apartment buildings, such as the beautiful Palazzina il Girasole (viale Bruno Buozzi 64).

three-dimensional treatment of walls. At **Santa Maria della Pace** (*see p100*) he combined opposing convex forms that, curving sharply at the ends, are nearly flat in the middle. The result is overwhelmingly theatrical.

Throughout the baroque period the patronage of popes, their families and the religious orders

sustained the explosion of architectural and artistic fervour. Popes commissioned the decoration of St Peter's (Urban VIII, 1623-44); the colonnade in front of it (Alexander VII, 1655-67); the layout of **piazza Navona** (*see p100*); and the redecoration of San Giovanni in Laterano (Innocent X, 1644-55). Their cardinal nephews

Borromini's **Sant'Ivo alla Sapienza** broke the rules of architecture. *See p26.*

inspired many lesser building schemes: the redecoration or restoration of existing churches, and private villas, gardens and palaces.

The religious orders were no less profligate. The Gesù, for example, though begun in the 1560s was completed decades later with a façade by early baroque master Giacomo della Porta. Then, from the 1640s, its interior walls – intended to be bare – started to acquire the alarming profusion of decoration we see today.

NEO-CLASSICISM AND UNIFICATION

During the 18th century the baroque gained something of a rococo gloss, as seen in Nicola Salvi's **Fontana di Trevi** (*see p80*), Francesco de Sanctis's **Spanish Steps** (*see p93*), and Fernando Fuga's hallucinatory **Palazzo della Consulta** on piazza del Quirinale. Giovanni Battista Piranesi imposed his neo-classical theories on the city in the later part of the 18th century, creating striking tableaux such as the **piazza dei Cavalieri di Malta**.

The French occupation of the city (1809-14) brought a flurry of Gallic blueprints for changes in town planning. Some plans – such as Giuseppe Valadier's magnificent reorganisation of **piazza del Popolo** (*see p93*) and the **Pincio** (*see p83*) – were carried out under French rule. Still others were adopted after 1815 by the restored papacy and claimed as its own.

In 1870 the city became capital of a united Italy, ruled by the northern Savoy dynasty, which sought to impose order on the chaotic cityscape, providing it with a road system and structures to house the burgeoning bureaucracy… even if this meant razing entire medieval and Renaissance quarters in the process. **Piazza Vittorio** (*see p136*), **Palazzo delle Esposizioni** (*see p84*) and the imperious, jingoistic **Vittoriano** monument (*see p62*) in piazza Venezia are fine examples.

Occasional relief from the pomposity comes in the shape of lovely Liberty (art nouveau) outcrops, such as the **Casina della Civette** (*see p157*), the palazzo housing the **Museo Hendrik Christian Andersen** (*see p85*), the frescoed **Galleria Sciarra** arcade at via Minghetti 10 and the whole, extraordinary **Coppedè district**, centred on piazza Mincio.

20TH CENTURY AND CONTEMPORARY

Italy's inter-war leader Benito Mussolini was obsessed with moving Italians out of cities and back to the countryside. He couldn't, however, stop Rome's urban spread. On the contrary, during the Fascist period (1922-43) the expansion of the city was given a further push by several large-scale projects.

One of the most impressive was the **Foro Italico** (*see p156*), a monumental sports complex complete with two stadiums and an army of towering statues of naked athletes.

To celebrate the 20th anniversary of the Fascist revolution – and to spearhead Rome's expansion towards the sea – construction also began on a whole new district, initially called E42 but later renamed *Esposizione universale romana* (**EUR** for short – *see p160*). It is one of the most striking examples of Fascist town planning anywhere in Europe.

With construction under way at EUR, Mussolini turned his attention to the *centro storico*: here, according to his Grand Plan, great chunks of the medieval and Renaissance urban fabric would be destroyed, making room for a network of boulevards to improve sight lines between major classical monuments. Thankfully, the outbreak of war stopped the Fascist leader wreaking too much havoc. He did, however, manage to bludgeon the **via dei Fori Imperiali** through the ruins of ancient fora from the Colosseum to piazza Venezia.

With Italians from all over the country drifting to the capital in the post-war period, a number of successful public housing projects were developed. Economic prosperity in the 1950s – halting at first, then rampant – allowed unfinished projects to be completed: **Termini** railway station was given a magnificent wave-like canopy over its concourse, and building resumed in EUR. Optimism fuelled by this prosperity encouraged the construction of many elegant modernist buildings, including the sports venues built by Pier Luigi Nervi for the 1960 Olympics and, in particular, his glorious reinforced-concrete **Palazzetto dello Sport** next to the **Stadio Flaminio** (*see p156*).

A growing population with money to spend on real estate was to have dire effects on the capital's outskirts, where property speculators had a field day as a very blind eye was turned on zoning regulations. From the 1960s to the '80s ugly high-rise blocks galloped across what had been unspoilt countryside.

The city centre, luckily, remained largely untouched by unscrupulous development: work on the first major post-war building project within the Aurelian Wall, the new **Ara Pacis** (*see p97*) pavilion, only began in 2000.

Today, thanks mainly to a municipal administration seriously committed to urban regeneration, the decades-long slump in new architecture is over. A string of competitions for new facilities have all been won by highly talented and original architects.

Rome's **mosque** (*see p312*), one of the largest in Europe, was completed in 1995 to a visionary design by Italian postmodernist Paolo Portoghesi. In December 2002 the last and largest of the three striking concert halls of Renzo Piano's **Parco della Musica** (*see p254* **Parco della Musica**) went into operation. Work continues on American Richard Meier's slick new 'container' for the Ara Pacis and huge **Dives in Misericordia** millennium church, though both of these controversial projects have been dogged by delays.

Work on Zaha Hadid's **MAXXI** (*see p156*) and on Odile Decq's new building for **MACRO** was scheduled to start in spring 2003 (*see p246* **MACRO**), while the building site for the **Centro Congressi Italia** at EUR, designed by local talent Massimiliano Fuksas in the shape of a cloud inside a gigantic glass box, is expected to become operational before the end of 2003.

Finally, love it or hate it (and for many locals it's the latter), the highly original new building for the **Es hotel** (*see p53*) next to Termini station suggests that things are moving on the commercial architecture front as well.

Women at work

If recent projects by established professionals such as **Renzo Piano** and **Richard Meier** (for both, *see above*) have put Rome back on the contemporary architecture map, the city is now being taken to new heights as a hotbed of revolutionary design thanks to schemes by female architects **Zaha Hadid** and **Odile Decq**.

London-based Anglo-Iraqi Hadid won a 1998 competition for MAXXI (*see p156*), with her spectacular plans immediately seized on by city hall to publicise its new-found fascination with all things architectural. Four years later, as the whole operation seemed likely to turn into a gigantic PR flop, the project finally got the go ahead. This building will no doubt be her most significant to date.

An important event in itself, the construction of Hadid's building was made even more extraordinary by the announcement of a project add an imposing new wing to the MACRO gallery (*see p246* **MACRO**), also designed by a cutting-edge architect of international repute: Parisian Odile Decq.

The two projects both represent a new current in architectural thinking that questions the traditional distinction between internal and external space, between rooms and circulation areas. Both are conceived as part of the urban landscape rather than just as smart containers. While Hadid's MAXXI unwinds organically to occupy all the recesses of a long, oddly shaped site, Decq's MACRO extension creates an architectural promenade that breaks the boundaries imposed by a dense urban fabric, reaching its climax in a terraced roof projecting the museum beyond its site.

As this guide went to press, both projects had reached the construction stage, with completion scheduled for winter 2005 (for Hadid) and autumn 2005 (for Decq). The former is funded by the centre-right national government, the latter by the centre-left city council: it's possible that political one-upmanship may mean that these deadlines are respected.

Dynamic Laocoön.
See p31.

Art in Rome

Rome is a compendium of Western art.

From the Renaissance until the Victorian age the primary objective of most Grand Tour visitors to Italy was to see with their own eyes the art of Rome. Despite hype in the forms of implausible descriptions and fanciful engravings many travellers happily surrendered in awe when confronted with the treasures of the Eternal City. On 2 April 1740 the English traveller Thomas Gray wrote home to his mother: 'As high as my expectation was raised, I confess, the magnificence of this city infinitely surpasses it.' Although in our own era some travellers to Rome may make nightlife a higher priority or prefer to acquire shoes rather than statuary, the artistic wealth of Rome rarely disappoints the visitor.

Art in Rome embraces both superlative quality and a stunning chronological range. That the city displays art covering nearly 3,000 years is staggering; that almost all of it was produced right here is even more amazing. No other city – not even the great museum centres of London, Paris and New York – can boast as much. Furthermore, many of the greatest paintings and pieces of sculpture are still in their original architectural settings, offering an authentic context museums can never duplicate.

Yet today, as in the 18th century, visitors can find Rome disorienting. After all there is no Louvre to offer one-stop museum shopping, nor an Uffizi to present a comprehensive survey of Italian painting. Moreover, the city's sprawling layout – with a dozen 'principal' squares – can frustrate the most intrepid traveller. Even those most closely involved with Rome's heritage can experience a sense of bewilderment: 'Being minister of culture here is like being minister of oil in Saudi Arabia,' said Giovanna Melandri, who headed Italy's Culture Ministry until 2001.

With a little planning, good walking shoes and a sense of adventure, however, the visitor can experience Rome's unique continuum of past and present: splendid monuments and intimate spaces, and the layered richness of a hundred generations of artists, patrons and collectors who basked in the absolute certainty that Rome was the centre of the civilised world.

Although the art of Rome has furthered the needs of the Catholic Church for nearly two millennia, the single strongest influence has always been the weighty legacy of the ancient world. In few cities are the remains of the past so palpable. Ancient Rome, as *caput mundi*, harvested or created much of the best art of antiquity. Those who successively sacked or occupied the city – from Alaric in 410 to Napoleon in 1808 (*see chapter* **History**) – have pillaged much of this patrimony, but the fraction that survived continues to astonish.

Egyptian obelisks transported across the Mediterranean still mark major squares and, while there are not many certain Greek originals in Rome today, the miracle of Greek art can be studied and appreciated in scores of important Roman copies. These marbles – often copies of bronze originals long since destroyed – display the Greek flair for endowing the body with beauty, purpose and a sense of movement. The classical ideal, combining striking naturalism with idealised body types, offered a standard of beauty that was hard to ignore.

Although the most famous Greek sculpture in Rome is the *Ludovisi Throne* – the centrepiece of the Ludovisi family collection housed in the Palazzo Altemps (*see p101*) – many works are transitional in nature, somewhere between Greek and Roman. An outstanding example in this category is the hulking *Belvedere Torso* – a superhuman physique from about 50 BC that inspired Michelangelo – now housed in the Vatican's Pio Clementino Museum (*see p147*).

The Etruscans, the pre-Roman peoples who dominated central Italy from the sixth to the third century BC, produced an exuberant, violent and sensuous art. One of the most pleasant museums in Rome is the newly refurbished Villa Giulia (*see p86*), which offers an extraordinary selection of Etruscan art, including life-sized terracotta sculptures from the Temple of Apollo at Veio (*see p282*), and a tender terracotta sarcophagus of a married couple. Equally important is the Etruscan work known as the *Lupa Capitolina* (the 'Capitoline She-Wolf'), a bronze treasure that can be found in the Musei Capitolini (*see p62*).

Beginning in the third century BC the Romans literally built upon this Greek and Etruscan legacy with an unprecedented construction boom. New structural techniques – notably the arch and poured concrete technology (*see also chapter* **Architecture**) – gave birth to daring and spacious buildings (*see* the Pantheon *p105*; Domus Aurea *p134*). The Romans were also responsible for monumental forms that blur the boundary between architecture and art, such as the triumphal arch ornamented with reliefs (particularly those of Septimus Severus and Titus in the Forum, *see p72*, and that of Constantine near the Colosseum, *see p69*) and the independent column ornamented with a spiral band (*see* Colonna di Traiano – Trajan's column *p75*; Colonna di Marco Aurelio *p96*). A further Roman innovation on a smaller scale was the portrait bust, which recorded facial features of the great and the average with arresting honesty.

Much of the best classical art is now concentrated in a few major museums. The Palazzo Altemps (*see p101*), which contains the statue of the *Gaul's Suicide*, is an ideal first stop. The Palazzo Massimo alle Terme (*see p138*) houses important works of Roman painting and sculpture, including a fine Augustus and two copies of the *Discus Thrower* by Myron. The large collections of the Musei Capitolini (*see p62*) feature the *Dying Gaul* and beautiful centaurs in dark marble from Hadrian's Villa (*see p288*). And though the sheer size of the classical collection of the Vatican Museums (*see p145*) can be demoralising, one Hellenistic work there never disappoints: the *Laocoön*, showing a powerful man and his two sons struggling for their lives against serpents, may be the most dynamic statue in the history of art.

ART MEETS CHRISTIANITY

Christian art flourished in Rome after AD 313, when Emperor Constantine's Edict of Milan legitimised the new religion. Rome was thus transformed from a city of temples to one of churches. Little portable early Christian art – the devotional apparatus of the newly recognised religion – survives, but stunning mosaics decorate a number of venerable churches: Santa Costanza (fourth century, *see p157*), Santa Maria Maggiore (fifth century, *see p139*), Santi Cosma e Damiano (sixth century, *see p76*), Santa Prassede (ninth century, *see p133*). Two of the most atmospheric early churches are the austere and lovely Santa Sabina (*see p122*) on the Aventine hill, and San Clemente (*see p126*) with its 12th-century mosaics and even earlier murals.

Later medieval art can be enjoyed in Santa Cecilia in Trastevere (*see p120*), which contains a ciborium (altar canopy; 1283) by **Arnolfo di Cambio** (best known as the architect of the Duomo in Florence) and a pioneering fresco of the *Last Judgment* (1293) by **Pietro Cavallini** above the nun's choir. The little-known artist

Cavallini – who perhaps deserves to rank with **Giotto** as an early initiator of the Renaissance – also impresses with his narrative mosaics (1291) in nearby Santa Maria in Trastevere (*see p118*).

'The definitive return of the papacy in 1420 permitted the Renaissance to take root.'

From 1309 to 1377 the papacy was based in Avignon; Rome withered, and only a fraction of the population remained. Thus the Gothic is largely absent in the Eternal City. The lack of late medieval art, however, is compensated by the wealth of Renaissance, and particularly High Renaissance, art of the 15th and 16th centuries.

The definitive return of the papacy in 1420 permitted the Renaissance and its doctrine of humanism to take root and eventually flourish in the primary seat of classical glory.

Humanism was preoccupied with reviving the language and art of the ancient Greeks and Romans, and reconciling this pagan heritage with Christianity. Renaissance ideas began to leave their mark on the city with architecture based on ancient examples, and sculpture and painting that assimilated the *contrapposto* grace and naturalism of the best classical statues. The papacy concluded that patronage of this new art could extend the faith: in 1455, on his deathbed, Pope Nicholas V informed his successors that 'noble edifices combining taste and beauty with imposing proportions would immensely conduce to the exaltation of the chair of St Peter'.

Nicholas's extant contribution to Vatican beautification – the little chapel of Nicholas V (*see p148*), frescoed by **Fra Angelico** and **Benozzo**

Style classics

When in Rome, artists have always done as the Romans did: used the art of classical antiquity as a constant point of reference. Yet artists didn't merely repeat the forms of antiquity. Rather, from the Renaissance through the Risorgimento, sculptors and painters attempted to undertake a complicated dialogue, even rivalry, with their antique predecessors.

The sheer quantity of surviving ancient art – as well as the availability of materials like marble and travertine – meant that it was hard to avoid working in a classical style. In architecture, the most striking buildings erected since the end of the Middle Ages – from Bramante's exquisite Tempietto (*see p121*) to the shamelessly overblown Vittoriano (*see p67*) – pay homage to the great buildings of the ancient Romans. Patrons from Renaissance popes to Mussolini associated classical architecture with grandeur and virility, and insisted on filling their own backyards with it.

In painting and sculpture, however, allusions to ancient art often seem to be the intentions of the artists themselves. Michelangelo found his muse in ancient marble statues, like the *Laocoön* and especially the *Belvedere Torso* (both in the Vatican Museums, *see p145*). Visitors can still marvel at the Michelangelo frescos in the Sistine Chapel (*see p147*), clearly based on the latter massive sculpture located a few hundred metres away; both the many

nude youths (*ignudi*) that flank the central spine of the vault (1508-12) and the central figures – particularly Christ, and St Bartholomew holding a flayed skin – of the altar wall's *Last Judgment* (1534-41) clearly cite the Torso.

Michelangelo's rival Raphael was particularly susceptible to ancient influence: the profile head of Socrates in the *School of Athens* (c1511, *see p145*) is directly taken from portrait busts of the Greek philosopher, and the format and figure types in the tapestries for the Sistine Chapel (now in the Vatican Pinacoteca, *see p147*) were adapted from reliefs from a destroyed arch of Marcus Aurelius (Musei Capitolini, *see p62*).

In the 17th century Bernini appropriately borrowed from the Vatican's *Belvedere Apollo* in his *Apollo and Daphne* (c1623) in the Galleria Borghese (*see p62*). He also energised the ancient Roman type of the River God, a reclining bearded man of great bulk, in his exuberant baroque *Fountain of the Four Rivers* (1651) in piazza Navona (*see p103*). Nearly two centuries later the greatest neo-classical artist, Canova, executed dozens of works that played upon ancient prototypes. Surely the most famous is his sculpture of Pauline Borghese as Venus (1804-8, Galleria Borghese, *see p85*), which not only depicts Napoleon's sister in the guise of the Roman goddess of love, but also has her reclining on a couch in the manner of the ancient *Sleeping Hermaphrodite*.

Gozzoli (1447-9) – may be modest in the light of his ambitions, but it remains an extraordinary jewel of the early Renaissance. Later popes undertook grander campaigns: Sixtus IV (1471-84) engaged the greatest painters of the day – **Perugino**, **Botticelli**, **Ghirlandaio** and **Cosimo Rosselli** – to fresco the walls of his Sistine Chapel from 1481-2. And think what you may of the morals of the Borgia pope, Alexander VI, his taste in art was exquisite, as seen in the frescos (1493-5) by **Pinturicchio** that perpetuate Perugino's sweet style throughout the many rooms of the Borgia Apartments (*see p146*).

Outside the Vatican the grace of 15th-century Florentine art can also be seen in the joyful and energetic frescos (1489-93) of **Filippino Lippi** in the Caraffa chapel in the church of Santa Maria sopra Minerva (*see p106*). In this and many other Roman churches coins are needed to operate the electric lights.

In the 16th century art and architecture took a monumental turn. In painting, the human figure grew in relation to the pictorial field: the busy backgrounds of 15th-century art were eliminated. Sculptors took their cue from ancient statues, making the human body newly heroic. **Michelangelo** (1475-1564), from Florence, first worked in Rome from 1496 to 1501 for clerics and businessmen. He carved his first *Pietà* (now in St Peter's, *see p143*) for a French cardinal; his 1498 contract challenged the supremacy of classical sculpture in promising to create a piece 'more beautiful than any work in marble to be seen in Rome today'. Michelangelo positioned the dead Christ gracefully in his mother's lap, creating an eternal meditation on death, and fulfilling his boastful pledge.

Under Julius II (1503-13) papal patronage called ever-greater artists to work on ever-larger projects at the Vatican, shifting the centre of the

Raphael's *School of Athens, see p34,* from the Vatican Museums.

Renaissance from Florence to Rome. Julius summoned Michelangelo back from Florence to begin work on the pope's own monumental tomb, a work destined for the choir of the old St Peter's and crammed with over-life-size statues. The headstrong Julius soon changed his mind, insisting that the young sculptor paint the ceiling of the Sistine Chapel. Complaining bitterly that he was 'no painter', Michelangelo rapidly frescoed the ceiling (1508-11), retelling the first nine chapters of Genesis with a grandeur and solidity previously associated with sculpture. Although the recent cleaning of the frescos provoked controversy, the vivid colours we now see are far closer to Michelangelo's intentions than the dark forms worshipped in the 19th and 20th centuries.

Although a later campaign to fresco the chapel's altar wall produced the triumphant and awe-inspiring *Last Judgment* (1534-41), the tomb for Julius limped to an unsatisfactory conclusion in the early 1540s in San Pietro in Vincoli (*see p135*), employing the powerful *Moses* (c1515) as its centrepiece.

Julius initiated his grandest plan of all when he called upon **Donato Bramante** (1444-1514) to design a new basilica of St Peter's. The stateliness of Bramante's style inspired painters as well as other architects. The most influential of the former was **Raphael** (1483-1520).

Julius would not deign to occupy the apartments of his dissolute Borgia predecessor; he insisted on a new suite of rooms – the so-called *Stanze* (*see p148*). These were decorated by Raphael from 1508. The presence of Michelangelo working next door on the Sistine ceiling was a spur to the young painter: the elegant *School of Athens* (1510-11) exemplifies the notion of the High Renaissance, with its re-creation of the great philosophers of ancient Greece against a backdrop of imaginary architecture borrowed from Bramante.

If Michelangelo was unsurpassed in depicting the human body in complex poses, the *Stanze* show Raphael's superiority in arranging poised compositions. The huge demand for this style forced Raphael to run an efficient workshop staffed with assistants. His success at delegation is most apparent in the delightful frescos in the Villa Farnesina (*see p119*), but one can measure the astonishingly swift development of the master himself in a single room of the Vatican Pinacoteca (*see p147*). There, three masterful altarpieces – *The Coronation of the Virgin* (1505), *The Madonna of Foligno* (c1511) and *The Transfiguration* (c1518-20) – chart the amazing shift from a sweetness reminiscent of Perugino to a brooding, dramatic late style. In the same room note the lavish tapestries, designed by Raphael for the lower walls of the Sistine Chapel.

DEMISE OF THE HIGH RENAISSANCE

The Sack of Rome in 1527 halted the artistic boom of the High Renaissance and frightened artists sought employment elsewhere. The simultaneous spread of the Protestant Reformation directly challenged the legitimacy of the pope and his worldly expenses. A more hardened, pessimistic spirit preferred the extraordinary forms of mannerist art, a style of exaggerated proportions and contorted poses that developed out of the mature work of Raphael and Michelangelo. Frescos (c1545) by Raphael's assistant **Perino del Vaga** (1501-47) in the Castel Sant'Angelo (*see p149*) depict both hyper-elegant humans and statues, playing with levels of reality.

'The cruelty often depicted in Caravaggio's paintings mirrored his violent life.'

By the second half of the 16th century mannerist style had lost its wit and energy. Baroque rescue came through the works of **Annibale Carracci** (1560-1609) of Bologna and the shocking naturalism of Michelangelo Merisi, better known as **Caravaggio** (1571-1610, *see p86* **More than tormented**). Caracci, who sought a buoyant version of High Renaissance harmony, is now hard to appreciate in Rome (apart from a lovely *Flight into Egypt* in the Galleria Doria Pamphili, *see p104*). Carracci's masterpiece, an ambitious fresco ceiling in the Palazzo Farnese (*see p110*), has been sadly inaccessible for years: the French embassy that occupies the building refuses access. On the other hand, his contemporary Caravaggio left paintings throughout the city during his stormy career. These works, with their extreme chiaroscuro (juxtaposition of light and dark), can be seen in the churches of Sant'Agostino (*see p104*) and Santa Maria del Popolo (*see p96*). His masterpiece may be the *Calling of St Matthew* (c1599-1602) in the church of San Luigi dei Francesi (*see p103*), where the beckoning finger of Christ recalls Michelangelo's *Creation of Adam* in the Sistine Chapel (*see p147*). The Galleria Borghese (*see p85*) houses a fine nucleus of Caravaggio paintings, from the coy secular works of his early years to the brooding religious canvases of his maturity, notably the extraordinary *David with the Head of Goliath* (c1609) in which the severed head is Caravaggio's self-portrait. The cruelty often depicted in Caravaggio's paintings mirrored his violent life, and altercations with police and patrons marked his Roman years. After losing a tennis match and killing his opponent, Caravaggio fled south. His bold style persisted for a generation,

Bernini's
*Apollo and
Daphne*, in the
Galleria Borghese.

sculpture, *The Ecstasy of St Theresa* (1647-52) in Santa Maria della Vittoria (*see p138*), with Michelangelo's *Pietà*. Michelangelo's mild Virgin shows perpetual, placid bereavement; Bernini's Theresa captures a split second of sensual rapture. The theatricality of sculptures like Bernini's *Apollo and Daphne* (1622-5) in the Galleria Borghese (*see p85*) pushed back the boundaries of sculpture; Bernini tried to capture whole narratives in a frozen instant, and describe textures more vividly than any previous carver. The Galleria Borghese contains many other Bernini statues, plus superb paintings.

Similarly, the Galleria Doria Pamphili (*see p104*) evokes the epoch with outstanding pictures in a magnificent setting. One small room forces a comparison of two portraits of the Pamphili Pope Innocent X (1644-55): a bust by Bernini and a canvas by the Spaniard **Diego Velázquez** (the pope found the painting 'too truthful'). Both museums are awash in aristocratic atmosphere.

EXPANDING ILLUSIONS

Subsequent generations pushed further the artistic unity of architecture, sculpture and painting pioneered by Bernini. Illusionistic ceiling decoration became more and more elaborate. Ceiling paintings – like those in the Palazzo Barberini (*see p79*) or the church of the Gesù (*see p109*) – depicted heavenly visions: assemblages of flying figures bathed in celestial light, as if the roof of the building had been removed. Perhaps the most inventive practitioner of ceiling painting was **Andrea Pozzo** (1642-1709), a Jesuit painter, architect and stage designer. In the church of Sant'Ignazio di Loyola (*see p106*) Pozzo painted both a fresco of the *Glory of St Ignatius Loyola* on the vault of the nave and a false dome on canvas. The latter fools the viewer only from the ideal viewing point, marked by a disc on the floor. The baroque style and the interest in illusionism persisted well into the 18th century.

The final great artistic movement born in Rome was neo-classicism, a nostalgic – some would say sentimental – celebration of ancient Greek art, expressed in stark white statues and reliefs. **Antonio Canova** (1757-1822) created enormous, muscular statues like *Hercules and Lichas*, which can be seen in the Galleria Nazionale d'Arte Moderna (*see p85*), and dignified tombs in St Peter's.

Later movements of the 19th and 20th centuries can be seen at the Galleria Nazionale d'Arte Moderna and the new MACRO (*see p246* **MACRO**). Modern art, regularly exhibited at the Scuderie Papali (*see p82*) and the Palazzo delle Esposizioni (*see p82*), offers a respite to overwhelmed tourists and proves that the city isn't (entirely) trapped by its own past.

though, as witnessed in the Vatican Pinacoteca's extraordinary room of baroque altarpieces by **Domenichino, Guido Reni** (*see p118* **Guido who?**) and **Nicolas Poussin** (taking their cues from altarpieces like Caravaggio's *Deposition* and Raphael's turbulent *Transfiguration*, both also in that museum). Equally weighty baroque altarpieces can be seen in the Pinacoteca of the Musei Capitolini (*see p62*), with **Guercino**'s *Burial of St Petronilla* (c1623) winning the prize.

The most faithful followers of Caravaggio's style were **Orazio Gentileschi** (1563-1639) and his daughter **Artemisia** (1593-1652), who perpetuated chiaroscuro, smooth surfaces and close-up viewpoints. Artemisia had to endure male prejudice (and much worse) to pursue her career, and both artists left Rome, resurfacing together in London in the late 1630s to work for Charles I. Canvases by father and daughter can be seen in the Galleria Spada (*see p108*).

The consummate artist of the Roman baroque, however, was primarily a sculptor: **Gian Lorenzo Bernini** (1598-1660). Bernini perhaps surpassed Michelangelo in the virtuosity of his marble carving. The confident energy inherent in baroque art is revealed by comparing Bernini's greatest religious

Accommodation

Accommodation

Bed in a palazzo, breakfast on a rooftop terrace – Rome goes to town on luxury sleeping options.

Rome's luxury hotel market has exploded recently, with the number of five-stars almost doubling to 20 in the last four years. This is due, in part, to an attempt by the city council to revamp enormous *palazzi* that no one knows what to do with in down-at-heel areas of town like the Esquilino (*see p136*). Hard by the main train station, the area is gradually being repackaged and the opening of the ultra-modern design-led Es Hotel (*see p53*) and the Hotel Boscolo Esedra (not listed; www.boscolohotels. it) in piazza della Repubblica are symbolic of the area's 'rebirth'.

There has also been development and investment further down the food chain. The majority of long-established hotels included in our selection have undergone recent renovations. The days of a cheap bed in Rome are lost in the mists of time: the maxim that you get what you pay for has never been truer, and you are as unlikely as ever to find a room with a view without haemorrhaging euros.

LOCATION

There are now three five-star hotels within a stone's throw of Termini station, but the vast majority of hotels in the area are cheap *pensioni* of dubious cleanliness swarming with penny-conscious backpackers. It's definitely worth looking further afield, even if it costs you a bit more: Termini is extremely well-connected, transport-wise, but it's probably not what you dreamt of for your Roman Holiday.

If you're staying for more than a few days, think about looking for a room in the *centro storico*. A shower before dinner and a wander (rather than a bus) back to the hotel afterwards can make all the difference. The area around **campo de' Fiori** offers low- to medium-priced hotels and bags of character, a lively market during the day and a cool Roman hangout in the evening. The area around the **Pantheon** and **piazza Navona** is generally a bit pricier, although there are good-value places around. Moving distinctly up the price range, Rome's top-end hotels have traditionally clustered around the once-chic **via Veneto**; scheduled for a makeover, this famous street is currently more Hard Rock Café than *dolce vita*. The **Tridente**, the area of designer shopping streets by the Spanish Steps, offers elegant, traditional

hotels, mostly in the upper price range. If you're looking for some peace, the **Celio** just beyond the Colosseum offers a break from the frantic activity of the *centro storico,* as does another of Rome's seven hills: the **Aventine**. Heading across the river, the ever-popular bar-packed quarter of **Trastevere** now has more accommodation options than formerly (*see p42* **Trastevere**). Just north of Trastevere, the medieval alleys around the Vatican give on to the busy retail thoroughfares of **Prati**: it's busy during the day but very hushed at night.

STANDARDS & PRICES

Italian hotels are classified on a star system, from one to five. One star usually indicates *pensioni*, which are cheap but have very few facilities – you may have to share a bathroom. The more stars, the more facilities a hotel will have, but bear in mind the fact that a higher rating is not a guarantee of friendliness, cleanliness or decent service.

A double room in a one-star will set you back €40-€100; a two-star, €45-€150; a three-star, €70-€300; a four-star, €200-€600. Five-star prices start at around €400, and don't stop until your bank manager starts to weep.

Prices generally rise by a relentless ten per cent a year, although it's worth keeping an eye out for special deals, particularly in low season. Hotel websites will have latest details. If you're staying in a group or for a longish period, it's worth asking about discounts.

If you're visiting with children, most hotels will be happy to squeeze a cot or camp bed into a room, but will probably charge 30 to 50 per cent extra for the privilege. Many offer triple or quadruple rooms, which tend to have a bit more space. Renting an apartment (*see p55*) could prove a cheaper and more flexible alternative.

BOOKING A ROOM

Always reserve a room well in advance, especially at peak times... which now means most of the year, with lulls during winter (January to March) and in the dog days of August. If you're coming at the same time as a major religious holiday (Christmas or Easter) it's wise to book weeks, or even months, ahead.

It is standard practice among larger hotels to ask you to fax confirmation of a booking, with a credit card number as deposit. In high season

Spear-heading the designer invasion: the **Es Hotel**. *See p53.*

smaller hotels may ask for a money order to secure rooms. The www.venere.com booking service offers many hotels in all price ranges.

If you arrive with nowhere to stay, the APT tourist office (*see p315*) provides a list of hotels; you have to do the booking yourself. The Enjoy Rome tourist information agency (*see p315*) will book a hotel for you at no extra charge. You should also try the Hotel Reservation service. Avoid the hotel touts that hang around Termini: you're likely to end up paying more than you should for a very grotty hotel.

Hotel Reservation

Fiumicino airport, arrivals halls Terminals A, B & C (06 699 1000/fax 06 678 1469/www. hotelreservation.it). **Open** *Terminals A & C* 7.30am-10.30pm daily. *Terminal B* 8.15am-midnight daily. **No credit cards.**
This agency has details on availability for numerous hotels at all prices. Staff speak English. **Branches**: *Apr-Nov* Ciampino airport (06 699 1000); Termini station, at the head of platforms 2-3 & 20 (06 699 1000).

OUR CHOICE

The hotels listed here have been chosen for their location, because they offer value for money or simply because they have bags of character. In the Deluxe category the emphasis is on opulence and luxury. Those in mid- to upper-price ranges are smaller, many in old *palazzi* with pretty, though often small, bedrooms. *Pensioni* are fairly basic, but those

listed here are friendly and usually family-run. Few Roman hotels have even heard of no-smoking areas, and not many have access for the disabled (*see p305*). Though staff are generally very willing to help guests with mobility difficulties, the real problem is that most places have so many stairs that there's not much they can do. As hotels renovate, they do tend to add a room for the disabled if they can.

Unless stated, prices are for rooms with bathrooms, and include breakfast.

The Trevi Fountain & the Quirinale

Mid-range

Residenza Cellini

Via Modena 5 (06 4782 5204/fax 06 4788 1806/ www.residenzacellini.it). Metro Repubblica/bus 40, 60, 64, 90, 170, 175, 492, 910. **Rates** €135-€185 double; €160-€240 junior suite. **Credit** AmEx, DC, MC, V. **Map** p335 2B.
A delightfully luminous and spacious *residenza* with three double rooms and three junior suites. The huge rooms are decorated in 'classic' style – faux-antique wooden furniture and stripes. Bathrooms have jacuzzis or showers with hydro-massage.
Hotel services *Air-conditioning. Dry-cleaning. Fax. Laundry. Non-smoking rooms. Parking (extra charge).* **Room services** *Air-conditioning. Dataport. Hairdryer. Jacuzzi. Minibar. Radio. Safe. TV (satellite).*

Via Veneto &
the Villa Borghese

Deluxe

Eden

*Via Ludovisi 49 (06 478 121/fax 06 482 1584/
www.hotel-eden.it). Metro Barberini/bus 52, 53, 61,
62, 63, 80, 95, 116, 119, 175, 492, 630.* **Rates**
(plus 10% tax) €435-€455 single; €645-€745 double;
€970 studio room; €1,800 single suite; €2,800
presidential suite; €3,300 penthouse suite; breakfast
€42. **Credit** AmEx, DC, MC, V. **Map** p335 1C.
Beautifully understated, the Eden is stylish yet
relaxed, offering the attentiveness and attention to
detail of a top-notch hotel without the stuffiness. Just
off via Veneto, it has elegant reception rooms, taste-
fully decorated bedrooms and a roof terrace with a
top-ranking restaurant and truly spectacular views.
The hotel is a favourite with the rich and famous.
Hotel services *Air-conditioning. Babysitting. Bar.
Business services. Conference facilities (70). Currency
exchange. Dry-cleaning. Fax. Gym. Laundry. Lifts.
Non-smoking rooms. Parking (nearby). Payphones.
Restaurant. Safe. Tours.* **Room services** *Air-
conditioning. Bathrobe and slippers. Dataport. Fax.
Hairdryer. Internet access. Iron. Minibar. PC point.
Radio. Room service (24hr). Safe. Telephone (2 lines).
TV (satellite/pay). VCR (suites only).*

Hassler Villa Medici

*Piazza Trinità dei Monti 6 (06 699 340/fax 06 678
9991/www.hotelhasslerroma.com). Metro Spagna/bus
52, 53, 61, 62, 63, 80, 95, 116, 119, 175, 492, 630.*
Rates €420-€479 single; €545-€860 double; suites
on request; breakfast €31-€41. **Credit** AmEx, DC,
MC, V. **Map** p335 1C.
Looking imperiously down from the top of the
Spanish Steps, the Hassler is easy to spot by the long
line of limousines parked out front. This is one of
Rome's classic hotels with all the trimmings you
might expect: chandeliers everywhere and oodles of
polished wood and marble.
Hotel services *Air-conditioning. Babysitting. Bars.
Beauty salon. Conference facilities (100). Currency
exchange. Dry-cleaning. Fax. Garden. Gym. Massage.
Laundry. Lifts. Limousine service. Parking (extra
charge). Restaurant. Safe.* **Room services** *Air-
conditioning. Dataport. Fax point. Hairdryer. Laptop
rent. Minibar. PC point. Radio. Room service (24hr).
Safe. Telephone. TV (satellite/cable).*

Majestic

*Via V Veneto 50 (06 421 441/fax 06 4880 0984/
www.hotelmajestic.com). Metro Barberini/bus 52, 53,
61, 62, 63, 80, 95, 116, 119, 175, 492, 630.* **Rates**
€370-€460 single; €490-€610 double; €730 junior
suite; other suites on request; breakfast €25-€40.
Credit AmEx, DC, MC, V. **Map** p335 1B.
The first hotel to open its doors on via Veneto, the
Majestic has been in business since 1889, and lives
up to its name. With its peaceful if formal atmosphere, silk settees and frescos in the reception room,

and marble in the bathrooms, it has long attracted
the great and the good, from Luciano Pavarotti to
Bill Gates and Madonna. According to the visitors'
book it's also where Carlos Menem spent time (and
presumably some of Argentina's fortune).
Hotel services *Air-conditioning. Babysitting. Bar.
Conference facilities (150). Currency exchange. Dry-
cleaning. Fax. Laptop (available on request). Laundry.
Lifts. Parking (extra charge). Restaurants (2). Safe.*
Room services *Air-conditioning. Dataport. Fax
point. Hair dryer. Jacuzzi. Minibar. Radio. Room
service. Safe. Telephone. TV (satellite). VCR.*

The Westin Excelsior

*Via V Veneto 125 (06 47 081/fax 06 482 6205/
www.starwood.com). Bus 52, 53, 61, 62, 63, 80,
95, 116, 119, 175, 492, 630.* **Rates** (plus 10% tax)
€275-€730 single; €495-€1,000 double; suites on
request; continental breakfast €30; buffet breakfast
€42. **Credit** AmEx, DC, MC, V. **Map** p335 1B.
This is a hotel where size really does matter: the
mind-boggling Villa La Cupola suite (two floors,
1,100 sq m/11,820 sq ft, eight-seat cinema…) is one
of the biggest in Europe, and the most expensive bed
in Rome at just over €9,000 a night. A wildly expensive renovation programme was completed in 2002,
providing a gym and marble bathrooms. The
entrance is lavish – and a bit gloomy if you arrive
in the daytime; rooms are a Hollywood-style fantasy. Staff are attentive in a slightly robotic way.
Hotel services *Air-conditioning. Babysitting. Bar.
Business services. Conference facilities (450).
Currency exchange. Dry-cleaning. Fax. Laundry.
Lifts. Multilingual staff. Non-smoking rooms.
Parking (nearby). Restaurant. Safe.* **Room services**
*Air-conditioning. Dataport. Fax point. Hairdryer.
Minibar. Radio. Room service (24hr). Telephone.
TV (satellite/pay).*

Expensive

Barocco

*Via della Purificazione 4 (06 487 2001/fax 06 485
994/www.hotelbarocco.com). Metro Barberini/bus
52, 53, 61, 62, 63, 80, 95, 116, 119, 175, 492, 630.*
Rates €164-€216 single; €246-€325 double; €330-
€390 triple; €360-€413 junior suite; €420-€516 suite.
Credit AmEx, DC, MC, V. **Map** p335 1C.
On a tiny street off piazza Barberini, the Barocco
combines calmness with a central location, not least
because its 41 rooms are soundproofed. The rooms
are stylish, with marble bathrooms, flouncy curtains
and enormous mirrors; some have balconies.
Hotel services *Air-conditioning. Babysitting (€15/
hr). Bar. Car parking and valeting (€26-€35/day).
Currency exchange. Dry-cleaning. Fax. Laundry.
Lifts. Non-smoking rooms. Payphone. Safe. TV room.*
Room services *Air-conditioning. Iron. Minibar. PC
connection. Radio. Room service. Safe. TV (satellite).*

Scalinata di Spagna

*Piazza Trinità dei Monti 17 (06 679 3006/06 6994
0896/fax 06 6994 0598/www.hotelscalinata.com).
Metro Spagna or Barberini/bus 52, 53, 61, 62, 63,*

Trastevere

Until recently, Trastevere was the enigma of Roman accommodation: packed with bars, restaurants and character, it had barely a hotel room on offer. Hotel density here is still not as great as across the river in the *centro storico*, but things are definitely changing.

Just off delightful piazza Santa Maria in Trastevere, the **Hotel Santa Maria** opened in 2000 on the site of a 16th-century convent. The bedrooms have cool tiled floors, slightly anonymous peach decor and spacious bathrooms. They all open on to charming, sunny central courtyards (*pictured*), planted with orange trees – the perfect spot for an *aperitivo* before ambling out to dinner.

Close by, the **Villa della Fonte** is a narrow townhouse with five cosy, wooden-beamed rooms (being renovated as we went to press). Breakfast is served on a small terrace in the warmer months, in your room during winter.

On the other side of piazza Santa Maria is the long-established **Hotel Trastevere**. Located opposite (not very attractive) Vatican offices, the hotel has nine rooms, some looking on to the market in piazza San Cosimato. The decor is strictly functional and some of the rooms are small, but the staff are friendly and helpful, and the hotel is good value in a great location.

On the quieter eastern side of viale Trastevere, the **San Francesco** opened in 2001 near San Francesco a Ripa (*see p119*). It has an attractive marble-floored entrance hall and a lovely roof terrace where breakfast is served when the weather's warm. Rooms are well-equipped and reasonably big, although they're all identical and have a slightly corporate feel. Some look over the internal courtyard of the adjacent convent.

Towards Stazione Trastevere, in what is definitely not the neighbourhood's most attractive corner, the minimalist **Ripa Hotel** is for those who value style over atmosphere. With 170 rooms, plus bar, gallery and artsy happenings of all kinds, it belongs to the same family that owns the startling new Es Hotel (*see p53*).

Hotel San Francesco
Via Jacopa de' Settesoli 7 (06 5830 0051/fax 06 5833 3413/www. hotelsanfrancesco.net). Bus 44, 75, 780, H/tram 3, 8. **Rates** €119-€145 single; €145-€205 double; €179-€229 triple. **Credit** AmEx, DC, MC, V. **Map** p337 2B.

Hotel Santa Maria
Vicolo del Piede 2 (06 589 4626/5474/ fax 06 589 4815/www.htlsantamaria.com). Bus 780, H/tram 8. **Credit** AmEx, DC, MC, V. **Rates** €124-€155 double as single; €145-€207 double; €166-€233 triple; €181-€259 junior suite/quad; €360 senior suite (up to 6 beds). **Map** p336 2B.

Hotel Trastevere
Via Luciano Manara 24/25 (06 581 4713/fax 06 588 1016/hoteltrastevere@ tiscalinet.it). Bus 780, H/tram 8. **Rates** €77 single; €98-€103 double; €129 triple; €154 quad. **Credit** AmEx, MC, V. **Map** p336 2C.

Ripa Hotel
Via degli Orti di Trastevere 1 (06 58 611/ fax 06 581 4550/www.ripahotel.com). Bus 780, H/tram 3, 8. **Rates** €300 single; €330 double; suite on request. **Credit** AmEx, DC, MC, V. **Map** p337 1B.

Villa della Fonte
Via della Fonte d'Olio 8 (06 580 3797/fax 06 580 3796/www.villafonte.com). Bus 780, H/tram 8. **Credit** AmEx, DC, MC, V. **Rates** €83-€95 single; €120-€145 double. **Credit** AmEx, DC, MC, V. **Map** p336 1C.

80, 95, 116, 119, 175, 492, 630. **Rates** €230-€290 single; €250-€350 double; €290-€380 triple; €340-€400 quadruple; €320-€420 junior suite. **Credit** AmEx, MC, V. **Map** p335 1C.

You could almost miss it, tucked romantically away into the corner of the piazza, a world away from the tourists and the constant stream of limousines to the Hassler (*see p41*) across the road. A charming, intimate hotel, the Scalinata has 16 rooms decorated in a rather enthusiastic yellow. Some rooms have private terraces. For those without a room with a view, the hotel's roof garden (where breakfast is served) offers a splendid panorama over the city.

Hotel services *Air-conditioning. Babysitting. Bar. Currency exchange. Dry-cleaning. Fax. Laundry. Parking (extra charge). Safe.* **Room services** *Air-conditioning. Hairdryer. Internet access. Minibar. PC connection. Radio. Room service. Safe. Telephone. TV (satellite).*

Moderate

Villa Borghese

Via Pinciana 31 (06 8530 0919/06 854 9648/fax 06 841 4100/www.hotelvillaborghese.it). Bus 52, 53, 910. **Rates** €113-€145 single; €157-€190 double; €190-€222 triple; €222-€250 suite. **Credit** AmEx, DC, MC, V. **Map** p334 2B.

The Villa Borghese was once the family home of writer Alberto Moravia but has been a hotel since the 1950s. It's separated from the Villa Borghese park (*see p83*) by a noisy road, although thankfully the rooms are all double-glazed. It's a family-run establishment with a cosy, if rather old-fashioned feel – sometimes too much so: some bathrooms and bedrooms can be a bit depressing.

Hotel services *Air-conditioning. Bar. Fax. Non-smoking rooms. Parking (extra charge). Payphone. Safe. TV room.* **Room services** *Air-conditioning. Hairdryer. Minibar. Safe. Telephone. TV (satellite).*

The Tridente

Deluxe

De Russie

Via del Babuino 9 (06 328 881/fax 06 3288 8888/ www.roccofortehotels.com). Metro Flaminio/bus 117, 119. **Rates** (plus 10% tax) €250-€510 single; €360-€620 double; suites on request; continental breakfast €9.50; buffet breakfast €24. **Credit** AmEx, DC, MC, V. **Map** p332 2A.

No chandeliers and gold cherubs here: the De Russie goes for a modern elegance a million miles away from the luxury-schmaltz hotels on via Veneto. Fabulous gardens and a state-of-the-art health centre make it a star magnet. Cameron Diaz and Leonardo DiCaprio stayed here while filming *Gangs of New York* at the Cinecittà studios.

Hotel services *Air-conditioning. Babysitting. Bar. Beauty salon. Business services. Concierge. Conference facilities (90). Currency exchange. Disabled rooms. Dry-cleaning. Fax. Garden. Gym.*

Laundry. Lifts. Limousine. Non-smoking rooms. Parking (extra charge). Restaurant. Safe. Sauna. Swimming pool. **Room services** *Air-conditioning. Dataport. Fax machine (on request). Hairdryer. Minibar. Radio. Room service (24hr). Safe. Telephone (2 lines). TV (satellite/pay/cable). VCR.*

Expensive

Fontanella Borghese

Largo Fontanella Borghese 84 (06 6880 9504/ 06 6880 9624/fax 06 686 1295/www. fontanellaborghese.com). Bus 81, 117, 119, 224, 628, 913, 926. **Rates** €114-€170 single; €170-€250 double. **Credit** AmEx, DC, MC, V. **Map** p333 1A.

On the second and third floors of a palazzo that once belonged to the noble Borghese family, this hotel is elegantly done out in relaxing cream and muted colours, brightened by a generous array of pot plants. Via del Corso and via Condotti are just around the corner: ideal for those who want to be in the thick of things but with somewhere to bolt to when the credit card starts to melt.

Hotel services *Air-conditioning. Bar. Dry-cleaning. Fax. Laundry. Lifts. Payphone. Safe.* **Room services** *Air-conditioning. Hairdryer. Mini bar. PC point. Room service. Safe. Telephone. TV (satellite).*

Valadier

Via della Fontanella 15 (06 361 1998/fax 06 320 1558/www.hotelvaladier.com). Bus 81, 117, 119, 224, 628, 913, 926. **Rates** €103-€268 single; €129-€351 double; €170-€387 triple; €206-€774 suite. **Credit** AmEx, DC, MC, V. **Map** p332 2A.

In the heart of shopping heaven, the Valadier was revamped a few years ago by Egyptian architect Sabah Hajar, giving it an exotic feel with more than a hint of cruise-liner; there are obelisks in the corridors and marble bathrooms. Bedrooms can be small but the mirrored ceilings mean most guests are too busy looking up at themselves to notice. The hotel's piano bar is straight out of *Casablanca*.

Hotel services *Air-conditioning. Babysitting. Bar. Conference facilities (50). Currency exchange. Dry-cleaning. Fax. Laundry. Lift. Payphone. Restaurant. Safe. TV room.* **Room services** *Air-conditioning. Dataport. Hairdryer. Minibar. Phone. Radio. Room service (24hr). Safe. Telephone. TV (satellite).*

Mid-range

Casa Howard

Via Capo le Case 18/via Sistina 149 (06 6992 4555/ fax 06 6794 6444/www.casahoward.com). Metro Spagna or Barberini/bus 52, 53, 61, 62, 63, 71, 80, 95, 116, 117, 119, 175, 492, 630. **Rates** €120-€160 single; €160-€190 double; breakfast €10. **Credit** MC, V. **Map** p335 1C.

Casa Howard ('Howard's End') is a beautifully decorated *residenza* near piazza di Spagna. In January 2003 Casa Howard Part II opened with five more rooms just round the corner. All rooms have been individually designed with a strong emphasis on

HOTEL NAPOLEON
★★★★

The Quietest, in the heart of the Eternal City

As a result of its distinctive structure, the Hotel Napoleon can boast a tranquillity perhaps unmatched in the historical centre. Indeed all the rooms look out onto large sunny courtyards from which it is impossible to hear any of the irritating sounds of the city.

The Friendly Atmosphere

The Hotel Napoleon, run for 40 years by the Cioce-Duranti family, will welcome you in a friendly atmosphere, with a kind and attentive staff, together with the style and the glamour of a 4 star Hotel: the elegant lounges, rich with antiques, the intimate bar and the small restaurant.

The Napoleon's cosy Bar

The right place to start your Roman evening with a good cocktail well prepared by Giacomino (James)

Piazza Vittorio Emanuele II, 105 - 00185 Roma
Tel. 064467264 - Fax 064467282
email: infobook@napoleon.it
http://www.napoleon.it

Don your kimono and flip-flop to the Turkish bath at **Casa Howard**. *See p43.*

quality. Whether you're in the exotic Chinese room or the more serious blue room, beds have been specially made and furniture designed by Ilaria Miani. All of the new (and slightly more expensive) rooms in via Sistina have en suite bathrooms; in via Capo le Case, you may have to go along the hall to your (private) bathroom. Either way, kimonos and slippers are provided so you can flip-flop to the Turkish bath. If you so require, a variety of services can be arranged on request, from hairdressing to massages. **Hotel services** *Air-conditioning. Courtesy phone. Dry-cleaning. Fax. Laundry and ironing service. Lifts. Non-smoking rooms. Safe. Turkish bath (extra charge).* **Room services** *Air-conditioning. Dataport. Hairdryer. PC with high-speed internet connection (Via Sistina only). TV (satellite).*

Locarno

Via della Penna 22 (06 361 0841/fax 06 321 5249/ www.hotellocarno.com). Metro Flaminio/bus 628, 926. **Rates** €120 single; €190-€200 double; €310 double deluxe; suites from €510. **Credit** AmEx, DC, MC, V. **Map** p332 2A.

The Locarno was founded in 1925 and the lobby still looks like an Agatha Christie film. It retains some original details: a Tiffany lamp, a grandfather clock, a wrought-iron cage lift. The lounge has a fire in winter, and there's a pretty patio with fountain. The lovely suites in the new wing across the patio make rooms in the main body of the hotel look decidedly dowdy. Regulars include director Peter Greenaway. **Hotel services** *Air-conditioning. Bar. Bicycles. Disabled room. Laundry. Lifts. Multilingual staff. Parking (extra charge). Safe. Non-smoking rooms (deluxe only).* **Room services** *Fax point. Hairdryer. Minibar. PC plug and modem. Radio. Safe. Telephone. TV (satellite).*

Marcus

Via del Clementino 94 (06 6830 0320/fax 06 6830 0312/www.hotelmarcus.com). Bus 81, 117, 119, 224, 628, 913, 926. **Rates** €65-€100 single; €83-€154 double; €120-€190 triple; €135-€206 quad. **Credit** AmEx, MC, V. **Map** p333 1A.

Descend the Spanish Steps and keep on walking to get to the peaceful and family-operated Marcus, which is in the heart of Rome but doesn't charge top-of-the-range prices. It's a bit shabby, with the decor an old-fashioned mix of bric-a-brac and ill-matched furniture. Offers cut-price entrance to a nearby gym. **Hotel services** *Air-conditioning. Bar. Fax. Lifts. Non-smoking rooms. Safe.* **Room services** *Air-conditioning (extra charge). Hairdryer. Minibar. Room service. Safe. Telephone. TV (satellite).*

The Pantheon & Piazza Navona

Expensive

Raphael

Largo Febo 2 (06 682 831/fax 06 687 8993/ www.raphaelhotel.com). Bus 30, 70, 81, 87, 116,

492, 628. **Rates** €260-€290 single; €390-€560 double; suites from €390; breakfast €28. **Credit** AmEx, DC, MC, V. **Map** p333 2A.

This ivy-draped hotel in a delightful little piazza is much more eccentric than its exterior suggests. The reception (being renovated as we go to press) is dotted with an eclectic mix of antiques including Picasso ceramics and an antique sleigh. Rooms are enthusiastically decorated in rich colours, some with marble pillars (convincing enough until you give them a knock). Close to the Senate, the Raphael has long been popular with politicians; PM Silvio Berlusconi has an apartment just round the corner. **Hotel services** *Air-conditioning. Babysitting. Bars. Conference facilities (30). Currency exchange. Dry-cleaning. Fax. Gym. Laundry. Lifts. Non-smoking rooms. Restaurants. Roof terrace. Safe. Sauna.* **Room services** *Air-conditioning. Dataport. Hairdryer. Minibar. Radio. Room service. Safe. Telephone. TV (satellite/pay).*

Sole al Pantheon

Piazza della Rotonda 63 (06 678 0441/fax 06 6994 0689/www.hotelsolealpantheon.com). Bus 30, 40, 46, 62, 63, 64, 70, 81, 87, 492, 628, 630, 780, 916/tram 8. **Rates** €220 single; €250 double as single; €340 double; €420 junior suite. **Credit** AmEx, DC, MC, V. **Map** p333 2A.

Dating back to the 15th century, the Sole is – management will tell you – the oldest hotel in Europe. Former guests range from Renaissance poet Ariosto to existentialist Jean-Paul Sartre. Rooms have a fresh feel, with tiles and pretty frescos. Ask for one of the rooms at the front for superb views over the Pantheon; if they're not available, console yourself by seeking out the glorious interior courtyard where breakfast is served in the warmer months. **Hotel services** *Air-conditioning. Babysitting. Bar. Business services. Conference facilities (10). Currency exchange. Dry-cleaning. Fax. Laundry. Lifts.* **Room services** *Air-conditioning. Hairdryer. Jacuzzi (most rooms). Iron. Minibar. Radio. Room service. Safe. Telephone. TV (satellite/pay).*

Mid-range

Due Torri

Vicolo del Leonetto 23/25 (06 6880 6956/06 687 6983/fax 06 686 5442/www.hotelduetorriroma.com). Bus 30, 70, 81, 87, 116, 492, 628. **Rates** €108-€114 single; €176-€185 double; €232-€270 suite for 3-4. **Credit** AmEx, DC, MC, V. **Map** p333 2A.

Well hidden among the labyrinth of cobbled streets in the *centro storico*, the Due Torri has a warm, welcoming atmosphere and a chequered past: once a Vatican-owned residence for cardinals, it was reincarnated as a brothel. The hotel was renovated in 2002: the red upholstery in the reception area was chosen to reflect both sides of its colourful history. The 26 rooms are cosy rather than spacious, and traditionally furnished with dark wooden furniture. If you're lucky or persistent, you might get one of the rooms with private terrace overlooking the rooftops.

Cool yet distinctive, the family-run **Lancelot**. *See p53.*

Hotel services *Air-conditioning. Bar. Currency exchange. Fax. Laundry. Lifts. Parking. TV room.* **Room services** *Air-conditioning. Hairdryer. Minibar. Radio. Room service. Safe. Telephone. TV (satellite).*

Navona
Via dei Sediari 8 (06 686 4203/fax 06 6880 3802/ www.hotelnavona.com). Bus 30, 70, 81, 87, 116, 492, 628. **Rates** €86 single; €110-€125 double; €160 triple. **Credit** MC, V. **Map** p333 2A.
Recently renovated, this hotel has a welcoming, communal atmosphere: a good choice for lone travellers. It's on the second floor of a palazzo, built on the site of the ancient baths of Agrippa, with the ground floor dating back to AD 1. The hotel's staff and Australian owners are friendly and helpful.
Hotel services *Air-conditioning. Car parking facilities. Currency exchange. Fax. Multilingual staff. Non-smoking rooms. Safe.* **Room services** *Air-conditioning. Hairdryer (on request).*

Residenza Zanardelli
Via G Zanardelli 7 (06 6821 1392/fax 06 6880 3802/www.hotelnavona.com). Bus 70, 87, 116, 204, 280. **Rates** €120-€140 double; €180 triple. **Credit** MC, V. **Map** p333 1B.
A quiet, pleasant place, the Zanardelli is just around the corner from piazza Navona and not far from St Peter's. With only seven rooms, it is a little more up-market and intimate than its sister hotel, the Navona (*see above*).
Hotel services *Air-conditioning. Fax. Lifts. Non-smoking rooms. Safe. TV room.* **Room services** *Air-conditioning. Hairdryer. Iron. Telephone. TV (satellite).*

Budget

Abruzzi
Piazza della Rotonda 69 (06 679 2021/www. hotelabruzzi.it). Bus 30, 40, 46, 62, 63, 64, 70, 81, 87, 492, 628, 630, 780, 916/tram 8. **Rates** €55-€75 single without bath; €125-€150 single; €90-€115 double without bath; €175-€195 double. **No credit cards. Map** p333 2A.
The splendid location is really this hotel's only selling point: many rooms have breathtaking views of the Pantheon, but you'd be hard-pressed to find anything more basic. At the time of writing some rooms were being equipped with bathrooms, air-conditioning, minibar, television and phone. Otherwise, it's a sink in the corner and a communal bathroom. The decor has a distinct 1970s Soviet bloc feel (lots of brown), the tiny entrance is grim and service is abrupt – at least the bedrooms are reasonably sized.
Hotel services Multilingual staff. Safe. **Room services** *(in some rooms) Air-conditioning (€10 extra). Telephone. Television.*

Mimosa
Via di Santa Chiara 61 (06 6880 1753/fax 06 683 3557/www.hotelmimosa.net). Bus 30, 40, 46, 62, 63, 64, 70, 81, 87, 492, 628, 630, 780, 916/tram 8. **Rates** €46-€77 single without bath; €67-€88 single; €60-€93 double without bath; €75-€108 double; breakfast included (high season only). **No credit cards. Map** p333 2A.
In medieval times this very central palazzo housed the Cavalieri della Croce, an order of crusading knights (for anyone wanting to go AWOL there was

a handy escape tunnel to the Tiber), and it's still like a barracks. Some rooms have been redecorated, but there's a hotchpotch of lino in the dark corridors. Breakfast is only included in high season; out of season don some dark glasses and mingle with the movers and shakers in the renowned Caffè Sant'Eustachio (*see p202*) down the road.
Hotel services *Fax. Non-smoking rooms. Telephone.* **Room services** *Telephone (2 rooms).*

The Ghetto & Campo de' Fiori

Mid-range

Teatro di Pompeo

Largo del Pallaro 8 (06 687 2812/06 6830 0170/fax 06 6880 5531/hotel.teatrodipompeo@tiscalinet.it). Bus 46, 62, 64, 916. **Rates** €130-€150 double as single; €170-€190 double; €200-€220 triple; €275 quad. **Credit** AmEx, DC, MC, V. **Map** p333 2A.

A long-established hotel near campo de' Fiori, the Teatro di Pompeo can claim, at least in part, to be the oldest hotel in Rome. Breakfast is served in what was a section of the first-century BC Teatro di Pompeo. The decor of the bar and 13 bedrooms is unfussy, verging on plain.
Hotel services *Air-conditioning. Bar. Fax. Laundry. Lift. Non-smoking rooms. Payphone. TV room.* **Room services** *Air-conditioning. Hairdryer. Minibar. Radio. Room service. Safe. Telephone. TV (satellite).*

Budget

Della Lunetta

Piazza del Paradiso 68 (06 686 1080/06 687 7630/ fax 06 689 2028). Bus 46, 62, 64, 916. **Rates** €55 single without bath; €65 single; €85 double without bath; €110 double. **Credit** MC, V. **Map** p333 2B.

B&B deluxe

Relatively new to the Rome accommodation scene, the B&B is flourishing, with some 1,000 now registered. From spare bedrooms in family flats in the sticks (check the location before booking) to rooms in aristocratic *palazzi*, there's a huge range to choose from for anyone seeking to avoid anonymous hotel rooms. In fact, some of Rome's most delightful accommodation – and best deals – are found at the top end of the B&B market.

Casa Banzo, tucked behind campo de' Fiori on the first floor of a pale blue palazzo complete with wide stone staircases and a small central courtyard, has three cool, light and reasonably large rooms. They are scattered about the palazzo's labyrinthine, statue-filled stairways and have been recently redecorated; all have private bathrooms. Breakfast is in the family dining room beneath frescos and coffered wooden ceilings.

The **Bed & Breakfast Italia** agency has 250 Roman options on their books, including luxury accommodation in *palazzi* – awarded four 'crowns' by the agency's vetters. One of the first to join the agency was a 60-something countess living in via degli Avignonesi, between Trevi Fountain (*see p78*) and the Palazzo Barberini gallery (*see p79*). The charming apartment is on the top two floors of a 19th-century palazzo; the decor is like a Visconti movie-set and the guest bedroom is large and bright with a fireplace; in summer breakfast is served on the terrace. The Naples-based **My Home Your Home**

agency (*see also p55* **Self-catering**) has extended operations to Rome, creating more of its distinctive accommodation options. In largo dei Chiavari, near campo de' Fiori (*see p78*), two fifth-floor rooms with a communal kitchen give out on to a terrace with a 360° view over Rome's glorious rooftops. On the river-side road near piazza del Popolo, the Domus Tiber offers three rooms in 'ethnic-eclectic' style with a kitchen and river views.

Bed and Breakfast Italia

Corso Vittorio Emanuele 284 (06 687 8618/ fax 06 687 8619/www.bbitalia.it). Bus 40, 46, 62, 64, 916. **Rates** (per person per night, min 2 nights) *2 crowns* €27.90-€37.70 single, €22.20-€30.50 double, €20.10-€28.40 triple; *3 crowns* €40.80-€50.60 single, €35.60-€43.40 double, €33.60-€40.80 triple; *4 crowns* €56.30-€66.60 single, €48.60-€57.80 double, €43.30-€51.10 triple. **Credit** MC, V. **Map** p336 1B.

Casa Banzo

Piazza Monte di Pietà 30 (06 683 3909/fax 06 686 4575/elptomas@tin.it). Bus 23, 63, 116, 280, 630, H/tram 8. **Rates** €100-€115 double. **Credit** (2.5% surcharge) MC, V. **Map** p336 1B.

My Home, Your Home

Lungotevere dei Mellini 35 (06 9761 3280/ www.myhomeyourhome.it). Bus 30, 34, 49, 70, 81, 87, 186, 492. **Rates** (for luxury B&B) €130-€200 double. **Credit** MC, V. **Map** p332 2C.

Built as it is on the foundations of the ancient Teatro di Pompeo, you could be forgiven for hoping that the Lunetta would live up to its former glory. But it has fallen into neglect since its last renovation 40 years ago: rooms are best described as functional. However, it's slap bang between campo de' Fiori and piazza Navona, and about as cheap as it gets. The hotel doesn't do breakfast, but the area is full of bars for a delicious cappuccino and *cornetto*.

Hotel services *Fax. Safe. TV room.* **Room services** *Telephone.*

Pomezia

Via dei Chiavari 13 (06 686 1371/fax 06 686 1371/ www.hotelpomezia.com). Bus 46, 62, 64, 916. **Rates** €70-€105 single; €80-€125 double; €140 triple. **Credit** AmEx, MC, V. **Map** p333 2A.

Downstairs, the family-run Pomezia's reception and breakfast room have been refurbished and a large disabled room added. Work was due to continue upstairs, with the addition of a lift and bathrooms for rooms without them. Bedrooms are small and very basic, but clean; staff are friendly and helpful.

Hotel services *Bar. Currency exchange. Disabled room. Dry-cleaning. Fax. Laundry. Multilingual staff.* **Room services** *Room service. Telephone.*

Smeraldo

Vicolo dei Chiodaroli 9 (06 687 5929/06 689 2121/ fax 06 6880 5495/www.hotelsmeraldoroma.com). Bus 46, 62, 64, 916. **Rates** €70-€90 single; €90-€120 double; breakfast €7. **Credit** AmEx, DC, MC, V. **Map** p333 2A.

Recently refurbished, the decor isn't particularly adventurous: the smallish rooms are identical and have rather a hotel-chain feel. Nevertheless all mod cons are provided, it's bang next to campo de' Fiori, well connected with the whole city and its terrace offers a pretty view across Rome's rooftops.

Hotel services *Air-conditioning. Bar. Currency exchange. Disabled room. English-speaking staff. Fax. Payphone. Roof terrace. Safe. TV room.* **Room services** *Air-conditioning. Hairdryer. Room service. Telephone. TV (satellite).*

Trastevere

See p42 **Trastevere**.

The Aventine

Mid-range

Villa San Pio, Sant'Anselmo & Aventino

Piazza Sant'Anselmo 2 (06 574 5231/fax 06 578 3604/www.aventinohotels.com). Metro Circo Massimo/bus 60, 75, 81, 118, 160, 175, 628, 673, 715. **Rates** (vary according to hotel) €83-€130 single; €114-€197 double; €130-€217 triple; €233 quad. **Credit** AmEx, DC, MC, V. **Map** p337 1A.

The three hotels in this group are all within a stone's throw of one another in a leafy residential area. The

Quiet pastels at **Sant'Anna**. *See p55.*

Villa San Pio consists of three separate buildings that share the same pretty gardens and an airy breakfast room; it has recently been refurbished, giving it a light feel and making it a very comfortable and pleasant place to stay. Ask for a room with a terrace for views either of the surrounding greenery or towards Monte Testaccio (*see p125*) with Fascist EUR (*see p159*) looming beyond. Its sister hotels the Sant'Anselmo and Aventino are less manicured and have yet to be refurbished. The management is loath to let you specify which hotel you'd like to stay in; but, where possible, go all out for the Villa San Pio.

Hotel services *Air-conditioning. Babysitting. Bar. Currency exchange. Disabled facilities. Fax. Garden. Laundry. Lifts. Parking. Safe.* **Room services** *Air-conditioning (not Sant'Anselmo). Hairdryer. Jacuzzi. Minibar. Room service. Telephone. TV (satellite).*

The Celio

Expensive

Celio

Via Santi Quattro 35C (06 7049 5333/fax 06 709 6377/www.hotelcelio.com). Metro Colosseo/bus 60, 75, 81, 85, 87, 117, 175, 673, 810, 850/tram 3. **Rates** €100-€230 single; €150-€310 double; €290-€490 ambassador suite; €380-€650 penthouse suite. **Credit** AmEx, DC, MC, V. **Map** p338 2B.

Down a quiet residential street by the Colosseum, the Celio's quite ordinary exterior hides a riot of madcap colours and styles. Mosaic floors, large sunray mirrors and sea scenes painted on the walls give the hotel an offbeat yet homely feel. Many of the rooms have frescoed details, erring on the kitsch. With just 19 rooms, it's intimate and welcoming. **Hotel services** *Air-conditioning. Babysitting. Currency exchange. Disabled room (though steps make access difficult). Dry-cleaning. Fax. Laundry. Non-smoking rooms. Parking (extra charge). TV room.* **Room services** *Air-conditioning. Dataport. Hairdryer. Minibar. Radio. Room service. Safe. Telephone. TV (satellite/pay). VCR (large selection of English and Italian films).*

Moderate

Lancelot

Via Capo d'Africa 47 (06 7045 0615/fax 06 7045 0640/www.lancelothotel.com). Metro Colosseo/bus 60, 75, 81, 85, 87, 117, 175, 673, 810, 850/tram 3. **Rates** €93 single; €145 double; €165 triple. **Credit** AmEx, DC, MC, V. **Map** p338 2B.

This beautifully kept and attractive family-run hotel has a cool yet distinctive Mediterranean feel, with elegant mixes of linen, wood and tiles used for the bedrooms, some of which have terraces looking towards the Palatine and the Colosseum. The reception has been given a personal feel with cool tiled floors and antique furniture, along with some unusual *objets*. Dinner is provided on advance request at an extra cost of €22 (wine and coffee included). **Hotel services** *Air-conditioning. Babysitting. Currency exchange. Dry-cleaning. English-speaking staff. Fax. Laundry. Lifts. Non-smoking rooms. Parking (on request). Restaurant. Disabled rooms (4). Safe. TV room.* **Room services** *Air-conditioning. Dataport. Hairdryer. Telephone. TV (satellite).*

Monti & Esquilino

Deluxe

Es Hotel

Via F Turati 171 (06 444 841/fax 06 4434 1396/www.eshotel.it). Metro Termini/bus 70, 71, 105/tram 5, 14. **Rates** (plus 10% tax) €380 double as single; €520 double; €826 junior suite; €955-€2,583 suite; breakfast €28. **Credit** AmEx, DC, MC, V. **Map** p338 1A.

A newcomer on Rome's luxury hotel scene, Es is a 'concept' hotel that avoids chandeliers, velvet and flounces like the plague. Seriously minimalist, it ain't Rome… but certainly is a very clear style statement. In each room the bed is on a low platform with bathroom incorporated behind, divided from the rest of the room by a glass screen. TVs are ultra-thin plasma screens, with DVD and internet connections. The rooftop bar has a great line in cocktails (*see p207*). **Hotel services** *Bar. Babysitting. Business centre. Car rental. Conference facilities (500). Gym. Laundry. Lifts. Multilingual staff. Non-smoking rooms. Parking. Restaurants. Rooftop swimming pool and terrace. Room service (24hr). Disabled rooms. Secretarial services.* **Room services** *Air-conditioning. DVD. Hairdryer. High-speed internet connection. Radio. Safe. Telephone. TV (satellite).*

St Regis Grand

Via VE Orlando 3 (06 47 091/reservations 06 4708 2740/2799/fax 06 474 7307/www.stregis.com/ GrandRome). Metro Repubblica/bus 40, 60, 61, 62, 64, 84, 86, 90, 170, 175, 492, 910, H. **Rates** (plus 10% tax) €685-€965 double as single or double; €1,440 junior suite; €2,275 suite; breakfast €29.70-€40.50. **Credit** AmEx, DC, MC, V. **Map** p335 1B.

Some 1,900 years after the Romans first stamped their mark on Europe, a new Caesar came to Rome: Caesar Ritz, the father of luxury. Ritz built the biggest and best hotel around: not only did it have working toilets, but each room had the previously unheard-of luxury of three electric lightbulbs. In 1999 the St Regis underwent a $35-million makeover to restore it to its former glory. Today the hotel's original chandeliers hang in massive reception rooms with acres of marble decorated in opulent gold, beige and red. Rooms have been individually designed using rich fabrics, and are filled with silk-covered Empire and Regency-style furnishings. **Hotel services** *Air-conditioning. Babysitting. Bar. Business services. Butler service. Concierge. Conference facilities (400). Currency exchange. Dry-cleaning. Fax. Gym. Laundry. Lifts. Limousine. Non-smoking rooms. Parking. Restaurants. Disabled rooms. Safe. Sauna. Wine cellar.* **Room services** *Air-conditioning. Dataport. Hairdryer. Minibar. Radio. Room service (24hr). Safe. Telephone. TV (satellite). VCR.*

Expensive

Bailey's

Via Flavia 39 (06 4202 0486/fax 06 4202 0170/www.hotelbailey.com). Bus 16, 36, 38, 60, 61, 62, 84, 86, 90, 92, 217, 360, 910. **Rates** €165-€181 single; €199-€284 double; €255-€352 triple; €372-€517 family room. **Credit** AmEx, DC, MC, V. **Map** p335 1A.

Bailey's opened in March 2001 in a charming 19th-century townhouse in the somewhat uninspiring area by via XX Settembre. But its stucco ceilings and the generous lashings of marble in its 29 rooms – some of which are very stripy – seem to have made it very popular.

Hotel services *Air-conditioning. Babysitting. Bar. Currency exchange. Disabled rooms. Dry-cleaning. Fax. Laundry. Lifts. Non-smoking rooms. Parking (extra charge). Payphone. Safe. TV room.* Room services *Air-conditioning. Dataport/modem. Fax point. Hairdryer. Minibar. Radio. Room service. Safe. Telephone. TV (satellite).*

Mid-range

Nerva

Via Tor de' Conti 3 (06 678 1835/fax 06 6992 2204/www.hotelnerva.com). Bus 60, 75, 84, 85, 87, 117, 175, 810, 850. Rates €90-€160 single; €120-€220 double; €150-€350 suite. Credit AmEx, DC, MC, V. Map p338 1C.

The family-run Nerva is right next to the Forum but there's not a view in sight… the hotel faces a wall. (Not just any wall: this wall formed part of the ancient Forum of Nerva, *see p75*). Nerva is very well-located, however, and the rooms have been nicely refurbished without losing their original features. The staff and proprietors are friendly.

Hotel services *Air-conditioning. Bar. Currency exchange. Laundry. Lift. Non-smoking rooms. Parking (extra charge). Disabled rooms. Safe. TV room.* Room services *Air-conditioning. Dataport. Hairdryer. Minibar. Safe. Telephone. Trouser-press. TV (satellite).*

Budget

Fawlty Towers

Via Magenta 39 (06 445 0374/4802/fax 06 4938 2878/www.fawltytowers.org). Metro Termini/bus 16, 36, 38, 40, 64, 75, 84, 86, 90, 92, 105, 170, 175, 217, 310, 360, 492, 649, 714, 910, H. Rates €18-€23 per person in dorm with shower-room; €44 single without bath; €51 single with shower; €62 double without bath; €67 double with shower; €77 double; €82-€90 triple. No credit cards. Map 335 1A.

This very popular 15-room hostel/hotel is close to Termini station and happily there's no sign of Basil. It's great value, with a relaxed communal atmosphere, and far more hotel services than you'd expect in this price range (and with this name). Book well in advance. The roof terrace provides a place to rest the feet after a hard day's sightseeing.

Hotel services *Common room with fridge. Internet access. English-speaking staff. Microwave. Roof terrace. TV (satellite). Walking tours.*

YWCA

Via Cesare Balbo 4 (06 488 0460/3917/fax 06 487 1028). Metro Cavour/bus 16, 70, 71, 75, 84, 360, 649, 714. Rates €37 single without bath; €47 single; €62 double without bath; €74 double; €26 per person triple/quad. No credit cards. Map p335 2B.

Exactly what it says on the tin: bedrooms for women with one to four beds in each and a midnight curfew. A little too close to Termini station for comfort, but women travelling alone may feel safer here than in mixed hostels/*pensioni*. You can get lunch for €11.

The Vatican & Prati

Expensive

Hotel dei Mellini

Via Muzio Clementi 81 (06 324 771/fax 06 3247 7801/www.hotelmellini.com). Bus 30, 34, 49, 70, 87, 224, 280, 492, 913, 926, 990. Rates €280 single; €320-€350 double; €420 junior suite; €520 Mellini suite. Credit AmEx, DC, MC, V. Map p332 2B.

The Hotel dei Mellini has 80 spacious rooms and suites elegantly decorated with neutral colours and occasional knick-knacks. Desks are provided for those who can't escape from duty, a sunny roof terrace for those who can. Children up to 12 years old sleep in their parents' room for free and complementary baby cribs are available.

Hotel services *Bar. Concierge service (24hr). Currency exchange. Disabled rooms. Dry-cleaning/ironing service. Non-smoking rooms. Parking (nearby). PC and mobile phone rental. Room service. Roof terrace.* Room services *Air-conditioning. Fax/modem lines. Hairdryer. Safe. Telephone. TV (satellite).*

Mid-range

Bramante

Vicolo delle Palline 24 (06 6880 6426/fax 06 687 9881/www.hotelbramante.com). Bus 23, 34, 40, 62, 280. Rates €110-€145 single; €160-€200 double; €216-€235 double deluxe; €190-€220 triple. Credit AmEx, DC, MC, V. Map p333 1C.

The Bramante is hidden down a cobbled street a couple of hundred metres from St Peter's. Home to 16th-century architect Domenico Fontana, it became an inn in 1873; it has since lost the horses and ale-swilling occupants and gained a large, pleasant reception and a little patio for the summer. The 16 rooms of varying sizes – some powder blue, others lemon – are simple yet elegant; most have high-beamed ceilings, some have wrought-iron beds.

Hotel services *Air-conditioning. Babysitting. Bar. Currency exchange. Dry-cleaning. Fax. Laundry. Non-smoking rooms. Payphone. Parking. Safe. TV room.* Room services *Air-conditioning. Dataport. Fax point. Hairdryer. Iron. Minibar. Telephone. TV (satellite).*

Franklin

Via Rodi 29 (06 3903 0165/fax 06 3975 1652/www.franklin.it). Metro Ottaviano/bus 23, 70. Rates €120-€160 single; €165-€230 double; €185-€260 triple. Credit AmEx, DC, MC, V. Map off p332 1C.

A bit out on a limb beyond the Vatican, the Franklin opened at the end of 2002 and so has yet to make its mark. There's a polished modern feel, and rooms are light and airy, if not particularly spacious. Every room has a state-of-the-art CD player, and guests can enjoy the hotel's extensive collection of vinyl LPs in the reception. The entire hotel is non-smoking.

Hotel services *Air-conditioning. Babysitting. Bar. Bicycle rental. Computer rental. Currency exchange.*

Bright, clean and near the Vatican: **Colors Hotel & Hostel**.

Laundry. Lift. Multilingual staff. No-smoking. Parking. Restaurant. Room service. Safe. **Room services** *CD player. Dataport connection/modem. Hairdryer. Minibar. Disabled rooms. Safe. Telephone. TV (satellite).*

Sant'Anna

Borgo Pio 133-4 (06 6880 1602/fax 06 6830 8717/ www.hotelsantanna.com). Bus 23, 34, 40, 62, 280. **Rates** €110-€130 single; €150-€195 double; €190-€205 triple. **Credit** AmEx, DC, MC, V. **Map** p333 1C.
A stone's throw from the Vatican wall, the Sant'Anna is a quiet hotel with 20 (fairly dated) rooms decorated in pastel shades. In summer you can have drinks in the small courtyard at the back; in winter, you can sip your cocktail under the stern gaze of Cardinal Borromeo in the reception.
Hotel services *Air-conditioning. Babysitting. Currency exchange. Disabled room. Fax. Laundry. Lift.* **Room services** *Air-conditioning. Fax point. Hairdryer. Minibar. PC point. Radio. Safe. Telephone.*

Budget

Colors Hotel & Hostel

Via Boezio 31 (06 687 4030/fax 06 686 7947/ www.colorshotel.com). Metro Ottaviano/bus 23, 34, 49, 492, 990. **Rates** €20 per person in dorm; €25 per person in dorm with shower (shared toilet); €73 double without bath; €83 double with shower (shared toilet); €89 double; €83 triple without bath; €89 triple with shower (shared toilet); €104 triple. **No credit cards. Map** p332 2C.
A short walk from St Peter's and the Vatican museums, Colors has bright, clean dorm and hotel accommodation, plus self-catering facilities. It's run by the ever-reliable Enjoy Rome agency (*see p315*); staff are multilingual and very helpful.
Hotel services *Kitchen. Internet access. Laundry facilities. Lounge. Terrace.*

The Suburbs

Budget

Ostello della Gioventù Foro Italico

Via delle Olimpiadi 61 (06 323 6267/fax 06 324 2613/www.ostellionline.org). Bus 32, 69, 224, 280. **Rates** €16 bed & breakfast; meals €8. **No credit cards. Map** p331
There are over 300 dormitory beds at this neo-brutalist building which is located handily near the Stadio Olimpico (*see chapter* **Sport**) if you're here for a football match, but a bit of a trek from the centre. The IYHF's main Rome hostel (standard category), it's open to members only, though you can join on the spot. Well adapted for wheelchairs, there's a garden, restaurant and bar too.

Self-catering

Consider renting an apartment if you're staying for more than a few days, particularly if there are more than two of you. Enjoy Rome (*see p315*) can find a flat for you, as can the IDEC agency (www.flatinrome.com) and My Home Your Home (06 687 6373/myhomeyourhome@ virgilio.it), while the London-based A Place in Rome (020 8543 2283/www.aplaceinrome.com) offers three delightful apartments in the heart of the *centro storico*.
The Landmark Trust (01628 825925/fax 01628 825417/www.landmarktrust.co.uk), which deals mostly with rented accommodation in the UK, rents an apartment in the Keats-Shelley House (*see p93*) that sleeps up to four. It costs £1,733 a week in high season, rather less in winter, but is full off lovely details including the original painted wooden ceilings.

Sightseeing

Features

Introduction

Take time to relax: you're in the world's most beautiful city.

Rome can seem like one big movie set. For a start, there are all those places that you'll recognise from *Roman Holiday*, *La dolce vita* – even *Gladiator*. Then you turn a corner and find yourself in the midst of bored-looking stars, rails of costumes, traffic chaos caused by on-set catering trucks and a man with a clapper board. No city in the world is as photogenic as Rome, no other city has such glamorous appeal.

It's also true that few cities in the world are as noisy, or as chaotic, or as much fun… or as exhausting. So before plunging into it, take an hour or two just to acclimatise yourself: sit in a café and watch the Roman world go by. It's going to take serious training to adopt Roman habits… so pace yourself. It's no easy job getting up with the lark, being immaculately dressed and made up from the moment you step out of the front door, and keeping going all morning on nothing more than a succession of half-inch-deep black espressos. And it takes a true expert to still look immaculate when *aperitivo* time rolls round at seven, dinner at nine and assorted social goings-on into the small hours.

To the uninitiated, *romani* give the impression that looking gorgeous and spending as much time as possible on their *telefonini* is the be-all and end-all of their existence. But they are also feverishly attached to their city, an attachment that recent city councils have done much to enhance. They are rightly proud of their recent steps forward in preserving their *patrimonio storico*: many historic buildings have been painstakingly restored and are illuminated at night to stunning effect; streets and squares have been repaved with traditional *sampietrini*; baroque fountains have been cleaned. Parts of the *centro storico* have been pedestrianised, there are clean green electric buses, and there's even a series of efficient tourist information kiosks (*see p315* **PIT**).

Despite euro-fuelled inflation, living costs in Rome still compare favourably with other European capitals. Hotels are expensive, local transport costs comparatively cheap, and eating out still an affordable pleasure.

ANCIENT SITES

The official heart of the ancient city, and the area with the greatest density of remains, lies between the Capitoline, Palatine, Esquiline and Quirinale hills. Located here are the Colosseum, the Roman Forum and ancient Rome's most desirable residential area, the Palatine, where – if ancient historians are to be believed – the sexual excesses of emperors and politicians were matched only by the passion with which they plotted against and poisoned one another.

CHURCHES

Central Rome has over 400 churches – excessive, perhaps, even for the headquarters of the Catholic Church. Across the centuries, popes, princes and aristocrats commissioned artists and architects to build, rebuild, adorn, fresco and paint their preferred places of worship. Motives were not wholly pious. For many it was a cynical means of assuring a place in heaven, securing temporal power, increasing prestige, or a combination of all three. Whatever the reasons, the results of all this munificence now form some of Rome's most spectacular sights.

Churches are places of worship. Though only the Vatican imposes its dress code strictly (both in St Peter's and the Vatican Museums), respect is appreciated and very short skirts or shorts are frowned upon. Many churches ask tourists to refrain from visiting during services; if you are admitted, you will be expected not to take photos, talk loudly or

Monday blues

Your long-awaited long weekend in Rome may be a let-down if you don't allow for Monday. Food shops are open on Monday mornings, but few other stores pull up their shutters until after lunch; hairdressers take the day off. Many museums – including such major sights as the Musei Capitolini (*see p62*) and the Galleria Borghese (*see p85*) – display the dreaded *lunedì chiuso* (closed Monday) sign.

So what *can* you do in Rome before you catch your Monday afternoon plane?

Well, for a start it's a great day for the Vatican. **St Peter's** – like all Rome's churches – is open on Mondays; so are **Musei Vaticani** (*see p144*). Two exceptions to the gallery-closing rule are the privately owned **Galleria Doria Pamphili**

wander around. A supply of coins for the meters to light up the most interesting art works is always handy.

MUSEUMS & GALLERIES

The days of closed doors, wildcat strikes and endless restoration programmes seem to be over. Opening hours are refreshingly longer, though still subject to seasonal changes that can vary at the last moment.

Opening hours

Winter hours (*orario invernale* – roughly October-May) are given in the listings in the following chapters. Summer hours (*orario estivo*) can vary significantly, especially at major museums and archaeological sites. Some keep doors open until 11pm. Check for current times at information kiosks (*see p315*). Many museums are closed on Mondays (*see p58* **Monday blues**). *Feriali* on timetables means Monday-Saturday; *festivi* means Sundays and public holidays.

Ticket offices at many museums, galleries and ancient sites stop issuing tickets some time before gates shut; where the gap is more than half an hour, this has been indicated in listings.

Church opening times should be taken as rough guidelines; most open and close an hour later in summer. Whether doors are open depends for many churches on the whims of national service youths assigned to help out; all but the principal churches close around noon, and remain firmly shut until late afternoon.

Tickets

See also p315 **Carry the card**.

Entrance to publicly owned museums and sites is free (*ingresso libero*) to EU citizens (and other countries with bilateral agreements) under 18 and over 65; check tariffs at entrances carefully. Under-25s in full-time education may also be eligible for discounts (*ingresso ridotto*), as may teachers, journalists and various others. Make sure you carry a range of ID.

One week each year, usually in the spring, is designated *Settimana dei beni culturali* (Cultural Heritage Week), when all publicly owned museums and sites – plus a few places rarely open to the public – are open long hours and free of charge (*see p232*).

Booking & cumulative tickets

Booking is mandatory for the Domus Aurea (*see p135*) and the Galleria Borghese (*see p85*), where visitors are admitted at specified times and in small groups, though if you turn up mid-week in low season, there's little chance of being turned away.

Booking is possible for many other sites and museums. Though this is recommended for very popular one-off exhibitions, the difficulties involved in getting through to the reservation phonelines may outweigh any benefits for regular museums and galleries.

In general, tickets must be picked up and paid for at the museum or site half an hour before your appointment. If you book, you'll

(*see p104*) and the **Galleria dell'Accademia di San Luca** (*see p78*). Or pop across to Trastevere to see the frescos at the **Villa Farnesina** (*see p119*). Archaeology is definitely a better bet than art on Mondays, with the **Colosseum** (see p69), the **Domus Aurea** (*see p135*) and various ancient burial places open: try the **Catacombe di Domitilla** (*see p153*), **Catacombe di San Callisto** (*see p153*) and **Catacombe di San Sebastiano** (*see p153*).

Other ideas? The stupendously wonderful/ awful **Vittoriano** (*see p67*) is open daily: admission is free and the view from the top is sensational. The **Pantheon** (*see p105*), being a church, is also open on Mondays. And if you're sitting on the Spanish Steps desperately waiting for the shops to open before you race to the airport, have a Romantic time at the **Keats-Shelley Memorial House** (*see p93*).

Sightseeing

be charged *diritti di prevendita* (pre-sale tax) of up to €2 on top of the ticket price. Note that calls to all numbers beginning 06 3996 are put through to the same private call centre operating for the Sovrintendenza, Rome's heritage board.

Call Centre della Sovrintendenza Archeologica

(06 3996 7700/www.pierreci.it). **Open** *Recorded information* 24hrs daily. *Booking line* 9am-6pm Mon-Fri; 9am-1pm Sat.

This service offers information in English on the following sights: Colosseum (*see p69*), Crypta Balbi (*see p109*), Domus Aurea (*see p135*), Foro Romano (*see p75*), Palatine (*see p71*), Palazzo Altemps (*see p101*), Palazzo Massimo alle Terme (*see p138*), Terme di Caracalla (*see p129*), Terme di Diocleziano (*see p140*), Tomba di Cecilia Metella (*see p154*) and Villa dei Quintili (*see p154*).

It also organises guided tours (*visite didattiche*). The phone booking service (if you want to talk to an operator, don't press 2 for information) offers tickets for individual sights, as well as the following cumulative tickets and services:

€20 – seven-day **Roma Archaeologia Card**. Covers the Colosseum, Palatino, Terme di Caracalla, Palazzo Altemps, Palazzo Massimo alle Terme, Terme di Diocleziano, Crypta Balbi, Tomba di Cecilia Metella, Villa dei Quintili.

€9 – seven-day **Museum Card** for the four Musei Nazionale Romano (MNR): Palazzo Massimo alle Terme, Terme di Diocleziano, Palazzo Altemps, Crypta Balbi.

Tickets booked on the phone can be paid for by credit card (AmEx, MC, V) and picked up at the sights

themselves. Alternatively, you can pick your tickets up (cash only) at the Terme di Diocleziano, via Enrico De Nicola 79, 9am-5pm Tue-Fri, 9am-noon Sat; *see p140*).

Galleria Borghese & Galleria Doria Pamphili

Visitors who have already 'done' the Galleria Borghese (*see p85*) are entitled to a discount if they visit the Galleria Doria Pamphili (*see p104*) within five days. Show your Galleria Borghese ticket and you'll be charged €5.70 instead of €7.30.

Sistema Musei Capitolini

(06 3996 7800/www.museicapitolini.org). **Open** *Recorded information* 24hrs daily. *Bookings & information* 9am-6pm Mon-Fri; 9.30am-1pm Sat.

This call-line handles the Musei Capitolini (*see p62*) and the Centrale Montemartini (*see p159*), dispensing information and organising bookings and guided tours. A cumulative ticket for the two museums, valid for one week and costing €8.26 (€7.75 concessions), can be purchased at the ticket office of either site.

Ticketeria

(06 32 810/fax 06 3265 1329/www.ticketeria.it). **Open** *Recorded information* 24hrs daily. *Bookings* 9am-6pm Mon-Fri; 9am-1pm Sat.

This service provides information on, and handles bookings for, Galleria Borghese (*see p85*), Palazzo Barberini (*see p79*), Galleria Doria Pamphili (*see p104*), Galleria Spada (*see p108*), Palazzo Corsini (*see p117*) and Villa Giulia (*see p86*), as well as the excavations at Ostia Antica (*see p276*), the Museo Nazionale at Tarquinia (*see p280*) and the Etruscan necropolis at Cerveteri (*see p280*). Collect tickets at the individual museums.

Ex-Rip.X

Many of Rome's minor archaeological sites can only be visited with prior permission from what used to be known as *Ripartizione X* but now seems to have become a nameless section within the heritage department.

The tourist with a passion for mini-mithraeums and fragments of faded fresco can arrange access by sending a fax in any major Western language to 06 679 0795. Remember to include a phone number (preferably in Rome) where you can be contacted to fix an appointment. Viewings are usually arranged within four or five days of application. If you haven't been contacted and are concerned, phone 06 6710 3819 during office hours to chase up your request. Price for admission depends on the site requested.

From the Capitoline to the Palatine

The dramatic heart of ancient Rome: fora, the Palatine and the Colosseum.

The most historically significant part of the city, the heart and hub of ancient Rome, lies beyond the Capitoline to the south-east. It was here that Rome was born, in the Foro Romano (Roman Forum) and the Palatino (Palatine), and it's here that you will find the city's best-recognised landmark: the **Colosseum**. Even for the most jaded of tourists, and those who have been to Rome many times, these dramatic, spectacular sights will remind you just why Rome continues to exert its magnetism.

The Capitoline & piazza Venezia

Il Campidoglio – the Capitoline – was, politically speaking, the most important of ancient Rome's seven hills and the site of the two major temples: to Jupiter Capitolinus, symbolic father of the city (whose cult chambers also included shrines to Minerva, goddess of wisdom, and Juno, wife of Jupiter), and to Juno Moneta, 'giver of advice'. The latter, the site of which is now occupied by the church of **Santa Maria in Aracoeli**, housed the sacred Capitoline geese, whose honking raised the alarm when Gauls attacked Rome in 390 BC. (Juno's temple was so well protected by the geese that Rome's first mint was built beside it; from *moneta* comes the word 'money'.)

The gorgeous piazza atop the Campidoglio was designed in the 1530s by Michelangelo for Pope Paul III. It took about 100 years to complete and some of Michelangelo's ideas were modified along the way, but it is still very much as he envisaged it. The best approach is via the great ramp of steps called the *cordonata*, also by Michelangelo, that sweeps up from via del Teatro di Marcello. At the top of the steps are two giant Roman statues of the mythical twins Castor and Pollux, placed here in 1583. The

Marcus Aurelius patrols the Capitoline.

building opposite the top of the steps is the Palazzo Senatorio, Rome's city hall, completed by Giacomo della Porta and Girolamo Rainaldi to a design by Michelangelo. Its bell tower, the Torre Campanaria (open by appointment, 06 3996 7800), offers perhaps the most stunning view in the whole city. To the left is the Palazzo Nuovo and to the right the Palazzo dei Conservatori, together forming the **Musei Capitolini** (Capitoline Museums). For four centuries the piazza's central pedestal supported a magnificent second-century gilded bronze equestrian statue of Emperor Marcus Aurelius, placed here by Michelangelo. The statue there now is a computer-generated copy from 1981, with the original (after years of restoration) behind glass in the Palazzo Nuovo.

Down the hill, to the north of the Campidoglio, piazza Venezia is a dizzying roundabout where six busy roads converge. It emerged as an important focus of business and power in the 15th century when the Venetian Pope Paul II had **Palazzo Venezia** constructed on its western side. Now an art museum, the palace was one of the first Renaissance buildings in Rome. Centuries later Mussolini would make it his headquarters, delivering orations from the balcony overlooking the piazza, where pedestrians were prevented from standing still by security-obsessed guards. To the south of the palazzo stands **San Marco**, a church founded in the fourth century and remodelled for Paul II.

Dominating the square is the glacial **Vittoriano** (aka l'Altare della patria), a piece of nationalistic kitsch that outdoes anything dreamed up by the ancients. This vast pile, entirely out of proportion with anything around it and made of unsuitably dazzling marble brought specially and at great cost from Brescia, was constructed between 1885 and 1911 to honour the first king of united Italy, Vittorio Emanuele II of Savoy. Centred on a colossal equestrian statue of the king (a banquet for 20 was once held in the horse's belly), it is also the home of the Eternal Flame, Italy's memorial to the unknown soldier. Right of the monument are remains of Roman and medieval houses razed to make way for the monstrosity.

Musei Capitolini

Piazza del Campidoglio 1 (06 6710 2071/www. museicapitolini.org). Bus 30, 40, 44, 46, 60, 62, 63, 64, 70, 81, 85, 87, 95, 117, 170, 175, 492, 628, 630, 780, 810, 850. **Open** *9.30am-8pm Tue-Sun; ticket office closes 7pm.* **Admission** *€6.20; €4.13 concessions; €7.45 special exhibitions; see also p59* **Tickets. No credit cards. Map p336 1A.*
Standing on opposite sides of Michelangelo's piazza del Campidoglio and housed in the twin palaces of Palazzo Nuovo and Palazzo dei Conservatori, the

Capitoline Museums are the oldest public museums in the world. The collection they house was initiated in 1471, when Pope Sixtus IV presented the Roman people with a group of classical sculptures. Until the creation of the Vatican Museums (*see p148*), Sixtus' successors continued to enrich the collection with examples of ancient art (mostly sculptures) and, at a later date, some important Renaissance and post-Renaissance paintings. The entire collection was finally opened to the public in 1734, by Pope Clement XII. The museums were overhauled in a massive restoration project that culminated in 2000; many statues remain frustratingly label-less. The most exciting innovation was the opening to the public of an artefact-lined tunnel passing beneath the square, joining the two *palazzi* but also allowing access to the **Tabularium** – ancient Rome's archive – which offers a spectacular view over the Foro Romano (*see p75*). Entrance to the Musei Capitolini is by the **Palazzo dei Conservatori**, on the right as you come up Michelangelo's stairs. The courtyard contains what's left (the rest was made of wood) of a colossal statue of Constantine that originally stood in the Basilica of Maxentius in the Forum (*see p76*).

Upstairs, the huge Sala degli Orazi e Curiazi (Room 1) is home to a statue (1635-40) by Bernini of his patron Urban VIII in which everything about the pope seems to be in motion. There's also a second-century BC gilded bronze Hercules. Room 2 (Sala dei Capitani) has late 16th-century frescos of great moments in ancient Roman history. In Room 3 (Sala dei Trionfi) the first-century BC bronze of a boy removing a thorn from his foot, known as the *Spinario*, is probably an original Greek work. There's also a rare bronze portrait bust from the fourth or third century BC, popularly believed to be of Rome's first consul, Brutus. Room 4 (Sala della Lupa) is home to the much-reproduced *She-Wolf*. This one is a fifth-century BC Etruscan bronze; the suckling twins were added during the Renaissance by, according to tradition, Antonio del Pollaiolo. In Room 5 (Sala delle Oche) is Bernini's touchingly pained-looking *Medusa* and an 18th-century bronze portrait of Michelangelo, believed to have been based on the great master's death mask. Room 6 (Sala delle Aquile) is frescoed with 16th-century Roman scenes amid faux-ancient 'grotesque' decorations. In Room 10 (Sala degli Arazzi) a marvellously well-preserved marble group shows the Emperor Commodus (of *Gladiator* fame) dressing up as Hercules and being adored by two Tritons. Room 11 (Sala di Annibale) still has original, early 16th-century frescos that show Hannibal riding an elephant of which Walt Disney would have been proud.

On the second floor the **Pinacoteca Capitolina** (Capitoline Art Gallery) contains a number of significant works. The most striking is Caravaggio's *St John the Baptist* (1596; in the Sala di Santa Petronilla), who has nothing even remotely saintly about him, but don't let it overshadow paintings by other greats: there's the weepiest of Penitent Magdalenes (c1598) by Tintoretto, a *Rape of Europa*

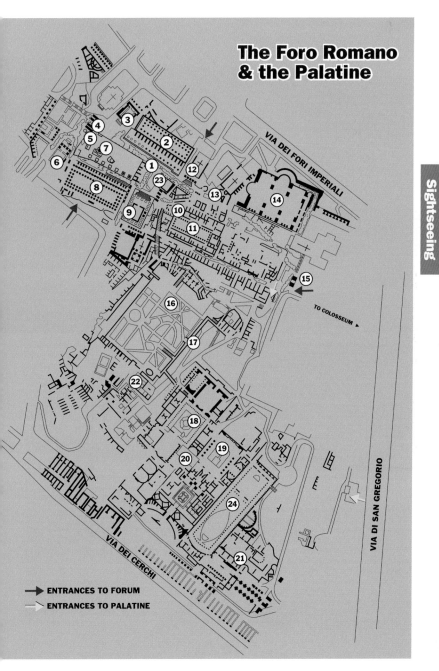

The Foro Romano & the Palatine

VIA DEI FORI IMPERIALI

TO COLOSSEUM ▶

VIA DI SAN GREGORIO

VIA DEI CERCHI

→ **ENTRANCES TO FORUM**

▷ **ENTRANCES TO PALATINE**

A Gaul expires in the **Musei Capitolini.**

by Veronese, and an early *Baptism of Christ* (c1512) by Titian in Room 3. There are also some strangely impressionistic works by Guido Reni (*see p118* **Guido who?**) in Room 6, various busy scenes by Pietro da Cortona in the room named after him, and some luscious portraits by Van Dyck in the Galleria Cini, which also contains a self-portrait by Velázquez (1649-51) and some lovely early 18th-century scenes of Rome by Gaspare Vanvitelli.

To get to the other side of the Musei Capitolini, housed in the **Palazzo Nuovo**, follow the signs to the Tabularium, the ancient Roman archive building upon which the Palazzo Senatorio was built. The tufa vaults of the Tabularium date back to 78 BC, and the view from here over the Forum is simply breathtaking, particularly in the evocative light around sunset. Also visible in this area are the ruins of the Temple of Veiovis ('underground Jupiter').

At the other end of the passageway and up some stairs, Palazzo Nuovo houses one of Europe's most significant collections of ancient sculpture. The three small ground-floor rooms contain portrait busts of Roman citizens, the endearing *Vecchio ubriacone* (or 'old drunk', part of Bacchus' entourage – perhaps a warning to those who indulge too much in the delights of Arcadia) and a huge sarcophagus with scenes from the life of Achilles, topped by two reclining second-century AD figures. Dominating the courtyard is the first-century AD river god, known as Marforio, reclining above his little fountain, and off to the right, behind glass, is the

much-celebrated second-century AD gilded bronze statue of Marcus Aurelius, all gravitas and imperium – which used to grace the square outside.

The collection continues upstairs. In the long gallery (Room 1), the wounded warrior falling to the ground with his shield, is probably a third-century BC discus thrower's top half, turned on its side and given a new pair of legs in the 17th century. Room 2 (Sala delle Colombe) contains a statue of a little girl protecting a dove from a snake, a much-reworked drunken old woman clutching an urn of wine, and a dove mosaic from Hadrian's villa (Villa Adriana; *see p286*) at Tivoli. Room 3 (Gabinetto della Venere) is home to the coy first-century BC *Capitoline Venus*. This was probably based on Praxiteles' *Venus of Cnodis*, considered so erotic by the fourth-century BC inhabitants of Kos that one desperate citizen was caught *in flagrante* with it. In Room 4 (Sala degli Imperatori) portrait busts of emperors, their consorts and children are arranged chronologically, providing a good insight into changing fashions and hairstyles. Next door in Room 5 (Sala dei Filosofi) are ancient portraits of philosophers and poets. Larger statues of mythical figures grace the huge Salone (Room 6). Room 7 (Sala del Fauno) is named after an inebriated faun in *rosso antico* marble, carved in the late second century BC. In Room 8 (Sala del Gladiatore) is the moving *Dying Gaul*, probably based on a third-century BC Greek original (but bearing a stunning resemblance to a '70s TV cop). Also in this room is the smirking, pointy-eared statue that inspired Nathaniel Hawthorne's *The Marble Faun*. Many ancient sculptures long hidden in the storerooms of the Musei Capitolini can now be seen at the Centrale Montemartini (*see p159*).

Museo di Palazzo Venezia

Via del Plebiscito 118 (06 6999 4243/4211). Bus 30, 40, 44, 46, 60, 62, 63, 64, 70, 81, 85, 87, 95, 117, 170, 175, 492, 628, 630, 780, 810, 850. **Open** 8.30am-7.30pm Tue-Sat; ticket office closes 6.30pm. **Admission** *Museum* €4; €2 concessions. *Special exhibitions* varies. **No credit cards. Map** p336 1A.

The interesting collection at Palazzo Venezia contains a hotchpotch of everything from terracotta models by Bernini to medieval decorative art. In Room 1 are Venetian odds and ends, including a double portrait by Giorgione; Room 4 has a glorious zodiac motif on the ceiling. Amid the early Renaissance canvasses and triptychs in Room 6 is a breastfeeding *Madonna dell'Umiltà* – quite a racy show of anatomy for the 14th century. Room 8 contains 18th-century aristos in pastel portraits, some of which look as if they've been acquired at the Porta Portese flea market (*see p225*). In the long corridor are collections of porcelain, including some Meissen, and Italian ceramics. In Rooms 18-26 are Bernini's terracotta musings for the Fontana del Tritone (*see p81*) and the angels on Ponte Sant'Angelo (built to link Castel Sant'Angelo with the *centro storico*). The eastern half of the palazzo often hosts major-sounding exhibitions that don't live up to expectations, but pay the extra fee if only to access Mussolini's old office, the huge Sala del Mappamondo, so-called because of an early map of the world that was kept there in the 16th century.

San Marco

Piazza San Marco (06 679 5205). Bus 30, 40, 44, 46, 60, 62, 63, 64, 70, 81, 85, 87, 95, 117, 170, 175, 492, 628, 630, 780, 810, 850. **Open** 7.30am-1pm, 4-7pm daily. **Map** p336 1A.

There's a strong Venetian flavour to this church, which, according to local lore, was founded in 336 on the site of the house where St Mark the Evangelist – the patron saint of Venice – stayed. There are medieval lions, the symbol of St Mark, by the main entrance door; inside are graves of Venetians and paintings of Venetian saints. Rebuilt during the fifth century, the church was further reorganised by Pope Paul II in the 15th century when the neighbouring Palazzo Venezia (*see above*) was built. San Marco was given its baroque look in the mid 18th century. Remaining from its earlier manifestations are the 11th-century bell tower, a portico attributed to that epitome of Renaissance man Leon Battista Alberti, the 15th-century ceiling with Paul II's coat of arms, and the rigid, Byzantine-style ninth-century mosaic of Christ in the apse. Among the figures below Christ is Gregory IV, who was pope when the mosaic was made: his square halo marks him out as bound for sainthood though still alive. In the portico is the gravestone of Vanozza Catanei, mistress of Rodrigo Borgia – Pope

Alexander VI – and mother of the notorious Cesare and Lucrezia. The chapel to the right at the end of the nave was designed by Pietro da Cortona and contains a funerary monument by neo-classical sculptor Antonio Canova.

Santa Maria in Aracoeli

Piazza del Campidoglio 4 (06 679 8155). Bus 30, 40, 44, 46, 60, 62, 63, 64, 70, 81, 85, 87, 95, 117, 170, 175, 492, 628, 630, 780, 810, 850. **Open** *Nov-Mar* 9am-12.30pm, 2.30-5.30pm daily. *Apr-Oct* 9am-12.30pm, 3.30-6.30pm daily. **Map** p338 1C.

Rising behind the Vittoriano monument (*see p67*), at the head of a daunting flight of 120 marble steps, the romanesque Aracoeli ('altar of heaven') stands on the site of an ancient temple to Juno Moneta. It was here, legend has it, that a sybil whispered to the Emperor Augustus *haec est ara primogeniti Dei* ('this is the altar of God's first-born'). Though there is an altar purporting to be the one erected by Augustus in the chapel of St Helena (to the left of the high altar), there's no record of a Christian church here until the sixth century. The current basilica-form church was designed (and reoriented to face St Peter's in the Vatican) for the Franciscan order in the late 13th century, perhaps by Arnolfo di Cambio.

Dividing the church into a nave and two aisles are 22 columns purloined from Roman buildings. There's a cosmatesque (*see p317* **Glossary**) floor punctuated by marble gravestones and a very gilded ceiling commemorating the Christian victory over the Turks at the Battle of Lepanto in 1571. Just inside the main door, on a pilaster to the right, is the worn tombstone of a certain Giovanni Crivelli, carved and signed (c1432) by Donatello. The first chapel on the right contains enchanting scenes by Pinturicchio from the life of St Francis of Assissi's helpmate St Bernardino (1486).

Approaching the main altar in the right aisle, the chapel of San Pasquale Baylon was decorated with dull 16th-century works until 2000, when parts were removed to reveal a huge fresco, probably by 13th-century genius Pietro Cavallini; restoration of the fresco was due to be completed in June 2003. The large chapel beside it, with scenes from the life of St Francis, contains a marvellous 13th-century mosaic-encrusted tomb: the upper section may be by Arnolfo di Cambio; the lower part is a third-century BC Roman sarcophagus.

On the main altar is a tenth-century image of Mary. Apse paintings by Cavallini were demolished in the mid 16th century. To the left of the altar, eight *giallo antico* columns mark the round chapel of St Helena, where relics of this redoubtable lady – mother of the Emperor Constantine and finder of the 'true' cross – are kept in a porphyry urn. An ancient stone altar, said to be that erected by Augustus, can be seen behind and beneath the altar.

Beyond the chapel, at the back of the transept, is the Chapel of the Holy Child. It contains a much-venerated disease-healing *bambinello* that is often whisked to the bedside of moribund Romans. The

Sightseeing

Indian Restaurant

Typical Indian cuisine in an elegant atmosphere,
located not far from the Colosseum. Special Indian dishes
include chicken tikka masala, lamb vindaloo, chicken maharaja
tandoori and makhani paneer. Attentive and courteous service.
Open every day

❖   ❖   ❖

Via dei Serpenti, 124 • 00184 Roma
Tel: 06/47.47.144 Fax: 06/47.88.53.93
In Venice: Maharani • Via G. Verdi, 97/99 • 30171 Mestre Venezia
Tel: 041/98.46.81 Fax: 041/95.86.98
email: maharajah@maharajah.it • www.maharajah.it

original – carved, it is said, in the 15th century from the wood of an olive tree from the Garden of Gethsemane – was stolen in 1994 and replaced by a copy, though the custodian is keen to impress upon any who question the *faux-bambinello*'s efficacy that the new one is even holier than the first. In any case, the wooden statue today excites the same fervent devotion as the original: each year thousands upon thousands of letters, their envelopes addressed as simply as 'Il Bambino, Roma', arrive from around the world, asking for the Christ-child's help.

The Gothic tomb opposite the Chapel of the Holy Child entrance is that of Matteo d'Acquasparta, who was mentioned by Dante in his *Paradiso*. Above is a *Madonna and Child with Two Saints* attributed to Cavallini. Three chapels from the main door on the left aisle, over the altar, is a fresco of St Anthony of Padua (c1449) by Benozzo Gozzoli. Rome's gypsy community flocks to this church on Christmas eve for a colourful, lively midnight mass.

At the base of the stairs leading to the church are the brick ruins of the Casa Romana dell'Aracoeli, an ancient apartment building whose interior can be visited by prior appointment through the Fori Imperiali visitors' centre (*see p72*).

Il Vittoriano

Piazza Venezia/via di San Pietro in Carcere/piazza Aracoeli (06 699 1718). Bus 30, 40, 44, 46, 60, 62, 63, 64, 70, 81, 85, 87, 95, 117, 170, 175, 492, 628, 630, 780, 810, 850. **Open** *Monument* 9.30am-4.30pm daily. *Sagrario delle Bandiere* 9am-1pm daily. *Museo Centrale del Risorgimento* 9.30am-6.30pm daily. *Complesso del Vittoriano* (open during exhibitions only, contact 06 678 0664) 9.30am-7.30pm Mon-Thur; 9.30am-11.30pm Fri-Sat; 9.30am-8.30pm Sun. **Admission** *Monument, Sagrario, Museo del Risorgimento* free. *Complesso del Vittoriano* depends on exhibition. **No credit cards. Map** p336 1A.

After many years of on-off restorations the Vittoriano is finally firing on all pistons: an eyesore it remains, but at least it's now a useful eyesore. The climb to the top of the monument is worthwhile not only to appreciate the enormity of the thing, but also to see the charmingly kitsch art nouveau propaganda mosaics in the colonnade, to visit the exhibition spaces inside, and – most importantly – to savour the view from the only place where you can see the whole city without the panorama being disturbed by the bulk of the Vittoriano itself. At the top of the first set of stairs two soldiers stand guard at the tomb of the *milite ignoto* ('unknown soldier'), placed here after World War I. Halfway up the terraces on the east side is the very pleasant outdoor Caffè Aracoeli, opened in 2002.

In the bowels of the building are various spaces: the **Museo Centrale del Risorgimento** (entrance through unmarked open doors halfway up the steps of the monument or from via San Pietro in Carcere) has all kinds of exhibits on the 19th-century struggle to unify Italy, including the rather fancy boot worn by Giuseppe Garibaldi (*see p16*) when he was shot in the foot at Aspromonte in 1862, and panels

(in English) explaining the key figures and events of the period. Some of the exhibitions held at the Vittoriano grant access from the entrance in piazza Aracoeli to a maze of Roman and medieval tunnels extending deep beneath the monument.

The **Sagrario delle Bandiere** (entrance in via dei Fori Imperiali) contains standards from many Italian navy vessels and the ornate chests in which they were kept. It also has a couple of torpedo boats, including a manned *Maiale* (Pig) torpedo, in what is a rather hushed 'don't-mention-the-war' collection. On the south-east side of the monument (entrance on via San Pietro in Carcere) is a building whose permanent sign reads 'Museo Centrale del Risorgimento'; it does in fact provide access to the museum, but most of the spaces here are used for special exhibitions of mostly modern art. (Any exhibition advertised as held at the **Complesso del Vittoriano** will be here.)

The Palatine & the Colosseum

This was where the Eternal City began, atop an easily defended rise – the Palatine hill – overlooking the Tiber at the point where an island made it easier to cross the river. Roman myth places the foundation of the city in the eighth century BC; in fact, proto-Romans were already settled here over a century before that, and maybe much earlier.

The presence of Rome's earliest temples on the Palatine hill made the area into desirable real estate, pushing commerce and bureaucracy down into the Foro Romano (*see p75*) as the Palatine became increasingly residential.

The valley to the north-west of the Palatine, where the Colosseum and Arco di Costantino now stand, was hemmed in by the Palatine, Celian and Oppian hills, as well as the Velia, the saddle of land that joined the Oppio to the Palatine. What was left of the Velia was bulldozed away by Mussolini when he drove his via dell'Impero (now via dei Fori Imperiali) through the Imperial Fora (*see p72*). The dwellings that had built up there from the seventh century BC were swept clean by the great fire of AD 64, leaving the area free to become the garden of Nero's **Domus Aurea** (*see p135*). To the south of the Palatine, the **Circo Massimo** opened for races in the fourth century BC, or maybe earlier.

Arco di Costantino

Piazza del Colosseo. Metro Colosseo/bus 60, 75, 81, 85, 87, 117, 175, 673, 810, 850/tram 3. **Map** p338 2C.

Standing beside the Colosseum, Constantine's triumphal arch was one of the last great Roman monuments, erected in AD 315, shortly before he

Triumphal arches

Sightseeing

When, in the course of routing an enemy army, the Romans killed more than 5,000 soldiers, they declared a 'triumph'. To make sure no one forgot these tip-top campaigns, they would erect monumental arches – either on the site of the victory or in Rome. In Rome arches straddled the via Triumphalis (now via di San Gregorio) or the via Sacra in the Roman Forum, along which triumphal parades would pass, dragging prisoners and hoisting aloft the spoils of war.

Triumphal arches could have one or three bays. Some were quadrifrons: square in plan, with four openings on to passages that met each other at right angles under the centre of the structure. Decoration followed a common pattern, with relief sculptures of key episodes from the campaign above the side arches or in the main passageway, and a depiction of the winged goddess of Victory in spandrels above the main arch.

In 1936 Mussolini thought he'd try out the ancient triumphal route. Having got his tanks through the Arch of Constantine (*see p67*), he decided the via Sacra would be too tricky and instead ploughed straight ahead, knocking down several monuments along the way.

In the archaeological area that stretches from the Forum to the Colosseum, the triumphal arches of Septimius Severus, Titus and Constantine are still as imposing today as they were in antiquity.

Arch of Septimius Severus

The upper decorations on this triple-bayed arch, built in AD 203 to commemorate the victory over Parthia (modern-day western Iran), have suffered from their 1,800 years of exposure and the scenes of military exploits are now blurred. The reliefs at the column bases, however, were buried until the 19th century and are thus in better condition. These show Roman soldiers (with no head-gear and wearing shoes) leading away their Parthian prisoners (identifiable by their downcast faces and floppy Smurf hats).

Arch of Titus

Dedicated to the emperor posthumously in AD 81, the Arch of Titus commemorated the sack of Jerusalem ten years previously. The remarkably preserved reliefs inside the west wall of the arch's single passageway depict Roman soldiers carrying away the spoils from the Temple of Herod (the menorah, the silver trumpets); the triumphal procession is shown on the east interior wall, with Titus himself accompanied by a winged Victory driving a four-horse chariot. In the ceiling of the vault there's a square panel that shows Titus riding to the heavens on the back of an eagle, an allusion to his apotheosis.

Arch of Constantine

The best preserved of all the triumphal arches in Rome, Constantine's was built in AD 315 to celebrate the Battle of the Milvian Bridge (*see p10* **History**). Most of the reliefs come from monuments to earlier emperors; those panels that are Constantinian (the narrow strips above the side arches, for example) give ample evidence of the decline in realism of late antique sculpture.

abandoned the city for Byzantium (*see chapter* **History**). Built to commemorate the Battle of the Milvian Bridge, a bloodbath in which Constantine fought under the sign of the cross and routed the army of his co-emperor Maxentius, Constantine's is the best preserved of Rome's triumphal arches. Its magnificent relief sculptures and statues were almost all lifted from earlier emperors' monuments around the city. In front of the arch, the round foundation sunk in the grass is all that remains of an ancient fountain called the Meta Sudans ('sweating cone'). Much more of this implausibly phallic object – almost all of it, in fact – would have been visible today if it hadn't been for Mussolini's avid bulldozing in the 1930s.

Circo Massimo

Via del Circo Massimo. Metro Circo Massimo/bus 60, 75, 81, 118, 175, 628, 673/tram 3. **Map** p327 1C.

Almost nothing of the actual structure remains at the Circus Maximus, ancient Rome's major chariot-racing venue, but rows of umbrella pines, strategically planted along the upper borders in the 1930s, lend the space a powerful and dignified air. It's still possible to visualise the flat base of the long, grassy basin as the racetrack, and the sloping sides as the stadium stands. At the southern end there are some brick remains of the original seating, although the tower there is medieval. The oldest and largest of Rome's ancient arenas, the Circus Maximus hosted chariot races from at least the fourth century BC. It was rebuilt by Julius Caesar, and could eventually hold as many as 300,000 people. Races involved up to twelve rigs of four horses each; the first charioteer to complete the seven treacherous, sabotage-ridden laps around the *spina* (ridge in the centre) won a hefty monetary prize and the adoration of the

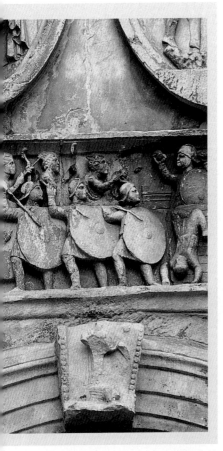

Built in AD 72 by Vespasian on the newly drained site of a lake in the grounds of Nero's Domus Aurea (*see p135*), the Colosseum hosted gory battles between various combinations of gladiators, slaves, prisoners and wild animals of all descriptions. Restoration carried out in 2001 opened up much larger areas of the arena to the public, including a reconstructed section of the sand-covered wood floor that allows visitors to walk a plank-type platform and look down into the elevator shafts through which animals emerged, via trapdoors, into the arena. The top rows of the Colosseum are the best vantage point from which to appreciate the truly massive scale of the building (and get a great view of the surrounding structures).

Properly called the Amphitheatrum Flavium (Flavian amphitheatre) by the ancients, the building was later known as the Colosseum not because it was big, but because of a gold-plated colossal statue, now lost, that stood alongside. The arena was about 500 metres (a third of a mile) in circumference, could seat over 50,000 people – some scholars estimate as many as 87,000 – and could be filled or emptied in ten minutes through a network of *vomitoria* (exits) that remains the basic model for stadium design today.

Nowhere in the world was there a larger or more glorious setting for the mass slaughter so loved by the brutal Romans. If costly, highly trained professional gladiators were often spared at the end of their bloody bouts, not so the slaves, criminals and assorted unfortunates roped in to do battle against them. Any combatant who disappointed the crowd by not showing enough grit was whipped until he fought more aggressively. When the combat was over, corpses were prodded with red-hot pokers to make sure no one tried to elude fate by playing dead. It was not only human life that was sacrificed to Roman blood-lust: wildlife, too, was legitimate fodder. Animals fought animals; people fought animals. In the 100 days of carnage held to inaugurate the amphitheatre in AD 80, 5,000 beasts perished. By the time wild-animal shows were finally banned in AD 523, the elephant and tiger were all but extinct in North Africa and Arabia. On occasion, however, the tables turned and the animals got to kill the people: a common sentence in the Roman criminal justice system was *damnatio ad bestias*, which involved bringing thieves and other miscreants to the Colosseum in the break between the morning and afternoon games and turning them loose, unarmed, into the arena, where hungry beasts would be waiting for them.

Entrance to the Colosseum was free for all, although a membership card was necessary, and a rigid seating plan kept the sexes and social classes in their rightful places. The emperor and senators occupied marble seats in the front rows; on benches higher up were the priests and magistrates, then above them the foreign diplomats. Women were confined to the upper reaches – all of them, that is, except the Vestal Virgins. Less addicted to blood-

Roman populace. The circus was also used for mock sea battles (with the arena flooded with millions of gallons of water), the ever-popular fights with wild animals and the occasional large-scale execution. Perhaps not accidentally, the furious, competitive flow of modern traffic around the circus goes in the same direction that the ancient chariots did.

Il Colosseo (The Colosseum)

Piazza del Colosseo (06 700 5469/06 3996 7700). Metro Colosseo/bus 60, 75, 81, 85, 87, 117, 175, 673, 810, 850/tram 3. **Open** 9am-sunset daily (as late as 7.30pm in summer, as early as 4.30pm in winter); ticket office closes 1hr earlier. **Admission** (includes Palatine) €8; €3.10 concessions; *see also p59* **Tickets. No credit cards. Map** p338 2B. **Note**: if the queue outside the Colosseum is daunting, you can buy tickets at the Palatine (*see p71*) and make straight for the turnstiles.

Sightseeing

Harry'S ®

ROMA

VIA VITTORIO VENETO, 150 - 00187 ROMA
TEL. +39 06 48 46 43/+39 06 47 42 103
FAX +39 06 48 83 117

OPEN 11.00-2.00 A.M. (MON-SAT)
LUNCH SERVED 12.30-3.00 P.M. DINNER SERVED 7.00 P.M.-1.00 A.M.
www.harrysbar.it

Canine concern or prostitute's pity?

The foundation myth of Rome tells of twin orphan boys, Romulus and Remus, who were discovered by a she-wolf on the slope of the Palatine hill in the eighth century BC. Luckily for the babes, the benevolent animal decided to nurse them instead of eating them. When strong enough, they were adopted by a local shepherd. (The story then loses its warmth and fuzziness, as Romulus kills his brother in order to proclaim himself first king of Rome.) This legend – the first part anyway – is so loved by Romans that the she-wolf has become the unofficial symbol of the city. But some scholars, pointing to the original language of the legend, raise the question of whether it was a wolf at all who found the boys. Lupa – the word for a she-wolf – was also a common Latin term for a prostitute.

letting than their fellow Romans, Suetonius reports that these hapless females often had to be carried out from their privileged seats near the emperor, having fainted in shock at the sight of so much gore.

By the sixth century, with the fall of the Roman Empire, the Colosseum registered a sad decline in the glory of its blood sports: chickens now pecked each other to death in the arena where rhinoceroses had once gored hippopotami. To spare themselves further ignominy, the Roman authorities discontinued the games and the Colosseum became little more than a big quarry for the stone and marble used to build and decorate Roman *palazzi*. The pockmarks all over the Colosseum's masonry date back to the ninth century, when Lombards pillaged the iron and lead clamps that until then had held the blocks together. This irreverence toward the Colosseum – whether by barbarians or Roman aristocracy – was not halted until the mid 18th century, when Pope Benedict XIV had stations of the cross built inside it and consecrated it as a church. For another century it was left to its own devices, becoming home to hundreds of species of flowers and plants, as well as to a fair number of Roman homeless who sheltered in the ruin's sturdy archways. After Unification in 1870 the flora was yanked up and the squatters kicked out, in what 19th-century English writer Augustus Hare described as 'aimless excavations'. 'In dragging out the roots of its shrubs,' he moaned in his *Walks in Rome* (1883), 'more of the building was destroyed than would have fallen naturally in five centuries.'

Il Palatino (The Palatine)

Via di San Gregorio 30/piazza di Santa Maria Nova 53 (06 699 0110/06 3996 7700). Metro Colosseo/bus 60, 75, 85, 87, 117, 175, 673, 810, 850/tram 3. **Open** 9am-sunset daily (as late as 7.30pm in summer, as early as 4.30pm in winter); ticket office closes 1hr earlier. *Museo Palatino* 9am-1hr before sunset. **Admission** (incl Colosseum) €8; €3.10 concessions; *see also p59* **Tickets. No credit cards. Map** p338 2C.
Numbers refer to the map on p63.
The Beverly Hills of ancient Rome, the Palatine hill was where the movers and shakers of both Republic and Empire built their palaces. The choice of

location was understandable: the Palatine overlooks the Foro Romano, yet is a comfortable distance from the disturbances and riff-raff down in the valley.

Entering the Palatine from the Roman Forum, you pass the Hortus Farnese (**16**), originally the Domus Tiberiana, on the right. These gardens, full of orange trees and burbling fountains, were laid out in the 16th century, making them one of the oldest botanical gardens in Europe. They were created for a member of a papal family, Cardinal Alessandro Farnese, who used them for lavish garden parties. The 17th-century pavilion at the top of the hill offers a good view over the Forum. Underneath the gardens, behind the pavilion, is the Cryptoporticus (**17**), a long semi-subterranean tunnel built by Nero either for hot-weather promenades or as a secret route between the Palatine buildings and his palace, the Domus Aurea (*see p135*). Lit only by slits in the walls, the Cryptoporticus is welcomingly cool in summer. At one end there are remnants of a stucco ceiling frieze and floor mosaics.

South of the gardens are the remains of the imperial palaces built by Domitian at the end of the first century AD, which became the principal residence of the emperors for the next three centuries. The nearest section, the Domus Flavia (**18**), contained the public rooms. According to Suetonius, Domitian was so terrified of assassination that he had the walls faced with shiny black selenite so he could see anybody creeping up behind him. It didn't work. The strange-looking room, with what appears to be a maze in the middle, was the courtyard; next to this was the dining room, where parts of the marble floor have survived, although it's usually covered for protection. The brick oval in the middle was probably a fountain. Next door is the emperor's private residence, the Domus Augustana (**19**). The oval building close to it may have been a garden or a miniature stadium for Domitian's private entertainment.

Sandwiched between the Domus Flavia and Domus Augustana is a tall grey building that houses the Museo Palatino (**20**). Downstairs are human remains and artefacts from the earliest communities of Rome, founded in the Forum and Palatine areas from the ninth century BC: Room 2 has a model of an eighth-century wattle-and-daub hut village. Emerging from the floor are the foundations of Domitian's dwelling. Upstairs are busts, gods and some fascinating eave-edgings from the first to the fourth centuries AD.

To the south of the Domus Augustana lie the remains of the comparatively small palace and baths of Septimius Severus (**21**), some of the best-preserved buildings in the area. Back towards the Farnese gardens is the Domus Livia (**22**), named after Augustus' wife. The wall paintings here date from the late Republic, and include trompe l'oeil marble panels and scenes from mythology.

The fora

The **Foro Romano**, the oldest of Rome's fora, began life as a swampy valley at the foot of the Palatine (*see p71*) that was used for burials. It was drained, according to legend, in the late seventh century BC by Rome's Etruscan king, Tarquinius Priscus, who had the Cloaca Maxima (*see p114*) built. The Forum was to become the centre of commerce, religion, state ceremony, law and bureaucracy.

As the existing fora became too small to cope with the legal, social and economic life of the city, the emperors combined philanthropy with propaganda and created new ones of their own: the **Fori imperiali** (Imperial Fora). All but one were built to celebrate military triumphs. Clearly visible on either side of the main road, there are five separate fora, each built by a different emperor. Mussolini saw fit to slice through them with the via dei Fori Imperiali (he was planning to create a bigger, better empire of his own after all), which connected his balcony at Palazzo Venezia (*see p65*) with the Colosseum. Since the 1990s work has been under way to recover tens of thousands of square metres of the ancient remains, turning the Fori imperiali into the world's biggest urban archaeological dig.

In his wisdom, Mussolini saved modern archaeologists the anguish of having to decide what to do with the medieval and early Renaissance buildings – including dozens of defence towers – that had grown up out of the Roman ruins: he bulldozed them. The recently restored **Torre delle Milizie** (*see p75*) behind the **Mercati di Traiano** is a picturesque memento. Between the Foro Romano and the Campidoglio (*see p61*) is the **Carcere Mamertino**.

Carcere Mamertino

Clivio Argentario 1 (06 679 2902). Bus 60, 81, 85, 87, 117, 175, 810, 850. **Open** *Nov-Mar* 9am-noon, 2-5pm daily. *Apr-Oct* 9am-noon, 2.30-6pm daily. **Admission** donation expected. **Map** p338 1C.
Anyone thought to pose a threat to the security of the ancient Roman state was thrown into the Mamertine Prison, a dank, dark and oppressive

little underground dungeon, squashed between the Foro Romano and via dei Fori Imperiali at the bottom of the steps up to the Capitoline. In those days the only way down to the lower level (built in the fourth century BC) was through a hole in the floor. The numberless prisoners who starved to death here were tossed into the Cloaca Maxima, the city's main sewer. The most famous of the prison's residents, legend has it, were Saints Peter and Paul. Peter head-butted the wall in the ground-level room, leaving his features impressed on the rock (at least that's what the plaque says). He also caused a miraculous well to bubble up downstairs in order to baptise his prison guards, whom he converted by his shining example.

Fori imperiali & Mercati di Traiano (Imperial Fora & Trajan's Market)

Visitors' centre: *via dei Fori Imperiali (06 679 7786/7702/www.capitolium.org). Metro Colosseo/bus 60, 75, 85, 87, 117, 175, 810, 850.* **Open** *Apr-Sept* 9am-7pm daily. *Oct-Mar* 9am-6pm daily. **Admission** (guided tour only) €7. **Map** p338 1C. **Mercati di Traiano**: *via IV Novembre 94 (06 679 0048/1620). Bus 40, 60, 64, 70, 117, 170.* **Open** (during exhibitions only) 9am-7pm Tue-Sun. **Admission** varies. **No credit cards**. **Map** p338 1C.
The recently opened visitors' centre, situated opposite the church of Santi Cosma e Damiano on the via dei Fori Imperiali, has literature about the Fori imperiali, a small exhibition area with emperors' busts and bits of pottery, as well as a bookshop, café and place to sit down.

Excavations carried out in the Imperial Fora in the 1990s opened up massive amounts of archaeological space to the public, but the work is far from over. City authorities are still debating whether to enclose Trajan's Market in Plexiglas – the very suggestion horrified almost everyone in 2000, but some of the higher-ups in Rome's archaeological superintendency say that some kind of casing is essential for the purpose of preservation – and sections of the excavations sometimes close (and open) to the public without warning. For now what has been uncovered of the five civic spaces that made up the Imperial Fora, built to the east of the Foro Romano over a period of about 200 years, is mostly visible from street level on either side of the via dei Fori Imperiali. An audio guide is available from the visitors' centre for €3.50.

To get down into more hidden corners you'll have to take a guided tour. Tours must be booked at least one day in advance, either by phone or at the visitors' centre. (The centre also books guided tours of the stadium of Domitian beneath piazza Navona, *see p103*, the Casa Romana dell'Aracoeli, *see p67*, and the mithraeum beneath Circo Massimo).

Trajan's Market, too, can be admired from street level or as part of one of the guided tours from the visitors' centre. Frequent exhibitions are held in the market, during which the site can be entered from via IV Novembre; on these occasions there's access to the rest of the ruins from the same entrance.

Ancient Romans shopped, gossiped and sued in the **Foro Romano**. *See p75.*

The earliest of the Fori imperiali, the **Forum of Caesar**, lies on the south-west side of via dei Fori Imperiali, closest to the Foro Romano. Begun by Julius Caesar in 51 BC after the Gallic wars (of *veni, vidi, vici* fame), the forum contained the temple of Venus Genetrix (three columns of which have been reconstructed) and the *basilica argentaria*, hall of the money-changers.

On the north-east side of via dei Fori Imperiali are the extensive remains of **Trajan's Forum**, the most recent of the fora, laid out in the early second century AD. At the northern extremity of this forum rises the white marble **Colonna traiana** (Trajan's Column), an amazingly well-preserved work of Roman sculpture, dedicated in AD 113 to celebrate the triumph over the Dacians. The spiral reliefs, containing over 2,500 figures, depict the campaigns against Dacia (more or less modern-day Romania) in marvellous detail, from the building of forts to the launching of catapults. The higher sections of the column are difficult to discern today, but would have been easily viewed by the ancients from galleries that used to stand nearby. (Plaster casts of the reliefs were made by Napoleon III and are now on display at the Museo della Civiltà Romana in EUR; *see p161*). At the top of the column is a bronze statue of St Peter, added in 1587 by Pope Sixtus V to replace the original one of Trajan (now lost). So beloved by the Roman people was Trajan that, when he died in AD 117, his funerary urn was placed in a chamber at the column base (covered with scaffolding at the time of writing); this made him and his wife, Plotina, the only Romans whose remains were allowed to be placed inside the city walls (*see p154* **Bring out yer**

dead). The height of the column, 38m (125ft), is believed to mark the elevation of that part of the Quirinale hill that extended into this area before it was cleared away to make room for Trajan's forum.

The Temple of Trajan, mentioned by ancient sources, was also around here, although the exact location is still unknown. The rectangular foundation to the south of Trajan's column, where several imposing granite columns still stand, was the *basilica Ulpia*, an administrative building whose once-imposing bulk is difficult to imagine today. To the west of Trajan's column and the *basilica Ulpia*, under the walls that support via dei Fori Imperiali, are the remains of one of the libraries that also formed part of Trajan's Forum. The most distinctive feature of the forum complex is the multistorey brick crescent to the south-east of the *basilica Ulpia*. This Great Hemicycle, forming part of the **Mercati di Traiano** (Trajan's Market), was built in AD 107, in part to shore up the slope of the Quirinale hill. Believed by many to have functioned like a modern shopping mall, some scholars say it was more of an administrative than a commercial space. The best way to appreciate its state of preservation is to visit the interior: entering from via IV Novembre, the first room is the Great Hall, a large space possibly used for the corn dole in antiquity (*see p10* **History**) but where one-off exhibitions are frequently held today. (Only during such exhibitions can this entrance be used to gain access to Trajan's Forum and the Forum of Augustus.) To the south of the Great Hall are the open-air terraces at the top of the Great Hemicycle, recently reopened after a lengthy restoration and offering spectacular views across to the Capitoline and Foro Romano. To the east of the Great Hall, stairs lead down to the so-called via Biberatica, an ancient street flanked by well-preserved shops. The shops here were probably *tabernae* (alcohol-serving bars), hence the name 'Biberatica' (*bibere* is Latin for 'to drink'). More stairs lead down through the various layers of the Great Hemicycle, where most of the 150 shops or offices are still in perfect condition, many with doorjambs still showing the grooves where shutters slid into place when the working day was over.

South of the Great Hemicycle, the structure with a loggia with five large arches is the 15th-century Casa dei Cavalieri di Rodi (House of the Knights of Rhodes); its somewhat Venetian look is due to having been built by Venetian Pope Paul II. The slightly leaning tower beyond the Great Hemicycle is the 13th-century **Torre delle Milizie** (Militia Tower), for years erroneously believed to be the place from which Nero watched Rome burn, after he had supposedly set fire to it. The chronology doesn't work, but try telling that to the poets.

To the south of the House of the Knights of Rhodes is the **Forum of Augustus**, the second of the Imperial Fora chronologically (inaugurated in 2 BC). The dominant feature here was the Temple of Mars Ultor ('the avenger'), built to commemorate the Battle of Philippi in 42 BC, in which Augustus (then

called Octavian) avenged Caesar's death. Three marble columns of the temple are visible on the right side, as is the towering tufa fire wall behind it, built to protect the imperial space from the Suburra (*see p135*) slum district just beyond.

The next forum to the south, which is bisected by via dei Fori Imperiali, is the **Forum of Nerva** (or Forum transitorium because of its connective function from the Suburra to the Foro Romano). It was dedicated by Nerva in AD 97. Some vestiges of a podium are all that remain of the Temple of Minerva that once stood at the east end of the elongated space, although the frieze around two marble columns of the portico (visible just before via Cavour) depicts Minerva, goddess of household skills, weaving and spinning.

The **Templum pacis**, third of the Fori imperiali to be built but the last to be unearthed (recognisable by the potted plants on the west side of via dei Fori Imperiali), was dedicated by Vespasian in AD 75 but devastated by a fire in 192. On display inside this 'Temple of Peace' were the spoils of various wars, including treasures looted from the Temple of Herod during the Sack of Jerusalem in AD 70. The temple's library is now part of the church of Santi Cosma e Damiano, and the immense *Forma Urbis*, a marble map of the city made in AD 193 by Septimius Severus, once adorned the brick wall to the left of the church's façade. Taking his cue (as always) from the ancient emperors, Mussolini made some maps of his own. Some 100 metres south along via dei Fori Imperiali, four white-and-black marble maps are still visible against the brick wall on the west side. They show an area that includes Europe, North Africa and the Near East, charting the growth of the Roman Empire through antiquity. There used to be a fifth map too, which showed Mussolini's Fascist 'empire', but it was removed after the war.

Foro Romano

Entrances from largo Romolo e Remo, via dei Fori Imperiali, piazza del Colosseo & via Foro Romano (06 699 0110). Metro Colosseo/bus 60, 75, 85, 87, 117, 175, 810, 850. **Open** 9am-1hr before sunset daily. **Admission** free. **Map** p338 2B&C.
Numbers refer to the map on p63.

In the earliest days of the Republic the Roman Forum was much like any Italian piazza today: an open space where people would shop, gossip, catch up on the latest news and perhaps visit a temple. In the second century BC, when Rome had become the capital of an empire that included Greece, Sicily and Carthage, it was decided the city needed a more dignified centre. The food stalls were moved out, and permanent law courts and offices were built. In time this centre was also deemed too small, and emperors began to build the new Imperial Fora (*see p72*). Nevertheless, the Foro Romano remained the symbolic heart of the Empire, and emperors continued to renovate and embellish it until the fourth century AD. (A recent decision to do away with the entry fee, thereby 'returning' the Forum to the Romans, was warmly welcomed by locals who can now be seen wandering through it on sunny weekends, looking very much at home.)

The area today consists of little more than the layouts of floors and a few columns, but with a bit of imagination a tour around the Forum can still give an accurate impression of what ancient Rome looked like. Before entering, look down over the Forum from behind the Capitoline for a view of its overall layout. Its main thoroughfare, the via Sacra (**1**), runs almost directly through the middle. Entering the Forum from the via dei Fori Imperiali entrance, the Temple of Antoninus and Faustina (*see below*) is on the left, and the remains of the *basilica Emilia* (**2**) are to the right. The basilica was a large hall, originally built for business and moneylending in 179 BC (what remains is mainly from later periods). The brown rusty marks dotted around the basilica at the end towards the Capitoline are bronze coins that fused into the floor during a fire in AD 410. The tall brick building at the coin end is a 1930s reconstruction of the Curia (**3**) or Senate House.

Standing out to the west of the Curia is the best-preserved monument in this part of the Forum, the massive Arch of Septimius Severus (**4**), built in AD 203 to celebrate a victory over the Parthians (*see p68* **Triumphal arches**). Near here was the *Milliarium aureum* ('Golden Milestone'), from which all distances to and from Rome were measured. Beyond the Arch of Septimius are the remains of the imperial *rostra* (**5**), a platform from which speeches and demonstrations of power were made, and from where Mark Antony supposedly asked the Roman populace to lend him its ears. Further back, the eight massive columns that formed part of the Temple of Saturn (**6**), built in the fifth century BC, stand out. The state treasury was housed underneath it. Also clearly visible is the solitary Column of Phocas (**7**), erected in AD 608 by Pope Boniface IV to thank the Byzantine emperor for giving him the Pantheon as a church. Visible on the other side of the via Sacra are the foundations of the *basilica Julia* (**8**), built by Julius Caesar in 55 BC and once a major – and by all accounts very noisy – law court. Ancient board games are carved into the steps.

Further into the Forum are three elegant columns that formed part of the Temple of Castor and Pollux (**9**), the saviours of Rome. According to legend, these twin giants and their horses appeared to the Roman forces during a battle in 499 BC, and helped the Republic to victory. Back towards the centre of the Forum is the podium of the Temple of Divus Julius (**23**), a nondescript mass of rubble-and-concrete masonry (*opus mixtum*) beneath a low-pitched green roof. According to tradition, this was the spot where Caesar was cremated; offerings of flowers, fruit and the occasional sonnet can still be found on the altar beneath the roof, added by Pope John Paul II.

Beyond the temple are the scant remains of the Arch of Augustus, built in 29 BC to commemorate the defeat of Antony and Cleopatra at Actium in 31 BC. Just beyond, three small columns arranged in a curve mark the round Temple of Vesta (**10**) and, within its garden, the rectangular House of the Vestal Virgins (**11**). On the via dei Fori Imperiali side of the via Sacra are the columns, atop a flight of steep steps, of the Temple of Antoninus and Faustina (**12**), built to honour a second-century emperor and his wife and, since the 11th century, part of the church of San Lorenzo in Miranda. The grooves cut into the tops of the columns are evidence of a failed attempt to dismantle the temple for its marble in the Middle Ages. The oldest graves ever unearthed in Rome were found here (in the grassy enclosure marked 'Sepolcreto arcaico'); the bodies are now housed in the Palatine Museum (*see p71*). The circular building further up the slope, on the left, is the Temple of Romulus (**13**), dating from the fourth century AD. It has nothing to do with the co-founder of Rome: this Romulus came along 1,000 years later, and was one of Emperor Maxentius' sons. The bronze doors of his temple are one of only four such sets surviving in Rome from the ancient period (the others being at the Pantheon, *p105*, San Giovanni, *p131*, and the Sancta Sanctorum, *p132*).

Looming above these temples are the remains of the massive Basilica of Maxentius (**14**), also known as the *basilica Nova*, begun in AD 306 and studied by Michelangelo and Bramante when they were designing St Peter's. The three vaults that remain are only one third of the basilica's original size, and the brick interior would have been covered with slabs of coloured marble. The southern end of the Forum is marked by the crest of a gentle hill, atop which stands the Arch of Titus (**15**), built in AD 81 to celebrate the Sack of Jerusalem (*see p68* **Triumphal arches**); the event is depicted in the elaborate relic panels (note the sacred seven-branched candelabra). A path to the right of this arch leads to the Palatine; another beyond leads down to the Colosseum.

Santi Cosma e Damiano

Via dei Fori Imperiali 1 (06 692 0441).
Metro Colosseo/bus 60, 75, 85, 87, 117, 175,
810, 850. **Open** 8am-12.45pm, 3-7pm daily.
Map p338 2C.
This small church on the fringe of the Forum incorporates the library of Vespasian's Temple of Peace and the Temple of Romulus (visible through the glass panel that forms the front wall). It has a wonderful sixth-century mosaic in the apse, representing the Second Coming, with the figure of Christ appearing huge against a blue setting as he descends a staircase of clouds. Notice how the heads of the lambs below are cocked upward at different angles, their attention caught by the action above. The coy lamb batting its eyelids in the centre – it represents Christ – looks as if it has just won an ovine beauty pageant. This massive style was the last phase in the development of late Roman mosaic, just before the Byzantine conquest brought the self-consciously classical mosaics of Santa Pudenziana (*see p135*).

The Trevi Fountain & the Quirinale

Come hither for fine art, stunning architecture, Anita's fountain… and a collection of pope innards.

Heavenly horse tamers by the **Palazzo del Quirinale**. *See p82*.

Italy's imposing presidential palace on the Quirinal hill has symbolised the changing forces of power in Rome down the centuries, from popes and kings to the present-day republic. Sitting atop the highest of Rome's original seven hills, it became a favourite of the popes: in summer they found it cooler and more salubrious than the Vatican palace, which was slightly too close to the malarial Tiber.

After the collapse of the papal states in 1870, Pope Pius IX, who was holed up inside the palace, refused to hand over his keys to the troops of King Victor Emanuel; they had to break down the doors. Just 76 years later the reigning Savoia family were forced to quit the palace following a referendum in which the monarchy, tainted by association with the Mussolini regime (*see p23* **Once, not future, kings**), was despatched into exile. Today a constant stream of motorcades swishing across the cobbles serves as a reminder that the Quirinale is still very much at the decision-making hub of 21st-century Italy.

Around the Trevi Fountain

The presidential palace walls tower over a tangle of medieval streets, all of which seem in the end to lead to the **Trevi Fountain**. There are still old people who remember mules carrying barrels of water from the fountain to the palace each day. It was, after all, said to be the best water in Rome: Grand Tourists used it to brew their tea.

Today's tourists hurl coins into it as they try to ignore the pressing sales patter of restaurant touts and tacky souvenir sellers. Few nip down via della Stamperia for an entertaining look at the Rome of the past in the paintings of the **Galleria dell'Accademia di San Luca**.

Playful **Triton** in piazza Barberini. *See p79.*

Names like via della Stamperia (Printing Works Street) and via della Dataria (Ecclesiastical Benefits Office Street) recall the era when the whole of the Trevi district acted as a service area for the palace: here were the printing presses, the bureaucratic departments and service industries that oiled the machinery of the papal state. Aristocratic families like the Odescalchis and Grimaldis built their palaces close by, as did the Barberinis and Colonnas whose superb art collections are now on view to the public.

The area's peculiarities include **Santi Anastasio e Vicenzo** – a church packed with popes' innards – and the **Museo Nazionale delle Paste Alimentari**, which will tell you everything that you ever wished to know (and more) about Italy's national food staple.

Fontana di Trevi
Piazza di Trevi. Bus 52, 53, 61, 62, 71, 80, 95, 116, 119, 175, 492, 630, 850. **Map** p335 2C.
Anita Ekberg made this fountain famous when she plunged in wearing a strapless black evening dress (and a pair of waders… but you don't notice those) in Federico Fellini's classic *La dolce vita*. Don't even think about it – wading, washing and splashing in fountains are strictly against local bylaws. You don't want to drink it either: the sparkling water is full of chlorine (though there's a chlorine-free spout hidden in a bird-bath-shaped affair at the back of the fountain to the right).

The Acqua Vergine was the finest water in the city, brought by Emperor Agrippa's mammoth 25km (15.5-mile) aqueduct to the foot of the Quirinal hill. Pope Urban VIII commissioned wunderkind

Gian Lorenzo Bernini to design a new fountain here, but died before work started. Urban's successor Innocent X had other plans, putting Bernini to work on his own pet project, the equally magnificent Fountain of the Four Rivers in piazza Navona (*see p103*). The Trevi Fountain as we know it (Trevi from *tre vie* – 'three roads' – though more than that meet here now) was finally built by Nicolo Salvi for another pope, Clement XII, in 1762.

Tucked away in a tiny piazza and surrounded day and night by crowds, the fountain's creamy travertine gleams beneath powerful torrents of water and constant camera flashes. The attention is justified: it's a magnificent rococo extravaganza of rearing sea horses, conch-blowing tritons, craggy rocks and flimsy trees, cavorting in front of the wall of the Palazzo Poli. Nobody can quite remember when the custom started of tossing coins in to ensure one's return to the Eternal City. The town council made such a poor job of collecting the coins that for 30 years a self-appointed collector waded in every morning and saved them the trouble. Now the money – all of it – goes to the Red Cross.

Galleria dell'Accademia di San Luca
Piazza dell'Accademia 77 (06 679 8850). Bus 52, 53, 61, 62, 71, 80, 95, 116, 119, 175, 492, 630, 850. **Open** 10am-12.30pm Mon-Sat. Closed July & Aug. **Admission** free. **Map** p335 2C.
Borromini's clever and very practical (at least for sedan chairs and mules) elliptical brickwork ramp to the upper floors of Palazzo Carpegno was inspired by the winding ramp inside Hadrian's mausoleum inside Castel Sant'Angelo (*see p149*). It was the final handsome touch to a palazzo that now houses the august institution founded in 1577 to train artists in the grand Renaissance style. Access to the gallery is concealed behind a virtuoso piece of stucco work: cornucopiae of overblown buttercups and daisies denote the riches of the earth, while crowns, mitres and chains symbolise what can be achieved by hard work in the course of a long and fortunate career. But without progeny, the allegory continues (a small child peers out of the herbiage), it is all worthless endeavour; it's not on record whether the few women members of the Academy, such as Lavinia Fontana (1551-1614) and Angelica Kauffman (1741-1807) agreed with the sentiments. This is a good place to track the changing face of Rome through the gallery's collection of artistically forgettable but nonetheless endearing portrayals of the Eternal City. There are works by Titian, Guido Reni (*see p118* **Guido who?**) and Van Dyck too.

Galleria Colonna
Via della Pilotta 17 (06 678 4350/www. galleriacolonna.it). Bus 40, 60, 64, 70, 117, 170, H. **Open** 9am-1pm Sat. Closed Aug. **Admission** €7; €5 concessions. **No credit cards. Map** p335 2C.
Saturday mornings are your only chance to see this stunning six-room gallery, completed in 1703 for the fabulously wealthy Colonna family, whose descen-

dants still live in the palace. The immense frescoed ceiling of the Great Hall pays tribute to family hero Marcantonio Colonna, who led the papal fleet to victory against the Turks in the great naval battle of Lepanto in 1571. There are more Turks, as well as evil cherubs and endangered maidens, on the ceiling of the next room, the Hall of the Desks, frescoed by Venetian artist Sebastiano Ricci. The gallery's most famous and much reproduced picture is probably Annibale Caracci's earthy peasant *Bean Eater*, but don't miss Bronzino's wonderfully sensuous *Venus and Cupid* from which restorers have just removed a few chaste little veils that were daubed on to the goddess in more prudish times. Included in the ticket price is a guided tour in English, which starts at 11.45am, but groups of ten or more can arrange guided tours of the gallery as well as the private apartments at other times during the week.

Museo Nazionale delle Paste Alimentari

Piazza Scanderbeg 117 (06 669 1119/www. pastainmuseum.it). Bus 52, 53, 61, 62, 71, 80, 95, 116, 119, 175, 492, 630, 850. **Open** 9.30am-5.30pm daily. **Admission** €9; €6 concessions. **No credit cards. Map** p335 2C.

It could be more snappily named, but this small museum is one of Rome's best-organised attractions. Portable CD players with explanations in six languages are issued to visitors to guide them through the sophistications of pasta-making: rolling and cutting techniques, the equipment, and the selection of ingredients. Publicity shots of famous devotees of the national dish doing battle with independently minded strands line the walls. If you're inspired to start rolling your own, there is a giftshop with all kinds of pasta-related items to take home with you.

Piazza Barberini & the Quattro Fontane

In ancient times, erotic dances were performed in elegant piazza Barberini to mark the coming of spring. Today, it's a deafening fume-filled chicane, funnelling traffic north into via Veneto (*see p83*) or south-east towards the Quattro Fontane (*see p81*). Keep carefully to the pavement, then, to observe the square's magnificent centrepiece: Bernini's playful **Fontana del Tritone**.

It's hard to imagine the time when this square was countryside and the great palace of the powerful Barberini family dominated all. There are bees – the Barberini family emblem – all over, including on Bernini's Triton. Carved out of local travertine stone, he sits amid the traffic with his two fish-tail legs tucked beneath him on a shell supported by four dolphins, blowing through a great conch shell, just as local fishermen used to do to summon their crews for a fishing trip.

North-east of the piazza, *vie* Barberini and Bissolati were redeveloped during the Fascist era when the urban fabric was relentlessly bulldozed. Most major airlines have offices in one of these two rather charmless streets.

Ringing with life-threatening *motorini*, narrow via Barberini climbs past the **Palazzo Barberini** gallery to the crossroads, which – for very obvious reasons – are known as the **Quattro Fontane** (four fountains).

Four delightful baroque fountains have stood here since 1593 (so no wonder they're grimy). They clearly represent four gods: the one accompanied by the she-wolf is undoubtedly the Tiber; the females are probably Juno (with duck) and Diana. But it's anybody's guess who the fourth figure is: some claim it's an allegory of the Nile while others make a case for the Florentine Arno. Some experts, who perhaps find hidden meaning in the duck, stoutly maintain that the two female figures represent Fidelity and Strength. Well, it's a theory.

From here the staggering view down both sides of the hill takes in three Egyptian obelisks. On one corner stands one of Carlo Borromini's great masterpieces: the superb church of **San Carlino alle Quattro Fontane**.

Palazzo Barberini – Galleria Nazionale d'Arte Antica

Via delle Quattro Fontane 13/via Barberini 18 (06 481 4591/bookings 06 32 810/www.galleria borghese.it). Metro Barberini/bus 52, 53, 61, 62, 63, 80, 95, 116, 119, 175, 492, 630. **Open** 9am-7.30pm Tue-Sun. **Admission** €5.12; €2.50 concessions; *see also p59* **Tickets. No credit cards. Map** p335 1B.

This vast baroque palace, built by the Barberini pope Urban VIII, houses one of Rome's most important art collections. It's undergoing an interminable restoration programme: so grit your teeth and ignore the cement mixers and piles of sand in the garden and general disarray before the magnificent entrance. The staggering trompe l'oeil frescoed ceiling of the Gran Salone on the *piano nobile* will transport you to baroque Rome in all its glory. Top architects like Maderno, Bernini and Borromini queued up to work on this pile, which was begun two years after Maffeo Barberini was elected pope and completed in a record five years (1627-33). Bernini did the main staircase on the left, a grand rectangular affair (marred by an ugly lift); Borromini, whose uncle Carlo Maderno was entrusted with the original palace plans, added a characteristically showy oval staircase on the right. When it was all finished Pietro da Cortona was called in to decorate the great papal throne room with a sumptuous *Triumph of Divine Providence*, one of the largest paintings in the world: its aim being to glorify the papacy and the Barberini family. Highlights of the collection (which tend to be shunted about from room to room as restoration work 'proceeds')

Sightseeing

Surya Mahal

Ristorante Indiano

Situato nel cuore di Trastevere, alle spalle dello splendido fontanone di P.zza Trilussa Surya Mahal Vi offre la magica opportunità di gustare in un meraviglioso giardino i migliori piatti "haute cuisine" indiana e una vasta scelta di specialità Tandoor. Infatti l'obiettivo di Surya Mahal è quello di preservare e perpetuare la ricca e genuina tradizione gastronomica dell'india del nord.

Surya Mahal with its lovely, enchanting garden and intimate atmosphere, set in Trastevere next to the fountain of P.zza Trilussa in the heart of old Rome, offers you an unforgettably magical, gastronomic and culturally rich experience of the "haute cuisine" and the more traditional Tandoor specialities of India. That you'll want to repeat again and again !...

Via di Ponte Sisto, 67 - P.zza Trilussa, 50
00153 Roma (Trastevere) Tel. +39 06 58 94 554
w w w . r i s t o r a n t e s u r y a m a h a l . c o m

River gods at the **Quattro Fontane**. *See p79.*

include Filippo Lippi's *Madonna* (with possibly the ugliest Christ-child ever painted); a recently restored, enigmatic portrait of a courtesan traditionally (although probably wrongly) believed to represent Raphael's mistress (*see p116* **Casa della Fornarina**); a *Nativity and Baptism of Christ* by El Greco; Tintoretto's dramatic *Christ and the Woman taken in Adultery*; Titian's *Venus and Adonis*; two Caravaggios, one of them showing Judith rather gingerly cutting off Holofernes' head; a Holbein portrait, *Henry VIII Dressed for his Wedding to Anne of Cleves* (although it has been suggested this may be a copy); Bronzino's forceful portrait of Stefano Colonna; Guido Reni's portrait of incest-victim Beatrice Cenci; a Bernini bust and painted portrait of Pope Urban VIII, who commissioned the palace; works by Raphael's best-known follower Sodoma (the nickname, apparently, was apt), including a *Rape of the Sabine Women* with predictably compliant subjects; and a self-assured self-portrait by Artemisia Gentileschi.

Part of the enormous palazzo still houses a grand old-fashioned Armed Forces officers club; at some point the club will vacate the premises and the plan is that this too will become gallery hanging-space. There are also plans to restore the formal gardens which, in their heyday, were famous for their rare plants. Meanwhile visitors have access to a suite of small private rooms, exquisitely painted and furnished for Princess Cornelia Costanza Barberini in the 18th century (note the charming natives in the room decorated with depictions of the discovery of America). Cornelia was the last of the Barberinis; the name died out when she was married off to one of the Colonna family at the age of 12. These rooms also house some Barberini family clothes and furniture.

San Carlino alle Quattro Fontane

Via del Quirinale 23 (06 488 3261/www.sancarlino-borromini.it). Metro Barberini/bus 40, 52, 53, 61, 62, 63, 64, 70, 71, 80, 95, 116, 119, 170, 175, 492, 630, H. **Open** *10am-1pm, 3-6pm daily.* **Map** *p335 2B.*

This was Carlo Borromini's first solo composition (1631-41), and the one he was most proud of. He was buried here in an unmarked grave after committing suicide. The most remarkable feature is the dizzying oval dome. The geometrical coffers in its decoration decrease in size towards the lantern to give the illusion of additional height – Borromini is all about illusion – and the illumination, through hidden windows, makes the dome appear to be floating in mid-air. Recently restored, this gem of a church has an austere adjoining courtyard and a simply beautiful library that open, occasionally, at the whim of the monastery's residents.

From the Quirinale to via Nazionale

Italians refer to it as the *colle* (hill) – there's no need to specify when you're referring to the all-important Quirinale. Legend has it that the area was first settled by the Sabines, who unwisely built their huts within calling distance of their rapacious neighbours, the Latins, across on the Palatine hill. Soon the huts were replaced by some of ancient Rome's most important temples.

The huge expanse in front of the presidential palace where the cavalry are put through their paces for visiting foreign heads of state has two names. More formally it is referred to as piazza del Quirinale, after the hill on which the palace is built, but for as long as anyone can remember locals have called it piazza di Monte Cavallo – Horse Hill Square – on account of the two towering Imperial-era equestrian statues. The giant horses rear up nervously beside the five-metre-high (16 feet) heavenly twins Castor and Pollux. The statues, which had been lying in the ruins of the Baths of Constantine, were dragged into an artistic arrangement by

Then what?

- There's standing room only in the tiny **Santa Maria dell'Archetto** in via San Marcello 41, which only opens for evening rosary (6.30-7.30pm daily, no phone). A miniature jewel casket dedicated to a particularly venerated image of the Virgin Mary, this chapel is the showcase of 19th-century artist Costantino Brumidi considered (rather exaggeratedly) the 'Michelangelo of the United States' for his later work on Capitol Hill.

- In 1286 a stone bearing an image of the Virgin's face floated to the surface of a well. The church of **Santa Maria in Via** (06 679 3841; open 7.30am-1pm, 4-8pm daily) now stands in the eponymous street on that very spot. The well allegedly has miraculous healing powers: for a small donation, you'll be handed a plastic cupful of the holy water.

- Stand in the presence of pope innards in **Santi Vincenzo ed Anastasio** (piazza di Trevi, open 7am-noon, 4-7pm daily): each pope from Sixtus V (1585-90) to Leo XIII (1878-1903) had his liver, spleen and pancreas preserved and interred in this church beneath the Quirinal palace, before the rest of him was buried somewhere grander. The papal offal is kept under lock and key, but an inventory is inscribed on a marble plaque by the altar.

Domenico Fontana, the favourite architect of the arch city planner Pope Sixtus V, and later flanked by a handy Egyptian obelisk that had stood outside Augustus' mausoleum (*see p97*), together with a big granite basin that had been a cattle trough in the Forum. On the far side of the square are the papal stables, transformed as part of Rome 2000 Holy Year make-over into the city's most elegant exhibition space, the **Scuderie del Quirinale**.

Across the road from the palace's long wing stands another Bernini marvel: the church of **Sant'Andrea al Quirinale**. Behind the church, the south-facing slope of the hill, which until Unification was still wooded and wild, is now very much a centre of official Rome, with its state buildings – police stations, court buildings and ministry offshoots – leading down towards the high-street shopping artery of via Nazionale and the **Palazzo delle Esposizioni**.

Palazzo delle Esposizioni
Via Nazionale 194 (www.palaexpo.it). Bus 40, 64, 70, 71, 170, H. **Map** p335 2B.
This imposing 19th-century purpose-built exhibition hall holds some of the city's best art, photography and unusual curiousity shows. Closed for major repairs and restoration as we went to press, it's scheduled to reopen some time in 2004.

Palazzo del Quirinale
Piazza del Quirinale (06 46 991/www.quirinale.it). Bus 40, 64, 70, 71, 170, H. **Open** 8.30am-12.30pm Sun. Closed July & Aug. **Admission** €5. **No credit cards. Map** p335 2C.
The popes still had not finished the new St Peter's when (in 1574) they started building a summer palace on the highest of Rome's seven hills. Given the possibility that one of the elderly popes might keel over during the holidays, it was decided to build somewhere suitable to hold the conclave to elect his successor. The Quirinale's Cappella Paolina is a faithful replica of the Vatican's Sistine chapel, minus the Michelangelos. Accommodation for the cardinals was provided in the Manica lunga, the immensely long wing that runs the length of via del Quirinale to the rear of the palace. On Sunday mornings, when parts of the presidential palace and gardens open to the public, you may be lucky enough to catch one of the concerts held in the Cappella Paolina.

Sant'Andrea al Quirinale
Via del Quirinale 29 (06 4890 3187). Bus 40, 64, 70, 71, 170, H. **Open** 8am-noon; 4-7pm Mon, Wed-Sun. **Map** p335 2C.
Bernini built this church for free as a gift to the Jesuits… then again, he was being pretty well paid at the time for his day job as chief architect of St Peter's. Pope Alexander VII (1655-67) was so pleased with this dazzling little church, built out of pale pink marble, that it became in effect the palace church. It is cunningly designed to create a sense of grandeur in a tiny space and every surface is lavishly decorated. The star turn is a plaster St Andrew floating through a broken pediment on his way to heaven.

Scuderie Papali al Quirinale
Via XXIV Maggio 16 (06 696 270/www. scuderiequirinale.it). Bus 40, 64, 70, 71, 170, H. **Open** varies with exhibitions. **Credit** (phone bookings only) AmEx, DC, MC, V. **Map** p335 2C.
Carved out of disused stables of the Quirinale palace, this large space for major exhibitions has been magnificently reworked by architect Gae Aulenti – she of Quai d'Orsay fame – who has taken care to preserve original features like the brickwork ramp to the upper floors but has laid down acres of chic marble flooring in the galleries and installed the very latest high-tech lighting. There is an excellent art bookshop, a café, a civilised little seating areas where you can chill out if the Stendhal syndrome seems about to strike, and – best of all – a breathtaking view of Rome's skyline glimpsed from the rear staircase as you leave.

Sightseeing

Via Veneto
& Villa Borghese

The *dolce vita* may have quit via Veneto, but don't miss the exceptional museums of Villa Borghese.

Row off cultural overload at the *laghetto* in **Villa Borghese**. *See p84.*

From the days of the Caesars right up to the building boom of the late 1800s, the area far to the north and north-east of the ancient settlement by the Tiber, stretching from what is now the Pincio to Porta Pia, was one of gardens, villas and religious orders. In the first century BC the Horti Sallustiani (*see p90*) were Rome's most extensive monumental gardens. From the Renaissance on, noble Roman families such as the Borghese and Ludovisi-Boncompagni embellished their sprawling estates here.

When Rome was made the capital of Italy in 1870, most of the greenery was carved up to build the kind of pompous *palazzi* (with the odd art nouveau touch, *see chapter* **Architecture**) so beloved of the new breed of upper-middle-class penpushers. Of the aristocratic estates, only the **Villa Borghese** was saved from post-Unification property speculators; it is now the city's most central public park.

Villa Borghese & the Pincio

In 1580 the wealthy and noble Borghese family bought a vineyard in a semi-rural area north of Rome. Two decades later the plot of land caught the fancy of pleasure-loving Cardinal Scipione Borghese, the favourite nephew of Pope Paul V, who was seeking a location for a *giardino delle delizie*, a garden of earthly delights. In 1608 he began buying up land all around it, and hired architects Flaminio Ponzio and Jan van Santen (Italianised to Giovanni Vasanzio) to produce a backdrop worthy of his sybaritic leisure activities and matchless collection of art.

Work on the magnificent gardens went on until Scipione's death in 1633. The result was a baroque amusement park, complete with trick fountains that sprayed unwitting passers-by, automata and erotic paintings, aviaries, menageries of wild beasts, and an alfresco

Museo Nazionale di Villa Giulia: a treasure house of Etruscan artefacts. *See p86.*

dining room (still visible to the right as you look at the façade of the Galleria Borghese) where the cardinal entertained his guests with due magnificence on warm summer evenings. At the centre of the park, flanked by formal gardens with exotic plants and fruit trees, rose the Casino (now the Galleria Borghese), an elaborate construction intended as a permanent home for Scipione's mushrooming collection of canvas and marble. Successive generations of the Borghese family altered Scipione's park according to changing fashions, and added to (or, tragically, partly sold off) his superlative art collection. When Rome became capital of a unified Italy, the clan looked set to sell off the estate to property speculators. In a rare example of civic far-sightedness the state stepped in in 1901, wresting possession of the Villa from the family in a bitter court battle and turning it into a public park.

Today the Borghese family's pleasure grounds are used for jogging, dog-walking, picnics and cruising. Bicycles and in-line skates can be hired in the park. Wandering around the Villa Borghese is a great way to recuperate from an overdose of sightseeing and carbon monoxide, although culture vultures can continue to sweat it out in three of Rome's greatest art depositories: the **Galleria Borghese** itself, the Etruscan museum at **Villa Giulia** and the **Galleria Nazionale d'Arte Moderna**. The park also houses the Dei Piccoli children's cinema, Rome's

Bioparco-Zoo (*see p240*) and **Museo Nazionale di Zoologia**. Other sights worth looking out for include the piazza di Siena, an elegantly shaped arena used for opera and showjumping, imitation ancient temples, and a lake with rowing boats (for hire from 9.30am to sunset daily). There is also a good view of the Muro Torto section of the Aurelian Wall from the bridge between the Pincio and Villa Borghese. Once a favourite suicide spot, this is now strung with nets to make sure depressed Romans no longer disturb the traffic below.

Overlooking piazza del Popolo (*see p96*), and now an integral part of the Villa Borghese, is one of the oldest gardens in Rome: the **Pincio**. The Pinci family commissioned the first gardens here in the fourth century, although the present layout was designed by Giuseppe Valadier in 1814. The garden is best known for its view of the Vatican at sunset, with the dome of St Peter's silhouetted in gold. The paved area behind the viewpoint is popular with cyclists (bikes can be hired nearby) and skaters.

To the south-east is the **Casino Valadier**; once a tearoom, it is now (after years of inactivity) undergoing a painfully slow revamp with the ostensible aim of becoming a classy eaterie. In the manicured green to the south-east sits the **Villa Medici** (*see p89* **Ivory towers**), the French academy in Rome, which for high-profile art exhibitions occasionally opens to the public; contact 06 67 711 or consult www. villamedici.it for programme information.

Between Villa Borghese and the river are two more museums: a striking art nouveau villa houses the **Museo Hendrik Christian Andersen** and the children's museum, **Explora – Museo dei Bambini di Roma** (*see p240*), is in a former bus depot.

Galleria Borghese

Piazzale Scipione Borghese 5 (information & bookings 06 32 810/www.galleriaborghese.it). Bus 52, 53, 95, 116, 910. **Open** 9am-7pm Tue-Sun. **Admission** €8.50; €5 concessions; *see also p59*. **Tickets**. **No credit cards**. **Map** p334 2B.
Note: booking, essential in high season, is always advisable (phone 9am-6pm Mon-Fri; 9am-1pm Sat). The Casino – a glorious case for some truly breath-taking gems – was designed in 1613 by Jan van Santen (Giovanni Vasanzio) to house Cardinal Scipione Borghese's art collection. One of Bernini's greatest patrons and collector of classical sculpture, the cardinal had as good an eye for a bargain as for a masterpiece: he picked up many works – even the odd Caravaggio – at bargain prices after they were rejected by the disappointed or shocked patrons who had commissioned them. After an ignominious 15-year closure, the gallery reopened in 1997 with decorations and artworks fully restored.

The imposing entrance salon has fourth-century AD floor mosaics, showing gladiators fighting wild animals, and ancient Roman statuary; next to it in Room 1 is one of the gallery's highlights: Canova's 1804 figure of Pauline, sister of Napoleon and wife of Prince Camillo Borghese, as a topless Venus; Prince Camillo thought the work so provocative that he forbade even the artist from seeing it after completion (asked by a shocked friend how she could bear to pose naked, the irascible Pauline is said to have snapped: 'The studio was heated').

Rooms 2-4 contain some spectacular sculptures by Bernini, made early in his career and already showing his genius: notice how Pluto's hand presses into Proserpine's marble thigh in *The Rape of Proserpine* (Room 4), and how her toes flex and spread in struggle. Bernini's *David*, not as famous but more dynamic than Michelangelo's, merits observation from different points of view in Room 2; the tense, concentrated face on the biblical hero is a self-portrait of the artist. Room 3 houses perhaps Bernini's most famous work: *Apollo and Daphne*. It shows the nymph fleeing the sun god's amorous pursuit, her desperate plea for help answered by her river-god father, who turns her – fingertips first – into a laurel tree. (The Latin inscription at the base reads: 'When we pursue fleeting pleasures, we reap only bitter fruits.') Bernini's virtuosity is especially evident in the cluster of paper-thin marble leaves separating the god and the girl.

Room 5 contains important pieces of classical sculpture, many of them Roman copies of Greek originals. Among the most renowned are a Roman copy of a Greek dancing faun and a copy of a sleeping hermaphrodite, displayed with his/her back

to the onlooker so that the breasts and genitals are invisible. Bernini's *Aeneas and Anchises* (not quite up to par with his works in the previous rooms) dominates Room 6, while the Egyptian-themed Room 7 contains more classical statues.

The six Caravaggio's in Room 8 include *David with the Head of Goliath*, the luscious *Boy with a Basket of Fruit*, an uncanny *Madonna of the Serpent* and *Sick Bacchus*, believed to be a self-portrait.

The first-floor picture gallery is packed with one masterpiece after another. Look out in particular for: Raphael's *Deposition* and Pinturicchio's *Crucifixion with Saints Jerome and Christopher* (Room 9); Lucas Cranach's *Venus and Cupid with Honeycomb* and Correggio's *Danaë*, commissioned as 16th-century soft porn for Charles V of Spain (as told in Ovid's *Metamorphoses*, Jupiter – disguised as a 'golden shower' – attempted to seduce the reclining, half-naked maiden) (both Room 10); a dark, brooding *Pietà* by Raphael's follower Sodoma (Room 12); two self-portraits and two sculpted busts of Cardinal Scipione Borghese by Bernini (Room 14); and Rubens's spectacular *Pietà* and *Susanna and the Elders* (Room 18). Titian's *Venus Blindfolding Cupid* and *Sacred and Profane Love*, recently restored but still difficult to interpret, are the centrepieces of Room 20, which also contains works by Veronese, Giorgione and Carpaccio, and a stunning *Portrait of a Man* by Antonello da Messina.

Galleria Nazionale d'Arte Moderna e Contemporanea

Viale delle Belle Arti 131 (06 322 981/www.gnam.arti.beniculturali.it/gnamco.htm). Bus 52, 95/tram 3, 19. **Open** 8.30am-7.30pm Tue-Sun; ticket office closes 6.40pm. **Admission** €6.50; €3.25 concessions. **No credit cards**. **Map** p334 1B.
Italy's national collection of modern art is housed in a massive neo-classical palace, built in 1912, with a recently opened modern wing. It covers Italian art of the 19th and 20th centuries, a period that is relatively unknown outside the country. Most of what's on display here will make you understand why, but a few works (and the cool, quiet elegance of the gallery itself) make it worth crossing Villa Borghese to take a look. The 19th-century collection contains works by the Macchiaioli, who used dots of colour to create their paintings. The 20th-century component is stronger, with works by De Chirico, Carrà, Sironi, Morandi, Marini and others, as well as representatives of movements like Arte povera and the Transavanguardia. There's an interesting assortment of works by international artists, among them Klimt, Kandinsky, Cézanne and Henry Moore. The museum has a well-stocked shop and pleasant café-restaurant, the Caffè delle Arti.

Museo Hendrik Christian Andersen

Via PS Mancini 20 (06 321 9089/www.gnam.arti.beniculturali.it). Metro Flaminio/bus 490, 495, 628/tram 2, 19. **Open** 9am-7.30pm Tue-Sun; ticket office closes 7pm. **Admission** free. **No credit cards**. **Map** p332 1A.

Sightseeing

In a striking art nouveau villa between the river and Villa Giulia (see p86), this offshoot of the Galleria Nazionale dell'Arte Moderna (see p86) was the studio-home of Hendrik Christian Andersen, a Norwegian-American whose artistic ambitions were monumental but whose fans were few. (One notable exception was Henry James who, reportedly, had his eye on the man rather than his works.) Andersen's fascistoid-homoerotic productions stride manfully across his studio; more interesting, perhaps, is his monumental plan for a modern ideal city. The terrace bar upstairs is a wonderful spot on a sunny day, and accessible without visiting the museum.

Museo Nazionale di Villa Giulia

Piazzale di Villa Giulia 9 (06 322 6571). Bus 52/tram 19. **Open** 8.30am-7.30pm Tue-Sun; ticket office closes 6.30pm. **Admission** €4; €2 concessions. **No credit cards. Map** p332 1A.

Built for pleasure-loving Pope Julius III in the mid 16th century, Villa Giulia's extensive gardens and pavilions were laid out by Vignola and Vasari, while Ammannati and Michelangelo both had a hand in the creation of the fountains. The villa was transformed into a museum in 1889, and houses Italy's richest collection of Etruscan art and artefacts (see p281 **Etruscans**). A fifth-century BC terracotta relief from a temple pediment from the port of Pyrgi depicts life-size episodes from the Theban cycle, indicating the Greek presence in Etruscan art. The Faliscan crater – an urn from the fourth century BC – depicts Dawn rising in her chariot, while the Chigi vase features hunting tales from the sixth century BC. Even the jewellery is covered with carved animals (note especially the masterful use of granulated gold), as are the hundreds of miniature vases, pieces of furniture and models of buildings made to accompany the dead to their eternal life. Red, black and white pottery shows scenes of dancing, hunting and more intimate pleasures. The sixth-century BC terracotta Sarcofago degli Sposi, presumably made as a tomb for a husband and wife, is adorned with a sculpture of the happy couple reclining on its lid. In the garden there is a reconstruction of an

More than tormented

Michelangelo Merisi – better known to the world as Caravaggio – was, as artistic geniuses go, more than tormented. In the 14 years he spent in Rome (1592-1606) he was arrested nearly a dozen times, served three prison terms and committed homicide. But while establishing this comprehensive criminal record, he also created nearly 30 spectacular paintings, of which 16 can still be seen today in Roman churches, museums and private collections.

Caravaggio's startlingly realistic painting style, capturing what art historians call the 'aesthetic of exclamation', was the most innovative and influential of its time. The strident contrasts of light and shadow in his painting reflect the artist's tumultuous personal life. Caravaggio ran with a tough crowd; this, combined with his loose-cannon temperament, led him to disturb the peace regularly. Unprovoked, he'd shout 'up your ass' to police he encountered on the street, and regularly picked fights. He was arrested several times for illegal possession of weapons, once for brandishing a sword and threatening innocent passers-by in piazza Navona. Once, when served a plate of artichokes at a Roman osteria, Caravaggio asked the waiter if they were cooked in oil or butter. The waiter suggested he smell the artichokes and figure it out for himself, to which a hyper-sensitive Caravaggio responded by throwing the plate in the waiter's face. After

being evicted from his apartment in vicolo del Divino Amore, he threw rocks at his landlady's apartment, breaking all the windows. Caravaggio's most serious display of lack of self-control was in May 1606, when he fatally stabbed a rival, Ranuccio Tomassoni, in an argument about a tennis match.

Until then Caravaggio's outbursts had been more or less tolerated by the authorities, as he was protected by noble families and high-ranking churchmen. But after the murder not even they could save him: Caravaggio was forced to flee Rome, never to return. He spent the last four years of his life between Naples, Malta (where he was again sent to prison but escaped) and Sicily, painting ever-darker canvasses that frequently feature his self-portrait in the faces of figures who are dead or dying. In 1610 he set sail from Naples, heading for Rome, but complications in the journey brought his felucca to Porto Ercole instead. There he died, at the age of 39, desperate, miserable and alone.

Where to find them...

Galleria Borghese (p85).
Galleria Doria Pamphilj (p104).
Musei Vaticani – Pinacoteca (p149).
Palazzo Barberini (p79).
Palazzo Corsini (p117).
San Luigi dei Francesi (p103).
Sant'Agostino (p104).
Santa Maria del Popolo (p96).

Paparazzi snapped on **via Veneto**.

Etruscan temple. Look out too for the frescos in the colonnaded loggia and, in the courtyard, a sunken nymphaeum (water garden) decorated with mosaics, fountains and statues. The Santa Cecilia academy (*see p252*) holds breathtaking summer concerts here.

Museo Nazionale di Zoologia

Via Aldrovandi 18 (06 6710 9270/www.comune. roma.it/museozoologia). Bus 217, 910/tram 3, 19. **Open** 9am-5pm Tue-Sun. **Admission** €4.13; €2.50 concessions; free under-18s. **No credit cards. Map** p334 1B.
On the north-east side of the zoo is the Museo di Zoologia, with brand new sections on animal reproduction, biodiversity and extreme habitats, plus a vast and glorious collection of dusty and moth-eaten stuffed animals in its old wing. Access is from via Aldrovandi or through the Bioparco-Zoo (*see p240*).

Via Veneto & the Quartiere Ludovisi

Rome's most famous modern street – officially via Vittorio Veneto (VEH-neto) – calls to mind, for some, the *dolce vita*. Still undeniably pretty, with its tree-lined slalom curve, the via Veneto's charm is now well hidden beneath big-name luxury hotels, insurance companies and an endless string of tourist- and expense account-oriented, glass-enclosed sidewalk cafés, almost

tragic in their attempt to convince unwitting middle-aged out-of-towners that dining or drinking here really is the Italian good life.

This area is also known as the Quartiere Ludovisi, after the 17th-century Villa Ludovisi whose palace and gardens were here until the late 1800s. Following the Unification of Italy in 1870 the Ludovisi family, like other aristocratic landowners of the day, sold their property off to building speculators; what had once been a slope of verdant tranquillity was gradually gobbled up by pompous Piedmontese *palazzi*. (Nearby Villa Borghese – *see p85* – only narrowly escaped the same dreadful fate.)

Prince Boncompagni-Ludovisi (whose surnames have been given to major roads in the vicinity) put the proceeds of the sale of his glorious estate towards building a massive palace on part of his former grounds. Crippled by running costs and the capital gains bill on the sale of his land, he sold his new abode to Margherita, King Umberto I's widow (who was to give her name to the classic pizza, as well as to this monument to the prince's lack of financial acumen). Halfway down via Veneto, Villa Margherita is now the US embassy.

As new *palazzi* sprang up, the area acquired the reputation for luxury that it retained until the mid 20th century. Its fame in the 1950s as the world's most happening place was largely due to the enormous American presence at Cinecittà (*see chapter* **Film**). Fellini's 1959 film *La dolce vita*, starring the late and much-lamented Marcello Mastroianni, consecrated the scene and originated the term 'paparazzo', the surname of a character in the film modelled on the legendary photographer Tazio Secchiaroli. Nowadays characterless cafés (where locals wouldn't be caught dead) and wildly expensive nightclubs with atrocious floorshows are a painful reminder of what the area is no longer.

The lower reaches of via Veneto are home to the eerie **Immacolata Concezione** and to Bernini's Fontana delle Api (Bee Fountain). Bees featured on the coat of arms of the Barberini family, from which Bernini's great patron Pope Urban VIII hailed.

L'Immacolata Concezione

Via Vittorio Veneto 27 (06 487 1185). Metro Barberini/bus 52, 53, 61, 62, 63, 71, 80, 95, 116, 119, 175. **Open** *Church* 7am-noon, 3.30-7pm daily. *Crypt* 9am-noon, 3-6pm daily. **Admission** *Crypt* donation expected. **Map** p335 1B.
Commonly known as *i Cappuccini* (the Capuchins) after the long-bearded, brown-clad Franciscan sub-order to which it belongs, this baroque church has a *St Michael* (1635) by Guido Reni (first chapel on the right) that was a major hit with English Grand Tourists (*see p118* **Guido who?**) and a fine *St Paul's Sight Being Restored* (1631) by Pietro da

TRAVEL THE TIMELINE OF HISTORY AND LIVE THE PAST!

Time Elevator is a motion-based cinematographic theatre that takes the audience on a simulated journey through the history of Rome from the legend of Romulus and Remus to the present day.

Special motion base and effects
Available in English, German, French, Spanish and Japanese
Open every day from 9.30 to midnight
Shows running every 15 minutes
Each sow lasts 45 minutes
Children from 5 years old
Ticket Price Adults € 11.00 – Children € 9.20
Fully air conditioned

Centrally located – Via dei SS Apostoli, 20
(just 3 minute-walk from Piazza Venezia through Via del Corso)
Tel + 39 06 6990053 · Web site: www.time-elevator.it

Ivory towers

There's no better place than Rome to absorb the history, art and culture of the past two millennia of Western civilisation, as dozens of nations – Western, Arab and Asian – have realised, establishing formal institutions here to take advantage of the city's infinite academic stimuli. Every year top students in the humanities and visual arts win prestigious fellowships to study and reside at the various *accademie* of Rome, many of which occupy the most prized real estate in the city.

The **Académie de France**, in spectacular Villa Medici atop the Pincio, is the oldest of the international academies (founded 1803) and has counted such masters as Canova among its guest teachers. Covering 45,000 square metres on the Gianicolo, with gardens designed by Russell Page, the **American Academy** is the largest; it holds frequent modern art exhibitions and regular series of arts-related lectures. Also on the Gianicolo are the Spanish and Norwegian academies, but most of the institutes are concentrated inside the Villa Borghese. In the area around via Omero, the academies of Belgium, Denmark, Egypt, Romania and Sweden form what insiders call the *ghetto delle accademie*. The

British School, an imposing pile designed by Edward Lutyens, is in the posh neighbourhood of Parioli, to the north of the park, along with the Austrian and Japanese academies.

When they aren't hosting exhibitions or public lectures, the *accademie* of Rome are a world unto themselves, rarefied communities where the only language you're likely to hear is the native tongue of that academy's nation and where residents often seem stuck in an 18th-century time warp, blissfully oblivious of 21st-century Rome outside their ivory towers.

Académie de France à Rome

Viale Trinità dei Monti 1A, Veneto & Borghese (06 6992 1653/www.villamedici.it). Metro Spagna/bus 116, 119, 490, 495. **Map** p335 1C.

American Academy in Rome

Via Angelo Masina 5, Gianicolo (06 58 461/ www.aarome.org). Bus 44, 75, 710, 870. **Map** p336 2C.

British School at Rome

Via Gramsci 61, Suburbs: north (06 326 4931/www.bsr.ac.uk). Bus 52, 231, 926/ tram 3, 19. **Map** p334 1C.

Sightseeing

All Rome's at your feet on the **Pincio**. *See p83.*

Cortona (first chapel on the left). Its real attraction, though, lies below in the crypt: the skeletons of generations of monks have been removed from the order's short supply of soil from Jerusalem, meticulously dismantled, and attractively arranged in swirls, sunbursts and curlicues through four subterranean chapels. Delicate ribs hang from the ceiling in the form of chandeliers and inverted pelvic bones make the shape of hourglasses, a reminder (as a notice states) that 'you will be what we now are'.

Piazza Sallustio & Porta Pia

East of Villa Borghese, street after street of imposing late 19th-century *palazzi* cover what was ancient Rome's greatest garden: the **Horti Sallustiani**, whose swathes of statues and huge villa occupied the valley between the Quirinale (*see p80*) and the Pincio (*see p84*) hills. The property passed from Julius Caesar via the historian Sallust into the hands of emperors Nero, Vespasian and Nerva. The Goths rampaged through it in 410, but enough was left for Renaissance writers to dwell on its clumps of picturesque ruins. Only in piazza Sallustio are ruins still visible: a hole in the middle of the square contains sufficient masonry to give an idea of lost grandeur (entry by appointment only, *see p60* **Ex-Rip.X**). Statues found here include the *Dying Gaul* (*see p64*) and the *Ludovisi Throne* (*see p101*).

Further east is the **Porta Pia**, its internal façade designed by Michelangelo. British schoolchildren are plagued by the breach Henry V urged his troops once more unto; Italian kids

have the *breccia* (breach) *di Porta Pia*: it was by this monumental entrance gate that a hole was blown, allowing Unification troops march along what is now via XX Settembre and evict the pope from his last stronghold in the Quirinale palace. Next to the gate the British embassy is a sadly out-of-place modern design by the now-unfashionable Sir Basil Spence, with a towering Henry Moore in the middle of its pool.

Then what?

● In the church of **Sant'Isidoro** (via degli Artisti 41, open 10am-noon, 3-6pm Mon-Sat, ring the bell for the custodian) the wonderful De Sylva chapel, to the right of the main altar, has cheeky high reliefs by Gian Lorenzo Bernini. Swathes of prudish 18th-century draperies were peeled off in a recent restoration, revealing Truth and Charity in all their buxom glory.

● For a heart-stopping cocktail, head for the rooftop La Terrazza bar of the **Eden** hotel (*see p41*). Go at sunset – preferably in romantic company.

● Seek out free exhibitions or glimpse classical scholarship at work and play with a stroll through the '**Academy Ghetto**' of viale delle Belle Arti and via Omero, where many nations have arts and humanities institutes (*see p91* **Ivory towers**).

The Tridente

High art and fine shopping in one triangular package.

Rather neglected: the **Mausoleum of Augustus**. *See p97.*

It is perfectly possible to visit Rome without ever straying out of the Tridente area. Many don't: increasing numbers of tourists come to the Eternal City just for the shopping, and that's what you do in the Tridente. Between one glorious fashion outlet and another, cosmopolitan shopaholics might do a spot of sightseeing, but they are more likely to admire the vistas from a café or restaurant table. Which is a pity – the area contains some of Rome's most fascinating sights.

The whole area was built as – and remains – a showpiece. Rome's finest square, **piazza del Popolo**, is the starting point of a three-pronged urban plan: leading out centrally from the square is the area's principal thoroughfare, the **via del Corso** (named after the hell-for-leather horse races – *corse* – that were held on it during *carnevale* until the 1870s); **via Ripetta** veers

off down the riverside, leading eventually to Emperor Augustus's mausoleum and the Ara Pacis; and the third street, chic **via del Babuino**, runs past a series of mouth-watering antique and designer stores to the Spanish Steps. Criss-crossing these three arteries (and punctuated by delectable restaurants and discreet hotels) are those streets, like **via Condotti**, that have given Rome its reputation as an international fashion centre.

Via del Babuino & piazza di Spagna

Piazza di Spagna is where everybody meets, congregating in the summer on whichever side of the grand staircase is in the shade. In spring the loafers, courting couples, exhausted tourists

Art at home

Take a cosy break from echoing marble galleries packed with badly labelled antiquities by viewing art at home... or rather in the homes of the artists that made it. Growing in number, Rome's case-museo recreate the artistic atmosphere with artists' last colours dried on to palettes and brushes, favourite reading material open on bedside tables and crowding library shelves, and well-worn props (including some frightful plastic fruit used by **Giorgio De Chirico**) still adorning light-filled studios.

His magnificent townhouse right by the Spanish Steps shows De Chirico was not of the artist-freezing-in-a-garret fraternity. Opened to the public on the 20th anniversary of his death in 1978, the master's attic-studio is now on show, as are some solidly bourgeois reception rooms liberally dotted with dozens of Metaphysical paintings.

The bizarrely fascinating works of Norwegian painter-sculptor **Hendrik Christian Andersen** (not to be confused with Danish story-teller Hans Christian Andersen, who also spent a fruitful period in Rome) are displayed in the beautiful Liberty (art-nouveau) villa (see p85 **Museo Henrik Christian Andersen**) where he lived for decades in a weird threesome with his mother and widowed sister-in-law. Despite the fact that Rome resolutely refused to have his works cluttering its public places, Andersen left his villa and entire opus (most of which – for reasons that will become obvious when you visit – remained unsold on his death in 1940) to the city, along with detailed plans for an ideal city.

A whole dynasty of sculptors worked in the fascinating Museo-Atelier Canova-Tadolini on via del Babuino. The studio originally belonged to the greatest of all 18th-century sculptors, **Antonio Canova**, who left it in his will (together with his sketches, models and tools) to his student and assistant Adamo Tadolini, from whom it passed to two more generations of Tadolini sculptors.

Writers too are commemorated in 'museum-houses', the best known and longest established being the small pink house where the English Romantic duo **John Keats** and **Percy Bysshe Shelley** lived a wretched few months in 1820-21. Who knows if they had time, in their poetical misery, to appreciate their spectacular view over the Spanish Steps? Bring a box of tissues to the **Keats-Shelley Memorial House** (see p93): even the hardest-hearted can be moved to tears by the sight of manuscripts written by consumptive poets with shaky hands. When Keats breathed his last in this house in 1821, he was only 25.

The German poet **Johann Wolfgang von Goethe**, who breezed into town from Weimar in 1786, had a much jollier time in the house on via del Corso that he shared with the painter Tischbein. The house preserves many of his diaries and letters, and hosts concerts, films and cultural events.

Casa-Museo Giorgio De Chirico

Piazza di Spagna 31 (06 679 6546). Metro Spagna/bus 52, 53, 61, 63, 71, 80, 85, 116, 119, 160, 850. **Open** 10am-1pm Tue-Sat; 1st Sun of mth. Closed Aug. **Admission** €5.16. **No credit cards. Map** p335 1C.

Museo-Atelier Canova-Tadolini

Via del Babuino 150 (06 3262 9336). Metro Spagna or Flaminio/bus 116, 119. **Open** by appointment only. **Admission** free. **No credit cards. Map** p332 2A.

Casa di Goethe

Via del Corso 18 (06 3265 0412/www. casadigoethe.it). Metro Spagna/bus 116, 119. **Open** 10am-6pm Tue-Sun. **Admission** €3; €2 concessions. **No credit cards. Map** p332 2A.

and those whose dates are seriously late are temporarily turfed off the steps while an army of gardeners arranges the display of pink azaleas. But they soon drift back again: park yourself for long enough on the steps and you'll meet everyone you know in Rome.

English 'milords' invented the whole place, creating Grand Tour agents, coffee shops, tearooms, libraries, elegant lodgings and a network of suppliers for all the prerequisites of civilised 18th-century living. Everyone's favourite Romantics stayed in what is now the **Keats-Shelley Memorial House** at the foot of the Spanish Steps. The Spanish have a magnificent embassy in the square, but got lucky when the area was named after them: it is the French who should be thanked for creating this sophisticated urban landscape, with its grand staircase leading down from the French preserve of Villa Medici (see p89 **Ivory towers**) and the **Trinità dei Monti** church and convent at the top. Don't be daunted by the steep climb to admire the sensational view from the Trinità dei Monti (though one of the best-kept secrets of the area is the passenger lift, cunningly concealed on the left just inside the main entrance to the Spagna metro station – this is also the easiest way up to the Villa Borghese, *see p83*).

From the top you can get the lie of the land: just beyond the **barcaccia**, a charming fountain in the shape of a half-sunken boat, is **via Condotti** with its super-smart boutiques, the Gucci and Prada emporia immediately recognisable even at this distance by the neat lines of Japanese tourists, clutching lengthy shopping lists for cult-status leather goods. Across the way is the legendary **Café Greco** (*see p200*), whose clientele included Casanova and mad King Ludwig of Bavaria. If it's tea you crave, try Babington's tea rooms on piazza di Spagna – that other august institution – which has been serving reviving beverages and English-style snacks for 110 years.

To the north-west the incongruously neo-Gothic spire of All Saints' English church (*see p311*) pokes up above the roof tops along via del Babuino. The origin of this oddly (and, to Roman ears, rudely) named street lies in the ugly statue draped over an old drinking trough, which reminded inhabitants of a member of the monkey family – another incongruity in the street to which all Rome's most beautiful people flock for their shopping.

Parallel to via del Babuino, tucked right under the Pincio hill, is the via Margutta, fondly remembered as the focus of the 1960s art scene. Federico Fellini lived here until his death in 1993. This was always the artists' quarter: artists' models would ply for business on the Spanish Steps, dressed in their favourite costumes. Once a year artists who still live here open their studios to the public (*see p233*). A collection of somewhat higher standard modern works can be seen at the **Galleria Comunale d'Arte Moderna e Contemporanea** south of piazza di Spagna.

Galleria Comunale d'Arte Moderna e Contemporanea

Via Francesco Crispi 24 (06 474 2848/ www.comune.roma.it.gal_com). Metro Barberini or Spagna/bus 52, 53, 61, 71, 80, 85, 95, 116, 160, 850. **Open** 10am-1.30, 2.30-6pm Tue-Sat; 9am-12.30pm Sun. **Admission** €2.58; €1.55 concessions. **No credit cards. Map** p335 1C.

Somewhat directionless since the opening of the contemporary (meaning post-1950) art centre in the old Peroni brewery (*see p246* **MACRO**), this three-floor gallery in a converted convent continues to show part of the city's permanent modern (1883-1948) collection, which contains works by Balla, De Chirico, De Pisis, Morandi and Guttuso.

Keats-Shelley Memorial House

Piazza di Spagna 26 (06 678 4235/www.keats-shelley-house.org). Metro Spagna/bus 52, 53, 61, 71, 80, 85, 95, 116, 160, 850. **Open** 9am-1pm, 3-6pm Mon-Fri; 11am-2pm, 3-6pm Sat. **Admission** €3. **No credit cards. Map** p335 1C.

The house at the bottom of the Spanish Steps where the 25-year-old John Keats died of tuberculosis in 1821 is crammed with mementos: a lock of Keats' hair and his death mask, a minuscule urn holding tiny pieces of Shelley's charred skeleton, copies of documents and letters, and a massive library make this a Romantics enthusiast's paradise. Devotees should also make the pilgrimage to the Cimitero Acattolico (Protestant Cemetery, *see p124*) in Testaccio, where both Keats and Shelley are buried. The apartment above the Keats-Shelley House can be rented for holidays (0162 882 5925/ bookings@landmarktrust.co.uk).

Piazza di Spagna & Spanish Steps

Metro Spagna/bus 52, 53, 61, 71, 80, 85, 95, 116, 160, 850. **Map** p335 1C.

Piazza di Spagna has been a compulsory stop for visitors to Rome ever since the 18th century, when a host of poets and musicians stayed nearby. The square takes its name from the Spanish Embassy to the Vatican, but is famous for the Spanish Steps (Scalinata di Trinità dei Monti), an elegant cascade down from the church of Trinità dei Monti. The steps (completed in 1725) could more accurately be called 'French': they were funded by French diplomat Etienne Gueffier, who felt the muddy slope leading up to the church – itself built with money from a French king – needed a revamp. At Christmas a crib is erected halfway up; in spring and summer the steps are adorned with huge tubs of azaleas; sometimes fashion shows are held here. At the foot of the stairs is a delightful boat-shaped fountain, the *barcaccia*, designed in 1627 by either Gian Lorenzo Bernini or perhaps his less-famous father Pietro; it's ingeniously sunk below ground level to compensate for the low pressure of the delicious Acqua Vergine that feeds it.

Via del Corso & piazza del Popolo

Via del Corso is the last urban stretch of the ancient via Flaminia, which linked Rome with the north Adriatic coast. Over the past 2,000 years it has been successively a processional route for Roman legions, a country lane, a track for *carnevale* races and, from the late 1800s, a showcase principal street for the capital.

The street's liveliest period began in the mid 15th century, when Pope Paul II began to fret over the debauched goings-on at the pre-Lenten *carnevale* celebrations in Testaccio (*see p123*). He decided to move the races and processions somewhere more central, where he and his

Sightseeing

Then what?

The fashion emporia of the Tridente exert a strong magnetic pull. But, if you're seeking to punctuate your retail routine with culture, there's plenty to do even after you've exhausted the major sights.

● Inspect the 24m-high (78ft) **obelisk** dedicated to the sun in piazza del Popolo. Augustus looted it from Heliopolis in 10 BC and erected it in the Circo Massimo (Circus Maximus, *see p68*) to commemorate his conquest of Egypt. The indefatigable obelisk-mover Pope Sixtus V had it dragged across town in 1589.

● Procure tickets for a concert in Rome's **conservatory** at via Vittoria 6. Or just listen at the windows as tomorrow's star soloists practise their party pieces.

● After the Seven Veils business, Salome convinced King Herod to cut off John the Baptist's head and present it to her on a silver tray. By tortuous routes the relic ended up in a side chapel of **San Silvestro** church in piazza San Silvestro, where it is still on display.

● If you've visited his studio museum (*see p92* **Art at home**), pay further respects to neo-classical sculptor **Antonio Canova** (his *Three Graces* are pictured, *right*) by walking past the exterior of his fragment-encrusted house in the street that bears his name. The great man's works are sadly out of fashion, but surely he's overdue for reappraisal?

● Join the politicians and media types from the Montecitorio parliament building to enjoy an old-fashioned ice-cream at **Giolitti's**, the city's most famous *gelateria* (via Uffici del

Vicario 40)... not the best ice-cream in Rome, but definitely the best connected.

● Sip a mood-setting aperitif at Fellini's former hangout **Canova** (*see p200*) or **Rosati** (*see p201*) in piazza del Popolo, then stroll up to the **Pincio** (*see p83*) to witness the extraordinary sunset over the Tridente.

troops could keep an eye on things. The obvious spot was the via Flaminia – then known simply as via Lata ('wide street') – at the end of which he built his Palazzo Venezia (*see p65*). The pope had the stretch of the street within the city walls paved (using funds from a tax on prostitutes) and renamed il Corso ('the avenue'). For over four centuries Romans flocked there at *carnevale* time to be entertained by such edifying spectacles as races between press-ganged Jews, hunchbacks, prostitutes and horses with hot pitch up their recta to make them run faster.

These grotesqueries only stopped after Italian Unification in the 1870s, when the new national government set up shop halfway along via del Corso. The cheap shops and eateries that lined the street were shut down, to be replaced by pompous neo-classical offices for banks and insurance companies. This set the tone for what remains the country's political heart: the Lower House (Camera dei Deputati) is in **Palazzo di Montecitorio**, in the piazza of the same name, and Palazzo Chigi, the prime minister's office, is next door in piazza Colonna, so named for the magnificent second-century AD **colonna di Marco Aurelio** (column of Marcus Aurelius) that graces it. Legends of Machiavellian wheeler-dealing cling to every restaurant and bar around the parliament building.

North from Palazzo Chigi imposing edifices such as **Palazzo Ruspoli** give way to lower-end clothing outlets, which attract a seething mass of suburban teenagers at weekends.

The pedestrianised piazza **San Lorenzo in Lucina**, with the church of the same name, is a welcome retreat from the fumes and crowds.

Beyond the retail crush is the symmetrically elegant **piazza del Popolo** – once the papacy's favourite place for executions – graced by the Caravaggio-packed church of **Santa Maria del Popolo**. The piazza has been gloriously restored and is virtually traffic-free.

Colonna di Marco Aurelio (Column of Marcus Aurelius)

Piazza Colonna. Bus 52, 53, 61, 63, 71, 80, 85, 95, 116, 119, 160, 850. **Map** p333 1A.

The 30m (100ft) column of Marcus Aurelius was built between AD 180 and 196 to commemorate the victories on the battlefield of that most intellectual of Roman emperors. Author of the famous *Meditations*, he died while campaigning in 180 (to be replaced by his son Commodus, who was largely forgotten until Ridley Scott resurrected him for his 2000 film *Gladiator*). The reliefs on the column, modelled on the earlier ones on Trajan's column (*see p73*) in the Imperial Fora, are vivid illustrations of Roman army life. In 1589 a statue of St Paul replaced that of Marcus Aurelius on top of the column.

Palazzo di Montecitorio

Piazza di Montecitorio (06 67 601/www.senato.it). Bus 52, 53, 61, 63, 71, 80, 85, 95, 116, 119, 160, 850. **Open** *Sept-July* 1st Sun of every mth; free guided tours (in Italian) 10am-5pm. **Admission** free. **Map** p333 1A.

Since 1871 this has been the Lower House of Italy's parliament, which is why police and barricades sometimes prevent you from getting near its elegantly curving façade. Designed by Bernini in 1650 for Pope Innocent X, much of the building has been greatly altered, but the clock tower, columns and window sills of rough-hewn stone are its originals. In piazza di Montecitorio stands the tenth-century BC obelisk of Psammeticus. It was brought from Heliopolis by Augustus to act as the gnomon (projecting piece) for the emperor's great sundial. In a recent refurbishment of the square a sundial of sorts was inlaid into the cobblestones.

Palazzo Ruspoli–Fondazione Memmo

Via del Corso 418 (06 6830 7344/www. palazzoruspoli.it). Bus 52, 53, 61, 63, 71, 80, 85, 95, 116, 119, 160, 850. **Open** exhibition times vary. **Admission** varies with exhibition. **Map** p333 1A.

The palace of one of Rome's old noble families is today used for touring exhibitions of photography, art, archaeology and history. It opens late at least one night a week. The basement rooms often host photo exhibitions, and admission is sometimes free.

Piazza del Popolo

Metro Flaminio/bus 88, 95, 117, 119, 490, 491, 495/tram 2. **Map** p332 2A.

For centuries piazza del Popolo was the first glimpse most travellers got of Rome, for it lies at the end of the ancient via Flaminia and directly inside the city's northern gate, the Porta del Popolo. If Grand Tourists arrived during *carnevale* time, they were likely to witness condemned criminals being tortured here for the edification and/or entertainment of the populace. The piazza was given its present oval form by Rome's leading neo-classical architect Giuseppe Valadier in the early 19th century (*see chapter* **Architecture**); the obelisk in the centre was brought from Egypt by Augustus and stood in the Circo Massimo (Circus Maximus, *see p68*) until 1589, when it was moved to its present site by Pope Sixtus V. It appears to stand at the apex of a perfect triangle formed by via Ripetta, via del Corso and via del Babuino, although this is an illusion. The churches on either side of via del Corso – Santa Maria dei Miracoli and Santa Maria di Monte Santo – appear to be twins, but are actually different sizes. Carlo Rainaldi, who designed them in the 1660s, made them and the angles of the adjacent streets appear symmetrical by giving one an oval dome and the other a round one. The immense Porta del Popolo gate was given a facelift by Bernini in 1655 to welcome Sweden's Queen Christina, who had shocked her subjects by abdicating her throne to become a Catholic. The plaque wishing *felice fausto ingressui* ('a happy and blessed arrival') was addressed to the Church's illustrious new signing. The piazza's greatest monument is the church of Santa Maria del Popolo, and the piazza contains those eternally fashionable meeting points: cafés Rosati (*see p201*) and Canova (*see p200*).

San Lorenzo in Lucina

Piazza San Lorenzo in Lucina 16A (06 687 1494). Bus 52, 53, 61, 63, 71, 80, 85, 95, 116, 119, 160, 850. **Open** *Church* 9am-noon, 5-7.30pm daily. *Roman remains* guided tour 4.30pm last Sat of each mth; other Sat by appointment for groups of 15 or more. **Admission** *Roman remains* €2. **Map** p333 1A.

This 12th-century church was built on the site of an early Christian place of worship, which in turn is believed to stand on the site of an ancient well sacred to Juno. The church's exterior incorporates Roman columns, while the 17th-century interior contains a wealth of treasures including Bernini portrait busts in the Fonseca Chapel, a kitsch 17th-century *Crucifixion* by Guido Reni and a monument to French artist Nicolas Poussin, who died in Rome in 1665. In the first chapel on the right is an ancient grill, reputed to be the one on which the martyr St Lawrence was roasted to death.

Santa Maria del Popolo

Piazza del Popolo 12 (06 361 0836). Metro Flaminio/bus 88, 95, 117, 119, 490, 491, 495/tram 2. **Open** 7am-noon, 4-7pm Mon-Sat; 8am-1.30pm, 4.30-7.30pm Sun. **Map** p332 2A.

According to legend, Santa Maria del Popolo occupies the site of a garden in which Nero's nurse and mistress secretly buried the hated emperor's corpse.

The site was still believed to be haunted by demons 1,000 years later, and in 1099 Pope Paschal II built a chapel there to dispel them. Nearly four centuries later, beginning in 1472, Pope Sixtus IV rebuilt the chapel as a church, financing it by taxing foreign churches and selling ecclesiastical jobs.

In the apse are Rome's first stained-glass windows, created by French artist Guillaume de Marcillat in 1509. The apse itself was designed by Bramante, while the choir ceiling and first and third chapels in the right aisle were frescoed by Pinturicchio, the favourite artist of the Borgias. In Pinturicchio's exquisite works, the Virgin and a host of saints keep company with some very pre-Christian sibyls. Most intriguing is the Chigi Chapel, designed by Raphael for wealthy banker Agostino Chigi. The mosaics in the dome depict God creating the sun and the seven planets, and Agostino's personal horoscope: with binoculars you can just about make out a crab, a bull, a lion and a pair of scales. The chapel was completed by Bernini, who, on the orders of Agostino's descendant Pope Alexander VII, added the two theatrical statues of Daniel and Habakkuk. The church's most-gawped-at possessions, however, are the two masterpieces by Caravaggio to the left of the main altar, in the Cerasi Chapel. On a vast scale, and suffused with lashings of the master's own particular light, they show the stories of Saints Peter and Paul. Note also the bizarre memorial of 17th-century notable GB Gisleni, left of the main door: grisly skeletons, chrysalids and butterflies remind us of our brief passage through this life before we exit the other end.

Via Ripetta

Halfway down the third arm of the Tridente, via Ripetta, is the emphatic piazza Augusto Imperatore, built by Mussolini around the rather neglected **Mausoleo di Augusto** – the family funeral mound of the Emperor Augustus – with the intention of having himself buried there with the Caesars. Above is the **Ara Pacis Augustae**, erected by Augustus to celebrate peace in the Mediterranean after his conquest of Gaul and Spain.

South of the square stand two fine churches: San Girolamo degli Illirici, serving Rome's Croatian community, and San Rocco, built for local innkeepers and Tiber boatmen by Alexander VI (1492-1503). Heading back towards via del Corso, the giant, curving walls of the Palazzo Borghese come into view; acquired in 1506 by Camillo Borghese, the future Pope Paul V, it was later the home of Napoleon's sister Pauline.

Ara Pacis Augustae
Via Ripetta/lungotevere in Augusta (06 6710 3887/fax 06 3600 3471/www.comune.roma.it/ arapacis). Bus 30, 70, 81, 87, 186, 492, 628, 913. **Open** closed for restoration. **Map** p332 2A.

Currently shrouded in scaffolding and corrugated iron, the Ara Pacis ('Altar of Peace') is one of the most artistically distinguished monuments of ancient Rome. It was inaugurated in 9 BC to celebrate the wealth and security that Augustus's victories had brought to the Empire. Originally located somewhere in the vicinity of piazza San Lorenzo in Lucina (map p333 1A), the altar was rebuilt on this site in the early 20th century from ancient fragments amassed through a fiendishly long and difficult excavation and a trawl through various museums.

The altar itself sits inside an enclosure carved with delicately realistic reliefs. The lower band of the frieze is decorated with a relief of swirling acanthus leaves and swans with outstretched wings; the upper band shows a procession, thought to depict the ceremonies surrounding the dedication of the altar. The carved faces of Augustus and his family have all been identified.

Heated public and political debate over the demolition of the earlier (1937-40) building that provided shelter for the Ara Pacis, American architect Richard Meier's design for an ultra-modern pavilion for the altar and attached exhibition space, and the proposed makeover of what is a stridently Fascist-era square plonked incongruously in central Rome have meant that completion targets for the whole project have slipped back and back – Romans scoff at the idea of work being finished by the latest target of spring 2004. Plans to pedestrianise the area and create a garden linking the Ara Pacis museum with the Mausoleo di Augusto are still on hold.

Mausoleo di Augusto (Mausoleum of Augustus)
Piazza Augusto Imperatore/via Ripetta. Bus 30, 70, 81, 87, 186, 492, 628, 913. **Open** with prior permission only (*see p60* **Ex-Rip.X**). **Map** p332 2A.

It's hard to believe that this forlorn-looking brick cylinder was one of the most important monuments of ancient Rome. It was originally covered with marble pillars and statues, all of which have long since been looted. Two obelisks that stood either side of the main entrance are now in the piazza del Quirinale (*see p81*) and piazza dell'Esquilino. The mausoleum was built in honour of Augustus, who had brought peace to the city and its Empire, and was begun in 28 BC. The first person buried here was Augustus's nephew, favourite son-in-law and heir apparent, Marcellus, also commemorated in the Teatro di Marcello (*see p115*). He died young in 23 BC. Augustus himself was laid to rest in the central chamber on his death in AD 14, and many more early Caesars went on to join him. In the Middle Ages the mausoleum was used as a fortress, and later hosted concerts, but Mussolini had it restored, reportedly because he thought it a fitting place for his own illustrious corpse. He also planted the cedars and built in Fascist-classical style the square that now surrounds the tomb.

The Pantheon & Piazza Navona

Squeeze in some Renaissance art and ecclesiastical architecture between the ancient military manoeuvres and late-night celebrity spotting.

In classical times the Campus Martius (Campo Marzio/Field of Mars), which covered a huge area around piazza Navona and the Pantheon, was given over to physical jerks, competitive sports and track events, including that forerunner of Formula One, chariot racing. To keep them fighting fit, the troops of the vast Roman army had the run of acres of verdant parkland stretching down to the Tiber, with luxurious marbled bathhouses to wash off the sweat, theatres for entertainment, and grand monuments and temples to inspire notions of Empire. You can glimpse something of its grandeur in the racetrack-shaped **piazza Navona** – built on the ruins of Domitian's stadium – which seated 30,000 spectators.

In the fifth century barbarians cut Rome's aqueducts, driving the city's Dark Age population down towards its alternative water supply: the Tiber. The Campo Marzio area started to be built over. For grander dwellings, dressed stone was filched from the disused military facilities; humbler souls too constructed their own little houses blithely among the ruins. In this area of haphazard development, every medieval wall tells a tale of primitive recycling.

Even today the area retains this admixture. Mink-coated contessas mingle with elderly pensioners, craftsmen and tradesmen; indeed, there's a good chance that they all live – or make a living – in various parts of the same palazzo. After dark this is a chic area with glitzy restaurants and sophisticated *enoteche* (wine bars). But in the daytime it's back to business: buying and selling, making and breaking against a stunning backdrop and with cacophonous sound effects.

West of piazza Navona

Via de' Coronari was Rome's original tourist trap. Pilgrims were funnelled along here after arriving at the northern entrance to the city at piazza del Popolo (*see p96*), and marched past a succession of hard-sell souvenir shops and rosary-makers (*coronari*) who vied to empty the

travellers' pockets before they set off across the Castel Sant'Angelo bridge to St Peter's. The 16th-century Banco di Santo Spirito – which is now a branch of the Banca di Roma – in via del Banco di Santo Spirito was handily placed to replenish them.

Corso Vittorio Emanuele II (known simply as corso Vittorio) was hacked through the area's medieval fabric after Unification in the 1870s, sparing only the most grandiose of homes – **Palazzo Massimo alle Colonne**, for instance, and Palazzo Braschi, which now contains the splendidly revamped **Museo di Roma**. Traffic here can be heavier at three in the morning than three in the afternoon, but don't get here too late or you'll miss the Rubens altarpieces in the magnificent **Chiesa Nuova**.

For more picturesque – though no less chaotic – nightlife activity, head east from corso Vittorio towards the church of **Santa Maria della Pace** and the *triangolo della Pace* around it: in this golden triangle movie stars and VIPs – real and would-be – cavort (though never before midnight) at the smart bars while the rest of humanity flows back and forth in a continuously moving wave. On a Saturday night you can forget eating if you haven't booked a table.

Chiesa Nuova/Santa Maria in Vallicella

Piazza della Chiesa Nuova (06 687 5289).
Bus 30, 40, 46, 62, 63, 64, 70, 81, 116, 492,
628, 630, 780, 916. **Open** 8am-noon, 4.30-7pm daily. **Map** p333 2B.
Filippo Neri (1515-95) was a Florentine businessman who gave up his career to live and work among the poor in Rome. He was a personable character, who danced on altars and played practical jokes on priests, and became one of the most popular figures in the city, his fame helping along by a miracle or two. He founded the Oratorian order to continue his mission. Work began on the Chiesa Nuova, the order's headquarters, in 1575, with funds raised by Neri's followers. He wanted a large and simple building, but after his death the whitewashed walls were covered with exuberant frescos and multicoloured marbles. Pietro da Cortona painted *Neri's Vision of*

the Virgin (1664-5) in the vault, the *Trinity in Glory* (1647) in the cupola and the *Assumption of the Virgin* (1650) in the apse; Rubens contributed three paintings, the *Virgin and Child* (1607) over the altar, and Saints Gregory and Domitilla, right and left respectively of the main altar (1607-8). The result is one of the most satisfying church interiors in Rome. The body of Neri, canonised in 1622, lies in a chapel ornately decorated with marble to the left of the main altar; his rooms are open to the public on 26 May (his feast day). Singing was an important part of Oratorian worship, and oratory as a musical form developed out of the order's services. Next to the church, Borromini designed the fine Oratorio dei Filippini, which is still used for concerts.

Museo di Roma

Palazzo Braschi, via di San Pantaleo 10 (06 6710 8346/www.museodiroma.comune.roma.it). Bus 30, 40, 46, 62, 63, 64, 70, 81, 116, 492, 628, 630, 780, *916.* **Open** 9am-7pm Tue-Sun; ticket office closes 6pm. **Admission** €6.20; €3.10 concessions. **No credit cards. Map** p333 2B.

The Museo di Roma remained inexplicably closed for 15 years until 2002, but it was worth waiting to see its stunning new setting. The building itself – which at the rear overlooks piazza Navona – was built in one of the last great flurries of nepotism by the nephew of 18th-century Pope Pius VI. Swallowed up by the Italian state in 1871 and intended to house the Interior Ministry, the palazzo later enjoyed a period of notoriety as Fascist party HQ. The city's treasures are displayed over two floors in magnificent frescoed rooms (the Egyptian motifs are particularly striking): rows of papal busts, topographical paintings, old photographs and costumes, as well as oddities like the Braschi family sedan chair (used by Pius VI) and the papal railway carriage (used by more recent pontiffs). On the ground floor is a bookshop and a study resource centre.

Vox pop

When Vatican walls had ears and you could lose your head for an offhand irreverent remark, Romans let off steam through 'talking' statues. There were six of them around the city where the populace would pin scurrilous verse, epigrams or ribald lampoons against the city's ecclesiastic or aristocratic establishment. The often sophisticated poems came to be called *pasquinate* (pasquinades) after **Pasquino**, the best known of the talking statues, whose armless classical form (pictured) – probably from the third century BC – still sprawls under the walls of Palazzo Braschi (*see above* **Museo di Roma**) where it was placed in 1501.

Pasquino may, or may not, have been a tailor to the Vatican who had a shop nearby from where much of papal Rome's insider gossip emanated. Legend says that after this tailor died, the gossip that would have been exchanged in his shop was pinned to the statue instead – sometimes in Latin, sometimes in Roman dialect. The tradition continued pretty much until the advent of television, with a real flurry during the 20 heavily censored years of Fascism. Even today Roman wits will pin satirical offerings to the much-eroded bit of marble.

Pasquino's foremost interlocutor, **Marforio**, became a political liability and was removed from his post in the Forum in 1587; he still languishes on the Campidoglio (*see p61*), where he was taken so that an eye could be kept on him. This repression led to a rash of 'talking' statues appearing: the hideous

Babuino (*see p93*) in via del Babuino; **Abate Luigi** in piazza Vidoni beside Sant'Andrea della Valle (*see p109*); the **facchino** (porter) on the corner of via Lata; and the busty **Madama Lucrezia**, next to the basilica di San Marco (*see p65*) in piazza Venezia.

Emperor and god: Hadrian is celebrated in the **Tempio di Adriano**. See p104.

Palazzo Massimo alle Colonne
*Corso Vittorio Emanuele 141 (06 6880 1545).
Bus 30, 40, 46, 62, 63, 64, 70, 81, 116, 492,
628, 630, 780, 916.* **Open** 8am-1pm, 16 Mar only.
Map p333 2A&B.
The aristocratic Massimo family is one of the city's oldest, claiming to trace descent from ancient Rome. When its palace was built in the 1530s by Baldassare Peruzzi, the unique design – curved walls with a portico built into the bend of the road that follows the stands of the ancient Stadium of Domitian (*see p103* piazza Navona) – aroused suitable admiration. The interior is only open to the public on one day each year, 16 March, in commemoration of the day in 1583 when a young Massimo was allegedly raised from the dead by St Filippo Neri. At the rear of the palace is the piazza de' Massimi, dominated by an ancient column originally from the Circus.

Santa Maria della Pace
Vicolo del Arco della Pace 5 (06 686 1156). Bus 30, 40, 46, 62, 63, 64, 70, 81, 116, 492, 628, 630, 780, 916. **Open** 10am-12.45pm Mon-Fri. **Map** p333 2B.
As the front door is usually locked, you're likely to enter this church via a simple, beautifully harmonious cloister by Bramante, his first work after arriving in Rome in the early 1500s. The church itself was built in 1482 for Pope Sixtus IV, while the theatrical baroque façade was added by Pietro da Cortona in 1656. The church's most famous artwork is Raphael's *Sybils*, just inside the door. It was painted in 1514 for Agostino Chigi, the playboy banker and first owner of the Villa Farnesina (*see p119*). Bramante's cloister is likely to be filled with exhibitions of works by contemporary artists.

Piazza Navona & east

The *centro*'s squares may have venerable histories and architecture, but they also have an endearingly self-deprecating character, providing wonderful sets for the less than grandiose happenings of everyday life. Pride of place has to go to the great theatre of baroque Rome: piazza Navona. For all its graceful sweep, with Bernini's fountains, Borromini's church of **Sant'Agnese in Agone** and picturesque pavement cafés, its denizens range from soothsayers, caricature artists, buskers and suburban smoothies to tourists, nuns, businessmen, ladies of leisure and anyone who simply wants a gossip or an ice-cream. At the south-western end, in little piazza Pasquino, stands the patron of the city's scandalmongers, a severely truncated classical statue lodged against one wall (*see p99* **Vox pop**).

In an attraction-packed area just to the north are **Palazzo Altemps**, with its spectacular collection of antique statuary; **Sant'Agostino** church and its Caravaggio masterpiece; and the **Museo Napoleonico** (*see p106* **Then what?**). On via dell'Orso, which in the Renaissance was inhabited mainly by upmarket courtesans, the **Osteria dell'Orso** (*see p175*) has been an eaterie since the 15th century.

Due east from the piazza, the Senate building – **Palazzo Madama** – is flanked by the church of **San Luigi dei Francesi**, which contains yet more Caravaggios, along with Borromini's extraordinary **Sant'Ivo alla Sapienza**.

True genius

Irascible, ascetic architect **Francesco Borromini** (1599-1667) did not achieve the same level of recognition in 17th-century Rome as his exuberant arch-rival Gian Lorenzo Bernini. Today, however, it's Borromini who is almost universally recognised as the true genius of Roman baroque architecture.

A good starting point for a tour of his most important buildings is the exquisite **San Carlino alle Quattro Fontane** (see p81), a church so small it occupies the same surface area as one of the columns supporting the dome of St Peter's. A few minutes' walk from San Carlino, beyond what would be a majestic front yard if it wasn't used as a car park, is **Palazzo Barberini** (see p79). Although considered one of Bernini's masterpieces, many believe that much of the credit for the Palazzo's beautiful proportions should go to Borromini, the assistant architect and a disciple of the building's original designer Carlo Maderno. Don't miss Borromini's oval staircase in the right wing.

From Palazzo Barberini walk down to the homonymous piazza and take via Sistina; turn into the second street on the left, then right on to via Capo le Case and you will come in full view of an under-regarded architectural jewels: the dome and bell tower of **Sant' Andrea delle Fratte**. As you walk closer, the

contrast between the dome's convex and concave walls – a typical Borromini feature – is striking. Around the corner in via di Propaganda is another Borromini masterpiece: the chapel of the **Palazzo di Propaganda Fide**. To build this chapel Borromini ordered – probably with glee – the demolition of an existing one, erected only a few years earlier by Bernini. The chapel's façade dominates the building's elevation on the narrow street with great theatrical effect.

Next stop in the tour is **Sant'Ivo alla Sapienza** (see p104). This small but grand church – built as the chapel of Rome University – stands at the end of a beautiful porticoed courtyard. From Sant'Ivo it's a short walk to the church of **Sant'Agnese in Agone** (see p103) in piazza Navona, probably Borromini's best-known building.

Last stop is the **Oratorio dei Filippini**. The Oratorio stands next to the Chiesa Nuova (see p98), its slightly concave façade almost embracing a large square off corso Vittorio Emanuele. To get here from piazza Navona, take via dei Banchi Vecchi and walk as far as piazza dell' Orologio (Clock Square), so-called because of the tower that dominates it. The tower marks the rear end of the Oratorio complex and, together with the dome of Sant'Andrea, is one of Borromini's most successful brick structures.

Museo Nazionale Romano – Palazzo Altemps

Piazza Sant'Apollinare 48 (06 683 3566).
Bus 30, 40, 46, 70, 81, 87, 116, 492, 628.
Open 9am-7.45pm Tue-Sun; ticket office closes 7pm. **Admission** €5; €2.50 concessions; *see also p59* **Tickets. No credit cards.**
Map p333 1A&B.

The 15th- to 16th-century Palazzo Altemps, which is just north of piazza Navona, has been beautifully restored to house part of the state-owned stock of Roman treasures (the rest of the collection is spread between the Palazzo Massimo alle Terme and the Terme di Diocleziano). Here, in perfectly lit salons, loggias and courtyards, you can admire gems of classical statuary that are originally from the private Boncompagni-Ludovisi, Altemps and Mattei collections.

The Ludovisis were great ones for having contemporary artists redo bits of statues that had dropped off over the ages or simply didn't appeal to the tastes of the day, as copious notes (in English) by each work explain. In Room 9, for example, is a stately *Athena with Serpent*, revamped in the 17th

century by Alessandro Algardi, who also had a hand in 'improving' the *Hermes Loghios* in Room 19 upstairs. In Room 20, the former dining room with pretty 15th-century frescos on foody themes, is an *Ares* touched up by Bernini. Room 21 has the museum's greatest treasure – or its greatest hoax if you subscribe to the theory of the late, great art historian and polemicist Federico Zeri – the 'Ludovisi throne'. On what may or then again may not be a fifth-century BC work from Magna Grecia (Zeri insisted it was a clumsy 19th-century copy of an original now in Boston), Aphrodite is being delicately and modestly lifted out of the sea spray from which she was born; on one side of her is a serious lady burning incense, and on the other is a naked one playing the flute. In Room 26 there is a Roman copy of a Greek *Gaul's Suicide*, which was commissioned, recent research has suggested, by Julius Caesar; also here is the Ludovisi sarcophagus, which bears some action-packed high-relief depictions of Roman soldiers thoroughly trouncing barbarians. Room 34 has a graceful *Bathing Aphrodite*, an Imperial Roman copy of a Greek bronze dating from the third century BC.

Piazza Navona

Bus 30, 40, 46, 62, 63, 64, 70, 81, 87, 116, 492, 628, 630, 780, 916. **Map** p321 2A&B.

This tremendous theatrical oval, dominated by the gleaming marble composition of Bernini's **Fontana dei Quattro Fiumi**, is the hub of the *centro storico*. The piazza owes its shape to an ancient stadium, built in AD 86 by the Emperor Domitian, which was the scene of at least one martyrdom (St Agnes was thrown to her death here for refusing to marry), as well as sporting events. Just north of the piazza, at piazza di Tor Sanguigna 16, you can still see some remains of the original arena, sunk below street level. These remains are partially visible from the street; they can also be visited on guided tours on Saturday and Sunday from 10am to 1pm (phone 06 6710 3819 for bookings and information).

The piazza acquired its current form in the mid 17th century. Its western side is dominated by Borromini's façade for the church of **Sant'Agnese in Agone** (*see p103*) and the adjacent Palazzo Pamphili, built for Pope Innocent X in 1644-50. The 'Fountain of the Four Rivers' at the centre of the piazza, finished in 1651, is one of the most extravagant masterpieces designed – though only partly sculpted – by Bernini. Its main figures represent the rivers Ganges, Nile, Danube and Plate, surrounded by geographically appropriate flora and fauna. The figure of the Nile is veiled, as its source was unknown. For centuries the story went that Bernini designed it that way so the river god appeared to be recoiling in horror from the façade of Sant'Agnese, designed by his arch-rival Borromini. In fact, the church was built after the fountain was finished. The obelisk in its centre came from the Circus of Maxentius on the via Appia Antica. The less spectacular Fontana del Moro is at the southern end of the piazza. The central figure (called the Moor, although he looks more like a portly sea god wrestling with a dolphin) was the only part designed by Bernini himself.

Palazzo Madama

Corso Rinascimento (06 67 061/www.senato.it). Bus 30, 70, 81, 87, 116, 204, 280, 492, 628. **Open** Guided tours only (in Italian) 10am-6pm 1st Sat of mth. **Admission** free. **Map** p333 2A.

Home to the Italian Senate since 1871, this palazzo was built by the Medici family in the 16th century as their Rome residence. Its rather twee façade, with a frieze of cherubs and bunches of fruit, was added a hundred years later. The Madama of its name refers to Margaret of Parma (1522-86), the illegitimate daughter of Emperor Charles V, who lived here in the 1560s before moving to the Netherlands, where she instigated some of the bloodiest excesses of the religious wars.

San Luigi dei Francesi

Piazza San Luigi dei Francesi (06 688 271). Bus 30, 70, 81, 87, 116, 204, 280, 492, 628. **Open** 8.30am-12.30pm, 3.30-7pm Mon-Wed, Fri-Sun; 8.30am-12.30pm Thur. **Map** p333 2A.

Dizzying **Sant'Ivo alla Sapienza**. *See p104.*

Completed in 1589, San Luigi/St Louis is the church of Rome's French community. That the interior (much of which was under restorers' scaffolding as this guide went to press) is lavish to the point of gaudiness goes unnoticed by most visitors, who are here for one thing: Caravaggio's spectacular scenes from the life of St Matthew in the fifth chapel on the left (not *in restauro*). Painted in 1600-02, they depict Christ singling out Matthew (left), Matthew being dragged to his execution (right) and an angel briefing the evangelist about what he should write in his gospel (over the altar). Don't let Caravaggio's brooding brilliance and dramatic effects of light and shade blind you to the lovely frescos of scenes from the life of St Cecilia by Domenichino (1615-17), which are in the second chapel on the right. Take change to feed the light meter.

Sant'Agnese in Agone

Piazza Navona (no phone). Bus 30, 40, 46, 62, 63, 64, 70, 81, 87, 116, 492, 628, 630, 780, 916. **Open** 10am-7pm Tue-Sun. **Map** p333 2B.

The virgin martyr St Agnes was stripped in public when she refused to abjure Christ, who kindly caused a miraculous growth of hair to cover her embarrassment; the flames of her execution pyre then failed to consume her, so her pagan persecutors lopped her head off, supposedly on the exact spot where the church of Sant'Agnese, which is the grandest building on piazza Navona, now stands.

Sant'Agnese was begun by Carlo and Girolamo Rainaldi for Pope Innocent X in 1652. It was intended to be their masterpiece, but they quarrelled with the pope, and Borromini was appointed in their place. He revised the design considerably, and added the concave façade that is one of his greatest achievements. The trompe l'oeil interior is typically Borromini, with pillars distributed irregularly to create the illusion that the apses are the same size.

Sant'Agostino

Piazza Sant'Agostino (06 6880 1962). Bus 30, 70, 81, 87, 116, 204, 280, 492, 628. **Open** 8am-noon, 4-7.30pm daily. **Map** p333 1A.

This 15th-century church stands on the site of a ninth-century one and has one of the earliest Renaissance façades in Rome, fashioned out of travertine limestone filched from the Colosseum. The third column on the left bears a fresco of *Isaiah* by Raphael (when its commissioner complained that the artist had charged him too much for the work, Michelangelo is said to have snapped: 'the knee alone is worth that'). Near this is a beautiful sculpture of Mary, her mother Anne and Jesus by Andrea Sansovino. In the first chapel on the left is Caravaggio's depiction of the grubbiest, most threadbare pilgrims ever to present themselves at the feet of the startlingly beautiful *Madonna of the Pilgrims* (1604). So dirty were they, in fact, that the church that originally commissioned the picture refused point-blank to have it. The main altar was designed by Bernini, who personally sculpted the two highest angels.

Sant'Ivo alla Sapienza

Corso Rinascimento 40 (06 686 4987). Bus 30, 70, 81, 87, 116, 204, 280, 492, 628. **Open** 9am-noon Sun. **Map** p333 2A.

This is perhaps the most imaginative geometrical design by tortured genius Francesco Borromini, with a concave façade countered by the convex bulk of the dome, which terminates in a bizarre corkscrew spire. The interior is based on a six-pointed star, but the opposition of convex and concave surfaces continues in the floor plan, on the walls and up into the dome, in a dizzying whirl.

From the Pantheon to via del Corso

Piazza della Rotonda, home to the **Pantheon**, is adorned with a central fountain whose steps provide an ever-popular hangout for hippies, punks, no-globals and other counter-cultural varieties. All seem oblivious of the well-heeled tourists paying over the odds for coffee at tables in the square, and to the smell that pervades when the wind blows the wrong way over the square's hamburger joint.

South of the Pantheon, Rome's only Gothic church, **Santa Maria sopra Minerva**, stands in piazza della Minerva. This otherwise unremarkable square-cum-car-park is home to **Il Pulcino della Minerva**, aka Bernini's elephant. This cuddly marble animal, with wrinkled bottom and benign expression, has stood here since 1667. It was designed by Bernini as a tribute to Pope Alexander VII: elephants were both a symbol of wisdom and a model of sexual abstinence. They were believed to be monogamous and to mate only once every five years, which, the Church felt, was the way things should be. The sixth-century BC Egyptian obelisk perched on its back was taken from an ancient temple to the goddess Isis.

Further east, piazza del Collegio Romano contains one of Rome's finest art collections, in the **Galleria Doria Pamphili**. The charmingly rococo piazza Sant'Ignazio has a severe Jesuit church, **Sant'Ignazio di Loyola**, while in piazza di Pietra the columns of the **Tempio di Adriano** (Hadrian's Temple) can be seen embedded in the walls of Rome's inactive stock exchange, now occasionally used for exhibitions. The quieter lanes close to via del Corso contain outposts of the Lower House in piazza del Montecitorio; journalists, MPs and assorted hangers-on haunt the area's bars. On the lower reaches of via del Corso is the privately owned **Museo del Corso** exhibition space.

Galleria Doria Pamphili

Piazza del Collegio Romano 2 (06 679 7323/www. doriapamphilj.it). Bus 62, 63, 81, 85, 95, 117, 119, 160, 175, 492, 628, 630, 850. **Open** 10am-5pm Mon-Wed, Fri-Sun; ticket office closes 4pm. **Admission** *Gallery (includes audio guide)* €7.30; €5.70 concessions; *see also p59* **Tickets**. **No credit cards. Map** p333 2A.

This is one of Rome's finest private art collections, housed in the rambling palace of the Doria Pamphili (also spelt Pamphilj) family, a pillar of Rome's aristocracy now headed by two half-British siblings. For many years the collection was crammed on to the walls of four corridors (Wings 1-4). It has now spilled into other areas of the palace, although the best is definitely still in the gallery proper.

A complete overhaul of the palazzo in 1996 restored it, as closely as possible, to the way it was arranged in the 18th century. Among the works on show are a portrait by Raphael of two gentlemen (1500s room); Correggio's unfinished *Allegory of Virtue* (Wing 3); four Titians, including *Religion Succoured by Spain* (Aldobrandini room) and a self-possessed *Salome holding the Head of John the Baptist* (1500s room). Caravaggio is represented by a *Penitent Magdalene* and the early *Rest During the Flight into Egypt* (both in the 1600s room). Of the paintings by Guercino, the martyred *St Agnes* (Wing 3), failing to catch light at the stake, stands out. There are also many works by the prolific Guido Reni (*see p118* **Guido who?**), darling of the Victorians but rarely to third-millennium tastes. The suite of rooms that leads off the far end of

Wing 2 houses Italian and some Flemish works, arranged chronologically by century; Wing 4 contains a number of works by Dutch and Flemish artists, including Brueghel. The collection's greatest jewel is arguably the extraordinary portrait by Velázquez of the Pamphili Pope Innocent X, displayed in a separate room of Wing 1 alongside a Bernini bust of the same pontiff. Landscapes by Carracci, Claude Lorraine and others are found in Wing 1. In the series of rooms en route to the gallery proper, a spectacular 18th-century ballroom leads into the Yellow Room, with its Gobelin tapestries, and then into a series of elegant rooms beyond. The chapel, by Carlo Fontana (1689), has been repeatedly altered, but has retained its original trompe l'oeil painted ceiling.

The private apartments, which also contain important pictures – such as a delicate *Annunciation* by Filippo Lippi, and Sebastiano del Piombo's portrait of the Genoese admiral and patriarch Andrea Doria as Neptune – are closed indefinitely for restoration.

Museo del Corso

Via del Corso 320 (06 678 6209/www.museo delcorso.it). Bus 62, 63, 81, 85, 95, 117, 119, 160, 175, 492, 628, 630. **Open** 10am-8pm Tue-Sun. **Admission** varies with exhibition. **No credit cards**. **Map** p333 2A.

This privately owned space stages exhibitions on artistic, historical and literary themes; the presentation is often more impressive than the content. There's also a handy café and internet access point.

Pantheon

Piazza della Rotonda (06 6830 0230). Bus 30, 40, 46, 62, 63, 64, 70, 81, 85, 87, 95, 117, 119, 160, 175, 492, 628, 630, 780, 850, 916/tram 8. **Open** 9am-7.30pm Mon-Sat; 9am-6pm Sun. 9am-1pm public holidays. **Admission** free. **Map** p333 2A.

The Pantheon is the best-preserved bit of ancient Rome. It was built by Hadrian in AD 119-128 as a temple to the 12 most important classical deities; the inscription on the pediment records an earlier Pantheon built a hundred years before by Augustus' general Marcus Agrippa, which confused historians for centuries. Its fine state of preservation is due to the building's conversion to a Christian church in 608, when it was presented to the pope by the Byzantine Emperor Phocas. The Pantheon has nevertheless suffered over the years – notably when bronze cladding was stripped from the roof in 667, and when Pope Urban VIII allowed Bernini to remove the remaining bronze from the beams in the portico to melt down for his *baldacchino* in St Peter's in the 1620s. The simplicity of the building's exterior, though, remains largely unchanged, and it retains its original Roman bronze doors.

Inside, the key to the Pantheon's extraordinary harmony is its dimensions. The radius of the dome is exactly equal to its height, so it could potentially accommodate a perfect sphere. At the centre of the dome is the oculus, a circular hole 9m (30ft) in diameter, the only source of light and a symbolic link between the temple and the heavens. The building

Lying with kings

Paris's Pantheon is a burial place of kings. Rome's Pantheon did less well in the royalty stakes (*see also p23* **Once, not future, kings**). Italy chalked up only four monarchs between Unification in the 1870s and the creation of the republic in 1946, and two of them inconveniently died in exile. Only Vittorio Emanuele II (d.1878), the first king of unified Italy, and his successor Umberto I, who was assassinated by an anarchist in 1900, are here, along with Umberto's widow Margherita (d.1926).

The Pantheon is a little short of illustrious artists too: they preferred as a rule to be buried in their home towns. But Raphael, who died in Rome in 1520, was laid to rest here. His tomb (pictured) bears some fine carving and an epitaph that Alexander Pope translated as: 'Living, great Nature feared he might outvie Her works, and dying, fears herself may die'. Other artists buried here are Annibale Caracci (d.1609), Baldassare Peruzzi (d.1536), Perin del Vaga (d.1547) and Taddeo Zuccari (d.1566).

Then what?

- Urbino-born architect Donato Bramante is credited with inventing the Roman High Renaissance. He began with the beautiful **Chiostro del Bramante** (Arco della Pace 5, 06 6880 9036/www.chiostrodelbramante.it) in 1500-04. From here he went on to the ground-breaking Tempietto at San Pietro in Montorio (*see p121*) and St Peter's too.
- Napoleon spent only a short time in Rome, but his *madame mère* Letizia and his sister Pauline took such a liking to the place that they settled down here. The **Museo Napoleonico** (piazza di Ponte Umberto I° 1, 06 6880 6286, closed Mon) contains art and memorabilia relating (albeit sometimes tenuously) to the family, including portraits, uniforms and a cast of Pauline's right breast.
- Along the south side of a building in the otherwise unremarkable piazza di Pietra are 11 Corinthian columns, each 15 metres (48 feet) high, that are now embedded in the grimy wall of Rome's inactive stock exchange. These originally formed part of a **temple** built to honour Emperor Hadrian (Adriano) by his designated heir, Antoninus Pius, in AD 145 (*see also p8* **Hadrian**).
- **Santa Maria dell'Anima** – in the street of the same name – is Rome's German church;

traditionally it's also the Flemish and Dutch church, hence the fine Renaissance tomb by Baldassare Peruzzi of Dutch Pope Adrian VI, who was the last non-Italian pontiff until a Pole was elected John Paul II in 1978. The high-minded Adriano only lasted a year as head of the Roman Church (1522-3). It's worth checking inside for the church's good concert programme.

- The church of **Sant'Eustachio** – found in the eponymous square – was (according to legend, at least) founded by Emperor Constantine on the site where Eustace was martyred. While out hunting one day this wealthy Roman landowner had a vision of a stag with a cross lodged between its antlers; he became the patron saint of hunters, and antlers figure on the church's current 18th-century façade.
- At via del Banco di Santo Spirito 31 is the ancient building (now a branch of the Banco di Roma) where Benvenuto Cellini worked as a goldsmith in the city mint. His famous autobiography *Una vita* gives an insight into the realities of life in Renaissance Rome, including a gruesome account of his imprisonment across the river in the Castel Sant'Angelo (*see p149*).

---

is still officially a church, but it's easy to overlook this, in spite of the tombs of eminent Italians, including the Renaissance artist Raphael and the first king of united Italy, Vittorio Emanuele II (*see p105* **Lying with kings**). Until the 18th century the portico was used as a market: supports for the stalls were inserted into the notches that can still be seen in the stonework of the columns.

Santa Maria sopra Minerva

Piazza della Minerva 42 (06 679 3926). Bus 30, 40, 46, 62, 63, 64, 70, 81, 87, 492, 628, 630, 780, 916/tram 8. **Open** 7am-7.30pm daily. **Map** p333 2A.
This is Rome's only Gothic church, built on the site of an ancient temple of Minerva. The best of its works of art are Renaissance: on the right of the transept is the superb Carafa chapel, with late 15th-century frescos by Filippino Lippi (1457-1504), commissioned by Cardinal Oliviero Carafa in honour of St Thomas Aquinas. Carafa took Renaissance self-assurance to extremes: the altar painting shows him being presented to the Virgin, right at the moment when Gabriel informs her she's going to give birth. The tomb of the Carafa Pope Paul IV (1555-9) is also in the chapel. He was one of the prime movers of the Counter-Reformation, chiefly remembered for persecuting the Jews and ordering Daniele

da Volterra to paint loincloths on the nudes of Michelangelo's *Last Judgment*. A bronze loincloth was also ordered to cover Christ's genitals on a work by Michelangelo here: the statue was finished by Pietro Urbano (1514-21) and depicts a heroic Christ holding up a cross. An early Renaissance work is the *Madonna and Child*, believed by some to be by Fra Angelico, in the chapel to the left of the altar, close to the artistic monk's own tomb. The father of modern astronomy, Galileo Galilei, who dared suggest in the early 16th century that the earth revolved around the sun, was tried for heresy in the adjoining monastery.

Sant'Ignazio di Loyola

Piazza Sant'Ignazio (06 679 4406). Bus 62, 63, 81, 85, 95, 117, 119, 160, 175, 492, 628, 630, 850. **Open** 7.30am-12.15pm, 4-7.15pm daily. **Map** p333 2A.
Sant'Ignazio was built to commemorate the canonisation of St Ignatius, founder of the Jesuit order, in 1626. Trompe l'oeil columns soar above the nave, and architraves by Andrea Pozzo open to a cloudy heaven. Trickery was also involved in creating the dome: the monks next door claimed that a real dome would rob them of light, so Pozzo simply painted a dome on the inside of the roof. The illusion is pretty convincing if you stand on the disc set in the floor of the nave. Walk away, however, and it dissolves.

The Ghetto
& Campo de' Fiori

A square where heretics were burnt, an island in the shape of a boat and the
oldest Jewish community in Europe.

Between fume-filled corso Vittorio Emanuele II
(known simply as corso Vittorio) and the river
lies the area that most people have in mind
when they imagine Rome. The area around
campo de' Fiori (*see p108*) and the old
Ghetto (*see p110*) is a picturesque tangle of
narrow cobbled streets, many named after the
trade carried on there in medieval times – the
hat-makers of via Cappellari, the trunk and later
umbrella-makers of via Baullari and the jerkin-
makers of via dei Giubbonari. All converge on
the city's liveliest market in campo de' Fiori.

All Roman life passed through this famous
square, which still has the look of a film set.
Then as now there were famous inns and
hostelries; one popular establishment – La
Vacca – was run by the mistress of Borgia pope
Alexander VI as a retirement investment. The
square is still a favourite place for noisy alfresco
drinking and dining. *Commedia dell'arte*
performances were staged in the campo for the
entertainment of the people, as were executions:
note the brooding bronze statue of the hooded
monk Giordano Bruno who got on the wrong
side of the Inquisition and burned at the stake
here in 1600. Any resemblance to Darth Vader is,
of course, coincidental.

Much of this area was part of the Campus
Martius – the Field of Mars – where sporting
events were held to keep Roman manhood
ready for war. Here too were the ancient city's
theatres. In the Dark Ages the area was built
over with little thought for urban planning.
Crooked, narrow streets are punctuated with
few open squares. Despite its restaurants and
high-density bars, there's a down-home lived-in
feel to the place, with calm echoing corners and
a high real-life quotient.

Giordano Bruno broods over
campo de' Fiori. *See p108.*

Campo de' Fiori & largo Argentina

The busy tram terminus and bus stops of largo Argentina sit oddly against the expanse of Roman ruins that fills the hole in the centre of the square, complete with a cat haven that has become a tourist attraction in its own right. Whether cat lover or just curious, you can visit the centre where, underneath the square's thundering traffic, the ladies of the **Rifugio Felino di Torre Argentina** (Argentina Cat Sanctuary, 06 687 2133, www.romancats.com, noon-6pm daily, guided tours 3pm Sun) battle to keep up with the annual influx of over 500 abandoned animals.

Officially called largo di Torre Argentina (nothing to do with the Latin American country: the name refers to a tower – *torre* – in a nearby street, plus the fact that the local diocese was called Argentoratum, a word derived from *argento*, 'silver'), this huge open space contained a narrow warren of streets that was bulldozed in 1885, then further obliterated in 1926-9, to reveal what is known as the Area Sacra Argentina ('sacred area'). Visible are columns, altars and foundations from one round and three rectangular temples, dating from mid third century BC to c100 BC. The frescos on the taller brickwork are from the 12th-century church of San Nicola de' Cesarini, which was built into one of the temples.

From largo Argentina buses stream east along via del Plebiscito past the **Gesù** church, and along via delle Botteghe Oscure past the **Crypta Balbi**, on their way to piazza Venezia.

Trek west along corso Vittorio, on the other hand, and you'll reach **Sant'Andrea della Valle**, with Rome's second-tallest dome, and the tiny **Museo Barracco** with its eclectic collection of antiquities. Set back off this fume-filled artery is the Vatican-owned **Palazzo della Cancelleria**, one of the area's most impressive Renaissance structures.

The high decibels and unbreathable air of those thoroughfares is a far cry from what lies to the west of largo Argentina, where cramped, crooked medieval streets converge on **campo de' Fiori**. South-west of the campo is **piazza Farnese**: elegant and operatic, the piazza is uncluttered apart from its two fountains, created in the 17th century out of granite tubs from the Terme di Caracalla (*see p129*) and topped with lilies – the Farnese family emblem. Overlooking them is the area's other major Renaissance pile, ponderous **Palazzo Farnese**, designed by Michelangelo and now home to the French embassy. Pretty **Palazzo Spada**, with its gallery, is nearby.

Campo de' Fiori

Bus 30, 40, 46, 62, 63, 64, 70, 81, 87, 116, 492, 628, 630, 780, 916/tram 8. **Map** p333 2B.

Home to Rome's most picturesque – although also most costly – food market in the mornings, campo de' Fiori, known to all as Il Campo, is surrounded by tall *palazzi*, many of whose once-worn walls and warped shutters have recently received colourful facelifts. The Campo has been a focus of Roman life since the 15th century. Lucrezia Borgia was born nearby, her brother was murdered down the road and Caravaggio played a game of tennis on the piazza, after which he murdered his opponent for having the temerity to beat him. The cowled statue in the centre is of Giordano Bruno, burned at the stake on this spot (*dove il rogo arse*, 'where the pyre burned', as the inscription reads) in 1600 for reaching the conclusion that philosophy and magic were superior to religion.

The market begins around 6am and packs up in the early afternoon, when people flow into the Campo's restaurants for lunch. Afternoons are quiet and slow, with things beginning to pick up around *aperitivo* time (*see p204* **Campo it up**). Much to the annoyance of residents, *alternativi* types with flea-bitten dogs, bongo drums and – locals will tell you bitterly – a flourishing sideline in drug dealing, gather beneath Giordano Bruno as the sun goes down. This, however, doesn't deter the diners who, by 9pm, have filled the restaurants again, nor the wine-sipping crowds that spill out from the bars to invade most of the square.

Galleria Spada

Piazza Capo di Ferro 3 (06 687 4896/www. galleriaborghese.it). Bus 23, 30, 40, 46, 62, 63, 64, 70, 81, 280, 492, 628, 630, 780, 916/tram 8. **Open** 8.30am-7.30pm Tue-Sun. **Admission** €5; €2.50 concessions; *see also p61* **Tickets. No credit cards. Map** p336 1B.

One of Rome's prettiest palaces, Palazzo Spada was built for Cardinal Girolamo Capo di Ferro in 1540 and acquired by Cardinal Bernardino Spada in 1632. Its most famous feature is Borromini's ingenious trompe l'oeil colonnade in the garden, which is 9m (30ft) long but appears much longer. Today the palace houses high court offices as well as the art collection of Cardinal Spada, displayed in its original setting. Spada's portrait by his protégé Guido Reni (*see p120* **Guido who?**) is on show in Room 1. More portraits follow in Room 2, including Titian's wonderful unfinished *Musician*. Don't miss the wacky-hatted *Cleopatra* by Lavinia Fontana in the same room. Room 3 contains massive, gloomy paintings such as Guercino's *Death of Dido* and Jan Brueghel the Elder's very un-Roman *Landscape with Windmill*, plus a couple of 17th-century Dutch globes. Room 4 has two powerful works by Artemisia Gentileschi – *St Cecilia Playing a Lute* and *Madonna and Child* – along with *Martyrdom of a Saint* by Domenichino. Copious notes in many languages are provided for each room.

Ponte Rotto: Rome's oldest bridge. *See p114.*

Il Gesù

Piazza del Gesù (06 697 001/Loyola's rooms 06 6920 5800). Bus 30, 40, 46, 62, 63, 64, 70, 81, 87, 492, 628, 630, 780, 916, H. **Open** *Church 6.30am-12.30pm, 4-7.30pm daily. Loyola's rooms Sept-June 4-6pm Mon-Sat; 10am-noon Sun; July & Aug 10am-noon Mon-Sat.* **Admission** *free.* **Map** p336 1A.

The huge Gesù is the principal church of the Jesuits, the order founded by Basque soldier Ignatius Loyola in the 1530s. Realising the power of a direct appeal to the emotions, Loyola devised a series of 'spiritual exercises' aimed at training devotees to experience the agony and ecstasy of the saints. The Gesù itself was designed to involve the congregation as closely as possible in the proceedings, with a nave unobstructed by aisles, offering a clear view of the main altar. Work began in 1568, with the façade by Giacomo della Porta added in 1575. His design was repeated ad nauseam on Jesuit churches across Italy (and the world) for decades afterwards. A large, bright fresco by Il Baciccia (1676-9) – one of Rome's great baroque masterpieces – decorates the gilded ceiling of the nave, which seems to dissolve on either side as stucco figures, by Antonio Raggi, and other painted images are sucked up into the dazzling light of the heavens. The figures falling back to earth are presumably Protestants. On the left is another spectacular baroque achievement: the chapel of Sant'Ignazio (1696-1700) by Andrea Pozzo, which is adorned with gold, silver and coloured marble. The statue of St Ignatius is by Antonio Canova. Towering above the altar is what was long believed to be the biggest lump of lapis lazuli in the world. In fact it's covered concrete. Outside the church, at piazza del Gesù 45, you can visit the rooms of St Ignatius, which contain a wonderful painted corridor with trompe l'oeil special effects by Pozzo, and mementoes of the saint, including his death mask.

Museo Barracco di Scultura Antica

Corso Vittorio 166 (06 6880 6848/06 687 5657). Bus 40, 46, 62, 64, 116, 916. **Open** *9am-7pm Tue-Sun.*

Admission €2.58; €1.55 concessions. **No credit cards. Map** p333 2B.

This small collection of mainly pre-Roman art (*in restauro* until August 2003) was amassed in the first half of the 20th century by Giovanni Barracco. His interests ran the gamut of ancient art; there are extraordinary Assyrian reliefs, Attic vases, sphinxes, bas-reliefs and Babylonian stone lions, as well as Roman and Etruscan exhibits and Greek sculptures. Don't miss the copy of the *Wounded Bitch* by Lysippus, on the second floor.

Museo Nazionale Romano – Crypta Balbi

Via delle Botteghe Oscure 31 (06 678 0167/www. archeorm.arti.beniculturali.it/sar2000/cripta/cripta. asp). Bus 46, 62, 64, 70, 87, 186, 492, 810, 916/ tram 8. **Open** *9am-7.45pm Tue-Sun; ticket office closes 6.45pm.* **Admission** *€4; €2 concessions; see also p61* **Tickets. No credit cards. Map** p336 1A.

In 1981 digging began in a down-at-heel city block on the northern fringe of the Ghetto, on what had been the southern fringes of the ancient Campus Martius. What was found went on show in 2000, in what is one of the most fascinating of Rome's new archaeological offerings. As well as being a fine sight in and of itself, the *crypta* (a large lobby) of the ancient Teatro di Balbo hosts displays documenting the changing faces of the palimpsest that is Rome. Here you can learn how accumulated detritus raised the street level, how the ancient fabric of Rome was incorporated first into the medieval city and then into its modern successor. There's a particularly rich section on Rome from the fifth-century fall of the Empire up to the tenth century.

Palazzo della Cancelleria

Piazza della Cancelleria. Bus 40, 46, 62, 64, 116, 916. **Open** *closed to the public.* **Map** p333 2B.

One of the most refined examples of Renaissance architecture in Rome, the Palazzo della Cancelleria was built, possibly by Bramante, between 1483 and

Locating Tosca

Giacomo Puccini, according to popular lore, was kneeling in prayer in the Barberini chapel of **Sant'Andrea della Valle** (*see below*) when he was struck by the idea for *Tosca*, that most dramatic of all Italian operas. And Act I – in which artist Cavaradossi paints a society beauty rather than his mistress Tosca (very much to Tosca's annoyance) – is set in that very chapel. Angelotti, a freedom fighter against papal rule, has escaped from prison and hides in the chapel where the artist is hard at work. By the time evil police chief Scarpia comes to nab him, however, Angelotti has fled. Scarpia picks up Tosca and her artist-lover instead, hoping to rid himself of the latter so that he can have his wicked way with the former.

Scarpia's office in the **Palazzo Farnese** (*see below*) is the setting for Act II, in which Cavaradossi is tortured off-stage just noisily enough to force Tosca to reveal the freedom fighter's whereabouts. Dragged back on stage, Cavaradossi makes the foolish mistake of cheering when news arrives

that Napoleon has scored a major military victory; he is arrested and sentenced to death. But Scarpia's evil knows no bounds: the police chief offers Tosca a reprieve for her lover if only she will give way to Scarpia's lust, and Tosca succumbs. Then thinks again. She takes a knife and stabs Scarpia with it, after he has written a safe-conduct note for the Tosca and Cavaradossi.

For Act III the action crosses the river to the **Castel Sant'Angelo** (*see p151*). Dawn is breaking over Hadrian's mausoleum; in the distance bells toll and a shepherd boy is singing. (Puccini conscientiously trekked up to the castle roof to study exactly which bells could be heard and incorporated their sounds into the score. As for the shepherd, the area around the castle was grazing land.) Double-crossed by the evil Scarpia, Tosca discovers that what was meant to be her lover's virtual execution proves to have been horribly real. Distraught, but still singing, Tosca hurls herself from the battlements of the castle and plunges to her death.

1513 for Raffaele Riario. He was the great-nephew of Pope Sixtus IV, who made him a cardinal at the age of 17, but Raffaele didn't allow his ecclesiastical duties to cramp his style. He is said to have raised a third of the cost of this palace with the winnings of a single night's gambling. He also got involved in plotting against the powerful Florentine Medici family; in retaliation the palace was confiscated for the Church when Giovanni de' Medici became Pope Leo X in 1513. It later became the Papal Chancellery, and is still Vatican property. The fourth-century church of San Lorenzo in Damaso was incorporated into one side of the building.

Palazzo Farnese

Piazza Farnese (06 6889 2818/visitefarnese@ getnet.it). Bus *30, 40, 46, 62, 63, 64, 70, 81, 87, 116, 492, 628, 630, 780, 916.* **Open** closed to the public. **Map** p336 1B.
This palazzo has housed the French embassy since the 1870s and is not generally open to the public, but guided tours in French can sometimes be arranged by appointment (preference is generally given to art historians). Considered by many to be the finest Renaissance palace in Rome, the huge building – recently and dramatically restored – was begun for Cardinal Alessandro Farnese (later Pope Paul III) in 1514 by Antonio da Sangallo the Younger. Sangallo died before it was completed, and in 1546 Michelangelo took over. He was responsible for most of the upper storeys and the grand cornice along the

roof. After his death the building was completed by Giacomo della Porta. Inside it has superb frescos by Annibale Carracci.

Sant'Andrea della Valle

Corso Vittorio 6 (06 686 1339). Bus 30, 40, 46, 62, 63, 64, 70, 81, 87, 116, 492, 628, 630, 780, 916. **Open** 8am-noon, 4.30-7.30pm daily. **Map** p336 1B.
Sant'Andrea was originally designed by Giacomo della Porta for the Theatine order in 1524, but its façade and dizzyingly frescoed dome both date from about a century later, when the Church was in a far more flamboyant frame of mind. The dome, by Carlo Maderno, is the second largest in Rome after St Peter's. Giovanni Lanfranco nearly died while painting the dome fresco – allegedly because his rival Domenichino had sabotaged the scaffolding on which he was working. Puccini set the opening act of *Tosca* (*see above* **Locating Tosca**) in the first chapel on the left inside the church.

The Ghetto

Rome's Jews occupy a unique place in the history of the diaspora, having maintained a presence in the city uninterrupted for over 2,000 years. This makes them Europe's longest-surviving Jewish community and one that enjoyed a surprising degree of security, even at times (such as in the years following the Black Death) when waves of anti-Semitism were sweeping the rest of Europe.

Some Italian Jews even applied a rather fanciful Hebrew etymology to 'Italia': they argued that the name was derived from it *I Tal Ya*, meaning 'island of the dew of God'.

It may seem odd that the city that was the great centre of power for the Christian Church represented such a safe haven for Jews, but their security came at a price. The popes took on the double role of protectors (curbing popular violence against Jews) and oppressors, bringing Jews under their direct jurisdiction and making sure they paid for the privilege. The first documented tax on Roman Jews dates back to 1310, and set the pattern for the tradition of blackmail that characterised the Church's relations with the Jewish community until the 19th century. Payment of this tax exempted Jews from the humiliating *carnevale* games, during which they were liable to be packed into barrels and rolled from the top of Monte Testaccio (*see p125*).

The historic memory of this kind of exploitation was revived during World War II. In September 1943 the German occupiers demanded 50 kilograms (110 pounds) of gold from the Jewish community, to be produced in 36 hours. After an appeal – to which both Jews and non-Jews responded – the target was reached, but this time accepting blackmail did not bring security. On 16 October over 1,000 Jews – mostly women and children – were rounded up and deported in cattle trucks to Auschwitz. A quarter of Rome's Jews died in concentration camps, a proportion that would

have been higher had it not been for the help given by wide sections of Roman society, including the Catholic priesthood (though not, many would argue, the Vatican).

Rome's Jews had originally settled in Trastevere (*see p116*), but by the 13th century they had started to cross the river into the area that would become the Jewish Ghetto, a cramped quarter in one corner of the *centro storico*, immediately north of the Tiber island. Its chief landmark today is the imposing synagogue, begun in 1874. This incorporates the **Museo d'Arte Ebraica**, a small museum of Roman Jewish life and ritual.

The Ghetto (the word is Venetian in origin) was walled off from the rest of the city in 1556 after the bull *Cum nimis absurdam*, issued by the anti-Semitic Pope Paul IV, ordered a physical separation between Jewish and Christian parts of cities. Many Jews actually welcomed the protection the walls and curfews afforded, despite the fact that they were also obliged periodically to attend mass to be lectured on their sinfulness. However, over-crowding, the loss of property rights and trade restrictions imposed on the community all took their toll, and the Ghetto experienced a long decline from the 16th to the 18th centuries.

By the time of Italian Unification in 1870, conditions for the more than 5,000 people who lived in the Ghetto had become desperately squalid. The new government ordered that the walls be destroyed and large sections of the district were rebuilt.

Sightseeing

The **Synagogue**, hub of Europe's oldest Jewish community.

Mosaic marble "La Colombe"

Inlaid work of marble "La Vittoria"

Marmi Line

Since 1933
Via dei Coronari, 113, 141/145
Tel. 06/6893795 - Fax 06/6832680

Pair of Moors

Marco Aurelio's bust

Situated at number 113 in Via dei Coronari, right in the heart of Rome's historic center, Marmi Line offers its customers a selection of antique and modern marble of superb workmanship. Talented designers and specialized craftsmen are in charge of the design and restoration of columns, bases, busts, vases, fountains and both inlaid and plain marble tables, still using production techniques which have been practiced for centuries.

Having antique, or even long-vanished varieties of marble at our disposal makes the products which we at "Marmi Line" have created for our customers, quite unique. Our window display has a vast assortment of gifts and ornaments as well as some exquisite pieces to add style to any interior décor.

The Four Seasons

http://marmiline.com

Giulio Cesare's bust

The Four Seasons

Inlaid work of marble

Packaged and delivered anywhere in the world

The via Portico d'Ottavia, an anarchic hotch-potch of ancient, medieval and Renaissance architecture leading to the **Portico d'Ottavia** itself, used to mark the boundary of the Ghetto. This street is still the centre of Rome's Jewish life, even though many of the people you'll see sitting around chatting in the evening or at weekends have come in from the suburbs. It's also a good place to sample a unique hybrid: Roman Jewish food. Restaurants like **Sora Margherita** (*see p179*) specialise in delicacies such as artichokes fried Jewish-style, while at one end of the street, in a tiny unmarked cornershop (the **Forno del Ghetto**, *see p221*), you'll find the bakery that turns out a *torta di ricotta e visciole* – ricotta and damson tart – that has achieved legendary status among Roman gourmets. The Ghetto's winding alleys also hide non-comestible gems that include the beautiful, delicate **Fontana delle Tartarughe** (Turtle Fountain).

Fontana delle Tartarughe

Piazza Mattei. Bus 30, 40, 46, 62, 63, 64, 70, 81, 87, 492, 628, 630, 780, 916/tram 8. **Map** p336 1A.
Four elegant boys cavort around the base of what is unquestionably one of Rome's loveliest fountains, gently hoisting tortoises up to the waters above them. According to legend, Giacomo della Porta and Taddeo Landini built the fountain for the Duke of Mattei at some point in the 1580s – in just a single night. The duke, so the story goes, had lost all his money and hence his fiancée, and wanted to prove to her father that he could still achieve great things. (The duke's family palazzo, packed with looted antiquities and now home to an American study cen-tre, is also in the square.) The tortoises, possibly by Bernini, were added in the following century.

Museo d'Arte Ebraica

Lungotevere Cenci 15 (06 6840 0661). Bus 23, 63, 280, 630, 780/tram 8. **Open** *Sept-Apr* 9am-4.30pm Mon-Thur; 9am-1.30pm Fri; 9am-12.30pm Sun. *May-Aug* 9am-7.30pm Mon-Thur; 9am-1.30pm Fri, Sun. Closed on Jewish holidays. **Admission** €6; €3 concessions. **No credit cards. Map** p336 2A.
As well as luxurious crowns, Torah mantles and silverware, the museum presents vivid reminders of the persecution suffered by Rome's Jewish community at various times during its long history. Copies of the 16th-century papal edicts that banned Jews from a progressively longer and longer list of activities are a disturbing foretaste of the horrors forced on them by the Nazis; the Nazi atrocities are in turn represented by stark photographs and heart-rending relics from the concentration camps. Admission to the museum includes a visit to the synagogue, which was built in the 1870s; it holds daily services (for contact details, *see p311*).

Portico d'Ottavia

Via Portico d'Ottavia. Bus 23, 30, 44, 63, 81, 95, 160, 170, 280, 628, 715, 716, 781. **Map** p336 2A.

These remains have been nonchalantly built around and into over the centuries. Now, held together by rusting braces, they form the porch of the church of Sant'Angelo in Pescheria, but they were originally the entrance to a massive colonnaded square that contained shops, libraries and temples. Emperor Augustus rebuilt the portico in the first century BC and dedicated it to his sister Octavia; the isolated columns outside belong to a later restoration, under-taken by Septimius Severus in AD 213. For centuries the portico also formed part of Rome's main fish market, hence the name of the church. A recent archaeological dig around the base of the portico has unearthed fascinating glimpses of ancient urban infrastructure, and walkways (which are open at all times) have been constructed to allow access to the site. Passers-by can inspect the towering walls of the adjoining Teatro di Marcello (*see p115*) before cut-ting through the archaeological area towards the Campidoglio (Capitoline, *see p61*).

The Tiber island & the bocca della verità

When the last Etruscan king was driven from Rome, the Romans uprooted the wheat from his fields and threw it in baskets into the river. There the baskets lay, with silt accumulating around them, until that silt formed an island. That, at least, is what legend says. The island – known quite simply as *l'isola Tiberina* (the Tiber island) – is the only one to disturb the stately flow of Rome's river, and it was transformed into a sanctuary dedicated to Aesculapius, god of medicine, in 291 BC. In the first century BC the island was shored up and given its present boat shape: on the wide footpath at river level, the remains of the ancient boat-shaped sculpture can still be seen, complete with the rod and snakes symbol of the god. The island's vocation to public health continues to this day: much of it is occupied by the Fatebenefratelli hospital.

Off the southern end of the Tiber island stand the scant remains of Rome's oldest bridge, which is prosaically – but accurately – known as the **Ponte Rotto** ('broken bridge'). Nearby, in the embankment, is the mouth of the ancient **Cloaca Maxima** sewer.

On the right bank, opposite the island's southern end, stood ancient Rome's *forum boarium* (cattle market) and *forum holitorium* (vegetable market). In addition to the striking remains of the **Teatro di Marcello**, it is now home to two delightful **temples** as well as a number of churches. These include **Santa Maria in Cosmedin** with its *bocca della verità* ('mouth of truth'); **San Nicola in Carcere**, which has market columns built into its walls; and **Santa Maria in Campitelli**.

Sightseeing

Teatro di Marcello: Renaissance palace and Roman ruin in one. *See p115.*

Ponte Rotto & Cloaca Maxima

Views from Ponte Palatino, isola Tiberina &
lungotevere Pierleoni. Bus 23, 63, 280, 630, 780,
H/tram 8. **Map** p336 2A.

The Broken Bridge – Pons Aemilius – was
the first stone bridge in Rome, dating back to 142
BC. It was rebuilt many times – even Michelangelo
had a go – before the greater part of the bridge finally collapsed into the muddy waters in 1598. Near its
west side there is a tunnel in the embankment, the
gaping mouth of the Cloaca Maxima, the city's 'great
sewer'. Built under the Tarquins (Rome's Etruscan
kings, *see p7*) in the sixth century BC to drain the
area round the Forum, it was given its final form in
the first century BC.

San Nicola in Carcere

Via del Teatro di Marcello 46 (06 6830 7198). Bus
30, 44, 63, 81, 95, 160, 170, 628, 715, 716, 781.
Open 7.30am-noon, 4-7pm Mon-Sat; 10am-1pm Sun.
Map p336 2A.

This church was built in the 11th century within the
ruins of three Republican-era temples, dedicated to
the two-faced god Janus, to the goddess Juno and to
Spes (Hope). The temples overlooked the city's fruit
and veg market (*forum holitorium*), the columns of
which can be seen embedded in the church wall.

Santa Maria in Campitelli

Piazza Campitelli 9 (06 6880 3978). Bus 30, 44,
63, 81, 95, 160, 170, 628, 715, 716, 781.
Open 7.30am-noon, 4-7pm daily. **Map** p336 1A.

Santa Maria in Campitelli was commissioned in 1656
to house the medieval icon of the Madonna del
Portico, to which the population had prayed (successfully) for a prompt release from a bout of the

plague. Completed in 1667, the church is Carlo
Rainaldi's masterpiece, a solemn, austere exercise in
mass and light. The floor plan is complex: basically
a Greek cross, it also has a (hidden) dome, apse and
series of side chapels. Inside are some fine baroque
paintings and a spectacularly over-the-top gilt altar
tabernacle by Giovanni Antonio de Rossi.

Santa Maria in Cosmedin

Piazza della Bocca della Verità 18 (06 678 1419).
Bus 44, 63, 81, 95, 170, 628, 715, 716, 781. **Open**
Apr-Sept 9am-6.30pm daily. *Oct-Mar* 9am-5pm daily.
Map p336 2A.

Santa Maria in Cosmedin was first built in the sixth
century. It was enlarged in the ninth century, and
given a beautiful campanile in the 12th. Between the
11th and 13th centuries much of the original
decoration was replaced with Cosmati work: the
spiralling floor, the throne, the choir and the 13th-
century *baldacchino*. This last is located above the
ultimate example of recycling – a Roman bathtub
used as an altar. If you want to prove a point, stick
your hand into the *bocca della verità* (the 'mouth of
truth'), a worn stone face under the portico that is
said to bite the hands of liars. According to legend,
it was much used by husbands to test the faithful-
ness of their wives; in fact, it was probably an ancient
drain cover. The scene in *Roman Holiday* where
Gregory Peck adlibs getting his hand bitten,
eliciting a (reportedly) unscripted shriek of genuine
alarm from Audrey Hepburn, is one of the most
delightful moments in cinema. In the sacristy is a
fragment of an eighth-century mosaic of the Holy
Family, brought here from the original St Peter's. At
half past ten on Sunday mornings a Byzantine rite
mass is sung in the church.

Teatro di Marcello

Via del Teatro di Marcello. Bus 30, 44, 63, 81, 95, 160, 170, 628, 715, 716, 781. **Open** with prior permission only; *see p61* **Ex-Rip.X. Map** p336 2A.

If you haven't had time to seek formal permission to enter the Theatre of Marcellus, don't give up: much of it is visible from the Portico d'Ottavia archaeological area (*see p113*) to the rear. It's one of the strangest and most impressive sights in Rome – a Renaissance palace grafted on to an ancient, time-worn circular theatre. Julius Caesar began building a massive theatre here to rival Pompey's in the Campus Martius, but it was finished in 11 BC by Augustus, who named it after his favourite nephew. At one time it was connected to the adjacent Portico d'Ottavia, and originally had three tiers in different styles (Ionic, Doric and Corinthian): the top one has collapsed. After the theatre was abandoned in the fourth century AD it had various uses before Baldassare Peruzzi built a palace for the Savelli family on top of the crumbling remains in the 16th century. To the north of the theatre are three columns that were part of the Temple of Apollo (dating from 433 BC).

'Tempio di Vesta' & 'Tempio di Fortuna Virilis' (Temples of Hercules Victor & Portunus)

Piazza della Bocca della Verità. Bus 44, 63, 81, 95, 170, 628, 715, 716, 781. **Map** p336 2A.

Like the Pantheon, these diminutive Republican-era temples both owe their fine state of preservation to their conversion into churches during the Middle Ages. The round one, which looks for all the world like an English folly, was built in the first century BC and dedicated to Hercules. Early archaeologists were confused by its round shape, which is similar to the Temple of Vesta in the Roman Forum, and mistakenly dubbed it the Temple of Vesta (Romans still tend to refer to it by this name). The second temple, which is square but similarly perfect in form, is a century older and was dedicated to Portunus, god of harbours (appropriately enough, as this was the port area of ancient Rome). The archaeologists got confused here too: the temple was understood to have been dedicated to 'manly fortune'. The two temples were deconsecrated and designated ancient monuments in the 1920s on orders from Mussolini.

Then what?

• The church of **San Bartolomeo** on the Tiber island was built atop an ancient temple to the god of medicine, Aesculapius. The lofty romanesque campanile is all that remains of the tenth-century structure built by Emperor Otto III, but recent restoration work on the magnificent ceiling has revealed the full baroque glory of the later church. Note the nave columns, which are thought to have come from the temple inaugurated in 293 BC.

• On a hot summer evening catch an open-air movie at the **cinema** set up on the island's embankment. Dab yourself with mosquito repellent, take a wrap and prepare for an unforgettable experience: whatever the film is like, this surely must be the most beautiful cinema in the world.

• Romans are notoriously unsentimental about animals, but fund-raising evenings for the **cat sanctuary** (*see p108*) picturesquely set amid the ruined temples of largo Argentina have proved a surprise hit with international society. Check upcoming events at www.romancats.com.

• The **Venerable English College** in via Monserrato (06 687 7258) has trained Catholic priests since 1579, but a pilgrim hostel has stood on this site since 1361. Many of its priests faced death when setting foot on English soil: 41 who were martyred for their faith during the turbulent 16th-century

persecutions are remembered in the college church dedicated to the Holy Trinity and St Thomas of Canterbury. Visit by prior appointment or catch mass at 10am daily from September to May.

• Michelangelo made detailed plans for a church worthy of the rich community of Florentine merchants in Rome, but **San Giovanni dei Fiorentini** in via Giulia/piazza dell'Oro was in the end entrusted to architect Antonio Sangallo, whose style better reflected the new austerity imposed by the Council of Trent. It's the perfect antidote to all that baroque excess.

• The **Oratorio del Gonfalone** at via del Gonfalone 32A, built in 1544, contains some of the most important mannerist frescos in the city. To get inside you'll have to catch a chamber music concert (*see p252*).

• Hidden deep in the Ghetto, the unassuming **Palazzo Cenci** in vicolo dei Cenci was home to the family of the same name, which gained notoriety in 1598 when Beatrice Cenci, her mother and two brothers were arrested for hiring thugs to murder her father. Popular opinion came to Beatrice's defence when it was revealed that her father had forced her to commit incest. It was not enough to save her, though: the pope condemned her to death and she was beheaded outside Castel Sant'Angelo in 1599.

Sightseeing

Trastevere & the Gianicolo

Trasteverini claim this is the real Rome. You might well agree.

All cities worth their salt have a *rive gauche*, a Left Bank where the jazz clubs and the cheaper restaurants are, where students and intellectuals live out bohemian fantasies in cheap but chic garrets with rooftop views. Trastevere is Rome's *rive gauche*.

Visitors begin their relationship with Trastevere with a pronunciation problem. Get it wrong, and taxi drivers will shake their heads and deny any knowledge of the place. To avoid embarrassment, remember that the stress in Trastevere (derived from the Latin *trans Tiberim*, 'across the Tiber') falls on the 'tev' bit (as in *Tevere*, the Italian for Tiber). Having overcome this initial hurdle, many foreigners develop a passionate love affair with the quarter – the wealthier ones to the point of acquiring a little *pied-à-terre* and a regular table in a picturesquely down-at-heel local bar.

Since ancient times the locals – *trasteverini* – have had an attitude problem. Over the last century or so an uncompromising 'them and us' attitude has developed into a fully fledged *noiantri* festival (see *p234*) celebrating those very characteristics that mark *trasteverini* out as different from, and – in their eyes – superior to, the Romans who live on the seven hills on the other side of the Tiber. These real Romans – as *trasteverini* like to think of themselves – are proud and tough, and reputedly quick-witted and quick-fisted. They revel in a robust, earthy sense of humour, and staunchly defend their rough dialect from the homogenized and alien Italian of national TV. Their favourite poets, Trilussa and Bella, combine these attributes in rollicking and oft-quoted local doggerel.

Trasteverini claim descent from slave stock, including first-century AD sailors lured up river from the port at Ostia with the promise of higher wages as operators of the heavy sailcloth sun-awnings that shaded spectators in the Colosseum. Through the Imperial period much of the *trans Tiberim* area was agricultural, with farms, vineyards, country villas and gardens laid out for the pleasure of the Caesars.

Later, Syrian and Jewish trading communities established themselves here before moving in the Middle Ages to the Ghetto area

(see *p110*) across the river. Trastevere was a working-class district in papal Rome and until well after Unification. But property prices have rocketed as the area has climbed steadily upmarket, with trendy winebars and restaurants sprouting amid the butchers, bakers, candlestick-makers and sundry other medieval trades that are still noisily plied in ground-floor workshops. For all that, Trastevere still retains much of its slightly louche charm. The traffic in the warren of alleys is chaotic, especially at night, and fur-coated Roman matrons venturing over from the other side of the Tiber instinctively transfer their designer bags on to the curbside shoulder beyond the reach of Vespa-borne opportunists.

North of viale Trastevere

The district is linked to Rome 'proper' by way of the elegant footbridge constructed by Pope Sixtus IV, the Ponte Sisto. Alternatively you can cross the heavily trafficked Ponte Garibaldi and take via della Lungaretta to the heart of Trastevere and to the area's main treasure, the exquisite church of **Santa Maria in Trastevere**. In nearby piazza Sant'Egidio the **Museo di Roma in Trastevere** is a sad and dusty 'tribute' to the area's colourful past.

Pope Sixtus V, who was heavily into urban planning, drove a handy road, via della Lungara (though it begins as via della Scala), through from here to the Vatican palaces. Along it, splendid Renaissance houses were built, including the **Villa Farnesina** with its frescos by Raphael, and the **Palazzo Corsini**, which houses part of the national art collection. En route is the humble **Casa della Fornarina**, where Raphael's mistress is said to have lived.

Casa della Fornarina

Via di Santa Dorotea 20. Bus 23, 280, 630, 780, H/tram 8. **Open** closed to the public. **Map** p336 2B. Just inside the Porta Settimiana, which was built in 1498, stands an unassuming house, now a restaurant, with a pretty window high on the façade and a granite column embedded in its wall. It is believed to have been that of Margherita *la Fornarina* (the Baker's Girl), Raphael's model and the great love of his life. Her portrait, with Raphael's signature proprietorially inscribed on a bangle on her naked arm, is one of the stars of the collection at the Palazzo Barberini (*see p79*). Contemporary gossips claimed that Sienese banker Agostino Chigi invited the baker's daughter to move in to the sumptuous riverside villa (now Villa Farnesina, *see p121*) that Raphael was frescoing for him in a desperate bid to keep the maestro's mind on his work. On his deathbed the 37-year-old Raphael sought to atone for his debauchery and sin by rejecting Margherita, who took herself off to the nearby convent of Sant'Apollonia in piazza Santa Margherita, just around the corner from her home.

Museo di Roma in Trastevere

Piazza Sant'Egidio 1B (06 589 9359/www.comune. roma.it/museodiroma.trastevere). Bus 23, 280, 630, 780, H/tram 8. **Open** 10am-8pm Tue-Sun; ticket office closes 7pm. **Admission** €2.58; €1.55 concessions. **No credit cards. Map** p336 2B.

There are worse places to take shelter than a cloudburst than Rome's folklore museum, housed in a 17th-century convent formerly occupied by Carmelite nuns. Under any other circumstances the temporary exhibitions of 'local interest' held in the pretty cloister may not be top of your must-see list, nor may the few faded watercolours of a long-vanished Rome. A series of whiskery waxwork tableaux evoking the life, work, pastimes and superstitions of 18th- and 19th-century Trastevere folk are more fun. There is also a room stuffed with the bric-a-brac of local dialect poet Trilussa.

Orto Botanico (Botanical Gardens)

Largo Cristina di Svezia 24 (06 4991 7106/7107). Bus 23, 280, 630, 780, H/tram 8. **Open** *Nov-Mar* 9am-5.30pm Tue-Sat. *Apr-Oct* 9am-6.30pm Tue-Sat. Closed Aug. **Admission** €2.06; €1.02 concessions. **Map** p336 2C.

Rome's Botanical Gardens were established here in 1883 within the gardens of what had been Queen Christina of Sweden's home (*see below* **Palazzo Corsini**). The place was already verdant: there were orange and lemon groves, and 200 fragrant jasmine bushes set in perfectly manicured grounds that stretched up the slopes of the Janiculum hill in a series of formal tableaux around sculptures and water features. Despite (or perhaps because of) its fairly dilapidated state as a botanical garden, this little park is still a welcome haven from the rigours of a dusty, hot city: plants tumble over steps and into fountains and fish ponds, creating luxuriant hidden corners that are now disturbed only by frolicking children, parked here by Trastevere mums.

Palazzo Corsini – Galleria Nazionale d'Arte Antica

Via della Lungara 10 (06 6880 2323/www. galleriaborghese.it). Bus 23, 280, 630, 780, H/tram 8. **Open** 8.30am-7.30pm Tue-Sun. **Admission** €4; €2 concessions; *see also p59* **Tickets. No credit cards. Map** p336 1C.

In the 1933 film *Queen Christina*, Greta Garbo played the former owner of this palace as a graceful tussler with existential angst: in real life the stout 17th-century Swedish monarch smoked a pipe, wore

Sightseeing

All that glitters

Forget frescos in Rome: the Eternal City glitters with mosaics. Directly descended from the artisans of classical Rome, mosaic artists arranged their tiny chips of marble or coloured glass into suitably pious matter when Christianity became the official religion of the Empire, and stayed busy over the next 1,000 years as countless new churches and basilicas were commissioned.

Some artists worked in both mosaic and fresco. Pietro Cavallini, who many believe to have been Giotto's master, made magnificent mosaics such as the *Life of the Virgin* (1291) in Santa Maria in Trastevere (*see p118; pictured*), while at the same time producing the dazzling fresco of the *Universal Judgment* for the nuns of Santa Cecilia nearby.

Fourth century Santa Costanza (*p158*); Santa Pudenziana (*p135*).

Fifth century Santa Maria Maggiore (*p139*).

Sixth century Santi Cosma e Damiano (*p76*).

Seventh century Sant'Agnese fuori le Mura (*p158*).

Ninth century Santa Maria in Domnica (*p127*); Santa Prassede (*p134*).

Twelfth century San Clemente (*p126*).

Thirteenth century Santa Maria Maggiore (*p139*); Santa Maria in Trastevere (*p120*).

Twentieth century Stadio dei Marmi (*p156*).

Guido who?

As surely as today's visitors to Rome head for the nearest Caravaggio, Grand Tourists of the 18th and 19th centuries made a beeline for the works of Guido Reni. Guido who? Yes, tastes in art change like tastes in fashion. And when that champion of clean strong lines, Victorian critic John Ruskin, gave the gushing Bolognese brush-wielder a big thumbs-down, Reni's star waned swiftly, never to rise again.

Mention Guido Reni (1575-1642) now and the average gallery-goer will look nonplussed. His soulful Madonnas, their eyes brimming with tears, his chocolate-boxy saints and his agonised martyrs gripped by spiritual ectasy are too over-the-top for 21st-century sensibilities. He is simply too emotional.

Or is he? His finer works are imbued with an extraordinary sense of drama, remarkably intense colours and unrivalled draughtsmanship. And while much of his huge output was snapped up by Grand Tourists to grace their Palladian-inspired stately homes back in chillier northern climes, plenty still remains here to mark Reni's 20-year Roman sojourn.

Today's tourists flock to see the ghoulish crypt decor created by Capuchin monks from handy piles of human bones in their monastery-cemetery, but scarcely bother to glance upstairs at the greatest treasure of the **Immacolata Concezione** (see p87): Reni's St Michael Trampling on the Devil (1626-7), which was long considered one of the finest paintings in Rome. In Trastevere, his Santa Cecilia graces the great church (see p122) dedicated to the patron saint of music; **Palazzo Corsini** (see p119) is home to his startling Salome with the Head of St John the Baptist and Christ Crowned with Thorns. Elsewhere in the city, there's more from the Bolognese master at **Palazzo Barberini** (see p79), the **Musei Capitolini** (see p62) and the **Vatican museums** (see p145).

trousers and entertained female – and a fair number of (ordained) male – lovers. 'Queen without a Realm, Christian without a Faith, And a woman without Shame' ran one of the political epithets attached to Pasquino, the 'talking' statue (see p99 **Vox pop**). But Christina was also one of the most cultured and influential women of her age. The 17th century's highest-profile convert to Catholicism, she abdicated her throne and established her court here in 1662, filling what was then Palazzo Riario with her fabled library and an ever-expanding collection of Old Masters. She threw the best parties in Rome and commissioned many of Scarlatti and Corelli's hit tunes before dying here in 1689. Today the palace, which was later redesigned by Ferdinand Fuga for the Corsini family, houses part of the national art collection. The galleries have beautiful frescos and trompe l'oeils, and contain the usual scores of Madonnas and Children (the most memorable a Madonna by Van Dyck). Other works include a pair of Annunciations by Guercino; two St Sebastians, one by Rubens, the other by Annibale Carracci; Caravaggio's unadorned Narcissus; and a triptych by Fra Angelico. There's a melancholy Salome by Guido Reni (see p120 **Guido who?**).

Santa Maria in Trastevere

Piazza Santa Maria in Trastevere (06 581 4802). Bus 23, 280, 630, 780, H/tram 8. **Open** *7.30am-9pm daily.* **Map** *p336 2B.*
Santa Maria in Trastevere, with its glorious 13th-century mosaics on the façade, is one of Rome's oldest churches. Overlooking a fountain designed by

Carlo Fontana in 1692, it stands in a traffic-free cobbled square, the heart and soul of Trastevere.

Legend has it that a miraculous well of oil sprang from the ground where the church now stands when Christ was born, and flowed to the Tiber all day. A small street leading out of the piazza, via della Fonte dell'Olio ('Oil Well Street'), commemorates the miracle. The earliest church on this site was begun in 337 by Pope Julius I, and was one of the first in Rome to be dedicated to the Virgin. The present building was erected for Pope Innocent II in the 12th century, and has wonderful mosaics. Those on the façade – from the 12th and 13th centuries – show Mary breast-feeding Christ, and ten women with crowns and lanterns on a gold background. Much altered over the years, their significance is now uncertain, but they may represent the parable of the wise and foolish virgins. Inside, the apse has a 12th-century mosaic of Jesus and his mother; the figure holding the church on the far left is Pope Innocent. Lower down, between the windows, there are beautiful 13th-century mosaics showing scenes from the life of the Virgin by Pietro Cavallini (see also p122 **Santa Cecilia**), whose relaxed, realistic figures represent the re-emergence of a Roman style after long years of the hegemony of Byzantine models. The Madonna and Child with rainbow overhead is also by Cavallini. Through the wooden door on the left, just before entering the transept, there are two tiny, exquisite fragments of first-century AD mosaics from Palestrina (see p291), and in the chapel immediately to the left of the high altar is a very rare sixth-century painting on wood of the Madonna.

Sightseeing

Villa Farnesina: pleasure palace for a papal banker.

Villa Farnesina

Via della Lungara 230 (06 6802 7268). Bus 23, 280, 630, 780, H/tram 8. **Open** *9am-1pm Mon-Sat.* **Admission** €4.50; €3.50 concessions. **No credit cards. Map** p336 1B.

This villa was built between 1508 and 1511 by Baldassare Peruzzi as a pleasure palace and holiday home for the rich papal banker and renowned party-thrower Agostino Chigi. The powerful Farnese family bought and renamed it in 1577 after the Chigis went bankrupt. Chigi was one of Raphael's principal patrons, and in its day the villa was stuffed to the rafters with great works of art, although many were later sold to pay off debts.

The stunning frescos in the ground-floor Loggia of Psyche were designed by Raphael but executed by his friends and followers, including Giulio Romano; according to local lore the master himself was too busy dallying with his mistress, La Fornarina (*see p118* **Casa della Fornarina**), to apply any more paint that was strictly necessary himself. The Grace with her back turned, to the right of the door, is attributed to him. Around the corner, in the Loggia of Galatea, Raphael took brush in hand to create the victorious goddess in her sea-shell chariot. Up the stairs is the Salone delle Prospettive, decorated by Baldassare Peruzzi with views of 16th-century Rome. Next to it is Agostino Chigi's bedroom, with a fresco of the *Marriage of Alexander the Great and Roxanne* by Raphael's follower Sodoma. Like most of his paintings this is a rather sordid number showing the couple being relieved of their clothes by vicious cherubs.

South of viale Trastevere

South of the viale Trastevere is a quiet, evocative enclave with a high concentration of genuine locals. The church of **San Francesco a Ripa** contains a startling Bernini statue. The warren of lanes around the church of **Santa Cecilia** is a good place to wander aimlessly, watching local craftsmen at work; behind anonymous doorways are architectural gems such as the **Chiostro dei Genovesi**. This area faces *l'isola tiberina* (the Tiber island, *see p113*).

Chiostro dei Genovesi

Via Anicia 12 (no phone). Bus 23, 280, 630, 780, H/tram 8. **Open** *Apr-Oct 3-6pm Tue, Thur. Nov-Mar 2-4pm Tue, Thur (ring the bell marked Sposito to get in).* **Admission** free. **Map** p336 2A.

To the right of the 16th-century church of Santa Maria dell'Orto – recognisable by its obelisks – is a wooden door opening into a glorious flower-filled cloister with a well, part of a 15th-century hospice for Genoese sailors designed by Baccio Pontelli. Concealed among the octagonal columns supporting the double loggia is a plaque commemorating Rome's first ever palm tree, planted here in 1588.

San Francesco a Ripa

Piazza San Francesco d'Assisi 88 (06 581 9020). Bus 23, 44, 280, H/tram 3, 8. **Open** *7.30am-noon, 4-7pm daily.* **Map** p337 1B.

This 17th-century church stands on the site of the hospice where St Francis of Assisi stayed when he visited Rome in 1219. The original church was built

Then what?

- Catch a **puppet show** in the open-air booth on the Gianicolo. The language is intractable but the sentiments limpid. Refrain (as the sign says) from throwing stones at Mr Punch.
- Clutch your wallet tightly early on Sunday morning and check seek out the amazing bargains among piles of tack at **Porta Portese flea market** (*see also p225*).
- Don't be fooled by the simple façade of **Santa Maria della Scala** in piazza della Scala. Built in 1592 around a miraculous image of the Virgin, this small church has extravagant baroque decor in coloured marble from all over Italy.
- Synchronise your watches, as Romans do, when a **cannon** is fired from the Gianicolo (*see below*) at noon... the perfect time for an *aperitivo*-with-a-view at the pavement café near the statue of Giuseppe Garibaldi.

- Ring ahead and make an appointment to view manuscripts and relics of one of Italy's foremost poets. Torquato Tasso, author of *Gerusalemme liberata*, died at piazza Sant'Onofrio 2 – now the **Museo Tassiano** (06 682 8121) – in 1598 and is buried in the adjoining church (map p333 2C).
- Join the expats and catch an English-language movie at the long-running **Pasquino** (*see chapter* **Film**), hub of Anglo social activity and Rome's only cinema showing exclusively non-dubbed films.
- The massive 12th-century church of **San Crisostogno** in piazza Sonnino was built over a *titulus* (private house used for secret Christian worship in Roman times). There are magnificent mosaics attributed to Cavallini in the apse and fascinating Roman remains in the crypt.

by Rodolfo Anguillara, one of Francis' richer followers, in the 13th century. It was entirely rebuilt in the 1680s, and today its unremarkable baroque interior rings to the guitar strumming of a thriving parish church. It's most visited for Bernini's sculpture of the *Beata Ludovica Albertoni* (1674), showing the aristocratic Franciscan nun dying in one of those agonised, sexually ambiguous baroque ecstasies (*see also p139* **Santa Maria della Vittoria**). A near-contemporary portrait of St Francis hangs in the cell said to have been occupied by the monk himself during a Roman stay; if the sacristan is feeling so inclined, he'll take you in and show you the rock that the ascetic Francis used as a pillow. The Ripa of the church's name refers to its position a stone's throw from what was Rome's main riverside port area, the Ripa Grande.

Santa Cecilia in Trastevere

Piazza Santa Cecilia (06 589 9289). Bus 23, 280, 630, 780, H/tram 8. **Open** *Church, excavations & crypt* 9.30am-12.30pm, 4-6.30pm daily. *Cavallini frescos* 10am-noon Tue, Thur; 11.30am-12.30pm Sun. **Admission** *Excavations & crypt* €2.50. *Cavallini frescos* €2. **No credit cards. Map** p336 2A.

This pretty church stands on the site of a fifth-century building that was itself built over an older Roman house, the bath and storerooms of which can still be visited beneath the church. According to legend it was the home of Valerio, a Roman patrician so impressed (or perhaps frustrated) by his Christian wife Cecilia maintaining her vow of chastity that he also converted. Valerio was martyred for his pains, and Cecilia was arrested while trying to bury his body. Her martyrdom was something of a botched job: after a failed attempt to suffocate her in the hot

steam baths of her house, her persecutors tried to behead her with three strokes of an axe (the maximum permitted). She took several days to die, which, the legend goes on, she spent singing. Hence she became the patron saint of music. Her tomb was opened in 1599, revealing her still-undecayed body. It rapidly disintegrated, but not before a sketch had been made, on which Stefano Maderna based the astonishingly delicate sculpture that lies below the high altar. Her sarcophagus can be seen in the crypt.

Make sure your visit to this church coincides with the very short periods when visitors can see a small remaining fragment of what must have been one of the world's greatest frescos. Pietro Cavallini's late 13th-century *Last Judgment* is high up in the gallery, and miraculously survived later rebuilding work in the church. While still working within a Byzantine framework, Cavallini floods the seated apostles with a totally new kind of light (note the depth of the faces) – the same light that was to reappear in Giotto's work and has led a growing number of scholars to believe that Cavallini, not Giotto, was responsible for the St Francis fresco cycle in the basilica di San Francesco in Assisi.

The Gianicolo

Looming above Trastevere – and above the Regina Coeli prison – the Gianicolo (Janiculum) hill offers unparalleled views over the city centre (and gives prisoners' spouses a chance to shout messages down to their locked-up loved ones during exercise hour). The tortuous via Garibaldi passes by Bramante's exquisite **Tempietto** and the baroque **Fontana Paola** on its way to an expanse of pine- and statue-dotted garden dominated by an enormous equestrian statue of Giuseppe Garibaldi. Every day at noon a cannon is fired from beneath the terrace on which the statue stands.

From the balcony of this terrace, views extend over the city and, on a clear day, to the mountains beyond. In 1849 it was the scene of one of the fiercest battles in the struggle for Italian unity, when freedom fighter Giuseppe Garibaldi and his makeshift army of *garibaldini* – a hotchpotch of former papal troops and starry-eyed young enthusiasts – defended the Roman Republic against French troops that had been sent to restore papal rule. The often noseless busts that line the roads through the park are those of the 1,000 martyrs of Italy's Risorgimento movement. Past the equestrian statue of Garibaldi's equally heroic wife Anita stands a curious lighthouse, the patriotic gift of Italian emigrants in Argentina. The view from this part of the hill takes in the ochre shades of medieval and baroque Rome. At the Vatican end of the walk, opposite the Bambin Gesù children's hospital, there's a good view over St Peter's basilica and the Castel Sant'Angelo.

Fontana Paola

Via Garibaldi. Bus 44, 75, 710, 870. **Map** p336 2C. This huge fountain on the Gianicolo hill was originally intended – like the Fontana dell'Acqua Felice (*see p138*) – to resemble a triumphal arch. The columns came from the original St Peter's basilica. The fountain was designed in 1612 by Flaminio Ponzio and Giovanni Fontana for Pope Paul V, from whom it takes its name. It was built to celebrate the reopening of an ancient aqueduct built by Emperor Trajan (AD 98-117) that brought water from Lake Bracciano.

Tempietto di Bramante & San Pietro in Montorio

Piazza San Pietro in Montorio 2 (06 581 3940).
Bus 870. **Open** *Church* 8am-noon, 4-6pm daily.
Tempietto 10am-noon, 2-4pm daily. **Map** p336 2C.
High up on the Gianicolo, on the spot where St Peter was believed to have been crucified, San Pietro in Montorio commands the finest view of any church in Rome. It also has one of Rome's greatest architectural gems in its courtyard: the Tempietto, designed by Bramante in 1508. This much-copied round construction was the first modern building to follow exactly the proportions of one of the classical orders (in this case, Doric; *see chapter* **Architecture**). Bernini got his hands on it in 1628, adding the staircase that leads down to the crypt. The church itself, founded in the ninth century and rebuilt in the late 15th, contains a chapel by Bernini (second on the left) and one by Vasari (fifth on the right). Paintings include Sebastiano del Piombo's *Flagellation* and a *Crucifixion of St Peter* by Guido Reni (*see p120* **Guido who?**).

Casa della Fornarina: pleasure palace for a lusty artist. *See p118.*

The Aventine & Testaccio

High living or hard graft? The extremes of Roman life were here.

Sightseeing

Lying south of the Capitoline hill, the Aventine and Testaccio districts are as much in contrast today as they were in antiquity. A luxurious calm still pervades the exclusive Aventine, the preferred residential area of ancient Rome's writers and thinkers (Cicero rented out flats here). At the foot of the hill, Testaccio – once a hive of warehouses around a busy river port – remains a bustling community populated by genuine, salt-of-the-earth *romani de Roma*.

The Aventine

The tranquil and leafy Aventine hill boasts Rome's highest property prices and hosts a sovereign passport-issuing territory in the headquarters of the **Knights of Malta** (on piazza dei Cavalieri di Malta). The delightful **Parco Savello** offers spectacular views, while some glorious churches (**Santa Sabina**, **Sant'Anselmo**, **Sant'Alessio** and **Santa Prisca**) are an added bonus.

There are still elderly people on the Aventine and its sister hill San Saba, just across the busy viale Aventino, who remember farmers herding sheep and goats into the area's *piazze* of an evening before taking them to market the next morning. Until very recently, when debris left by transvestite prostitutes made it a health hazard, old ladies on piccolo Aventino could be seen picking *rughetta* (rocket) for salads from the foot of the Aurelian Wall (*see p155* **Walls**).

Parco Savello
Via di Santa Sabina. Bus 60, 75, 81, 118, 175, 628, 673/tram 3. **Open** dawn to dusk daily. **Map** p337 1A.
Inside the walled area of the 12th-century fortress of the Savello family is a garden, full of orange trees and massive terracotta pots of oleander. Marred only by sloppy upkeep, the garden ends in a terrace from which a sweeping view of Rome opens up: facing west, the sunset can be spectacular. Nearby, on via di Valle Murcia, is the city *roseto* (rose garden). It smells lovely – but gets very crowded – when briefly open to the public in late spring/early summer.

Santa Sabina
Piazza Pietro d'Illiria 1 (06 57 941). Bus 60, 75, 81, 118, 175, 628, 673. **Open** 6.30am-12.45pm, 3.30-7pm daily. **Map** p337 1A.

This magnificent, solemn basilica was built in the fifth century over an early Christian *titulus* (*see p317* **Glossary**). Added to and decorated over the centuries, it was shorn of later accretions in a merciless restoration in the 1930s: what you see today is arguably the closest thing – give or take a 16th-century fresco or two – to an unadulterated ancient church that Rome has to offer. The high nave's towering, elegant Corinthian columns support an arcade decorated with original marble inlay work. The late fifth-century wooden doors are carved with scenes from the New Testament, including one of the earliest renderings of the crucifixion. Selenite (thin, translucent sheets of crystallised gypsum) has been placed in the windows, as it would have been in the ninth century; the choir is the genuine article. In the floor in the middle of the nave is the mosaic tombstone of Brother Muñoz de Zamora (died 1300). Above the entrance a fifth-century mosaic recalls that the priest Peter of Illyria built the church while Celestine was pope; two figures on either side of the inscription represent the *ecclesia ex gentibus* and the *ecclesia ex circumcisione*, church members who hailed from the pagan world and those descended from Jews. Later additions remaining in the church include Taddeo Zuccari's 16th-century fresco in the apse (said to have been inspired by the original mosaic). A tiny window in the entrance porch looks on to where St Dominic was said to have planted an orange tree. The adjoining monastery contains a cell (usually closed) where the saint stayed; a peaceful 13th-century cloister, reached by a sloping corridor near the main door, is sometimes open.

Villa Magistrale dei Cavalieri di Malta
Piazza Cavalieri di Malta 3 (06 6758 1234/ www.smominfo.org/www.orderofmalta.org). Bus 60, 75, 81, 118, 175, 628, 673/tram 3. **Map** p337 1A.
Designed by the great fantasist Gian Battista Piranesi in the 18th century, the piazza's mysterious reliefs and orderly cypress trees make it into some kind of surrealist mise en scène. Villa Magistrale is the priory of the Knights of Malta, from whom the piazza takes its name; it is on the western side. If you look through the little hole in the priory doorway, you'll see one of Piranesi's most spectacular illusions: at the end of a neat avenue of trees sits the dome of St Peter's, apparently only a few metres away. This is probably the only keyhole in the world

through which you can see three sovereign territories: those of Italy, the Vatican and the aristocratic, theocratic Knights of Malta, a sovereign order with extraterritorial rights that has its own head of state, and issues its own number plates (starting SMOM), stamps and passports. Large groups can visit the priory by appointment.

Testaccio

Further south, though still within the ancient Wall, is the wedge-shaped Testaccio, hemmed in by the Tiber to the north-west, via

Marmorata to the north and via Campo Boario to the east. While other parts of town boast baroque fountains, Renaissance *palazzi* and streets named after Latin poets, Testaccio has an ancient rubbish heap, a defunct slaughterhouse and streets named for modern inventors: via Beniamino Franklin, or via Alessandro Volta (he invented the battery and gave his name to the volt). One of the few areas of central Rome where a sense of community is strongly felt, the line between courtyard and street is blurred enough to allow old ladies to pop into the local *alimentari* in dressing gown

The yellow Tiber

Today Rome has almost forgotten about its river, but the Tiber was a lifeline in antiquity, providing not only drinking water but also a vital trade link with the sea. The bustle along its banks rivalled that of the Roman Forum. Barges carrying columns and obelisks, or amphitheatre-bound elephants and lions, arrived daily at the Porto Fluviale ('river port', *see p124*) in Testaccio. As nearby Monte Testaccio (*see p125*) attests, the port also saw the delivery of some 53 million amphorae of olive oil between the second century BC and the fourth century AD.

Despite supplying the *urbs* with its basic needs – for construction, entertainment and sustenance – the Tiber was a treacherous ally, flooding often and catastrophically. Julius Caesar proposed diverting its course to the west, behind the Gianicolo, but the project was never carried out and, century after century, high water-levels continued to take the city by surprise: 3,000 people died in the flood of 1598. As the waters rose, the city's sewers would regurgitate any waste that had recently been washed down; combined with other silt, this detritus accounts for the seven metre (25 foot) difference between ancient and modern ground levels. Today the Tiber is kept in check – and is sadly isolated from the city – by imposing walls, built between 1871 and 1926.

The river's silty bed has yielded many treasures of Roman sculpture. According to tradition, the golden menorah from the temple in Jerusalem is still trapped somewhere in the Tiber's mucky bottom. Poets charitably described the colour of the river as *biondo* (blond), but *verdastro opaco* (murky green) would be more accurate. No longer potable in the late 1800s, the water was deemed unfit for swimming by the

mid-1900s (though some foolhardy souls still challenge law and possible infection on hot summer days). Industrial waste from the feeder river Aniene to the east has not helped, but the city council plans to revive the Tiber: four treatment plants have been installed in areas north of the city and a fleet of water shuttles and luxury boats, aimed at commuters and tourists, recently went into service (*see below*).

Tiber travel today is a sedate affair. Gone are the ancient river ports and medieval mills. Being so much lower than the rest of the city, all you see are the flood walls, some riverside sport facilities and the occasional coypu. Some stretches, however, are thick with vegetation; here the Tiber looks as primitive today as it would have in the eighth century BC – you can almost picture Romulus and Remus floating along in their basket.

The **Compagnia Navigazione Ponte Sant'Angelo** (information & bookings 06 6938 0264/06 6929 4147, credit MC, V) operates *bateaux-mouches*-like craft from a jetty at the southern end of Ponte Sant'Angelo opposite the Castel Sant'Angelo (*see p148*). Guided boat tours (€10; 1hr 30min) and boat-plus-minibus tours (€32; 2hr 30min) leave at 9am, 10.30am, 3pm and 4.30pm; boat tours with dinner included (€43; 2hr 30min) depart at 7.30pm. Booking is always advisable and can be done by phone, but tickets can be bought at the jetty or the Hotel Reservation desks (*see p39*). Passengers are asked to be at the jetty 15 minutes before departure.

A regular commuter service was due to go into operation in mid 2003, stopping at eight jetties between the Duca D'Aosta bridge in the north and Ponte Marconi in EUR (tickets €1.50).

and slippers. It may lack famous monuments, but Testaccio revels in its authenticity: a visit here is one of the best ways to get a sense of 21st-century *romanitas*.

Begin in piazza Testaccio, home to one of Rome's best-stocked and liveliest food markets. Once a desperately poor area, Testaccio has reaped the benefits of post-war prosperity without losing either its character or its original residents, who remain resolutely salt-of-the-earth despite encroaching health-food shops, sushi bars and other trappings of gentrification. Many of the apartment blocks are still publicly owned and let at controlled rents. At the beginning of the 20th century a quarter of all families here slept in their kitchens, and tenants were forced to brave the suspended walkways (*ballatoi*) connecting the apartments on each floor. These can still be glimpsed from the recently restored courtyard of the block at piazza Testaccio 20.

You'll meet few non-residents in Testaccio by day: the only tourist destination is **Cimitero Acattolico** (the Protestant Cemetery), and the more obscure **Piramide di Caio Cestio** (Pyramid of Gaius Cestius), **Museo di Via Ostiense**, **Emporium** and **Monte Testaccio** draw only connoisseurs. By night, however, the area is inundated with outsiders flocking to hip restaurants and myriad clubs burrowed into the flanks of Monte Testaccio (*see p261*), opposite the huge **Mattatoio**.

Cimitero Acattolico

Via Caio Cestio 6 (06 574 1900). Metro Piramide/bus 23, 75, 95, 280/tram 3. **Open** *Oct-Mar* 8am-4.30pm Tue-Sun. *Apr-Sept* 9am-5.30pm Tue-Sun. **Admission** free (donation expected). **Map** p337 2A.

'It might make one in love with death to know that one should be buried in so sweet a place.' So Shelley described the Protestant Cemetery, final resting place of his friend John Keats, in the preface to his poem *Adonais*, little knowing that he too would be taking up residence here after a boating accident just a year later. Only a wall divides it from the chaos of piazza di Porta San Paolo, but miraculously it remains a haven of peace. The inhabitants of the cemetery – its official title is 'Cimitero acattolico', the non-Catholic cemetery – are not limited to Protestants: there are Russian Orthodox, Chinese, Buddhist and even atheist tombs. A map is available at the entrance to help you find the graves of distinguished residents such as Goethe's son Julius, Keat's companion Joseph Severn, and Antonio Gramsci, founder of the Italian Communist Party.

Emporio-Porto Fluviale

Lungotevere Testaccio. Bus 23, 30, 75, 95, 170, 280/tram 3. **Open** by prior appointment only, *see p60* **Ex-Rip.X**; visible from lungotevere Testaccio and Ponte Sublicio. **Map** p337 1A.

From the second century BC the bank just south of the modern Ponte Sublicio (built in 1919) was Rome's Emporium, the ancient wharf area, from which steps led up to the Porticus Emilia, a huge covered warehouse 60m (200ft) wide and almost 500m (1,600ft) long. Behind the Porticus were the *horrea* (grain warehouses), built under Tiberius (AD 14-37) to help control the imperial grain monopoly: the occasional outcrop of bricks from these can still be seen among Testaccio's apartment blocks in *vie* Vespucci and Florio. The 20th-century Fontana delle Anfore on the river bank recalls Testaccio's commercial past.

Il Mattatoio

Piazza Giustiniani/via di Monte Testaccio. Bus 23, 30, 75, 95, 170, 280, 673/tram 3. **Map** p337 2B.

Then what?

● A high concentration of clubs and restaurants makes **Monte Testaccio** a night-time destination for most, but take a walk around here during the day and you'll see goats grazing peacefully above discos where techno beats were booming a few hours before.

● Send your postcards from via Marmorata's **Ufficio Postale**, an architectural gem from the Fascist era by Adalberto Libera (*see also p49* **Modernism the Roman way**). Mussolini would have been proud to know that this is one of the most efficient branches of the Poste Italiane in the city... or was, until a 'time-saving' system of *numeretti* was introduced recently.

● Stroll the piccolo Aventino's **via di Villa Pepoli** (above the Terme di Caracalla, *see p129*) – one of the most exclusive residential streets in Rome.
● Trace the most ancient boundaries of the city in piazza Albania and on the Aventine's via Sant'Anselmo, where chunks of the fifth-century BC **Servian Walls** are still visible, hunkering under more modern structures.
● The Persian god Mithras ran Jesus a close race for Top Deity in fourth-century Rome. Pay your respects at the Aventine's **Mitreo di Santa Prisca**, the best-preserved mithraic shrine in Rome, beneath the church of the same name. (By prior appointment only; *see p60* **Ex-Rip.X**).

The lofty, leafy Aventine looks down over vibrant, workaday Testaccio.

Recognisable by the bizarre statue of a winged hero slaughtering an ox on top of its façade, the Mattatoio (municipal slaughterhouse) was Europe's most advanced abattoir when it opened in 1891. The 24-acre complex coped with an eightfold increase in the population, and provided Testaccio's residents with work (not to mention noise and smells) until it was pensioned off in 1975. For decades bickering between politicians, architects and planners over what to do with the structure caused stasis: now, the whole area, including the Campo Boario cattleyards next door, is destined for (tasteful) redevelopment, with spaces allotted to the university architecture department, to multimedia projects, for exhibition space (*see p246* **MACRO**) and to art-inclined commercial activities. The changes are under way, but the Mattatoio complex is still home to tourist-carriage-drawing horses, and the homeless, who rent mattresses in the stables.

Monte Testaccio

Via Zabaglia 24. Bus 23, 30, 75, 95, 280, 673/tram 3. **Open** by appointment only, *see p60* **Ex-Rip.X**. **Map** p337 2A.

Known locally as the 'Monte dei cocci' – the hill of shards – Monte Testaccio is just that: although it's covered by soil and scrubby plants, underneath the 'hill' is nothing but a pile of broken amphorae (ancient earthenware jars), flung here between AD 140 and 255 after being unloaded at the Porto Fluviale (*see p124*). Most came from the Roman province of Betica (Andalucia) and contained olive oil. In the Middle Ages Monte Testaccio and the area below it were famous as the site of the pre-Lenten *carnevale* celebrations, with the horse races and religious pageants of the nobility vying with the less refined sport of the people. Pigs, bulls and wild boar were packed into carts at the top of the hill and sent careering down: survivors of the impact were finished off with spears. Jews too were subjected to indignities of all kinds, although they were spared the *coup de grâce*. Some of the buzzing clubs and

restaurants built into the base of the hill (*see chapter* **Nightlife**) have glass walls to afford glimpses of the tightly stacked potsherds beyond. (The district's symbiotic relationship with the amphora is also recalled in a 20th-century statue in piazza dell'Emporio and amphora-shaped details in the wrought-iron gates of some *palazzi*.)

Museo di Via Ostiense

Via R Persichetti 3 (06 574 3193). Metro Piramide/bus 23, 30, 60, 75, 95, 175, 280/tram 3. **Open** 9am-1.30pm Wed, Fri-Sun; 9am-1.30pm, 2.30-4.30pm Tue, Thur. **Admission** free. **Map** p337 2A.

A visit to this small museum (in the middle of a daunting traffic roundabout, just opposite the train station for Ostia Antica) can be handily combined with one to the excavations of the ancient port city (*see p276*). The third-century AD gatehouse, called Porta Ostiensis in antiquity and Porta San Paolo today, contains artefacts and prints describing the story of the via Ostiense – the Ostian Way – built in the third century BC to join Rome to its port and the vital saltpans at the Tiber's mouth, plus large-scale models of old Ostia and the port of Trajan (*see p277*). Porta San Paolo also houses an apartment in which an elderly lady still resides: her laundry lines are visible from the tower.

Piramide di Caio Cestio

Piazza di Porta San Paolo. Metro Piramide/bus 23, 30, 60, 75, 95, 175, 280/tram 3. **Open** by prior appointment only, *see p60* **Ex-Rip.X**; visible from piazza di Porta San Paolo. **Map** p337 2A.

Lodged in the Aurelian Wall is a steep white pyramid. It was built by Gaius Cestius, an obscure first-century BC magistrate and tribune who, caught up in the *aegyptomania* that was then sweeping Rome, decided he wanted his tomb to look like a pharaoh's. He did not build it with as much care as the Egyptians (it's made of brick and only clad in marble), but has survived remarkably well since Cestius was buried here in 12 BC.

The Celio & San Giovanni

Ancient baths and churches within churches in Rome's green south-east.

Greener and less touristed than other parts of the *centro storico*, the south-east side of old Rome contains some of the most fascinating, unusual and spectacular sights in the city, from the massive remains of the **Terme di Caracalla** (Baths of Caracalla, *see p129*) to the ancient buildings hidden beneath the churches of **San Clemente** (*see below*) and **Santi Giovanni e Paolo** (*see p128*). But other churches also make this area well worth a visit: **San Giovanni in Laterano** (*see p131*) and the relic-heavy **Santa Croce in Gerusalemme** (*see p132*) were two of Christian Rome's first major churches – the former donated by the Emperor Constantine, the latter by his mother.

The Celio

For a taste of what large swathes of Rome must have been like as the barbarians swept in and sent the locals fleeing towards the Tiber, head for the Celio, where the atmosphere is still wonderfully thick with antiquity.

One of the seven hills of Rome (*see p134* **The full Monti**), the lush and unkempt Celio spreads eastward from the **Terme di Caracalla** and the sprawling white marble cuboids of the UN's Food and Agriculture Organisation – built to house Mussolini's Colonies Ministry. Among the area's unusual sights is the false-fronted church of **San Gregorio Magno**, with its picturesquely overgrown vegetable garden tended by nuns from Mother Theresa's order. From here St Augustine was despatched to convert the pagans of far-off Britain in the sixth century. Nearby is the **Antiquarium Comunale**, an endearing collection of ancient artefacts unearthed locally (closed indefinitely for restoration at the time of writing).

An ancient arcaded street leads up the hill past the church of **Santi Giovanni e Paolo**, which was built over a street of Roman houses, to **Santa Maria in Domnica**, with its pretty mosaic, and the **Villa Celimontana** park. The grid of narrow streets on the hill's lower slopes contains three ancient churches: the somewhat

gruesome **Santo Stefano Rotondo**, the secluded **Santi Quattro Coronati** and the multi-layered **San Clemente**.

Antiquarium Comunale

Viale del Parco del Celio 22 (06 700 1569). Bus 60, 75, 81, 175/tram 3. **Closed** indefinitely for restoration. **Map** p338 2B.

There's something charmingly provincial about this quiet museum in a villa on the Celio hill. Like any local museum, it houses the ancient finds of the area; this being Rome, however, the collection is rather better than you would get elsewhere. Many of the exhibits were unearthed as the city expanded at the end of the 19th century. Big collections took the pick of the finds, but this little museum hung on to a wonderful range of domestic artefacts, tools and kitchen equipment, many of which look surprisingly similar to their modern equivalents. Perhaps most touching is a jointed doll, a sort of ancient (small-busted) Barbie, found in the tomb of a young girl who died shortly before she was due to be married; it's exquisitely carved, even detailing the complicated hairstyle fashionable in the second century AD. At the time of printing, the authorities could not say when the Antiquarium would reopen, but if you're in the vicinity, do check to see if by some miracle the restoration has been completed.

San Clemente

Via San Giovanni in Laterano (06 7045 1018/ www.sanclemente.it). Metro Colosseo/bus 60, 85, 87, 117, 810, 850/tram 3. **Open** 9am-12.30pm, 3-6pm Mon-Sat; 10am-12.30pm, 3-6pm Sun. **Admission** *Church* free. *Excavations* €3. **No credit cards.** **Map** p338 2B.

Arguably Rome's most fun-packed basilica, San Clemente is a church on top of a church on top of even older, Imperial Roman buildings; the composite is one of the best examples of Rome's chequered architectural past, though you'd never know it by simply walking past the outside. Due to excavations begun in 1857 by the Irish Dominicans who have been in charge of the church since the 17th century, visitors can descend through all three layers. The existing 12th-century basilica is a smaller copy of its fourth-century predecessor, which in turn was built over an early Christian *titulus* (a church built over, and named for, a site where early saints were martyred and/or buried). The original church waburnt down when the Normans sacked Rome in

Porta Maggiore. *See p131.*

1084, but the *schola cantorum* (a walled marble choir) survived and was moved upstairs to the new church, where it still stands. The most striking feature, however, is a vivid 12th-century mosaic in the apse, showing the vine of life spiralling around delightful pastoral scenes. Peasants tend their flocks and crops among interspersed saints and prophets, and the whole mosaic centres on the crucified Christ. The chapel of St Catherine of Alexandria (facing the altar) has frescos by Masolino (possibly helped by Masaccio) showing scenes from the life of the saint, who was tortured to death strapped to a wheel (giving her name, much later, to the firework).

Steps lead down from the sacristy to the fourth-century basilica, the layout of which is much obscured by walls built to support the church above. Faded frescos illustrate episodes from St Clement's miracle-packed life. According to legend, Clement – the fourth pope – was exiled to the Crimea by the Emperor Trajan, but continued his proselytising undaunted and so was hurled into the sea, tied to an anchor. A year later the sea receded, to reveal a tomb containing the saint's body; after that, the sea would recede once each year and another miracle occur.

At the end of the underground basilica, past the strange modern Slavic memorial to St Cyril – inventor of Cyrillic script, he was a great figure of the Orthodox churches and responsible for bringing Clement's body back to Rome – a stairway leads down to an ancient Roman lane. On one side are the remains of a second-century apartment block or *insula*, where the cult of the god Mithras was celebrated. Mithraism, Christianity's main rival in the late Empire, was a complex mystical religion of Persian origin, with rituals and symbolism involving bulls, scorpions, snakes and testicles. Three rooms have been excavated in the Mithraic area: the anteroom, with benches and stucco ceiling; the sanctuary, with an altar depicting Mithras killing a bull; and a schoolroom. On the other side of the lane are the ground-floor rooms of a Roman house that was used by early Christians as a *titulus*.

San Gregorio Magno

Piazza di San Gregorio 1 (06 700 8227). Metro Circo Massimo/bus 60, 75, 81, 118, 160, 175, 628/tram 3. **Open** 9am-12.30pm, 3-6pm daily. **Map** p338 2B.
Now essentially a baroque building, finished by Giovanni Battista Soria in 1633, this church is famous as the starting point for St Augustine's sixth-century mission to convert heathen Britain to Christianity. It was originally the family home of one of the most remarkable popes, Gregory the Great (*see p11*), who had it converted into a monastery in 575. In the chapel to the right of the altar is a marble chair dating from the first century BC, reputed to have been used by Gregory as his papal throne. Also here is the tomb of Tudor diplomat Sir Edward Carne, who came to Rome several times to try to persuade the pope to annul the marriage of Henry VIII and Catherine of Aragon, so that the king could marry Anne Boleyn. You may need to ring the bell to get in during the week. Across the vegetable garden stand three small chapels and, behind them, some remains of Roman shops that lined the Clivus Scauri (beside Santi Giovanni e Paolo, *see p128*). The chapels of Santa Barbara and Sant'Andrea are medieval structures, both heavily restored in the early 17th century and both popularly believed to have been part of the house of Gregory the Great and his mother St Sylvia. The cappella di Sant'Andrea has frescos by Guido Reni (*see p118* **Guido who?**) and Domenichino. The chapel of Santa Silvia dates from the 17th century.

Santa Maria in Domnica

Via della Navicella 10 (06 700 1519). Bus 81, 117. **Open** 9am-noon, 3.30-6pm daily. **Map** p3391B.
Known to locals as the Navicella ('little ship', after the Roman statue that stands outside), Santa Maria dates from the ninth century, but its 16th-century

Peaceful **Terme di Caracalla**. *See p129*.

portico and ceiling were added by Pope Leo X. In the apse, behind a modern altar, is one of the most charming mosaics in Rome. Commissioned in the ninth century by Pope Paschal I, it shows the Virgin and Child surrounded by a crowd of saints. The pope kneels at their feet, with a square halo to indicate that he was still living at the time. Above their heads, the apostles are apparently skipping through a flower-filled meadow, with Christ in the centre.

Santi Giovanni e Paolo

Piazza Santi Giovanni e Paolo 13 (church 06 700 5745/excavations 06 7045 4544/www.caseromane.it). Bus 60, 75, 81, 175/tram 3. **Open** *Church* 8.30am-noon, 3.30-6pm daily. *Excavations* (booking required) 10am-1pm, 3-6pm Mon, Thur-Sun. **Admission** *Excavations* €6; €4 concessions; €3.50 extra per person for guided tours. **No credit cards**. **Map** p338 2B.

Goths and Normans did their worst to the original church, built here in the fourth century. What's left can be seen embedded in the 12th-century façade of the current construction; the square has scarcely changed since medieval times. Within, heavy-handed decorating in the 18th century left the church looking like a luxury banqueting hall, with creamy stucco work and extravagant chandeliers.

Excavations beneath the church have revealed first- and second-century Roman houses, evidently used as places of Christian worship, and a cellar used for secret Christian burials. The site has been identified as the home of Pammachius, a senator

who gave all his money to the poor and embraced Christianity, converting his house into the original church; his story was recorded by his friend St Jerome. Extensive restoration was completed in 2002, returning wall frescos to their original splendour and opening up extensive subterranean Roman areas to the public. Ask the sacristan for permission to view the impressive remains of the Temple of Claudius (separate from the church, accessed through a metal door to the right of the façade), which once dominated the Celian hill and is now hidden under the church, monastery and bell tower. Down the left of the church runs the Clivus Scauri, a lane that bears the same name as it did in Roman times; it is crossed by buttresses that were built to shore up the church between the fifth century and 14th century.

Santi Quattro Coronati

Via dei Santi Quattro 20 (06 7047 5427). Bus 85, 87, 117, 810, 850/tram 3. **Open** *Church & Oratory* 7.30am-8pm Mon-Sat (sometimes closes 1-3pm); 7.30am-12.30pm, 3-7.30pm Sun. *Cloister* closed for restoration; due to reopen mid 2003. **Map** p3382B.

This basilica dates from the fourth century but, like San Clemente (*see p126*) and Santi Giovanni e Paolo (*see above*), was burnt down by rampaging Normans in 1084. It was rebuilt as a fortified monastery, with the church itself reduced to half its original size; the outsize apse, visible as you look uphill along via dei Santi Quattro, remains from the original church. The early basilica form is still discernible, and the columns that once ran along the aisles are embedded in the walls of the innermost courtyard. The church has a fine cosmatesque floor. There is also a beautiful cloister, from about 1220, with a 12th-century fountain playing amid its flowerbeds.

In the oratory next to the church (ring the bell and ask the nuns for the key) is a fresco cycle depicting the Donation of Constantine – the legend put forward by the papacy for centuries as a primary source of its authority. The legend has it that an early pope, Sylvester, cured Emperor Constantine of leprosy (or another similarly unpleasant disease), after which the august personage was so grateful that he granted the Bishops of Rome spiritual and worldly authority over the whole Empire. The frescos, painted in the 13th century as a defence of the popes' temporal power, show a pox-ridden Constantine being healed by Sylvester, crowning him with a tiara and giving him a cap to symbolise the pope's spiritual and earthly authority. Just to make sure there are no lingering doubts about Sylvester's capacity for heroics, he resuscitates a bull killed as a sacrifice and frees the Romans from a dragon. Visitors should be as silent as possible: the monastery is still home to an enclosed order of nuns.

Santo Stefano Rotondo

Via di Santo Stefano Rotondo 7 (06 421 191). Bus 81, 117. **Open** *Nov-Mar* 1.50-4.20pm Mon; 9am-1pm, 1.50-4.20pm Tue-Sat. *Apr-Oct* 3.30-6pm Mon-Sat. **Map** p339 1B.

Obelisks

Roman emperors were crazy about obelisks. They had slaves drag them through Egypt, loaded them on to vast barges, and brought them across the Mediterranean and up the Tiber. The best came from the Nile-side Temple of the Sun in Heliopolis. Some have inscriptions in stylish hieroglyphics; others are blank. Some had fake inscriptions hacked into them when they arrived in Rome.

Emperor Augustus celebrated his conquest of Egypt by lugging back a 235-ton monster to stand in the middle of the Circo Massimo (*see p68*). It's 23 metres (76 feet) high and was carved in about 1300 BC. (Pope Sixtus V, a keen re-erecter of obelisks, later decided it would look nicer outside the new church he was building in piazza del Popolo; *see p96*.) Augustus set up another big'un in the Campus Martius, where the Roman army did their physical jerks; it now stands in front of the Italian parliament building, Palazzo Montecitorio (*see p95*). The obelisk in the centre of St Peter's square (*see p143*) once adorned Emperor Caligula's circus, where it was illuminated by burning Christians.

Less looming is the five-ton baby in front of Santa Maria sopra Minerva (*see p106*), which Bernini wittily mounted on top of a marble elephant. With its twin, now atop the fountain in front of the Pantheon (*see p105*), it once guarded a Roman temple to Isis and Serapis.

Fascist dictators had a weak spot for obelisks too: note the fine Ethiopian one by the UN Food and Agriculture Organisation HQ (*see p126*). It's the subject of an ongoing dispute between the former colony and the Italian government, which has so far reneged

on its undertaking to return Mussolini's war booty. Equally controversial is the modern obelisk, still proudly inscribed 'Mussolini Dux', that continues to throw a shadow over the Foro dei Marmi (*see p156*) sports complex.

One of very few round churches in Rome, Santo Stefano dates from the fifth century. Many mystics believed it had been modelled on the Holy Sepulchre in Jerusalem; in its measurements, they argued, lie the secret of the Holy Number of God. The church originally had three concentric naves separated by antique columns; the simplicity of the place was disturbed when arches were built to shore it up in the 12th century, and the outer ring was walled-in in 1450. The haunting peace diminished in the 16th century when the outer interior wall was frescoed with graphic scenes of ghastly martyrdoms, from lapidations to decapitations. A mithraeum beneath the church can be visited on the fourth Saturday of the month (booking is essential on 06 3996 7700). An appointment can also be made through the city council (*see p61* **Ex-Rip.X**).

Terme di Caracalla (Baths of Caracalla)

Viale delle Terme di Caracalla 52 (06 575 8626). Metro Circo Massimo/bus 60, 75, 81, 118, 175, 628, 714. **Open** 9am-1pm Mon; 9am-1hr before sunset Tue-Sun; ticket office closes 2hrs before sunset. **Admission** €5. **No credit cards. Map** p339 2B.

The high-vaulted ruins of the Baths of Caracalla, surrounded by trees and grass, are pleasantly peaceful today, but were anything but tranquil in their heyday, when up to 1,600 Romans could sweat it out at any one time in the baths and gyms. You can get some idea of the original splendour of baths from the fragments of mosaic and statuary littering the ground, although the more impressive finds are in the Vatican Museums (*see p148*) and the Museo Archeologico in Naples. The baths were built

Sightseeing

Bits and bobs

Endow your church with the bones of saints and the instruments of their martyrdoms and the faithful will come in droves. Emperor Constantine's mother, Helena, was among the most avid early relic-hunters, setting sail from Rome for the Holy Land in the fourth century AD and returning with a heavy-laden ship containing (among other things) a chunk of True Cross.

Relic-dealing was a seller's market. Business-wise residents of Jerusalem and Bethlehem knew well the price a nail from Christ's crucifixion, say, would fetch. Hundreds of years after the supply of those nails could reasonably be expected to have been exhausted, 'newly discovered' nails were still being gobbled up by a credulous clientele. Today the churches of Rome are home to some of the, er, most authentic relics gleaned from the Holy Land, and those of local martyrs, attracting devotion… and morbid curiosity.

between AD 213 and 216, although Caracalla, who died during military campaigns abroad in 217, never saw them completed. Also known as the Thermae Antoninianae, Caracalla's were the fifth largest ever built in Rome and the largest of their era. The two cavernous rooms down the sides were the *gymnasia*, where Romans engaged in such strenuous sports as toss-the-beanbag. There was also a large open-air *natatio* (pool) for lap-swimming. After exercising, they cleansed themselves in saunas and a series of baths of varying temperatures. The baths were usually open from noon until sunset, and were opulent social centres where people came to relax after work. The complex also contained a library (still identifiable on one side of the baths), a garden, shops and stalls. Underneath it all was a network of tunnels, totalling 9.5km (six miles) in length, where maintenance workers (read: slaves) scurried about, treading the giant hamster-wheels that pumped clean water up to the bathers and tending to the huge braziers that heated the various chambers from below the tiles and through pipes in the walls. Caracalla's baths were in use for more than 300 years until the fun dried up abruptly in 537 when the Visigoths sacked Rome and severed the city's aqueducts. For years the baths hosted classical concerts in summer, including the Three Tenors' performance during the 1990 World Cup. Gone, alas, are the days of full-scale productions of *Aida* – spoilsport archaeologists determined that the trampling of elephants did not enhance the structural stability of the 1,800-year-old ruins.

Villa Celimontana

Via della Navicella (no phone). Bus 60, 75, 81, 117, 175, 628/tram 3. **Open** dawn to dusk daily. **Admission** free. **Map** p339 2B.

This is a pretty, leafy, walled garden, with swings and climbing frames that swarm with local kids. The lawns are packed with bits of ancient marble from the collection of the Mattei family, which owned the property from 1553 until 1928 when it became a public park. The best examples from the Mattei collection can now be admired in the Palazzo Altemps (*see p101*), although the park still contains an Egyptian obelisk (one of 13 in Rome; *see p129* **Obelisks**) that was transferred here from the Capitoline hill in the 16th century. In summer the villa becomes the gorgeous venue for big-name evening jazz concerts (*see p265*).

From San Giovanni to Santa Croce in Gerusalemme

Concealed among the drab post-Unification apartment buildings filling this neighbourhood are some key Christian spaces and relics (*see p131* **Bits and bobs**). Before that lumpen architecture changed the look of the area, this was a largely rural zone both inside and outside the walls around the Porta di San Giovanni, occupied by those ancient residents (including Christians wishing to keep a low profile) who preferred quiet anonymity and a patch of land for tilling to the hubbub of central Rome by the Forum and along the riverbanks.

The massive basilica of **San Giovanni in Laterano**, immediately recognisable by the host of gigantic statue-saints partying atop its façade, dominates the cityscape here. This is Rome's cathedral and the world's first-ever basilica church: note that even Emperor Constantine, who donated the land for the basilica, preferred to hedge his bets by allotting the new sect out-of-the-way terrain, rather than upset the pagan powers-that-were by giving them a high-profile position in the centre.

To the south of the façade of San Giovanni are the sunken brick remains of the **Porta Asinaria**, an ancient gate belonging to the third-century AD Aurelian Wall. On the eastern side of piazza San Giovanni are the remaining sections of the former papal residence, the Lateran Palace. Across the street, to the north of the basilica stands the recently restored **Sancta Sanctorum** – formerly the pope's private chapel – at the top of the **Scala Santa** (Holy Stairs). Once the ceremonial staircase of the old palace, these 28 steps are traditionally believed to be those Christ climbed on his way to trial at Pontius Pilate's house in Jerusalem. Gracing the middle of the piazza to the west of the basilica is Rome's oldest, tallest obelisk, made in the 15th century BC and imported in AD 357 to be placed in the Circo Massimo (*see p68*). Pope Sixtus V had it moved here in 1588.

In a narrow street to the north of here, the little-visited **Museo Storico della Liberazione di Roma** contains grim reminders of the city's wartime tribulations, while between San Giovanni and Santa Croce is a stretch of green park, where children will appreciate see-sawing and swinging after a morning's sightseeing.

Constantine's redoubtable relic-collecting mother St Helena converted part of her private palace into the church of **Santa Croce in Gerusalemme**. Nearby stands the quaint **Museo Nazionale degli Strumenti Musicali**. Further north is the **Porta Maggiore**, a monumental travertine archway built by the Emperor Claudius in the first century AD to mark the triumphal entrance of the aqueducts into the city and later

Top five Relics

St Agnes's head (Sant'Agnese in Agone, *see p103*)
Tradition says Agnes was 14 when she died, but the skull looks more the size of a teenage chimpanzee's.

St Lawrence's grill (San Lorenzo in Lucina, *see p95*)
The very gridiron upon which this patron saint of Rome (and of outdoor cooking) sizzled is to be found under the altar in the first chapel on the right, though it's not visible in its entirety.

St Thomas's finger (Santa Croce in Gerusalemme, *see p154*)
There's a great postcard of the bending, doubting digit available for purchase from the sacristy bookshop.

St Sebastian's arrow (San Sebastiano, *see p154*)
Having provoked the wrath of the emperor in the third century by defending Christians, Sebastian was sentenced to a pot-pourri of tortures on the Palatine hill, including being tied to a column (also here) and perforated by Imperial arrows.

The Holy Stairs (Scala Santa, *see p132*)
Among the most ambitious of St Helena's imports, these 28 stone stairs were brought to Rome from Pontius Pilate's house. Now covered with walnut planks, the faithful climb them on their knees.

incorporated into the Aurelian Walls. Visible in the attic level of the gate and in the brick structures nearby are the channels (*speci*) that carried the water. The ancient via Prenestina's original paving (*see also p291*) can be seen under the arches, while the curious and well-preserved Tomb of Eurysaces, an ancient Roman baker, lies just to the east.

Museo Nazionale degli Strumenti Musicali
Piazza Santa Croce in Gerusalemme 9A (06 701 4796). Metro Manzoni/bus 649/tram 3. **Open** 8.30am-7.30pm Tue-Sun. **Admission** €2; €1 concessions. **No credit cards. Map** off p339 1A.
In the early 20th century opera singer Evan Gorga put together this collection of over 800 rare and beautiful musical instruments. The collection gives a comprehensive overview of the history of European music since ancient times, rounded out with fascinating pieces from Asia and the Americas. Look out for mandolins with armadillo-carapace resonance boxes, an early 18th-century piano built by the instrument's inventor Bartolomeo Cristofori, and the exquisite, triple-stringed Barberini harp.

Museo Storico della Liberazione di Roma
Via Tasso 145 (06 700 3866). Metro Manzoni/bus 810/tram 3. **Open** 4-7pm Tue, Thur, Fri; 9.30am-12.30pm Sat, Sun. **Admission** free. **Map** p338 2A.
Prisoners of the Nazis were brought to this grim building for interrogation during the occupation of Rome in 1943-4; this is a truly haunting tribute to those resistance fighters, civilians taken in reprisal, and members of the Nazis' proscribed groups such as Jews, homosexuals, gypsies and Communists. The walls are covered with pictures and biographies of those who passed through on their way to die; display cases contain remnants of their blood-stained clothing. On the second and third floors several cells have been preserved, complete with prisoners' farewell messages to their families scratched into the walls. Even if your Italian isn't good enough to understand the words, it's a moving and a chilling place, not forgotten in a hurry.

San Giovanni in Laterano
Piazza di San Giovanni in Laterano 4 (06 6988 6433). Metro San Giovanni/bus 85, 87, 117, 218, 714, 850/tram 3. **Open** *Church* 7am-6.30pm daily. *Baptistery* 9am-noon, 4-7pm daily. *Cloister & museum* 9am-6pm daily. **Admission** *Cloister & museum* €2. **No credit cards. Map** p339 1A.
San Giovanni was built around 313, on a site given to Pope Melchiades for the purpose by the Emperor Constantine himself. Little remains of the original basilica, which has been sacked, destroyed by fire and earthquake, and heavily restored and rebuilt over the centuries. The façade, surmounted by 15 huge statues, dates from the final rebuilding and was designed by Alessandro Gallei in 1735. The interior was last transformed in 1646 by Borromini,

Sightseeing

who encased the original columns in pillars and stucco. The enormous bronze doors in the main entrance came originally from the Senate House in the Foro Romano (*see p75*). A 13th-century mosaic in the apse survived the revamp, as did a fragment of fresco attributed to Giotto (behind the first column on the right); it shows Pope Boniface VIII announcing the first Holy Year in 1300 (*see p13*). Another survivor is the Gothic *baldacchino* over the main altar; the two busts behind the grille were once believed to contain the heads of Saints Peter and Paul. Off the left aisle is the 13th-century cloister: the twisted columns, studded with mosaics, were made by the Vassalletto family. Remains from the original basilica also appear around the walls. The central well is ninth century. A small museum off the cloister contains vestments, along with manuscripts of music by Palestrina. The north façade was added in 1586 by Domenico Fontana. On its right is the octagonal baptistery, founded by Constantine but rebuilt in 432 and again in 1637. Restored after a bomb exploded nearby in 1993, it has fine fifth- and seventh-century mosaics, as well as a charming little chapel accessed through a door to the left of the baptismal font. Access to the ancient structures beneath the church can be arranged through the Vatican excavations office (*see p144*).

Santa Croce in Gerusalemme

Piazza Santa Croce in Gerusalemme 12 (06 701 4769/www.basilicasantacroce.it). Metro Manzoni/bus 81, 649/tram 3. **Open** 7am-7pm daily. **Map** off p339 1A.
Founded in 320 by St Helena, mother of the Emperor Constantine, this church began as a hall in her home, the Palatium Sessorianum. It was rebuilt and extended in the 12th century, and again in 1743-4. The outline of the original building can be seen from the grounds of the Museo Nazionale degli Strumenti Musicali (*see p131*). It was built to house the fragments of the passion of Christ brought back from the Holy Land by St Helena; these are now behind glass in a chapel at the end of a hall off the left side of the nave. The first part of the hall is Fascist era, with lashings of grey marble, and houses a large piece of old wood behind glass – don't get too excited, however: this is a fragment of the good thief's cross, not Christ's. At the end of this hall to the right is the chapel containing the holier relics: as well as three pieces of *the* cross and a nail, there are two thorns from Christ's crown and the finger of St Thomas – allegedly the very one the doubting saint stuck into Christ's wound. As if that weren't enough, bagfuls of soil from Calvary lie under the tiles in the charming lower chapel beneath the altar. The chapel's mosaics were originally laid in the fifth century, but were redesigned around 1484 by Melozzo da Forlì.

Scala Santa (Holy Stairs) & Sancta Sanctorum

Piazza di San Giovanni in Laterano 8 (06 772 6641). Metro San Giovanni/bus 85, 87, 714/tram 3. **Open** *Scala Santa* Oct-Mar 6.30am-noon, 3-6pm

daily; Apr-Sept 6.30pm-noon, 3.30-6.30pm daily. *Sancta Sanctorum* Oct-Mar 10.30-11.30am, 3-4pm Tue, Thur, Sat; Apr-Sept 10.30-11.30am, 3.30-4.30pm Tue, Thur, Sat. **Admission** *Scala Santa* free. *Sancta Sanctorum* €3. **No credit cards. Map** p338 2B.
According to tradition, these stone stairs (now covered with walnut planks) are the very ones that Jesus climbed in Pontius Pilate's house before being sent to his crucifixion. Brought to Rome from Jerusalem by St Helena in the fourth century, a crawl up the Scala Santa has been a fixture on every serious pilgrim's list ever since. In 1510 Martin Luther gave this a go, but halfway up he decided that relics were a theological irrelevance and walked back down again. Don't climb them unless you know 28 different prayers (one for each step) and have kneepads (no walking up). Prepare for a queue on Good Friday. At the top of the Holy Stairs (but also accessible by non-holy stairs to the left) is the beautifully restored Sancta Sanctorum ('holy of holies'), once – when all things Church-related were headquartered at the nearby Lateran Palace – the *privatissima* chapel of the popes. What made the chapel so holy was the fact that important relics of early Christianity – including the heads of the apostles Peter and Paul, as well as that of the young St Agnes – were kept in the crypt beneath the altar. Most of the relics have since been distributed to other basilicas around the city, but displayed in a glass case on the left wall is a fragment of the table on which the Last Supper was served. The real treasures here, however, are the exquisite 13th-century frescos in the lunettes and on the ceiling, attributed to Cimabue. For a time, no one but the pontifex maximus himself was allowed to set foot in the Sancta Sanctorum, but the exclusive entry policy has been relaxed nowadays: anyone with three euros is welcome.

Then what?

● Take a peek at where the gladiators lived and trained: the first-century AD **Ludus Magnus**, partially excavated between via San Giovanni in Laterano, via Labicana and piazza del Colosseo. Access to the ruins is by appointment with **Ex-Rip.X** (*see p60*).
● Dating from the first century AD and used by adherents of a cult to Pythagoras, the subterranean meeting hall of the fascinating **Basilica di Porta Maggiore** looks like something Indiana Jones might drop into at any moment. Book ahead through **Ex-Rip.X** (*see p60*).
● Give the kids a break at the Celio's brand-new **playground**. You'll find it between via Claudia and piazza della Sanità Militare.

Monti & Esquilino

Impoverished poets swooned below, while their patrons partied in *palazzi* above.

A single *rione* (city district) until 1874, Monti and Esquilino encompassed some of the ancient city's most exclusive residential areas on its higher ground and its worst slum, the Suburra, lower down the hill.

On the Esquiline hill, Maecenas – that great patron of first-century Rome – lived in style in a sumptuous villa, entertaining guests in his private auditorium (*see p139* **Then what?**) with performances of works by his pet poets, Horace, Ovid and Propertius. And so did Felice Peretti, aka Pope Sixtus V, whose exquisite villa was demolished and eventually replaced by Termini railway station. On the neighbouring Colle Oppio (Oppian hill), Nero fiddled in his **Domus Aurea** (*see p134*) entertaining his guests with his imperial twanging.

Much of what remained of these urban idylls fell prey to the property developers who swooped down on the new capital after Unification in the 1870s, creating residential districts that are, architecturally speaking, all of a piece: ponderous *palazzi* fronting wide boulevards – a gross incongruity in twisting, narrow Rome. Over the years, what was fashionable and stately has grown tacky and down-at-heel. In an ironic twist of fate, the alleys of what was the Suburra – where once the most determined developers feared to go – are now some of Rome's liveliest and trendiest.

Monti

Throughout history, the rich always occupied Rome's salubrious higher ground; the urban poor – and out-of-work poets – were confined to the steamy Suburra, an ancient shanty town on marshy ground between the Quirinale, Viminale and Esquiline hills (*see p135* **The full Monti**). Propertius fondly recalls nightly assignations here with his mistress Cynthia, who climbed out of a first-floor window, down a rope and into his arms. Fellow poet Juvenal, who lived in the heart of this hottest, noisiest, dirtiest and most chaotic quarter of the city, reported in his *Satires* that the most common cause of death in the Suburra was insomnia.

But then Rome always was the noisiest city on earth, and the area of present-day Monti that was the Suburra – the enclave stretching east from the Forum between *vie* Nazionale and

Cavour – is just as noisy, cosmopolitan and full of life today as it was 2,000 years ago. Streets may be cleaner, property prices are unquestionably higher, but the narrow, chaotic streets full of funky clothes shops, wild bars and ethnic restaurants pulsate with the same kind of frenetic activity.

Monti did not avoid the post-Unification developers altogether: there are bureaucratic monstrosities in the shape of the Sisde secret police HQ on via Lanza, the lumpen Bank of Italy HQ in Palazzo Koch on via Nazionale, and the lab on undulating via Panisperna where in 1934 Enrico Fermi and Ettore Majorana first split the atom (*see p140* **Splitting atoms**).

There's relief in the streets south of **Santa Maria Maggiore** (*see p139*), where two stunning early churches, **Santa Prassede** and **Santa Pudenziana**, glow with extraordinary mosaics. For a verdant break, head for the **Villa Aldobrandini** gardens at the south-western end of via Nazionale, a traffic artery lined with carbon-copy high-street fashion emporia.

Santa Prassede

Via Santa Prassede 9A (06 488 2456/www. santaprassede.org). Bus 16, 70, 71, 75, 84, 360, 649, 714. **Open** 7.30am-noon, 4-6pm Mon-Sat; 7.30am-noon, 4-6.30pm Sun. **Map** p338 1B.
This church is a scaled-down copy of the old St Peter's, a ninth-century attempt to recreate an early Christian basilica. But, as the uneven brickwork shows, the Romans had lost the knack. The home-grown mosaic artists were no better, so Pope Paschal I decided to import mosaicists from Byzantium to decorate the church. The results are exotic and rich, and what the mosaics lack in subtle modelling they make up for in glorious colours, flowing drapery and fluid movement. In the apse, Christ riding on a cloud is being introduced to the martyr St Praxedes by St Paul on the right, while St Peter is doing the honours on the left for her sister St Pudenziana. Pope Paschal is there too, holding a model of the church and sporting a square halo signifying that he was alive when the mosaic was made. Beneath, 12 lambs represent the apostles. The triumphal arch shows the heavenly Jerusalem, with palm-frond-toting martyrs heading for glory.

Off the right side of the nave is the chapel of San Zeno, with some of Rome's most spectacular mosaics. Entered beneath a carved architrave pilfered from an ancient site, the chapel is a dazzling swirl of Byzantine blue and gold, punctuated with saints,

Santa Prassede. *See p133.*

animals and depictions of Christ and his mother. The wall and ceiling mosaics are ninth-century; the jolly Mary clutching a dwarf-like Jesus and flanked by sister-saints Praxedes and Pudenziana in the niche above the altar is 13th century. In a room to the right is a portion of column, said to be part of the very one that Jesus was tied to for scourging.

Santa Pudenziana

Via Urbana 160 (06 481 4622). Metro Cavour/ bus 16, 70, 71, 75, 84, 360, 649, 714. **Open** 8am-6.30pm Mon-Sat; 8.30am-7pm Sun. **Map** p338 1B.
The mosaic in the apse of Santa Pudenziana dates from the fourth century (although it was hacked about in a brutal restoration in the 16th century), and so pre-dates the arrival in Rome of the stiffer Byzantine style. It is a remarkable example of the continuity between pagan and Christian art, depicting Christ and the apostles as wealthy Roman citizens, framed by very Roman architectural details and wearing togas, against an ancient Roman cityscape and a glorious Turneresque sunset. Were it not for Christ's halo and symbols of the four evangelists in the sky, it could be a portrait of senators.

Villa Aldobrandini

Via Mazzarino 11. Bus 40, 60, 64, 70, 117, 170. **Open** 7am-dusk daily. **Map** p338 1C.
This villa was built in the 16th century for the Dukes of Urbino, and later bought by the Aldobrandini Pope Clement VIII. It's now state property and closed to the public, but the gardens remain open. Reached through a gate off via Mazzarino and up a

steep flight of stairs, the formality of the gardens' lawns and gravel paths is disturbed only by tramps sleeping on benches. During renovations the gardens were raised some 30m (100ft) above street level, behind the high wall that dominates the southern end of via Nazionale. A picturesque place with splendid views over the city, somewhat marred by the thundering traffic below.

Colle Oppio

The serene, green Colle Oppio was the site of Nero's **Domus Aurea**, an all-too-vivid reminder of the hated emperor that was torn down, filled in and replaced with Trajan's baths complex soon after the tyrant's death. Nowadays the Colle Oppio park is peopled by swarms of Roman mums and their toddlers during the day. A string of unpleasant incidents involving far-right local youths, homeless immigrants and a sprinkling of the city's more foolhardy gays has resulted in the park being firmly locked after darkness falls.

On the western slope, **San Pietro in Vincoli** contains important relics and a mighty Michelangelo. Further north, on the border with Monti (*see p133*), the church of **Santi Silvestro e Martino ai Monti** stands above a Roman house. Nearby, on via Merulana, the **Museo Nazionale d'Arte Orientale** provides an exotic break from ancient Rome.

Domus Aurea (Golden House)

Viale della Domus Aurea (06 3996 7700). Metro Colosseo/bus 60, 75, 81, 85, 87, 117, 175, 186, 204, 673, 810, 850/tram 3. **Open** 9am-7.45pm Mon, Wed-Sun; ticket office closes 6.45pm. **Admission** €5; €2.50 concessions; plus €1 booking fee; *see also p59* **Tickets**. **No credit cards**. **Map** p338 2B.
Note: visits must be booked in advance.
In the summer of AD 64 a fire devastated a large part of central Rome. The ashes of patrician palaces mingled with those of slums. Afterwards anything in the area east of the Forum left unsinged was knocked down to make way for a home fit for the sun-god that Nero liked to think he was.

Work began on the emperor's Domus Aurea (Golden House) immediately after the fire had died down. A three-storey structure, its main façade faced south and was entirely clad in gold; inside, every inch not faced with mother-of-pearl or inlaid with gems was frescoed by Nero's pet aesthete Fabullus. Fountains squirted rich perfumes, and baths could be filled with sea or mineral water. In one room, wrote Suetonius, an immense ceiling painted with the sun, stars and signs of the zodiac revolved constantly, keeping perfect time with the heavens.

The house stood in parkland. Lakes were dug, forests planted and a gilded bronze statue of Nero 35m (116ft) high erected. The moment Nero was in his grave in AD 68, however, work began to eradicate every vestige of the hated tyrant. Vespasian drained the lake to build his amphitheatre (the tight-fisted emperor kept Nero's colossus, simply putting a new head on it, and so the stadium became known as the Colosseum), and Trajan used the brickwork as a foundation for his baths. So thorough was the cover-up job that for decades after the house's frescos were rediscovered in 1480, no one realised it was the Domus Aurea that they had stumbled across. The frescoed 'grottos' became an obligatory stopover for Renaissance artists, inspiring – among many other things – Raphael's weird and wonderful frescos in the Vatican (and incidentally giving us the word 'grotesque'). The artists' signatures, scratched into the ancient stucco, can still be seen on the ceiling. After decades of digging and restoration, some 30 rooms of the Domus Aurea reopened in June 1999. Over 100 rooms remain off-limits, and a further 200-odd still wait to be excavated.

Museo Nazionale d'Arte Orientale

Via Merulana 248 (06 487 4415). Bus 16, 85, 87, 714, 810, 850/tram 3. **Open** 8.30am-2pm Mon, Wed, Fri, Sat; 8.30am-7.30pm Tue, Thur, Sun. Closed 1st & 3rd Mon of mth. **Admission** €4; €2 concessions. **No credit cards. Map** p338 1A.

For a break from unrelenting Roman artefacts try this impressive collection of oriental art, in a gloomy palazzo near Santa Maria Maggiore. It's arranged geographically and roughly chronologically. First are ancient artefacts from the Near East – pottery, gold, votive offerings – some from the third millennium BC. Then come 11th- to 18th-century painted fans from Tibet, sacred sculptures, and some Chinese pottery from the 15th century. Perhaps most unusual are artefacts from the Swat culture, from Italian-funded excavations in Pakistan.

San Pietro in Vincoli

Piazza di San Pietro in Vincoli 4A (06 488 2865). Metro Cavour/bus 16, 70, 71, 75, 84, 360, 649, 714. **Open** 7am-12.30pm, 3.30-6pm daily. **Map** p338 1B.

Built in the fifth century over an earlier church and third-century BC ruins, St Peter in Chains was touched up in the eighth, 11th and 15th centuries, and baroque-ified in the 18th. Dominating the church are the monument to Pope Julius II and Michelangelo's imposing *Moses* (1515). Julius wanted a final resting place five times this size, with 40 statues, in the larger and more prestigious St Peter's, but he died too soon to check that Michelangelo had

The full Monti

As you trudge the streets of Monti (which means 'mountains') you won't be aware of scaling great heights. Yet this *rione* (district) contains sections of four of Rome's 'official' seven hills – the Quirinal, the Viminal, the Caelian (Celio) and the Esquiline.

Popes, kings and later the presidents of Italy chose to live on the airy, awe-inspiring **Quirinale** (*see p81*). Even today a politician who is 'going up to the Quirinale' is on his way to be promoted or given marching orders by the head of state.

'**Viminale**' is political shorthand for the interior ministry, which is housed in the uncharming Fascist-era Palazzo del Viminale off via Nazionale.

The **Celio**, home to many medieval monasteries, climbs steeply to the south of the Colosseum. The Villa Celimontana (*see p130*), far from the cut and thrust of modern city life, is one of the city's prettiest parks.

At the summit of the **Esquilino** is the great basilica of Santa Maria Maggiore (*see p139*). It was formerly the site of a temple to Juno and thus has always been a place where women were venerated.

And the others?

The most famous hill is the **Campidoglio** (*see p61*) or Capitol, the ancient citadel and site of the city's most important temples. The

mayor of Rome's grand Michelangelo-styled office is now on the Campidoglio, where local law is handed down by a city council that still stamps SPQR – *Senatus populusque romanus* – on rubbish bins and drain covers.

Legend recounts that Iron Age twins Romulus and Remus set up hut on the **Palatino**; by classical times it was a palazzo-filled hill of Rome's movers and shakers.

The **Aventino** has historical resonance too: politicians who 'withdraw to the Aventine' recall the desperate stand of a brave group of Roman plebs, led by Gaius Gracchus, who holed up on the hill in second century BC in an attempt to get parliamentary government restored to Rome. In 1924 150 politicians 'withdrew to the Aventine', storming out of Mussolini's lower house in protest over the political assassination of an opposition MP. Italian MPs with their hackles up still threaten to head Aventino-wards from time to time, though it doesn't usually last for long.

Oddly, Rome's highest hill – the **Gianicolo** (Janiculum, *see p120*) – doesn't feature among the official seven. Neither does the **Colle Oppio** (Oppian hill), the only one still always called *colle* (hill) by Romans. And nor does the **Velia** (Velian hill), which joined the Colle Oppio to the Palatine until Mussolini bulldozed the via dei Fori Imperiali through it.

put in the required work (the artist was otherwise engaged in the Sistine Chapel at the time). His successors were less ambitious. As a result the mighty Moses (his horns prompted by a bad translation of the Old Testament, where the old Hebrew word for 'radiant' was mistaken for 'horned') is wildly out of proportion with everything else, and infinitely better than the offerings of Michelangelo's students who threw together the rest.

The master's hand can be seen in the statues of Leah and Rachel either side of the patriarch. He clearly had nothing to do with the statue of poor Julius himself, by Maso del Bosco. Julius was never placed in his tomb, ending up in an unmarked grave across in the Vatican. In November 2000 what was billed as a 'nine-month' restoration of *Moses* got under way; the impressive scaffolding was still there as this guide went to press, and had a decidedly permanent air to it. Work was going on, however, behind perspex screens in order to keep *Moses* visible at all times, and progress could be followed on the www.progettomose.org website.

If tourists flock here for Michelangelo, believers come for the chains. Eudoxia, wife of Emperor Valentinian III (445-55), was given a set of chains said to have been used to shackle St Peter in Jerusalem; when she gave them to Pope Sixtus III, the story goes, he placed them next to others used on the saint in the Mamertine Prison (*see p72*) and they became miraculously entangled. They are now conserved in a reliquary on the main altar. There chains are the most venerated St Peter-related relic in Rome; they are paraded every 1 August.

Santi Silvestro e Martino ai Monti

Viale del Monte Oppio 28 (06 478 4701). Metro Cavour or Vittorio/bus 16, 70, 71, 75, 84, 360, 649, 714. **Open** 7.30-11.30am, 4-6.30pm Mon-Sat; 8am-noon, 4.30-7pm Sun. **Admission** *Excavation* donation expected. **Map** p338 1B.

The main reason to visit here is to see the third-century *titulus* (early Christian meeting house) beneath the ninth-century church; ask the sacristan to unlock the gate for you. It's a spooky and rarely visited place, littered with bits of sculpture, decaying mosaics and frescos. It does not have the usual jungle of newer foundations sunk through Roman brickwork, so it's not difficult to picture this as an ancient dwelling and/or place of worship. The church above the *titulus* is chiefly remarkable for two frescos: one showing San Giovanni in Laterano (*see p131*) as it was before Borromini's changes (by Dughet, to the left of the entrance), and the other portraying the interior of the original St Peter's (*see p143*; by Gagliardi, left of the altar).

Esquilino

If you've come to Rome on a budget package or picked up a last-minute deal, chances are you'll end up in a hotel on the Esquilino, around Termini railway station. It may come

as a shock. For despite heroic efforts by the municipal authorities to convince us that a 'renaissance' is under way here, the Esquilino's grimy *palazzi* and questionable after-dark denizens may not be what you expected of the Eternal City. Don't despair. They're well hidden, but the Esquilino's charms and attractions are there – in droves.

The ancient ruins and Renaissance villas that dotted the area were swept away, and a whole new city-within-a-city built in the grid mode favoured by the Turinese planners who accompanied Italy's new royal family from that city to the capital after Italian Unification in the 1870s. Piazza Vittorio Emanuele II – by far the city's biggest square and always known simply as **piazza Vittorio** – was the new capital's showcase residential area. You'd never know it. A steady decline into characterless slumhood was halted in the 1980s by the arrival of a multi-ethnic community, which injected life and colour but no prosperity at all into the run-down streets around the square. The noisy, smelly and infinitely characterful market that once occupied the pavements around the garden at the centre of the square was finally moved in 2002 into covered quarters in a former army barracks in via Lamarmora (*see p222*), losing in charm what it gained in hygiene. The pavement where the market once stood has been refurbished with benches from which to observe activity in the piazza. The gardens at the heart of the piazza – victim of an unfortunate revamp by Gruppo GRAU in the '80s and '90s – offer a cooler place to rest in the shade of palm and plane trees. As you do so, have a go at breaking the still-encoded recipe for changing base metal into gold on the Porta Magica in the northern corner of the square; this curious door, with hermetic inscriptions dating from 1688, is all that remains of the Villa Palombara, an estate that once occupied this site. The gardens' benches are occupied by assorted down-at-heel Eastern European immigrants who clearly haven't cracked the code; the flat travertine paving is perfect for early-morning ballroom-dancing lessons attended by droves of Chinese.

North-west of the piazza, **Santa Maria Maggiore** – its ceiling gilded with the first gold brought from the New World – is a fine example of the Christian basilica style.

Due north of piazza Vittorio is **Termini railway station**. The railway reached Termini in the 1860s. The first station building (1864-71) was demolished to make way for what is one of Italy's most remarkable modern buildings, a triumph of undulating horizontal geometry built in a two-stage operation. Architect Angiolo Mazzoni designed the lateral wings,

Art nouveau nymphs cavort in **piazza della Repubblica**.

complete with tubular towers of metaphysical grace straight out of a De Chirico painting; building began in 1937 as a key part of feverish preparations for the Fascist Universal Expo planned for 1942, but the war – and history – intervened and the Expo never took place. In 1947 a judging commission hedged its bets by selecting two projects in a competition for the design for a new main station building. Despite the compromise, the result is staggering. The great reinforced concrete 'wave' was completed in time for the 1950 Holy Year. In the late '90s the station – and piazza dei Cinquecento in which it stands – underwent a major facelift (*see 219* **On track**).

Proximity to the railway terminus made the surrounding area particularly interesting to the developers. Architect Gaetano Koch designed a ministerial and administrative district, focusing on the semicircular, arcaded **piazza della Repubblica** (1888), once the *esedra* (or exedra) of the massive Terme di Diocleziano complex (*see p140*) and still frequently referred to as piazza Esedra by locals. After a recent renovation, Koch's *palazzi* are stunningly white.

This heavily trafficked roundabout is the traditional starting point for major demonstrations, and a favourite hangout for the motley overflow from Stazione Termini.

The **Fontana delle Naiadi** at its centre was due for unveiling in 1901, but the nudity of the art nouveau nymphs cavorting seductively with sea monsters so shocked the authorities that it was boarded up again for years. Locals, fed up with the eyesore, eventually tore the planks down – a rather undignified inauguration. Sculptor Mario Rutelli is said to have returned to Rome once a year for the rest of his life just to take his buxom models out to dinner.

The extraordinary Museo Nazionale Romano collection of ancient artefacts, which used to be confined to the Terme di Diocleziano, has spilled over into the **Palazzo Massimo alle Terme** on the south-east fringe of the square. To the north-west is the church of **Santa Maria della Vittoria**, containing one of Bernini's most extraordinary sculptures, and the **Fontana dell'Acqua Felice**. Designed by Domenico Fontana in the form of a triumphal arch, this fountain was completed in 1589. It was one of many urban improvements that were commissioned in Rome by Pope Sixtus V, and provided this district with clean water from an ancient aqueduct. The statue of Moses in the central niche of the fountain, by Leonardo Sormani, has been roundly condemned as an atrocity against taste ever since it was unveiled in 1586.

Taste atrocity at the **Acqua Felice**.
See p137.

To the south-west of piazza della Repubblica,
via Nazionale descends to the old centre,
passing the American church of **San Paolo
entro le Mura**, with its art nouveau mosaics,
along the way. If you've had your fill of the
picturesque and need a shot of the Kafkaesque,
take a look at such monolithic examples of
Italian public architecture as the interior
ministry in piazza del Viminale or the Teatro
dell'Opera (*see p253*) in via Firenze.

Museo Nazionale Romano –
Palazzo Massimo alle Terme

*Largo di Villa Peretti 1 (06 4890 3501/bookings
06 3996 7700/www.archeorm.arti.beniculturali.it/
sar2000/Museo_romano/Pal_massimo.asp). Metro
Repubblica/bus 16, 36, 38, 40, 64, 86, 90, 92, 105,
157, 170, 175, 204, 217, 310, 360, 492, 590, 649,
714, 910, C, H.* **Open** 9am-7.45pm Tue-Sun; ticket
office closes 7pm. **Admission** €6; €3 concessions; *see
also p59* **Tickets**. **No credit cards**. **Map** p335 2A.

The Italian state's spectacular collection of ancient
art and artefacts underwent a radical reorganisation
in the run-up to 2000. It is now divided between
the Terme di Diocleziano (Baths of Diocletian, *see
p140*), Palazzo Altemps (*see p101*) and here at the
Palazzo Massimo alle Terme.

In the basement of Palazzo Massimo is an
extensive collection of coins from earliest times,
Roman luxuries, descriptions of trade routes and

audio-visual aids (all of which make this floor
especially appealing to kids). On the ground and first
floors are busts of emperors, their families and
lesser mortals, in chronological order (allowing you
to track changing fashions in Roman hairstyles). The
ground floor covers the period up to AD 69. In Room
5 is a magnificent statue of Augustus as pontifex
maximus; Room 8 has a very graceful Muse.

The first floor begins from the age of Vespasian
(AD 69-79), the first of the Flavians: his pugilistic
portrait bust can be seen in Room 1. Room 5 contains statues of Apollo and of a young girl holding
a tray, both from Nero's villa south of Rome in Anzio
(*see p295*), and a gracefully crouching Aphrodite
from Hadrian's Villa at Tivoli (*see p288*). Room 6
has a marble Roman copy of a Greek discus thrower, cast in bronze in the fifth century BC. In Room 7
is a peacefully sleeping hermaphrodite, which is a
second-century AD copy of a Greek original.

The real highlight of the Palazzo Massimo,
though, lies on the second floor, where rare wall
paintings from assorted villas have been reassem-
bled (you will be assigned a time for a guided visit
when you buy your ticket). The spectacular fresco
from the triclinium (dining room) of the villa of
Augustus's wife Livia in Prima Porta, just north of
Rome, shows a fruit-filled garden bustling with animal life and displays a use of perspective that was
rarely seen again until the Renaissance. A triclinium from the Roman Villa Farnesina (in Room 3) has
delicate white sketches on a black background, surmounted by scenes of courts handing down sen-
tences that have had experts baffled for centuries.
Also in Room 3 is a lively naval battle, from a frescoed corridor in the same villa. The three cubicoli
(bedrooms) in Room 5 all have decorative stuccoed
ceilings. Room 10 contains Botero-like larger than
life (megalographic) paintings, and Room 11 has
dazzlingly bright marble intarsio works. On the
ground floor is an excellent gift- and bookshop, with
many titles in English and a fine range for children.

San Paolo entro le Mura

*Via Napoli 58 (06 488 3339). Bus 40, 60, 64,
70, 71, 170.* **Open** 10am-4pm Mon-Fri; Sun for
services. **Map** p335 2B.

The Episcopalian church of St Paul's Within the
Walls, fronting on to via Nazionale, is one of English
Gothic-revivalist architect GE Street's happier creations: a light, airy space made radiant by graceful,
glowing Pre-Raphaelite mosaics by Edward Burne-
Jones. The Arab-inspired wall tiles may be the work
of his Arts & Crafts Society buddy William Morris.

Santa Maria della Vittoria

*Via XX Settembre 17 (06 4274 0571). Metro
Repubblica/bus 16, 36, 38, 60, 61, 62, 84, 86, 90,
92, 217, 360, 910.* **Open** 8.30-11am, 3.30-6pm Mon-
Sat; 8.30-10am, 3.30-6pm Sun. **Map** p335 1B.

This modest-looking baroque church, its interior
cosily candlelit and lovingly adorned with marble
and gilt, holds one of Bernini's most famous works.
The Ecstasy of St Teresa, in the Cornaro chapel (the

Then what?

● According to the poet Horace, poetry-loving billionaire Maecenas cleared an extensive part of the east side of the Esquiline hill and built a villa surrounded by acres of gardens and vineyards there. At the bottom of his garden Maecenas built an auditorium. Of the villa there is no trace. The **Auditorium di Mecenate** (largo Leopardi, 06 6710 3819), on the other hand, can be visited by appointment.

● Wedged tightly between the Forum and the Suburra, the **salita del Grillo** is a rare and quite overlooked remnant of Gothic Rome. You can't ascend the great Torre della Milizia (1227-41), but you can admire the exterior of the remarkable Casa dei Cavalieri di Rodi (House of the Knights of Rhodes), a Crusaders' HQ.

● When things were at their nastiest in medieval Rome, rival clans – powerful families like the Conti, Frangipani, Annibali, Capocci and Caetani – took to their **towers** and pulled up the ladders. By the 13th century, when anarchy had reached its peak, the city bristled with over 200 towers.

Of these about a dozen remain standing, and half of these are in Monti. The Torre dei Conti, erected in 1203, stands skyscraper-close to the famous Torre della Milizia (*see p75*). Another pair of towers – built by the Graziani and Capocci families – stands in piazza San Martino ai Monti. The Torre dei Margani was transformed into the belfry of the church of San Francesco di Paola in the piazza of the same name.

● **Via San Francesco di Paola** is a dark, dank staircase that passes beneath a palazzo believed to have belonged to the formidable Vanozza Catanei, mother of dastardly Cesare Borgia. What more suitable place for Cesare's hated brother Juan to meet a grisly end, stabbed by an unidentified assassin as he left a party *chez* Catanei?

● Every surface inside **Madonna dei Monti** (piazza Madonna dei Monti) is colourfully marbled or frescoed. The design of this small but exquisite church by Giacomo della Porta (1580) marks the moment of transition between Renaissance and baroque styles.

fourth on the left), shows the Spanish mystic floating on a cloud in a supposedly spiritual trance after a teasing, androgynous angel has pierced her with a burning arrow. The result is more than a little ambiguous. (Writing of the angel incident in her *Life*, Teresa recalled: 'So intense was the pain I uttered several moans; so great was the sweetness caused by the pain that I never wanted to lose it.') When the chapel is seen as a whole, with the heavens painted in the dome, the light filters through a hidden window, reflecting gilded rays and bathing Teresa in a heavenly glow. She is surrounded by a row of witnesses – members of the Cornaro family sitting in a balcony and earnestly discussing the spectacle.

Santa Maria Maggiore

Piazza Santa Maria Maggiore (06 483 195/museum 06 483 058/www.prtour.it). Bus 16, 70, 71, 75, 84, 105, 204, 360, 590, 649, 714/tram 5, 14. **Open** *Church* 7am-7pm daily. *Museum & loggia* (guided tours only) Mar-Oct 9am-6.30pm daily; Nov-Feb 9am-1pm, 4-6.30pm daily. **Admission** *Museum & loggia* €2.60. **No credit cards. Map** p338 1B.

Behind this blowsy baroque façade is one of the most striking basilica-form churches in Rome. Local tradition says a church was built on this spot c366; documents place it almost 100 years later. The fifth-century church was first extended in the 13th century, then again prior to the 1750 Holy Year, when Ferdinando Fuga overhauled the interior and attached the façade that we see today. Inside, a flat-roofed nave shoots between two aisles to a triumphal arch and apse. Above the columns of the nave, heavily restored fifth-century mosaics show scenes from the Old Testament. Thirteenth-century mosaics in the apse by Jacopo Torriti show Mary, dressed as a Byzantine empress, being crowned Queen of Heaven by Christ.

The Virgin theme continues in fifth-century mosaics on the triumphal arch. The ceiling in the main nave is said to have been made from the first shipment of gold extracted from the Americas by Ferdinand and Isabella of Spain, and was presented to the church by the Borgia Pope Alexander VI. The Borgias' heraldic device of a bull is very much in evidence. In the 16th and 17th centuries two incredibly flamboyant chapels were added. The first was the Cappella Sistina (last chapel on the right of the nave), designed by Domenico Fontana for Sixtus V (1585-90), and decorated with multicoloured marble, gilt and precious stones. Sixtus had ancient buildings ransacked for materials and employed virtually every sculptor working in the city.

Directly opposite is the Cappella Paolina, an even gaudier Greek-cross chapel, designed in 1611 by Flaminio Ponzio for Paul V to house on its altar an icon of the Madonna dating from the ninth (or possibly the 12th) century.

To the right of the main altar a plaque marks the burial place of Rome's great baroque genius Gian Lorenzo Bernini and his father Pietro. In the loggia high up on the front of the church (tours leave the baptistery about every ten minutes; notes are provided in English) are glorious 13th-century mosaics that decorated the façade of the old basilica, showing the legend of the foundation of Santa Maria Maggiore. The lower row shows Mary appearing to Giovanni the Patrician who, with Pope Liberius, then sketches the plan for the basilica. The legend goes that the Virgin told Giovanni to build a church on the spot where snow would fall the next morning. The snow fell on 5 August 352, a miracle that is commemorated on that day every year, when thousands of flower petals are released from the roof of the church in the Festa della Madonna delle Neve (*see p234*). The Cappella Paolina also contains a relief (1612) by Stefano Maderno showing Liberius tracing the plan of the basilica in the snow.

Terme di Diocleziano

Via Enrico De Nicola 79 (06 3996 7700/www. archeorm.arti.beniculturali.it/sar2000/diocleziano). Metro Repubblica/bus 36, 38, 40, 64, 86, 90, 92, 105, 157, 170, 175, 217, 310, 714, 910. **Open** 9am-7.45pm Tue-Sun; ticket office closes 7pm. **Admission** €5; €2.50 concessions; *see also p59* **Tickets**. **No credit cards**. **Map** p335 1A.

Diocletian's baths, built from AD 298-306, were the largest in Rome, covering over a hectare (2.5 acres) and able to accommodate 3,000 people at a time. For an idea of the immense size of the structure, tour the remaining fragments: the tepidarium and part of the central hall are in the church of Santa Maria degli Angeli (piazza della Repubblica, map p335 1A); a circular hall can be seen in the church of San Bernardo alle Terme (piazza San Bernardo, map p335 1B); and the beautifully restored Aula Ottagona (octagonal hall) – which used to house Rome's planetarium and now has a tasteful sprinkling of large classical sculptures – is in via Romita (free admission; 9am-2pm Tue-Sat, 9am-1pm Sun).

A convent complex was built around the largest surviving chunk of the baths by Michelangelo in the 1560s: freshly restored and now containing stone inscriptions and other minor items from the Museo Nazionale Romano ancient artefacts collection, the Terme di Diocleziano reopened to the public in 2000. The collection is sufficiently low-key to allow you to concentrate on admiring the massive Roman bath buildings themselves and on Michelangelo's 16th-century restoration of the place, including its magnificent central cloister.

Splitting atoms

The atomic bomb was born in a convent on via Panisperna. Its father was the Pope.

Enrico Fermi, who would direct the first sustained nuclear chain reaction in a squash court on the campus of the University of Chicago in December 1942, earned the pontifical nickname in the 1920s not just because he was such a charismatic leader, but also because the quantum theory he propounded was for many years considered to be a matter of faith rather than of scientific record. Either you believed or you didn't; in order to believe, you had to accept that Enrico Fermi was infallible. Ergo, he was the Pope.

Fermi was appointed to the newly created chair of Theoretical Physics in Rome in 1926, when he was only 25. The institute was the brainchild of Sicilian senator Orso Mario Corbino – one of the few parliamentarians who were not members of the Fascist party. Himself a respected physicist, Corbino wanted to rescue Italian physics from the swamp of tradition, and he saw the dynamic Fermi as the right man for the task.

In the days before Mussolini built the central campus of the Città Universitaria (*see p158*), Rome's La Sapienza university was spread across the city in a series of ad hoc homes. Space was found for the new

institute in the grounds of the former convent of San Lorenzo at the top of the via Panisperna switchback. Here Fermi assembled the team of young physicists who became known as *i ragazzi di via Panisperna* (the via Panisperna boys): among them were his deputy Franco Rasetti, known as 'the Cardinal Vicar'; Emilio Segrè, whose fiery temper earned him the moniker 'the Basilisk'; and the brilliant Enrico Majorana, 'the Great Inquisitor', a moody young Sicilian who would later vanish, never to be found again.

It was on via Panisperna, in March 1934, that Fermi's team carried out their momentous experiment on radioactivity induced by neutron bombardment. The irradiation equipment was at one end of the second floor and the Geiger counters at the other; Fermi and his assistant Edoardo Amaldi would race each other down the corridor in order to test the short-lived isotopes before they disappeared. Today the corridors are more sedate places: the building – which can still be glimpsed behind a high-security gate next to the church of San Lorenzo at No.90 – is part of Italy's Interior Ministry. Plans to turn part of it into a museum celebrating the *ragazzi* have so far come to naught.

The Vatican & Prati

Whether you come to kiss St Peter's big toe or to worship Michelangelo's *Pietà*, the Vatican's got to be on the itinerary.

Family tomb, pope bunker and gallery: **Castel Sant'Angelo**. *See p149.*

It is almost impossible now to imagine the trauma the Catholic Church suffered in 1870 when Italian troops breached the walls of the papal city-stronghold at Porta Pia (*see p90*), putting an end to centuries of unchallenged and authoritarian rule by the occupant of the throne of St Peter. Over the years foreign despots, including Napoleon, had been either seen off or paid off; but in 1870 it all went wrong: the pope lost control of a vast, rich swathe of central Italy and was ignominiously forced back into the Vatican palace behind the *mura leonina* (Leonine Wall) to emerge only at the invitation of the newly formed Italian state.

The meadows (*prati*) around the Renaissance ramparts suddenly became real-estate opportunities as the secular city expanded beyond the Tiber. The biggest piazza by the Vatican walls was provocatively named after the Risorgimento – the movement that had destroyed the papacy's hold on Italy. Broad avenues were laid out and named after historic freedom fighters like Cola di Rienzo, or heroes from an even earlier – and pointedly pre-Christian – classical past. The Borgo – the

medieval warren outside the Vatican walls – adapted as best it could: after all, there was a tidy living to made out of servicing the now-stranded papal administration.

The Vatican state

Having made the trains run on time, Italy's pre-war Fascist leader Benito Mussolini turned his attention to the unresolved problems of Church and State. In 1929 he drew up the Lateran Pact, a treaty designed to sort out the status of the Vatican once and for all. From the Vatican's point of view, the terms of the reconciliation treaty ('La Conciliazione' as it came to be known) awarded the Church a huge cash payment, tax-free status and an important continuing moral influence over future legislation on social issues like education and divorce. To commemorate the historic agreement, Mussolini demolished a particularly picturesque part of the medieval Borgo (including the house where Raphael had lived), replacing it with a short but 'modern' approach road to St Peter's: via della Conciliazione.

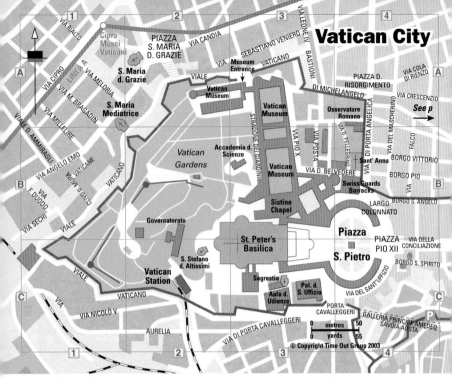

With barely 400 residents, and occupying an area of less than half a square kilometre, the Vatican City is the smallest state in the world. It has its own diplomatic service, judiciary, postal service, army (the Swiss Guard), heliport, railway station, supermarket, and radio and TV stations. It has observer status at the UN, and issues its own stamps and currency (Vatican euros – limited by the European Central Bank to a tiny circulation, the Holy See keeps a few knowledgeable collectors happy with occasional issues of coins that increase exponentially in value, fast). It also contains one of the world's finest collections of art and antiquities.

When the Pope is in Rome, crowds gather after mass in St Peter's square at noon on Sunday to hear him address pilgrims from the window of his study in the Apostolic Palace. On Wednesday mornings he holds a general audience in St Peter's square, if the weather is fine, or in the modern 8,000-seat Sala Nervi audience hall (see p143 **Papal audiences**).

The first basilica in memory of St Peter was built on the site of the martyred saint's tomb by Emperor Constantine in the mid fourth century, and quickly became a place of pilgrimage. Before that the area had been occupied by an infamous circus (now evoked in Bernini's great elliptical colonnade) built

by Emperors Nero and Caligula, in which the Christian victims of religious persecution were buried around the race track.

While the residence of the pontifex maximus remained across the city at the Lateran (see p131), pilgrims continued to flock to the tomb of the founder of the Roman Church. All around, the Borgo grew up to service the burgeoning Dark Age tourist industry.

Pope Leo IV enclosed the Borgo with the 12m-high (40ft) Leonine Wall, following a series of Saracen and Lombard raids in the eighth and ninth centuries. Pope Nicholas III extended the walls and provided a papal escape route, linking the Vatican to the impregnable Castel Sant'Angelo by way of a long Passetto (covered walkway). He never had cause to use his getaway, but Clement VII did in 1527 during fierce fighting with the troops of Emperor Charles V (see chapter **History**). The nine-month siege and subsequent Sack of Rome was a watershed: things in the papal stronghold were never the same again. Almost the whole papal army was slaughtered. The city was burned and looted. The popes withdrew back across town to the old Lateran Palace, and then to the grand new Quirinale palace (see p84) where they stayed until the troubles of 1870 sent them back across the Tiber once more.

Note: Dress with decorum: anyone wearing shorts or a short skirt, or with bare shoulders and midriff, will be turned away or forced to suffer the indignity of being wrapped in green kitchen towelling. **Credit cards** are not accepted anywhere in the Vatican state.

Tourist Information Office

Piazza San Pietro (Tourist Information Office 06 6988 1662/www.vatican.va). Metro Ottaviano/ bus 23, 40, 62, 64. **Open** 8.30am-6.45pm Mon-Sat. **Map** p333 1C & p142.

This office dispenses information, organises guided tours, has a bureau de change, offers postal and philatelic services, and sells souvenirs and publications. The number for the Vatican's switchboard is 06 6982.

Papal audiences

(06 6988 3273/3114/fax 06 6988 5863). **Open** *Prefettura office* 9am-1pm Mon-Sat.

Apply to the Prefettura della Casa Pontificia for tickets, which are free. They can also be collected on Tuesdays from 3-8pm. Entry is through the bronze door at the basilica end of Bernini's colonnade. For a private audience, your local bishop has to make a written request, which can take between three months and a year to be granted.

St Peter's basilica

After 120 years as the world's most elegant building site, the current St Peter's was consecrated on 18 November 1626 by Urban VIII – exactly 1,300 years after the consecration of the first basilica on the site. The earlier building was a five-aisled classical basilica, fronted by a large courtyard and four porticoes. Steadily enlarged and enriched, it became the finest church in Christendom.

By the mid 15th century, however, its south wall was collapsing. Pope Nicholas V had 2,500 wagonloads of masonry from the Colosseum carted across the Tiber, but never got further than repairs. No one wanted to take responsibility for demolishing the most sacred church in Christendom. It took the arrogance of Pope Julius II and his pet architect Donato Bramante to get things moving. In 1506 some 2,500 workers tore down the 1,000-year-old basilica, and Julius laid the foundation stone for its replacement.

Following Bramante's death in 1514, Raphael took over the work and scrapped his predecessor's plan for a basilica with a Greek-cross plan, opting for an elongated Latin cross. In 1547 Michelangelo took command and reverted to a Greek design. He died in 1564, aged 87, but not before coming up with a plan for a massive dome and supporting drum. This was completed in 1590, the largest brick dome ever constructed.

In 1607 Carlo Maderno won the consent of Pope Paul V to demolish the remaining fragments of the old basilica and put up a new façade, crowned by enormous statues of Christ

Sightseeing

Brits abroad The pilgrims

Intrepid pilgrims criss-crossed Europe to score heavenly brownie points by visiting St Peter's shrine in Rome at least once in their lives. Some, including British King Alfred, made the trip more than once. So many Brits descended from the north that the hostel and church established around 726 by King Ine of Wessex to house and heal exhausted travellers became the nucleus of the world's first purpose-built hospital. The *burgus saxonum* around it gave its name to this area – in Sassia – south-east of the basilica.

British funds for the hospice were cut off when the Normans invaded in 1066, after which it passed into papal hands and thence to the Templar knight Guy de Montpellier, who set up a hospital and founded the Order of the Holy Spirit (Santo Spirito). A few rooms of the modern hospital of Santo Spirito house a gruesome collection of medical artefacts, dating from ancient times to the 19th century. As well as the predictable collection of

skeletons, organs, anatomical charts and surgical instruments, there are wax votive offerings that were left at churches and shrines to encourage God to cure parts of the body conventional medicine could not reach. There are also reconstructions of a 17th-century pharmacy and an alchemist's laboratory.

The two massive 15th-century frescoed wards, the gloriously elegant fruit of a rebuilding programme in Renaissance times, have only comparatively recently been emptied of their beds to provide space for itinerant exhibitions. Any rare opportunity to visit them should be seized.

Museo Storico Nazionale dell'Arte Sanitaria

Lungotevere in Sassia 3 (06 6835 2353). Bus 23, 40, 62, 280. **Open** 10am-noon Mon, Wed, Fri. **Admission** €2.58; €1.55 concessions. **No credit cards**. **Map** p333 1C.

Bernini's elaborately curving colonnade.

and the apostles. After Maderno's death Bernini took over and, despite nearly destroying both the façade and his reputation by erecting towers on either end (one of which fell down), he became the hero of the hour with his sumptuous *baldacchino* and famous elliptical piazza. This latter was built between 1656 and 1667, its colonnaded arms reaching out towards the Catholic world in a symbolic embrace. The main oval measures 340 by 240 metres (1,115 by 787 feet), and is punctuated by the central Egyptian obelisk (dragged from Nero's Circus in 1586) and two symmetrical fountains by Maderno and Bernini. The 284-column, 88-pillar colonnade is topped by 140 statues of saints.

In the portico (1612), opposite the main portal, is a mosaic by Giotto (c1298), a survivor from the original basilica. There are five doors leading into the basilica: the central ones come from the earlier church, while the others are all 20th century. The last door on the right is opened only in Holy Years by the pope himself.

Inside, the basilica's size is emphasised on the marble floor, where a boastful series of brass lines measure the lengths of other churches around the world that haven't made the grade. But it is Bernini's huge curlicued *baldacchino* (1633), hovering over the high altar, that is the real focal point. This was cast from brass purloined from the Pantheon (prompting local wits to quip *quod non fecerunt barbari, fecerunt Barberini*, 'what the barbarians didn't do, the Barberini did': Bernini's patron, Pope Urban VII, was a Barberini) and is bathed in light flooding in from windows in the dome above. The canopy stands over the traditional

site of St Peter's tomb; two flights of stairs lead beneath the altar to the *confessio*, where a niche contains a ninth-century mosaic of Christ, the only thing from old St Peter's that stayed in the same place when the new church was built.

Catholic pilgrims head straight for the last pilaster on the right before the main altar, to kiss the big toe of Arnolfo da Cambio's brass statue of St Peter (c1296), worn down by centuries of pious lips, or to say a prayer before the crystal casket containing the mummified remains of much-loved Pope John XXIII, who was beatified in 2002. Tourists, on the other hand, make a beeline for the first chapel on the right, where bullet-proof glass now protects Michelangelo's *Pietà* (1499). This is the only work that he ever bothered to sign, on the band across the Virgin's chest. Proceeding around the basilica in an anti-clockwise direction, notice Carlo Fontana's highly flattering monument to the unprepossessing Queen Christina of Sweden, a convert to Catholicism in 1655 (*see also p117* **Palazzo Corsini**), to the left of the Pietà chapel. The third chapel has a tabernacle and two angels by Bernini, plus St Peter's only remaining painting: a Trinity by Pietro da Cortona (the others have been replaced by mosaic copies). In the first chapel beyond the right transept is a tear-jerker of a neo-classical tomb (1792), the last resting place of Pope Clement XIII, by Antonio Canova.

Bernini's Throne of St Peter (1665), flanked by papal tombs, stands at the far end of the nave beyond the high altar, under an almost psychedelic stained-glass window. Encased within Bernini's creation there is a wood and ivory chair, probably dating from the ninth century but for many years believed to have belonged to Peter himself. To the right of the throne is Bernini's 1644 monument to his patron Urban VIII, who commissioned the bronze portrait (between statues of Charity and Justice) before his death. On the pillars supporting the main dome are much-venerated relics, including a chip off the True Cross.

Near the portico end of the left aisle is a group of monuments to the Old Pretender James Edward Stuart (the 18th-century claimant to the throne of England and Scotland), his wife Maria Clementina Sobieski and their sons Charles Edward (Bonnie Prince Charlie) and Henry Benedict. They are buried in the grottos below.

The **Vatican Grottos** – Renaissance crypts containing more papal tombs – are beneath the basilica, and the **Necropolis**, where St Peter is believed to be buried, lies under the grottos. The small **treasury museum** off the left nave of the basilica contains some stunning liturgical relics. The **dome**, reached via hundreds of stairs (there's a cramped lift as far as the basilica roof), offers fabulous views of the **Vatican Gardens**.

Basilica

Open *Oct-Mar* 7am-6pm daily. *Apr-Sept* 7am-7pm daily. **Admission** free.
Free guided tours in English set off from the tourist office. In theory they leave at 2.15pm and 3pm on Monday, Thursday and Friday, but they depend on the goodwill of volunteers and so do not always take place. Phone ahead to check.

Dome

Open *Oct-Mar* 8am-4.45pm daily. *Apr-Sept* 8am-5.45pm daily. **Admission** €4. *With lift* €5.
Note that there are 320 steps to climb even after the lift has taken you to the first level.

Grottos

Open *Oct-Mar* 7am-5pm daily. *Apr-Sept* 7am-6pm daily. **Admission** free.

Necropolis

Apply at the Uffizio degli Scavi (06 6988 5318/fax 06 6988 5518 or 06 6987 3017/scavi@fsp.va). **Open** *Guided tours* 9am-5pm Mon-Sat. **Admission** €9.
English-language tours must be booked at least 25 days in advance. Under-15s are not admitted.

Treasury Museum

Open *Oct-Mar* 9am-5pm daily. *Apr-Sept* 9am-6pm daily. **Admission** €5; €3 concessions.

Vatican Gardens

(06 6988 4466/4587). **Guided tours** *Low season* 10am Tue, Thur-Sat (depending on the weather). *High season* 10am Sat only. **Admission** €9; €7 concessions.
Phone at least one week in advance to book.

The Vatican Museums

It's a brisk ten-minute walk northwards around the Vatican walls from St Peter's to the entrance of the Vatican Museums.

Begun in 1506 by Pope Julius II, this immense, stunning collection represents the accumulated fancies and obsessions of a long line of strong, often contradictory personalities. The popes' unique position allowed them to obtain treasures on favourable terms from other collectors, and artists often had little choice as to whether they accepted papal commissions.

Musei Vaticani

Viale del Vaticano (06 6988 3333). Metro Ottaviano/bus 23, 32, 34, 49, 81, 492/tram 19. **Open** *Mar-Oct* 8.45am-3.20pm Mon-Fri; 8.45am-1.45pm Sat. *Nov-Feb* 8.45am-12.20pm Mon-Sat. Last Sun of each mth 8.45am-12.20pm. **Admission** €10; €7 concessions; free last Sun of mth. **No credit cards. Map** p142.
Note: The Vatican revises its opening times from year to year; phone ahead to avoid disappointment. The collections are so vast that it's impossible to take

Sightseeing

Vatican wisdom

For full immersion in St Peter's and the Vatican Museums, comfortable footwear is the order of the day (essential if you are to attempt the ascent of the dome: the 320 marble stairs after you emerge from the lift are very slippery).

Access to the Sistine Chapel, as well as the magnificent papal apartments, is solely through the Vatican Museums and **not** through St Peter's itself. Note too that opening times for the museums are much shorter than those for the basilica.

Covering the distance between St Peter's square and the entrance to the Vatican Museums shouldn't take you much more than ten minutes if you're reasonably fit and it isn't high summer; queuing to get through the museum door, however, is another matter. At busy times you should come prepared for a long, long wait, and if you're dead set on seeing the *Last Judgment* but not endowed with endless patience... **get up early!**

Take binoculars. You'll need them for viewing the details of frescos in the barn-like Sistine Chapel, as well as for appreciating the view if you're planning an ascent of the dome.

The Vatican Museums audio tour is highly recommended.

in more than a small part on one visit, but four colour-coded routes cater for a dash to the Sistine Chapel through to a five-hour plod around the lot. There are also itineraries for wheelchair users, with disabled toilets en route. Wheelchairs can be borrowed at the museum: you can't book them, but call ahead (06 6988 3860) to check there's one free. The following are selected highlights from the collections.

Appartamento Borgia

This six-room suite, known as the Borgia Rooms, was adapted for the Borgia Pope Alexander VI (1492-1503) and decorated by Pinturicchio with a series of frescos on biblical and classical themes. In 1973 some 50 rooms adjoining the Borgia Apartments were renovated to house the Collezione d'Arte Religiosa Moderna.

Galleria Chiaramonte

Founded by Pius VII in the early 19th century and laid out by the sculptor Canova, this is an eclectic collection of Roman statues, reliefs and busts. Don't miss the replica of a Greek statue by Polyeuctos of stuttering orator Demosthenes and a copy of a *Resting Satyr* by the Greek sculptor Praxiteles.

Gallerie dei Candelabri & degli Arazzi

The long gallery studded with candelabra contains Roman marble statues, while the next gallery has ten huge tapestries (*arazzi*), woven by Flemish mas-

ter Pieter van Aelst from the cartoons by Raphael that are now in London's Victoria & Albert Museum.

Galleria delle Carte Geografiche

Pope Gregory XIII (of Gregorian calendar fame) had a craze for astronomy, and was responsible for this 120m (394ft) long gallery, with its Tower of the Winds observation point at the north end. Ignazio Danti of Perugia drew the maps (1580-3), which show each Italian region, city and island with extraordinary precision.

Museo Egiziano

Founded by Gregory XVI in 1839, in rooms partly decorated in Egyptian style, this is a representative selection of ancient Egyptian art from 3,000-600 BC. It includes statues of a baboon god, painted mummy cases and a marble statue of Antinous, Emperor Hadrian's lover, who drowned in Egypt and was declared divine by the emperor. A couple of real mummies help make this the most exciting bit of the whole Vatican if you have grisly-minded kids in tow.

Museo Etrusco

Founded in 1837 by Gregory XVI, and enlarged in the 20th century, this collection contains Greek and Roman art as well as Etruscan masterpieces, including the contents of the Regolini-Galassi Tomb (c650 BC), the Greek-inspired fourth-century BC *Mars*, and the fifth-century BC *Young Man and Small Slave*.

Conclave

It is considered very bad form, as well as pointless, to speculate on who the next pope might be: after all, it's the Holy Spirit who'll decide who next occupies the throne of St Peter. Nevertheless, there's an army of people – journalists, academics and even bookmakers – who make a living by studying possible voting patterns. And each claims to know for sure what the outcome of the next conclave will be.

Despite his failing health, the octogenarian former actor and playwright Pope John Paul II keeps up a punishing schedule. Yet there is no denying the 'end of an era' atmosphere that has been hanging over the world's smallest state for some time.

What exactly happens as the cardinals huddle before Michelangelo's *Last Judgment* and Catholics wait eagerly in St Peter's square for as many days as it takes for a decision to be reached? Ask any churchman and he'll tell you the Holy Spirit moves among his modern-day apostles until the best candidate is found. But the Holy Spirit has to preside over much frantic politicking and several null ballots before the right man for the job emerges.

Cardinals are kept incommunicado inside the Vatican for the duration of the conclave (albeit in smart guest quarters these days, rather than camping inside the Sistine Chapel). Smoke signals from a particular chimney – black smoke for a null vote, white smoke for a successful one – are the only indication to the outside world of how the election is going. When a unanimous decision is finally made, a handful of straw placed on the fire produces white smoke and thus proclaims the good news to the world.

So who is the most likely man to become the 265th successor of St Peter? With half the world's Catholics concentrated in Latin America, many people are putting their money on *papabili* (papal possibles) from that continent. The powerful Italian lobby, on the other hand, wants one of its own men back in this traditionally Italian job.

Whoever wins, the event will have the kind of coverage no previous papal election has had: for years now, each papal sneeze or tumble has prompted major American networks to fly in camera crews and spend small fortunes in hotel rooms and rooftop accommodation with Vatican views.

Museo Paolino

This collection of Roman and neo-Attic sculpture has been housed here since 1970. Highlights include the beautifully draped statue of Sophocles from Terracina, a trompe l'oeil mosaic of an unswept floor and the wonderfully elaborate Altar of Vicomagistri.

Museo Pio-Clementino

In the late 18th century Pope Clement XIV and his successor Pius VI began the world's largest collection of classical statues; it now fills 16 rooms. Don't miss the first-century BC *Belvedere Torso* by Apollonius of Athens; the *Apollo Sauroctonos*, a Roman copy of the bronze *Lizard Killer* by Praxiteles; and, in the octagonal Belvedere Courtyard, the exquisite *Belvedere Apollo* and *Laocoön*, the latter being throttled by the sea serpents Athena had sent as punishment (he had warned the Trojans to beware the wooden horse).

Pinacoteca

Founded by Pius VI in the late 18th century, the Pinacoteca (picture gallery) includes many of the pictures that the Vatican hierarchy managed to recover from Napoleon after their forced sojourn in France in the early 19th century. The collection ranges from early paintings of the Byzantine School and Italian primitives to 18th-century Dutch and French old masters, and includes Giotto's *Stefaneschi Triptych*, a Pietà by Lucas Cranach the Elder, several delicate Madonnas by Fra Filippo Lippi, Fra Angelico, Raphael and Titian, Raphael's very last work *The Transfiguration*, Caravaggio's *Entombment* and a chiaroscuro *St Jerome* by Leonardo.

Pio Cristiano Museum

The upper floor of the Museo Paolino is devoted to a collection of early Christian antiquities, mostly sarcophagi carved with reliefs of biblical scenes.

Sistine Chapel

The world's most famous frescos cover the ceiling and one immense wall of the Cappella Sistina, built by Sixtus IV in 1473-84. For centuries it has been used for popes' private prayers and papal elections (see *p148* **Conclave**). In the 1980s and '90s the 930 sq m (10,000 sq ft) of *Creation* – on the ceiling – and the *Last Judgment* – on the wall behind the altar – were subjected to the most controversial restoration job of all time.

In 1508 Michelangelo was commissioned to paint some kind of undemanding decoration on the ceiling of the Sistine Chapel. Julius II may have been egged on to employ a sculptor with no experience in fresco by his architect Bramante, who was jealous of the pope's admiration for Michelangelo and desperately wanted to see him fail. Michelangelo responded by offering to do far more than mere decoration, and embarked upon his massive venture alone. He spent the next four years on top of scaffolding on his back, with paint and plaster dripping into his eyes; his pay arrived so infrequently that he complained to his brother in 1511, 'I could well say that I go naked and barefoot.'

St Peter's square.

The work, completed in 1512 (so Michelangelo was working a short corridor away from Raphael), was done in the heady days of the High Renaissance when optimistic artists were nobly bent on the pursuit of beauty. Beginning at the *Last Judgment* end, scenes depict the *Separation of Light from Darkness*, the *Creation of Sun, Moon and Planets*, the *Separation of Land and Sea* and the *Creation of Fishes and Birds*, the *Creation of Adam*, the *Creation of Eve*, the *Temptation and Expulsion from Paradise*, the *Sacrifice of Noah* (which should have appeared after the *Flood*, but for lack of space), the *Flood*, and the *Drunkenness of Noah*. Michelangelo painted these scenes in reverse order, beginning with Noah's drunkenness. They are framed by monumental figures of Old Testament prophets and classical sibyls.

Twenty-two years after completing this masterpiece, the aged and embittered artist rolled up his sleeves again and started work on the *Last Judgment* to fill the altar wall. In the interim Rome had been sacked (see *p15*) – an episode seen by many, including Michelangelo, as the wrath of God descending on the corrupt city – and the atmosphere was gloomy and pessimistic. Taking him seven years, the work (completed in 1541) is altogether more doom-laden, as befits its subject. Hidden among the larger-than-life figures that stare, leer and cry out from their brilliant blue background, Michelangelo painted his own frowning, miserable face on the

Sightseeing

Popes ammassed artistic treasures in the **Vatican Museums**. *See p145.*

wrinkled human skin held by St Bartholomew, below and to the right of the powerful figure of Christ the Judge. Pius IV objected to so much nudity and wanted to destroy the fresco; thankfully he was persuaded to settle for modest loincloths, most of which were removed in the recent restoration.

Dwarfed by Michelangelo's work – which they preceded – the sorely neglected paintings on the side walls of the chapel are a who's who of Renaissance greats. On the left-hand wall as you look at the *Last Judgment* are: the *Journey of Moses* by Perugino; *Events from the Life of Moses* by Botticelli; *Crossing the Red Sea* and *Moses Receives the Tablets of the Law* by Cosimo Rosselli; *The Testament of Moses* by Luca Signorelli; *The Dispute over Moses' Body* by Matteo da Lecce; *The Resurrection* by Arrigo Paludano; *The Last Supper* by Cosimo Rosselli; *Handing over the Keys* by Perugino; *The Sermon on the Mount* by Cosimo Rosselli; *The Calling of the Apostles* by Ghirlandaio; *The Temptations of Christ* by Botticelli; and *Baptism of Christ* by Perugino. The papal portraits are by the same masters.

Stanze di Raffaello, Loggia di Raffaello, Cappella di Niccolò V

The Raphael Rooms were part of Nicholas V's palace, and were originally decorated by Piero della Francesca. Julius II then let Perugino, Lorenzo Lotto and other Renaissance masters loose on them. Then he discovered Raphael, whereupon he gave the young artistic genius *carte blanche* to redesign four rooms of the Papal Suite.

The order of the visit changes from time to time, but it makes sense, if possible, to see the rooms in the order in which they were painted. The Study (Stanza della Segnatura) was Raphael's first bash (1508-11), and features philosophical and spiritual themes – the *Triumph of Truth, Good and Beauty*. Best known is the star-packed *School of Athens* fres-

co, with contemporary artists as classical figures: Plato is Leonardo; the thinker on the steps – Heraclitus – is Michelangelo; Euclid is Bramante (note the letters RUSM, Raphael's signature, on his gold collar); and Raphael himself stands to the left of a capped man, believed to be his pupil Sodoma. Raphael next turned his hand to the Waiting Room (Stanza di Eliodoro, 1512-14), frescoed with political themes such as *The Expulsion of Heliodorus*, a re-reading of a biblical episode designed to highlight Pope Julius II's supreme political savvy.

The Dining Room (Stanza dell'Incendio, 1514-17) is devoted to the feats of popes Leo III and IV, including *The Fire in the Borgo*, which Leo IV halted with the sign of the cross. The Reception Room (Sala di Constantino, 1523-5) was completed by Giulio Romano after Raphael's death in 1520, but was based on Raphael's sketches of the Church's triumph over paganism.

The long Loggia di Raffaello, with a beautiful view over Rome, was started by Bramante in 1513 and finished by Raphael and his assistants. It features 52 small paintings on biblical themes, and leads into the Sala dei Chiaroscuri (Gregory XIII obliterated Raphael's frescos here, but the magnificent ceiling remains). The adjacent Cappella di Niccolò V (Chapel of Nicholas V), has outstanding frescos of scenes from the lives of saints Lawrence and Stephen by Fra Angelico (1448-50).

The Vatican Library

Founded by Pope Nicholas V in 1450, this is one of the world's most extraordinary libraries, containing 100,000 medieval manuscripts and books, and over a million other volumes. It is open to students and specialists on application to the Prefettura (06 6988 3273). *See also p308.*

Borgo & Prati

Leading up to the Vatican is via della Conciliazione, an austere foil to Bernini's elaborate curves. Until the 1930s – when Mussolini did the demolition job that popes had planned for centuries – this was a fascinating warren of medieval streets, only a few of which remain in the Borgo quarter. Here salt-of-the-earth Romans mingle with off-duty Swiss Guards and immaculately robed priests from the Vatican Curia (administration). In medieval Rome's British enclave you'll also find the **Museo Storico Nazionale dell'Arte Sanitaria** (*see p145* **Brits abroad: the pilgrims**). Cutting through Borgo is the raised, covered Passetto, the 13th-century escape route to **Castel Sant'Angelo** (*see below*).

Further north, the sedately bourgeois Prati residential area was built in the late 19th century. A spot of retail therapy down Prati's main drag, via Cola di Rienzo, is a good antidote to a surfeit of culture. Otherwise, there are the endless military barracks lining viale delle Milizie; some quiet, tree-lined streets close to the river; and the massive, bombastic Palazzo di Giustizia – popularly known as *il palazzaccio*, 'the big ugly building' – between piazza Cavour and the Tiber. On the river bank is one of Catholic Rome's truly weird experiences: the **Museo delle Anime dei Defunti**.

Castel Sant'Angelo

Lungotevere Castello 50 (06 681 9111). Bus 23, 40, 49, 87, 280, 926. **Open** 9am-8pm Tue-Sun; ticket office closes 7pm. **Admission** €5; €2.50 concessions. **No credit cards. Map** p333 1B.

Begun by the Emperor Hadrian in AD 135 (*see also p8* **Hadrian**) as his own mausoleum, Castel Sant'Angelo has since functioned as a fortress, a prison and a papal residence. Although it now plays host to temporary art shows (displays of stolen paintings and artefacts recovered by the police are a regular choice), the real pleasure of a visit to Castel Sant'Angelo lies in wandering from Hadrian's original spiralling ramp entrance to the upper terraces, with their superb views of the city and beyond.

In between there is much to see: the lavish Renaissance salons, decorated with spectacular frescos and trompe l'oeils; the glorious chapel in the Cortile d'Onore, designed by Michelangelo for Leo X; and, halfway up an easily missed staircase, Clement VII's surprisingly tiny personal bathroom, painted by Giulio Romano. Puccini had Tosca hurl herself from the top of Castel Sant'Angelo (*see p110* **Locating Tosca**).

Museo delle Anime dei Defunti

Lungotevere Prati 12 (06 6880 6517). Bus 23, 30, 34, 40, 49, 70, 80, 81, 87, 280, 492, 913, 926. **Open** *Oct-June* 7.30-11am, 4.30-7pm daily. *July-Sept* 7.30-10am, 5.30-7.30pm daily. **Admission** free. **Map** p333 1B.

This macabre collection, attached to the startlingly neo-Gothic church of Sacro Cuore del Suffragio, contains hand- and fingerprints left on the prayer books and clothes of the living by dead loved ones, urging those left in the temporal world to say mass to release their souls from purgatory. Begun just over a century ago, the collection is intended to convince the sceptical of life after death. Among other uncanny exhibits, there's an incandescent handprint supposedly left by Sister Clara Scholers on the habit of a fellow-nun in Westphalia in 1696, and hand-scorched bank notes left by a dead soul outside a church where he wanted mass to be said.

Then what?

● Classicists may get a kick out of translating the long plaque put up to mark the inauguration of the massive and highly controversial **multi-storey car park** built beneath the Gianicolo hill for the 2000 Holy Year. All official Vatican documents are still written in the language of the Caesars, though words like 'car park' can pose something of a challenge.

● Pass by the **AS Roma Store** at via Cola di Rienzo 136 (06 320 3471/www.asroma.it) and book tickets for a football match. Consume a very reasonable buffet lunch while watching the team's heroic exploits on video.

● Learn the secrets of the world's most nattily dressed police force in the **Museo Storico dell'Arma dei Carabinieri** at piazza

del Risorgimento 46 (06 689 6696, open 8.30am-12.30pm Tue-Sun, admission free).

● The summer-long (June-Sept) **literary festival** in the gardens of the Castel Sant'Angelo has become a tradition. A blissful breeze blows up from the Tiber on hot summer evenings; you can sit and eat outdoors, attend a reading, catch a late-night movie, take tango or cookery lessons, or just buy books.

● The city's wholesale **flower market** (Mercato dei Fiori, via Trionfale 45, 06 3973 3326) opens its doors to the public once a week, from 10am until 1pm on Tuesday mornings only. Come with porters and bearers to carry away your bargain-priced camellias, orchids and palm trees.

The Appian Way

Allow yourself to be enchanted by the Queen of Roads.

The Appia Antica: somewhat quieter in modern times.

Map p151

Begun in the late fourth century BC by the statesman, lawmaker and sometime official censor Appius Claudius Caecus, the via Appia Antica is the oldest Roman military road. (It's called the 'old Appian Way' to distinguish it from the modern via Appia Nuova to the east.) Designed to make possible the rapid movement of troops and supplies, it originally stretched from the city centre to Capua near Naples, and was gradually lengthened as Roman control extended south. By the time it reached Brindisi on the Adriatic coast in 121 BC, it was the Romans' main route to the eastern Empire: the via Appia was now so important it called the *regina viarum*, 'the Queen of Roads'.

The via Appia originally began at the Porta Capena, near the Circo Massimo (*see p68*), and ran south through the valley where the Terme di Caracalla (*see p129*) stand. With the construction of the Aurelian Wall (*see p155* **Walls**) around AD 270, its point of departure was considered to be the Porta Appia, now called the Porta San Sebastiano.

Spruced up and made into the centrepiece of an extensive new park, the **Parco della Caffarella-Parco dell'Appia Antica** (*see p152* **Country ways**), the via Appia has become ever more popular as a destination for strolling families – especially on Sundays, when the road is closed off to all but local traffic. After dusk, it remains a favoured retreat for lovers in trembling parked cars; at the Grande Raccordo (ring-road) end, a handful of elderly prostitutes sit by their braziers.

Despite Fiats and Vespas, the atmosphere along the Appia Antica is thick with antiquity, the motorised traffic just a modern echo of a thousands years of comings and goings.

GETTING THERE

The municipal transport company's Archeobus (information and bookings 06 4695 2343) is an eco-friendly air-conditioned minibus that departs on the hour from piazza Venezia between 9am and 5pm daily, stopping at the Circo Massimo, Terme di Caracalla, Museo delle Mura, Parco dell'Appia Antica visitors' centre, the church of Domine Quo Vadis?, the catacombs of San Callisto and San Sebastiano, Circo di Massenzio and Tomba di Cecilia Metella, and the Villa dei Quintili. An all-day ticket costs €7.75 (under-6s free; no credit cards) and allows you to hop on and off wherever you like along the route.

Alternatively, use the regular bus services listed below, each of which cover some section of the Appian Way.

118 viale Aventino–Terme di Caracalla–Porta San Sebastiano–along via Appia Antica to Domine Quo Vadis? and Catacombe di San Callisto and San Sebastiano–via Appia Pignatelli

218 piazza San Giovanni – Porta San Sebastiano–along via Appia Antica to Domine Quo Vadis?–along via Ardeatina to Fosse Ardeatine and, with a bit of a hike, the Catacombe di Domitilla

660 from metro station Colli Albani: along via Appia Antica from Circo di Massenzio to Tomba di Cecilia Metella

664 from metro station Colli Albani: along via Appia Nuova to Villa dei Quintili

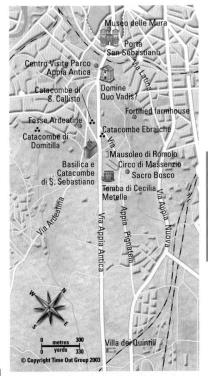

© Copyright Time Out Group 2003

Along the Appian Way

The via Appia Antica begins at the formidable Porta San Sebastiano, the largest and best-preserved of the gates that were built by Aurelian when he walled the city in the third century AD (see p155 **Walls**). The Porta San Sebastiano also houses the **Museo delle Mura**; access to the ramparts of Aurelian's fortifications from the museum has been suspended indefinitely since the collapse of a nearby section of the wall in 2001.

The first kilometre or so of the via Appia Antica is not particularly attractive: sights to look forward to here include an ugly viaduct and a Hyundai body shop. But little bits of antiquities peek out here and there, hinting at the via Appia's rich history.

On the right, a former paper mill has been transformed into the **Centro Visite Parco Appia Antica** (visitors' centre, see p152). On the left is the austere church of **Domine Quo Vadis?** (open 7am-7pm daily). Inside the door are the imprints of two long flat feet that are supposed to have been left by Christ when he appeared to St Peter, who was running away

from Rome and crucifixion. (These footprints are in fact a copy; the originals are housed in the church of San Sebastiano, see p153.) Christ told Peter that he was going back to Rome to be crucified again himself, thus shaming Peter into returning too. A bad painting to the left side of the altar depicts Peter's martyrdom.

A right fork outside the church along the via Ardeatina leads to the **Catacombe di Domitilla** (access from via delle Sette Chiese) and the **Fosse Ardeatine** (via Ardeatina 174, 06 513 6742, open 8.15am-5pm daily), a memorial to a more recent act of barbarity. Formerly a quarry, this latter is where 335 Italians were shot by the Nazis in 1944 in revenge for a Resistance ambush. A left fork past the Domine Quo Vadis? church along via della Caffarella leads into the **Parco della Caffarella-Parco dell'Appia Antica** proper.

Past the Caffarella turn-off, the Appia Antica gets narrower – with Renaissance retaining walls on either side – and the traffic more nerve-racking. If you're on foot, cut through the grounds of the **Catacombe di San Callisto** (you'll find the entrance further up the hill

Circo di Massenzio. *See p153.*

between the *vie* Ardeatina and Appia Antica). Here the beautiful cypress-lined lanes lead you to the largest catacombs in Rome, but don't neglect the smaller and equally fascinating **Catacombe di San Sebastiano** that lie further to the south.

Beyond the catacombs the countryside opens up, offering wide vistas across fields punctuated by three of the road's most famous ancient sites: the **Mausoleo di Romolo**, the **Circo di Massenzio** and the **Tomba di Cecilia Metella**. The Circo di Massenzio was built by Romulus' father Maxentius for chariot racing; its red-brick ruins now rise up behind the **Mausoleo di Romolo**.

Beyond, a long, dead-straight stretch of road still retains, in parts, the original flagstones used by the Romans. Like all Roman roads, the via Appia had a standard width of 14 Roman feet (4.2 metres/13.7 feet), which allowed two carriages to pass each other, or five infantry-men to march abreast. You can sneak a peek through the locked gates that line the road here for a glimpse of some swish private villas. Further along, the villas become more sparse and the grassy sides of the via Appia are dotted with picturesquely overgrown ruins. At the fifth Roman mile is the second-century AD **Villa dei Quintili** (access from via Appia Nuova only). Beyond this point the road is quieter and the landscape wilder, with fragments of aqueduct standing in the fields. Any turning to the left will take you eventually to the modern via Appia Nuova. Between the Appia Nuova and the Tuscolana, the **Parco degli Acquedotti** (*see p291*) has striking remains of Roman aqueducts.

Catacombs

There are some 300km (200 miles) of catacombs running through the soft volcanic rock beneath suburban Rome, including three major burial places along the via Appia Antica – the **catacombe di San Sebastiano**, **Domitilla** and **San Callisto**. Most date from between the first and fifth centuries AD. Most of the tombs were Christian, but there were also several Jewish catacombs (including those at Vigna Rondanini, via Appia Antica 119A; open by prior permission only, *see p61* **Ex-Rip.X**). For the Christians, however, the catacombs offered one special advantage: in the under-ground chambers ceremonies could be carried out and the dead buried far from the prying and vindictive eyes of pagan persecutors.

The standard form of burial was in a niche (*loculus*) carved in the rock. The body was wrapped in linen and laid in the niche, which was then sealed with tiles or slabs of marble. The name, age and a character-description-cum-eulogy of the deceased were inscribed on the slabs by catacomb staff – not always

the most literate of people, as poignant misspellings of names and adjectives reveal. The grander arched niches (*arcosolia*) tend to be the graves of martyrs or other important members of the flock, while some families with a little extra cash could upgrade to a private crypt where generations could all be buried together. Frescos on the walls illustrate biblical episodes with a common theme: the indomitability of faith. Popular symbols include representations of Christ as a fish or as a shepherd, while a lamb or a sheep represents humanity.

Included in the admission fee at the catacombs is an obligatory guided tour. This is (a) so you don't get lost and (b) so you don't pilfer any bones that might still be around. The guides are mostly priests or theologians from all over the world, whose English-language skills are generally much weaker than their religious convictions.

See also **Catacombe di Priscilla** (*p157*) *and* **Sant'Agnese Fuori le Mura** (*p158*).

Country ways

The **Parco della Caffarella-Parco dell'Appia Antica** has been painstakingly reclaimed – from property developers, subsistence farmers and drug dealers – over decades, and the 25-plus square km (ten square miles) are now Rome's closest amenable countryside.

The Valle della Caffarella – between via Appia Antica and via Latina, another ancient road – was the first stretch of *campagna romana* ('Roman countryside') and lauded by Grand Tour visitors to the Eternal City in the 18th and 19th centuries. In earlier and more dangerous times, with barbarians apt to descend unannounced, its proximity to the safety of Rome's walls made it the city's breadbasket, fruit orchard and vegetable garden. Easily reachable on foot or by bike are ancient ruins, a sacred wood and a fortified 16th-century farmhouse where toothless peasants – looking for all the world like they were planted there by the local tourist board – make and sell cheese.

The visitors' centre has bikes for rent, maps and information. It also organises tours (phone or check the website for details).

Centro Visite Parco Appia Antica
Via Appia Antica 42 (06 512 6314/www. parcoappiaantica.org). **Open** 10.30am-noon, 3-5pm daily. *Information line* 9am-6pm Mon-Fri. **Admission** *Park* free. *Guided tours* free. **No credit cards**.

Catacombe di Domitilla
Via delle Sette Chiese 282 (06 511 0342). **Open** 8.30am-noon, 2.30-5pm Mon, Wed-Sun; ticket office closes 4.50pm. Closed Jan. **Admission** €5; €3 concessions. **No credit cards**.
Package-tour companies have a bulk-rate agreement with the operators of these catacombs, which means tourist groups can be an overwhelming presence and individual travellers may be treated like second-class citizens. There are some excellent frescos, however, and in the off-peak months (Nov-Feb) and hours Domitilla's catacombs are quite pleasant.

Catacombe di San Callisto
Via Appia Antica 78, 110 or 126 (06 513 0151/ www.catacombe.roma.it). **Open** 8.30am-noon, 2.30-5pm Mon, Tue, Thur-Sun. Closed Feb. **Admission** €5; €3 concessions. **Credit** MC, V.
These are the largest and most impressive of Rome's catacombs, with 20km (12.5 miles) of tunnels and 500,000 tombs. Make sure your guide takes you through the 'labyrinth'.

Catacombe di San Sebastiano
Via Appia Antica 136 (06 785 0350). **Open** 9am-noon, 2.30-5pm Mon-Sat. Closed mid Nov-mid Dec. **Admission** €5; €3 concessions. **No credit cards**.
The word 'catacomb' started here, at an underground burial complex built near a tufa quarry: *kata kymbas*, in Greek, means 'near the quarry'. The guided tour here also takes you through the *piazzuola*, an interesting cluster of pagan tombs; they are now underground, but were built at street level before the catacombs were dug.

Circo di Massenzio & Mausoleo di Romolo
Via Appia Antica 153 (06 780 1324). **Open** 9am-5pm (until 7pm Apr-Oct) Tue-Sun. **Admission** €2.58; €1.55 concessions. **No credit cards**.
Built by the Emperor Maxentius in the early years of the fourth century AD, this chariot racetrack could seat 10,000 people. Notice the interesting use of earthenware jugs (amphorae) in the upper part of the long walls; the empty volume helped lighten the load of the vaults. The emperor had his beloved son Romulus buried in the mausoleum (indefinitely *in restauro* as this guide went to press) just north of the circus. The brick ruins of the villa are visible enough from the road, but if you go inside the site you're rewarded by an unforgettable panorama of umbrella pines, rolling hills and the tomb of Cecilia Metella (*see p154*). Prepare to swoon.

Museo delle Mura
Via di Porta San Sebastiano 18 (06 7047 5284). **Open** 9am-7pm (until 7pm Apr-Oct) Tue-Sat; 9am-5pm Sun. **Admission** €2.58; €1.55 concessions. **No credit cards**.
Housed in the ancient Porta San Sebastiano, the little Museum of the Walls has a smallish collection of artefacts associated with Roman walls and roads. The museum's greatest attraction used to be the access it gave visitors to a walkway on top of a substantial stretch of the Aurelian Wall itself, but this *passeggiata* was closed indefinitely in 2001.

San Sebastiano (church)
Via Appia Antica 136 (06 780 8847). **Open** 8.30am-5.30pm Mon-Sat; 8.30am-12.30pm Sun.
Above the catacombs of the same name, the basilica of St Sebastian is ignored by most visitors. It was commissioned in the fourth century by Emperor Constantine (but almost completely rebuilt in the baroque period) and originally called the Basilica Apostolorum, because the bodies of apostles Peter and Paul were supposedly temporarily transferred to the catacombs here in the third century. The church was renamed for St Sebastian, a third-century Roman martyr best known for suffering

Sightseeing

death by imperial arrow, though lapidation actually finished him off. Two relics of the saint – one of the arrows and the column he was tied to while the arrows were being shot – are in the first chapel on the right. Also on display is the marble slab in which Christ left his footprints during his miraculous apparition at Domine Quo Vadis? (*see p151*).

Tomba di Cecilia Metella

Via Appia Antica 161 (06 780 2465). **Open** 9am-30min before sunset Tue-Sun; ticket office closes 4pm. **Admission** €2; €1 concessions; *see also p61* **Tickets**. **No credit cards**.

This squat cylinder from the 40s BC was the final resting place of a woman who had married into the wealthy Metella family; despite being related only by marriage, the family gave her this unusually lavish mausoleum. During the 14th century the Caetani family, relatives of Pope Boniface VIII, incorporated the tomb into a fortress, adding the crenellations around its top, and proceeded to extract tolls from passers-by. Across the street from the tomb are the ruins of the church of San Nicola, a rare example of Gothic architecture in Rome, surrounded by further walls of the fortress, which once straddled the road.

Villa dei Quintili

Via Appia Nuova 1092 (06 718 2273). **Open** 9am-4pm Tue-Sun. **Admission** €4; €2 concessions; *see also p61* **Tickets**. **No credit cards**.

Built in the second century AD by the brothers Quintili (consuls who would later be executed by Emperor Commodus of *Gladiator* fame), this was the biggest country villa outside Rome's city walls. Many of the fittings and statues were removed during digs in the 18th and 19th centuries; what opened to the public in 2000 was the vast structure itself, set in splendid isolation amid fields strewn with fragments of the many-coloured marble that once faced its mighty halls. At the villa's gate on to the via Appia Antica there is a pretty nymphaeum (*in restauro* as this guide went to press).

Bring out yer dead

Whether pagan or Christian, subterranean or above ground, all tombs in ancient Rome had one thing in common: they were outside the city walls. In the fifth century BC burials within a sacred boundary, called the *pomerium*, were banned – the law was enacted for religious reasons but, by chance, also benefited public health. So the Romans took their dead to the roads leading out of the city. The grandest of ancient Rome's roads, the Appian Way, was the chic-est place to spend eternity. Although the Appia today is most famous for its Christian catacombs, it was originally studded with splendid – and competitive – funerary monuments for pagans. Barbarian and papal pickaxes dismantled most of these in the Middle Ages, reducing once-imposing mausoleums and pyramids to stumps of unrecognisable masonry. A few, like the tomb of Cecilia Metella (*see p154*), have survived, giving visitors an idea of the former grandeur of funerary architecture on the Queen of Roads. Of course, only the wealthiest could afford a flashy sepulchre like Cecilia's; most Romans had to settle for something more modest. Depending on the wealth and religion of the deceased, tomb types varied widely.

Catacomb: system of tunnels on multiple levels, up to 40m (130ft) underground, intended for mass burials of Christians and Jews; both religions favoured inhumation to the common pagan practice of cremation.

Columbarium: literally 'dovecote', so-called because of the small niches lining the walls where cinerary urns were placed. *Columbaria* were communal underground tombs for working-class Romans and slaves, and the most economical of the pagan funerary options. The Columbarium of Pomponius Hylas, at via di Porta Latina 10, can be visited with prior permission (*see p61* **Ex-Rip.X**).

Mausoleum: named after Mausolus, who built the prototype in Halicarnassus, this was the preferred tomb of the platinum-card-holding Roman. The traditional mausoleum was a squat masonry cylinder, often with a mound of earth on top where trees were planted. The tomb of Cecilia Metella, Hadrian's tomb – now **Castel Sant'Angelo** (*see p151*) – and the **Mausoleum of Augustus** (*see p96*) are the most famous examples in Rome. The two latter are now in the city centre, but were outside the *pomerium* when they were built.

Necropolis: A 'city of the dead' was for those pagans who wanted something a little showier than a common *columbarium* but were still several rungs below mausoleum-class. Necropolises were neighbourhoods of family tombs, miniature houses in which the urns of the dead were arranged on the floor; the walls often had fresco or mosaic decoration. A visit to the Vatican necropolis, under St Peter's, is an unforgettable descent into early Christian history (*see p147*).

Walls

In the fourth century BC the Servian walls were built to protect Rome from vengeful Etruscans (*see p281* **Etruscans**) and invading Gauls. The circuit stretched north to modern-day Termini station (where ruins of the walls are visible at the lower-level McDonald's) and south to the Aventine, encompassing the original seven hills. But as the city's population – and sense of invincibility – grew, large stretches of these walls were demolished. For half a millennium Rome's power over the Mediterranean was unchallenged and no defensive measures were necessary in the city.

In what historians call the 'troubled century' – the third century AD – this confidence began to ebb. News that Rome was being ruled by a series of lame-duck emperors reached the barbarian hordes, who began advancing south towards the Italian peninsula.

By AD 270 the barbarian threat was an emergency. Emperor Aurelian decided to build a new set of walls, Rome's first fortifications in 600 years. Construction of the *mura aureliane*, in no-frills brick-faced concrete, was swift. In under five years the 18km (11 mile) circuit was complete. The project was expedited by incorporating pre-existing structures, like the Piramide Cestia near the Porta Ostiense (*see p125*) and the aqueducts at Porta Maggiore (*see p131*). Army engineers designed the walls to follow the lie of the land, including hills like the Pincio (*see p84*) – whose height would help watchmen keep an eye on points north – and the Gianicolo (*see p120*) – whose bulk protected the important commercial district of Trastevere below. Though on the outskirts and at a lower elevation, Testaccio's grain warehouses (*see p124*) were an essential inclusion.

The walls were 8m (26ft) tall, 4m (13ft) thick, with towers every 30m (98ft). There were 18 main gates corresponding with the major roads; nine still stand. The gates were normally open, with guards stationed outside. In times of alarm the wooden doors were bolted shut and iron portcullises lowered.

Though the remains are still imposing, the Aurelian walls ultimately failed to protect the city. Even major reinforcements carried out in the fourth and fifth centuries were of little use: in AD 410 Alaric the Goth entered the city and Rome's role as predator of the world abruptly changed to that of barbarians' prey.

Sightseeing

The Suburbs

Ancient or modern, Rome's suburbs are truly monumental.

After a brusque introduction to suburban Rome from incoming trains or taxis, visitors may well fail to see the point of straying from the museum- and monument-packed *centro storico*. If the *palazzi* that went up immediately around the *centro* after Italian Unification in the 1870s are monotonous, the tower blocks that straggled out across the *campagna romana* during the post-war 'economic miracle' are downright grim.

There are, however, notable exceptions to the anti-aesthetic impact of 'modern' Rome: the elegant Liberty (art-nouveau) *palazzi* along the *vie* Salaria and Nomentana to the north, for example, and the memorably Fascist urban planning in EUR to the south. Elsewhere, even the most architecturally uninspired districts boast some wonderful surprises worth hopping on a bus or metro for, whether an undervisited catacomb, a charming museum, a sprawling park or just a slice of what life is like for the 90 per cent of modern Romans who live a world away from what the tourist sees.

Flaminia

The dead-straight via Flaminia shoots north from piazza del Popolo, passing through affluent residential *Roma nord* with its myriad sports facilities: the **Stadio Flaminio** and Acqua Acetosa running tracks in the east, and the **Foro Italico** and **Stadio Olimpico** football stadium (*see chapter* **Sport**) to the west. It also crosses a mushrooming cultural zone, containing Renzo Piano's daring new **Auditorium** (*see p254*) and **MAXXI**, and allows a fleeting glimpse of Paolo Portoghesi's graceful if anomalous **mosque**, on a hill to the east. The via Flaminia crosses the river at the ancient Ponte Milvio, where Emperor Constantine had his battle-winning vision (*see p10*); now open to pedestrians only, the second-century BC bridge offers a good view of the neighbouring Ponte Flaminio, a glorious example of Fascist rhetorical architecture.

MAXXI

Ex-Caserma Montello, via Guido Reni 10 (06 320 2438/www.gnam.arti.beniculturali.it). Bus 53, 280, 910/tram 2. **Open** (during exhibitions only) 11am-7pm Tue-Sun. **Admission** free. Free guided tours 6pm Wed. **No credit cards.**

This enormous hangar-like space in a former army barracks is to be transformed – to a design by Anglo-Iraqi architect Zaha Hadid – into the Eternal City's cutting-edge centre – the Museo delle arti del XXI secolo, MAXXI – for anything to do with the arts of the 21st century. Until Hadid's project is completed towards the end of 2005 (and maybe even after: conservative Rome is unlikely to rival the Tate Modern phenomenon), it will host occasional, low-profile temporary exhibitions.

Foro Italico & Stadio Olimpico

Piazza de Bosis/via del Foro Italico. Bus 32, 280, 910/tram 2. **Map** p331.

A marble obelisk, 36.3m (120ft) high, with the words 'Mussolini' and 'Dux' inscribed in it, greets visitors to the Foro Italico, a sports complex conceived in the late 1920s by prominent Fascist architect Enrico Del Debbio. The avenue leading west of the obelisk is paved with black-and-white mosaics of good Fascists doing Fascist things – flying warplanes, saluting the Duce and engaging in all kinds of athletic activity, including difficult gymnastic manoeuvres like the 'Iron Cross'. It's a wonderfully camp sight today, and amazingly well preserved considering the thousands of feet that trample the tiles every weekend on their way to the Stadio Olimpico beyond (built in the 1950s but modified for the 1990 World Cup), where AS Roma and SS Lazio both play (*see chapter* **Sport**). The glorification of athleticism continues to the north, at the Stadio dei Marmi, also by Del Debbio. Surrounding the track here are 60 marble statues of naked athletes, each with some kind of sports apparatus, from crossbows to *bocce* (bowling) balls. The statues' exaggerated flaunting of musculature is amusingly camp, although their earnest sculptors probably intended them to be taken perfectly seriously. Other facilities at the Foro Italico include tennis courts, where the Italian Open is held each May, and two swimming pools.

Parioli

Called somewhat pretentiously *i Parioli* in the plural by locals – though it's not clear what a singular *pariolo* is – this is one of the most expensive residential areas in the city, located north of the Villa Borghese and west of the Villa Ada. Built over the hilltop estates of some of baroque Rome's finest private villas, the atmosphere here is rather dull, and the late 19th- and early 20th-century architecture not consistently impressive. For Romans, however, a Parioli address is the ultimate status symbol;

Art nouveau charm in the **Coppedè** district.

the consummate *pariolino*, in local parlance, is a rich kid who drives a spotless Jeep or BMW, takes for granted the family's summer property in Sardinia, and wears clothes – purchased at Davide Cenci – pressed by a Filipina maid.

Salaria

The via Salaria – the salt road – existed before Rome, when ancient tribes brought vital salt supplies along it from saltpans on the east coast. Today the road begins its northeasterly itinerary across the Italian peninsula from piazza Fiume. The modern district on either side of the Salaria is called Trieste, home to upmarket post-Unification apartment blocks and a bevy of embassies, but the real treasures of the area are the delightful Coppedè quarter – a cluster of art nouveau buildings centred around piazza Mincio – as well as the leafy shade of the Villa Ada public gardens and the **Catacombe di Priscilla**. In via della Moschea, between the *vie* Salaria and Flaminia, lies Paolo Portoghesi's **mosque** (*see p312*), built from 1984-92.

Catacombe di Priscilla

Via Salaria 430 (06 8620 6272). Bus 63, 92, 310, 630. **Open** *Oct-Mar* 8.30am-noon, 2.30-5pm Tue-Sun. *Apr-Sept* 8.30am-noon, 2.30-5.30pm Tue-Sun. Closed Jan. **Admission** €5; €3 concessions. **No credit cards**.
This two-storey second century AD burial place, contains bas-reliefs and frescos, including what is believed to be the first depiction of Mary.

Nomentana

Via Nomentana, one tick of the clock past the Salaria, leads out of Rome to the north-east, flanked on either side by another middle-class

residential area, with some charming art nouveau buildings. It has its green lung in the Villa Torlonia (again with a touch of art nouveau in the **Casina delle Civette**), its art fest in the **MACRO** contemporary art gallery (*see p246*) and perhaps the earliest Christian mosaics in **Santa Costanza**, by the church and catacombs of **Sant'Agnese fuori le Mura**. To the south-east, the area around the via Tiburtina is more low-rent.

Casina delle Civette & Villa Torlonia

Via Nomentana 70 (06 4425 0072). Bus 36, 60, 61, 62, 490, 495, 649. **Open** *Oct-Mar* 9am-4pm Tue-Sun. *Apr-Sept* 9am-5pm Tue-Sun. Ticket office closes 1hr earlier. **Admission** €2.58; €1.55 concessions. **No credit cards**.
The Villa Torlonia, with its pretty park, was glorified as Mussolini's suburban HQ in the 1930s, trashed by Anglo-American forces when they made it their HQ from 1944-7, and bought by Rome city council in 1978 in a disastrous state, after which the main house and its outbuildings disappeared for years behind scaffolding. Unquestionably the best thing to emerge from this long *restauro* is the Casina delle Civette, a wacky Swiss-chalet-meets-faux-medieval-folly shed that was bestowed with all kinds of stupendous stained glass and *boiseries* in 1916-20. The Casina's own art nouveau fittings have been beautifully restored and supplemented with many other works in stained glass from the same period. Underneath the park, and accessible only by prior appointment (*see p60* **Ex-Rip.X**), is one of the few Jewish catacombs in Rome.

Sant'Agnese fuori le Mura & mausoleum of Santa Costanza

Via Nomentana 349 (06 861 0840/www.santagnese. net). Bus 36, 60, 90. **Open** *Church* 7.30am-noon, 4-7.30pm daily. *Catacombs & Santa Costanza* 9am-noon Mon; 9am-noon, 4-6pm Tue-Sat; 4-6pm Sun. **Admission** €5 (catacombs). **No credit cards**. Unique in Rome, the circular fourth-century mausoleum of Santa Costanza, 2km (1.4 miles) beyond the beginning of the via Nomentana at Porta Pia (*see p90*), was built for Constantine's daughters, Constance (a saint only by popular tradition, never having been canonised) and Helen. The purple sarcophagus here, containing the remains of Constance, is a plaster cast of the porphyry original, now in the Vatican Museums. The barrel-vaulted ambulatory, whose arcades rest on exquisite 'pillows' of marble, is decorated with perhaps the world's earliest surviving Christian mosaics. They look more pagan than Christian – simple pastoral scenes with a spiralling vine encircling figures collecting and treading grapes – but historians insist the wine-making motifs represent Christ's blood, not the pastimes of Bacchus. In the adjoining church of Sant'Agnese, also dating from Constantine's time, is a seventh-century apse mosaic showing a diminutive figure of St Agnes standing on the flames of her martyrdom, flanked by two popes. St Agnes was almost certainly buried in the catacombs below this church, though her skull was later moved to the church of Sant'Agnese in Agone, in what is now piazza Navona (*see p103*). The catacombs are among Rome's least-visited and most atmospheric, but beware: they're are closed each year for one month, usually January. In the back of the church-and-mausoleum complex is the Circolo Bocciofilo (bowling club), where you can often drop in on high-intensity *bocce* tournaments, get a *caffè* at the bar and admire the *circolo*'s trophies in the club room.

East

San Lorenzo

Map p159.
Badly built, densely populated and still showing wounds from World War II, San Lorenzo is scarred like an alley cat. It's also one of Rome's liveliest neighbourhoods, full of restaurants, artists, graffiti and cultural diversity, plus the spillover from the nearby La Sapienza university. The area has a history of rebellion. It was 'designed' in the 1880s as a working-class ghetto, with few public services or amenities, and soon developed into Rome's most radical area, where anarchist workers bravely resisted the rising tide of Fascism. The street battles of the 1920s between *squadracce fasciste* and the *sanlorenzini* form part of Italian left-wing legend. Bordering the district to the north-east is the vast Verano cemetery, which explains why every other shop window in San Lorenzo, an otherwise vital community, advertises *onoranze funebri* (funeral services). At the entrance of the Verano stands the ancient basilica of **San Lorenzo fuori le**

Mura. To the north-west the **Città Universitaria** (the main campus of Europe's biggest university, La Sapienza), with buildings designed in the 1930s by Piacentini and Foschini, is an example of the Fascist take on the architecture of higher education.

San Lorenzo fuori le Mura
Piazzale del Verano 3 (06 491 511). Bus 71, 492, 649/tram 3, 19. **Open** *Oct-Mar* 7.30am-12.30pm, 3-7pm daily. *Apr-Sept* 7.30am-12.30pm, 3-8pm daily.
This basilica on the ancient via Tiburtina was donated by Constantine to house the remains of St Lawrence after the saint met his fiery end on a griddle. Rebuilt in the sixth century by Pope Pelagius II, it was later united with a neighbouring church, using Pelagius's church as the chancel. Successive restorations were undone in the 1860s, when some unfortunate frescos were added. A couple of wayward bombs plunged through the roof in 1943, making San Lorenzo the only Roman church to suffer war damage, but it had been painstakingly reconstructed by 1949. On the right side of the 13th-century portico are frescos from the same period, showing scenes from the life of St Lawrence. Inside the triumphal arch are sixth-century mosaics reflecting Byzantine influence. The figures are flat, stiff and outlined in black, floating motionless against a gold ground. There is little modelling or play of light and shade, and the colouring is not as subtle as in the earlier mosaics. This is partly due to the Greek-inspired use of marble squares instead of the glass normally favoured by the Romans.

South

Ostiense, Garbatella & San Paolo
These districts south of Testaccio (*see p123*) are similarly interesting areas of late 19th- and early 20th-century workers' housing: many of their apartment blocks are architecturally outstanding. Despite some urban blight, they have a strong community feel.
On via Ostiense lurks the wonderful but undervisited **Centrale Montemartini**. Further down the road is one of Rome's major basilicas, **San Paolo fuori le Mura**. Between them is a dense concentration of some of Rome's most happening nightspots, especially around via Libetta (*see chapter **Nightlife***).

Centrale Montemartini
Via Ostiense 106 (06 574 8030/www. euromusees2001.org). Bus 23, 769. **Open** 9.30am-7pm Tue-Sun; ticket office closes 6.30pm.
Admission €4.13; €2.58 concessions; *see also p59* **Tickets**. **No credit cards**.
It may be true that the Centrale Montemartini contains merely the leftover ancient statuary from the Musei Capitolini (*see p62*), but this being Rome the dregs are pretty impressive; moreover, the setting

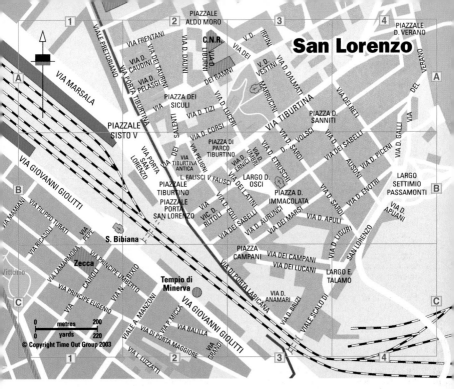

itself makes this wonderful spot worth a visit. You enter through the headquarters of Rome's electricity company, beneath the skeleton of its old gasworks. Inside are fauns and Minervas, bacchic revellers and Apollos, all starkly white but oddly at home against the gleaming black machinery of the decommissioned generating station.

San Paolo fuori le Mura

Via Ostiense 184 (06 541 0341). Metro San Paolo/ bus 23, 170, 769. **Open** *Basilica* 7am-6.30pm Mon-Fri; 7am-7pm Sat, Sun. *Cloister* 9am-1pm, 3-6.30pm daily. Constantine founded San Paolo to commemorate the martyrdom of St Paul at nearby Tre Fontane (*see p160*). The church, 3km (two miles) beyond the Porta San Paolo along the via Ostiense, has been destroyed, rebuilt and restored several times; the present basilica – the largest in Rome after St Peter's – is only 150 years old, although a few details and a wonderful cloister survive from its ancient beginnings. The greatest damage to the building occurred in a fire in 1823, but subsequent restorers have also contributed to the destruction of the older church. Features that have survived include 11th-century doors decorated with biblical scenes; a strange 12th-century Easter candlestick, featuring human-, lion- and goat-headed beasts spewing the vine of life from their mouths; and the elegant 13th-century *ciborio* (painted canopy) above the altar, by Arnolfo di Cambio. In the *confessio* beneath the altar is the

tomb of St Paul, topped by a stone slab pierced with two holes through which devotees stuff bits of cloth to imbue them with the apostle's holiness.

The cloister is a good example of cosmatesque work (*see p317* **Glossary**), its twisted columns inlaid with mosaic and supporting an elaborate arcade of sculpted reliefs. In the sacristy are the remnants of a series of papal portraits that once lined the nave. The modern church has carried on this tradition, replacing the originals with mosaic portraits of all the popes from Peter to the present incumbent. There are only eight spaces left; once they are filled the world, apparently, will end.

EUR

Italian Fascism managed to be simultaneously monstrous and absurd, but its delusions of grandeur helped produce some of the most interesting European architecture and town planning of this century.

In the early 1930s Giuseppe Bottai, Mussolini's governor of Rome and the leading arbiter of Fascist taste, had the bright idea of expanding landbound Rome along the via Ostiense towards the sea, some 20km (12.5 miles) away. Imperial Rome had its monuments, Papal Rome had its churches and Fascist Rome (*la Terza Roma*), Bottai thought, should have its very own architectural spaces as well. He combined this with the notion of a universal exhibition, pencilled in for 1942 and intended to combine permanent cultural exhibition spaces with a monument to the regime.

Popular Fascist architect Marcello Piacentini was charged with co-ordinating the vastly ambitious project, but in the event few of the original designs were ever built. The planning committee became so bogged down in argument that little had been achieved by the outbreak of World War II, when work was suspended. After the war, it was resumed, but with a different spirit. Still known as EUR (*Esposizione universale romana*), the project went ahead disassociated from its Fascist ambitions, uniting some of Italy's best architects – Giovanni Muzio, Mario de Renzi, Ludovico Quaroni and partners Luigi Figini and Gino Pollini. With its unrelieved planes of icy travertine and its forbidding reinterpretations of classical monuments, the bombastic modernism of EUR lets you know you're not in Kansas any more. (As do all the manhole covers, which read 'EVR' or 'E42' in this part of town, as opposed 'SPQR' elsewhere in Rome.) On either side of the axial via Cristoforo Colombo, laid out in Mussolini's day and originally called via Imperiale, Fascist-inspired buildings such as Guerrini's Palazzo della Civiltà del Lavoro, popularly known as *il colosseo quadrato* (the square Colosseum), and Arnaldo Foschini's toy-town church of Santi Pietro e Paolo (piazzale Santi Pietro e Paolo) can be seen alongside post-war *palazzi* like Adalberto Libera's original Palazzo dei Congressi (piazza JF Kennedy) and Studio BBPR's superbly functional post office in viale Beethoven.

A slew of fittingly didactic museums (the **Museo dell'Alto Medioevo**, the **Museo della Civiltà Romana**, the **Museo delle Arti e Tradizioni Popolari**, the **Museo Preistorico ed Etnografico**) allows a glimpse inside these grandiose monuments to Fascist grandeur.

The 1960 Olympics offered another stimulus for filling out the area. The masterpiece is Nervi and Piacentini's flying saucer-like **Palazzo dello Sport** (in piazza dello Sport), hovering over EUR's artificial lake and now often used for big rock concerts (*see chapter* **Nightlife**) and political conventions. The area contains several other attractions, such as the LUNEUR Park funfair (*see p240*) and the Piscina delle Rose swimming pool (*see chapter* **Sport**).

Most Romans never visit EUR except on business or for concerts. At night, however, and especially in summer, it becomes the playground of fun-loving, suntanned, wealthy brats. Rome's desire to be a little bit of California finds its most eloquent expression

in EUR's relatively unsnarled, tree-lined boulevards, and there's a definite whiff of rich-kid, good-time culture in the air. For relief from EUR's relentless modernity, head for the leafy charm of the **Abbazia delle Tre Fontane**.

GETTING THERE

The quickest way from the city centre to EUR is by underground (Metro line B; get off at EUR Fermi), but approaching the district from the surface, along the via Cristoforo Colombo (bus 30, 170, 714), is the best way to experience the isolated, emerging-from-greenery feel of EUR, which was a significant part of the original architects' design. (They didn't, naturally, envisage the funfair off to the left.)

Abbazia delle Tre Fontane

Via Acque Salvie 1 (06 540 1655/shop 06 540 2309/ tre.fontane@flashnet.it). Bus 671, 707, 716, 761, 767. **Open** *San Vincenzo Anastasio* 6.45am-12.30pm, 3-8pm daily. *Other churches* 8am-12.30pm, 2.30-6.30pm daily. *Shop* 9am-1pm, 3.30-6.30pm daily.

To the east of EUR's extensive Tre Fontane sports facilities lies a haven of ancient, eucalyptus-scented green, dotted with three churches commemorating the three points hereabouts where St Paul's head supposedly bounced after it was severed from his body in AD 67. (Being a Roman citizen, Paul was eligible for the relatively quick and painless head-chop, as opposed to the long-drawn-out crucifixion.) This is the Trappist monastery of Tre Fontane, where water has gurgled and birds have sung since the fifth century. The church of San Paolo delle Tre Fontane is said to be built on the very spot where the apostle was executed; apart from a column in one corner to which Paul is supposed to have been tied, all traces of the fifth-century church were done away with in 1599 by architect Giacomo della Porta, who was also responsible for the two other churches. Monks planted the eucalyptus trees in the 1860s, believing they would drive away the malarial mosquitoes endemic there; they now brew a liqueur from the trees and sell it in a little shop (no credit cards) along with their chocolate and remedies for all ills.

Museo dell'Alto Medioevo

Viale Lincoln 3 (06 5422 8199). Metro EUR Fermi/ bus 30, 170, 714. **Open** 9am-8pm Tue-Sun. **Admission** €2; €1 concessions. **No credit cards**. Focusing on the decorative arts between the fall of the Roman Empire and the Renaissance, this museum has intricate gold- and silver-decorated swords, buckles and horse tackle are more mundane objects: painted ceramic bead jewellery and the metal frames of what may be Europe's earliest folding chairs.

Museo della Civiltà Romana

Piazza G Agnelli 10 (06 592 6135/6041). Metro EUR Fermi/bus 30, 170, 714. **Open** 9am-7pm Tue-Sat; 9am-1pm Sun (ticket office closes 30min before). **Admission** €4.13; €2.58 concessions. **No credit cards.**

Destroyed, rebuilt and restored: **San Paolo fuori le Mura**. *See p159*.

This museum dates from 1937, when Mussolini mounted a massive celebration to mark the bi-millennium of Augustus becoming the first emperor. The fact that the celebration came about 35 years too early was overlooked by *il Duce*, who was eager to draw parallels between Augustus' glory and his own. With its blank white walls and lofty, echoing corridors, the building is Fascist-classical at its most grandiloquent. There are detailed models of ancient Rome's main buildings, and a fascinating cutaway model of the Colosseum's maze of tunnels and lifts, as well as full-scale casts of the intricate reliefs on Trajan's column (*see p73*). The centrepiece is a giant model of Rome in the fourth century AD, that puts Rome's scattered fragments and artefacts into context very helpfully.

Museo delle Arti e Tradizioni Popolari

Piazza G Marconi 8 (06 592 6148/06 591 2669). Metro EUR Fermi/bus 30, 170, 714. **Open** 9am-6pm Tue-Fri; 9am-8pm Sat, Sun. **Admission** €4; €2 concessions. **No credit cards**.
This enormous collection is dedicated to Italian folk art and rural tradition. Exhibits include elaborately decorated carts and horse tack, as well as craft-related implements, and a bizarre collection of votive offerings left to local saints. Malevolent-looking puppets fill one room; another has costumes and *carnevale* artefacts.

Museo Preistorico ed Etnografico L Pigorini

Piazza G Marconi 14 (06 549 521). Metro EUR Fermi/bus 30, 170, 714. **Open** 9am-8pm daily. **Admission** €4; €2 concessions. **No credit cards**.
This museum displays prehistoric Italian artefacts together with ethnological material from a range of world cultures. The lobby contains a reconstruction of the prehistoric Guattari cave near Monte Circeo (*see p295*), with a genuine Neanderthal skull. On the first floor is the ethnological collection, with an all-too-predictable range of hut-urns, arrowheads, pottery, jewellery, masks and a couple of shrunken heads. The second floor has archaeological finds from digs all over Italy, including mammoth tusks and teeth, and some human bones.

West

Monteverde

Climbing the steep hill behind Trastevere and the Gianicolo is **Monteverde Vecchio**, a leafy, well-heeled suburb that is home to the vast, green, tree-filled expanses of the **Villa Pamphili** park (map p331). There children will enjoy feeding the turtles – if you can find the pond – and riding the ponies, which, if not here, are probably at their other haunt, the Gianicolo (*see p120*). Underneath the park lie the catacombs of **San Pancrazio** (piazza San Pancrazio, 10am-noon, 4pm-6pm daily). Nearby, to the south-east, is the smaller but equally lovely **Villa Sciarra** garden (map p337 1C), with its rose arbours, children's play area and miniature big dipper.

From here, spare yourself any further wandering to the south: all you get is Monteverde Nuovo, a charmless, more downmarket, predominantly post-war addition of high rise flats and heavily trafficked streets.

New and newer

Some of Rome's most exciting 21st-century architectural projects are going up north of the centre in an area already transformed by the leading architects of the 20th century. Renzo Piano's **Parco della Musica** (*see p254*) alone makes a trip up via Flaminia worthwhile. But it's not the whole story.

Hop on the number 2 tram at piazzale Flaminio and alight at the **Stadio Flaminio** (Pierluigi Nervi, 1957-9), the most imposing structure of the **Villaggio Olimpico**, a district of sports venues and residential buildings constructed for the 1960 Olympics.

From the stadium entrance, walk along the side of the building up viale Tiziano, taking note of the spectacular repetition of elegant diagonal beams supporting the terraces. Take the first street to the right (via D Pietri) and, as you approach the northern end of the stadium, there's an impressive view of the Parco della Musica skyline.

To get to the Parco della Musica entrance gate (viale P De Coubertin 15), cross the car park to your left and walk under the corso Francia flyover. For an in-depth explanation of the niceties of concert-hall design, take a guided tour (*see p254*) of the auditoria; alternatively, there's plenty you can see by yourself, including the ruins of a Roman villa-farm unearthed during construction and (after causing major delays) integrated into the complex.

One of the most original features of Parco della Musica is the roof garden, from which you can enjoy not only great views of the beetle-shaped auditoria but also of the northern part of Rome. To the east is the green mound of Villa Glori park. The brick-clad blocks to the north – part of the Villaggio Olimpico, and an interesting example of 1950s low-cost residential architecture – were designed by a group of renowned modernist architects, including Adalberto Libera and Luigi Moretti (*see also p27* **Modernism the Roman way**), as dwellings for Olympic athletes. To visit the area, leave the Parco della Musica from the main gate, turn left, walk past the flyover and turn right into via dell' Unione Sovietica. Crescent-shaped blocks have brick cylinders on their flat rooftops, the development's most frequently recurring feature.

Heading back towards the Stadio Flaminio, in the middle of piazza Apollodoro, is the flying saucer-like **Palazzetto dello Sport** (1956-8; *pictured below*).

Like the Stadio Flaminio and the **corso Francia flyover** towering above it, the Palazzetto was designed and built by civil engineer Pierluigi Nervi, one of the most innovative designers of the 20th century and a man firmly convinced of the intrinsic beauty of concrete. Look in through the upper glazing to catch a glimpse of the magnificent beehive structure of the Palazzetto's dome and you may find you share his conviction.

From the Palazzetto it's a short walk west down via Guido Reni to the **MAXXI** (*see p29* **Women at work**).

Conscious of the very poor quality of the landscaping around what are destined to become two of the city's major cultural venues, the city council has recently appointed Renzo Piano to design a green corridor stretching from Villa Glori, through Parco della Musica, to MAXXI.

Eat, Drink, Shop

Eating Out

Test *mamma*'s cooking in a neighbourhood trat or live the high life at Rome's new designer restaurants.

Try seafood alfresco at **San Teodoro**. *See p168.*

In the last few years a scattering of design-led restaurants has opened in Rome and the fusion gospel that seems positively Old Testament in London or New York has finally gained a foothold in the Eternal City (*see p176* **The design crew**).

But those who come to Rome to avoid the triumph of style over substance, to flee the sad northern predominance of menu description over the dish it describes, need not despair. Though they grab the attention of food critics

and the fashion crowd, eateries like **Reef**, **Supper Club** or **Ketumbar** (*for all see p176* **The design crew**) are still very much in the minority. In any case, these arrivistes take their food seriously. Eating out is still central to the Roman way of life, whether you're a web designer or a tram driver.

Most of this eating out is still done in that pillar of the local culinary temple, the neighbourhood trattoria. The great majority of these fine establishments are still family-run, with *mamma* in the kitchen, aided and abetted by the rest of the household. You can be fairly sure that she will be cooking up the same traditional Roman dishes, such as *spaghetti all'amatriciana* or *saltimbocca* (for food terms, *see p184* **Reading the menu**), that were on the menu last time you visited. Italian cuisine in general – and the Roman version in particular – is nothing if not conservative.

If there is one specifically Roman contribution to the Italian culinary tradition, it's creativity with offal. Traditional Roman restaurants rely heavily on the *quinto quarto* or 'fifth quarter' – those parts of the beast that were left over after the prime cuts of meat, plus the liver and kidneys, were sold off. That means brain (*cervello*), spinal marrow (*schienale*), nerves (*nervetti*), stomach and intestines (*trippa* or *pajata*), hooves (*zampi*), the thymus and pancreas glands (*animelle*). Even tails are highly thought of by Roman gourmets, as in the classic slaughterhouse worker's dish *coda alla vaccinara*. The once working-class areas of Testaccio and Trastevere are peppered with *trattorie* that serve these delicacies. They seem to have weathered the BSE scare – though *schienale* and *animelle* have now been banned by the EU, and one of the most Roman dishes of them all, *pajata* (baby calf's intestines with the mother's milk still inside), is now made with sheep's intestines rather than veal.

In terms of quality, eating out in Rome is better than at any time in the last 20 years, but the Eternal City is no longer a paradise of budget restaurants. The advent of the euro at the beginning of 2001 has pushed prices up by as much as 50 per cent. US visitors in particular will be shocked by how expensive everything has become – though this is explained as much by the exchange rate as by Roman inflation.

Take heart, though: there are still bargains to be found – particularly if you are prepared to forsake the *centro storico* for the suburbs, where running costs are lower and the clientele less tolerant of *fregature* (rip-offs). The other advantage of seeking out more far-flung hostelries like **Al Ponte della Ranocchia** (*see p196*), **Osteria del Velodromo Vecchio** (*see p197*) or **Marcello** (*see p196*) is a warmer welcome than one can expect in the tourist-weary centre, and the frisson of being the only *straniero* in the house.

GOING THE COURSE

The standard Roman (and Italian) running order is: *antipasto* (hors-d'oeuvre), *primo* (usually pasta, occasionally soup), *secondo* (the meat or fish course) with optional *contorno* (vegetables or salad, served separately) and *dolce* (dessert). You're under no obligation to

order four courses – few locals do. It's perfectly normal, for example, to order a first course followed by a simple *contorno* (often the only option for vegetarians). If you choose, you can even invert the usual order by ordering an *antipasto* after the pasta course. Fixed-price meals are a rarity. Top-flight establishments occasionally offer a *menu degustazione* (taster menu), but any establishment offering a *menu turistico* should be avoided, especially if it is written in several languages.

DRINKS

Most top-of-the-range restaurants have respectable wine lists, but more humble *trattorie* and *osterie* tend to have a limited selection. House wine is often an uninspiring Castelli romani white or equally unimpressive Montepulciano d'Abruzzo red, but there are exceptions, especially in more upmarket places (for an overview of the up-and-coming Lazio wine scene, *see p171* **Beyond Frascati**). In *pizzerie*, the drink of choice is *birra* (beer) or a variety of soft drinks. Mineral water – *acqua minerale* – is either *gassata* (sparkling) or *naturale* (still) and usually comes by the litre. If you have a full meal, and they like you, you may be offered free *amaro* or *grappa* at the end.

PRICES, TIPPING & TIMES

Restaurants are no longer allowed to add *pane e coperto* (bread and cover) to the bill. Some restaurants ignore the ban; others get round it by charging just for the bread.

Service is a grey area. Places that add it to the bill as a fixed item are still in the minority, so it's usually safe to assume it isn't included. Romans themselves tend not to tip much, especially in *pizzerie* and family-run places.

Eat, Drink, Shop

Prices

Average restaurant prices in this chapter are based on three courses; they have been rounded up to allow for service, but do not include wine. Unless you go for the full blow-out, you will almost always eat more cheaply than we have indicated. For *pizzerie*, the prices given are for a standard pizza, a beer and one extra, such as a *bruschetta*. Wine bar and gastropub averages are based on two courses and a glass of wine or beer. Snack and quick meal outlets vary so much as to what they offer that we have tried, wherever relevant, to include average prices in the text of the review.

HOTEL EDEN

ROMA

RESTAURANT

"LA TERRAZZA DELL'EDEN"

Via Ludovisi, 49 · 00187 Roma · Italia

Tel. (39) 06 47812752 · 06 4814473

www.hotel-eden.it

A good rule of thumb is to leave around five per cent in a pizzeria or humble trattoria, slightly more in more upmarket places – but never more than ten per cent. If service has been slack or rude, don't feel ashamed to leave nothing – or to check the bill in detail, as there is still the occasional restaurateur who becomes strangely innumerate when dealing with tourists.

Italy is still a cash society, so never assume you can use cards or travellers' cheques. By law, when you pay the bill (*il conto*) you must be given a detailed receipt (*una ricevuta fiscale*). In theory, if you leave a restaurant without it you can incur a fine; but the law is chiefly aimed at tax-dodging restaurateurs.

Opening times can change according to time of year and the owners' whim. Times given are for the kitchen – in other words, when you can actually turn up and order a hot meal – but many restaurants stay open for an hour or more after the cook goes home. In the evening, few proper restaurants open before 8pm, though *pizzerie* often kick off at least an hour earlier.

KIDS, WOMEN & DRESS

Taking children into restaurants – even the smartest – is never a problem in Rome. Waiters will usually produce a high chair (*un seggiolone*) on request and are generally happy to bring a *mezza porzione* – a half-portion. Also, just about any kitchen in the city will do those two off-menu standbys, *pasta al pomodoro* (with tomato sauce) or *pasta in bianco* (plain, to be dressed with oil and parmesan).

Though attitudes are changing, women dining alone may still occasionally attract unwelcome attention – most of it in the form of frank stares. Single diners of either sex can have trouble getting a table in cheaper places at busy times: eating out is a communal experience here, and few proprietors want to waste a table that could hold four diners.

Very few places impose a dress code, although shorts and T-shirts go down badly in formal, upmarket restaurants. Some restaurants now ban mobile phones; a surprising number of restaurants have taken anti-smoking by-laws seriously. Booking, once unusual, is becoming more of a habit, even in places that might appear to be spit-and-sawdust – especially so on Friday and Saturday evenings.

PIZZA

The city's *pizzaioli* have always been proud of their thinner, flatter *pizza romana*, but recently the fickle public has started to defect to the puffier Neapolitan variety. Either way, make sure your pizza comes from a wood-fired brick oven (*forno a legna*); pizzas from electric or gas-fired ovens just don't have the same flavour.

So orthodox is the range of toppings in Roman *pizzerie*, so eyebrow-raising any departure from the norm, that it's worth learning the main varieties by heart. For these, and for the various gap-fillers that it is customary to order while you're waiting for your pizza to come out of the oven, *see p184* **Reading the menu**.

Takeaway pizza – generally referred to as *pizza rustica* or *pizza a taglio* – is not prepared while you wait, but the best outlets (including all those listed) have a fast turnover and take quality seriously. Sit-down *pizzerie* usually only open in the evenings, but generally begin serving from 7pm (early by Roman standards).

WINE BARS

Neighbourhood *enoteche* (wine shops) and *vini e olii* (wine and oil) outlets have been around in Rome since time immemorial, complete with their huddle of old men drinking wine by the glass (*al bicchiere* or *alla mescita*). For a selection of places in which drinking is the main point of the exercise, *see chapter* **Cafés, Bars & Gelaterie**. Recently, a number of upmarket, international-style wine bars have also sprung up, offering snacks and even full meals to go with their wines. Those included in this chapter range from places that lay out tables among the bottle-lined shelves at lunch to full-blown wine-oriented restaurants like **Il Simposio** (*see p192*).

SNACKS

The Roman habit of sitting down to two full meals each day is fast disappearing; as a result places designed for eating on the run are on the increase. Roman snack culture, though, lurks in unlikely places. Few new arrivals, for example, consider stepping into a humble *alimentari* (grocer's) to have their picnic lunch prepared on the spot – and yet for fresh bread and high-quality fillings this is invariably the best option. Favourite casing is the ubiquitous white Roman roll, *la rosetta*, or a slice of *pizza bianca* (plain oiled and salted pizza base, eaten as is or filled); fillings are generally ham, salami or cheese, as *alimentari* do not sell fruit and veg. *See also p191* **Gastronomy on a shoestring**.

INTERNATIONAL

If you don't like Italian food, you're in the wrong town: Rome is not a good place to indulge in a gastronomic world tour. True, Chinese restaurants abound, and Indian, Thai, Korean and Mexican food can be tracked down, but the standard is far lower than in London, Paris or New York. The one exception to the rule – a consequence of Italy's murky colonial history – is a range of good Eritrean, Somali and Ethiopian cuisine.

Eat, Drink, Shop

VEGETARIANS

The city has few bona fide vegetarian restaurants; but, even in traditional *trattorie*, waiters will no longer look blank when you say *non mangio la carne* ('I don't eat meat'). They'll just assume you're a mad-cow worrier – and offer lamb, chicken or *prosciutto* (ham) instead. Despair not: the message will eventually sink in, and there's plenty left to try – from *penne all'arrabbiata* (pasta in a tomato and chili sauce) through *tonnarelli cacio e pepe* (thick spaghetti with crumbly sheep's cheese and plenty of black pepper) to *carciofi alla giudia* (deep-fried artichokes, a Roman Jewish speciality). If you are at all unsure about the ingredients of any dish, ask.

Capitoline & Palatine

Restaurants

San Teodoro

Via dei Fienili 49/51 (06 678 0933). Bus 30, 44, 63, 81, 95, 160, 170, 628, 715, 716, 781, 916. **Open** *Nov-Apr* 12.30-3.30pm, 7.30pm-12.30am Mon-Sat. *May-Sept* 12.30-3.30pm, 7.30pm-12.30am daily. Closed mid Jan-mid Feb. **Average** €48. **Credit** AmEx, DC, MC, V. **Map** p338 2C.

This is a marvellous place for a seafood-oriented alfresco meal: tables are arranged in a square amid the medieval houses of a residential enclave in the shadow of the Forum. Come prepared to splash out, though: it's decidedly upmarket. Still, dishes like *raviolini di broccolo in brodo di arzilla* (broccoli ravioli in skate broth) or *coda di rospo* (angler fish) with courgette flowers, served in a *piccante* sauce, are top-notch; service is unobtrusively professional, and the once rather skeletal wine list improving. Don't miss the *gelato di cassata*: an ice-cream take on the classic Sicilian ricotta and candied fruit cake.

Trevi & Quirinale

Restaurants

Al Presidente

Via in Arcione 94-5 (06 679 7342). Bus 52, 53, 61, 62, 63, 71, 80, 95, 116, 119, 175, 490, 630. **Open** 7.30-11.30pm Tue-Fri; 1-3.30pm, 7.30-11.30pm Sat, Sun. Closed 3wks Aug. **Average** €50. **Credit** DC, MC, V. **Map** p335 2C.

This born-again family restaurant under the towering walls of the Quirinale palace is one of the few really reliable addresses in the *menu-turistico*-dominated Trevi Fountain area. In elegant but restrained surroundings, the Petruccioli family offers a balance between creativity and tradition on a menu that is strong on seafood. *Primi* include a deliciously creamy asparagus and squid soup; the *secondo* of turbot au gratin with crunchy artichokes is excellent; the fine desserts equally convincing. Bonuses

include a good selection of wines by the glass, an intelligent range of taster menus (€45-€60), and a pretty pergola for the summer.

Wine bars & gastropubs

Antica Birreria

Via di San Marcello 19 (06 679 5310). Bus 62, 63, 81, 85, 95, 117, 119, 160, 175, 492, 628, 630, 850. **Open** noon-midnight Mon-Sat. Closed 1wk Aug. **Average** €17. **Credit** AmEx, MC, V. **Map** p335 2C.

Better known by its traditional name, Birreria Peroni, this is the perfect place for a quick lunch or dinner. Service is rough-and-Roman but friendly, and the food – three or four hot pastas, salmon, sausages, caprese salad – is good and relatively cheap. The *birreria* still retains its original art nouveau decor, with a chiaroscuro frieze featuring slogans like 'drink beer and you'll live to be 100'. Avoid the 1-2.30pm rush, when you have to push past the row of regulars eating their pasta standing up at the bar. There are four Peroni beers on draught, including the excellent lager: ask for '*una birra chiara*'.

Vineria il Chianti

Via del Lavatore 81-2 (06 678 7550). Bus 52, 53, 61, 62, 63, 71, 80, 95, 116, 119, 175, 490, 630. **Open** 10am-2.30am Mon-Sat. *Meals served* 12.30-3.30pm, 7.15-11pm Mon-Sat. Closed Aug. **Average** €20. **Credit** AmEx, DC, MC, V. **Map** p335 2C.

In the middle of the Trevi Fountain souvenir belt, this wine bar offers welcome relief from the surrounding tack. As the name suggests, wine, food and decor all have a Tuscan slant – though the service is young, brisk and Roman. The typical lunch menu might feature a couple of filling grain and bean soups, a pasta dish such as *ravioli con i fiori di zucca* (ravioli topped with courgette flowers) and meaty *secondi* such as *abbacchio scottadito* (grilled lamb chops); pizzas make an appearance in the evening. Seating is cosy, not to say cramped. In summer, tables fill the little piazzetta outside.

Snacks & quick meals

For **Antica Birreria**, *see above*; *see also p199* **News Café**.

Caffetteria Borromini

Via XX Settembre 124 (06 488 0866). Metro Barberini/bus 40, 52, 53, 60, 61, 62, 63, 64, 70, 71, 80, 95, 116, 119, 170, 175, 490, 630. **Open** 7.30am-8pm Mon-Fri. *Lunch served* 12.30-3pm Mon-Fri. Closed 1wk Aug. **Credit** AmEx, MC, V. **Map** p335 1B.

This is cheap Italian fast food at its best, with two pasta choices, plenty of *secondi* – from salads to *scamorza al salmone* (grilled cheese with smoked salmon) and real wood-fired pizza, a rarity at lunchtime. All is served up with breathtaking efficiency to hordes of hungry office workers. Allow €10-€12 for two courses and a glass of wine.

Restaurants

For all-round dining pleasure at a fair price
Antico Arco, p183; Al Presidente, p168; Tuttifrutti, p188; Uno e Bino, p197.

For eating outside
Baja, p195; Cecilia Metella, p196; Ar Galletto, p179; Santa Lucia, p175; San Teodoro, p168.

For seeing and being seen
Fiaschetteria Beltramme, p171; Hostaria dell'Orso, p171; Ketumbar, p176; Santa Lucia, p175; Supper Club, p177.

For a cheap lunch
Antica Birreria, p168; Buccone, p223; Caffetteria Borromini, p168; Enoteca Corsi, p175; Osteria del Rione, p177; Sora Margherita, p180; Vic's, p172.

For creative Italian cooking
Agata e Romeo, p189; Al Ponte della Ranocchia, p196; Antico Arco, p183; Boccondivino, p173; Il Convivio, p173; Uno e Bino, p197.

For traditional Roman cooking
Agustarello, p185; Alfredo e Ada, p172; Checchino dal 1887, p185; Marcello, p196;

Osteria dell'Angelo, p192; Osteria del Velodromo Vecchio, p197.

For Italian regional cooking
Hosteria degli Artisti, p189 (Campania); L'Ortica, p196 (Naples); Papà Baccus, p168 (Tuscany); Velando, p195 (Val Camonica).

For fish & seafood
Alberto Ciarla, p181; Osteria del Pesce, p180; Cantina Cantarini, p169.

For vegetarians
Arancia Blu, p195; Il Margutta, p172.

For pizza
Dar Poeta, p183; Da Remo, p188.

For international cuisine
Hang Zhou, p191; Jaipur, p183; Zen, p195.

For wine
Del Frate, p195; Antico Arco, p183; Cavour 313, p192; Checchino dal 1887, p185; Cul de Sac, p175; Ditirambo, p177; Enoteca Ferrara, p184; Il Simposio, p192; Tramonti e Muffati, p197; Uno e Bino, p197.

For aspiring gladiators
Magna Roma, p189.

Eat, Drink, Shop

Veneto & Borghese

Restaurants

Cantina Cantarini
Piazza Sallustio 12 (06 485 528/06 474 3341). Bus 36, 60, 62, 63, 80, 86, 360, 630. **Open** 12.30-3pm, 7.30-10.30pm Mon-Sat. Closed 4wks Aug, 1wk Dec-Jan. **Average** €24. **Credit** AmEx, DC, MC, V. **Map** p335 1A.
This high-quality trattoria in a smart district, offers very reasonable prices to a faithful local clientele. Meat-based for the first part of the week, it turns fishy thereafter. The atmosphere is as *allegro* as seating is tight – though outside tables take off some of the pressure in summer. But the excellent *coniglio al cacciatore* (stewed rabbit), *fritto misto di pesce* (fried mixed fish) and *spaghetti al nero di seppia* (with squid ink) should quell any concerns about comfort.

Papà Baccus
Via Toscana 36 (06 4274 2808). Bus 52, 53, 63, 80, 630. **Open** 12.30-3pm, 7.30-11.30pm Mon-Fri daily. Closed 1wk Aug. **Average** €45. **Credit** AmEx, DC, MC, V. **Map** p334 2B.
If Tuscany isn't on your holiday itinerary, head for Papà Baccus to sample Tuscan cuisine at its best. All the raw materials, from the olive oil to the excellent hams and salamis, are imported from owner Italo Cipriani's native Casentino valley. For starters, try the *ribollita*, a delicious soup made from beans, fresh vegetables and bread, or the tasty *sfoglia di caciotta toscana primosale* (layers of cheese and anchovy with a spinach, pear and walnut salad). There are fishy main courses, but the real forte of Papà Baccus is the *chianina* beefsteak, served with zolfino beans or simply seared. The mark-up on wine is more than reasonable, but staff are attentive without being overbearing.

Where every experience is a common path for tradition and innovation, for design and architecture, for spirit and music and for all that talks of a multisensorial attitude to life.

Frascati & Falesco

The wines of Lazio (the region of which Rome is the capital) have traditionally been looked down on – not without justification – as low-grade fuel for the city's numerous *osterie* and *trattorie*. The local wine industry centres on the rolling, villa-strewn hills of the Castelli romani (*see p292*) east of the city, around the towns of Frascati and Marino; its preference for quantity over quality long acted as a brake on the development of a serious regional wine culture. It has to be said, though, that the poor reputation of wine from the Castelli has also historically been the fault of crafty Roman innkeepers and restaurateurs, who would cut Frascati with cheap Sicilian white to produce a cloudy, urine-coloured brew that at its best could be described as '*onesto*' and at its worst was a handy paint-stripper substitute.

Things have changed, though, as Lazio responds to the general Italian demand for quality wine. The Frascati area still has a small army of farmer-winemakers, who hang a vine branch over the cellar door to show that the new wine is ready to drink straight from the barrel. But it also has some more serious players, ranging from huge industrial wineries in the **Fontana Candida** mould to medium-scale family estates like **Di Mauro (Colli Picchioni)**, **Villa Simone** and **Castel De Paolis**, which have started producing wines of some stature. Fontana Candida's Santa Teresa *cru* is a model of the new clean, lean style of Frascati, while Villa Simone's

Vigneto Filonardi stands up for a more traditional approach: full, fruity and just slightly *abboccato* (tending to sweet).

But compared to the pace of the quality wine explosion further south in Campania or Puglia, things are still moving slowly in Lazio. Perhaps the most interesting developments come from the far north of the region, on the shores of Lake Bolsena, where a single producer, **Falesco**, has overturned the strictly-for-tourists reputation of the curiously named Est Est Est and turned it into an eminently quaffable white that reaches levels of true finesse in the single-vineyard *cru* Poggio dei Gelsi. Falesco also produces a Merlot-based red, Montiano, which has earned a place among the great Italian reds – and is a lot cheaper than many of its rivals. In Falesco's wake, other producers in the same area, from **Sergio Mottura** to **Paolo d'Amico**, are achieving good results. D'Amico's two Chardonnays (Falesia and Calanchi di Vaiano) are among the few really successful Italian manifestations of the international *über*-grape. In the south of the region, the **Casale del Giglio** winery in Aprilia is a rare oasis in the wine desert. Purists sniff at the wide range of non-native grape varieties planted here, but owner Antonio Santarelli is vindicated by some of his convincing reds – notably Mater Matuta (Syrah, Petit Verdot) and Madreselva (Merlot, Cabernet Sauvignon).

Eat, Drink, Shop

The Tridente

Restaurants

See also **Reef** *in p176* **The design crew.**

Fiaschetteria Beltramme

Via della Croce 39 (no phone). Metro Spagna/bus 52, 53, 61, 62, 63, 71, 80, 95, 116, 119, 175, 490, 630. **Open** noon-3pm, 8-11pm Mon-Sat. Closed 2wks Aug. **Average** €28. **No credit cards. Map** p332 2A.
Don't be fooled by the 'no phone, no credit cards' line and the grandma's-front-room decor. This historic trattoria is hugely trendy; Madonna once fled a gala dinner to eat here. Specialities include *tonnarelli cacio e pepe* and *pollo con i peperoni* (chicken with peppers). No bookings (unless you're Madonna).

Gino in vicolo Rosini

Vicolo Rosini 4 (06 687 3434). Bus 52, 53, 61, 62, 63, 71, 80, 95, 116, 119, 175, 490, 630. **Open**

1-2.45pm, 8-10.30pm Mon-Sat. Closed Aug. **Average** €26. **No credit cards. Map** p333 1A.
In a hard-to-find lane around the back of the parliament building, off piazza del Parlamento this unreconstructed neighbourhood osteria is always filled to bursting with MPs, and accompanying political hacks and hangers-on. The cuisine champions the lighter side of the Roman tradition in dishes like *coniglio al vino bianco* (rabbit in white wine) and *zucchine ripiene* (stuffed courgettes); desserts include home-made *crostate* (jam tarts) and an excellent *tiramisù*. Come early, or be prepared to wait for one of the hotly contested tables.

'Gusto

Piazza Augusto Imperatore 9 (06 322 6273). Bus 81, 117, 119, 628, 913, 926. **Open** *Restaurant* 1-3pm, 8pm-midnight daily. *Pizzeria* 12.30-3pm, 7.30pm-1am daily. *Wine bar* 11am-2am daily. **Average** *Restaurant* €47. *Pizzeria* €18. **Credit** AmEx, DC, MC, V. **Map** p333 1A.

The granddaddy of the new breed of Roman designer diners (see p176 **The design crew**), 'Gusto is a multi-purpose, split-level pizzeria, restaurant and wine bar, with a cook's shop (see p214) and bookshop next door. The ground-floor pizza and salad bar is packed with staff from surrounding offices at lunchtime, and with just about everyone in the evening. The wicker-and-beige decor may make you yearn for something more Roman, but the decent pizzas and abundant salads are reasonably priced. Upstairs, the more expensive and pretentious restaurant blends stir-fry with Italian staples, not always convincingly. Service is brisk downstairs, verging on the incompetent upstairs. Perhaps the part that works best is the wine bar out back – buzzing, stylish, and with a good selection of wines by the glass.

Il Margutta

Via Margutta 118 (06 3265 0577). Metro Spagna or Flaminio/bus 117, 119. **Open** 12.30-3.30pm, 7.30-11pm daily. **Average** €34. **Credit** AmEx, DC, MC, V. **Map** p332 2A.
Rome's historic vegetarian diner occupies a large plant-filled space on artsy, exclusive via Margutta. The decor pays homage to the area, with plenty of modern art; on some Tuesday evenings there is live jazz. At lunch, a set-price one-plate buffet (€15, with water and dessert) is an alternative to the more formal restaurant, which offers a meatless slant on modern Italian cuisine, with one or two oriental touches. On Saturday and Sunday there's a filling all-you-can-eat brunch for €25.

Matricianella

Via del Leone 3-4 (06 683 2100). Bus 70, 81, 117, 119, 629. **Open** 12.30-3pm, 7.30-11pm Mon-Sat. Closed Aug. **Average** €34. **Credit** AmEx, DC, MC, V. **Map** p333 1A.
A good example of how to upgrade the Roman family trattoria without betraying its roots. Spread over three cosy rooms, this is a friendly, bustling place with great prices. The Roman imprint is most evident in classics such as *bucatini all'amatriciana*, but there are plenty of more creative options, including a tasty *risotto mantecato* (creamy risotto with courgette flowers) and some great *fritti* (fried dishes), including *bucce di patate* (potato peel). The well-chosen wine list is a model of honest pricing; service is no-nonsense, verging on the abrupt. But once you've eaten here, you'll understand why it's almost always packed. Be sure to book ahead.

Pizzerie

Pizza Ciro

Via della Mercede 43 (06 678 6015). Metro Spagna/bus 52, 53, 61, 62, 63, 71, 80, 95, 116, 119, 175, 490, 630. **Open** 11.30am-1.30am daily. **Average** €18. **Credit cards** AmEx, DC, MC, V. **Map** p335 2C.
From outside it looks like a modest, vaguely touristy pizza parlour. But Ciro is in fact a huge dining factory with 150 covers, many of them in a large back room that houses the pizza oven. The pizzas – of the high-crust Neapolitan variety – are not at all bad, and *primi* such as *tubetti alla Ciro* (with rocket and mussels) provide a decent alternative for those who are doughed out. Technicolor Bay of Naples murals set the design tone; the service is brisk but efficient.

Wine bars & gastropubs

See p201 **Shaki** *and p223* **Buccone**.

Snacks & quick meals

For **Il Margutta**, *see above*; *see also p223* **Buccone**.

Le Pain Quotidien

Via Tomacelli 24-5 (06 6880 7727). Bus 81, 117, 119, 628, 913, 926. **Open** 9am-midnight Tue-Sun. **Credit** AmEx, DC, MC, V. **Map** p333 1A.
The first Italian outlet of the Belgian Le Pain Quotidien chain has been a resounding success. 'Our daily bread' is an organic bakery with dining facilities; but in the Roman branch, the shelves of stone-ground bread and white-capped doughboys are a backdrop to the main act, which is the feeding of hordes of hungry style-bunnies around huge, communal wooden tables. Salads, cheese platters and pâtés dominate the menu, which is supplemented on Saturdays and Sundays by the latest Roman *fighetto* (rich Prada kid) craze: the American brunch. Allow €22 per person for a filling lunch with wine.

Vic's

Vicolo della Torretta 60 (06 687 1445). Bus 52, 53, 61, 62, 63, 71, 80, 95, 116, 119, 175, 490, 630. **Open** 12.30-3pm, 7.30-11pm Mon-Sat. Closed 2wks Aug. **No credit cards**. **Map** p333 1A.
This new-but-old wine and salad bar offers a range of creative salads (€7.50 standard, €9 mega) such as radicchio, pine nuts, sultanas and parmesan. There are also one or two hot pasta or soup dishes, plus *crostini* (toasted bread) with mozzarella and various other toppings, and a good selection of crêpes. Pared-back Roman osteria decor, friendly service and an excellently priced wine list.

Pantheon & Navona

Restaurants

See also p175 **Il Bichiere di Mastai**; **Experanto** *and* **Supper Club** *in p176* **The design crew**.

Alfredo e Ada

Via dei Banchi Nuovi 14 (06 687 8842). Bus 40, 46, 62, 64, 916. **Open** 1-3.30pm, 8-10.30pm Mon-Fri. Closed Aug, 1wk Dec-Jan. **Average** €20. **No credit cards**. **Map** p333 2B.
Zia Ada (Auntie Ada) has been bustling among this restaurant's eight tables since the 1940s. The day's set-price menu is chalked on a board; it generally

includes simple dishes such as *spaghetti aglio e olio* and *spezzatino di vitello con piselli* (veal stew with peas) or *salsiccia con fagioli* (sausage with beans). Dessert consists of a plateful of home-made biscuits that Ada fishes out of a battered tin box.

Armando al Pantheon

Salita de' Crescenzi 31 (06 6880 3034). Bus 30, 40, 46, 62, 63, 64, 70, 81, 87, 116, 492, 628, 780, H/tram 8. **Open** 12.30-3pm, 7.30-11pm Mon-Fri, 12.30-3pm Sat. Closed Aug. **Average** €30. **Credit** AmEx, DC, MC, V. **Map** p333 2A.
Armando is a simple, no-frills trattoria a few yards from the Pantheon, with all the hallmarks of authenticity: cork walls, indifferent artworks, a pretty stained-glass entrance. The menu is almost unchanging (we can vouch personally for the last 19 years), with classics like *fettucine all'Armando* (with mushrooms, peas and tomatoes) or *ossobuco* done reliably but with few pretensions to the major league. The only concessions to changing times are some not always successful vegetarian dishes. Service is friendly, the wine list small but navigable.

Boccondivino

Piazza Campo Marzio 6 (06 6830 8626). Bus 52, 53, 61, 62, 63, 71, 80, 95, 116, 119, 175, 490, 630. **Open** 1-3.30pm, 7.45-11.30pm Mon-Sat. Closed 2wks Aug. **Average** €52. **Credit** AmEx, DC, MC, V. **Map** p333 1A.
A convincing attempt to combine design flair with culinary excellence. The entrance, flanked by two columns from an ancient Roman temple to Mars, give on to a jazzy space with faux-marble walls, a creeper-forest of high-tech lights and zebra-striped wire bucket chairs. The food's good too, with a mod-Med fusion approach that shines with a main-course squid on a bed of potatoes mashed in oil with mullet *bottarga*, or a duck breast with caramelised vegetables and honey sauce. Dinner is à la carte, but at lunch there's a good-value two-course business menu – more traditional Italian than fusion – which is offered with mineral water and house wine at €18.

Il Convivio

Vicolo dei Soldati 31 (06 686 9432/www. ilconviviotroiani.com). Bus 30, 70, 81, 87, 116, 492, 628. **Open** 8-10.30pm Mon; 1-2.30pm, 8-10.30pm Tue-Sat. Closed 1wk Aug. **Average** €82. **Credit** AmEx, DC, MC, V. **Map** p333 1B.
The three Troiani brothers run a high-class act in this temple of foodie excellence just north of piazza Navona. The menu changes with the season and the latest experiments of chef Angelo. An antipasto of *polpettine di seppia con carciofo alla romana* (cuttlefish rissoles with artichoke) is a good example of his approach: a dish from the popular tradition brought into sharp relief by the addition of something a little nouvelle. First courses are equally fine, and the high standard is maintained through the *secondi* – where fresh vegetables, meat, game and seafood all take equal billing – and the spectacular desserts (don't miss the *zabaione* ice-cream with praline almonds and balsamic vinegar). The cellar is

Sicilian influences at **Il Fico**.

extensive (but expensive), with a wide range of non-Italian labels. For Convivio beginners, there is a six-dish taster menu, priced at €75.

Il Fico

Piazza del Fico 25 (06 687 5568). Bus 40, 46, 62, 64, 916. **Open** *Apr-Oct* noon-2.30pm, 6.30pm-1am Tue-Thur; 6.30pm-1am Fri-Sun. *Oct-Apr* noon-2.30pm, 6.30pm-1am Fri-Sun. **Credit** AmEx, DC, MC, V. **Average** €20. **Map** p333 2B.
Next to the bar of the same name but no longer under the same management, the 'Fig Tree' specialises in seafood but in winter can have as many meat dishes as fish *piatti*. A southern influence is evident in dishes like Sicilian-style *pesce spada* (swordfish in a tomato, caper and olive sauce) and *caponata*, a vegetable ratatouille. The seafood lasagna is tasty, if a bit heavy and oversauced. Outdoor seating on a lovely piazza in the summer is a plus. Otherwise, try the very back room to avoid the neglected suburban trattoria-style front room.

Hostaria dell'Orso

Via dei Soldati 25C (06 6830 1192/www. hostariadellorso.it). Bus 30, 70, 81, 87, 116, 492, 628. **Open** 8-11.30pm Mon; 1-3pm, 8-11.30pm Tue-

IL BACARO ROMA

sfizi ai fornelli

Via degli Spagnoli, 27
Roma
tel.06 6864110
www.ilbacaro.com

**OPEN
TO LATE NIGHT**
(closed Sunday)
Reservations advisable

Sat. **Average** €100. Closed 2wks Aug. **Credit** AmEx, DC, MC, V. **Map** p333 1B.

Milanese superchef Gualtiero Marchesi rose to fame in the 1970s and 1980s with a series of flashy signature dishes like *riso oro e zafferano* (saffron risotto with gold leaf on top). In an attempt to boost some top-rank glamour into Rome's dining scene, the city council brought Marchesi in when this 15th-century palazzo was restored in 2002, but this pricey 'Bar-Restaurant-Discotheque' is showing signs of tarnish and fatigue before it has even got up to speed. Under Renaissance beams and friezes, a bare scene is enlivened only by bright orange leather chairs. A pyramid of rice, blackened with squid ink and spiced up with ginger is typical of the Marchesi approach: a tasty, showy, but unexalted talking point for the VIP (or aspiring VIP) clientele this place is obviously angling for. You can opt for a €135 evening *menu degustazione*; but if famous chefs are your thing, you'll eat much better for the same money chez Heinz Beck at La Pergola (*see p196*).

Santa Lucia

Largo Febo 12 (06 6880 2427). Bus 30, 70, 81, 87, 116, 492, 628. **Open** 12.30-3pm, 8pm-midnight Mon, Wed-Sun. Closed 2wks Aug. **Average** €40. **Credit** MC, V. **Map** p333 2B.

The most recent venture of mover 'n' shaker Bar della Pace (*see p201*) founder Bartolo Cuomo is this late-opening bar/restaurant in a pretty, shady square next to piazza Navona. The decor is a stylish collision between a Roman antique shop and a Moroccan hotel; outside, when the weather permits, tables are arranged in the lovely raised piazza. The food has a vaguely Neapolitan slant – *antipasti* like *pizzelle* (puffy mini-pizzas) and *gattò di patate* (potato flan) are followed by good seafood and vegetable pasta dishes; most clients then skip straight to the succulent desserts. It pays to book ahead, though a few tables are always reserved for those who just want a drink and room can always be found for passing film stars.

Pizzerie

Da Francesco

Piazza del Fico 29 (06 686 4009). Bus 40, 46, 62, 64, 916. **Open** noon-2.55pm, 7pm-12.45am Mon, Wed-Sun; 7pm-12.45am Tue. **Average** €18. **No credit cards. Map** p333 2B.

Accept no imitations: Da Francesco is the genuine *centro storico* pizzeria article. No bookings are taken: if you get there before 8pm, you generally walk right on in; if you get there much after, you join the huge, milling throng. The reasons for this popularity are very simple: tasty pizzas; a warm, traditional ambience; brisk but friendly service; and a range of competent, classic *primi* and *secondi* for those who can't face a doughy disc. You often get the distinct feeling that they are rushing you through to free up the table – but that's the price you pay for such a central bargain diner.

Wine bars & gastropubs

Il Bicchiere di Mastai

Via dei Banchi Nuovi 52 (06 6819 2228). Bus 40, 46, 62, 64, 916. **Open** 11am-1am Tue-Sun. **Open** noon-3pm, 7pm-1am Tue-Sun. **Average** €45. **Credit** AmEx, DC, MC, V. **Map** p333 2B.

This new gourmet wine bar is a good place if your're looking for an affordably high-class lunch or dinner without indulging in all the traditional meal trappings. The atmosphere is relaxing, the decor country-house chic and the food decidedly ambitious. A selection of enoteca staples – cheese and cured meats – serve as the permanent *antipasti*, but the rest of the menu changes every week. The approach is creative Italian: dishes like broccoli mousse with onions and smoked duck, or *cavatelli* pasta with aubergine and pesto sauce are mostly (though not invariably) convincing. At via dei Banchi Nuovi 54, a restaurant branch (open dinner only, Tue-Sat) is a more four-course blow-out affair.

Casa Bleve

Via del Teatro Valle 48-9 (06 686 5970). **Open** 8am-10pm Mon-Sat. Closed Aug. **Average** €22. **Credit** AmEx, DC, MC, V. **Map** p336 1B.

Once squeezed in among the bottle-laden shelves of one of the best *centro storico* wine shops (La Bottega del Vino da Anacleto Bleve, via Santa Maria del Pianto 9-11, Ghetto, open 8am-8pm Mon-Sat), this high-class lunchtime buffet operation has moved into new premises near the Senate building. The food is fresh and simple, with mixed salads, plates of *formaggi misti* (mixed cheeses) or salami and carpaccio, plus one or two daily specials. The menu of wines by the glass is select, but prices can be a tad steep compared to other venues.

Cul de Sac

Piazza Pasquino 73 (06 6880 1094). Bus 30, 40, 46, 62, 63, 64, 70, 81, 87, 492, 628, 780, H/tram 8. **Open** noon-4pm, 7pm-12.30am daily. **Average** €16. **Credit** MC, V. **Map** p333 2B.

This was Rome's first-ever wine bar, a major breakthrough on Rome's eating scene when it was founded in 1968. Looking fairly traditional nowadays, it's cramped inside and out: pine benches and tables, and decidedly no frills. But the location – just off piazza Navona, with a ringside view of the 'talking statue' of Pasquino (*see p99* **Vox pop**) – coupled with reasonable prices and an encyclopaedic wine list ensure full occupancy all the time. Food is standard wine-bar fare, with mainly cold dishes: the generous Greek salad and the signature lentil soup stand out from the rest.

Enoteca Corsi

Via del Gesù 87-8 (06 679 0821). Bus 30, 40, 46, 62, 63, 64, 70, 81, 87, 492, 628, 780, H. **Open** noon-3pm Mon-Sat. Closed 4wks Aug. **Average** €18. **Credit** AmEx, DC, MC, V. **Map** p336 1A.

This 1940s wine shop was the first in Rome to begin serving lunch, and is now more trattoria than

The design crew

Why has the designer restaurant bug taken so long to infect Rome? Easy: because for Romans, what's on the plate always takes precedence over what's on the walls. British designer-eats guru Terence Conran once said that he was spurred on by the challenge of bringing visual stimuli to bear on what was essentially a literary culture (note: no mention of food). Those trying to shake up the Roman restaurant scene are faced by a different challenge: convincing people that cutting-edge design and culinary excellence really can go together.

But the resistance to new-fangled dining experiences is giving way. Spearheaded by design hotels like the **Es Hotel** (see p53), where rooftop restaurants have attracted plenty of outside custom, a cohort of stand-alone restaurants has opened in the last three or four years. These are five of the best.

Experanto

Corso Rinascimento 66, Pantheon & Navona (06 686 1312). Bus 30, 70, 81, 87, 116, 492, 628. **Open** *8pm-midnight Mon-Sat.* **Credit** *AmEx, DC, MC, V.* **Fixed price** *€40 or €50.* **Map** *p333 2A.*
This restaurant with white chairs and colourful place settings (*pictured*) has a maitre d' who could pass for Austin Powers' Italian uncle. The food, though, is eclectic Mediterranean. The daily changing *menù al buio* ('shot in the dark') is a five- or six-course taster affair: you choose meat or fish then take what comes. On our visit, the seafood soup with zabaglione was a rich mix of salty and sweet, the baked ricotta with radicchio was boring and the pan-seared halibut was well prepared if a bit bland. The *mousse al fico d'india* (prickly pear) was an interesting closing dish.

enoteca. The daily-changing menu is written up on the board at the entrance. Dishes on offer follow the traditional Roman culinary calendar – potato *gnocchi* on Thursdays and stewed *baccalà* (salt cod) on Fridays. A slice of ricotta tart followed by an espresso make a fitting end to a hearty meal. No bookings are taken, so get there early or be prepared to queue on workdays.

Snacks & quick lunches

See also p175 **Cul de Sac**; *p175* **Enoteca Corsi**; *p181* **L'Insalata Ricca**; *p202* **Trinity College**.

Ketumbar

Via Galvani 24, Testaccio (06 5730 5338). Bus 95, 170, 673/tram 3. **Open** *8-11.30pm daily. Closed Aug.* **Average** *€46.* **Credit** *AmEx, DC, MC, V.* **Map** *p337 2A.*
The setting couldn't be more Roman, in the flank of Monte Testaccio (see p125), but the decor is modern Buddha Bar-ethnic. Ever-trendy Ketumbar actually works better now than it did during its frenetic, air-kissing early days. The fusion fare has its ups and downs: the ups on our most recent visit were the spaghetti with courgettes, mint, red mullet and ginger, and the gilthead bream and vegetables wrapped in sweetcorn leaves and grilled Vietnamese-style. The wine list is small but decently priced and service is surprisingly affable. Best of all, the resident DJ has turned down his ambient music so you can hear yourself speak. If you're in a rush, down a plate of pasta and glass of wine at the bar, which stays open until around 2am.

ReD

Via P De Coubertin 30, Suburbs: north (06 8069 1630). Bus 53, 217, 910. **Open** *Bar 10am-3am daily. Restaurant 12.30-2.30pm, 8pm-midnight daily.* **Average** *€45.* **Credit** *AmEx, DC, MC, V.*
The name stands for 'Restaurant and Design', which aptly describes this new locale inside the Parco della Musica (see p254). There's a vast selection of wines, cheese and *salumi* at the bar. The restaurant – run by veterans of restaurants, *enoteche*, public relations and interior design – successfully fuses high style and haute cuisine at reasonable prices. Pasta dishes include *cappellaci* of buffalo milk ricotta with home-made butter and balsamic vinegar. For

Lo Zozzone

Via del Teatro Pace 32 (06 6880 8575). Bus 40, 46, 62, 64, 916. **Open** *9am-9pm Mon-Sat. Closed Aug.* **No credit cards. Map** *p333 2B.*
Now in new, more spacious premises with (gasp!) outside tables, the 'dirty old man' (an affectionate Roman nickname that became official with the move) serves up Rome's best *pizza bianca ripiena* – which, as a sign explains, is 'White Pizza With Any Thing You Like Inside' – a variety of hams, cheeses, fresh figs, dried tomatoes and other delights. Pay at the till for a regular (€2), large (€2.50) or huge (€3) piece; then join the receipt-waving hordes to get served. There are plans to open on Sundays too.

secondi, try the shrimp with rosemary, garlic and chilli pepper on a bed of cheesy pecorino polenta. Instead of a doggy bag, take home a chair: the furniture is for sale.

Reef
Piazza Augusto Imperatore 47, Tridente (06 6830 1430). Bus 81, 117, 119, 628, 913, 926. **Open** *8-11.30pm Mon-Fri; 1-3pm, 8-11.30pm Sat, Sun. Closed 3wks Aug.* **Average** €55. **Credit** AmEx, DC, MC, V. **Map** p332 2A.

With its cracked-glass walls, pale wood and soaring ceilings, Reef is a hip, sleek novelty – more London in feel than Rome. While by no means good value, it does offers decent, Med-Asian seafood cooking in original surroundings. The raw seafood *antipasto* for two is fresh, if a bit bland; but the *zuppa di ceci, polpo e rosmarino* (puréed chickpea soup with octopus and rosemary) sings with flavour and velvety texture. Mains run from sushi and sashimi to creative Italian dishes like swordfish baked in a sesame crust.

Supper Club
Via dei Nari 14, Pantheon & Navona (06 6880 7207/www.supperclub.com). Bus 30, 40, 46, 62, 63, 64, 70, 81, 87, 492, 628, 780, H/tram 8. **Open** *9pm-midnight Mon-Sat. Closed 1wk Aug.* **Fixed price** €55, not incl drinks. **Credit** AmEx, DC, MC, V. **Map** p333 2A.

This designer diner shares its name and inspiration with Amsterdam's Supper Club, but this is a much more Roman experience. A former warehouse has been turned into a series of interconnecting chill-out caverns. The evening's guests – who must book ahead – are ushered into the bar; then at 9pm, they proceed to the main dining area, a vaulted space with a huge central divan-raft beneath faded baroque frescos. Climb over the back of the sofa to your table, then sit cross-legged or recline while the waiters prowl the perimeter, trying and mostly failing to reach the tables. A DJ in the corner mixes ambient sounds, backed up around half-time by a sultry torch singer or other live acts. The fixed (but daily changing) four-course fusion menu has its hits (on a recent visit, a starter of vegetable rissoles with Parma ham and rocket sorbet) and misses (the *mezzelune* of celeriac and seafood), and the wine list has too few bottles at too steep a mark-up. But this is hardly the point: you come for the ambience.

Ghetto & Campo de' Fiori

Restaurants

Ditirambo
Piazza della Cancelleria 74 (06 687 1626). Bus 30, 40, 46, 62, 63, 64, 70, 81, 87, 492, 628, 780, H/tram 8. **Open** *8-11.30pm Mon; 1-3pm, 8-11.30pm Tue-Sun. Closed 3wks Aug.* **Average** €30. **Credit** MC, V. **Map** p336 1B.

This funky trattoria around the corner from campo de' Fiori has good-value food based on fresh, mainly organic ingredients. It does traditional fare with a creative kick, as in the *malfatti* pasta with courgette flowers. Meaty *secondi* include a decent fillet steak with balsamic vinegar. The brusque service doesn't put off the local punters, so do book ahead.

Filetti di Baccalà
Largo Librai 88 (06 686 4018). Bus 63, 630, 780, H/tram 8. **Open** *5-10.30pm Mon-Sat.* **Average** €15. **No credit cards. Map** p336 1B.

The official name is Dar Filettaro a Santa Barbara, but the general public takes its cue from the sign over the door, which promises exactly what you get: fried, battered salt cod fillets. But *what* fillets… perfectly crispy outside and tender inside, this quin-

The Drunken Ship

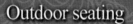

Enjoy a narghile, ful and backgammon at **Sciam**. *See p180.*

tessentially Roman dish is served with sides like fried courgettes rather than chips. Service is brisk and ambience lacking, but the prices can't be beat.

Ar Galletto

Piazza Farnese 102 (06 686 1714). Bus 30, 40, 46, 62, 63, 64, 70, 81, 87, 492, 628, 780, H/ tram 8. **Open** 12.15-3pm, 7.30-11.15pm Mon-Sat. Closed 10 days Aug. **Average** €28. **Credit** AmEx, DC, MC, V. **Map** p336 1B.

You don't need to pay the inflated prices charged by other trats around here for a ringside view of piazza Farnese. Humbler than the competition, Ar Galletto has tables on the square in summer. The food is standard Roman, but dishes like *penne all'arrabbiata* or *spaghetti alle vongole* are appetising and – for the location – well priced.

Da Giggetto

Via Portico d'Ottavia 21A-22 (06 686 1105). Bus 23, 63, 280, 630, 780, H/tram 8. **Open** 12.30-3pm, 7.30-11pm Tue-Sun. Closed 2wks July. **Average** €30. **Credit** AmEx, DC, MC, V. **Map** p336 1A.

In this standby in the Jewish Ghetto, a troop of old-fashioned waiters serves up decent versions of the classics of *cucina ebraica* like *carciofi alla giudia* (fried whole artichokes) and fried *baccalà* (salt cod). The atmosphere is warm and bustling, with large tables of tourists – both Italian and foreign – enjoying the ambience and the plentiful helpings. The unexpectedly extensive wine list has reasonable mark-ups. In warm weather, outside tables have a view of first-century Portico d'Ottavia (*see p113*).

Il Gonfalone

Via del Gonfalone 7 (06 6880 1269). Bus 23, 40, 46, 62, 64, 116, 280, 916. **Open** 7.45-11pm Tue-Sun. Closed 2wks Aug. **Average** €32. **Credit** AmEx, DC, MC, V. **Map** p333 2B.

In this reasonably priced creative Italian restaurant housed in a Renaissance palazzo, Chilean chef Victor Hugo (yes, that's his real name) changes the menu every two weeks. So you're unlikely to find the pasta with swordfish, sultanas and pine nuts, or the antipasto of *bresaola* (thinly sliced dried beef) with pink grapefruit in a honey vinaigrette that we enjoyed on our last visit; but whatever is on offer should be good. In summer, the little piazza outside is a charming place for an alfresco meal. A well-chosen wine list is overseen by one of the owners of the Cavour 313 wine bar (*see p192*). Book ahead.

Osteria del Pesce

Via di Monserrato 32 (06 686 5617). Bus 46, 64, 116. **Open** 7.30pm-midnight Mon-Sat. **Credit** AmEx, DC, MC, V. **Average** €57. **Map** p333 2B.

Despite the name ('Fish Inn') this is no spit and sawdust trat-with-fish but a hip restaurant with an 'in' clientele, serving nothing but simply prepared, super-fresh seafood. Quality fish in Rome costs, but you can certainly pay more elsewhere. The atmosphere is casual – all dark wood and terracotta, subtle lighting, and a huge red chilli pepper behind the bar. Relax and enjoy a tuna carpaccio appetiser, then proceed to a seafood pasta, or skip to *secondi* like fresh langoustines, sea bass or snapper prepared to order (sautéed or grilled). The wine list is white-only, but the selection of liqueurs and *digestivi* vast.

Sora Lella

Via Ponte Quattro Capi 16 (06 686 1601). Bus 23, 63, 280. **Open** 12.50-2.20pm, 7.50-10.45pm Mon-Sat. Closed Aug. **Average** €45. **Credit** AmEx, DC, MC, V. **Map** p336 2A.

Sora Lella was a sort of Roman celebrity Queen Mum and TV star. Her son set up this upmarket trattoria on the Tiber island in her honour after she died in 1993. It avoids folksy kitsch and offers good Roman cooking, with filling classics such as *pasta e patate* (pasta and potatoes) or *gnocchi all'amatriciana* playing off against more creative options like *paccheri al sugo di pesce* (pasta in fish sauce) or *filetto al Cesanese del Piglio* (beef fillet in a sauce made from a red Lazio wine). Some dishes fail to reach the peaks and prices are a little high for what you get, but the ambience is warm and welcoming, service efficient and the wine cellar well stocked.

Sora Margherita

Piazza delle Cinque Scole 30 (06 687 4216). Bus 23, 63, 280, 630, 780, H/tram 8. **Open** 12.30-3pm Tue-Fri, Sun; 12.30-3pm, 8-10.30pm Sat. Closed Aug (maybe). **Average** €20. **No credit cards**. **Map** p336 1A.

A long shut-down had aficionados worrying about makeovers, but this wonderful Ghetto osteria is back, looking just as splendidly down-at-heel as before. The only difference is the new extended opening hours, which now stretch to dinner on Saturdays, when guests have to become members of the restaurant's *associazione sportiva* (it costs, and means, nothing... just a licensing arrangement). Sora Margherita is not for health freaks, but no one argues with serious Roman Jewish cooking at these prices. The classic pasta and meat dishes on offer include a superlative *pasta e fagioli, tonnarelli cacio e pepe* and *ossobuco* washed down with rough-and-ready house wine. Dessert consists of good, home-made *crostate* (jam or ricotta tarts).

International

Sciam

Via del Pellegrino 56 (06 6830 8957). Bus 40, 46, 62, 64, 916. **Open** 2pm-2am daily. **Average** €20. **Credit** AmEx, MC, V. **Map** p333 2B.

Next to a shop that restores Persian rugs and sells Middle Eastern glass tableware and baubles is an Ottoman café: entering here feels like leaving 21st-century Rome and stumbling into 19th-century Constantinople. The food is simple meze fare: tabouleh, houmous, ful damasco (fava beans with olive oil, lemon, tomato and parsley) and other Syrian classics – all entirely vegetarian. They average €4 a portion, but you get six for the price of five. There's no alcohol – have a mint tea or mango juice instead. Or if you really want to get in the mood, order a narghile (hubble-bubble pipe) and commandeer the backgammon board.

Wine bars & gastropubs

L'Angolo Divino

Via dei Balestrari 12 (06 686 4413). Bus 30, 40, 46, 62, 63, 64, 70, 81, 87, 116, 492, 628, 780, H/tram 8. **Open** *Oct-Mar* 10am-2.30pm Mon; 10am-2.30pm, 5.30pm-1am Tue-Sun. *Apr-Sept* 10am-2.30pm Mon; 10am-2.30pm, 5.30pm-1am Tue-Sat; 5.30pm-1am Sun. Closed 1wk Aug. **Average** €15. **Credit** MC, V. **Map** p333 2B.

Over 20 reds, whites and dessert wines are available by the glass, many more by the bottle, at this punningly named bar on a quiet street near campo de' Fiori. There's a good range of smoked fish, salami and salads, a vast selection of cheeses, plus some hot dishes in winter. The furniture is basic, the mood – stoked by a gentle jazz soundtrack – laid-back.

Snacks & quick lunches

Bruschetteria degli Angeli

Piazza B Cairoli 2A (06 6880 5789). Bus 23, 63, 280, 630, 780, H/tram 8. **Open** 12.30-3pm, 7.30pm-1am Mon-Sat. Closed 1wk Aug. **Credit** AmEx, DC, MC, V. **Map** p336 1B.

This unpretentious, pub-like diner overlooks a dusty park, set back from via Arenula. As the name suggests, the star turns are *bruschette* (average €7.50) – thick toasted bread, here in mega format, with various toppings from red chicory and bacon to grilled courgettes and mozzarella. There's also pasta, grilled steaks and a good range of draught beers.

Da Giovanni

Campo de' Fiori 39 (06 687 7992). Bus 30, 40, 46, 62, 63, 64, 70, 81, 87, 116, 492, 628, 780, H/tram 8. **Open** *Nov-Apr* 9am-3pm, 5-9pm Mon-Sat. *May-Oct* 9am-3pm, 5pm-2am Mon-Sat. Closed Aug. **No credit cards**. **Map** p333 2B.

Giovanni does the best takeaway sliced pizza in the campo de' Fiori area. Check out the one with *fiori di zucca* (courgette flowers).

Pasta burn-out? Grab a kebab at **Le Piramidi**.

L'Insalata Ricca

Largo dei Chiavari 85 (06 6880 3656). Bus 30, 40,
46, 62, 63, 64, 70, 81, 87, 116, 492, 628, 780,
H/tram 8. **Open** noon-3.30pm, 6.30-11.30pm daily.
Credit AmEx, DC, MC, V. **Map** p333 2A&B.
L'Insalata Ricca is a good answer to that classic
Roman dilemma – where to go when you're dying
for a decent salad. The Anglo-Italian menu lists over
30 different types, from *baires* (walnuts, apple and
melted gorgonzola) to *speck* (with ham, fontina
cheese and croutons). The success of L'Insalata
Ricca has led to a rash of lookalikes scattered around
the city; the mothership remains the best.
Branch: piazza Pasquino 72 (06 6830 7881).

Le Piramidi

Vicolo del Gallo 11 (06 687 9061). Bus 30, 40, 46,
62, 63, 64, 70, 81, 87, 116, 492, 628, 780, H/
tram 8. **Open** 10.30am-11pm Tue-Sun. Closed 3wks
Aug. **No credit cards. Map** p336 1B.
Around the corner from campo de' Fiori, Le Piramidi
makes for a welcome change from takeaway pizza.
The range of Middle Eastern takeaway fare is small,
but it's all fresh, cheap and tasty.

Zi' Fenizia

Via Santa Maria del Pianto 64 (06 689 6976). Bus
23, 63, 280, 630, 780, H/tram 8. **Open** 9am-7pm
Mon-Thur, Sun; 9am-3.30pm Fri. Closed Jewish
holidays. **No credit cards. Map** p336 1A.
Rome's only kosher pizza outlet. Auntie Fenizia does
over 40 flavours, including the house speciality: *aliciotti e indivia* (anchovies and endives).

Trastevere & Gianicolo

Restaurants

Alberto Ciarla

Piazza San Cosimato 40 (06 581 8668/www.
albertociarla.com). Bus 780, H/tram 8. **Open**
8.30pm-midnight Mon-Sat. Closed 1wk Aug,
1wk Jan. **Average** €68. **Credit** AmEx, DC, MC, V.
Map p336 2B.
The reputation of this restaurant is stuck in the same
1960s time warp as the decor. But Alberto Ciarla is
still one of Rome's best fish restaurants – and a meal
here is not prohibitive, especially if you opt for one
of the taster menus. A trademark dish like *spigola
con le erbe* (sea bass with herbs) strikes the right balance between art and nature, while a *primo* of *pasta
e fagioli con le cozze* (pasta and beans with mussels)
is strong, decisive and very Roman. The menu is a
triumph of *dolce vita* typography, the overriding
mood one of charmingly courteous camp.

Alle Fratte di Trastevere

Via delle Fratte di Trastevere 49-50 (06 583 5775).
Bus 23, 280, 780, H/tram 8. **Open** *Sept-Apr* 12.30-
3pm, 6.30-11.30pm Mon, Tue, Thur-Sun. *May-Aug*
6.30pm-1.30am Mon, Tue, Thur-Sun. Closed 2wks
Aug. **Average** €25. **Credit** AmEx, DC, MC, V.
Map p336 2B.
Trastevere has its fair share of traditional, family-
run *trattorie*, but the cheap and cheerful Alle Fratte
has got to be one of the best. It does honest Roman

trattoria fare with Neapolitan influences and the service is friendly, attentive and bilingual (the owner's wife is from Long Island). First courses like *pennette alla sorrentina* (penne pasta with tomatoes and mozzarella) are served up in generous portions. *Secondi* include oven-roast sea bream, veal escalopes in marsala and a good grilled beef fillet. Desserts are home-made; the post-prandial *digestivi* flow freely.

Antico Arco

Piazzale Aurelio 7 (06 581 5274). Bus 44, 75, 710, 870. **Open** *7.30pm-midnight Mon-Sat. Closed 3wks Aug.* **Average** *€47.* **Credit** *AmEx, DC, MC, V.* **Map** *p336 2C.*
Dinner at this relaxed creative Italian restaurant on the Gianicolo hill – right behind Porta San Pancrazio – is always a pleasure, and still represents excellent value for money. The soothing modern decor makes up for the lack of a view and the service is mostly attentive – though it can get a little terse at peak periods. The menu is strong on all fronts, from the *antipasti*, which include an outstanding onion flan with a piccant grana cheese sauce, to the *primi*, where Antico Arco classics like the risotto with castelmagno cheese are flanked by recent innovations such as the ravioli filled with potatoes and squid in an olive broth. The *secondi* cover the board from meat to fish to game and the choreographic desserts are no letdown. Maurizio, the *sommelier*, can help you steer a course through an extensive, well-priced wine list. It's hugely popular, so book at least a couple of days in advance.

Paris

Piazza San Callisto 7A (06 581 5378). Bus 780, H/tram 8. **Open** *12.30-2.50pm, 7.45-11pm Tue-Sat; 12.30-3pm Sun. Closed 3wks Aug.* **Average** *€45.* **Credit** *AmEx, DC, MC, V.* **Map** *p336 2B.*
Don't be fooled by the name: this upmarket restaurant is militantly Roman. It's one of the few places where you can still sample *minestra di arzilla ai broccoli* (skate soup with broccoli). Paris highlights the Jewish side of the city's culinary traditions, most obviously in the succulent *gran fritto vegetale con bacalà* (a fry-up of artichokes, courgettes and their flowers and salt cod). Service is a little slow at times, but reassuringly old-fashioned, like the decor. In summer, there are a few tables outside in the square.

Vizi Capitali

Vicolo della Renella 94 (06 581 8840/www. vizicapitali.com). Buses 23, 280, 780, H/tram 8. **Open** *7pm-midnight Mon-Sat.* **Average** *€30.* **Credit** *AmEx, DC, MC, V.* **Map** *p336 2B.*
Neither break-the-bank nor trattoria casual, this recent opening shoots for a sophisticated clientele with an interesting mix of dishes and flavours. The tasty shellfish and crustacean soup with cherry tomatoes and grilled bread is a tasty starter. Pastas are flavourful, like the *tonnarelli* with scampi, pears and parmesan. Stick with straightforward *secondi* like the Argentinian beef or the *gran misto di mare* (mixed seafood grill). The dessert menu is extensive

and all made *à la minute*, so indulge in a molten chocolate cake or the delicious apple strudel. Service is a bit slow, but enthusiastic and gracious.

International

Jaipur

Via di San Francesco a Ripa 56 (06 580 3992). Bus 780, H/tram 8. **Open** *7pm-midnight Mon; noon-3pm, 7pm-midnight Tue-Sun.* **Average** *€28.* **Credit** *DC, MC, V.* **Map** *p337 1B.*
Jaipur does some of Rome's best Indian food, and it's good value too – which helps make up for this recent arrival's garish lighting and colour scheme. The menu ranges from basic starters to a large selection of tandoori specials, curries and murghs (the *murgh maccan*, charcoal-grilled chicken with a butter-tomato gravy, is particularly tasty). There are two pages of vegetarian dishes, including an outstanding *baighan bharta* (aubergine purée cooked in a clay oven, dressed with spices).

Pizzerie

Da Ivo

Via di San Francesco a Ripa 158 (06 581 7082). Bus 780, H/tram 8. **Open** *6pm-1am Mon, Wed-Sat; 12.30-3pm, 6pm-1am Sun. Closed 2wks Sept.* **Average** *€15.* **Credit** *AmEx, DC, MC, V.* **Map** *p336 2B.*
Throngs of waiting clients in the narrow street outside flag what must be one of Rome's most famous pizzerias. Inside, 200 hungry souls are jammed into a space that would be very tight for half that number, but the atmosphere is electric (especially on match days, when conversation-stopping TV absorbs all sight lines), the pizza's acceptable and the service prompt if inelegant. There's also a decent range of pasta dishes too.

Dar Poeta

Vicolo del Bologna 45 (06 588 0516). Bus 23, 280, 780, H/tram 8. **Open** *7.30pm-midnight daily.* **Average** *€20.* **Credit** *AmEx, MC, V.* **Map** *p336 2B.*
Dar Poeta's offerings have fluffy bases and creative toppings, including the namesake pizza (with courgettes, sausage and spicy pepper) and the *bodrilla* (with apples and Grand Marnier). The varied *bruschette* are first-rate and healthy salads offer a break from pastry. Leave room for dessert, as the sweet *calzone* stuffed with Nutella and ricotta is to die for. You can eat till late and the waiters are genuinely friendly, but be prepared to queue, as they don't take bookings.

Da Vittorio

Via di San Cosimato 14A (06 580 0353). Bus 780, H/tram 8. **Open** *7.30pm-midnight Mon-Sat.* **Average** *€18.* **Credit** *MC, V.* **Map** *p336 2B.*
Vittorio was here way before Neapolitan pizzas caught on in Rome and will no doubt still be here when the fad has passed. He's as expansively

Eat, Drink, Shop

Reading the menu

Pasti – *meals*
prima colazione breakfast; **pranzo** lunch;
cena supper; **uno spuntino** a snack.

Materie prime – basic ingredients
aceto vinegar; **latte** milk; **limone** lemon;
olio d'oliva olive oil; **pane** bread; **pepe**
pepper; **sale** salt; **zucchero** sugar.

Modi di cottura – *cooking techniques*
al dente cooked, but still firm; **al forno**
baked; **al sangue** rare (for steaks); **al vapore**
steamed; **alla griglia, grigliato, alla piastra**
grilled; **bollito** boiled; **cotto** cooked; **crudo**
raw; **fritto** fried; **in bianco** plain, just with oil
or butter (rice, pasta) or no tomato (pizza);
in brodo in clear meat broth; **all'acqua**
pazza (of fish) in thin broth; **ripassato in**
padella (of vegetables) fried with garlic and
chilli after boiling or steaming; **in umido**
poached; **stufato** stewed; **brasato** braised.

Antipasti – *hors-d'oeuvres*
alici marinati marinated anchovies;
antipasto di mare seafood hors-d'oeuvre;
antipasto misto mixed hors-d'oeuvre (usually
marinated vegetables and cold cuts);
bresaola dry-cured beef; **bruschetta** toast

with garlic, oil and optional tomatoes; **fiori**
di zucca fried courgette flowers stuffed with
mozzarella and anchovy; **olive ascolane**
olives in breadcrumb-and-mincemeat coats;
prosciutto cotto/crudo/con melone cured
ham/raw (Parma) ham/ham with melon;
salumi charcuterie.

Pasta, sughi e condimenti – *pasta, sauces*
and toppings
spaghetti alle vongole spaghetti with clams
(usually *in bianco*, without tomatoes); **ravioli**
ricotta e spinaci ravioli stuffed with cottage
cheese and spinach, often served with *burro*
e salvia (butter and sage); **agnolotti, tortellini**
similar to ravioli but usually meat-filled;
fettucine long flat pasta strips; **tonnarelli**
like large spaghetti, square in cross-section;
cannelloni long pasta rolls, designed
for filling; **rigatoni** short pasta tubes;
orecchiette ear- or hat-shaped pasta discs,
often served with a broccoli sauce; **al pesto**
with a sauce of pine nuts, pecorino and basil;
al pomodoro fresco with fresh, raw tomatoes;
al ragù 'bolognese' (this term is not used
by Italians), ie with minced meat and
tomatoes; **al sugo** with puréed cooked

napoletano as they come and so are his succulent
pizzas, which include the self-celebratory Vittorio
(mozzarella, parmesan, fresh tomato and basil). Kids
will delight in his heart-shaped junior specials. The
place is minute, but bursts with exuberance.

Wine bars & gastropubs

Enoteca Ferrara

Piazza Trilussa 41A (06 5833 3920). Bus 23, 280,
780, H/tram 8. **Open** *Wine shop* 10am-3pm, 5.30pm-
2am daily. *Meals served* Oct-Apr 12.30-3pm, 7.30-
11.30pm daily; May-Sept 12.30-3pm, 7.30-11.30pm
Mon-Sat. **Average** €38. **Credit** DC, MC, V.
Map p336 2B.
In a surprisingly large space for Trastevere,
the Paolillo sisters run a tasteful imbibery with an
850-label cellar. The apartheid wine lists (one book
for whites, one for reds) provide a happy evening's
reading. Some punters come to Ferrara to buy a
bottle, some for a pre- or post-dinner glass of wine,
some overcome the slight diffidence of the bar staff
and succumb to one of the wholesome-looking
dishes on the counter. The more serious eater, however, books in advance and takes advantage of the
restaurant's inventive offerings, including mussel
and clam soup and fried fillet of perch, served with
red cabbage and lemon. Most days there's a set

menu too (€55, without wine). Expect to spend
around €12 for a glass of wine and a quick snack.
From May to September you can wine and dine in a
pretty garden at the back.

Snacks & quick meals

See also *p205* **Enoteca Trastevere**, *p203*
Friends Art Café, *p205* **Ombre Rosse**.

I Dolci di Checco er Carrettiere

Via Benedetta 7 (06 581 1413). Bus 23, 280, 780,
H/tram 8. **Open** 6.30am-2am Tue-Sun. **No credit**
cards. Map p336 2B.
Located behind piazza Trilussa, this small bar,
annexed to one of Trastevere's oldest restaurants,
has outstanding cakes and pastries, plus fresh
quiches, crisp *crocchette* and, usually, tasty baked
pasta. There's a savvy selection of malt whiskies too,
and some of the best *gelato* this side of the Tiber.

Sisini

Via San Francesco a Ripa 137 (06 589 7110).
Bus 780, H/tram 8. **Open** 9am-9pm Mon-Sat.
Closed 3wks Aug. **No credit cards. Map** p336 2B.
Probably Trastevere's best *pizza rustica* (takeaway
pizza) outfit. The flavours are fairly conservative,
but there's a wide range and they're all delicious.
Roast chicken is another forte.

Eat, Drink, Shop

tomatoes; **all'amatriciana** with tomato, chilli, onion and sausage; **alla gricia** the same without the tomato; **all'arrabbiata** with tomato and chilli; **alla carbonara** with bacon, egg and parmesan; **alla puttanesca** with olives, capers and garlic in hot oil; **cacio e pepe** with sheep's cheese and black pepper.

Carne – meat
abbacchio, agnello lamb; **capra, capretto** goat, kid; **coniglio** rabbit; **maiale, maialino** pork, piglet; **manzo** beef; **pancetta** similar to bacon; **pollo** chicken; **prosciutto cotto, prosciutto crudo** 'cooked' ham, Parma ham; **tacchino** turkey; **vitello, vitella, vitellone** veal.

Roman offal specialities
coda alla vaccinara oxtail braised in a celery broth; **pajata** intestines with the mother's milk still inside; **fagioli con le cotiche** beans with pork scratchings; **insalata di zampi** hoof jelly salad; **animelle** the spongy white pancreas and thymus glands, generally fried; **tripa** tripe; **cervello** brain; **lingua** tongue; **guanciale** pig's cheek cured in salt and pepper; **nervetti** strips of cartilage.

Piatti di carne – meat dishes
bollito con salsa verde boiled meat with parsley in vinegar sauce; **carpaccio,**

bresaola very thinly sliced types of cured beef; **ossobuco** beef shins with marrow jelly inside; **polpette, polpettine** meatballs; **porchetta** roast piglet; **rognoni trifolati** stir-fried chopped kidneys, usually with mushrooms; **salsicce** sausages; **saltimbocca** veal strips and ham; **spezzatino** casseroled meat; **spiedini** anything on a spit; **straccetti** strips of beef or veal, stir-fried.

Formaggi – cheeses
cacio, caciotta young, coarse-tasting cheese; **gorgonzola** strong blue cheese, in creamy (*dolce*) or crumbly (*piccante*) varieties; **parmigiano** parmesan; **pecorino** hard, tangy Roman cheese used instead of parmesan; **ricotta** crumbly white cheese, often used in desserts; **stracchino** creamy, soft white cheese.

Pesce – fish
Sarago, dentice, marmora, orata, fragolino all bream of various kinds; **alici, acciughe** anchovies; **baccalà** salt cod; **branzino, spigola** sea bass; **cernia** grouper; **merluzzo** cod; **pesce San Pietro** John Dory; **pesce spada** swordfish; **razza, arzilla** skate or thornback ray; **rombo** turbot; **salmone** salmon; **sarde, sardine** sardines; **sogliola** sole; **tonno** tuna; **trota** trout.

Aventine & Testaccio

Restaurants

See also **Ketumbar** *in p176* **The design crew.**

Agustarello
Via Giovanni Branca 100 (06 574 6585). Bus 23, 75, 95, 170, 716, 781/tram 3. **Open** 7.30-11.30pm Mon; 12.30-3pm, 7.30-11.30pm Tue-Sat. Closed 3wks Aug. **Average** €25. **No credit cards. Map** p337 2B.
This pared-back Testaccio trattoria pays homage to the Roman tradition in all its anatomical detail. Dishes like *rigatoni con la pajata* (with baby veal intestines) were briefly rocked by the BSE scare, but are now defiantly back on the menu; if you prefer to play safe, the *tonnarelli cacio e pepe* (with sheep's cheese and black pepper) are equally fine. Agustarello's flagship *secondo* is the succulent *involtini con il sedano* (veal rolls with celery stuffing). Finding a table here at short notice is a desperate task. In summer, tables extend into a courtyard.

Checchino dal 1887
Via di Monte Testaccio 30 (06 574 6318). Bus 95, 170, 673/tram 3. **Open** 12.30-3pm, 8pm-midnight Tue-Sat. Closed Aug; 1wk Dec. **Average** €52. **Credit** AmEx, DC, MC, V. **Map** p337 2A.

Nestling among the trendy bars and clubs opposite Testaccio's former slaughterhouse, the Mariani family's historic restaurant is Rome's leading temple of authentic *cucina romana*. Imagine a chippie rising to become one of London's leading restaurants, and the odd mix of humble decor, elegant service, hearty food and one of the most extensive wine cellars in Rome falls into place. Vegetarians should give this place a wide berth: specialities include *trippa* and *coda alla vaccinara*. Pasta dishes like the traditional *bucatini all'amatriciana* are delicious. Desserts feature a delicious *stracciatella* cake with ricotta, almonds and chocolate chips.

Luna Piena
Via Luca della Robbia 15/17 (06 575 0279). Bus 23, 30, 75, 95, 170, 716, 781/tram 3. **Open** 7.30-11.30pm Tue, Wed; 12.30-2.50pm, 7.30-11.30pm Mon, Thur-Sun. Closed mid June-mid July. **Average** €25. **Credit** AmEx, DC, MC, V. **Map** p337 2A.
This local trattoria with updated, artsy decor serves a good range of culinary classics. The *bucatini alla gricia* (pasta in a bacon and pecorino sauce) and *saltimbocca* are hard to beat, while the more adventurous might opt for the home-made pumpkin-filled ravioli. Space is rather cramped and staff often tetchy, but the wallet-friendly bill makes Luna Piena a value-for-money creative trattoria. There are a few tables outside in the street during the summer.

▶ # Reading the menu
(continued)

Frutti di mare – seafood
astice, **aragosta** lobster, spiny lobster;
calamari, **calamaretti** squid, baby squid;
cozze mussels; **crostacei** shellfish; **gamberi**,
gamberetti shrimps, prawns; **granchio** crab;
mazzancolle king prawns; **moscardini** baby
octopus; **ostriche** oysters; **polipo**, **polpo**
octopus; **seppie**, **seppiette**, **seppioline**
cuttlefish; **telline** wedge shells (small clams);
totani baby flying squid; **vongole** clams.

*Verdura/il contorno – vegetables/
the side dish*
aglio garlic; **asparagi** asparagus; **basilico**
basil; **broccoli siciliani** broccoli; **broccolo**
green cauliflower; **broccoletti** tiny broccoli
sprigs, cooked with the leaves; **carciofi**
artichokes; **carote** carrots; **cavolfiore**
cauliflower; **cetriolo** cucumber; **cicoria**
green leaf vegetable, resembling dandelion;
cipolle onions; **fagioli** haricot or borlotti
beans; **fagiolini** green beans; **fave** broad
beans; **funghi** mushrooms; **funghi porcini**
boletus mushrooms; **indivia** endive; **insalata**
salad; **lattuga** lettuce; **melanzane** aubergine;
patate potatoes; **patatine fritte** french fries;
peperoncino chilli; **peperoni** peppers; **piselli**
peas; **pomodori** tomatoes; **porri** leeks;
prezzemolo parsley; **puntarelle** bitter Roman
salad usually dressed with an anchovy sauce;
radicchio bitter purple lettuce; **rughetta**,
rucola rocket; **scalogna** shallots; **sedano**
celery; **spinaci** spinach; **verza** cabbage;
zucchine courgettes.

Frutta – fruit
albicocche apricots; **ananas** pineapple;
arance oranges; **cachi** persimmons; **ciliege**
cherries; **coccomero**, **anguria** watermelon;
fichi figs; **fragole**, **fragoline** strawberries,
wild strawberries; **frutti di bosco** woodland
berries; **mele** apples; **nespole** loquats;
pere pears; **pesche** peaches; **prugne**, **susine**
plums; **uva** grapes.

Dolci/il dessert – desserts
gelato ice cream; **montebianco** cream,
meringue and marron glacé; **pannacotta**
'cooked cream', a very thick, blancmange-
like cream, often served with chocolate
(*cioccolata*), caramel or wild berry (*frutti
di bosco*) sauce; **sorbetto** sorbet; **tiramisù**
mascarpone and coffee sponge; **torta della
nonna** flan of pâtisserie cream and pine
nuts; **torta di mele** apple flan; **millefoglie**
flaky pastry cake.

Pizza
calzone a doubled-over pizza, usually filled
with cheese, tomato and ham; **capricciosa**
ham, hard-boiled or fried egg, artichokes
and olives; **funghi** mushrooms; **marinara** plain
tomato, sometimes with anchovies;
margherita tomato and mozzarella; **napoli**,
napoletana tomato, anchovies and
sometimes mozzarella; **quattro formaggi**
four cheeses (in theory); **quattro stagioni**
mozzarella, artichoke, egg, mushrooms.

Pizzeria extras
bruschetta toast with garlic rubbed into it and
oil on top, and usually diced raw tomatoes;
crochette potato croquettes, often with a
cheesy centre; **crostini** slices of toast, usually
with a grilled cheese and anchovy topping;
filetto di baccalà deep-fried salt cod in batter;
olive ascolane deep-fried olives stuffed with
sausage meat; **supplì** deep-fried rice balls held
together by tomato sauce, with mozzarella
inside; may also contain mincemeat.

Veggie options
orechiette ai broccoletti/cima di rape
ear-shaped pasta with broccoli sprigs/green
turnip-tops; **pasta e ceci** soup with pasta and
chickpeas; **pasta e fagioli** soup with pasta
and borlotti beans; **pasta alla puttanesca/
alla checca** (literally, 'à la whore' or 'à la
raging queen') based on olives, capers and
tomatoes, though anchovies (*alici*) are
sometimes slipped into the former; **penne
all'arrabbiata** pasta with tomato sauce and
lots of chilli; **ravioli** OK if filled with *ricotta
e spinaci* (soft cheese and spinach) and
served *con burro e salvia* (with butter and
sage) or a simple *sugo di pomodoro* (tomato
sauce); **risotto ai quattro formaggi** risotto
made with four types of cheese; **spaghetti
aglio, olio e peperoncino** with garlic and
olive oil; **spaghetti cacio e pepe** with
crumbled salty sheep's cheese and lots
of black pepper.

Veggie main courses (secondi)
Second courses are more of a problem;
you'll often have to make do with something
uninspiring. Among the standard options
are: **carciofi alla giudia** deep-fried artichokes;
fagioli all'uccelletto haricot beans with
tomato, garlic and olive oil (strictly speaking
a *contorno*, but substantial enough to take
the place of a main course); **melanzane
alla parmigiana** aubergine with parmesan
(this occasionally has meat in the topping);
scamorza grilled cheese – specify without
ham (*senza prosciutto*) or without anchovies
(*senza alici*).

Eat, Drink, Shop

Artsy **Luna Piena**. *See p185.*

Tuttifrutti

Via Luca della Robbia 3A (06 575 7902). Bus 23, 30, 75, 95, 170, 716, 781/tram 3. **Open** 8-11pm Tue-Sun. **Average** €25. Closed Aug. **Credit** AmEx, MC, V. **Map** p337 2A.

Behind an anonymous frosted-glass door, this *circolo culturale* is one of Testaccio's best-value dining experiences – pipping its neighbour, Luna Piena (see p185), on the gastronomic side. Once past the free 'membership card' formality (it's a licensing law thing), you can concentrate on the daily changing menu of creative pan-Italian fare that might include an antipasto of *pecorino di fossa* cheese with honey and pears, followed by tonnarelli with dandelion leaves and rosemary, and baked lamb with potatoes and rosemary. You'll be talked through it by the earnest, welcoming crew that runs the place, who will also be happy to recommend a bottle from a limited but well-priced wine list. The kitchen stays open late, so you can sashay straight from dinner to one of Testaccio's many clubs.

International

Court Delicati

Viale Aventino 39 (06 574 6108). Metro Circo Massimo/bus 60, 75, 673/tram 3. **Open** noon-2.45pm, 7.30-11pm Tue-Sun. Closed Aug. **Average** €30. **Credit** AmEx, DC, MC, V. **Map** p339 1C.

Court Delicati is basically just a decent Chinese restaurant, but it has gained some renown as one of the few places to add a few Thai and Indonesian

dishes to the usual repertoire. So as well as better-than-average steamed dumplings and hot crispy beef, regulars can also enjoy the violently spicy *tomyam* (seafood) soup and a very passable *nasi goreng*. Beer and wine are as reasonably priced as everything else on the menu.

Pizzerie

Remo

Piazza Santa Maria Liberatrice 44 (06 574 6270). Bus 23, 75, 95, 170, 716, 781/tram 3. **Open** 7pm-12.30am Mon-Sat. Closed Aug. **Average** €12. **No credit cards. Map** p337 1A.

The best place in town for authentic *pizza romana*, Remo is a Testaccio institution, with a prime location on the district's main piazza. You can sit at wonky tables balanced on the pavement, or in the cavernous interior, overseen by Lazio team photos. The *bruschette al pomodoro* are the finest in Rome.

Wine bars & gastropubs

L'Oasi della Birra

Piazza Testaccio 41 (06 574 6122). Bus 23, 75, 95, 170, 716, 781/tram 3. **Open** 7.30pm-1am Mon-Sat. Closed 2wks Aug. **Average** €22. **Credit** MC, V. **Map** p337 2A.

In the basement of a modest enoteca on Testaccio's market square, the 'Oasis of Beer' has over 500 brews on offer, from Belgian Trappist to Jamaican

Red Stripe. It's one of the few places where you can track down the products of Italian microbreweries such as the award-winning Menabrea, and the selection of wines by the bottle is almost as impressive. The accompanying food ranges from snacks (*crostini, bruschette*, a well-stocked cheeseboard) to full-scale meals with a Teutonic-Magyar slant (goulash, wurstel, krauti). Booking is always a good idea, especially at weekends. The outside tables operate year round, weather permitting.

Snacks & quick meals

Il Seme e la Foglia
Via Galvani 18 (06 574 3008). Bus 95, 170, 673/ tram 3. **Open** 7.45am-1.30am Mon-Sat; 6pm-1.30am Sun. Closed 3wks Aug. **No credit cards. Map** p337 2A.
Once a po-faced macrobiotic affair, this has become a lively daytime snack bar and evening pre-club stop. At midday there's always a pasta dish, plus large salads (around €7) and exotic filled rolls.

Celio & San Giovanni

Restaurants

Hosteria degli Artisti
Via G Sommeiller 6 (06 701 8148). Metro Manzoni/bus 105/tram 3, 5, 14, 19. **Open** 12.30-3.30pm, 7.30-11.30pm daily. Closed Sun in Aug. **Average** €27. **Credit** MC, V. **Map** off p339 1A.
In a nondescript residential street not far from Porta Maggiore, this good-value southern Italian restaurant is a hidden gem. It looks like the inside of a Neapolitan Christmas crib, but the food is serious, with an accent on the cuisine of northern Campania (south of Rome, north of Naples): *'mpepata di cozze* (a peppery mussel soup), *pasta e patate con provola affumicata* (pasta and potato bake with smoked cheese), *alici fritte* (fried anchovies).

Magna Roma
Via Capo d'Africa 26 (06 700 9800/www. magnaroma.com). Metro Colosseo/bus 60, 75, 81, 117, 175, 673/tram 3. **Open** Oct-Mar 6-8pm, 8.30-11.30pm Tue-Sat; 12-2.30pm, 6-8pm, 8.30-11.30pm Sun. *Apr-Sept* 7.30-11pm Mon-Sat. Closed 2wks Aug. **Average** €50. **Credit** AmEx, DC, MC, V. **Map** p338 2B.
Modern Rome's first ancient Roman restaurant (*thermopolium*) is no tourist toga party: Magna Roma takes its task extremely seriously. At dinner (8.30-11.30pm), guests are greeted by English-speaking owner Luciano Marino and archaeologist Franco Nicastro, who spiel an introduction to the meal while damsels in 1970s-style togas hand out beakers of *muslum* (grape must, sweetened with honey). *Aperitivum nibblums* are followed by a fixed (but seasonally changing) succession of dishes such as *lenticulam de castaineis* (lentil and chestnut soup) and the delicious *oplontis*, a ricotta, honey

and candied fruit dessert reconstructed from a wall painting in the eponymous Roman town. Even the cutlery is Roman. The house wine – billed as the legendary Roman 'falernum' – is an uninspiring Frascati. The price per head – which includes food, water, house wine and service – goes down the larger your party. At lunch and during the early dinner *gustaticium* (6-8pm), a lighter (and cheaper) buffet-style meal is offered. Dinner should be booked ahead, and any special dietary requirements mentioned beforehand.

Wine bars & gastropubs

Divinare
Via Ostilia 4 (06 709 6381). Metro Colosseo/bus 60, 75, 81, 85, 87, 117, 175, 673, 810, 850/ tram 3. **Open** 10.30am-3.30pm, 5-9pm Mon-Thur; 10.30am-3.30pm, 5pm-midnight Fri, Sat. **Average** €20. **Credit** AmEx, DC, MC, V. **Map** p338 2B.
For years this was the neighbourhood watering hole, with rough wine from the barrel and a few tables where old men played cards over a simple plate of pasta. Now it's a sophisticated wine bar, with a good choice of wine by the glass and an interesting range of enoteca fare, including cheese platters, cured meats, wild game carpaccio and unusual salads. Bottles are stacked to the ceiling: more than 700 different crus are available to drink in or take away, plus small-farm olive oils, hand-made pasta and organic jams.

Monti & Esquilino

Restaurants

Agata e Romeo
Via Carlo Alberto 45 (06 446 6115). Metro Vittorio/bus 16, 70, 71, 75, 84, 360/tram 5, 14. **Open** 1-2.30pm, 7.30-10.30pm Mon-Fri. Closed 3wks Aug, 2wks Jan. **Average** €80. **Credit** AmEx, DC, MC, V. **Map** p338 1A.
This intimate cordon bleu haven near Santa Maria Maggiore is a family affair, with Romeo presiding over the dining room and extensive wine list, while his wife Agata takes traditional Roman cuisine to a new level in the kitchen. Among the *primi*, the cannelloni filled with a white duck *ragù* are memorable, their thin home-made pasta gratinéed to a delectable crispness, and the terrine of oxtail stew with cream of celeriac elates: the oxtail gives carnivorous bite; the celeriac is puréed for the sophisticate, julienned and fried for the inner child. The dessert list includes a triple-whammy of semi-sweet chocolate cake with chocolate sorbet and chocolate *semifreddo*.

La Piazzetta
Vicolo del Buon Consiglio 23A (06 699 1640). Metro Cavour/bus 75, 84, 117. **Open** noon-3pm, 7-11pm Mon-Sat. Closed 2wks Aug. **Average** €30. **Credit** MC, V. **Map** p338 1C.

Eat, Drink, Shop

MUSIC LIVES HERE!

Hard Rock CAFE

Hard Rock CAFE

VIA VITTORIO VENETO 62 a/b
00187 ROMA
Tel. 064203051
rome_sales@hardrock.com

ROME

Gastronomy on a shoestring

Doing Europe on €25 a day? Want to indulge without slipping into the red? Then you've come to the right city. Rome has many a temple dedicated to the joys of eating and drinking that is just as much worth visiting as any classical ruin. And, just like the entrance-free Forum, many cannot be bettered for love nor money. Here, then, is our essentially democratic, €3-pegged, gastronomic Top Ten:

1. Coffee at **Sant'Eustachio** (*p202*) for that mid-morning lift or after-dinner hit. Order the house speciality: espresso served cappuccino-style.

2. **Lo Zozzone** (*p176*) provides one of Rome's best lunches: warm *pizza bianco*, split and filled with whatever ingredients you point at. Try the brie, grilled aubergine and rocket combo or stick to the classic prosciutto and mozzarella.

3. For heaven in a tub, order any flavour that takes your fancy at **San Crispino** (*p200*) – you'll soon be back to try the rest.

4. Cannoli at **Dagnino** (*p207*). If Sicily isn't on your itinerary, then don't miss these sweet ricotta and chocolate-chip filled goodies.

5. Most local *alimentari* (grocer's) still make up fresh rolls and sandwiches on the spot. Ask for '*un panino con...*' and point to whatever cold cuts, cheese or sun-dried vegetables take your fancy.

6. *Granita di caffè con panna* – iced coffee and whipped cream – at the **Tazza d'Oro** (*p202*). Consume sitting on the wall overlooking the Pantheon and muse on the glory that is Rome.

7. No fine-palated tippler should miss **L'Angolo Divino**'s (*p180*) generous happy hour (10am-8pm Mon-Fri) and vintages from all over Italy.

8. A trip to Rome isn't complete without trying the deep-fried salted cod at the **Filetti di Baccalà** (*p177*). Diet when you get home.

9. The **Vineria** (*p204*) is the place to start the evening. But enjoy your prosecco at the bar – a table outside can triple the bill.

10. Forget restaurant desserts. You can't beat a *tartufo* (cherry-centred chocolate ice-cream swathed in whipped cream) at the **Tre Scalini** (*p202*). It may tip you over the €3 limit, but it's worth the extravagance.

Eat, Drink, Shop

Franco Bartolini opened this elegant little restaurant in a medieval lane tucked in behind the Colosseum a couple of years ago. Always popular, its outside tables book up days in advance as soon as the weather gets warmer. Pasta dishes come in generous portions: try the *vermicelli alla tarantina* with mussels, clams, cherry tomatoes and fresh basil. *Secondi* include perfectly cooked fish like oven-baked turbot (*rombo*) with potatoes. But make sure you leave space for dessert: Sicilian pastry-chef Enrico Lalicata does an excellent selection of home-made cakes and biscuits, plus what is probably the best *crème brûlée* in town.

International

Africa

Via Gaeta 26-8 (06 494 1077). Metro Castro Pretorio/bus 36, 38, 75, 217, 310, 360, 492, 649. **Open** noon-4pm, 7-11.30pm Tue-Sun. Closed 2wks Aug. **Average** €15. **Credit** MC, V. **Map** p335 1A.

Cheerfully casual, Africa serves up filling Eritrean and Ethiopian cuisine. After a starter of falafel served with a spicy dip, you can tuck into spongy, whole-wheat *taita* bread: the idea is to break pieces off and use them to scoop up the meat or vegetables (though there are forks for those who prefer them). Try the mixed vegetarian plate, which comes with delicious stewed lentils. The *tibsi* – grilled veal with

spicy sauce – is also good. Deliciously sweet sesame halwa, served with a cup of spicy tea, makes a perfect end to the meal.

Il Guru

Via Cimarra 4-6 (06 474 4110). Bus 40, 60, 64, 70, 170, H. **Open** 7pm-midnight daily. **Average** €22. **Credit** AmEx, DC, MC, V. **Map** p338 1B.

If you're dying for an Indian, Il Guru will fill the gap... though no better than your local curry house back home. The cuisine is standard pan-Indian, done at a decidedly standard level of competence. But there's a proper tandoori oven, staff are friendly and it's cheap even by Roman standards. There are three fixed menus: vegetarian (€16), meat (€18) and fish (€20). But, as the menu says, 'no sharing please'.

Hang Zhou

Via San Martino ai Monti 33C (06 487 2732). Metro Cavour/bus 16, 75, 84, 360, 649, 714. **Open** noon-3.30pm, 7-11.30pm daily. **Average** €15. **Credit** MC, V. **Map** p338 1B.

The vast majority of Rome's Chinese restaurants are cheap and mediocre. Hang Zhou is cheap and decidedly special: not so much for the food (though the menu does make an effort to rise above the herd with a series of daily specials) as for the verve of its media-savvy owner, Sonia, who appears in hundreds of photos plastered on the wall of this shoe-box of a restaurant, beaming next to anyone who is remotely famous… and quite a few who aren't. It's colourful, friendly, theatrical and incredibly good value: the average price given above is for a full spread, but you can easily eat here for €10 a head. Book for dinner, or be prepared to queue.

Hasekura

Via dei Serpenti 27 (06 483 648). Bus 40, 60, 64, 70, 117, 170, H. **Open** *noon-2.30pm, 7-10.30pm Mon-Sat. Closed Aug.* **Average** €35. **Credit** AmEx, DC, MC, V. **Map** p338 1C.

The decor might not be old Kyoto, but the food at Hasekura is about the most authentically Japanese in Rome. Partners Ito Kimiji (kitchen) and Franca Palma (up front) serve beautifully presented dishes to tourists and curious Italians alike. Good bets are the fixed-price set menus (from €31 to €44 in the evening; from €15.50 to €34 at lunch). The soba and tempura options are excellent, though for fish lovers the sushi and sashimi are hard to resist.

Wine bars & gastropubs

See also p206 **Al Vino al Vino**.

Cavour 313

Via Cavour 313 (06 678 5496). Metro Cavour/bus 75, 84, 117. **Open** *Oct-May 12.30-2.30pm, 7.30pm-12.30am Mon-Sat; 7.30pm-12.30am Sun. June & July, Sept 12.30-2.30pm, 7.30pm-12.30am Mon-Sat. Closed Aug.* **Credit** AmEx, DC, MC, V. **Map** p338 1C.

A friendly atmosphere (despite the gloomy dark wood decor), a serious cellar and good snacks explain the eternal popularity of this wine bar near the Forum. Prices are reasonable, and there's a selection of hot and cold snacks; in winter, it's especially strong on soups. With over 500 bottles on the wine list, choice is the only problem.

Snacks & quick meals

Indian Fast Food

Via Mamiani 11 (06 446 0792). Metro Vittorio/bus 70, 71, 360, 649/tram 5, 14. **Open** *11am-4pm, 5-10pm Mon-Sat; noon-11pm Sun.* **No credit cards. Map** p338 1A.

Rome's only Indian takeaway is just off piazza Vittorio. You can eat in too, accompanied by gloriously kitsch Indian music videos. While noshing on those vegetable samosas, you can even send a moneygram to Mumbai. Does life get any better?

Pizzeria Leonina

Via Leonina 84 (06 482 7744). Metro Cavour/bus 40, 60, 64, 70, 117, 170, H. **Open** *8am-9pm daily.* **No credit cards. Map** p338 1B.

This has long been considered one of the best *pizzerie a taglio* in Rome (though new management have yet to prove themselves up to the same standards). Avoid peak times, as the queue is endless (you have to take a number). It's not as cheap as one might hope, but with toppings like spicy beans, tuna salad and even apple strudel, it's worth it.

Shawerma Express

Via Calatafimi 7 (06 481 8791). Metro Termini/bus 16, 36, 38, 75, 217, 360. **Open** *11am-10pm daily.* **No credit cards. Map** p335 1A.

Good-value Arab and Middle Eastern specialities such as falafel, fuul (spicy beans), couscous and kebabs, served with pitta bread, to take away or eat in. There are tables outside in summer.
Branches: via Natale del Grande 17, Trastevere (06 581 9863); via dei Sabelli 37-8, Suburbs: south (06 445 7611).

The Vatican & Prati

Restaurants

Borgo Antico

Borgo Pio 21 (06 686 5967). Bus 23, 34, 40, 62, 64, 280. **Open** *12.30-3pm, 8pm-midnight Mon-Sat; 12.30-3pm Sun. Closed 3wks Aug.* **Average** €30. **Credit** AmEx, DC, V, MC. **Map** p333 1C.

Goethe's belief that life's too short to drink mediocre wines is taken seriously at Borgo Antico. This rustic, wood-beamed hostelry offers an extensive selection of wines, many also available by the glass, to be savoured together with a selection of gastronomic delights. No pasta or pizza here: cold platters include salamis from Umbria and Friuli, cheeses that have been matured in a variety of interesting ways and smoked raw fish. Hot dishes might take in *polenta* served with porcini mushrooms, truffles, wild boar or hare sauce; or a range of fondues (minimum two people). At lunch, a €12 *prezzo fisso* menu includes a *primo*, a salad and a glass of wine.

Osteria dell'Angelo

Via G Bettolo 24 (06 372 9470). Metro Ottaviano/bus 23, 32, 70, 490, 913/tram 19. **Open** *8-11pm Mon, Wed, Thur-Sat; 1-2.30pm, 8-11pm Tue, Fri. Closed Aug.* **Average** €18 lunch, €23 (fixed price) dinner. **No credit cards. Map** p332 2C.

Five minutes' walk north of the Vatican, Angelo Croce's neighbourhood trattoria is a real one-off, just like the man himself. The decor consists of photos of boxers and rugby players – the two sporting passions of Angelo and his culinary helpmates, who have cauliflower ears but hearts of gold. The menu – which, in the evening, comes at a fixed price of €23 a head, rough-and-ready house wine included – celebrates the Roman tradition in dishes like *tonnarelli cacio e pepe* (among the best in town) and meatballs flavoured with nutmeg, pine nuts and sultanas. Dessert consists of a glass of sweet wine and *ciambelline* (aniseed biscuits).

Il Simposio

Piazza Cavour 16 (06 321 1502). Bus 30, 34, 49, 70, 87, 90, 280, 492, 913, 926. **Open** *1-2.30pm, 8-11.15pm Mon-Fri; 8-11.15pm Sat. Closed Aug.* **Average** €50. **Credit** AmEx, DC, MC, V. **Map** p333 1C.

Though annexed to Costantini (a glorious art nouveau enoteca), Il Simposio is more a full-scale restaurant – complete with plush seats and *belle époque*

Refuel by the river at **Baja**. *See p195*.

mirrors – than a humble wine bar. The menu depends largely on what's in season: in spring, one might opt for the simple but tasty double artichoke *antipasto* – one served *alla romana* (braised and stuffed with a minty mixture of herbs), the other *alla giudia* (deep fried). The *primi* juxtapose traditional dishes like *spaghetti all'amatriciana* with the more innovative, like the potato and white bean soup with goat's cheese croutons. Main courses are mostly meat- and game-based. Desserts include a daring, but delicious, molten chocolate cake with double-malt beer sauce. The wine list is as authoritative as one would expect given the pedigree.

Taverna Angelica

Piazza A Capponi 6 (06 687 4514). Bus 23, 34, 40, 49, 62, 64, 81, 492. **Open** 7.30pm-12.30am daily. Closed 2wks Aug. **Average** €40. **Credit** AmEx, MC, V. **Map** p333 1B.

One of the few stylishly creative eateries within easy range of the Vatican. The acoustics are not conducive to a quiet evening out, but the food is imaginative and well presented, the wine list extensive, and the service friendly and efficient. Tasty starters include a triptych of marinated or smoked fish (swordfish, octopus and salmon) or duck (tartare, smoked breast and roast), while the *primi* include

risotto with smoked eel (*anguilla affumicata*) or with wild endive and sausage (*scarola e luganica*). There is also a wide selection of cheeses and some delicious and unusual desserts, including fresh dates filled with coffee cream.

Velando

Borgo Vittorio 26 (06 6880 9955). Bus 23, 34, 40, 62, 64, 280. **Open** noon-3pm, 7.30-11.30pm Mon-Sat. Closed 1wk Aug. **Average** €30. **Credit** AmEx, DC, MC, V. **Map** p333 1C.

The traditional dishes and nouvelle cuisine from the Val Camonica area of northern Italy served in this refinedly minimalist resturant are popular with bishops and cardinals from the large religious organisation up the street. Be prepared to expand your mind and your taste buds with delicacies like *risotto alle fragoline di bosco* (wild strawberry risotto) and *strudel con rana e verdure* (yes, that's frog and vegetable strudel), or stick to more traditional recipes based on freshwater fish or *caprino* goat's cheese. Leave room for one of the rich and creamy desserts. The extensive wine list focuses on north Italy, with several varieties available by the glass.

International

Zen

Via degli Scipioni 243 (06 321 3420/www. zenworld.it). Metro Lepanto/bus 30, 70, 280, 913. **Open** 1-2.30pm, 8.30-11pm Tue-Fri, Sun; 8.30-11pm Sat. Closed 2wks Aug. **Average** €35. **Credit** AmEx, DC, MC, V. **Map** p332 2B.

This recently opened offshoot of a successful Milanese sushi bar was a hit from day one. The decor is refreshingly modern. In the centre is Rome's first sushi and sashimi conveyor belt (for which no bookings are taken); there are tables around the side and in a large back room: head for these if you want a more substantial meal – which might consist of a sushi or sashimi boat, or seared tuna, or an excellent, light tempura. Zen has set a new standard for high-quality affordable Japanese food in Rome – so come early if you want to be sure of a place at the conveyor belt, or book ahead for a table.

Wine bars & gastropubs

Del Frate

Via degli Scipioni 118 (06 323 6437). Metro Ottaviano/bus 32, 70, 913/tram 19. **Open** 12.30pm-1am Mon-Sat; 6.30pm-1am Sun. Closed 10 days Aug. **Average** €24. **Credit** AmEx, DC, MC, V. **Map** p332 2C.

This historic Prati bottle shop expanded into a wine bar annexe a couple of years ago, and has since built up a loyal local following. Of an evening, tables spill over into the enoteca itself, amid tall wooden shelves crammed with bottles. The menu offers a series of hot and cold dishes – served all day long – that can be combined in various ways. The oven-baked ravioli with salmon and courgette sauce is a good

demonstration of the modern Italian flair of young chef Cecilia Miraglia, who is equally strong on desserts. The only off-note is the steep mark-up on wines: almost triple what the same bottle would cost to take away (especially painful if you happen to be staring at it on the shelf).

Snacks & quick meals

NapulArte

Via Fabio Massimo 113 (06 323 1005). Metro Ottaviano/bus 23, 49, 81, 492. **Open** *Apr-Oct* 7am-2am daily. *Nov-Mar* 7am-11pm daily. **Credit** AmEx, DC, MC, V. **Map** p332 2C.

Opened at the end of 2001, this subterranean Neapolitan bar/pizzeria is run by a lively though rather gruff family. They do a good range of Neapolitan cakes such as *sfogliatelle* (layers of crispy pastry with ricotta inside) and *pastiera napoletana* (a flan filled with ricotta, softened cereal grains and orange-water – definitely an acquired taste). You can also pop in for a cheap light meal based on a range of pasta dishes or thick-crust Neapolitan pizzas.

The Suburbs

Restaurants

Arancia Blu

Via dei Latini 55-65, East (06 445 4105). Bus 71, 492/tram 3, 19. **Open** 8.30-11.45pm Mon-Sat; 12.30-3pm Sun. **Average** €30. **No credit cards**. **Map** p159.

The nouvelle approach of this upmarket vegetarian restaurant in bohemian San Lorenzo is seen in a salad of *puntarelle* (chicory stems) with a walnut-balsamic vinegar dressing and aged piave cheese shavings: an interesting twist on a Roman classic. Onion stuffed with ricotta, pecorino, pine nuts and parsley with a carrot and Humebashi vinegar sauce is also tasty; other offerings are less convincing and lack flavour, like the *crema di porri e patate* (potato and leek soup) with fried artichokes. Still, the large cheese selection and wine list are pluses, and the extensive dessert list – including a chocolate tasting menu with accompanying rum – is an original touch. The service is sometimes rude, but the owners are enthusiastic and passionate about their work, offering cooking and wine-tasting classes too.

Baja

Lungotevere Arnaldo da Brescia, North (06 3260 0118). Metro Flaminio/bus 81, 224, 628, 926. **Open** 8pm-midnight Tue-Sun. *Bar open* 10pm-2am Tue-Sun. **Average** €42. **Credit** AmEx, DC, MC, V. **Map** p332 2B.

In the *dolce vita* years, converted Tiber barges were *the* place to eat, drink and party. Recently, Romans have begun to rediscover their river, and Baja – the city's first floating restaurant – is one of the results. Access is from a badly lit flight of steps at the Ponte Margherita end of the riverside road. The menu is

Italian with Latin American touches, including a decent selection of Argentinian beef dishes. Seafood dominates, however, with a salmon carpaccio marinated in pink grapefruit followed by black olive *gnocchetti* in tomato and shrimp sauce. The crustless pie of sea bass with vegetables is a fresh alternative to a basic fish fillet. Afterwards, slip downstairs, where a bar packed with twenty- and thirty-somethings keeps going until late. In summer, tables spill out on to the deck.

Cecilia Metella

Via Appia Antica 127/129, South (06 513 6743).
Bus 118, 660. **Open** noon-3pm, 7-10.30pm Tue-Sun.
Average €38. **Credit** AmEx, DC, MC, V. **Map** p151.
Just across the street from the catacombs of San Sebastiano, this long-established restaurant is one of the few to combine an obvious tourist orientation with an equally obvious concern for quality. Perched on top of a low hill, with a vine-covered terrace for outdoor dining, Cecilia Metella is ideal for a lazy lunch after a visit to the catacombs or nearby Circus of Maxentius (*see p153*). Service is swift and professional; specialities include *scrigno alla Cecilia* (baked green noodles in cheese sauce) and *pollo al Nerone* (flambéed chicken). The *polenta ai porcini* (polenta with porcini mushrooms) is also very tasty.

Marcello

Via dei Campani 12 (06 446 3311), East. Bus
71, 492/tram 3, 19. **Open** 7.30pm-midnight Mon-
Fri. Closed Aug. **Average** €20. **No credit cards.**
Map p159.
From the outside it looks like one of those spit and sawdust places that Romans refer to as *un buco* – a hole in the wall. There's no name, just a sign saying 'Cucina'. Inside, old wooden tables are occupied by hordes of hungry students from the nearby university. Alongside Roman offal specialities like tripe and *pajata* are lighter and more creative dishes such as *straccetti ai carciofi* – strips of veal with artichokes. The same goes for pasta: as well as reliable traditional recipes (*spaghetti alla carbonara, all'amatriciana* or *alla gricia*), you can also order homemade *ravioloni* filled with fresh cheese, ricotta and walnuts. A surprisingly extensive wine list, strong on big reds, confirms that Da Marcello – now run by Marcello's son, Isidoro – is a lot more than a *buco*.

La Pergola dell'Hotel Hilton

Via Cadlolo 101, North (06 3509 2211). Bus
907, 913, 991, 999. **Open** 7.30-10.30pm Tue-Sat.
Closed 4wks Jan; 2wks Aug. **Average** €105.
Credit AmEx, DC, MC, V.
Vado a mangiare da Beck ('I'm going to eat chez Beck') has become the Roman gourmet's favourite phrase. Heinz Beck is the German chef who was summoned in the mid 1990s to revitalise the rooftop restaurant of the Hilton hotel. The plaudits are fully merited: he is a chef who marries technical dexterity with an inspired understanding of taste and texture. Long known as 'the chef who doesn't do pasta', Beck is letting Italy get to him slowly: on the

evening we visited three out of seven *primi* were pasta dishes – including some melt-in-the-mouth *tortellini di ricotta e pecorino con fave* (pasta parcels filled with ricotta and pecorino cheese, served with shelled broad beans), which demonstrate the lighter side of the chef's repertoire. Alongside the main menu and the dessert menu, there is also a water list, a tea and herbal infusion list, and a wine list in two volumes – one Italian, the other international. Markups on wine seem pretty steep – sometimes over five times *enoteca* prices. But La Pergola as a whole is not overpriced. It may sound odd to claim that €260 for a full meal for two with a decent bottle of wine represents good value for money, but there are at least half a dozen places in Rome that charge similar prices for meals that are in a far lower league. And there are plenty of gourmets willing to pay the price: so be sure to book at least a week in advance.

Al Ponte della Ranocchia

Circonvallazione Appia 29, South (06 785 6712).
Metro Ponte Lungo/bus 87, 671, 673. **Open** 12.30-
2.30pm, 8-11.30pm Mon-Sat. Closed 1wk Aug.
Average €28. **Credit** AmEx, DC, MC, V.
Don't be fooled by the simple trattoria decor. 'At the Bridge of the Frog' uses Jewish and Levantine influences to put a welcome spin on the local tradition, with much emphasis on fresh ingredients and a well-priced wine list. House speciality is the *ruota del faraone* (for two or more), a lightly fried wheel of fettuccine with meat stock, goose, sultanas and pinenuts. Among the other *primi*, the *pappardelle con crema di cipolle, porcini e reggiano* (pasta with onion sauce, porcini mushrooms and parmesan) are excellent. *Secondi* include the Roman-Jewish classic *aliciotti con l'indivia* (anchovies with endives). Finish off with a plate of walnut-filled *cannoncini alla romana* biscuits, served with a glass of dessert wine. It's in a residential area of town where tourists rarely tread, but is easily reached by metro.

L'Ortica

Via Flaminia Vecchia 573L, North (06 333 8709).
Bus 32, 224. **Open** 8-11pm Mon-Sat. Closed 2wks
Aug. **Average** €48. **Credit** AmEx, DC, MC, V.
If there was a prize for the oddest Roman gourmet restaurant location, L'Ortica would win it hands down. To get there, head north across the resoundingly still-Fascist-after-all-these-years Ponte Flaminio into busy corso Francia, and locate the Standa supermarket on your right. On the terrace above it – next door to a seedy billiard parlour – stands Vittorio Virno's oasis of culinary excellence. The accent is Neapolitan – militantly so, with all the ingredients brought in fresh from trusted southern suppliers and put to excellent use in dishes such as squid stuffed with endive, sultanas and pinenuts. Virno is a discerning kleptomaniac, and his collection of copper pans, irons, wicker baskets and other domestic antiques adorns a series of elegant, spacious rooms. Outside, the verdant terrace is screened from the surrounding suburban chaos for alfresco dining when the weather warms up.

Osteria del Rione

Via Basento 20, North (06 855 1057). Bus 52, 53, 63, 86, 217, 360, 630, 913. **Open** *12.30-2.30pm, 7-11.30pm Mon-Fri; 7-11.30pm Sat. Closed Aug .* **Fixed price** €16. **No credit cards. Map** p334 1A.

A short walk from Villa Borghese, the Osteria del Rione ('neighbourhood hostelry') is ideal for those sick of nouvelle cuisine who want to eat like a horse and drink like a fish for a total of €16 per head (the price of the *menù fisso*). If your Italian is a little shaky, bearded owner Bruno will recite the menu in his charming English. It always includes an array of *antipasti* such as *bruschette*, grilled vegetables and 'strong cheese' (a sort of Italian cheddar), plus a choice of three pasta dishes, followed by 'meat-a-balls' and other forms of beef. The fixed menu includes all the wine you can drink, and if you are not too hammered by the time the home-made dessert arrives, Bruno will suggest rounding things off with a glass of grappa. You can order à la carte, but unless you're on some sort of weird Californian diet, go for the ultra-cheap *menù fisso* experience.

Osteria del Velodromo Vecchio

Via Genzano 139, South (06 7886 793). Metro Colli Albani/bus 85, 87, 671. **Open** *12.30-3pm Mon-Wed; 12.30-3pm, 8-11pm Thur-Sat. Closed Aug.* **Average** €26. **Credit** MC, V.

A really friendly, good-value osteria near a former cycling stadium – hence the name. Inside is one small room with eight tables; in summer, a few more are arranged outside on a sheltered patio. The cooking is solidly Roman, but alongside old favourites like *pasta e fagioli* or *rigatoni con la pajata*, there are a few more creative dishes, like *fettucine tonno e zucchine* (with tuna and courgettes). One or two dishes – like *aliciotti e indivia* (anchovies and endives) – reflect the Jewish contribution to the local tradition. Desserts consist of home-made *crostate* (pastry tarts), or aniseed biscuits with a glass of sweet wine. The wine list is small but surprisingly adventurous.

Tram Tram

Via dei Reti 44-6, East (06 490 416). Bus 71, 492/tram 3, 19. **Open** *12.30-3pm, 7.30-11.30pm Tue-Sun. Closed 2wks Aug.* **Average** €28. **Credit** AmEx, DC, MC, V. **Map** p159.

Taking its name from its proximity to the tram tracks, this good-value nouvelle trattoria attracts a young crowd, who are not fazed by the waiters' rather hassled manner or the lack of elbow room. The menu derives its inspiration from Puglia (the heel of Italy) and is strong on fish and vegetables, as in the *tagliolini calamaretti e pesto* (pasta strips with baby squid and pesto). There are a few vegetarian main courses. The wine list is small but well chosen, with very reasonable mark-ups.

Uno e Bino

Via degli Equi 58, East (06 446 0702). Bus 71, 492/tram 3, 19. **Open** *8.30-11.30pm Tue-Sun. Closed 2wks Aug.* **Average** €32. **Credit** DC, MC, V. **Map** p159.

Behind an unassuming façade lies one of Rome's best-value gourmet dinners. The decor is stylishly minimal: bare walls with long mirrors, simple square tables and rough paper placemats. The back wall is all bottles: the result of the oenological peregrinations of host Giampaolo Gravina. Though you can simply order a bottle from the well-priced list, it's worth asking for advice – if only to hear him talk knowledgeably but above all lovingly about wine. In the kitchen, Sicilian chef Andrea Buscema betrays his origins in audacious combinations of vegetables and herbs with fish, meat and game: as in the *animelle tostate al timo e fagioli cannellini* (toasted innards with thyme and cannellini beans). Pasta courses tend to be more rustic, but in the best sense of the word: the wide buckwheat *tagliatelle* with fontina cheese, potatoes and spinach is flavourful. The desserts are good too, and there's a well-stocked cheese board. Book well in advance.

International

Bishoku Kobo

Via Ostiense 110B, South (06 574 4190). Metro Garbatella/bus 23. **Open** *7.30-10.30pm Mon-Sat. Closed 1wk Aug.* **Average** €25. **No credit cards.**

This Japanese restaurant on via Ostiense is well placed for visitors to the collection of antique statues in the adjacent Centrale Montemartini (*see p158*). Though the food is classic Japanese, the ambience is pure neighbourhood trattoria – except details like a gloriously kitsch sushi clock. The sashimi, sushi and stuffed vegetables are all good, and the tempura is well worth the extra wait. Prices are low, and it's always packed with locals – book ahead.

Wine bars & gastropubs

Tramonti e Muffati

Via Santa Maria Ausiliatrice 105, South (06 780 1342). Metro Colli Albani/bus 16, 85. **Open** *Meals served 8.30pm-midnight Mon-Sat. Wine bar/deli 4.30-8.30pm Mon-Sat. Closed Aug.* **Average** €24. **Credit** AmEx, DC, MC, V.

This tiny wine bar and delicatessen just off the via Appia Nuova has built up a solid reputation. Behind the small shopfront are a total of five rustic tables for evening dining: book well ahead. The secret of Marco Berardi's success is an obsessive hunt for the very best Italian wines, bakery goodies and farm products. These delicacies (most of which can also be bought here to take away) are supplemented by a few hot dishes such as *testaroli della Lunigiana* (spongy pasta squares) with pesto sauce and *pinoli* (pine nuts), or a cheese fondue flavoured with truffle shavings. But wine is the real point of the exercise – to the extent that the items on the menu are organised not by courses, but on the basis of what type of wine they best suit. The well-priced list features a number of small but interesting regional producers; if in doubt, ask signor Berardi for advice.

Cafés, Bars & *Gelaterie*

From breakfast-time crush to *aperitivo* and *digestivo*, life in Rome revolves around the bar.

At the height of the Empire, ancient Rome's citizens did their mass socialising at the Colosseum. Sure, the blood and gore were a big draw. But it was the human interaction that Romans really craved – the yelling, the joking, the fighting, the chaos. Romans still excel at the art of public socialising. The difference now is the forum: anyone still hankering after sweat and violence heads for the football stadium; others settle for the breakfast-time crush in their neighbourhood bar.

The old-school Roman bar where old men in hats down a coffee and a *digestivo*, then stamp out their cigarette on a sawdust-covered floor, is a vanishing breed. You'll probably need to schlep out into the suburbs if you want to escape stainless steel and pierced and tattooed staff pumping up the fashion TV.

So faint is the line between 'bar' and 'café' in Rome that the words are generally interchangeable. Bar tends to refer to places where you knock back your *caffè* at the counter; cafés tend to have seating and may offer a more extensive drink and food menu. But both bars and cafés, traditional and newly established, are slowly becoming jacks of all trades: witness the numerous cafés on piazza Navona, where upwards of 15 establishments strive to be all things to all tourists: café, pizza parlour, wine bar and fully fledged restaurant.

Whether bar or café, the etiquette is the same: non-regulars are expected to pay at the *cassa* (cash desk) before consuming. Identify what you want, then pay. When you order at the bar, placing a 10¢ or 20¢ coin on your *scontrino* (receipt) will get the bartender's attention. If you sit down, you will be served by a waiter and charged at least double for the privilege.

Besides coffee, which comes in many different forms (*see p201* **Caffè variations**), most bars have *cornetti* (croissants), which vary widely in quality, *tramezzini* (good if fresh, but usually to be avoided by the afternoon) and *pizza romana* (a slab of topping-less pizza brushed with olive oil, sliced through the middle and filled). Sandwiches and pizza can be toasted (ask, *me lo può scaldare, per favore?*).

To accompany your snack, bars generally offer *spremute* (freshly squeezed juice) and some have *frullati* (fruit shakes) and *centrifughe* (juiced carrots or apples) too. All offer a range

of sodas, juices and mineral waters. Tap water (*acqua semplice, acqua dal rubinetto*) is free; a glass of mineral water (*acqua minerale naturale* or *gassata*) costs around 30¢-50¢. Wine, beer and some liqueurs are also often on offer. *Digestivi* like *amari* ('bitters', infused aromatic liqueurs) and *limoncello* (lemon liqueur) will help you digest your meal and should be sipped, rather than downed like shots.

By law, all bars must have a *bagno* (lavatory), which can be used by anyone, whether or not they buy anything in the bar. The *bagno* may be locked; ask the cashier for the key (*la chiave per il bagno*). Bars must also provide dehydrated passers-by with a glass of tap water, again with no obligation to buy.

PUBS & ENOTECHE

Rome's *enoteche* and *vini e olii* (bottle shops) have historically been meccas and meeting places for old men who like to down a glass or two straight from the barrel before wending their way home. Many of these places have recently become, at the very least, charming places to grab a drink and a slice of the *vita romana*. At best, they are chic wine bars or bars with a late-night *dopo cena* (after dinner) scene, offering a wide variety of drinks – from a glass of Falanghina or Chianti to caipirinhas, caipiroskas and mojitos – and a beautiful crowd for people-watching. Some *enoteche* have developed into fully fledged eateries: for these, *see chapter* **Eating Out**. The ones we list below have remained predominantly watering holes. Rome's pubs are divided between a handful of long-standing UK-style institutions and a host of newer casual 'joints'. The best of both categories have been listed in this chapter.

PASTICCERIE & GELATERIE

Every neighbourhood of Rome has its own *pasticcerie* (cake shops); most of these (but not all, *see p222* **Shopping: Confectionery & cakes**) are bars where freshly baked goodies can be consumed *in situ* with a coffee or some other drink. The range of items on offer rarely varies: choux pastry *bignè* with creamy fillings, *semifreddi* ice-cream cakes, fruit tarts and a large assortment of biscuits. There can be huge variations, however, in the quality and freshness of the produce: the *pasticcerie* listed below are always reliable.

Sleek, minimalist style at the **Zest Bar**. See p207.

For a change from the usual offerings, try feast-day seasonal delicacies. *Panettoni* – sponge cakes with raisins and candied fruit – are ubiquitous around Christmas. The Easter variation is vaguely bird-shaped and called a *colomba* (dove). Around the feast of San Giuseppe (19 March), *pasticcerie* fill up with fried batter-balls filled with custard. During *carnevale* – in the run-up to Lent – you'll find compact balls of fried dough called *castagnole* and crispy pastry strips (generally fried too) dusted with sugar called *frappe*.

Many bars in Rome boast a well-stocked freezer cabinet with a sign promising *produzione artigianale* (home-made ice-creams). This is often a con. And while this doesn't necessarily mean the ice-cream will be bad – indeed, in some cases this not-so-genuine article can be very good – it's good to be selective if you're seeking a truly unique *gelato* experience. Look at the fruit *gelati*: if the colours seem too bright to be real, they probably aren't. Banana should be cream-coloured with a tinge of grey, not electric yellow... you get the picture.

Ice-cream to take away is served in a *cono* (cone) or *coppetta* (tub) of varying sizes, usually costing from €1 to €3. As well as the two main categories, *frutta* or *crema* (fruit-based or cream-based ice-creams), there's also *sorbetto* or the rougher *granita* (water ices). As a general rule, ice-creams kept in aluminium tubs are a safer bet than those in plastic ones.

When you've exhausted the *gelato*, you should sample a *grattachecca*. It's the Roman version of water ice, and consists of grated ice with flavoured syrup poured over it. The city was once full of kiosks selling this treat, but now only a handful remains. They are almost always on street corners (hence *angolo* in the addresses below), and most will be closed if you're visiting in winter; even in summer, opening hours are erratic.

Trevi & Quirinale

Cafés & bars

News Café

Via della Stamperia 72 (06 6992 3473). Metro Barberini/bus 52, 53, 61, 62, 63, 71, 80, 95, 116, 119, 175, 492, 630. **Open** *Oct-Mar* 7.30am-9pm Mon-Thur; 7.30am-1am Fri; 9am-1am Sat; 11am-8pm Sun. *Apr-Sept* 7am-1am daily. **Credit** AmEx, DC, MC, V. **Map** p335 2C.

This is a New York-style bar with modern steel and wood decor that pays lip service to the 'news' theme with racks of papers and a 24-hour satellite news screen. But behind the façade it's a regular Roman bar with better-than-average lunch options (salads, soups, pastas, filled rolls) and cakes – including those notorious Roman classics muffins and brownies. The seating is cramped – unless you manage to secure one of the few outside tables – and the service can be a little offhand. But don't miss out on the loo... amazing.

Gelaterie

Il Gelato di San Crispino

Via della Panetteria 42 (06 679 3924). Bus 52, 53, 61, 62, 63, 71, 80, 95, 116, 119, 175, 490, 630. **Open** noon-12.30am Mon, Wed, Sun; noon-1.30am Fri, Sat. Closed mid Jan-mid Feb. **No credit cards.** **Map** p335 2C.

Il Gelato di San Crispino has far and away the best ice-cream in Rome – some say the best ice-cream in the world. The secret is the makers' obsessive control over the whole process. Flavours change according to what's in season – in summer the *lampone* (raspberry) and *susine* (yellow plum) are really fabulous. Don't even think of asking for a cone, though: only cups or tubs are allowed. True devotees shun this Trevi Fountain branch and instead head out into the suburbs, where the miracle of San Crispino first occurred. In truth the product is equally exceptional at each of the branches, and the central branch has the additional advantage – over and above its location – of offering exquisite Jamaican coffee.

Branches: via Acaia 56 (06 7045 0412); via Bevagna 90 (06 3322 1075).

Veneto & Borghese

Cafés & bars

Café de Paris

Via Veneto 90 (06 4201 2257). Bus 52, 53, 63, 80, 95, 116, 119, 630. **Open** 8am-1am daily. **Credit** AmEx, DC, MC, V. **Map** p335 1B.

When via Veneto was in its *dolce vita* heyday many moons ago, this was the epicentre of laid-back cool. Here you could be served in your jeans (which was really quite something in those days) and eavesdrop on the paparazzi as they badmouthed their prey. But times have changed: the via Veneto is now very passé and this is just another rather bland café. Nonetheless, there's an English tea hour for those who are homesick, and in the evenings you can sup at the wine bar in the refurbished interior.

Doney

Via Veneto 145 (06 4708 2805). Bus 52, 53, 63, 80, 95, 116, 119, 630. **Open** 8am-2am daily. **Credit** AmEx, DC, MC, V. **Map** p335 1B.

Doney used to provide competition for the Café de Paris across the street. At its peak in the 1950s and 1960s it was a key meeting point for the Cinecittà set (including such luminaries as Ava Gardner, Marcello Mastroianni, Tyrone Power, Anita Ekberg) and the Roman intelligentsia. After a slow couple of decades, it's been polished up and relaunched by the nightlife PR ladies who are also behind the success of La Suite (*see p261*). It's red, it's sexy… and it's expensive, as befits the café of the upmarket Westin Excelsior hotel (*see p41*). But it's popular with both tourists and locals, and the *aperitivi* pull in a swanky set from further afield in the city too.

Il Tridente

Cafés & bars

Antico Caffè Greco

Via Condotti 86 (06 679 1700). Metro Spagna/bus 52, 53, 61, 71, 80, 85, 95, 116, 119, 160, 850. **Open** 8.30am-8pm daily. **Credit** AmEx, DC, MC, V. **Map** p335 1C.

Founded in 1760, this venerable café was once the hangout of Casanova, Goethe, Wagner, Stendhal, Baudelaire, Shelley and Byron. Opposition to the French Occupation of 1849-70 was planned here. Today it has its sofas packed with tourists, while locals cram the foyer. Literary and musical evenings with a light dinner hark back to its artistic past.

Café Notegen

Via del Babuino 159 (06 320 0855). Metro Spagna/bus 117, 119. **Open** 7.30am-midnight daily. **Credit** DC, MC, V. **Map** p332 2A.

An historic gathering spot for theatre people, artists and intellectuals, this century-old café prides itself on being a café 'in the French sense', serving hot and cold dishes and great cakes at any hour to sophisticated customers seated in velvet booths. Downstairs, live cabaret, music and the odd play are performed on an irregular basis.

Canova

Piazza del Popolo 16 (06 361 2231). Metro Flaminio/buses 95, 117, 119, 491. **Open** 8am-midnight daily. **Credit** AmEx, DC, MC, V. **Map** p332 2A.

Traditionally, Canova's clientele was right-wing and at daggers drawn with the left-wing rabble at Rosati (*see below*) across the square, though there little evidence of this now. It's a characterless, all-purpose spot (even selling kitschy souvenirs), but does catch the late afternoon sun. On summer evenings, it stays open until the last night owl heads home.

Ciampini al Café du Jardin

Viale Trinità dei Monti (06 678 5678). Metro Spagna/bus 52, 53, 61, 71, 80, 85, 95, 116, 119, 160, 850. **Open** *Mid Mar-mid May, mid Sept-mid Oct* 8am-8pm daily. *Mid May-mid Sept* 8am-1am Mon, Tue, Thur-Sun. Closed mid Oct-mid Mar. **Credit** AmEx, DC, MC, V. **Map** p335 1C.

This open-air café near the top of the Spanish Steps is an oasis surrounded by creeper-curtained trellises, with a pond in the centre. There's a selection of sandwiches, salads, pastas, cocktails and ices, and it also serves a good breakfast. There's a stunning view, especially at sunset, so whet your appetite by sipping an *aperitivo* in true Italian style.

Dolci e Doni

Via delle Carrozze 85B (06 6992 5001). Metro Spagna/bus 52, 53, 61, 71, 80, 85, 95, 116, 119, 160, 850. **Open** *Oct-Apr* 9am-9pm daily. *May-Sept* 9am-11pm daily. Closed 1wk Aug. **Credit** AmEx, DC, MC, V. **Map** p333 1A.

Caffè variations

To get a short, thick espresso ask for *un caffè*. A cappuccino is an espresso with steamed, frothy milk added. It is rarely consumed after 11am; Romans wouldn't be caught dead drinking it after a meal.

caffè macchiato with a dash of milk
caffè monichella with whipped cream
caffè ristretto coffee essence lining the bottom of the cup – a tooth-enamel remover
caffè al vetro in a glass

Variations on the espresso

caffè americano with a lot more water
caffè corretto with a dash of either liqueur or spirits (indicate which)
caffè freddo iced espresso; comes sugared unless you ask for *caffè freddo amaro*
caffè Hag espresso decaf
caffè lungo a bit more water than usual

Variations on the cappuccino

caffè latte more hot milk and less coffee
caffè corretto iced coffee with cold milk; will come sugared unless you specifically ask for *cappuccino freddo amaro*
cappuccino senza schiuma without froth
latte macchiato hot milk with just a dash of coffee for flavour

This bijou tearoom, renowned for its cakes and chocolates, also specialises in breakfasts, brunches and quick quiche-and-salad lunches. There are cakes to take away, and catering can be arranged.

Gina

Via San Sebastianello 7A (06 678 0251). Metro Spagna/bus 52, 53, 61, 71, 80, 85, 95, 116, 119, 160, 850. **Open** 9am-9pm Mon-Wed, Sun; 9am-midnight Thur-Sat. Closed 1wk Aug. **Credit** AmEx, MC, V. **Map** p335 1C.
Finally – a brand new, modern locale in this part of town… quite a relief from the area's posh tearooms and over-decorated cafés. The décor is clean and ultra-white, with delicate touches like votive candles and single pink roses in miniature Mason jars. The menu, divided into sections ('Be Warm' – soups, melted brie; 'Be Light' – salads; 'Be Classic' – Italian staples), offers lunch and light fare, plus a selection of great ice-creams and even chocolate fondue. The owners have cleverly used their location, on the street leading up to the Villa Borghese park, to 'Be Romantic': they prepare gourmet picnic baskets complete with blanket, wine, cheese, fruit and chocolates. Hours were due to be extended until 2am.

Rosati

Piazza del Popolo 5 (06 322 5859). Metro Flaminio/ bus 95, 117, 119, 491. **Open** 7.30am-11.30pm daily. **Credit** AmEx, DC, MC, V. **Map** p332 2A.
Rosati is the traditional haunt of Rome's intellectual left: Calvino, Moravia and Pasolini were regulars. The art nouveau interior has remained unchanged since its opening in 1922. Try the Sogni romani cocktail: orange juice with four kinds of liqueur in red and yellow – the colours of the city. *Cornetti* and sandwiches are fresh and good; an ample brunch is served from 1pm to 4pm on Sundays.

Shaki

Via Mario de' Fiori 29A (06 679 1694). Metro Spagna/bus 52, 53, 61, 71, 80, 85, 95, 116, 119, 160, 850. **Open** *Mar-Sept* 9.30am-midnight daily.

Oct-Feb 10.30am-10.30pm daily. **Credit** AmEx, DC, MC, V. **Map** p335 1C.
Deep in designer territory, this ultra-stylish wine bar looks like it has landed from some distant land (namely, Milan). Design is cool, modern and Japanese-influenced; the food, however, is unrepentantly Mediterranean. There are no hot dishes, only a selection of *panini* and salads made with fresh ingredients. Prices are high for what's on offer.

Pubs & *enoteche*

See also p223 **Buccone.**

Antica Enoteca di Via della Croce

Via della Croce 76B (06 679 0896). Metro Spagna/bus 52, 53, 61, 71, 80, 85, 95, 116, 119, 160, 628, 850. **Open** 11.30am-1am daily. Closed 1wk Aug. **Credit** AmEx, DC, MC, V. **Map** p332 2A.
When this place opened in 1842 it was the favourite haunt of Scandinavian painters who lived on nearby via Margutta. A tasteful revamp has retained most of the original fittings, including the marble wine vats and a venerable wooden cash desk, making it a great place to sip one of many wines offered by the glass. There's a cold *antipasto* buffet at the bar and a restaurant with tables in the long back room offering a full range of hot dishes at meal times. It also operates as an off-licence.

Navona & Pantheon

Cafés & bars

Bar della Pace

Via della Pace 3/7 (06 686 1216). Bus 30, 40, 46, 62, 64, 70, 81, 87, 116, 492, 628. **Open** 3pm-2am Mon; 9am-2am Tue-Sun. **Credit** MC, V. **Map** p333 2B.
Rome's Antico Caffè della Pace (which is known to all and sundry as Bar della Pace) is eternally à la mode. It continues to be a great (though expensive) place from which to survey passing fashion victims.

Eat, Drink, Shop

Pick a pavement table of a summer evening and watch the square, always overflowing with revellers in their trendy togs.

Sant'Eustachio
Piazza Sant'Eustachio 82 (06 6880 2048). Bus 30, 40, 46, 62, 63, 64, 70, 81, 87, 492, 628, 630, 780, H. **Open** *8.30am-1am daily.* **No credit cards.** **Map** p333 2A.
This is one of the city's most famous coffee bars and its walls are plastered with celebrity testimonials. The coffee is quite extraordinary, if expensive; the barmen turn their backs while whipping up a cup so as not to let their secret out. Try the *gran caffè*: the *schiuma* (froth) can be slurped out afterwards with spoon or fingers. Unless you specify (*amaro* means 'no sugar'; *poco zucchero* means 'a little sugar'), it comes very sweet.

La Tazza d'Oro
Via degli Orfani 84 (06 678 9792). Bus 30, 40, 46, 62, 63, 64, 70, 81, 87, 492, 628, 630, 780, H. **Open** *8am-8pm Mon-Sat. Closed 1wk Aug.* **Credit** AmEx, DC, MC, V. **Map** p333 2A.
The powerful aroma wafting from this ancient *torrefazione* (coffee-grinder's) overlooking the Pantheon is a siren call to coffee lovers. It's packed with coffee sacks, tourists and regulars who flock for *granita di caffè* (coffee sorbet) in summer, and *cioccolata calda con panna* (hot chocolate with whipped cream) in winter.

I Tre Scalini
Piazza Navona 28-32 (06 6880 1996). Bus 30, 40, 46, 62, 64, 70, 81, 87, 116, 492, 628. **Open** *9am-12.30am Mon, Tue, Thur-Sun. Closed Jan.* **No credit cards.** **Map** p333 2A&B.
This bar is famous for its *tartufo* – a calorie-bomb chocolate ice-cream concoction with huge lumps of chocolate inside. There are tables outside at which to enjoy food from a wide-ranging menu and a tearoom on the first floor. Beware: sit down, and the price mark-up is massive. Take your ice-cream away and enjoy it next to Bernini's fountain (*see p103*).

Pubs & *enoteche*

La Trinchetta
Via dei Banchi Nuovi 4 (06 6830 0133). Bus 40, 64, 70, 492. **Open** *8pm-2am Mon-Sat. Closed Aug.* **Credit** DC, MC, V. **Map** p333 2B.
This nook is a hidden gem: it's not only an enoteca, it's a *grapperia* as well, with a huge range of different labels. To sate the appetite, a selection of cheese and *salumi* are available as well as hot, fresh dishes like lasagna and various *torte salate* (quiches). La Trinchetta also has theme evenings: Thursday, for example, is a very popular sushi night... so book.

Trinity College
Via del Collegio Romano 6 (06 678 6472). Bus 62, 63, 81, 85, 95, 117, 119, 160, 175, 492, 628, 630, 850. **Open** *noon-2am daily.* **Credit** AmEx, DC, MC, V. **Map** p333 2A.

This is a city-centre pub much frequented by thirsty employees of the Cultural Heritage Ministry opposite. It has a more authentic feel than many of the capital's Irish pubs, although the thirsty packs of American college students prove 'tis all an illusion.

Pasticcerie & *gelaterie*

La Caffettiera
Piazza di Pietra 65 (06 679 8147). Bus 62, 63, 81, 85, 95, 117, 119, 160, 175, 492, 628, 630, 850. **Open** *Oct-May 7am-9pm daily. June-Sept 7am-9pm Mon-Sat.* **Credit** AmEx, DC, MC, V. **Map** p333 2A.
Politicians and mandarins from the nearby parliament buildings lounge in the sumptuous tearoom of this temple to Neapolitan goodies, while lesser mortals – such as parliamentary hacks – bolt coffees at the bar. The rum babà reigns supreme, but ricotta lovers rave over the crunchy *sfogliatella*, delicately flavoured with cinnamon and orange peel, and the *pastiera*, a rich tart filled with ricotta, orange-flower water, citrus peel and whole grains of wheat.

Cremeria Monteforte
Via della Rotonda 22 (06 686 7720). Bus 30, 40, 46, 62, 63, 64, 70, 81, 87, 492, 628, 630, 780, H. **Open** *10am-11pm Tue-Sun. Closed mid Dec-Jan.* **No credit cards.** **Map** p333 2A.
This *gelateria*, handily situated around the corner from the Pantheon, is a cut above the many others in the area. The *stracciatella* and after eight (mint) flavours have lumps of chocolate in them, and are creamy, light and delicious.

Ghetto & Campo de' Fiori
See also p204 **Campo it up.**

Cafés & bars

Da Vezio
Via dei Delfini 23 (06 678 6036). Bus 30, 40, 46, 62, 63, 64, 70, 81, 87, 492, 628, 630, 780, H. **Open** *7am-8.30pm Mon-Sat. Closed 3wks Aug.* **No credit cards.** **Map** p336 1A.
Vezio Bagazzini is a legendary figure in the Ghetto area, on account of his bar behind the former Communist party HQ. Every square centimetre is filled with Communist icons and trophies – not just Italian, but Soviet and Cuban too. Every Italian leftist leader worth his or her salt arrives here at some point for a photo with Vezio, as evident from the walls. As this guide went to press, Vezio was fighting an eviction order.

Pubs & *enoteche*
See also p180 **L'Angolo Divino.**

Il Goccetto
Via dei Banchi Vecchi 14 (06 686 4268). Buses 40, 46, 62, 64, 916. **Open** *11.30am-2pm, 5.30-11pm*

Mon-Sat. Closed 3wks Aug. **Credit** AmEx, MC, V. **Map** p333 2B.

One of the more serious *centro storico* wine bars, occupying part of a medieval bishop's house, with original painted ceilings and a cosy, private-club feel. Wine is the main point, with a satisfying range by the glass from €2.50, but there's a choice of cheeses, salamis and salads too. Closes early afternoon on Saturdays in July.

Lot 87
*Via del Pellegrino 87 (06 9761 8344/www.lot87.com).
Bus 40, 46, 62, 64, 916.* **Open** 8am-2am Mon-Fri;
9am-2am Sat; 11am-2am Sun. Closed 1wk Aug.
Credit AmEx, MC, V. **Map** p333 2B.
This new-for-2003 bar follows the 'international aesthetic' popping up around Rome: steel and blond wood, minimalist design and flat-screen TVs. Fairly funky, what it lacks in atmosphere it makes up for with warm, friendly service – and a long list of cocktails for only €5 that will warm your, erm, heart. From 7-9pm there's an *aperitivo* hour during which, for that same €5, you can drink and munch your way down the snack-laden bar. Also serves an American-style bacon-and-egg breakfast.

Mad Jack's
*Via Arenula 20 (06 6880 8223). Bus 63, 630, 780,
H/tram 8.* **Open** 11am-2am daily. Closed 2wks Aug.
Credit AmEx, DC, MC, V. **Map** p336 1B.
A formulaic but reliable Irish pub in a very central location that's open through the day, every day. At night and especially on weekends, crowds of young Italians and Anglos spill out on to the pavement. The beverages of choice are beer or cider – both available on draught in a range of versions – but there is also an array of wines and cocktails, plus a small selection of standard bar nibbles. But beware: late in the evening this can be a depressing place if you're over 25.

Pasticcerie & gelaterie

See also p222 **Dolceroma** and **Forno del Ghetto**.

Alberto Pica
*Via della Seggiola 12 (06 686 8405). Bus 23, 63, 280,
630, 780, H/tram 8.* **Open** *Oct-Mar* 8am-2am Mon-
Sat. *Apr-Sept* 8am-2am Mon-Sat; 4pm-3am Sun. Closed
10 days Aug. **No credit cards. Map** p336 1B.
Alongside the regular bar is an excellent selection of ice-creams, among which the rice specialities stand out: imagine eating frozen, partially cooked rice pudding and you'll get the picture. *Riso alla cannella* (cinnamon rice) is particularly delicious.

Bernasconi
*Piazza Cairoli 16 (06 6880 6264). Bus 63, 630, 780,
H/tram 8.* **Open** 7am-8.30pm Tue-Sun. Closed Aug.
No credit cards. Map p336 1B.
Cramped and inconspicuous like so many of Rome's best cake shops, it's well worth fighting your way inside for *lieviti* (breakfast yeast buns). Bernasconi's

cornetti are unbeatable: the real vintage variety. Close to the synagogue, this spot straddles Rome's Jewish and Catholic worlds, with kosher sweets and Lenten *quaresimale* cookies.

Trastevere & Gianicolo

Cafés & bars

Bar Gianicolo
Piazzale Aurelio 5 (06 580 6275). Bus 870. **Open**
6am-1am Tue-Sun. **No credit cards. Map** p336 2C.
Wooden panels and benches lend this tiny bar on the hill above Trastevere, at the site of Garibaldi's doomed battle with the French (*see p17*), an intimate and chatty feel that's unusual in Rome. Carrots and apples are juiced on the spot and a good range of interesting sandwiches and light meals – along with outside tables overlooking the Porta di San Pancrazio – make it a good spot for a drink or a snack after a walk in Villa Pamphili (*see p161*).

Bar San Calisto
*Piazza San Calisto (06 589 5678). Bus 780, H/tram
8.* **Open** 5.30am-2am Mon-Sat. **No credit cards.**
Map p336 2B.
Green tourists get their coffee or beer on piazza Santa Maria in Trastevere; locals who know better go to this bar. Its harsh lighting would make Sophia Loren look wan and the dingy space – inside and out – is no picture postcard. But it's dirt cheap and as such it has always been the haunt of arty and fringe types (plus many questionable characters after sundown). They're here downing beers or an *affogato* (ice-cream swamped with liqueur), or savouring some of the best chocolate in Rome: hot and thick with fresh whipped cream in winter and in the form of creamy *gelato* in warmer months.

Di Marzio
*Piazza Santa Maria in Trastevere 15 (06 581 6095).
Bus 780, H/tram 8.* **Open** 7am-2am Tue-Sun. Closed
10 days Jan, 10 days Aug. **Credit** MC, V.
Map p336 2B.
Piazza Santa Maria is not the cheapest place in Rome to sit out and have a drink, but if you do want to admire this square with drink in hand, Di Marzio is where the locals go. It has great *cornetti* in the morning and good sun in the afternoon, and is a central stop in the evening for a quick drink or coffee pre- or post-dinner, before heading on to bigger and better bars in the neighbourhood.

Friends Art Café
*Piazza Trilussa 34 (06 581 6111). Bus 23, 280, 780,
H/tram 8.* **Open** 7am-2am Mon-Sat; 6pm-2am Sun.
Closed 1wk Aug. **Credit** AmEx, DC, MC, V.
Map p336 1B.
This lively, modern bar is a popular place where habitués meet for everything from a morning *cornetto* and cappuccino to after-dinner cocktails. The chrome detailing and brightly coloured plastic chairs in the dining room, coupled with the constant

Campo it up

Situated along the route for papal processions from St Peter's (*see p143*) to San Giovanni in Laterano (*see p131*), this erstwhile 'field of flowers' – campo de' Fiori – was the hub of an area packed with inns that serviced the bodily rather than the spiritual needs of medieval pilgrims. Through the centuries, ladies of the night (and day) presided over bawdy inns where drinking was the priority.

The same priority applies in the Campo today. Since 1869 a colourful, boisterous (albeit overpriced) food market has hampered drinking activities from early morning until 2pm, Monday to Saturday. After that, garbage trucks descend on the square, holding up business for a little longer. But by 4pm locals and tourists alike are drifting into the freshly swept Campo, ready to tackle its bars.

By *aperitivo* time, it's a dog-eat-dog battle to grab a table at the watering holes that line the Campo. The longest-running wine bar on the piazza, **La Vineria** is the authentic local thing, where Romans flock to chat and plan the evening ahead over good wines by the glass starting at a remarkably cheap €1. The **Taverna del Campo** supplements its liquid offerings with a range of snacks.

The scene gets livelier/rowdier from 10pm, when the 'program'-attending denizens of US university-owned accommodation around the Campo descend on bars such as **Sloppy Sam's**, which is also very popular with the obnoxiously drunken participants of organised bar-crawls. **The Drunken Ship** is a student favourite too, perhaps because of its student discounts and DJs of an evening. If you're looking for a quieter drink, try the Ship's happy hour from 5pm to 8pm.

Decidedly more Roman in atmosphere, the newly opened **Bottiglieria Il Nolano** is rustic indoors in the winter. But in warmer weather, it sets old-fashioned cinema-style seats on the pavement outside, perfect for watching the Campo's colourful parade of characters.

Bottiglieria Il Nolano
Campo de' Fiori 11-12 (06 687 9344).
Open 6pm-2am Tue-Sat; noon-2am Sun.
No credit cards.

The Drunken Ship
Campo de' Fiori 20-21 (06 6830 0535).
Open 5pm-2am daily. **Credit** MC, V.

Sloppy Sam's
Campo de' Fiori 10 (06 6880 2637).
Open 4pm-2am daily. **Credit** MC, V.

Taverna del Campo
Campo de' Fiori 16 (06 687 4402). **Open** 9am-2am Tue-Sun. **Credit** AmEx, DC, MC, V.

La Vineria
Campo de' Fiori 15 (06 6880 3268).
Open 9am-1am Mon-Sat; 5pm-1am Sun.
Closed 10 days Aug. **Credit** AmEx, DC, MC, V.

din of fashion TV in the background, lend the place a retro-'80s funhouse feel. Lunch and dinner menus offer the usual suspects (*bruschette*, salads, pastas) at reasonable prices.

Ombre Rosse

Piazza Sant'Egidio 12 (06 588 4155). Bus 780, H/tram 8. **Open** 8am-2am Mon-Sat; 5pm-2am Sun. **Credit** AmEx, MC, V. **Map** p336 2B.
In the heart of Trastevere on a scenic piazza, this café is a meeting spot day and night. With no midday closure, it's perfect for morning coffee, a late lunch or a light dinner (try the chicken salad or fresh soups). It fills to bursting point pre- and post-dinner, when snagging one of the coveted outside tables is a coup. Service is slow but friendly: as the bartender hand-crushes the ice for your next caipiroska, you have plenty of time to watch the Trastevere menagerie go by.

Pubs & *enoteche*

Artù

Largo MD Fumasoni Biondi 5 (06 588 0398). Bus 23, 280, 870. **Open** 6pm-2am Tue-Sun. Closed 3wks Aug. **Credit** MC, V. **Map** p336 1B.
This friendly place, in a little square that's an extension of piazza Sant'Egidio, hovers somewhere between Italian bar and English pub. The stained-glass windows, selection of high-quality brews, polished wood bar and smattering of English-speaking regulars lean towards the UK; the wine list, fashion TV and *aperitivo* buffet (from 6.30-9pm) are reminders that we're still in *bella Italia*. There's also a full menu of 'pub' fare, with sandwiches, pasta and meat courses. A handy spot for a nibble before or after a film at the Pasquino (*see p241*).

Enoteca Trastevere

Via della Lungaretta 86 (06 588 5659). Bus 780, H/tram 8. **Open** 5pm-2am Mon, Tue, Thur-Sat; 11am-1am Sun. Closed 3wks Jan. **Credit** AmEx, MC, V. **Map** p336 2B.
The usual enoteca decor prevails at this neighbourhood favourite: wooden tables and chairs, walls lined with hundreds of bottles of mostly Italian wine and a menu that offers an assortment of cheese, cured meats, *bruschette* and *crostini*, salads and desserts. But this enoteca has a couple of less obvious selling points too: a large selection of grappas, distilled liqueurs and *amari* by the glass at reasonable prices, plus a good selection of organic wines.

Stardust

Vicolo de' Renzi 4 (06 5832 0875). Bus 23, 280, 780/tram 8. **Open** 3.30pm-2am Mon-Sat; noon-2am Sun. **No credit cards**. **Map** p336 2B.
This tiny space with a handful of tables and cushioned benches lining the walls is an institution for local night owls. From 3.30pm to 7pm it's a tearoom; from 7pm to 10pm it's a bistro, perfect for an *aperitivo* and snack. But it really comes alive after 10pm, when it becomes a raucous, smoky bar/pub where

bartenders blast anything from Lenny Kravitz to Cuban jazz, Euro-rap to Czech polkas and owner Anna's favourite: Italian opera. The crowd is a colourful mix of locals, out-of-work actors and expats. Sunday from noon to 5pm there's a great international brunch (often themed) with eggs, bacon, pancakes, home-made bagels and a shake-those-Sunday-blues atmosphere.

Pasticcerie & gelaterie

See also p203 **Bar San Calisto**.

Doppia Coppia

Via della Scala 51 (no phone). Bus 23, 280, 780, H/tram 8. **Open** *Nov, Feb-Mar* 1-8pm Mon-Fri; 1-10pm Sat, Sun. *Apr-Oct* 1pm-midnight Mon-Fri; 1pm-1am Sat, Sun. Closed Dec, Jan. **No credit cards**. **Map** p336 2B.
This tiny *gelateria* on a corner in Trastevere dishes out a fantastic *stracciatella* (chocolate chip), along with about 20 other equally delicious flavours. In summer months, it also offers *granita* (water ice) in refreshingly tart lemon, tangerine, coffee or mint.

Sora Mirella

Lungotevere degli Anguillara, angolo Ponte Cestio (no phone). Bus 23, 280, 780, H/tram 8. **Open** *Mar-Sept* 10am-3am daily. **No credit cards**. **Map** p336 2A.
Mirella styles herself *la regina della grattacheccia* (the Queen of Water Ices) and there seems no reason to disagree. Sit on the Tiber embankment wall as you tuck into the *speciale superfrutta* – fresh melon, kiwi fruit and strawberry (or whatever is in season) with syrups served in a special glass.

Aventine & Testaccio

Cafés & bars

Bar del Mattatoio

Piazza O Giustiniani 3 (06 574 6017). Bus 95, 170, 673, 719, 781/tram 3. **Open** 6am-8.30pm Mon-Sat. Closed 2wks Aug. **No credit cards**. **Map** p337 2B.
This is a brick-built doll's house of a bar, with Gothic recesses in the front. It's also one of the earliest-opening bars in Rome, once upon a time catering for the early-bird workers from the slaughterhouse opposite. Nowadays the bar's constituency is mainly dawn revellers limping home from Testaccio's clubs (*see chapter* **Nightlife & Music**).

Pubs & *enoteche*

L'Oasi della Birra

Piazza Testaccio 41 (06 574 6122). Bus 23, 30, 75, 95, 170, 280, 716, 781/tram 3. **Open** 7.30pm-1am Mon-Sat. Closed 2wks Aug. **Credit** MC, V. **Map** p337 2A.
In the basement of an enoteca on Testaccio's market square, this 'Oasis of Beer' has over 500 brews on offer. It's one of the few places in Rome where

you can track down the products of Italian micro-breweries such as the award-winning Menabrea; the selection of wines by the bottle is almost as impressive. The food ranges from full-scale meals with a Germanic/Eastern slant (goulash, wurstel, krauti) to snacks (*crostini, bruschette*). The outside tables operate year round, weather permitting. Booking is a good idea.

Pasticcerie & gelaterie

Chiosco Testaccio
Via G Branca, angolo via Beniamino Franklin (no phone). Bus 95, 170, 781/tram 3. **Open** *May-mid Sept* noon-1.30am daily. **No credit cards. Map** p337 2B.
Still going strong after over 80 years in this working-class neighbourhood, the kiosk is painted a different colour each year. Ice is hand-grated and the unusual flavours of tamarind and *limoncocco* (lemon-coconut) are specialities.

Celio & San Giovanni

Cafés & bars

Café Café
Via dei Santi Quattro 44 (06 700 8743). Metro Colosseo/bus 85, 87, 117, 810, 850/tram 3. **Open** 10am-1am Tue-Sun. Closed 2wks Aug. **Credit** MC, V. **Map** p338 2B.
A pleasant change from the usual chrome-and-glass counters, this attractive place offers teas, wines, salads and sandwiches for travellers weary after a romp around the Colosseum. There's a brunch buffet from 11.30am to 4pm on Sundays.

Monti & Esquilino

Cafés & bars

Antico Caffè del Brasile
Via dei Serpenti 23 (06 488 2319). Bus 40, 64, 70, 117, 170, H. **Open** *Sept-June* 5.30am-8.30pm Mon-Sat; 7am-2pm Sun. *July, Aug* 5.30am-8.30pm Mon-Sat. Closed 2wks Aug. **No credit cards. Map** p338 1C.
Its giant coffee-roaster no longer functions, but this bar on the characterful main street of Monti retains its traditional atmosphere. The current pope – when he was still humble Cardinal Wojtyla – could once be counted among their clientele.

Pubs & enoteche

The Druid's Den
Via San Martino ai Monti 28 (06 4890 4781). Metro Cavour/bus 16, 75, 84, 360, 649. **Open** 6pm-1.30am Mon-Thur, Sun; 6pm-3am Fri, Sat. **No credit cards. Map** p338 1C.
Like its rival the Fiddler's Elbow (*see below*), this pub was already well established before the current

craze for all things Irish developed in Rome. It serves a decent pint of Liffey water, as well as beaming football in from the British Isles.

The Fiddler's Elbow
Via dell'Olmata 43 (06 487 2110). Metro Cavour/bus 16, 75, 84, 360, 649. **Open** 5pm-1.15am Mon-Sat; 3pm-1.30am Sun. **No credit cards. Map** p338 1B.
One of the oldest, best-known pubs in Rome, the Fiddler's Elbow has been unchanged for years. Its narrow, basic wood-and-bench interior is smoky as ever, making it popular with students.

Tazio
Piazza Repubblica (06 489 381). Metro Repubblica/ bus 40, 64, 70, 170, H. **Open** 9am-1am daily. **Credit** AmEx, DC, MC, V. **Map** p335 2B.
Named after the king of paparazzi, Tazio Secchiaroli, this *champagnerie* and café in the posh new Hotel Exedra has a glitzy '80s-style red-and-black champagne-sipping room, with proseccos and spumantes ranging from €5 to €10 a glass. Bottles on the extensive list start at €50 and head into the stratosphere. Nibbles here are gratis, but you can head into the more subtly decorated bar rooms for interesting sandwiches and classic champagne accompaniments (fois gras, truffles, caviar). Decorations include photos by the master himself.

Al Vino al Vino
Via dei Serpenti 19 (06 485 803). Bus 40, 64, 70, 117, 170, H. **Open** 11.30am-1.30pm, 5pm-12.30am daily. Closed 3wks Aug. **Credit** DC, MC, V. **Map** p338 1C.
This wine bar on lively via dei Serpenti has a range of more than 500 wines, with 25 available by the glass. But its real speciality are *distillati*: dozens of fine grappas, whiskies and other strong spirits. In

Retro '80s funhouse at Friends Art Café. See p203.

the back room are pretty cast-iron tables, topped with volcanic stone and ceramics. The menu here is strong on Sicilian specialities such as *caponata* (Sicilian ratatouille) and eggplant *parmigiana*.

Zest Bar

Es Hotel, via F Turati 171 (06 444 841/ www.eshotel.it). Metro Termini/bus 70, 71, 105. **Open** 10am-1.30am daily. **Credit** AmEx, DC, MC, V. **Map** p338 1A.

This seventh-floor bar in the cool new Es Hotel (*see p53*) is the first Schrager-type hotel and bar in Rome. You'll either love or hate the view – over the De Chirico-esque forms and tracks of Termini railway station – but if you're among the latter, turn your gaze inward to the sleek ergonomic chairs, black lacquer and minimalist bar. And the crowd, of course. It's an attractive mix of slim, tanned thirty-something Romans and foreign business folk. Prices are high (€13 for a cocktail) but hell – you're paying for style. Visit in warm weather, when the roof deck opens for poolside partying.

Pasticcerie & gelaterie

Dagnino

Galleria Esedra, via VE Orlando 75 (06 481 8660). Metro Repubblica/bus 40, 64, 70, 170, H. **Open** 7am-10.30pm daily. **Credit** MC, V. **Map** p335 1B.

Stunning 1950s decor and a chronic oversupply of tables set the scene for this corner of Sicily in the heart of Rome. If it's Sicilian and edible, it's here: ice-cream in buns, life-like marzipan fruits. Regulars come for crisp *cannoli siciliani* filled with ricotta and, above all, the splendour of shiny green-iced *cassata*, uniting all the flavours of the south: the perfume of citrus, almond paste and fresh ricotta.

Il Palazzo del Freddo di Giovanni Fassi

Via Principe Eugenio 65/67 (06 446 4740). Metro Vittorio/bus 70, 71, 105/tram 5, 14. **Open** noon-midnight Tue-Thur; noon-1am Fri, Sat; 10am-midnight Sun. **No credit cards**. **Map** p336 1A.

With its pompous name, breathtakingly kitsch interior and splendid ices, Fassi nothing less than a Roman institution. Founded in 1880, its walls are adorned with Edwardian adverts and Fascist-era posters that extol the virtues of the shop's wares. Service is as unfailingly irascible as ever and the crowds can be difficult to elbow your way through, but the ices are never less than sublime: best of all are *riso* – the English translation, 'rice pudding', hardly does it justice – and the Palazzo's own invention, *la caterinetta*, a mysterious concoction of whipped honey and vanilla.

Vatican & Prati

Cafés & bars

Antonini

Via Sabotino 19/29 (06 3751 7845). Bus 30, 224, 280, 628. **Open** 7am-9pm daily. **Credit** MC, V. **Map** p332 1C.

In winter you can't move for fur coats in this high-class *pasticceria*. It's the place to come to buy cakes to take to that important lunch or dinner party. Alternatively, eat them *in situ*: one *montebianco* (meringue, marron glacé, spaghetti and cream) is a meal in itself. It also does a great line in *tartine* – canapés topped with pâté, smoked salmon or caviar. Sitting outside is a good way to observe life in high-rent residential Rome.

Aperitivi

When it comes to having an *aperitivo*, Milan is undoubtedly the capital city of Italian quaffing. But the good people of Rome are never slow to adopt habits that involve additional socialising, and there's been a marked move towards easing your way into the evening with a glass of something alcoholic among the bronzed and beautifully attired residents of the Italian capital proper.

Where to go

● **Antica Enoteca di Via della Croce** (*p201*): perfect post-shopping refresher or pre-dinner locale for wine and cheese
● **Ciampini al Café du Jardin** (*p200*): lovely view, particularly at sunset
● **Doney** (*p200*): chic crowd and lots of outdoor tables on via Veneto
● **Friends Art Café** (*p203*): central Trastevere location and free nibbles
● **Lot 87** (*p203*): inexpensive cocktails and free bar snacks near campo de' Fiori

● **Tazio** (*p206*): an elegant place to start the evening, with a tremendous range of bubbly
● **La Vineria** (*see p204* **Campo it up**): classic location for prosecco and people-watching

What to drink

● **Prosecco**: the classic Italian pre-dinner bubbly – try a Valdobiàddene or Cartizze
● **Bellini**: the famous invention of Harry's Bar in Venice – half prosecco and half peach nectar
● **Wine**: try a Greco di Tufo or Falanghina, varietals from the southern Campania region popular since ancient times, or a warming red in colder weather
● **Campari**: the bitter, bright red soda, or the cocktail of Campari mixed with soda water; over ice, with a slice of orange
● **Mojito**: becoming all the rage, with crushed ice, crushed mint, sugar and rum
● **Caipirinha/caipiroska**: straight from Brazil, sugar and limes crushed with ice and either cachaça (-inha) or vodka (-oska)

Faggiani

Via G Ferrari 23/9 (06 3973 9742). Bus 30, 70, 224, 280, 628. **Open** *6.30am-9pm Mon, Tue, Thur-Sun. Closed 3wks Aug.* **Credit** AmEx, DC, MC, V. **Map** p332 1C.
Faggiani is as pleasant a place for breakfast as it is for an evening *aperitivo*: it's not just a classic family bar with excellent coffee, but also has one of northern Rome's finest *pasticcerie* attached. Indeed it's worth making the trip up to Prati simply to sample the *cornetti* and *budino di riso* (rice dessert) – probably the best in Rome.

Pasticcerie & gelaterie

Pellaccia

Via Cola di Rienzo 103 (06 321 0807). Bus 30, 70, 81, 224, 280. **Open** *6.30am-1am Tue-Sun. Closed 1wk Aug.* **No credit cards. Map** p332 2B.
This bar on Prati's busiest street produces some of the best ice-cream north of the river. It's the perfect place to recover after slogging around the Vatican.

The Suburbs

Cafés & bars

Palombini

Piazzale Adenauer 12, EUR (06 591 1700). Metro Magliana/bus 30, 170. **Open** *7am-midnight daily. Closed 2wks Aug.* **Credit** AmEx, DC, MC, V.
In the imposing shadow of the Palazzo del Civiltà

del Lavoro (*see p160*) stands this airy pavilion, surrounded by sweeping gardens. The huge patio area, covered by a steel and plastic tent, makes it a favourite meeting point for young Romans. As a *gelateria, pasticceria* and supplier of tasty snacks, it's also first-rate.

Pasticcerie & gelaterie

See also p200 **Il Gelato di San Crispino**.

Mondi

Via Flaminia 468A, North (06 333 6466). Bus 910/tram 2. **Open** *Oct-May 7am-10pm Tue-Sun. June-Sept 7am-1am.* **Credit** AmEx, DC, MC, V.
Looking for the best bar/*pasticceria* in town? Residents of the Cassia-Flaminia area swear this is it. The cakes and luscious *semifreddi* (frozen ice-cream-based desserts) are more like works of art than mere confectionery.

San Filippo

Via di Villa San Filippo 2/10, North (06 807 9314). Bus 53, 360. **Open** *Nov-Apr 7am-10pm Tue-Thur; 7am-midnight Fri-Sun. May-Oct 7am-midnight Tue-Sun. Closed 3wks Aug.* **No credit cards**.
From the outside, this looks like just another local *bar-latteria*, but make sure you drop in if you're in the well-heeled Parioli district. San Filippo is home to some wicked ice-cream. The places to start are probably the *nocciola* (hazelnut) and *cioccolato* (chocolate), but there is also a wide range of seasonal fruit flavours: try the watermelon (*anguria*), peach (*pesca*) or melon (*melone*).

Shops & Services

Throw off the chains! Shopping in Rome is an idiosyncratic pleasure.

The steady encroachment of chain stores and international brands has failed to make any real impact on the incredibly varied Roman shopping scene. Avoid the major arteries and you'll find Rome's cobbled streets are still full of surprises: the craft workshops and aromas from ancient delis around campo de' Fiori (*see p108*) or Trastevere (*see p116*), or around piazza Navona (*see p100*) the centuries-old herbalists and antique bookshops thriving next to sparkling design stores and innovative, high-quality boutiques purveying the handbags and shoes that Italy is famous for. Even uninspired high streets like via Nazionale (*see p133*) or via del Corso (*see p93*) conceal a few gems.

If big-name designers are what you're after, the classic window-shopping area is around via Condotti (**map** p333 1A; *see also p215* **Big guns**). Independent designers are crowded on to via del Governo Vecchio (**map** p333 2B). For posh high-street and deli shopping head to via Cola di Rienzo (**map** p323 2B-C), a busy street near the Vatican. And don't forget to take a rest: the shopping-in-Rome experience isn't complete without spending time seeing and being seen in one of the city's many pavement cafés (*see chapter* **Cafés, Bars & Gelaterie**).

In many of Rome's shops the assistants pretend customers don't exist; others think their vocation in life is to intimidate shoppers. Perfect the essential lines *mi può aiutare, per favore?* ('Can you help me please?') and *volevo solo dare un'occhiata* ('I'm just looking') and you're ready for any eventuality. Beware: although legally bound to accept goods that are returned unused within seven days of purchase, shops do everything in their power to refuse.

PAYING

Many Roman shops have used the introduction of the euro as an excuse for a hike in prices, but designer togs are still more purse-accessible here than outside Italy. Unless you're in the flea market, don't try bargaining: prices are fixed. If you're not given a *scontrino* (receipt), then ask for it: shops are required by law to provide one, and they and you are liable for a fine in the (unlikely) event of your being caught without it. Small food shops and delis tend not to accept credit cards, but most other places do.

TAX REBATES

Non-EU residents are entitled to a value-added tax (IVA) rebate on purchases of personal goods over €155, providing they are exported unused and bought from a shop with the Europe Tax Free sticker. The shop will give you a form to show to customs when leaving Italy; you must keep your receipt.

OPENING TIMES

Due to recent liberalisation of opening hours, an increasing number of city-centre shops stay open non-stop from 9.30am or 10am to around 7.30pm or 8pm, Monday to Saturday. Many central shops, especially chains and those on major shopping streets, also open on Sunday, though for shorter periods (generally 11am-1pm, 4-7.30pm). Among shops that do still shut for lunch, the traditional 1-4pm shutdown is getting rarer: shops more often close for an hour or so. Small neighbourhood and corner shops tend to stay open later (often after 8pm) or close for longer hours at lunch.

Times given below are winter opening hours; in summer (approximately July to September), shops that opt for long lunches tend to reopen later, at 5pm or 5.30pm, staying open until 8-8.30pm. Most food stores close on Thursday afternoons in winter, and on Saturday afternoons in summer. Most non-food shops are closed on Monday mornings. Note that many shops shut down for at least two weeks each summer, generally in August. Almost all are shut for two or three days around the August 15 public holiday. If you want to avoid finding a particular shop *chiuso per ferie* ('closed for holidays'), be sure to ring ahead.

One-stop shopping

Malls and hypermarkets, a relative novelty in Rome, are usually confined to the outskirts.

COIN

Piazzale Appio 7, San Giovanni (06 708 0020). Metro San Giovanni/bus 16, 81, 85, 87, 186, 218, 810, 850. **Open** 9.30am-8pm Mon-Sat. **Credit** AmEx, DC, MC, V. **Map** off p339 1A.
A reliable department store, with some bargains – especially at the make-up counter. Romans go there for sensible skirts or sheets that last, but also for mid-range high-street fashion. There's an excellent houseware department, and sturdy kids' clothes. The Cola di Rienzo branch has a supermarket.

Branches: via Mantova 1B (06 841 6279); via Cola di Rienzo 173 (06 3600 4298); viale Libia 61 (06 8621 4660); Centro Commerciale Cinecittà Due, viale Palmiro Togliatti 2 (06 722 1724).

MAS

Via dello Statuto 11, Esquilino (06 446 8078). Metro Vittorio/bus 105, 360, 649/tram 5, 14. **Open** 9am-12.45pm, 3.45-7.45pm Mon-Sat; 10am-1pm, 3.45-7.30pm Sun. **Credit** MC, V. **Map** p338 1A.

This Roman institution has a mind-boggling (and often strikingly ugly) assortment of clothes, shoes, luggage, jewellery and linen. But there are some great finds if you've got the patience to rummage through four floors of bargain bins and racks.

La Rinascente

Largo Chigi 20, Tridente (06 679 7691). Bus 52, 53, 61, 62, 63, 71, 80, 85, 116, 117, 119, 160, 850. **Open** 9.30am-10pm Mon-Sat; 10.30am-8pm Sun. **Credit** AmEx, DC, MC, V. **Map** p333 1A.

This large-scale store is good for classy jewellery and accessories, designer and off-the-peg clothing; there's also an extensive selection of lingerie at accessible prices. The beautiful art nouveau interiors make it worth a visit even for non-shoppers. There are English-language desks at both shops. **Branch**: piazza Fiume (06 884 1231).

UPIM

Piazza Santa Maria Maggiore, Esquilino (06 446 5579). Bus 16, 70, 71, 75, 204, 360, 590, 649, 714. **Open** 9am-8.30pm Mon-Sat; 10.30am-8.30pm Sun. **Credit** AmEx, DC, MC, V. **Map** p335 2A.

Lower-end fashion and cheap household accessories, plus cosmetics, toiletries and household goods. **Branch**: via del Tritone 172 (06 678 3336).

Antiques

See also p226 **Marmi Line**.

Some of the best areas to look for (pricey) antiques are via del Babuino, via Giulia and via dei Coronari, where there are antiques fairs in May and October. The dealers-cum-restorers thronging via del Pellegrino may be cheaper, but quality dips too. A bargain can be picked up occasionally in the flea markets (*see p225*).

Artists' supplies & stationery

Ditta G Poggi

Via del Gesù 74-5, Pantheon & Navona (06 678 4477/www.poggi1825.it). Bus 30, 40, 46, 62, 63, 64, 70, 81, 87, 186, 492, 628, 810, 916/tram 8. **Open** 9am-1pm, 4-7.30pm Mon-Sat. Closed 2wks Aug. **Credit** AmEx, MC, V. **Map** p333 2A.

Poggi has been selling paints and colours, brushes, pencils, chalk, canvases and paper in many formats since 1825. This spacious shop is heaven for artists. **Branch**: via Cardinale Merry del Val 18-19 (06 581 2531).

Officina della Carta

Via Benedetta 26B, Trastevere (06 589 5557). Bus 23, 280, 780, H/tram 3. **Open** 9.30am-1pm, 3.30-7pm Mon-Sat. Closed 3wks Aug. **Credit** AmEx, DC, MC, V. **Map** p336 2B.

Beautiful handmade paper is incorporated into albums, gift boxes, notebooks and a host of other items by the ladies of this hole-in-the-wall shop.

Il Papiro

Via del Pantheon 50, Pantheon & Navona (06 679 5597/www.ilpapirofirenze.it). Bus 30, 40, 46, 62, 63, 64, 70, 81, 87, 186, 492, 628, 810, 916/tram 8. **Open** 10am-8pm daily. **Credit** AmEx, DC, MC, V. **Map** p333 2A.

Florentine writing paper, paper-covered boxes, picture frames, pens, photo albums and more. **Branches**: via dei Crociferi 17 (06 6992 0537); salita de' Crescenzi 28 (06 686 8463).

Pineider

Via dei Due Macelli 68, Tridente (06 679 5884). Metro Spagna/bus 52, 53, 61, 62, 63, 71, 80, 85, 116, 117, 119, 160, 850. **Open** 3-7pm Mon; 10am-7.30pm Tue-Sat. Closed 1wk Aug. **Credit** AmEx, DC MC, V. **Map** p335 1C.

Francesco Pineider opened his first custom stationery shop in 1770s Florence, fast becoming stationer of choice for princes and poets. Wonderful gifts for the discriminating – the finest papers, writing sets and leather goods designed by Italy's master craftsmen. Prices are high, of course. **Branch**: via della Fontanella di Borghese 22 (06 687 8369).

Bookshops

Amore e Psiche

Via Santa Caterina da Siena 61, Pantheon & Navona (06 678 3908). Bus 30, 40, 46, 62, 63, 64, 70, 81, 87, 186, 492, 628, 810, 916/tram 8. **Open** 3-8pm Mon; 9am-2pm, 3-8pm Tue-Fri; 10am-8pm Sat, Sun. Closed 1wk Aug. **Credit** AmEx, MC, V. **Map** p333 2A.

A beautifully designed store specialising in psychology, with a good range of poetry and art books (some in English) and friendly staff. Holds readings for kids on Sundays and book presentations.

Bibli

Via dei Fienaroli 28, Trastevere (06 588 4097/www.bibli.it). Bus 23, 280, 780, H/tram 8. **Open** 5.30pm-midnight Mon; 11am-midnight Tue-Sun. **Credit** AmEx, DC, MC, V. **Map** p336 2B.

Perfect for book-junkies: more than 30,000 books to browse (some in English), a cosy café for brunch, lunch or tea, and frequent presentations in the conference room. Internet access and comfy chairs too.

Feltrinelli

Largo Argentina 5A, Ghetto & Campo de' Fiori (06 6880 3248). Bus 30, 40, 46, 62, 63, 64, 70, 81, 87, 186, 492, 628, 810, 916/tram 8. **Open** 9am-8pm Mon-Sat; 10am-1.30pm, 4-7.30pm Sun. **Credit** AmEx, DC, MC, V. **Map** p336 1A.

An outlet for the publishing house, Feltrinelli has large selections of art, literature, history, philosophy, politics and comic books, plus videos, DVDs, rare magazines, maps, postcards, posters, arty T-shirts and stationery.
Branches: via del Babuino 39-41 (06 3600 1842); via VE Orlando 78-81 (06 487 0171).

Al Ferro di Cavallo
Via Ripetta 67, Tridente (06 322 7303). Bus 81, 116, 119, 204, 224, 590, 628, 926. **Open** 9.30am-7.30pm Mon-Sat. Closed 2wks Aug. **Credit** AmEx, DC, MC, V. **Map** p332 2A.
Located in front of Rome's Art Academy, this is not only the ultimate bookshop for art, architecture and graphic design (with books in French and English too), but also a gallery for emerging artists.

Mel Giannino Stoppani
Piazza dei SS Apostoli 59A-65, Trevi & Quirinale (06 6994 1045). Bus 40, 60, 64, 70, 117, 170. **Open** 9.30am-7.30pm Mon-Sat; 10am-1.30pm, 4-7.30pm Sun. **Credit** AmEx, DC, MC, V. **Map** p335 2C.

Rome's only children's bookshop, stocking over 15,000 titles in Italian and other languages (and creative toys). It offers an array of kiddie activities, such as organising birthday parties in the colourful shop.

Odradek
Via dei Banchi Vecchi 57, Ghetto & Campo de' Fiori (06 683 3451). Bus 40, 46, 62, 64, 916. **Open** 9.30am-8pm Mon-Sat. **Credit** AmEx, DC, MC, V. **Map** p333 2B.
Named after Kafka's character, this shop focuses on alternative books, comics, mass media, philosophy, political movements, sci-fi and the artistic avant-garde. It also stocks some foreign-language books.

Rinascita
Via delle Botteghe Oscure 1-2, Ghetto (06 679 7637). Bus 30, 40, 46, 62, 63, 64, 70, 87, 186, 204, 492, 630, 780, 810, 916. **Open** 10am-8pm Mon-Sat; 10am-2pm, 4-8pm Sun. **Credit** AmEx, DC, MC, V. **Map** p336 1A.
A temple of left-wing culture, Rinascita offers modern literature, comic books, history, art and politics. The record department is next door (*see p229*).

Il Tempo Ritrovato-Libreria delle Donne
Via dei Fienaroli 31D, Trastevere (06 581 7724). Bus 23, 280, 780, H/tram 8. **Open** 3.30-7.30pm Mon; 10am-1pm, 3.30-7.30pm Tue-Sat. Closed 2wks Aug. **Credit** MC, V. **Map** p336 2B.
The staff at Rome's only women's bookshop are helpful and friendly; the stock covers women writers, writers on women, sexuality, gender politics…

English-language

Anglo-American Book Co
Via della Vite 102, Tridente (06 679 5222). Bus 52, 53, 61, 62, 63, 71, 80, 85, 116, 117, 119, 160, 850. **Open** 3.30-7.30pm Mon; 10am-7.30pm Tue-Sat. Closed 2wks Aug. **Credit** AmEx, DC, MC, V. **Map** p335 1C.
A good selection of books in English, including a vast range of scientific and technical texts for university students. What isn't in stock, staff will order.

The Corner Bookshop
Via del Moro 45, Trastevere (06 583 6942). Bus 23, 280, 780, H/tram 8. **Open** 10am-1.30pm, 3.30-8pm Mon-Sat; 11am-1.30pm, 3.30-8pm Sun. Closed Sun in Aug. **Credit** AmEx, MC, V. **Map** p336 2B.
This small store is known for its interesting selection of fiction, non-fiction and general interest titles. It recently changed owner and moved to this slightly bigger space three doors up the road.

Economy Book & Video Center
Via Torino 136, Esquilino (06 474 6877/www.fineideas.it). Metro Repubblica/bus 40, 60, 64, 70, 170, 116T, H. **Open** 9am-8pm Mon-Sat. Closed 1wk Aug. **Credit** AmEx, DC, MC, V. **Map** p335 2B.
The limited selection of books here includes second-hand titles, lots of books and videos for rent. A good noticeboard offers work, shelter and Italian lessons.

Antica Erboristeria.
See p213.

The English Bookshop
Via Ripetta 248, Tridente (06 320 3301/theenglish bookshop@katamail.com). Metro Flaminio/bus 117, 119, 590. **Open** 10am-7.30pm Mon-Sat. Closed 2wks Aug. **Credit** AmEx, DC, MC, V. **Map** p332 2A.
A general bookshop with plenty of non-fiction and a good children's selection. Opens on Sundays in the run-up to Christmas.

Feltrinelli International
Via VE Orlando 84, Esquilino (06 482 7878). Metro Repubblica/bus 36, 60, 61, 62, 84, 175, 492, 590, 910. **Open** 9am-8pm Mon-Sat; 10am-1.30pm, 4-7.30pm Sun. **Credit** AmEx, DC, MC, V. **Map** p335 1B.
Don't subsidise other, overpriced English-language bookshops before trying this attractive store: fiction, non-fiction, magazines and guidebooks in English, French, Spanish and other languages.

The Lion Bookshop
Via dei Greci 33, Tridente (06 3265 4007). Metro Spagna/bus 52, 53, 61, 62, 63, 71, 80, 85, 116, 117, 119, 160, 850. **Open** 3.30-7.30pm Mon; 10am-7.30pm Tue-Sun. **Credit** AmEx, DC, MC, V. **Map** p332 2A.
Long a point of reference for expats, you can browse in the reading room while sipping tea or coffee.

Cosmetics & perfumes

Antica Erboristeria Romana
Via di Torre Argentina 15, Pantheon & Navona (06 687 9493). Bus 30, 40, 46, 62, 63, 64, 70, 81, 87, 186, 492, 628, 810, 916/tram 8. **Open** 8.30am-1.30pm, 2.30-7.30pm Mon-Sat. Closed 2wks Aug. **Credit** AmEx, DC, MC, V. **Map** p336 1A.
This charming 18th-century shop has banks of tiny wooden drawers, some marked with skull and crossbones, and ceilings of carved wood. Herbal remedies, scented paper, liquorice and hellbane are all in stock.

L'Olfattorio – Bar à Parfums
Via Ripetta 34, Tridente (06 361 2325/www.olfattorio.it). Metro Flaminio/bus 81, 117, 119, 204, 224, 628, 926. **Open** 3.30pm-7.30pm Tue-Sat. Closed Aug. **Map** p332 2A.
This luscious sanctuary of handcrafted scents is pure joy: nothing's for sale, so you can test the products at will. 'Bartender' Stefania will awaken your olfactory organs with perfumes that make industrially produced scents pale in comparison. You are then handed a list of outlets that sell the heavenly potions.

Profumeria Materozzoli
Piazza San Lorenzo in Lucina 5, Tridente (06 6889 2686). Bus 52, 53, 61, 62, 63, 71, 80, 85, 116, 117, 119, 160, 850. **Open** 3.30-7.30pm Mon; 10am-1.30pm, 3-7.30pm Tue-Sat. Closed 3wks Aug. **Credit** AmEx, DC, MC, V. **Map** p333 1A.
Founded in 1870, this elegant *profumeria* stocks the sought-after Acqua di Parma line and an array of the most difficult-to-find hair and body products (their rarity is reflected in the prices).

Pro Fumum
Via della Colonna Antonina 30, Pantheon & Navona (06 679 5982). Bus 52, 53, 61, 62, 63, 71, 80, 85, 116, 117, 119, 160, 850. **Open** 3.30-7.30pm Mon; 9.30am-7.30pm Tue-Sat. Closed 2wks Aug. **Credit** AmEx, DC, MC, V. **Map** p333 1A.
Appeals to well-off creative types with handmade or rare-brand creams, lotions and perfumes. Try the *bacchette*: wooden sticks to be immersed in scents which then perfume the house for months.
Branches: viale Angelico 87-9 (06 372 5791); piazza Mazzini 4 (06 321 7920).

Roma – Store
Via della Lungaretta 63, Trastevere (06 581 8789). Bus 23, 280, 780, H/tram 8. **Open** 10am-8pm Mon-Sat (until midnight Fri & Sat in Mar-Sept); 11am-8pm Sun. **Credit** AmEx, DC, MC, V. **Map** p336 2B.
Don't let the boring name deter you: this temple of lotions and potions specialises in sophisticated French and English scents (Diptyque, Crabtree & Evelyn, L'Occitane, Creed, Penhaligon). Crest toothpaste and Listerine mouthwash lurk in a corner.

Design & household

The area around via delle Botteghe Oscure and via Arenula (map p333 2A) is packed with shops selling linen, fabric, knitting wool, buttons, laces, curtain ribbons… many Romans remember being dragged here as kids by mum and granny on a Saturday. Rome is also has a good selection of contemporary design shops.

Arredamento Contemporaneo (ArCon)
Via della Scrofa 104-108, Tridente (06 683 3728). Bus 52, 53, 61, 71, 80, 85, 116, 160, 850. **Open** 3.30-7.30pm Mon; 9am-1pm, 3.30-7.30pm Tue-Sat. Closed Aug. **Credit** AmEx, DC, MC, V. **Map** p333 1B.
This store sells the best of Italian 1970s and contemporary home design, from furniture to accessories like the neo-pop lamps and chairs of Vico Magistretti, Flos and Artemide, trendy couches by Zanotta, Cassina furniture, at non-rip-off prices.

Celsa
Via delle Botteghe Oscure 44, Ghetto (06 6994 0872). Bus 30, 40, 46, 62, 63, 64, 70, 87, 186, 204, 492, 630, 780, 810, 916. **Open** 9am-1pm, 3.30-7.30pm Mon-Sat. **Credit** AmEx, MC, V, DC. **Map** p333 2A.
Fabric, linen, wool, cotton, blankets and tailoring odds and ends in great quantity are sold in this reliable shop on the outskirts of the Ghetto.

CUCINA
Via Mario de' Fiori 65, Tridente (06 679 1275/www.cucinastore.com). Metro Spagna/bus 52, 53, 61, 62, 63, 71, 80, 85, 116, 117, 119, 160, 850. **Open** 3.30-7.30pm Mon; 10am-7.30pm Tue-Sat. **Credit** AmEx, DC, MC, V. **Map** p332 2A.
Everything a cook might need or miss from home, including turkey basters, bamboo rice-steamers, and a selection of eccentric muffin and baking moulds.

Eat, Drink, Shop

You can try but you can't buy at **L'Olfattorio – Bar à Parfums**. *See p213.*

D CUBE

Piazza Mignanelli 24, Tridente (06 678 9054).
Metro Spagna/bus 116, 117, 119, 590. **Open**
10am-8pm Mon-Sat. Closed 2wks Aug. **Credit**
AmEx, DC, MC, V. **Map** p335 1C.
On two floors of creative design complements, this
shop stocks all the essentials for a trendy home life
– at a price. There are golden breakfast tablecloths,
slick cutlery and extravagant bathroom accessories.
Branches: via della Pace 38 (06 686 1218); via dei
Crociferi 42 (06 6920 0911).

'Gusto

Piazza Augusto Imperatore 7, Tridente (06 323
6363). Bus 81, 204, 224, 628, 926. **Open** 10.30am-
2am daily. **Credit** AmEx, DC, MC, V. **Map** p332 2A.
Attached to the popular fusion restaurant of the
same name (*see p171*), this *enoteca*/culinary store has
a wide selection of food books in many languages.
Gadget-lovers have a field day with the pricey but
wonderfully designed wine and kitchen accessories
– all those things they never knew they needed.

Italia Garipoli

Borgo Vittorio 91A, Vatican & Prati (06 6880
2196). Bus 23, 32, 49, 81, 492, 590, 982/tram
19. **Open** 10am-1pm, 4-7pm Mon-Sat. Closed Aug.
No credit cards. **Map** p333 1C.
This wonderful, old-fashioned shop preserves the
waning art of embroidery – linen, lingerie, tablecloths, layettes and bride's dresses. There's little for
immediate sale, as much is made to order. Prices are
reasonable, but delivery times are long.

Leone Limentani

Via del Portico d'Ottavia 47, Ghetto (06 6880 6686).
Bus 30, 40, 46, 62, 63, 64, 70, 81, 87, 186, 492,
628, 810, 916/tram 8. **Open** 4-8pm Mon; 9am-1pm,
3.30-7.30pm Tue-Sat. Closed 2wks Aug. **Credit**
AmEx, DC, MC, V. **Map** p336 1&2A.
If you can't match your broken plate, cup or vase in
this subterranean Aladdin's cave of high-piled
crockery, chances are you won't find it anywhere.
Many brand names are discounted by about 10%.

Stock Market

Via dei Banchi Vecchi 51-2, Ghetto & Campo de'
Fiori (06 686 4238). Bus 40, 46, 62, 64, 916. **Open**
3.30-8pm Mon; 10am-8pm Tue-Sat. Closed 2wks Aug.
Credit AmEx, DC, MC, V. **Map** p333 2B.
This curious emporium shifts end-of-line kitchen
goods, quirky light fittings and other odd articles
that no one else can – or wants to – sell. Film directors have been known to slouch in looking for props.
Branches: via Appia Nuova 147 (06 7030 5305); via
EQ Visconti 96 (06 3600 2343); via Alessandria 133
(06 8535 6593).

Too Much

Via Santa Maria dell'Anima 29, Pantheon & Navona
(06 6830 1187/www.toomuch.it). Bus 30, 70, 81, 87,
116, 186, 204, 628, 491. **Open** noon-midnight
daily. **Credit** AmEx, MC, V. **Map** p333 2B.
This two-storey shop is covered from floor to ceiling with curious (and mostly useless) design and
household objects. It is almost too much indeed for
lovers of kitsch gadgets.

Eat, Drink, Shop

Branches: piazza Trevi 82 (06 678 6816); piazza del Popolo 20 (06 323 3353).

Fashion

Accessories & leatherwear

Borini
Via dei Pettinari 86, Ghetto & Campo de' Fiori (06 687 5670). Bus 23, 40, 46, 62, 64, 280, 916/tram 8. **Open** 3.30-7.30pm Mon; 9am-1pm, 3.30-7.30pm Tue-Sat. Closed 2wks Aug. **Credit** AmEx, MC, V. **Map** p336 1B.
Borini's shoes – all made in the family workshop – are elegant, created with an eye on current fashion trends, and very, very durable. In view of which, the price tags are surprisingly restrained.

Borsalino
Via di Campo Marzio 72A, Tridente (06 679 6120). Bus 52, 53, 61, 71, 80, 85, 160, 116, 850. **Open** 3.30-7.30pm Mon; 10am-2pm, 3.30-7.30pm Tue-Sat. Closed 3wks Aug. **Credit** AmEx, DC, MC, V. **Map** p333 1A.
Italy's hat-maker *per eccellenza*, the Borsalino firm has been making the world's most famous men's felt hat for over a century. Now the renowned house also designs women's hats and belts, gloves and scarves.

Elisheva
Via de' Baullari 19, Ghetto & Campo de' Fiori (06 687 1747). Bus 30, 40, 46, 62, 64, 70, 81, 87, 116, 186, 204, 491, 628, 916. **Open** 10am-8pm Mon-Thur, Sun; 10am-5pm Fri; 6-9pm Sat. **Credit** AmEx, DC, MC, V. **Map** p333 2B.
Elisheva shoes, created by Giorgio Moresco, are comfortable, fashionable and feminine too, and come with a touch of eccentricity and humane prices. Some vintage clothes and bags to match the shoes are also stocked.

Fausto Santini
Via Frattina 120, Tridente (06 678 4114). Metro Spagna/bus 52, 53, 61, 62, 63, 71, 80, 85, 116, 117, 119, 160, 850. **Open** 10am-7.30pm Mon-Sat; noon-7pm Sun. **Credit** AmEx, DC, MC, V. **Map** p335 1C.
Santini's shoes and bags are a cut above the rest. They follow a trend of their own, refusing to pander to passing fads. Innovative designs coupled with the highest quality make the price tag less painful.

Big guns

All crowded cosily together in the grid of streets at the bottom of the Spanish Steps, the emporia of the big guns of Italian fashion can be reached from the Spagna metro station or by any bus to piazza San Silvestro. They all take major credit cards.

Dolce e Gabbana
Via Condotti 51-2 (06 6992 4999). **Open** 1-7.30pm Mon; 10am-7.30pm Tue-Sat. **Map** p335 1C.
Branch: piazza di Spagna 93 (06 6938 0870).

Fendi
Via Borgognona 36A-38B, 39-40 (06 696 661). **Open** 10am-7.30pm Mon-Sat; 11am-2pm, 3-7pm Sun. **Map** p335 1C.

Gianfranco Ferrè
Via Borgognona 5B, 6, 6A (06 679 7445). **Open** 1pm-7.30pm Mon; 10am-7.30pm Tue-Sat. **Map** p335 1C.

Gianni Versace
Via Borgognona 24-5 (06 679 5037). **Open** 10am-7.30pm Mon-Sat. **Map** p335 1C.
Branches: via Bocca di Leone 26 (06 678 0521).

Giorgio Armani
Via Condotti 77 (06 699 1460). **Open** 3-7pm Mon; 10am-7pm Tue-Sat. **Map** p333 A1.

Branches: Emporio Armani, via del Babuino 140 (06 3600 2197); Armani Jeans, via del Babuino 70A (06 3600 1848).

Max Mara
Via Condotti 17-19A (06 6992 2104). **Open** 10am-7.30pm Mon-Sat. **Map** p333 A1.
Branches: via Frattina 28 (06 679 3638); Max&Co, via Condotti 46 (06 678 7946); via del Corso 488 (06 322 7266).

Prada
Via Condotti 92/95 (06 679 0897). **Open** 3-7pm Mon; 10am-7pm Tue-Sat. **Map** p333 A1.

Valentino
Via Condotti 13 (06 679 5862). **Open** 3-7pm Mon; 10am-7pmTue-Sat. **Map** p333 A1.
Branches: via del Babuino 61 (06 3600 1906); menswear: via Bocca di Leone 15 (06 678 3656); haute couture: piazza Mignanelli 22 (06 67 391).

Davide Cenci
Via Campo Marzio 1/8 (06 699 0681). Bus 62, 63, 81, 85, 95, 117, 119, 160, 175, 492, 628, 630, 850. **Open** 3.30-7.30pm Mon; 9.30am-1.30pm, 3.30-7.30pm Tue-Fri; 10am-7.30pm Sat. Closed 1wk Aug. **Map** p333 A1.

Furla

Piazza di Spagna 22, Tridente (06 6920 0363/www. furla.com). Metro Spagna/bus 52, 53, 61, 62, 63, 71, 80, 85, 116, 117, 119, 160, 850. **Open** 10am-8pm Mon-Sat; 10.30am-8pm Sun. **Credit** AmEx, DC, MC, V. **Map** p335 1C.

The number of Furla shops might make you feel like one of the masses for buying here, but their curvy, creative and classic bright colours are great. **Branches:** via Condotti 55-6 (06 679 1973); via del Corso 481 (06 3600 3619); via Tomacelli 136 (06 687 8230).

Ibiz

Via dei Chiavari 39, Ghetto & Campo de' Fiori (06 6830 7297). Bus 30, 40, 46, 62, 64, 70, 81, 87, 116, 186, 204, 491, 628, 916. **Open** 9.30am-7.30pm Mon-Sat. Closed 10 days Aug. **Credit** AmEx, DC, MC, V. **Map** p336 1B.

Ibiz makes trendy and functional bags for work or leisure. Choose the one you want while watching others being made next door.

Loco

Via dei Baullari 22, Ghetto & Campo de' Fiori (06 6880 8216). Bus 30, 40, 46, 62, 64, 70, 81, 87, 116, 186, 204, 491, 628, 916. **Open** 3-8pm Mon; 10.30am-8pm Tue-Sat. Closed 2wks Aug. **Credit** AmEx, DC, MC, V. **Map** p333 2B.

This small store stocks some of the funkiest shoes around. From classy to wild and eccentric, its pieces are always one step ahead of mass fashion.

Sermoneta Ties

Via Borgognona 9-10, Tridente (06 678 3879). Metro Spagna/bus 52, 53, 61, 62, 64, 70, 81, 85, 116, 117, 119, 160, 850. **Open** 10am-8pm Mon-Sat. **Credit** AmEx, DC, MC, V. **Map** p335 1C.

An incredible selection of ties and scarves by Giorgio Sermoneta and other top-name designers.

Settimio Mieli

Via San Claudio 70, Tridente (06 678 5979). Bus 52, 53, 61, 62, 63, 71, 80, 85, 116, 117, 119, 160, 850. **Open** 1-7.30pm Mon; 10am-7.30pm Tue-Sat. Closed 2wks Aug. **Credit** AmEx, DC, MC, V. **Map** p333 1A.

Maker of leather gloves since 1924, Settimio Mieli used to supply all manner of designs and colours to the *dolce vita* divas whose pictures fill the walls. The shop is the size of a glove-compartment.

Boutiques

Alan Journo

Via Fontanella Borghese 59A, Tridente (06 6830 1540). Metro Spagna/bus 52, 53, 61, 62, 63, 71, 80, 85, 116, 117, 119, 160, 850. **Open** 3-7pm Mon; 10.30am-2pm, 3-7pm Tue-Sat. **Credit** AmEx, DC, MC, V. **Map** p333 1A.

Milan-based designer Alan Journo makes stunning, elegant clothes – inspired by the '30s and '50s – in cutting-edge fabrics. Eccentric purses and hats are also here. Expensive but hard to resist.

Arsenale

Via del Governo Vecchio 64, Pantheon & Navona (06 686 1380). Bus 30, 40, 46, 62, 64, 70, 81, 87, 116, 186, 204, 491, 628, 916. **Open** 3.30-7.30pm Mon; 10am-7.30pm Tue-Sat. Closed 2wks Aug. **Credit** AmEx, DC, MC, V. **Map** p333 2B.

Patrizia Pieroni's wonderful designs make great window displays – not to mention successful party conversation pieces.

Baco della Seta

Via Vittoria 75, Tridente (06 679 3907). Metro Spagna/bus 81, 204, 224, 628, 926. **Open** 3.30-7.30pm Mon; 10am-2pm, 3.30-7.30pm Tue-Sat. Closed 2wks Aug. **Credit** AmEx, DC, MC, V. **Map** p332 2A.

Beautiful, elegant women's day and evening wear – all in pure silks of glorious hues. Prices, given the fabrics, are not exorbitant.

Maga Morgana

Via del Governo Vecchio 27 (06 687 9995). Bus 30, 40, 46, 62, 64, 70, 81, 87, 116, 186, 204, 491, 628, 916. **Open** 10am-7.30pm Mon-Sat. **Credit** AmEx, DC, MC, V. **Map** p333 2B.

Designer Luciana Iannace makes one-of-a-kind women's clothes, including hand-knitted sweaters, skirts and dresses. Knitted and woollen items are sold down the road at via del Governo Vecchio 98.

NuYorica

Piazza Pollarola 36-7, Ghetto & Campo de' Fiori (06 6889 1243/www.nuyorica.it). Bus 30, 40, 46, 62, 64, 70, 81, 87, 116, 186, 204, 491, 628, 916. **Open** 10.30am-8pm Mon-Sat. Closed 2wks Aug. **Credit** AmEx, DC, MC, V. **Map** p333 2B.

Extravagant but stylish clothes and shoes by the most trendy designers. The shoe selection is totally irresistible: creative and different but elegant and classy at the same time. The prices are high… but the clothes are unique. **Branch:** (shoes only) TAD, via del Babuino 155A (06 3269 5127).

Osvaldo Testa

Via Frattina 42, Tridente (06 679 1296). Metro Spagna/bus 52, 53, 61, 62, 63, 71, 80, 85, 116, 117, 119, 160, 850. **Open** 4-7.30pm Mon; 10am-1.30pm, 3.30-7.30pm Tue-Thur; 10am-2pm, 3-7.30pm Fri, Sat. Closed Aug. **Credit** AmEx, DC, MC, V. **Map** p335 1C.

Classic men's knitwear and suits, off-the-peg (at less than big-name-designer prices) or bespoke. **Branch:** via Borgognona 13 (06 679 6174).

Rubinacci

Via della Fontanella Borghese 33, Tridente (06 6889 2943). Metro Spagna/bus 52, 53, 61, 62, 63, 71, 80, 85, 116, 117, 119, 160, 850. **Open** 3-7pm Mon; 10am-1.30pm, 3-7.30pm Tue-Sat. **Credit** AmEx, DC, MC, V. **Map** p333 1A.

Superb handmade suits at sky-high prices. Step into the warm, retro shop and its elegant staff make you feel special enough to seriously consider spending the €2,200-odd to have a suit made to order.

Eat, Drink, Shop

NuYorica.
See p217.

TAD

*Via del Babuino 155A, Tridente (06 3269 5122/
www.taditaly.com). Metro Spagna or Flaminio/bus
117, 119, 590.* **Open** *noon-7.30pm Mon, Sun;
10.30am-7.30pm Tue-Sat. Closed 2wks Aug.*
Credit *AmEx, DC, MC, V.* **Map** *p332 2A.*
The concept behind this 'concept store' is that you can
shop for clothes, shoes, flowers, household accessories, CDs, mags and perfumes, get your hair done,
eat and drink all in one super-pop place where contemporary design and ancient architecture are beautifully mixed. Eccentric hotshot designers, at a price.

Victory

*Via San Francesco a Ripa 19, Trastevere (06 581
2437). Bus 780, H/tram 8.* **Open** *4-8pm Mon;
9.30am-1.30pm, 4-8pm Tue-Sat.* **Credit** *AmEx,
DC, MC, V.* **Map** *p336 2B.*
For Italian and French boutique-chic designs that
will take you from thank-God-it's-Friday to Monday.
Menswear is at piazza San Callisto 10 (06 583 5935).

Lingerie

A recent spate of new lingerie chains has
made it easier to buy inexpensive undies
along all retail streets. Upmarket lingerie
shops cluster around via Condotti , while
most open markets have at least one
bancarella selling inexpensive underwear.
Rinascente (*see p210*) is a good bet for
middle-range items, while the **Intimissimi**
chain (at via del Corso 167 and many other
places) caters for men and women looking
for inexpensive, reliable undies.

Brighenti

*Via Frattina 7, Tridente (06 679 1484). Metro
Spagna/bus 52, 53, 61, 62, 63, 71, 80, 85, 116,
117, 119, 160, 850.* **Open** *9.30am-1.30pm, 3.30-7.30pm Tue-Thur; 9.30am-
7.30pm Fri, Sat. Closed 2wks Aug.* **Credit** *AmEx,
DC, MC, V.* **Map** *p335 1C.*
Lingerie in glorious, silky shades by major names
(the likes of Dior, Nina Ricci, and Ferrè), is sold in a
beautiful, pastel-hued temple to luxury. The own-
name brand offers opulence at slightly lower
(though not low) prices.
Branch: via Borgognona 27 (06 678 3898).

Demoiselle

*Via Frattina 93, Tridente (06 679 3752). Metro
Spagna/bus 52, 53, 61, 62, 63, 71, 80, 85, 116,
117, 119, 160, 850.* **Open** *10am-8pm Mon-Sat.
Closed 1wk Aug.* **Credit** *AmEx, DC, MC, V.*
Map *p335 1C.*
Luscious, sexy and classy lingerie by La Perla.
Delicious temptations are displayed in cream-
coloured surroundings, lit by chandeliers.

Simona

*Via del Corso 82-3, Tridente (06 361 3742).
Metro Spagna/bus 52, 53, 61, 62, 63, 71, 80, 85,
116, 117, 119, 160, 850.* **Open** *3.30-7.30pm Mon;
10am-7.30pm Tue-Sat.* **Credit** *AmEx, DC, MC, V.*
Map *p332 2A.*
Simona is the shop for those well-endowed women
who have always longed for sexy, lacy bras: staff
will alter bra straps and bands until you go home
singing Barry White tunes. A good selection of
undies, sleepwear and 'non-sleepwear' at prices that
aren't too painful.

Mid-range

The Butcher

Via L Manara 9, Trastevere (06 5832 0376). Bus 780, H/tram 8. **Open** 10am-1.30pm, 4-7.30pm Mon-Sat; 4-7.30pm Sun. Closed 1wk Aug. **Credit** AmEx, DC, MC, V. **Map** p336 2B.

Superb menswear shop with trendy, elegant trousers, jumpers, shirts and shoes by young designers.

Ethic

Piazza Cairoli 11-12, Ghetto & Campo de' Fiori (06 6830 1063). Bus 30, 40, 46, 62, 63, 64, 70, 81, 87, 186, 492, 628, 810, 916/tram 8. **Open** noon-8pm Mon, Sun; 10am-8pm Tue-Sat. Closed 1wk Aug. **Credit** AmEx, DC, MC, V. **Map** p336 1B.

Creative clothes in bright or natural colours from acid greens to browns and blacks; evening dresses complemented by lovely shoes, bags and jewellery. **Branches**: via del Corso 85 (06 3600 2191); via del Pantheon 50 (06 6880 3167).

Eventi

Via della Fontanella 8, Tridente (06 3600 2533). Metro Flaminio/bus 117, 119, 590. **Open** 3.30-8pm Mon; 10am-1pm, 3.30-8pm Tue-Sat. Closed 2wks Aug. **Credit** AmEx, MC, V. **Map** p332 2A.

Disco-days garb for a daring clientele. If the clothes don't grab you, visit for the decor: you change in shower units, and try on shoes sitting on the loo. **Branch**: via dei Serpenti 134 (06 484 960).

Fiorucci

Via Nazionale 236, Esquilino (06 488 3175). Metro Repubblica/bus 36, 60, 61, 62, 84, 175, 492, 590, 910. **Open** 9.30am-8pm Mon-Sat. **Credit** AmEx, DC, MC, V. **Map** p335 2B.

Don't let the pushy staff put you off – in fact this store caters for everyone. Apart from selling the eccentric Fiorucci designs, it also stocks Dolce & Gabbana lingerie as well as Miss Sixty and Kookaï at accessible prices.
Branch: via Mario de' Fiori 54 (06 679 2946).

Iron G

Via Cola di Rienzo 50, Prati (06 321 6798). Bus 30, 70, 81, 186, 224, 280, 590, 913. **Open** 11am-7.30pm Mon-Sat. Closed 1wk Aug. **Credit** AmEx, MC, V. **Map** p335 1C.

The hippest labels and expensive shoes for the fashion victims of this well-heeled neighbourhood. Creatively designed surroundings, but an intimidating place to shop.

Pellegrino

Via dei Serpenti 153, Monti (06 482 4979). Metro Cavour/bus 40, 60, 64, 70, 117, 170. **Open** 4-7.30pm Mon; 10am-1pm, 4-7.30pm Tue-Sat. Closed Aug. **No credit cards. Map** p338 1B.

For €100 you can have a shirt made to order by this tailor with a history. For €10 more, he'll embroider your initials. Orders take a week, but speedy deliveries can be arranged for departing tourists.

Vintage and second-hand

The bargains aren't what they used to be, but **Porta Portese** on Sunday mornings and **via Sannio** all week (for both, *see p225* **Flea Markets**) always have some vintage treasures (you need to get there early to find the best stuff). The *heimat* of second-hand clothes shops is via del Governo Vecchio, but don't necessarily expect prices to be restrained.

On track

For anyone only familiar with Termini railway station pre-1998, the idea of spending a pleasant afternoon's shopping, coffee-sipping and art-admiring there would elicit loud guffaws. But in a make-over that began in that year and was completed in 2000, this stunning example of post-war architecture (*see p29*) shed the grime and sleaze of decades to emerge as a shining, multifunctional space hosting a dozen restaurants and cafés, and over 60 shops and boutiques... not to mention the **Temporaneo Contemporaneo** art gallery (*see p246*), which is off the long walkway from the main concourse to the platform for the Fiumicino airport express.

Most of the station's shopping opportunities are below ground in what is now called Forum Termini – once a major

drug-dealing hub and unofficial shelter for the city's homeless. The space now holds clothes shops, shoe shops, opticians, bookstores, jewellers (most shops are open 8am to 8pm or 10pm and take major credit cards) and a useful supermarket, Termini Drugstore. Tired shoppers can rest at the colourful Acafè in Forum Termini or head to the Ciao or Autogrill self-services above the ticket hall for a bird's-eye view of hassled travellers.

Travellers with time to kill can stock up for their journeys at all hours in the Termini Drugstore (06 8740 6055, credit AmEx, MC, V), which is open from 6am to midnight daily. Be warned, though: old habits die hard, and in the wee hours the company you'll find yourself in is still not all that salubrious. *See also p302. Information www. romatermini.it.* **Map** p335 2A.

Eat, Drink, Shop

People

*Piazza Teatro di Pompeo 4A, Ghetto & Campo de'
Fiori (06 687 4040). Bus 30, 40, 46, 62, 64, 70,
81, 87, 116, 186, 204, 491, 628, 916.* **Open**
10.30am-2.30pm, 3.30-8pm Mon-Sat. Closed 3wks
Aug. **Credit** AmEx, DC, MC, V. **Map** p336 1B.

Tastily furnished with 1960s furniture, this tiny
vintage clothes store is the best in town. As well as
quality second-hand coats and men's suits, it sells
cool '60s- and '70s-style garments made in period
fabrics but designed by Germana and the other
girls running the shop: one-of-a-kind dresses in
Pucci style, bell-bottoms, blouses, shirts, jeans and
flares, scarves and accessories – at bargain prices.

Pulp

*Via del Boschetto 140, Monti (06 485 511). Metro
Cavour/bus 40, 60, 64, 70, 117, 170.* **Open** 4-8pm
Mon; 10am-1pm, 4-8pm Tue-Sun. **Credit** MC, V.
Map p338 1B.

This colourful store stocks selected second-hand
clothing, as well as garments designed in-house with
vintage fabrics. Visit here for that particularly flow-
ery shirt or feather boa and matching gown…

Vestiti Usati Cinzia

*Via del Governo Vecchio 45, Pantheon & Navona
(06 686 1791). Bus 30, 40, 46, 62, 64, 70, 81, 87,
116, 186, 204, 491, 628, 916.* **Open** 10am-2pm,
3.30-7.30pm Mon-Sat. **Credit** AmEx, DC, MC, V.
Map p333 2B.

The best of the Governo Vecchio stores.

Food & drink

It used to be hard work finding a supermarket
in the *centro storico*: dwellers had to rely on
produce markets or take long treks. But a recent
flurry of mini-markets opening has made things
easier. These are good for packed food – pasta,
tinned tomatoes, biscuits, cleaning products –
but don't generally do much in the way of fruit
and veg. So open markets are still best for fresh
produce. If you hanker after mouth-watering
Italian specialities, head for stores like
Volpetti or **Castroni** (*see below*). For fresh (as
opposed to long-life) milk or cream, your best
bet is not a shop, but any bar labelled *latteria*.
Most deli products are sold by the *etto* (100g)
rather than the kilo: ask for *un etto, due etti* and
so on. *Enoteche* (off-licences) often have counter
bars for downing a glass or two. *See also
p171* **Beyond Frascati**; for cakes, *see p222*.

Delis

Ai Monasteri

*Corso Rinascimento 72, Pantheon & Navona
(06 6880 2783). Bus 30, 70, 81, 87, 116, 186,
204, 491, 628.* **Open** 9am-1pm, 4.30-7.30pm Mon-
Wed, Fri, Sat; 9am-1.30pm Thur. Closed Aug.
Credit MC, V. **Map** p333 2A.

Endowed with an air of holiness, this shop sells
honey, preserves, liqueurs and other interesting
foodie oddities made in monasteries across Italy.
They include an elixir for long life (no guarantee).

Castroni

*Via Cola di Rienzo 196, Prati (06 687 4383).
Metro Ottaviano/bus 23, 32, 49, 81, 492, 590,
982/tram 19.* **Open** 8am-8pm Mon-Sat. **Credit**
MC, V. **Map** p332 2C.

This wonderful shop has lots of Italian regional specialities and imported international foodstuffs:
everything from Chinese noodles to Vegemite. The
place to go to for that special something from home
or to taste some obscure Italian regional produce.

Innocenzi

*Via Natale del Grande 31, Trastevere (06 581 2725).
Bus 780, H/tram 8.* **Open** 7.30am-1.30pm, 4.30-8pm
Mon-Wed, Fri, Sat; 7.30am-1.30pm Thur. Closed
2wks Aug. **No credit cards. Map** p336 2B.

Pulses spill from great sacks stacked around this
treasure trove of foodie specialities from all over the
world. Currants for your Christmas pud? Crunchy
peanut butter? Look no further.

Viola

*Campo de' Fiori 42, Ghetto & Campo de' Fiori
(06 6880 6114). Bus 30, 40, 46, 62, 63, 64, 70, 81,
87, 186, 492, 628, 810, 916.* **Open** 7.30am-1.30pm,
4.30-8pm Mon-Wed, Fri, Sat; 7.30am-1.30pm Thur.
Credit AmEx, DC, MC, V. **Map** p336 1B.

This 19th-century establishment is dedicated exclusively to pork products. Connoisseurs say they're
the best in the city; lovers swear by the aphrodisiac
properties of the dried, spicy *coppiette di maiale*.

Volpetti

*Via Marmorata 47, Testaccio (06 574 2352/www.
fooditaly.com). Metro Piramide/bus 23, 30, 75, 280,
716/tram 3.* **Open** 8am-2pm, 5-8pm Mon-Sat.
Credit AmEx, DC, MC, V. **Map** p337 2A.

One of the best delis in Rome, with exceptional
cheese, hams and salamis. It's hard to get away without one of the jolly assistants loading you up with
samples of their wares – pleasant, but painful on the
wallet. If you can't get to Testaccio, check the website: staff will dispatch all over the world.

Produce markets

If you're feeling sad and lonely, a stroll through
an animated, colourful produce market has to
be the best antidote. Every neighbourhood in
Rome has at least one (those in the *centro
storico* tend to be more expensive), opening
Monday to Saturday from around 6am until
2pm. Some stay open on Tuesday and
Thursday afternoons, but much depends on
the whims of individual stallholders. None
accepts credit cards.

Apart from the bigger ones listed below,
there is a handful of tiny central(ish) street

Eat, Drink, Shop

markets. They can be found in via dei Santi Quattro (map p338 2B), a stone's throw from the Colosseum; via Milazzo (map p335 2A), near Termini station; and piazza Bernini on the San Saba side of the Aventine hill (map p339 2C).

Piazza dell'Unità
Via Cola di Rienzo, Prati. Metro Ottaviano/bus 23, 32, 49, 81, 492, 590, 982/tram 19. **Map** p332 2C.
Prices at this covered market reflect the tone of its posh neighbourhood near the Vatican.

Piazza Vittorio
Via Lamarmora, Esquilino. Metro Vittorio/bus 105, 360, 590, 649/tram 5, 14. **Map** p338 1A.
This chaotic market, which used to fill piazza Vittorio near Termini station, has recently been moved to more salubrious but less picturesque quarters in a former barracks. The usual Italian fresh produce, cheese and meats are supplemented by pulses, halal meat, spices, African fruits, Asian food and flea market junk.

Piazza San Cosimato
Trastevere. Bus 780, H/tram 8. **Map** p336 2B.
Despite the hordes of tourists, this market retains some of its neighbourhood feel.

Piazza Testaccio
Testaccio. Bus 23, 30, 75, 95, 170, 280, 716, 781/tram 3. **Map** p337 2A.
A stroll through the true heart of Rome: prices are considerably lower than at more central markets too.

Confectionery & cakes
See also p198 **Pasticcerie**.

La Bottega del Cioccolato
Via Leonina 82, Monti (06 482 1473). Metro Cavour/bus 75, 84, 117. **Open** 9.30am-7.30pm Mon-Sat. Closed June-Aug. **Credit** AmEx, DC, MC, V. **Map** p338 1B.
A feast for the senses, selling mouth-watering pralines and chocolate things of all kinds, including handmade marron glacé mousse.

Ciardi
Via Cavour 267, Monti (347 065 5468). Metro Cavour/bus 75, 84, 117. **Open** 5am-8pm daily. **No credit cards. Map** p338 1C.
Don't be deterred by its anonymous appearance: this is one of Rome's best *pasticcerie*. Just one bite of the *tramezzini* (sandwiches) opens the door to a brave new world.

Dolceroma
Via Portico d'Ottavia 20B, Ghetto (06 689 2196). Bus 23, 63, 280, 630, 780, H/tram 8. **Open** 8am-1.30pm, 3.30-8pm Tue-Sat; 10am-1pm Sun. Closed Aug. **No credit cards. Map** p336 1A.
Though it specialises in Viennese cakes, this is also the place for American-style carrot cake and choc chip cookies. Don't get hooked: prices are high.

Forno del Ghetto
Via Portico d'Ottavia 1, Ghetto (06 687 8637). Bus 30, 40, 46, 62, 63, 64, 70, 81, 87, 186, 492, 628, 810, 916/tram 8. **Open** 8am-8pm Mon-Thur; 8am-sunset Fri. Closed 3wks Aug & Jewish holidays. **No credit cards. Map** p336 1A.

Trading on history

Sky-rocketing rents, muscular franchising chains and the pressures of globalisation all present a threat to Rome's historic shops. Now, however, they can turn to the city council for help in keeping their heads above water. Pieces of Roman retail history that have been open for 50 years or more (and many have been open a lot longer than that) in historic buildings with original or seriously old furnishings and a long same-trade tradition are now eligible for *bottega storica* (historic shop) status, which gives them access to special funding. Museums in their own right, these shops are perfect for salving the guilty consciences of those to whom shopping appeals more than sightseeing.

Pharmacies and herbalists are about the best represented on the list of *botteghe storiche.* They include the **Antica Farmacia Reale**, founded in 1687 (via del Gambero 13, Tridente, 06 679 2220); the **Antica**

Erboristeria Romana, founded in 1790 (*see p213*); and the **Pontificia Erboristeria** (via Pozzo delle Cornacchie 26, Pantheon & Navona, 06 686 1201).

Historic bookshops are numerous too, and include the wonderfully musty **Libreria Tombolini** (via IV Novembre 146, Trevi & Quirinale, 06 679 5719) and the **Antica Libreria Scienze e Lettere** (piazza Madama 8, Pantheon & Navona, 06 686 1141).

Passamanerie Crocianelli (via dei Prefetti 37/40, Pantheon & Navona, 06 687 3592) is the kind of haberdasher's that your grandmother frequented, with a dazzling array of tapes and tassels. **Catello D'Auria** (via Due Macelli 55, Tridente, 06 679 3364) is an historic purveyor of leather goods and handbags, while **Cesaretti** (via Magnanapoli 9, Capitoline & Palatine, 06 679 0058) patches up broken dolls in his rather eerie 'hospital'.

Pacific Trading Co
Viale Principe Eugenio 17-21, Esquilino (06 446 8406). Metro Vittorio/bus 105, 360, 649/tram 5, 14. **Open** 9am-8pm Mon-Sat. **Credit** MC, V. **Map** p338 1A.
Sells an enormous variety of Asian foodstuffs.

Health foods

Il Canestro
Via Luca della Robbia 12, Testaccio (06 574 6287). Bus 23, 30, 75, 280, 716/tram 3. **Open** 9am-8pm Mon-Sat. **No credit cards**. **Map** p337 2A.
Il Canestro offers a huge range of natural health foods, cosmetics and medicines, including some organic versions of Italian regional specialities. The branch on via San Francesco a Ripa also offers nutrition-related courses and alternative medicine.
Branches: via San Francesco a Ripa 106 (06 581 2621); via Gorizia 51 (06 854 1991).

Drink

See also p171 **Beyond Frascati**. For wine bars, *see chapters* **Eating Out** and **Cafés, Bars & Gelaterie**.

Buccone
Via Ripetta 19-20, Tridente (06 361 2154). Bus 81, 204, 224, 628, 926. **Open** 9am-8.30pm Mon-Thur; 9am-midnight Fri, Sat; 10am-5pm Sun. Closed 3wks Aug. **Credit** AmEx, DC, MC, V. **Map** p332 2A.
In a 17th-century palazzo, this *enoteca* is filled from floor to arched ceiling with wines and spirits, all subdivided by region – from cheap Valpolicella to Brunello Riserva at over €500.

Costantini
Piazza Cavour 16, Prati (06 321 3210). Bus 34, 49, 87, 280, 926, 990. **Open** *Shop* 4.30-8pm Mon; 9am-1pm, 4.30-8pm Tue-Sat. *Wine bar* noon-3pm, 6.30pm-midnight Mon-Fri; 6.30pm-midnight Sat. Closed Aug. **Credit** AmEx, DC, MC, V. **Map** p333 1B.
This vast, cavernous cellar contains just about any Italian wine you want, divided by region.

Enoteca al Parlamento
Via dei Prefetti 15, Tridente (06 687 3446/www.enotecaalparlamento.it). Bus 81, 116, 117, 204, 590, 628, 913, 926. **Open** 9am-2pm, 4-8.30pm Mon-Sat. Closed 2wks Aug. **Credit** AmEx, MC, V. **Map** p333 1A.
Hundreds of bottles of spirits and the best Italian wine fill the wooden selves of this warm shop, which also stocks delectable honey, jams, regional specialities and balsamic vinegar. Wine tasting at the counter is accompanied by delicious *tartine*.

Il Giardino del Tè
Via del Boschetto 107, Monti (06 474 6888/www.ilgiardinodelte.it). Metro Cavour/bus 40, 60, 64, 70, 170, 116T, H. **Open** 4-7.30pm Mon; 10.30am-2.30pm, 4-7.30pm Tue-Fri; 10am-1.30pm, 4-7.30pm Sat. Closed Aug. **Credit** AmEx, DC, MC, V. **Map** p338 1C.

Wine-packed: **Buccone.**

Run by three unwelcoming women, this tiny shop has no sign but is immediately recognisable by the line of slavering regulars outside. Sells unforgettable damson and ricotta (or chocolate and ricotta) pies and *pizze* – bricks of moist dough and dried fruit.

Valzani
Via del Moro 37B, Trastevere (06 580 3792). Bus 23, 280, 780, H/tram 8. **Open** noon-8.30pm Mon, Tue; 10am-8.30pm Wed-Sun. Closed June-Aug. **Credit** AmEx, MC, V. **Map** p336 2B.
A Trastevere institution, surviving eviction orders and the vicissitudes of sweet-eating fashion. Sachertorte and spicy, nutty *pangiallo* are specialities, but form the tip of an iceberg of chocolatey delights, including out-of-this-world chocolate eggs.

Ethnic foods

The best place for Indian, Korean, Chinese or African foodstuffs is the area around piazza Vittorio, now home to a large slice of Rome's recent-immigrant population. The market there (*see p136*) has stalls selling halal and kosher meat, along with many other products hailing from everywhere from Asia to Africa. There are also kosher shops in the Ghetto (*see p110*).

Eat, Drink, Shop

Flea markets

With Romans discovering the potential of second-hand clothes, design classics and bric-a-brac, prices at the many weekly and monthly flea markets have risen. But bargains can still be found, especially at suburban markets. In larger markets, such as the mythical Porta Portese and via Sannio, it's de rigueur to haggle. This doesn't necessarily require a great deal of Italian. Pigeon English and/or gestures will suffice for most deals. No credit cards.

Borghetto Flaminio
Piazza della Marina 32, Suburbs: north (06 588 0517). Bus *88, 204, 231, 490, 495, 628/tram 2, 19*. **Open** *Sept-mid June* 10am-7pm Sun. *Mid June-mid July* 5pm-midnight Sun. **Admission** €1.60. **Map** p332 1A.
Although this garage sale is held in a well-heeled part of the city, stallholders are required to keep prices relatively low. *Objets* and curios from the Fascist period.

La Soffitta Sotto i Portici
Piazza Augusto Imperatore, Tridente (06 3600 5345). Bus *81, 116, 117, 204, 590, 628, 913, 926*. **Open** 10am-7pm 3rd Sun of mth. **Map** p333 1A.
Lots of antiques, collector's items and oldies of all kinds from magazines to painted boxes at non-bargain prices.

Porta Portese
Via Portuense from Porta Portese to via Ettore Rolli, Trastevere (no phone). Bus *23, 44, 170, 280, 781, H/tram 3, 8/train to Trastevere*. **Open** 5am-2pm Sun.
Map p337 1&2B.
Porta Portese is Rome's biggest and most famous flea market. On Sundays streets between Porta Portese, Ponte Testaccio and viale Trastevere are full of dealers selling everything under the sun: antique furniture, carpets, canework and mirrors, clothes, pirated cassettes, glass, china, houseware, CDs, records, kitchenware, jeans, fake Lacoste shirts and leather goods. Somebody may well try to pick your bag or pocket as you rummage.

Via Sannio
San Giovanni (no phone). Metro *San Giovanni/bus 16, 81, 85, 87, 186, 218, 650, 850*. **Open** *May-Oct* 10am-1.30pm Mon-Fri; 10am-2pm Sat. *Nov-Apr* 10am-1.30pm Mon-Fri; 10am-6pm Sat. **Map** p339 1A.
Less frenetic than Porta Portese, Via Sannio is a better bet for good second-hand clothes. The main section consists of three covered corridors, a bit like an Arab bazaar, offering new clothes and shoes at reasonable prices; behind them are used and retro.

Good tea is a rare find in Rome, but don't despair: this tiny shop stocks teas from all over the world, scented coffee and sugar, and a collection of tea pots, some hand-coloured by a local artist.

Trimani
Via Goito 20, Esquilino (06 446 9661). Metro *Termini/bus 75, 86, 92, 217, 360*. **Open** 8.30am-1.30pm, 3.30-8pm Mon-Sat. Closed 1wk Aug. **Credit** AmEx, DC, MC, V. **Map** p335 1A.
Rome's oldest and best wine shop was founded in 1821 by Francesco Trimani; his descendant Marco now presides. Purchases can be shipped anywhere.

Gifts

Jewellery & watches

Federico Buccellati
Via Condotti 31, Tridente (06 679 0329). Metro *Spagna/bus 52, 53, 61, 62, 63, 71, 80, 85, 116, 117, 119, 160, 850*. **Open** 3.15-7pm Mon; 10am-1.30pm, 3-7pm Tue-Fri; 10am-6pm Sat. **Credit** AmEx, DC, MC, V. **Map** p335 1C.

One of the most talented gold- and silversmiths in Italy, Buccellati's creations speak for themselves.

Bulgari
Via Condotti 10, Tridente (06 679 3876). Metro *Spagna/bus 52, 53, 61, 62, 63, 71, 80, 85, 116, 117, 119, 160, 850*. **Open** 3-7pm Mon; 10am-7pm Tue-Sat. Closed Sat in Aug. **Credit** AmEx, DC, MC, V. **Map** p335 1C.
Rome's most traditional citadel of extravagant jewellery. You may collapse in the straight-backed antique chairs on hearing how much the watches cost.

Pomellato
Via del Babuino 63, Tridente (06 324 1623). Metro *Spagna/bus 116, 117, 590*. **Open** 4-7.20pm Mon; 10.30am-7.20pm Tue-Sat. **Credit** AmEx, DC, MC, V. **Map** p332 2A.
Exquisitely designed jewellery and talismans.

Siragusa
Via delle Carrozze 64, Tridente (06 679 7085). Bus *52, 53, 61, 62, 63, 71, 80, 85, 116, 117, 119, 160, 850*. **Open** 9.30am-1pm, 3.30-7.30pm Mon-Fri. Closed last wk July-1st wk Sept. **Credit** AmEx, DC, MC, V. **Map** p333 1A.

Eat, Drink, Shop

Treasures on vinyl

Rome may not be the world's music capital, but there's lots of incredible vinyl here at better prices than you'd ever find in London. Gone are the days when Roman record dealers practically gave old records away, unaware of the fact that Italian easy listening, orchestral and soundtrack music were being rediscovered around the world, and that their bargain-basement goods would end up with inflated price tags in London or New York. For the patient vinyl-stalker, though, the Eternal City still offers finds galore.

The **Porta Portese** flea market (see p225 **Flea Markets**) is the first obligatory stop in any LP hunt. As in any market, success depends on luck: you may leave with a bag full of bargains or with just one record. But you'll always find something. Pass beneath the Porta Portese gate and walk about 500 metres along via Portuense for the best stalls; there are more in via Ippolito Nievo. Most stall-owners have bigger selections stashed in a garage or warehouse elsewhere: feel free to ask them for an appointment to browse. But these are dealers who know what they're dealing in. If you're really lucky, you'll pay nothing for a true gem lying between a pair of crumpled shoes and a couple of Chinese-made calculators on an old blanket on or near Ponte Testaccio.

Every month or so, a **Mostra Mercato del Disco** (record fair) is set up in the San Paolo sports centre, next to the Basilica di San Paolo (see p159). This is a paradise for record collectors, with dozens of stalls selling second-hand, vintage vinyl; but beware, this stuff is generally far from cheap. Check local media for dates and venues, which can change.

If your vinyl-lust hasn't been sated, or you don't feel like sifting through piles of junk, head for a record store. **Transmission**, in the studenty district of San Lorenzo (see p158), has a wide selection, as does **Pink Moon**, located near the Porta Portese market. Other good bets are **Soul Food** (see p229) and **Goodfellas** (see p228); this latter doesn't deal in second-hand discs, but stocks piles of vinyl.

Pink Moon
Via Antonio Pacinotti 3D, Suburbs: south (06 557 3868/www.pinkmoonrecords.com). Train to Trastevere/bus 170, 766, 780, 781. **Open** 10am-1pm, 4-8pm Mon-Sat. Closed 1wk Aug. **No credit cards. Map** off p337 2B.

Transmission
Via dei Salentini 27, Suburbs: east (06 4470 4370/www.transmission.it). Bus 71, 204, 492/tram 3, 19. **Open** 10am-8pm Mon-Sat. Closed 2wks Aug. **Credit** DC, MC, V. **Map** p159.

Original Greek, Roman and Etruscan coins, stones and tiny artefacts, in modern gold and oxidised silver settings based on models from antiquity.

Marble

If you want a more dignified souvenir of the Eternal City than a pope-on-a-rope, you can pick up marble bits and pieces, ancient or (inspired by the classical world) modern.

La Bottega del Marmoraro
Via Margutta 53B, Tridente (06 320 7660). Metro Spagna/bus 81, 116, 117, 204, 590, 628, 913, 926. **Open** 9am-1pm, 3.30-7.30pm Mon-Sat. **No credit cards. Map** p332 2A.
Everything marble, from small pseudo-Roman inscriptions (can be made to order) to full-sized modern and ancient headless statues.

Marmi Line
Via dei Coronari 113 & 141-145, Pantheon & Navona (06 689 3795). Bus 40, 46, 62, 64, 280, 916. **Open** 10am-8pm Mon-Sat. Closed 1wk Aug. **Credit** AmEx, DC, MC, V. **Map** p333 1B.

Ancient busts, columns, vases and tables, as well as reproductions in Numidian and *rosso antico* marble, and more. Can be shipped worldwide.

Studio Massoni
Via Canova 23, Tridente (06 322 7207). Bus 81, 204, 590, 628, 913, 926. **Open** 9am-1pm, 3-7pm Mon-Fri. Closed Aug. **Credit** AmEx, DC, MC, V. **Map** p332 2A.
Made-to-order plaster casts of just about any well-known statue or object you care to have copied. A lot lighter to carry home than the real thing.

Miscellaneous

Eclectica
Via in Aquiro 70, Pantheon & Navona (06 678 4228). Bus 52, 53, 61, 62, 63, 80, 85, 116, 117, 119, 850. **Open** 4.30-7.30pm Mon; 10.30am-1pm, 4.30-7.30pm Tue-Sat. **Credit** AmEx, MC, DC, V. **Map** p333 1A.
Specialising in antique toys and militaria, Eclectica also has an array of *objets* including tricks, hats and mantles for the professional magician, and juggling gear. It's all quite expensive though.

Transmission: record collectors' heaven. *See p226.*

Linearia-Museum Store

Corso Vittorio Emanuele 5, Pantheon & Navona (06 6920 0722). Bus 30, 40, 46, 62, 63, 64, 70, 81, 87, 186, 492, 628, 810, 916/tram 8. **Open** 10.30am-7.30pm Mon-Sat; 11am-2pm, 4-7.30pm Sun. **Credit** AmEx, DC, MC, V. **Map** p333 2A.

Two floors of postcards, posters, books and gadgets from all Rome's major museums and others in Milan, Venice, Florence and across the world.

Music: CDs & records

See also p226 **Treasures on vinyl**.
For larger outlets head to **Messaggerie Musicali** (via del Corso 472, 06 684 401) or

Ricordi (via Cesare Battisti 120, 06 679 8022; via del Corso 506, 06 361 2370). The latter also sells musical instruments, scores and concert tickets, and offers sound equipment for sale or hire.

Disfunzioni Musicali

Via degli Etruschi 4-14, Suburbs: east (06 446 1984/www.disfu.com). Bus 71, 204, 492/tram 3, 19. **Open** 3.30-7.30pm Mon; 10.30am-8pm Tue-Sat. **Credit** DC, MC, V. **Map** p153.

The selection's not as wide as it used to be, but this San Lorenzo shop is still one of the best places in Rome to buy underground and rare records, new and second-hand, including recent US and British indie.

Eat, Drink, Shop

Holy trade

If you've always hankered after a cardinal's hat or a communion chalice, make for the aptly named largo delle Stimmate (Stigmata Square, **map** p333 2A) and elbow your way through window-shopping clergy along via dei Cestari. There, in shop window after shop window, are displays of vestments in luxuriously fabrics, as well as sacred art and everything required for a well-laid altar table.

For life-sized wooden or plaster statues of the Virgin Mary, Jesus and the Archangel Gabriel, as well as cherubs of all ilks, stop in at the **Galleria d'Arte Sacra** (via dei Cestari 15, 06 678 0203) or **Gaudenzi** (at the end of the street at piazza della Minerva 69A, 06 679 0431). For a peek at intimidating gold crosses, clerical robes, fabric and church ornaments (not to mention nuns' 'sensible' shoes and pyjamas) head for **De Ritis** (via dei Cestari 48, 06 686 5843) or **Barbiconi** (via Santa Caterina da Siena 59, 06 679 4985).

But unless you're bona fide church personnel, the chances are you'll not be allowed to make any purchases. For this, you'll be forced to visit the lower-tone places around the Vatican itself – in via del Mascherino, via di Porta Angelica and Borgo Pio (all **map** p333 1C) – and content yourself with a St Peter's in a snowstorm-bubble, a blinking Christ postcard or a plaster cast of the saint who rivals even the BVM in the Catholic popularity stakes: Padre Pio.

Goodfellas

Via Fortebraccio 20A, Suburbs: east (06 214 8346/ 800 901 168/www.goodfellas.it). Bus 81, 412, 810/ tram 5, 14, 19. **Open** *10.30am-7.30pm Mon-Sat. Closed 2wks Aug.* **Credit** *MC, V.*
Rome's ultimate shop for all that's new and fresh in international music. It's especially good on hard-to-find alternative labels, rivalling the best London record shops – what's not in stock can be ordered. Well worth the trek (it's not *all* that far from Termini).

One Love Music Corner

Via di Porta Labicana 38, Suburbs: east (06 4470 2335/www.onelovehp.com). Bus 71, 204, 492/tram 3, 19. **Open** *3.30-8pm Mon; 10.30am-1.30pm, 3.30-8pm Tue-Sat. Closed 10 days Aug.* **Credit** *AmEx, DC, MC, V.* **Map** *p159.*
This all-reggae treasure chest in San Lorenzo has piles of fresh imports from Jamaica in stock. The owners do six-month buying stints there, and also produce local artists.

Rinascita

*Via delle Botteghe Oscure 5-6, Ghetto & Campo de'
Fiori (06 6992 2436). Bus 30, 40, 46, 62, 63, 64,
70, 87, 186, 204, 492, 630, 780, 810, 916.* **Open**
10am-8pm Mon-Sat; 10am-2pm, 4-8pm Sun. **Credit**
AmEx, DC, MC, V. **Map** p336 1A.

All the basics, plus a good collection of world music,
Latin American and the latest on the electronic fron-
tier. There are videos and DVDs too, many in
English. (For the next-door bookshop, *see p211*.)

Soul Food

*Via San Giovanni in Laterano 192-4, San Giovanni
(06 7045 2025). Metro Colosseo/bus 85, 117, 650,
850.* **Open** 3.30-8pm Mon; 10.30am-1.30pm, 3.30-8pm
Tue-Sat. Closed 2wks Aug. **Credit** AmEx, MC, V.
Map p338 2A.

A cool vintage record shop, stocking punk, '60s
garage, beat, exotica, lounge, rockabilly and rarities
of all kinds, many Italian. Record collectors' heaven.

Services

Dry-cleaning & laundries

The city is bristling with *tintorie monoprezzo*
(one-price dry-cleaners) that, despite the name,
don't charge the same for all items: tariffs
generally start at €3, rising stiffly if there's a
pleat to iron in. Most laundries do the washing
for you (charging by the kilo), but the following
are self-service.

Onda Blu

*Via Lamarmora 12, Esquilino (06 446 4172). Metro
Vittorio/bus 105, 360, 590, 649/tram 5, 14.* **Open**
8am-10pm daily. **No credit cards. Map** p338 1A.

Six kilos (13lb) of clothes can be washed and dried
for €4; 16 kilos for €12. Bright and friendly.

Wash & Dry

*Via della Pelliccia 35, Trastevere (800 231 172). Bus
780, H/tram 8.* **Open** 8am-9pm daily. **No credit
cards. Map** p336 2B.

A spanking-clean self-service launderette: €3.50 to
wash eight kilos (17lb) and the same to tumble-dry.
Branch: via della Chiesa Nuova 15 (800 231 172).

Hairdressers & beauticians

Rome's hairdressers shut up shop on Mondays.
Appointments are not usually necessary, but be
prepared to wait if you don't book.

Biancaneve e i Sette Nani

*Via Metastasio 17, Tridente (06 686 5409). Bus 81,
116, 117, 204, 590, 628, 913, 926.* **Open** 9am-1pm,
3.30-7pm Tue-Sat. Closed 2wks Aug. **No credit
cards. Map** p333 1A.

A unique, old-fashioned hairdresser for kids,
equipped with toys and chairs shaped like rocking
horses. Washes and cuts your child's hair for about
€20. It'll open on Sunday if you book.

Concept Hair & Make-Up

*Via Cimarra 60, Monti (06 481 7149). Metro
Cavour/bus 40, 60, 64, 70, 116T, 170, H.* **Open**
10.30am-7.30pm Tue-Sat. **Credit** AmEx, DC, MC, V.
Map p338 1B.

Forget hectic Rome in this little light-wood heaven
with a charming back garden. Bianca and Marcello
(both speak good English and German) take care of
you with trendy haircuts, make-up and a cup of
herbal tea.

Femme Sistina

*Via Sistina 75A, Tridente (06 678 0260). Metro
Spagna/bus 52, 53, 61, 62, 63, 71, 80, 85, 116,
117, 119, 160, 850.* **Open** 10am-7pm Tue-Sat;
11am-6pm Mon, Sun. **Credit** AmEx, DC, MC, V.
Map p335 1C.

Don't be put off by the frozen-in-the-'60s look
upstairs: the hairdressers downstairs have styled the
locks of such notables as Anna Maria of Greece,
Nicole Kidman and Audrey Hepburn. They also
offer facials, leg waxing and lash tinting.

Metamorfosi

*Via Giovanni Branca 94, Testaccio (06 574 7576).
Bus 23, 75, 95, 170, 280, 716/tram 3.* **Open** 9am-
7.30pm Mon-Fri. Closed 2wks Aug. **Credit** MC, V.
Map p337 2B.

This friendly no-frills neighbourhood beautician will
do you one of Rome's cheapest leg waxes, plus massages, make-up and pampering of all sorts.

Opticians

Replacement lenses can usually be fitted
overnight, and most opticians will replace
a missing screw on the spot (perhaps
gracelessly, but nearly always for free).
If you're having prescription lenses fitted,
it's normal to get a discount on frame prices;
if it isn't offered, ask for one. See also *Ottica*
in the Yellow Pages.

Grand Vision Optical

*Via del Tritone 115 (06 4201 4565). Metro
Barberini/bus 52, 53, 61, 62, 63, 80, 95, 116, 119,
175, 204, 590, 630.* **Open** 9.30am-8pm Mon-Sat; 2-
8pm Sun. Closed Sun in Aug. **Credit** AmEx, DC, MC,
V. **Map** p335 1C.

A grand staircase dominates this large shop selling
a wide variety of designer frames and sunglasses.

Mondello Ottica

*Via del Pellegrino 97-8, Ghetto & Campo de' Fiori
(06 686 1955). Bus 40, 46, 62, 64, 916.* **Open**
9.30am-1pm, 4-7.30pm Tue-Sat. Closed 3wks Aug.
Credit AmEx, DC, MC, V. **Map** p336 1B.

Giancarlo and Rosaria will frame your face with the
most prestigious international designer eyewear.
It's worth visiting this gallery-like store just to gog-
gle at the clever window installations by local
artists. Lenses can often be replaced on the spot; and
adjustments and repairs are done for free and
executed with a smile.

Eat, Drink, Shop

Photocopying

In addition to specialised shops, some *tabacchi* (tobacconists) and *cartolerie* (stationers) do photocopies: as a rule, give them a miss if you need crisp, clear copies. Around the university, many copy centres offer discounts to students.

B&M
Via Marmorata 79-81 (06 5728 7289). Bus 23, 30, 75, 95, 170, 280, 716/tram 3. **Open** 9am-1pm, 2.30-7pm Mon-Fri. **Credit** MC, V. **Map** p337 2A.
Excellent photocopying, and plotter and CAD services for architects. You can also send faxes.

Xeromania
Viale Trastevere 119, Trastevere (06 581 4433). Bus 780, H/tram 8. **Open** 9am-1pm, 3-7.30pm Mon-Fri; 9am-1pm Sat. **No credit cards. Map** p337 1B.
A general copy shop, which also has a reliable fax sending and receiving service.

Photo developers

Film can be bought in specialist camera shops, opticians and most tobacconists. Lots of one-hour developing services are scattered around town, but they are not always reliable.

Foto-Cine di Pennetta
Via Dandolo 2, Trastevere (06 589 6648). Bus 780, H/tram 8. **Open** 9am-7.45pm Mon-Fri; 9am-1pm, 4-7.30pm Sat. Closed 1wk Aug. **Credit** MC, V. **Map** p337 1B.
High-quality photo shop with one-day developing and digital processing; camera repairs too.

Fotocolor Lab
Piazza Buenos Aires 20, Suburbs: north (06 884 0670). Bus 63, 86, 92, 630/tram 3, 19. **Open** 8.30am-1pm, 3.30-7pm Mon-Fri. Closed 2wks Aug. **Credit** MC, V. **Map** p334 1A.
A professional developer, specialising in slides and black-and-white. Does good colour prints as well.

Repairs

F Pratesi (Clinica della Borsa)
Piazza Firenze 22, Tridente (06 6880 3720). Bus 52, 53, 61, 62, 63, 71, 80, 85, 116, 117, 119, 160, 850. **Open** 9.30am-1pm, 3.30-7.30pm Mon-Fri; 9.30am-1pm Sat. Closed Aug. **Credit** MC, V. **Map** p333 1A.
Specialises in repairing bags slit open by thieves. Repairs take up to three days.

Vecchia Sartoria
Via dei Banchi Vecchi 19, Ghetto & Campo de' Fiori (06 6830 7180). Bus 40, 46, 62, 64, 916. **Open** 8am-1pm, 3-7pm Mon-Sat. Closed 3wks Aug. **No credit cards. Map** p333 2B.
Run by a skilled traditional tailor and a seamstress, the Vecchia Sartoria does clothing repairs quickly and at reasonable prices.

Ticket agencies

Expect to pay *diritti di prevendita* (pre-sales supplement) on tickets bought anywhere except at the venue on the night. **Ricordi** (*see p227*) sells tickets for classical concerts and for many rock, jazz and other events.

Orbis
Piazza Esquilino 37, Esquilino (06 482 7403). Bus 16, 70, 75, 84, 105, 204, 360, 590, 649, 714. **Open** 9.30am-1pm, 4-7.30pm Mon-Sat. Closed 3wks Aug. **No credit cards. Map** p335 2A.
Tickets for most concerts, theatre and sporting events.

Travel agencies

Centro Turistico Studentesco (CTS Student Travel Centre)
Via Genova 16, Monti (06 462 0431). Bus 40, 60, 64, 70, 71, 116T, 170, H. **Open** 9.30am-1pm, 2.30-6.30pm Mon-Fri; 9.30am-1pm Sat. **Credit** MC, V. **Map** p335 2B.
This agency offers discounts on air, rail and coach tickets for all those in full-time education. CTS services can also be used by non-students.
Branches: corso Vittorio Emanuele 297 (06 687 2672/2673/2674); via degli Ausoni 5 (06 445 0141).

Elsy Viaggi
Via di Torre Argentina 80, Pantheon & Navona (06 683 2096/www.elsyviaggi.com). Bus 30, 40, 46, 62, 63, 64, 70, 81, 87, 186, 492, 628, 810, 916/tram 8. **Open** 9.30am-1.30pm, 2.30-6pm. **Credit** DC, MC, V. **Map** p336 1A.
Centrally located travel agency that accepts credit cards for air and train tickets.
Branch: via Prenestina 172B (06 275 7581).

Video rental

The **Economy Book & Video Center** (*see p211*) has over 2,000 English-language titles for rent. Membership costs €25 a year.

Hollywood
Via Monserrato 107, Ghetto & Campo de' Fiori (06 686 9197/www.hollywood-video.it). Bus 40, 46, 62, 64, 916/tram 8. **Open** 3-7.30pm Mon; 10am-7.30pm Tue-Sat. Closed Aug. **Credit** MC, V. **Map** p333 2B.
A wide selection of auteur cinema and about 400 original-language films. Lots of set photos and original film posters are for sale. Lifetime membership costs €25 and two-day rental €3.10.

Videoteca Navona
Corso Rinascimento 13-15, Pantheon & Navona (06 686 9823). Bus 30, 70, 81, 87, 116, 186, 204, 491, 628. **Open** 10am-1.30pm, 2-8.30pm Mon-Sat. Closed 2wks Aug. **Credit** AmEx, MC, V. **Map** p333 2A.
A huge selection of Italian- and English-language films. Lifetime membership costs €18 (or leave a €50 deposit); a two-day rental costs €3.10 for older films and €3.65 for novelties.

Arts & Entertainment

Festivals & Events

When festivities are called for, Romans know how to make a day of it. Or four.

Today's ten annual public holidays pale into insignificance beside the 150 days ancient Rome allowed itself for R&R, but Romans still enjoy their free time to the full. The first watery sun will drive citizens *fuori porta* (outside the city gates), gallantly braving huge tailbacks at motorway tollbooths for a breath of fresh air. And any holiday that falls midweek is taken as an invitation to *fare il ponte* ('do a bridge') – take an extra day or two off between the official holiday and the nearest weekend.

Different districts of Rome celebrate their own patron saints with anything from a bit of limp bunting on a church to days of parading and feasting. For really special events makeshift stages are erected in squares and occupied far into the night by lusty crooners.

Spring

Festa di Santa Francesca Romana

Monastero Oblate di Santa Francesca Romana, via Teatro di Marcello 32 & 40 (06 679 3565). Bus 30, 44, 63, 81, 95, 160, 170, 628, 715, 716, 781. **Date** 9 Mar & Sun in Mar: times vary. **Map** p336 1A.
The battered wife of a Trastevere gang leader, Francesca (1384-1440) sublimated her frustrations in tending to the bodies and souls of the poor and sick. In 1433 she founded the Oblate di Maria, an order of nuns who never took final vows and could come and go from the convent as they wished. (Their unusual status so confused Napoleon that he failed to close the convent down along with Italy's other religious orders, making it the only one with an uninterrupted history.) Francesca's medieval palazzo of Tor de' Specchi became the order's headquarters and was magnificently frescoed after her death. Francesca was believed to have the gift of dislocation – being in several places at the same time – which endeared her to Italy's pioneer motorists, who adopted her as their patron saint in the early 1900s. Motor vehicles of all descriptions are blessed on 9 March at her church in the Foro Romano (*see p75*).

Palazzo Massimo alle Colonne

See p100. **Open** 16 Mar only: 8am-1pm.
The Massimo family is one of the oldest in Rome: its name is recorded from the start of the 11th century. This family palazzo dates from 1532. In one of its rooms – now the family church (not chapel: this is Rome's only privately owned church) – San Filippo Neri performed one of his most celebrated miracles. Called to administer the last rites to young Paolo Massimo, the saint found the boy already dead; nothing daunted, he brought him back to life, chatted for a while, and then – when Paolo declared he was finally ready to meet his maker – commended him to God. On the anniversary, after a private mass, a procession of family, servants and altar boys escorts the presiding cardinal or archbishop to a room – off-limits to visiting plebs – where the remnants of Rome's nobility are treated to a buffet. To see the spectacle in all its Felliniesque glory, turn up around 11.30am.

Festa di San Giuseppe

Around via Trionfale. Metro Ottaviano/bus 23, 32, 49, 81, 492/tram 19. **Date** 19 Mar. **Map** p332 2C.
Although no longer an official public holiday, the feast of St Joseph remains popular, especially in the Trionfale district. And carpenters and woodworkers still get the day off. In the run-up to the feast, the city's cafés and *pasticcerie* are piled high with deep-fried batter-balls called *bigne di San Giuseppe*.

Maratona della Città di Roma

Information 06 406 5064/fax 06 406 5063/ www.maratonadiroma.it. **Date** 3rd Sun in Mar.
Rome's annual marathon has a growing reputation and now attracts big-name runners. The serious race begins and ends in the via dei Fori Imperiali. The Stracittadina fun-run is a 5km jog through the *centro storico*. Sign up online.

Settimana dei Beni Culturali

Information tollfree 800 991 199/06 8833 6060/ www.beniculturali.it. **Dates** vary, usually spring.
During Cultural Heritage Week all public museums and monuments are open to the public without charge. Many museums and sites that are usually closed are opened up for the occasion.

Festa di Primavera – Mostra delle Azalee

Piazza di Spagna. Metro Spagna/bus 52, 53, 61, 62, 63, 71, 80, 81, 85, 95, 116, 117, 119, 160, 175, 492, 628, 630, 850. **Dates** end Mar, early Apr.
Map p335 1C.
Spring arrives early in Rome, bringing masses of flowers. When the azaleas come out, some 3,000 vases of them are arranged on the Spanish Steps.

Settimana Santa & Pasqua (Holy Week & Easter)

Vatican: *bus 23, 34, 40, 62, 280.* **Map** p333 1C.
Colosseum: *Metro Colosseo/bus 60, 75, 85, 87, 117, 810, 850/tram 3.* **Dates** Mar, Apr. **Map** p338 2B&C.
On the Saturday before Palm Sunday the city is flooded with tour groups from around the world.

Arts & Entertainment

Carnevale – a riotous pagan farewell to winter. *See p235.*

The draw is open-air mass in St Peter's square. Thereafter the non-stop services of Holy Week are Christendom's nearest equivalent to the collective fervour of Mecca. Events culminate in the pope's Stations of the Cross (Via Crucis) and mass at the Colosseum late on the evening of Good Friday. On Pasquetta (Easter Monday) the city empties again, as Romans traditionally have their first picnic *fuori le porte* (outside the city gates): scoffing *porchetta* (roast suckling pig) and *torta pasqualina* (cheesy bread, with salami and hard-boiled eggs).

Natale di Roma

Campidoglio. Bus 30, 40, 44, 46, 60, 62, 63, 64, 70, 81, 85, 87, 95, 117, 170, 175, 492, 628, 630, 780, 810, 850. **Date** 21 Apr. **Map** p336 1A.
It may seem odd for a city to have a birthday, but it's not funny to Romans, whose city was 'born' in 753 BC (*see p7*). The spectacular main celebrations take place at the Campidoglio (*see p61*). The city hall and the other *palazzi* on the hill are illuminated, and enormous quantities of fireworks are set off.

Giornate FAI

Information: Fondo per l'Ambiente Italiano (FAI), via delle Botteghe Oscure 32 (06 6880 4789/www. fondoambiente.it). Bus 30, 40, 46, 62, 63, 64, 70, 81, 87, 492, 628, 630, 780, 916/tram 8. **Open** 9.30am-1pm Mon, Wed, Fri; 9.30am-1pm, 3-6pm Tue, Thur. **Map** p336 1A.
For one weekend each spring, the non-profit FAI (contact details above) persuades institutional and private owners of historic properties to open their firmly locked doors. Unmissable opportunities.

Fiera d'Arte di via Margutta

Via Margutta (06 812 3340). Metro Spagna/bus 88, 95, 117, 119, 628, 926/tram 2. **Dates** 4-5 days Apr/May; 4-5 days Oct/Nov. **Map** p332 2A.
If via Veneto was where the *dolce vita* set hung out at night, via Margutta was where they did their daubing. Few active painters still live here, but the

street is still chock-full of art galleries. High points of their year are the two art fairs, each four days long. The paintings range from so-so to terrible.

Mostra dell'Antiquariato

Via de' Coronari (06 6880 6052/06 361 2322/ www.assviadeicoronari.it). Bus 30, 40, 46, 70, 81, 87, 116, 492, 628. **Dates** 2wks Apr/May; 2wks Oct/Nov. **Map** p333 1B.
Via de' Coronari is the hub of Rome's antiques trade. During its bi-annual antiques fair, shops stay open late, allowing you to browse to your heart's content.

Concorso Ippico Internazionale di Piazza di Siena

Piazza di Siena, Villa Borghese (www.fise.it). Metro Spagna or Flaminio/bus 88, 95, 117, 490, 496. **Dates** end Apr-beg May. **Map** p334 2C.
This international show-jumping event is one of Rome's truly jet-set occasions; it's as smart and self-consciously *all'inglese* as can be imagined.

Primo Maggio

Piazza San Giovanni. Metro San Giovanni/bus 16, 81, 85, 87, 117, 850/tram 3. **Date** 1 May. **Map** p339 1A.
Trades unions celebrate May Day by organising a huge free rock concert, traditionally held in front of the basilica of San Giovanni in Laterano (*see p131*). Top Italian, and some international, acts perform from mid afternoon into the night. In recent years, however, organisers have faced an uphill struggle to avoid having the gig transferred to a soulless field in the suburbs: check local press for venue.

Campionato Internazionale di Tennis (Italian Open)

Foro Italico, viale dei Gladiatori (www.masters-series.com/roma/). Bus 32, 224, 280/tram 2. **Date** 10 days in May.
Italy's annual tennis championships is one of the first big events in the European tennis season.

Arts & Entertainment

RomaEuropa Festival

From its humble, if stylish, origins in 1986 as a small summer happening at the Villa Medici – the French Academy (*see p89* **Ivory towers**) – the RomaEuropa Festival has mushroomed into Rome's trendiest, most prestigious performing arts festival, offering a packed programme of major international dates throughout autumn.

Globalisation is the philosophy behind this slew of ethnic events and multimedia performances: East meets West and old meets new in dance and dance/theatre happenings, and events where the concept of 'music' is pushed to its limits. But the festival also caters to hedge-sitters – those music lovers who like loads of atmosphere and tunes they can sink their teeth into.

Because of that there are ancient music concert cycles and a host of events staged against the backdrops of some of Rome's most beautiful sights and monuments, as well as a sprinkling of techno music and jazz events in nightclubs and alternative venues.

Tickets can be purchased by credit card on the tollfree number (800 795 525; AmEx, MC, V) or directly at the individual venues, though many events sell out well ahead of time. Check local press or the festival's website (www.romaeuropa.net) for programme details. The festival office is on via XX Settembre 3 (information 06 4890 4024/booking 06 474 2308/fax 06 4890 4030) and the season runs from September to November.

Summer

Estate Romana
Various locations (www.estateromana.it).
Dates June-Sept.
The Estate Romana (Roman Summer) festival brings an embarrassment of cultural riches to the city. *Piazze, palazzi*, parks and courtyards come alive with music from local jazz and pop bands, and films are shown on outdoor screens late into the night.

Festa di San Giovanni
San Giovanni in Laterano. Metro San Giovanni/ bus 16, 81, 85, 87, 117, 850/tram 3. **Date** 23 June. **Map** p338 2A.
This saint's day may have lost its resonance elsewhere, but in the San Giovanni district the singing, dancing and games go on all night. It's de rigueur to eat *lumache in umido* (stewed snails) and *porchetta* (roast suckling pig). The religious highlight is a candlelit procession, usually led by the pope, to San Giovanni in Laterano (*see p131*).

San Pietro e San Paolo
San Paolo fuori le Mura. Metro San Paolo/bus 23. **Date** 29 June.
The two founders of Catholicism share the honours as the twin patron saints of Rome, and each is honoured in his own basilica. At St Peter's (*see p143*) a solemn mass is the highlight; celebrations at San Paolo fuori le Mura (*see p159*) focus outside the church with an all-night street fair on via Ostiense.

Roma Alta Moda
Information 06 678 1313/fax 06 692 0303/ www.altaroma.it. **Venues** vary. **Dates** 5 days July; 5 days Jan.
Rome's fashion community has long been overshadowed by trendier Milan, but it strikes back with Alta Moda, when the coming year's collections by Roman designers and other top labels are sneak-previewed against dramatic historical and cultural backdrops around the city.

Festa di Noantri
Piazza Santa Maria in Trastevere, piazza Mastai. Bus 780, H/tram 8. **Dates** mid July. **Map** p336 2B.
Roughly translatable as 'a knees-up for us plebs' – theoretically in honour of the Madonna del Carmine, whose procession kicks things off – the Festa di Noantri is one of the last surviving glimmers of Trastevere's old working-class culture. For two weeks sections of Trastevere are closed to traffic and filled with stalls, open into the small hours. Spectacular fireworks round off the closing night.

Festa delle Catene
Chiesa di San Pietro in Vincoli, piazza di San Pietro in Vincoli 4A (06 488 2865). Metro Cavour/bus 16, 70, 71, 75, 84, 360, 649, 714. **Date** 1 Aug. **Map** p338 1B.
Chains alleged to be those with which St Peter was bound in prison in Jerusalem, and those with which he was shackled in a Roman prison, are displayed in a special mass at San Pietro in Vincoli (*see p135*).

Festa della Madonna della Neve
Basilica di Santa Maria Maggiore, piazza Santa Maria Maggiore (06 483 195). Bus 16, 70, 71, 75, 84, 105, 204, 360, 590, 649, 714/tram 5, 14. **Date** 5 Aug. **Map** p335 2A.
For Romans sweating through a sticky August, snow is an enticing thought. Perhaps that's why the legend of the snowfall over the Esquiline hill on 5 August 352 still has such resonance. It is commemorated when a deluge of rose petals flutters down on to festive mass-goers in the basilica of Santa Maria Maggiore (*see p139*).

Ferragosto
(Feast of the Assumption)
Date 15 Aug.

The Feast of the Assumption is the high point of summer; those few who haven't fled Rome for the whole of August take a long weekend, and practically everything is closed. The very few restaurants that stay open serve the traditional Ferragosto dish of *pollo con i peperoni* (chicken with peppers).

Autumn

See also p233 **Fiera d'Arte di via Margutta,** *p233* **Mostra dell'Antiquariato** and *p234* **RomaEuropa Festival.**

Ognissanti/Giornata dei Defunti
Cimitero del Verano, piazzale del Verano. Bus 71, 163, 492/tram 3, 19. **Dates** 1, 2 Nov. **Map** p159.

Otherwise known as Tutti santi, All Saints' Day (Ognissanti) is followed by La commemorazioni dei defunti (or Tutti i morti), when the pope celebrates mass at the vast Verano cemetery. Romans travel en masse to visit family graves.

Winter

See also p234 **Roma Alta Moda.**

Immacolata Concezione
Piazza di Spagna. Metro Spagna/bus 52, 53, 61, 62, 63, 71, 80, 81, 85, 95, 116, 117, 119, 160, 175, 492, 628, 630, 850. **Date** 8 Dec. **Map** p335 1C.

The statue of the Madonna in piazza di Spagna is the day's focal point, when, with the pope looking on, the fire brigade runs a ladder up Mary's column and a lucky fireman gets to place a wreath over her outstretched arm (in times past, popes themselves did the climbing). At the base of the column locals and dignitaries deposit mounds of flowers.

Natale & Santo Stefano
(Christmas & Boxing Day)
Dates 25, 26 Dec.

The world centre of Catholicism is no great shakes at Christmas. The trappings of northern Yuletide consumerism have asserted themselves strongly in recent years: stores now feature extra-long opening hours, Sunday shopping and classy street decorations. These are recent imports, though: a few years ago it was Epiphany (*see below*) that really counted. For a taste of a more traditional Roman Christmas, get tickets to the papal midnight mass in St Peter's (from the Prefettura, *see p143*; put your request in months ahead) or visit the cribs: you'll find one in most churches. There's a good example halfway up the Spanish Steps; but piazza San Pietro has the biggest crib of all, plus a huge Christmas tree.

San Silvestro & Capodanno
(New Year's Eve &
New Year's Day)
Dates 31 Dec, 1 Jan.

Nowadays thousands of Romans gather in piazza del Popolo (*see p96*) to see the year out with a free concert, disco and mighty firework display. But in a tradition that is far from a thing of the past, they made their own hullabaloo with home-grown firework displays that were as riotous as they were limb-threatening. The mayhem builds to a crescendo in the minutes around midnight – unforgettable from a hotel window, but reminiscent of a war zone if you're caught up in it at street level. It's best experienced in down-home areas such as Testaccio or San Lorenzo, but beware: some older residents still honour the tradition of chucking unwanted consumer durables off their balconies.

Epifania – La Befana
Piazza Navona. Bus 30, 70, 81, 87, 116, 492, 628. **Date** 6 Jan. **Map** p333 2A&B.

Reflecting Rome's pagan spirit, the Feast of the Epiphany is better known by the name of La Befana – the old witch. As the legend goes, this Mother Christmas only brought presents to good children; bad ones found their shoes filled with bits of coal. Today all Roman *bambini* get their presents anyway, as 'coal' comes in the form of a cloying black sweet. From mid December to 6 January, piazza Navona fills with market stalls selling sweets and cheap tat. The climax comes late on 5 January, when La Befana herself touches down in the piazza.

Sant'Eusebio
Via Napoleone III. Metro Vittorio/bus 70, 71, 105, 360/tram 5, 14. **Date** 17 Jan. **Map** p338 1A.

Animal lovers keen to ensure their pets get a place in heaven have them blessed at the little church of Sant'Eusebio. This ceremony used to go on for days and was loved by tourists, who used to cause traffic jams as they cooed over what is a rare example of Italian devotion to animal welfare.

Carnevale
Date week before Ash Wednesday and Lent (usually late Feb-Mar).

In the Middle Ages, this riotous pagan farewell to winter before the rigours of Lent was celebrated with lurid abandon outside the city walls on Monte Testaccio (*see p125*). Anxious to keep a check on their libidinous subjects, Renaissance popes brought the ceremony back within the walls to via del Corso (*see p93*). Nowadays the young'uns dress up in pretty colours and swarm about the city with their proud parents by day, while older kids shower the streets with shaving foam and confetti by night.

▶ See also *p316* When to Go: public holidays.
▶ For rock, roots and jazz festivals, *see p264*; for classical music and opera festivals, *see p255*;
▶ for film festivals, *see p243*;
▶ for theatre and dance festivals, *see p272*.

Arts & Entertainment

Children

History comes to life in Rome – but for the here and now there are parks, books and puppets too.

Rome's museums are resolutely hands-off...

Like so many aspects of the Rome 'experience', visiting the city with children can be both exhilarating and extremely frustrating.

Where else in the world can you see gladiators with gleaming swords in an ancient arena where hapless Christians were thrown to the lions? Where else can you find triumphal arches and pagan temples, towering statues and emperors' tombs that have changed little over the last 2,000 years? With a bit of imagination Rome can bring those dull history lessons to life like no other city. On the other hand, most of Rome's museums and galleries are among the least user-friendly (let alone child-friendly) of any Western metropolis. Exhibits are often unlabelled, badly lit and definitely hands-off.

Traditionally, when mum and dad went out, Italian tots were left at home with granny. Consequently, there's not much in the way of facilities for small children in shops (supermarket checkouts are often too narrow for buggies), at cinemas (no special showings for parents and toddlers here) or in restaurants (no children's menus and most places don't start

serving before 8pm). Negotiating cars parked on pavements and avoiding the ubiquitous mad moped-drivers can also bring on a headache.

That said, things are changing in the Eternal City. A children's museum, **Explora** (*see p241*), opened its doors here in 2001; an increasing number of children's workshops, shows and other activities are now listed in weekly 'what's on' mags like *Roma C'è* and *Trovaroma* (*see p310*); and special kiddy events supported by the city council abound during the long, hot summer holidays (mid June to mid September).

The secret of a successful family holiday is forward planning. This is the time to brush up on your history: spin a good yarn to your kids about why the Christians were hiding in the catacombs or how long Michelangelo lay supine while decorating the ceiling of the Sistine Chapel (*see p147*) and your offspring may not only survive the experience, but even remember some of it afterwards.

If you're visiting in the heat and humidity of the summer months, you'll have to slog far from the centre to find leisure centres or public pools *(see chapter* **Sport & Fitness***).* But you can take advantage of the drinking fountains located on street corners and in *piazze* all over the city: unless they say *non potabile*, they all have excellent quality drinking water. Though climbing into fountains will earn you a sharp reprimand from local police, there are few better ways to revive your flagging youngsters than letting them cool off, splash around and fill up their water bottles from a spout while you plan the next stage of your tour.

You can also, of course, always beguile them with food. Rome has all the usual fast-food chains, peddling bland supra-national chicken nuggets, burgers and chips. But even the hardest-to-please child may enjoy fresh pasta, pizza and ice-cream instead. You needn't even worry if they run riot around the restaurant while you try to interpret the menu: Italians love children (other people's children anyway) and are more than likely to find your bored and noisy offspring utterly charming.

GETTING AROUND

If you're only staying a day or two, you could give your children (and yourself) a feel for Rome with a bus tour *(see p301)*. Otherwise, the best way to see the city is on foot. When this palls, electric mini-buses (116, 117, 119) connect some of the central sights (though they're often packed). Regular buses have nowhere to stash a pushchair, but some kind soul will usually give up their seat to you if you have toddlers in tow. Children under ten travel free on city transport; older children pay the full price for single-journey and one- or three-day bus passes; if you're here longer term, invest in a cheaper monthly travel pass for school-age children.

Sightseeing

If you've neglected to visit the history department of your local library before departure, you could begin your sightseeing with a whirlwind trip through the past three millennia at the **Time Elevator**. After taking part in a game-show-type quiz to reveal the depth of their ignorance about Rome's art and architecture, time travellers are invited to take their flight-simulator seats and don the appropriate language headphones for their jolting journey back in time. Starting with brothers Remus and Romulus, who founded Rome some time around 753 BC, this half-hour video touches briefly on some of the key people (Caesar, Nero, Michelangelo) and events (the advent of Christianity, the birth of baroque) that marked the city for better or for worse. It's pricey, and not recommended for the under fives (or anyone who's had a large meal

recently), but it's a slick performance that will grab your children's attention. After the virtual tour, it's time to tackle ancient Rome for real, starting a stroll away at the **Foro Romano** *(see p75)*. As there's a high risk of the kids refusing point-blank to waste time looking at heaps of old stones, you could do worse than invest in one of the 'then and now' guidebooks on sale from the many souvenir stalls around the area: they may seem tacky to you, but they could help bring the place to life for your children.

The **Colosseum** *(see p69)* is a little further down the via dei Fori Imperiali. (Beat the lengthy queues by buying your ticket en route at the entrance to the Palatine.) There's always an enthusiastic team of ersatz gladiators and centurions in full regalia to evoke the good ancient days and pose for your holiday snapshots in exchange for a few euros.

Remember Ben-Hur? The **Circo Massimo** *(see p68)* – once a grandiose track for chariot races – is now an elongated expanse of patchy grass that's less than salubrious after dark. But during the day it's a perfect (if unshaded) place to let your kids work off excess energy while re-enacting the Hollywood epic.

A short walk away at the Tiber end of the track, the front porch of the church of **Santa Maria in Cosmedin** *(see p114)* is home to the *bocca della verità* ('mouth of truth'), an ancient drain cover that is supposed to chomp off the hand of anyone unwise enough to tell a fib.

The Vatican is, of course, a 'must do'. Kids may get a kick out of the Swiss Guards' brightly coloured costumes. While you admire Bernini's magnificent square outside **St Peter's** *(see p143)*, keep the kids amused by telling them to find and stand on the small round plaques embedded in the pavement in front of each 'arm' of the colonnade: they'll be amazed to see the three tiers of columns perfectly aligned to form a single row. Once inside the church, challenge them to find the foot on the statue of St Peter that has been worn away by the lips of devout pilgrims or the boastful brass markers set into the floor that show how much bigger this basilica is than any other church. A trip up to the dome is always a favourite (don't try this with babes in arms or bulky pushchairs), with wonderful views both down into the church and out across Rome.

The **Vatican Museums** *(see p144)* offer nothing in the way of children's itineraries, so decide yourself what might catch their attention: the well-preserved mummies in the Egyptian section, or the grisly, tormented faces of Michelangelo's figures descending into hell on the wall behind the altar of the Sistine Chapel. If you're looking for a bribe or some extra energy as you trudge the 15-minute walk

Arts & Entertainment

along the Vatican walls from St Peter's to the museum entrance, stop in at the Old Bridge ice-cream shop, just past piazza Risorgimento.

Nearby **Castel Sant'Angelo** (*see p149*) has handy swings and slides in the gardens outside (not to mention some spectacular frescos and trompe l'oeils inside).

If it's art you're after, then take heart: both the imposing **Palazzo Barberini** (*see p79*) and the elegant **Galleria Borghese** (*see p85*) are well situated for a picnic in **Villa Borghese** (*see p83*), where you can recover from cultural overload by hiring bikes or, on the artificial lake, a rowing boat.

On the northern side of Villa Borghese is the recently revamped **Bioparco** – formerly the plain old Zoo – and the nearby **Museo di Zoologia** (*see p87*), complete with a mock-up of a bear cave that will scare your little kids silly if they venture into its depths. The zoo's facelift has sent ticket prices up without doing much in the way of improving animal facilities, but a train ride around the grounds, a snazzy, well-stocked reptile house and a decent-size picnic and play area make it a safe bet for the younger ones who won't keep comparing it to bigger, better versions they've visited in other cities.

Situated half a kilometre from the Villa Borghese is Rome's long-awaited children's museum: **Explora – Museo dei Bambini di Roma**. Housed inside a disused bus depot with energy-generating solar panels on the roof, this hands-on play-city has been designed for the under-12s, with activities from plumbing and car maintenance to commerce and communications. Younger ones will be fascinated to watch what happens when you flush a toilet, while older visitors can try their hands with real television cameras. There's also a good gift- and bookshop, a restaurant and a terrace bar from which you can keep an eye on the adventure playground while waiting for your session to begin.

Other museums that may entertain include the **Crypta Balbi** (*see p109*), which supplements its fascinating displays on Rome in the Dark Ages with computer games to show how the ancient city was gradually incorporated into the modern.

And the **Museo della Civiltà Romana** (*see p161*), which is a hike out into the southern suburb of EUR, but rewarding for its huge plaster models of how ancient Rome looked before the rot set in. The museum is also conveniently close to the rather run-down **LUNEUR Park** funfair (www.luneur.it) and the **Piscina delle Rose** swimming pool (*see chapter* **Sport & Fitness**).

Last but not least, don't forget to pass by the **Trevi Fountain** (*see p78*) and let your kids join the crowds lobbing small change over their shoulders to ensure a return visit some day.

So many books, so little time

If you've had your fill of the sights and want to enjoy more serious things like shopping, why not stop in at one of the bookshops that also offers workshops for children?

The **Lion Bookshop and Café** (*see p213*) is just a minute away from the Spanish Steps and its adjacent designer stores. Armchairs and proper cuppas make it the perfect place for a rest when your feet (and your wallet) have had enough. It also offers classes (€8 per hour), in English, where kids can try their hands at bookbinding, fabric painting, mask-making and sculpting. To book, call Sarah on 06 700 5347 or 328 086 5660.

Mel Giannino Stoppani (*see p211*) is an intimidating name for a children's bookshop, but it has a well-stocked foreign section and a comfortable play area where children and parents can sit and browse. It runs workshops and other activities in Italian only.

Biblioteca Centrale per i Ragazzi (via San Paolo alla Regola 16, 06 686 5116, www.bibliotechediroma.it, closed Mon, Sat pm & Sun, map p336 1B), Rome's main children's library, is housed on two floors of an ancient palazzo, complete with bits of fresco on the walls. Downstairs is well designed to encourage toddlers and first readers, while the first floor has a selection of English, French, German and Spanish books for older kids, as well as a computer room, a video library and an events notice board. Non-residents can use the library, but not borrow books. The library usually moves to a tent in a park for most of the summer.

If you're staying any length of time with little ones, check out the **Ladybirds** mums and toddlers group that meets in All Saints' English church (*see p311; www. allsaintsrome.org*) on the first and third Wednesday afternoon of each month. The church also runs a Sunday School and crèche during the 10.30am service and has a good selection of children's books, cards and videos on sale at the end of the service. For details contact Marjorie at joemarj@mclink.it.

Bioparco-Zoo
Piazzale del Giardino Zoologico 1 (06 360 8211/www. bioparco.it). Bus 217, 910/tram 3, 19. **Open** 9.30am-5pm daily; ticket office closes 4pm. **Admission** €8; €6 4-12s. **No credit cards. Map** p334 1B-C.

Explora – Museo dei Bambini di Roma
Via Flaminia 82 (06 361 3776/www.mdbr.it). Metro Flaminia/bus 88, 95, 204, 490, 491, 495/tram 2, 19. **Open** 1hr 45min sessions at 9.30am, 11.30am, 3pm, 5pm Tue-Fri; 10am, noon, 3pm, 5pm Sat, Sun. **Admission** €6; under-3s free. **Credit** MC, V. **Map** p332 1A.
Booking is essential at weekends and strongly advised other days.

Time Elevator
Via dei Santissimi Apostoli 20 (06 699 0053/www. time-elevator.it). Bus 62, 63, 81, 85, 95, 117, 119, 160, 175, 492, 628, 630. **Open** 10am-midnight daily. **Admission** €11; €9.20 under-12s. **Credit** MC, V. **Map** p336 1A.

Parks & gardens

Besides the central **Villa Borghese** (*see p83*), with its bikes, skates and rowing boats for hire, other parks with children's attractions include:

● **Villa Celimontana** (*see p130*) with swings, a cycle/skating track for tinies and a fishpond that can double (against all rules) as a paddling pool – in lush green shade dotted with classical marble fragments.

● **Villa Pamphili** (*see p161*), Rome's biggest park, replete with swings, lakes, woods, pony rides: you name it, they've got it. The only problem is whether you can find the particular attraction you're looking for – not always an easy task in 1.5 square kilometres (one square mile) of parkland.

● **Villa Sciarra** (*see p161*), a little gem of a park, with lots of swings and climbing frames, a mini-big dipper, rides, fountains, manicured lawns and a pigeon-filled aviary.

● **Villa Ada** (*see p157*), on the north side of the city, recently restored with swings, rides, ponies and basic exercise equipment.

Puppets & theatre

Italy's long and glorious puppet tradition centres on Sicily and Naples, but Rome also offers some good productions. One of the best-known *burattinai* (puppeteers) operates up on the Gianicolo and is identifiable by the sign *Non Tirate Sassi!* (Don't throw stones!). Another is in Largo K Ataturk, EUR, conveniently near a Giolitti ice-cream emporium. Both serve up Pulcinella, just as violent and misogynistic as

...but there's plenty of fun to be had.

his English descendant Mr Punch, delivered in a Neapolitan accent so thick that most local kids understand it no better than foreigners do: it's the whacks on the head that count, anyway.

Puppet Theatre (piazza dei Satiri, 06 589 6201) stages performances of popular fairy tales at 5pm each Sunday. If you make an advance group booking, they'll do it in English.

Teatro Verde (circonvallazione Gianicolense 10, 06 588 2034, www. teatroverde.it, closed May-mid Oct, tickets €6.80), Rome's best-known children's theatre, offers puppet shows and plays, mostly in Italian. Visit the costume and prop workshop half an hour before the curtain goes up.

Teatro Vittoria (*p272*) often stages variety-cum-acrobatic acts popular with children.

Babysitters/childcare

Higher-range hotels have their own babysitting services, and all but the most basic hotels will arrange a babysitter for you.

Angels
Via dei Fienili 98 (06 678 2877/338 667 9718/ fax 06 678 9246/http://web.tiscali.it/angelsstaff/).
Tried and tested English-speaking babysitters are provided by Brit Rebecca Harden, who also provides domestic staff, teachers, secretaries and waitresses for longer-term visitors in Rome and all over Italy.

Film

Roman cinema has a noble history – and a bustling present.

You'd think that all that history, all that ancient stone, would crush such a fragile medium as film, made of plastic and light. But Rome has never had any problems dealing with surfaces. Ever since September 1905, when the first Italian feature film – *The Fall of Rome* – was projected on a screen right next to the Porta Pia (*see p90*), the city gate where the victorious Garibaldini troops portrayed in the film had entered the capital, historical reality and celluloid fiction have learnt to cohabit.

In the studios of Cinecittà, inaugurated with Fascist pomp in 1937, the 'white telephone' (an object of unthinkable luxury) romances of the 1930s and '40s gave way – after the neo-realist interlude – to the great season of Hollywood-on-the-Tiber, when US producers discovered just how cheap it was to film here. The Christians-thrown-to-the-lions romp *Quo Vadis?* (1952) – MGM's biggest grossing film after *Gone With the Wind* – opened the floodgates to *gli americani*, much to the delight of the post-war Roman public and nascent paparazzi. *Roman Holiday* (1953) brought Cary Grant and Audrey Hepburn; *The Barefoot Contessa* (1954) drew Ava Gardner and Humphrey Bogart; Charles Vidor's *Farewell to Arms* (1957) brought Rock Hudson and Jennifer Jones. Meanwhile, Fellini was consecrating his elaborate visions in Teatro 5, the largest of Cinecittà's studio sheds, sandwiching his startlingly modern *La dolce vita* (1960) between two US sword-and-sandal blockbusters, *Ben-Hur* (1959) and *Cleopatra* (1963). Spaghetti Westerns and Viscontian epics kept the place riding high through to the mid '60s, but thereafter its decline was as rapid as its Hollywood-fuelled ascent: by 1971 the state-controlled studio was several million dollars in the red. Soon Fellini's second home was churning out Fellini's greatest bugbear: low-grade TV variety shows.

The 1990s saw something of a revival, with the return of big Hollywood productions from Sylvester Stallone (*Cliffhanger, Daylight*) to Anthony Minghella (*The Talented Mr Ripley*). There was even a reprise of the way-over-budget glory days of *Cleopatra* when Martin Scorsese's *Gangs of New York* roadshow rolled into town with Leonardo DiCaprio and Cameron Diaz – much to the joy of local paparazzi. Since then, the Exorcist prequel *Exorcist: The Beginning* and Mel Gibson's über-Catholic

The Passion – shot in Latin and Aramaic – have kept the studio's technicians busy. And it's not just foreign directors whose cameras are rolling in Rome. Though it's not always obvious abroad, Italians are still making around 100 films a year. For an overview of the current Italian film scene, *see p242* **Beyond Benigni**.

MOVIE-GOING IN ROME

Italians are enthusiastic movie-goers. Rome especially has seen a picture palace renaissance in recent years: in the 1990s the number of screens in the city more than doubled, and audiences have kept pace. This has been due partly to the conversion of older cinemas into two- or three-screen miniplexes, but also to the creation of purpose-built mega-cinemas, especially in the outer suburbs.

Arthouse fans are well served by the **Circuito Cinema** chain, which controls six first-run outlets (including Quattro Fontane), and the first-run independent **Nuovo Sacher**, owned by cult director Nanni Moretti, which looks set to weather a recent eviction threat. The most recent addition to the arthouse scene is the **Filmstudio** – a two-screen reincarnation of the club that launched a thousand earnest film buffs in the 1960s and '70s.

The downside is the dubbing. Italian dubbers are widely recognised as the world's best, but that's no consolation for anyone who likes to hear films in the original language (*lingua* or *versione originale* – VO in newspaper listings). Anything that moves is dubbed and subtitles are virtually unheard of. This said, Rome currently offers more opportunities to see films in English than ever before. One cinema, the historic **Pasquino**, is entirely given up to *versione originale*. Other cinemas that often show films in English are the **Quirinale**, **Metropolitan** and **Warner Village Moderno**. The **Alcazar** and **Nuovo Sacher** frequently show *lingua originale* films on one or two days a week, and the **Nuovo Olimpia** (via in Lucina 164, 06 686 1068) has occasional VO screenings.

For a standard 90-minute film, the four daily screenings will generally be at 4.30pm, 6.30pm, 8.30pm and 10.30pm; the box office usually opens half an hour before the first showing. Some screens now accept payment by credit card, but this is still a rarity. Nowadays, most larger cinemas stay open all year, but many cinemas and most cineclubs still close down completely in July and August. Compensation is found in the open-air cinemas and festivals around the city (*see p243*).

The best source of information on what's on, including summer venues, are the local sections of the dailies *La Repubblica* and *Il Messaggero*, while www.trovacinema.it provides programme details for almost all first-run cinemas in Italy.

First-run cinemas

All first-run cinemas offer lower prices for the first two screenings on Monday, Tuesday, Thursday and Friday (generally 4.30pm and 6.30pm), and all day Wednesday. Programmes generally change on Friday.

Alcazar

Via Cardinal Merry del Val 14, Trastevere (06 588 0099). Bus 780, H/tram 8. **Tickets** €7; €4.50 reductions. **No credit cards**. **Map** p336 2B.
All red and plush, this was one of the first major Rome cinemas to screen VO films on Mondays. For the last two showings it's wise to book ahead (tickets must be picked up 30min beforehand).

Filmstudio

Via degli Orti di Alibert 1C, Trastevere (06 6819 2987). Bus 23, 280. **Tickets** €7; €4.50 reductions. **No credit cards**. **Map** p336 1C.
This historic Rome film club returned from oblivion to its old home at the end of 2000 with new, comfortable seats and state-of-the-art screening facilities. It alternates first-run arthouse films with more recherché treats and themed seasons, which include the occasional film in *lingua originale*.

Metropolitan

Via del Corso 7, Tridente (06 3260 0500/www. medusamulticinema.com). Metro Flaminio/bus 88, 95, 117, 119, 495, 628, 926/tram 2. **Tickets** €7.25; €5 reductions. **Credit** AmEx, DC, MC, V. **Map** p332 2A.
This modern miniplex at the piazza del Popolo end of via del Corso has all today's cinema-goer could want, from popcorn to automatic ticketing and Dolby sound. Anything from blockbusters to the artier edge of Hollywood often run in *lingua originale* on one of the four screens. You can book online.

Nuovo Sacher

Largo Ascianghi 1, Trastevere (06 581 8116). Bus 44, 75, 780, H/tram 3, 8. **Tickets** €7; €4.50 reductions. **No credit cards**. **Map** p337 1B.
The Nuovo Sacher is owned and run by Nanni Moretti (*see p242* **Beyond Benigni**), who bought it out of irritation at the poor state of film distribution in Rome. A meeting place for local cinematic talent, it supports independent Italian filmmakers – with initiatives such as a short-film festival in July, in the open-air arena alongside the cinema – as well as presenting foreign arthouse titles on long runs. VO films are usually shown on Mondays and Tuesdays. There's a small bar and bookshop.

Pasquino

Piazza Sant'Egidio 10, Trastevere (06 581 5208/ www.multisalapasquino.com). Bus 780, H/tram 8. **Tickets** €6.20; €4.15 reductions. **No credit cards**. **Map** p336 2B.
Rome's historic English-language cinema – a point of reference for all English-speaking newcomers – used to be a fleapit with dodgy sound, but a 1998 refurbishment has turned it into a modern three-screen cinema with dodgy sound. Screens 1 and 2 tend to show first-run Hollywood mainstream films, while the shoebox-sized Screen 3 is given over to French or Spanish arthouse fare.

Quattro Fontane

Via Quattro Fontane 23, Trevi & Quirinale (06 474 1515). Bus 40, 60, 64, 70, 170. **Tickets** €7; €4.50 reductions. **No credit cards**. **Map** p335 2B.
The designer showcase miniplex of new indie distribution cartel Circuito Cinema, with state-of-the-art sound system and a small bar. Small domestic indies often get their only Italian outing in Sala 4.

Quirinale

Via Nazionale 190A, Trevi & Quirinale (06 488 2653). Bus 40, 60, 64, 70, 170. **Tickets** €6; €4/€5 reductions. **No credit cards**. **Map** p335 2C.
Sala 2 of this central miniplex has taken over the function of the late but unlamented Quirinetta as Rome's other permanent English-language showcase. The films tend to be on the more artistic edge of the Hollywood spectrum.

Warner Village Moderno

Piazza della Repubblica 45-6, Esquilino (reservations 06 477 7911/information 06 4777 9202). Metro Repubblica/bus 40, 60, 61, 62, 64, 90, 170, 175, 492, 910. **Tickets** €7.50; €5.50 reductions. **Credit** AmEx, DC, MC, V. **Map** p335 2B.
The full-on American Movie-going Experience; it's enough to make you nostalgic for the grubby but venerable porn palace that used to be here. Warner Village has two outposts in Rome: the other is a huge 18-screen multiplex at Parco de' Medici, just off the Fiumicino airport road. This more restrained five-screen central branch is remarkable only for occasional original-language Hollywood blockbusters.

Cinema d'essai & cineclubs

Generally small and cheap, *cinema d'essai* mainly features classics or contemporary arthouse cinema, occasionally in *versione originale*. It is in these cinemas and the still smaller cineclubs that the full range of international cinema and the best of the Italian cinema heritage can be seen. Certain *centri sociali* (*see chapter* **Nightlife**) also offer screenings of alternative or difficult-to-see films. A membership card (*tessera*) is required by many clubs, but these are cards are either free or carry only a minimal charge. (*See also p241* **Filmstudio**.)

Beyond Benigni

Of the hundred or so Italian films produced each year (2002 was a boom year, with 130 including co-productions), only a handful are seen abroad. The filmmakers complain about the unfairness of the Hollywood-oriented global distribution system, but the plain fact is that Italian cinema has lost the power to shock, amaze and delight that it had in the 1960s, when directors like Fellini, Pasolini and Bertolucci were at their peak.

In recent years, the only real success story in international terms has been Roberto Benigni, whose Holocaust weepie *La vita è bella* (*Life is Beautiful*) stormed its way to three Oscars in 1999. For many, Benigni's walk to the stage over the chair backs and acceptance speech ('I don't deserve this, but I hope to win some other Oscars') were more enjoyable than the film itself; others, though, find the Tuscan actor-director's mix of humour and schmaltz as affecting as a good Frank Capra. Benigni then won Miramax backing for one of his pet projects, a live-action take on the Italian children's classic *Pinocchio*, which was to be much closer to Carlo Collodi's dark 1883 book than the bowdlerized Disney animated version. With a budget of $40 million, this is the most expensive Italian film to date. But huge success in Italy was not repeated in the States, where the film flopped on its Christmas 2002 release.

For those who still have time for the cinema of the *bel paese* in its darkest hour, there are signs of life beyond Benigni. Some of it is represented by old-guard cineastes like Marco Bellocchio, with his fascinatingly opaque religious satire *L'ora di religione* (*The Divinity Lesson*, 2002). Nanni Moretti too – a sort of Roman Woody-Allen-meets-Ken-Loach – is ageing gracefully, as demonstrated by *La stanza del figlio* (*The Son's Room*), his most serious film to date, which picked up the Palme d'Or at the 2001 Cannes film festival. Even Bernardo Bertolucci – who many cineastes had marked down as a defector after his Hollwood ethno-pap phase (from *The Last Emperor* to *Little Buddha*) – made a decided return to arthouse form with *L'assedio* (*Besieged*, 1998), a powerful, low-budget tale of repressed passions and amorous sacrifices.

The real star of the younger generation is Gabriele Muccino, whose fragile, indulgent and rather too glossy parables of contemporary Italian twenty- and thirty-something malaise – *L'ultimo bacio* (*The Last Kiss*, 2001) or *Ricordati di me* (*Remember Me*, 2003; pictured) – strike a chord with the generation they portray, perhaps because they hold up a mirror that flatters as much as it criticises. Mining the same seam in a more mature and sexually ambivalent way is Italo-Turkish

Azzurro Scipioni

Via degli Scipioni 82, Prati (06 3973 7161). Metro Lepanto/bus 30, 70, 81, 280, 913. **Tickets** €5; €3 reductions. **No credit cards. Map** p332 2C.

Azzurro Scipioni is the best-known of the *d'essai* cinemas, and is run by director Silvio Agosti. It has two screens: the Sala Chaplin shows more recent art-house successes, while Sala Lumière, with a video projector, is devoted to cinema classics and themed seasons. Streetsweepers get in free.

Detour

Via Urbana 47A, Monti (06 487 2368/www. cinedetour.it). Metro Cavour/bus 75, 84, 117. **Tickets** €3.50 with annual membership card (€1.50). **No credit cards. Map** p335 2B.

A small but committed cineclub with an eclectic programme alternating cinema classics, world cinema, shorts and more. Workshops, debates and art exhibitions are also organised.

Grauco Film Ricerca

Via Perugia 34, Suburbs: south (06 782 4167). Bus 81/tram 5, 14, 19. **Tickets** €5; €4 reductions

(obligatory annual membership €5; incl 1 ticket). **No credit cards.**

The tiny Grauco concentrates on powerful independent cinema from around the world, sometimes in *versione originale*, with a particular day of the week often devoted to one country. On Saturday and Sunday afternoons, kids' classics are screened (in Italian). Films are usually shown at 7pm and 9pm.

Sala Trevi 'Alberto Sordi'

Vicolo del Puttarello 25, Trevi & Quirinale (06 678 1206). Bus 52, 53, 61, 63, 71, 80, 85, 95, 116, 119, 160, 850. **Admission** €4; €3 reductions. Closed Mon. **No credit cards. Map** p335 2C.

This brand new 100-seater art cinema belongs to the Cineteca Nazionale, Italy's national film archive. Named after the late, great Alberto Sordi, the cinema is dedicated to restored Italian classics by Fellini, Pasolini, Sergio Leone and others, plus the occasional foreign interloper. It shares its basement location with a 400sq m (4,300sq ft) archaeological site based around two ancient Roman *insulae* (apartment blocks), which can be seen through glass panels at the side of the main screening room.

director Fernan Ozpetek, whose *Le fati ignoranti* (*Ignorant Fairies*, 2001) was one of the first Italian films to deal with gay characters in ways that go beyond the clichés of low-grade local comedy. The follow-up, *La finistra di fronte* (*Facing Windows*, 2003), was not entirely successful: a hodge-podge of Big Scenes in the lives of angst-ridden thirty-something Romans. Giuseppe Piccioni made one of the best and most perceptive social dramas of recent years with *Fuori dal mondo* (*Out of this World*, 1998), though his follow-up, *Luce dei miei occhi* (*Light of My Eyes*, 2001), was too mannered a study of suburban unhappiness to be really convincing. *Il cinema d'impegno*, or committed political filmmaking, has thrown up a couple of decent films in recent years – in particular, Marco Tullio Giordano's strong anti-Mafia stand in *I cento passi* (*The Hundred Steps*, 2000).

For real vitality, though, you'll have to check out the vibrant regional cinema that has been developing in southern Italy over the last decade. Directors like Edoardo Winspeare and Alessandro Piva (Puglia), Antonio Capuano and Franco Paternò (Naples) or the Sicilian duo Daniele Ciprí and Franco Maresco (imagine David Lynch gone High Catholic) suggest that the Italian cinematic renaissance, when it finally gets off the ground, may well be piloted from outside the capital.

Festivals & summer programmes

Around the beginning of July, as cinemas are closing and box-office figures take a nosedive, Rome unexpectedly becomes a great place to take in a movie. A raft of second-run or art-house open-air cinema feasts is launched as part of the Estate Romana (Roman Summer) festivities (*see p234*), many of them in breath-taking settings. In addition, several *arene* (open-air screens) provide a chance to catch that blockbuster you missed or take in an underground classic.

There are also two regular mini-festivals in Rome: **Cannes a Roma** and **Venezia a Roma**. These show a selection of original-language films from the Cannes and Venice film festivals a few days after the festivals themselves close (in May and September respectively). Festivals and *arene* come and go, so always check local press for details of

what's on when you visit. The following are, however, regular summer fixtures.

Cineporto

Parco della Farnesina, Suburbs: north (06 3600 5556/www.cineporto.com). Bus 32, 224, 280. **Dates** July, Aug. **Tickets** €6. **No credit cards.** One of the most successful and popular summer festivals is in the park by the Stadio Olimpico. There are two separate screens, each showing two dubbed films a night, often recent releases. Live concerts are presented between shows on many nights.

Massenzio

Information 06 700 1719/www.massenzio.it. **Dates** July, Aug. **Tickets** €6. **No credit cards.** The biggest and most politically correct of all Rome's open-air film festivals, featuring about 200 films every year. The venue changes annually (in 2002 it was in EUR, *see p159*), so check the details when you arrive. The imaginative programmes are organised around directors, actors, countries, genres or themes; there's usually a large viewing area for the more commercial films and a smaller arthouse space.

Galleries

Look lively: Rome's contemporary art scene is beginning to flourish.

In the space of a few years Rome's modern and contemporary art scene has gone from second-rate to excellent. This is largely due to the commitment of the current city administration and its predecessor (*see also* **Rome Today**) to cultural development. As well as new spaces for old art – such as the striking Centrale Montemartini (*see p158*) – they funded the expansion of the Galleria Comunale d'Arte Moderna e Contemporanea (*see p246* **MACRO**), a space dedicated to recent and new art.

The success of this initiative encouraged major public and private investment in the arts, with the result that the city now boasts an ever-increasing number of exhibition spaces, some of which are world class. The most impressive is set to be **MAXXI** – the Museo del XXI Secolo ('Museum of the 21st Century'), the construction of which is currently under way to an uncompromisingly modern design by Anglo-Iraqi architect Zaha Hadid (*see p29* **Women at work**). MAXXI, scheduled for completion by 2005, will comprise a museum of modern architecture, workshops and spaces for exhibitions, live shows and conferences. Part of the complex is already open to the public, hosting an ambitious programme of celebrated contemporary artists and new names.

The starting point for checking out the artistic output of recent decades remains the **Galleria Nazionale d'Arte Moderna** (GNAM, *see p85*) on the northern fringe of Villa Borghese. GNAM houses the national collection of modern art and still hosts major contemporary art shows, although this may change if the most recent part of the collection moves to MAXXI. Even so, GNAM is investing in a revamp of its early 20th-century building and in the construction of a new wing.

To find out more about recent Italian art, head for the **Temporaneo Contemporaneo** (*see p246*) gallery: it's inside the beautifully refurbished Ala Mazzoniana by platform 24 at Termini railway station. The gallery is the first remarkable attempt to create a space dedicated to the arts inside an Italian public transport hub. It has a brilliant selection of works by upcoming Italian artists and members of the commercially successful 1980s Transavanguardia movement.

Important temporary shows of modern and contemporary art and photography are also held at the **Palazzo delle Esposizioni** (*see p82*),

the **Museo di Palazzo Venezia** (*see p65*) and inside the **Vittoriano** complex (*see p67*). Other large central venues for temporary art shows include the **Scuderie del Quirinale** (*see p82*), **Palazzo Ruspoli** (*see p96*), the **Museo del Corso** (*see p105*) and the **Chiostro del Bramante** in Santa Maria della Pace (*see p100*). The exhibitions held inside **Palazzo di Montecitorio** (*see p96*) are always worth checking out: they are free, generally of very good quality and will give you a chance to get into the parliament building without making a booking. (Avoid weekends: queues can be hours-long.) Cultural events at foreign academies (*see p89* **Ivory towers**) can also include top-class shows. Check out in particular the British School, Goethe Institut, Accademia di Spagna, Istituto Cervantes, Accademia d'Ungheria, Académie de France (Villa Medici) and the American Academy.

With so much competition from the public sector, the quality of Rome's private galleries has also improved. A cluster of hip new spaces around the Regina Coeli prison has turned Trastevere into the new mecca for art lovers. Other established art-packed streets include via Margutta and via Giulia. Only the most renowned and/or most reliable galleries are listed below. Note that opening times and summer closures can vary from year to year.

To find out what's going on at any given time, pick up *The Art Guide* (www.artguide.it), a free handout available in most galleries. It provides not only listings of exhibitions, but also information about openings in case you feel moved to mingle with Rome's artsy set. The *Trovaroma* supplement of Thursday's *La Repubblica* has a comprehensive arts section with reliable reviews; there's an English-language summary at the back.

The Tridente

Associazione Culturale Valentina Moncada

Via Margutta 54 (06 320 7956/www. valentinamoncada.com). Metro Spagna/bus 117, 119. **Open** 4-8pm Mon-Fri. Closed 2wks July; Aug; 1wk Sept. **No credit cards. Map** p332 2A.
A picturesque garden conceals a series of purpose-built 19th-century artists' studios: Wagner, Liszt and Fortuny visited. The exhibitions programme ranges from 20th-century masters to radical young artists.

Galleria Gian Enzo Sperone

Via di Pallacorda 15 (06 689 3525/www.
speronewestwater.com). Bus 52, 53, 61, 71, 80,
81, 85, 117, 119, 160, 590, 628, 850. **Open**
(by appointment only) Oct-Apr 4-8pm Mon; 10am-
1pm, 4-8pm Tue-Sat. *May-Sept* 4-8pm Mon; 10am-
1pm, 4-8pm Tue-Fri. Closed Aug. **No credit cards**.
Map p333 1A.
One of Rome's most prestigious promoters, Sperone
now frequently holds unusual, experimental shows.

Magazzino d'Arte Moderna

Via dei Prefetti 17 (06 687 5951/www.
magazzinoartemoderna.com). Bus 62, 63, 81, 85,
95, 116, 117, 119, 160, 175, 492, 628, 630, 850.
Open 11am-3pm, 4-8pm Tue-Fri; 11am-1pm, 4-8pm
Sat. Closed Aug. **No credit cards. Map** p333 1A.
This gallery works very closely with the artists
it promotes. It's strong on installations and videos.

Monogramma Arte Contemporanea

Via Margutta 57 (06 3265 0297/www.
monogramma.it). Metro Spagna or Flaminio/
bus 117, 119. **Open** 4-9.30pm Mon; 10am-1pm,
4-7.30pm Tue-Sat. Closed Aug. **Credit** AmEx,
MC, V. **Map** p332 2A.
One of the most interesting galleries on artsy
via Margutta, Monogramma has often hosted the
first Italian shows of upcoming international artists.

La Nuova Pesa

Via del Corso 530 (06 361 0892/nuovapesa@
farm.it). Metro Flaminio/bus 117, 119. **Open**
3-7pm Mon-Fri. Closed Aug. **No credit cards**.
Map p333 1A.
In the '50s La Nuova Pesa organised the first post-
war Italian shows of Picasso, Gris and Léger.
The gallery now works with upcoming Roman
artists and established international names alike.

Ghetto & Campo de' Fiori

Associazione Culturale L'Attico

Via del Paradiso 41 (06 686 9846). Bus 40, 46, 62,
64, 116, 916/tram 8. **Open** 5-8pm Mon-Sat. Closed
Aug. **No credit cards. Map** p336 1B.
One of the most innovative galleries in Rome, a
starting point for new artists and a place for known
names to introduce new directions in their work.

Galleria Giulia

Via Giulia 148 (06 686 1443/fax 06 6880 2061).
Bus 23, 116, 280, 870. **Open** 4-7.30pm Mon; 11am-
1pm, 4-7.30pm Tue-Sat. Closed mid July-mid Sept.
No credit cards. Map p333 2B.
This gallery has found its niche with shows by
German expressionists and Italian contemporary
artists. Strong on graphic arts and sculpture.

Il Ponte Contemporanea

Via di Montoro 10 (06 6880 1351/www.
ilpontecontemporanea.com). Bus 40, 46, 62, 64,
116, 916. **Open** *Sept-Mar* noon-7pm Tue-Sat.
Apr-July noon-8pm Mon-Fri. Closed Aug.
No credit cards. Map p333 2B.

Room to create at **MACRO**. *See246*.

This stylish gallery focuses mostly on photography
and installation art. Pierre&Gilles and Tracey
Moffat had their first Italian shows here.

Valentina Bonomo Arte Contemporanea

Via del Portico d'Ottavia 13 (06 683 2766/www.
galleriabonomo.com). Bus 23, 63, 280, 630, 780,
H/tram 8. **Open** 3.30-7.30pm Mon-Sat. Closed
Aug-mid Sept. **No credit cards. Map** p336 1A.
A new gallery directed by one of Rome's most
experienced art promoters. It consistently shows
new work by well-known Italian artists.

Trastevere

Galleria Lorcan O'Neill

Via Orti d'Alibert 1E (06 6889 2980/www.
lorcanoneill.com). Bus 23, 280. **Open** *Oct-Apr* noon-
8pm Tue-Fri; 2-8pm Sat. *May-July, Sept* noon-8pm
Tue-Fri. Closed Aug. **No credit cards. Map** p336 C1.

Galleria SALES

Via di San Francesco di Sales 16A (06 6880
6212/sales@getnet.it). Bus 23, 280. **Open** *Oct-Apr*
3.30-7.30pm Tue-Sat. *May-Sept* 3.30-7.30pm Mon-Fri.
Closed mid July-mid Sept. **No credit cards**.
Map p336 C1.

...O

...teractive contemporary art scene ...n a shot in the arm in the late 1990s ...he opening of Galleria Comunale d'Arte ...derna e Contemporanea in a stunningly ...onverted brewery. Re-christened **MACRO** (Museo d'Arte Contemporaneo di Roma), this space will grow by 2005 to cover 10,000 square metres (107,500 square feet), due to an extension designed by superstar architect Odile Decq (*see p29* **Women at work**).

With more room and improved facilities MACRO will be able to do what it already does, only better. It will bring big international names to Rome, give space to young artists experimenting in new media, showcase local artists engaged in the production of place-specific art, and work on extending what is at present a fairly limited permanent collection. Under Danilo Eccher, one of Italy's most respected curators, MACRO has already extended into over 3,000 square metres (32,300 square feet) of carcass-storage space inside Rome's former slaughterhouse, the Mattatoio (*see 124*). Shows will be held here as construction work goes into its final phase at MACRO HQ, after which the two abbatoir buildings will revert to their intended purpose: a gigantic evening workshop for alternative art forms, tapping into the creative energy of Testaccio's nightlife (*see chapter* **Nightlife & Music**).

At first glance, city-owned MACRO seems to be on a collision course with nationally owned MAXXI (*see p244*), also due for completion in 2005. Optimists hope that the two spaces will form part of the same long-term project for giving Rome what it has long needed: a network of important venues for new art.

MACRO
Via Reggio Emilia 54, Suburbs: north (06 6710 7900/www.comune.roma.it/ macro). Bus 36, 60, 62, 80, 84, 90. **Open** 9am-7pm Tue-Sun. **Admission** €5.16; €4.13 concessions. **No credit cards. Map** p334 2A.

Mattatoio
Piazza Giustiniani, Testaccio. Bus 23, 30, 75, 95, 170, 280, 673/tram 3. **Open/admission** depends on exhibition. **No credit cards. Map** p337 2B.

Possibly the best known of the slew of hip new galleries in northern Trastevere.

Stefania Miscetti
Via delle Mantellate 14 (06 6880 5880). Bus 23, 280. **Open** *Oct-Mar* 4-8pm Tue-Sat. *Apr-June* 4-8pm Mon-Fri. Closed July-Sept. **No credit cards. Map** p336 1C.

Another of the more established Trastevere galleries, Miscetti holds unusual shows of sculpture and installations. While you're there, check out 2CR Edizioni d'Arte next door.

Volume!
Via di San Francesco di Sales 86 (06 7030 1433/ www.volumefnucci.it). Bus 23, 280. **Open** 6-8pm Tue-Sat. Closed mid July-mid Sept. **Map** p333 2C.

Not so much a gallery as a meeting place for those passionate about experimental art, Volume! is a welcome addition to the area's thriving art scene (it's in the road parallel to Miscetti and 2CR).

Monti & Esquilino

Temporaneo Contemporaneo
Inside Termini railway station, by platform 24 (06 4782 6414). Metro Termini/bus 36, 38, 40, 64, 75, 84, 105, 170, 175, 360, 492, 910. **Open** 10.30am-9.30pm Mon, Wed-Sun. **Admission** €2; €1 concessions. **Map** p335 2A.

In a recently restored wing of Termini station, this gallery currently houses part of the Galleria Nazionale d'Arte Moderna (GNAM, *see p85*) collection. It also runs a stimulating programme of temporary shows by upcoming Italian artists.

Vatican & Prati

Galleria d'Arte Mascherino
Via del Mascherino 24 (06 6880 3820/www. thanitart.com). Bus 23, 32, 49, 81, 492, 982, 990/tram 19. **Open** 4.30-7.30pm Tue-Sat. Closed mid July-Aug. **No credit cards. Map** p333 2B.

Mascherino specialises in underground artists whose work involves experimentation with video and digital production techniques.

The Suburbs

Studio d'Arte Contemporanea Pino Casagrande
Via degli Ausoni 7A, South (06 446 3480/ gallcasagrande@libero.it). Bus 71, 204, 492, C/ tram 3, 19. **Open** 5-8pm Mon-Fri. Closed mid July-mid Sept. **No credit cards. Map** p159.

In the hip area of San Lorenzo, Casagrande's loft-like exhibition space hosts some of Rome's most challenging exhibitions.

Gay & Lesbian

There's more on offer for Rome's increasingly visible gay and lesbian community.

'Go forth and multiply' is the rallying cry for Rome's gay community at the start of the third millennium. New organisations, venues and facilities have appeared, giving increasing space to different takes on being gay or lesbian in the Eternal City.

The historic Mario Mieli group, which organises much of the city's social and welfare programme, as well as an enjoyable Pride Week, is now flanked by the hyperactive Di'Gay Project, a younger, more apolitical outfit that is doing an excellent job of adding yet more social goodies to the shopping trolley.

As for venues, the market continues to diversify and cater for distinct clienteles, with restaurants, pubs, clubs and bars attracting punters of all ages. Whether you're into afternoon tea-sipping, dining in the pink, dancing till you're dizzy or prowling the dankest dark room, you won't be disappointed.

A proliferation of mixed one-nighters mirrors the increasing number of venues opening in Rome where men and women can have fun under the same roof. Or, for that matter, in the open air: one of the big successes in Rome's summer calendar is **Gay Village** (see p250), which is held at the erstwhile abattoir in Testaccio. With concerts, various dancefloors and bars, it's now worth staying in the city for the traditionally becalmed month of August.

THE GREAT OUTDOORS

Once upon a time the gay scene in Rome was synonymous with outdoor cruising, and there are still hedonistic delights to be had on the Monte Caprino side of the Capitoline hill and in the *galoppatoio* (yes, it does mean horse-riding) section of the Villa Borghese gardens. Rome's nudist beach also survives as one of the community's alfresco glories. Il Buco ('the hole') is a short stretch of sandy dunes unexpectedly located between the family-fun resorts of Ostia and Torvaianica (see p277). Gay men and women of all ages flock to the Buco from June to September, enjoying sun, sand and (unfortunately less than crystal-clear) sea. Nudism was once the order of the day, but swimming costumes are now tolerated. To get there by car, take via Cristoforo Colombo to Ostia, turn left at the coast and drive for about five miles (an '8km' milestone marks

the spot). Alternatively, take the train from the Roma-Ostia Lido station (Metro Piramide) to Lido di Ostia-Cristoforo Colombo, then the 061 bus (summer months only) from outside the station to the last stop. From there it's only a ten- or 15-minute walk further south.

PERSONAL SAFETY

Discretion is the keyword. Although Romans pride themselves on their worldly acceptance of human variety, public effusions are best avoided. The police are as likely to protect you as they are to harass, but caution is recommended at all outdoor cruising sites.

Bars, clubs & restaurants

Rome's gay venues open and close at an alarming rate, so a phone call to check the establishment still exists is a good idea before you slip into something sexy.

Some bars charge no entrance fee but oblige you to buy a drink. A growing number of venues ask for an Arci Uno Club card. This costs €14 for annual membership, can be bought at any venue that requires it and gives admission to many venues throughout Italy. Some places, though, have their own membership cards, valid only in the individual venue. In most bars you are given a printed slip on which the bar staff tick off what you consume; you pay the total amount on leaving. Be careful not to lose your slip, or you'll have to pay a stiff penalty.

Rome now has a few rainbow-flagged restaurants. At the **Asinocotto** (via dei Vascellari 48, 06 589 8985, closed Mon, average €35) – literally 'cooked ass' – cook Giuliano Brenna has impressed as much with his right-on political stance as with his culinary skills, while **La Taverna di Edoardo II** (vicolo Margana 14, 06 6994 2419, closed Tue, average €30) serves up specialities like their Orgasmo dessert, an OTT creation that the ill-fated monarch would surely have appreciated.

L'Alibi

Via di Monte Testaccio 40/44, Testaccio (06 574 3448). Metro Piramide/bus 23, 95, 716/tram 3. **Open** 11.30pm-5am Tue-Sun. **Admission** free Tue-Thur, Sun; €10 Fri (incl 1 drink); €15 Sat (incl 1 drink). **Credit** AmEx, MC, V. **Map** p337 2B.

Good shepherd

In a city that still has no women-only bars and clubs, the **Casa Internazionale delle Donne** stands out like a beacon. Originally a separatist squat in an abandoned 17th-century convent, it is still known as the Centro Buon Pastore (Good Shepherd Centre), it was recently given a multi-million euro makeover. The results are simply superb: original features have been respected, but this vast riverside complex now has the potential to cater for many more women's needs.

Over 50 associations use the building, from the original separatist sisterhood to newer groups created by women from the various immigrant communities in the city. Buon Pastore organises study workshops and meetings, and boasts its own book-shop and a library housing its historic feminist archives. There's a conference centre and hotel facilities (06 6840 1724) too. But space is also given to letting the collective hair down, with shows, exhibitions and film events (like the recent Lesbollywood season), plus Le Sorellastre café and restaurant (*see p251*).

Casa Internazionale delle Donne
Via della Lungara 19, Trastevere (06 6880 9723/www.casadelledonne.org). Bus 23, 280. **Map** p336 1C.

The Alibi paved the way for Testaccio's boom as a quarter with an alternative feel (*see p123; see also* chapter **Nightlife & Music**) and is still one of Rome's few full-time gay discos. Just as well it's good. Two floors in winter, three in summer – with the roof garden is its best feature. There's a well-oiled sound system, occasional floor shows and a noticeably competitive atmosphere.

Coming Out
Via San Giovanni in Laterano 8, Celio & San Giovanni (06 700 9871/www.comingout.com). Metro Colosseo/bus 85, 850. **Open** 5pm-5am daily. **No credit cards. Map** p338 2A.
This unassuming pub is the latest addition to the thriving scene that's developing in the Colosseum area. Coming Out offers beers, cocktails and a fair range of snacks to a predominantly youthful crowd of men and women. It is also a useful address to bear in mind if you need a place to meet before you head out after something a bit more frantic; given the closing time, it's good for a friendly night-cap too. There are occasional live acts on Thursdays.

Hangar
Via in Selci 69A, Monti (06 488 1397/www. hangaronline.it). Metro Cavour/bus 75, 84. **Open** 10.30pm-2.30am Mon, Wed-Sun. Closed 3wks Aug. **Admission** free with Arci Uno Club card (*see p247*). **No credit cards. Map** p338 1B.
American John Moss has been at the helm of Rome's oldest gay bar since it opened two decades ago. Hangar maintains its friendly but sexy atmosphere whether it's half full (occasionally in the middle of the week) or packed (at weekends and for the Monday porn shows). The two bars here are linked by a long, dark passage, which is designed for cruising before consuming. The venue's latest addition, much to the delight of its twenty-something clientele, is a small dark area.

K Men's Club
Via Amato Amati 6/8, Suburbs: south (06 2780 0292). Bus 105. **Open** 10pm-4am Mon-Thur, Sun; 10pm-5am Fri, Sat. **Admission** €6 with annual membership card (€5). **No credit cards.**
K (pronounced Kappa) once blazed the trail as Rome's first sex and S&M cellar, though these days there's not much fetishwear in this far-flung den of iniquity. The main attraction remains its variety of well-equipped dark areas and the occasional mid-week 'total naked' party. If you're after raunch 'n' sleaze, look no further.

Max's Bar
Via A Grandi 7A, Monti (06 7030 1599/www. maxsbarrome.net). Metro Manzoni/tram 3, 5, 14, 19. **Open** 10.30pm-3.30am Mon, Tue, Thur, Sun; 10.30pm-5am Fri, Sat. **Admission** free Mon; €8 Tue, Thur, Sun; €10 Fri; €11 Sat (prices incl 1 drink). **No credit cards. Map** off p339 1A.
Max's is a fairly relaxed, mainstream venue near Porta Maggiore. Its dancefloor (disco-commercial) and bars are popular with all ages and walks of life, which may explain its chummy charm – and why it attracts its fair share of Roman silver foxes.

Shelter
Via dei Vascellari 35, Trastevere (no phone). Bus 23, 280/tram 8. **Open** 9pm-3am daily. **Admission** with membership card (free). **No credit cards. Map** p336 2A.
The atmosphere here tends towards coffee and chat rather than cruise and choose. One of the growing number of places where gay men and women relax together and enjoy cocktails and desserts.

Side
Via Labicana 50A, Monti (348 6929 472). Metro Colosseo/bus 85, 87/tram 3. **Open** 8.30pm-2.30am Tue-Sun. **No credit cards. Map** p338 2B.
Side is a minor success story: an unpretentious gay bar that doesn't hide behind reinforced doors and a windowless façade – which is courageous, given its location on the edge of a traditional stronghold of neo-Fascists. Warm evenings see the predominantly young crowd spill out on to the pavement, making a tiny Marais of this corner of town.

New (and ancient) venues abound for Rome's gays and lesbians.

Skyline

Via degli Aurunci 26/28, Suburbs: south (06 444 0817/www.skylineclub.it). Bus 71/tram 3, 19. **Open** *Oct-Mar* 10.30pm-2am Tue-Thur; 10.30pm-3am Fri, Sat; 6.30pm-2am Sun. *Apr-Sept* 10.30pm-2am Tue-Thur, Sun; 10.30pm-3am Fri, Sat. **Admission** free with Arci Uno Club card *(see p247)*. **No credit cards. Map** p159.

The decor of this compact club is a strange hybrid, somewhere between military fatigues and stainless steel slick, but the crowd is relaxed and mixed, with constant movement between the bar and the cruisy balcony and tiny dark areas. Occasionally hosts XXL Saturday nights dedicated to Italian bears.

Sphinx

Piazza M Fanti 40, Esquilino (06 444 1312/www. sphinx40.it). Metro Termini/bus 70, 71/tram 5, 14. **Open** 10.30pm-3.30am Tue-Fri; 10.30pm-5am Sat, Sun. **Admission** free with Arci Uno Club card *(see p247)*. **No credit cards. Map** p338 1A.

This new venue is aimed at the leather and bear community, but gay men of any age should feel welcome. The cavernous bar area is flanked by dark rooms, which fill up as the night progresses. Dress code is not strictly enforced except for the special Leather Club Roma nights *(see p250)* when it's best to dust off the boots and/or fetish gear.

Residencies/one-nighters

Mucca Assassina (Killer Cow), the DJ crew based at the Mario Mieli gay centre, run the largest and best one-nighters around Rome. On Fridays from October to June they're usually at the Qube *(see p264)*, after which they sometimes transfer outdoors to the Buco *(see p247)*. The crew mixes a standard disco diet with novelty theme evenings; it's worth calling the Circolo Mario Mieli *(see p250)* to check details.

Sweat and romance at the **Europa Multiclub**.

Following their lead is the Di'Gay Project, with its rival Friday night event **Omogenic** at the Circolo degli Artisti (via Casilina Vecchia 42, 06 7030 5684) and its monthly women-only event **Venus Rising** (*see p251*). Otherwise straight clubs that also have gay nights include Goa and the (appropriately named) Mount Gay bar, while Caffè Latino (*see p261*) now has a bisexual night on Sundays. Check local listings for the latest venues to jump on the bandwagon.

Saunas

Europa Multiclub

Via Aureliana 40, Veneto & Borghese (06 482 3650/ www.gaysauna.it). Metro Repubblica/bus 36, 60.
Open 2pm-midnight Mon-Thur, Sun; 2pm-6am Fri, Sat. **Admission** (with Arci Uno Club card, *see p247*) €13; €11 after 11pm Fri, Sat. **No credit cards.**
Map p335 1B.
Rome's largest sauna boasts 1,300 sq m (4,335 sq ft) of gym facilities and pools, complete with waterfalls. Leave your togs in multicoloured lockers and cruise to the steam, sweat and romantically star-lit booths. A mixed crowd, with young, muscled tendencies.

Mediterraneo Sauna

Via Villari 3, Esquilino (06 7720 5934). Metro Manzoni/bus 85, 87/tram 3. **Open** 2pm-midnight daily. **Admission** (with Arci Uno Club card, *see p247*) €12 Mon-Fri; €13 Sat, Sun. **No credit cards.**
Map p338 2A.

Tasteful decor and an emphasis on hygiene distinguish this sauna from many others. The steam room and maxi jacuzzi provide repose prior to exertion in the 'relax rooms' on the upper and lower levels. All body types and ages.

Information/organisations

There are about 30 gay activist organisations in Italy, mostly in the north. Foremost is the Bologna-based Arcigay network.

Arcigay Nazionale

Via Don Minzoni 18, 40121 Bologna (051 649 3055/www.arcigay.it).

Arcigay Ora

Via Goito 35B, Esquilino (333 687 9939/ atrinchieri@libero.it). Metro Termini.
As we went to press, the Arcigay network's Rome branch was being evicted; phone for its new address.

Circolo Mario Mieli di Cultura Omosessuale

Via Efeso 2A, Suburbs: south (06 541 3985/ fax 06 541 3971/www.mariomieli.org). Metro San Paolo/bus 23. **Open** 10am-6.30pm Mon-Fri.
This is the most important gay, lesbian and trans-gender group in Rome, named after the pioneer author and thinker Mario Mieli. It also provides a base for debates and events. Its one-nighters, run by Mucca Assassina (*see p249*), are highly popular. The centre also offers counselling and care facilities.

Di'Gay Project

Via G Rocca 59, Suburbs: south (06 574 2693/www. digayproject.org). Bus 23. **Open** Sept-June 3.30-8pm Mon-Fri. **Meetings** 9-11pm Thur.
Hosts a series of events and one-nighters, as well as the summer Gay Village. Check out the website.

Gay Village

Ex-Mattatoio, via Monte Testaccio, Testaccio (06 574 2693/347 666 9547/www.gayvillage.it). Metro Piramide/bus 23, 95, 280/tram 3. **Open** 26 June-31 Aug. **Admission** €15 per wk. **No credit cards.**
A six-week open-air bonanza that makes August the gayest month of the year: bars, restaurants, live acts, discos, cinema – and lots of seeing and being seen.

Leather Club Roma

338 847 9424 after 6pm daily/www.lcroma.com.
This group devoted to leather and fetish lifestyles holds dress-code-only parties on the second Saturday of the month at the Sphinx club (*see p249*).

Websites, publications & outlets

For up-to-date information on happenings and events, consult www.gay.it. Click on 'Lazio' for listings, news and chatrooms in and around Rome. *Edicole* (newsstands) are often good for gay books and videos, while the *edicole* in *piazze* dei Cinquecento (map p335 1-2A) or Colonna (map p333 1A) are good for porn: by day discreet amounts are displayed, but piles of it come out at night.

Aut

A monthly magazine published by the Circolo Mario Mieli (*see above*), with interesting articles and up-to-date listings; available free at many gay venues.

Edizioni Babilonia

Via Astura 8, 20141 Milan (02 569 6468/ www.babiloniaweb.it).
Italy's principal gay publishing house, responsible for the fairly lively monthly magazine *Babilonia* (€5.16 at selected newsstands), which contains a detailed listings guide for the whole of Italy.

Libreria Babele

Via dei Banchi Vecchi 116, Ghetto & Campo de' Fiori (06 687 6628/babelecla@tiscalinet.it). Bus 40, 46, 62, 64, 916. **Open** 3.30-7.30pm Mon; 10am-2pm, 3.30-7.30pm Tue-Sat. Closed 2wks Aug. **Credit** AmEx, DC, MC, V. **Map** p333 2B.
The largest exclusively gay and lesbian bookshop in Rome. As well as a large selection of books, videos, guides and magazines, there's a cabinet of small leather goods and a useful noticeboard.

Pride

Free glossy monthly magazine. Contains the usual listings, but not always bang up to date.

Studio Know How

Via San Gallicano 13, Trastevere (06 5833 5692). Bus 23, 280/tram 8. **Open** 11.30am-9.30pm Mon-Sat. Closed 2wks Aug. **Credit** AmEx, DC, MC, V. **Map** p336 2B.
Roman branch of a Milanese sex-shop chain, focusing exclusively on gay and lesbian accoutrements.

Lesbian Rome

There are still two identifiable factions in *Roma lesbica*: older lesbian groups, which meet at the **Buon Pastore** centre (*see p248* **Good Shepherd**), have their roots in 1970s feminism and continue to claim separate identity from men, gay or straight; younger lesbians, on the other hand, tend to join the less separatist Arci-Lesbica association or meet the lads at Circolo Mario Mieli or the Di'Gay Project. Joint ventures like Mucca Assassina get a good turnout from gay men and lesbians, and Shelter Café (*see p248*) is also popular with women.

Rome has yet to host a permanent lesbian club or disco, but there are occasional one-nighters and other events: check noticeboards at gay and women's bookshops, stop by the Buon Pastore or ring Arci-Lesbica or Circolo Mario Mieli for the latest. Try www.listalesbica.it too.

See also p248 **Shelter**.

Le Sorellastre

Via San Francesco di Sales 1B, Trastevere (349 762 2845). Bus 23, 280. **Open** 7pm-midnight Tue-Sat. **No credit cards. Map** p336 1C.
A bar and small restaurant within the walls of the historic Buon Pastore women's centre (*see p248* **Good Shepherd**). No male diners.

Venus Rising at Goa

Via Libetta 13, Suburbs: south (339 772 5619/ www.digayproject.org). Metro Garbatella/bus 29, 769, 770. **Open** 10.30pm-late one Fri per mth. **No credit cards.**
A successful one-nighter at the trendy Goa club. Women-only, with occasional erotic entertainment.

Arci-Lesbica Roma

Viale Stefanini 15, Suburbs: north (06 418 0211/ www.arcilesbicaroma.org). Metro Santa Maria del Soccorso. **Open** for events.
Often working in close association with the Circolo Mario Mieli (*see above*), Arci-Lesbica offers a helpline (6.30-9pm Tue) and organises midweek get-togethers, country walks, pub evenings and occasional residencies at local nightspots: phone or consult the website for information.

Collegamento lesbiche italiane (CLI)

Casa Internazionale delle Donne, via San Francesco di Sales 1B, Trastevere (06 686 4201/www.clrbp.it). Bus 23, 280. **Open** 7.30-11pm Tue. **Map** p336 1C.
Formed in 1981, this separatist group meets in the Buon Pastore women's centre (*see p248* **Good shepherd**) once a week to discuss politics. It's strictly women-only, but you don't need to be a member to take part. Organises conferences, literary evenings, concerts, dances, holidays and an annual masked ball. The Coordinamento lesbiche italiane, little sister of the CLI, meets here on Tuesdays between 7pm and 9pm.

Libreria delle Donne: Al Tempo Ritrovato

Via dei Fienaroli 31D, Trastevere (06 581 7724/ libreriadelledonne@libero.it). Bus 23, 280/tram 8. **Open** 3.30-8pm Mon; 10am-1pm, 3.30-8pm Tue-Sat. **Credit** MC, V. **Map** p336 2B.
Bookshop with a well-stocked lesbian section (including some English titles) and helpful noticeboard. Organises debates and Friday get-togethers.

Zipper Travel Association

Via Castelfidardo 18, Esquilino (06 488 2730/www. zippertravel.it). Metro Castro Pretorio/bus 75. **Open** 9.30am-6pm Mon-Fri. **Credit** MC, V. **Map** p335 1A.
One of the few travel agencies in Italy to offer customised travel for gay women.

Arts & Entertainment

Music: Classical & Opera

It's quiet, it's understated... but classical music *does* feature in Rome's treasury of cultural riches.

Exciting opera doesn't feature among Rome's top ten cultural attractions, but in its quiet way the classical music scene is alive and well, with the city's understated range of interesting contemporary music getting better each year.

THE SCENE

The top job in Roman classical music is the directorship of the **Accademia Nazionale di Santa Cecilia** (*see p254* **Parco della Musica**), founded in the 16th century by no less a person than Palestrina. Composer Luciano Berio is the current director of the academy. Inflexible and rigorous in his pursuit of perfection, he has blown away some of the Academy's cobwebs, opening it up to 'non-classical' music: recent cross-genre happenings have involved Richard Galliano, Michael Nyman, Caetano Veloso and Jan Garbarek. Meanwhile, in-house conductor Myung-Whung Chung has drilled his orchestra mercilessly,

elevating it to world standards. Santa Cecilia also continues to attract some of the world's greatest conductors for its symphonic season.

Many other institutions large and small also make their voices heard. The **Accademia Filarmonica Romana** (06 320 1752, www.filarmonicaromana.org), founded in 1821, is smaller than Santa Cecilia, but boasts composers such as Rossini, Donizetti, Paganini and Verdi among its founders. It offers a varied programme of chamber music, ancient music, ballet and chamber opera. It is particularly active in co-producing large multimedia events with big-name stage directors such as Bob Wilson and modern composers like Philip Glass, who has become a habitué of the Accademia's **Teatro Olimpico** (*see p255*).

Another major concert provider is the **Istituzione Universitaria dei Concerti** (IUC, 06 361 0051, www.concertiiuc.it/ bigliet.htm), founded after World War II to inject some into

Organics

In the darker corners of many of Rome's churches lurk original baroque mechanical pipe organs of the type preferred by 17th-century composers. After decades of neglect, many have been painstakingly brought back to life, using handcrafted spare parts that are perfect replicas of the worn-out originals.

The organs currently most in use are in the **Oratorio del Gonfalone** (via del Gonfalone 32A, 06 687 5952/www.oratoriodelgonfalone.it); in the church of **San Giovanni de' Fiorentini** (via Acciaioli 2, 06 6889 2059), which is played for mass at noon on Sundays; and in **San Giovanni in Laterano** (*see p131*), where the Luca Blasi organ is played after 10am mass. There are also concerts at **San Marcello al Corso** (piazza San Marcello 5, 06 699 301), **San Carlo ai Catinari** (piazza Cairoli 117, 06 6880 3554; one Sunday a month) and in **Santa Maria in Trastevere** (*see p118*).

But alongside these period pieces, the Eternal City boasts some fine modern instruments. A German-built organ recently presented to Pope John Paul II is used mainly for liturgical celebrations in the Sistine Chapel (private services only), but can be whisked around the Vatican's august halls to other venues on a kind of railway-track contraption. The giant mechanical organ in sprawling **Santa Maria degli Angeli** (*see p139*) was another gift to the current pope, in this case built by Bartelemie Formentelli to mark the 2000 Holy Year.

Some of Rome's smaller private musical organisations also organise cycles of organ recitals. The Associazione Musicale La Stravaganza (06 7707 2842) and the Associazione Romana d'Organo César Franck (www.coralecesarfranck.wxs.org) are among the most prominent of these groups.

Teatro dell'Opera: acoustically perfect, artistically patchy.

life Rome's culturally dead university campus. The IUC now offers a varied season with often outstanding – and frequently experimental – international and Italian recitals and chamber music at La Sapienza's main auditorium, the rather stark **Aula Magna** (*see p255*).

The 16th-century **Oratorio del Gonfalone** (06 687 5952, *see p252* **Organics**) hosts a chamber music season that reflects the joyous personality of director Angelo Persichilli. Every concert and recital on the programme, which runs from December to May, seems to have been lovingly chosen to fit the beautiful surroundings, and to show off the Oratorio's magnificent 18th-century organ.

At the genteelly decaying **Teatro Ghione** (*see p255*), director Christopher Axworthy is behind the surprising Euromusica Master Series, studded each year with some brilliant jewels, such as Gyorgy Sandor, Shura Cherkassky, Fou Ts'ong, Mikhail Pletnev and Alicia De Laroccha. Notwithstanding the stellar programme, the theatre and staff remain approachable and ticket prices extremely reasonable. Many of the artists are elderly personal friends of Axworthy, some of whom rarely perform because of their advanced age.

For ticket agencies, *see p230*.

THE OPERA
Of course, there's the **Teatro dell'Opera** (*see p255*) too. Its glorious opening in 1880 – as the Teatro Costanzi – included premieres of

Cavalleria Rusticana, L'Amico Fritz, Iris and *Tosca*, conducted by such figures as Pietro Mascagni, Igor Stravinsky and Riccardo Zandonai. A change of name to Teatro Reale dell'Opera di Roma, in 1928, was meant to make the opera house sound more serious, but it has always lagged behind Milan's Teatro alla Scala – and even the 'provincial' houses in Bologna, Palermo, Naples and Venice. Acoustically, the building is close to perfect, and singers claim to love it. But the state-run institution is still struggling to overcome decades of scandalously bad administration that left it with a staggering budget deficit and even worse reputation.

Conductor Gianluigi Gelmetti has been at the helm since 2001. Working hand-in-hand with super-bureaucrat Francesco Ernani, he is managing to serve up a dignified – if uneven – bill of fare. Belt-tightening forced Ernani to cut back on opulent new opera productions, so he has opted to fill the house with many smaller – often contemporary – offerings. These include opera triptychs, ballets and concerts, plus some larger co-productions with other Italian opera houses. Top-name singers rarely stay around after the opening night, so keep an eye on cast lists to avoid second-rate substitutes.

CHURCHES
There is nothing in Rome to compare with the church-music traditions of Vienna or London: some of the city's most famous and beautiful churches are dreadful places to hear concerts.

Arts & Entertainment

St Peter's (*see p143*) has the acoustics of a football stadium and lousy choirs to match. Among the city's monasteries and convents, only **Sant'Anselmo** (piazza dei Cavalieri di Malta 5, 06 57 911) manages decent plainchant. Kitsch amplification in places like **San Giovanni in Laterano** (*see p131*) completely destroys the effect. The only truly outstanding church choir is that of the Russicum (via Carlo Alberto 2, 06 446 1104), the Eastern Rite church opposite Santa Maria Maggiore.

Santa Maria degli Angeli (piazza della Repubblica, 06 488 0812) has become a popular venue for concerts of sacred music, thanks to its

Parco della Musica

Arts & Entertainment

Much to the surprise of the sceptics, Rome kept its promise and, after years of set-backs, proudly celebrated its 'birthday' (*see p233*) on 21 April 2002 with the grand opening of a new auditorium. Baptised Parco della Musica, it gave the Eternal City the world-class concert venue it had lacked for decades.

Architect Renzo Piano (famous for creating the Pompidou Centre and Kansai Airport) designed the three main halls in the shape of lutes, with an open-air arena in the middle and the remains of a Roman villa peeping up between the brick and glass walls. Critics describe the complex as looking like three menacing grey bugs, but a luxurious garden of olive trees and other Mediterranean flora will soften the stark contours of the '70s-looking red-brick buildings, and Piano is certain that the lead roof tiles will fade to fit in with mellow Roman tones.

Acoustically, it's perfect. The three concert halls are lined in layers of soft cherry wood and are the perfect sizes for full symphonic orchestra and choir, chamber music orchestra and recital. The largest hall – which can seat 2,800 people – is the domain of the **Accademia Nazionale di Santa Cecilia**, which now holds its winter season here; the Sala Sinopoli holds nearly 1,300 people, and the smallest hall some 700.

The outside *cavea*, with room for 3,000, was conceived as a venue for rock and pop concerts. All in all, the complex sprawls over 55,000 square metres (590,000 square feet) and hosts five rehearsal rooms, a library, a book and CD shop, offices, bars and restaurants (*see ReD, p176* **The design crew**).

Accademia Nazionale di Santa Cecilia

Via della Conciliazione 2, Vatican & Prati (06 6880 1044/www.santacecilia.it). **Box office** 11am-6pm Mon, Tue, Thur, Fri; 11am-4pm Sat, Sun. **Credit** MC, V. **Map** p333 1C.

Parco della Musica

Via P de Coubertin 15, Suburbs: north (06 80 242/box office 06 808 2058/fax 06 8024 1211/www.musicaperroma.it). **Open** *Complex* 10am-6pm daily (admission free). **Box office** *Oct-June* 11am-6pm Mon, Tue, Thur-Sun; until interval on concert days. *July-Sept* 11am-6pm Mon-Fri. **Credit** MC, V. Tickets for single concerts are sold in two phases: from mid October (Oct-Jan concerts) and from February (Feb-June concerts); they can be booked online. Guided tours cost €10 (€5 concessions; no credit cards) and take place several times a day. Times change frequently so call ahead or check the website.

sprawling interior and fine organ (*see p252* **Organics**). The church often hosts the Festival di Pasqua (*see p232*) and you can sometimes catch singers like José Carreras or Montserrat Caballé on important church holidays. The church hierarchy does not allow paying concerts on consecrated ground, so events are free and very popular. Make sure you arrive early or call ahead to find out if it is possible to book. There are also occasional free performances by visiting choirs, so it's worth keeping an eye on posters at church entrances all over the city. In winter, churches tend to be bone-chillingly cold.

Auditoria

See also p254 **Parco della Musica**.

Aula Magna dell'Università la Sapienza

Piazzale Aldo Moro, Esquilino (06 361 0051/fax 06 3600 1511/www.concertiiuc.it/bigliet.htm). Metro Policlinico/bus 61, 490, 495/tram 3, 19. **Concerts** Oct-Apr. **Box office** up to 1hr before concerts. **Credit** MC, V. **Map** p159.
With kitsch Fascist decor but reasonable acoustics, this is the main auditorium for the IUC season (*see p252*). Tickets are also available from agencies (*see p230*) or online.

Teatro dell'Opera di Roma

Piazza B Gigli 1, Esquilino (06 481 601/7003/ www. opera.roma.it). Metro Repubblica/bus 40, 60, 64, 70, 117, 170. **Box office** 9am-5pm Tue-Sat; 9am-1.30pm Sun; until 15min after performances begin. **Credit** AmEx, DC, MC, V. **Map** p335 2B.
The lavish late 19th-century *teatro all'italiana* interior is quite a surprise after Mussolini's angular façade and its tacky potted palms. There are towering rows of boxes, loads of stucco, frescos and gilding everywhere. The acoustics vary greatly: the higher (cheaper) seats are unsatisfactory, so splash out on a box... it's all part of the experience. Bookings can be made online at www.chartanet.it.

Teatro Ghione

Via delle Fornaci 37, Vatican & Prati (06 637 2294/ www.ghione.it). Bus 34, 46, 64, 916. **Box office** 10am-1pm, 4-7.30pm daily. **Credit** MC, V.
This plush little red and gold theatre regales its faithful public with extraordinary recitals by legendary – and mostly ancient – performers.

Teatro Olimpico

Piazza Gentile da Fabriano, Suburbs: north (06 3265 9917/www.teatroolimpico.it). Bus 53, 280, 910/tram 2, 19. **Concerts** Oct-May. **Box office** 11am-7pm daily; from 8pm on concert days. **Credit** MC, V. **Map** p332 1B.
Great for all types of performances, the Olimpico has good acoustics – even for cheaper seats. Owned by the Accademia Filarmonica (*see p252*) and used for

their Thursday concerts, it also hosts many of the event making up the RomaEuropa Festival (*see p234* **RomaEuropa Festival**).

Festivals

See also p234 **RomaEuropa Festival**.
Most of Rome's summer festivals take place under the **EstateRomana** umbrella. This overwhelming event-fest runs from June to September and provides such quantities of entertainment of all descriptions that it's difficult to know where to start. The city council website (www. comune.roma.it) posts a complete programme in the spring.
   As this guide went to press it was unclear whether the Accademia Nazionale di Santa Cecilia's brief summer season of quality crowd-pleasers (international orchestras and classical/ popular cross-overs) would take place in **Terme di Caracalla** (*see p129*) or the outside *cavea* of the Parco della Musica (*see p254* **Parco della Musica**). Phone 06 328 171 or tollfree 800 907 080, or check the Parco della Musica website for details.

Concerti all'Orto Botanico

Largo Cristina di Svezia 24, Trastevere (06 686 8441/06 3936 6322/fax 06 3936 6229/www. assmusrom.it). Bus 23, 280, 630, 780, H/tram 8. **Season** July. **Box office** at venue before concerts. **No credit cards. Map** p.336 2C.
Organised by the Associazione Musicale Romana, these concerts – which include Gershwin and Piazzola as well as mainstream chamber music – take place in the beautiful botanical gardens where a natural amphitheatre makes for a lovely venue for a limited number of spectators. Booking essential.

Concerti del Tempietto

Various venues (06 8713 1590/06 8720 1523/fax 06 2332 26360/www.tempietto.com). **Box office** at venues from 1hr before concerts. **No credit cards**.
From November to July, the Associazione Il Tempietto organises concerts in various city venues, mainly the Sala Baldini (piazza Campitelli 9), the church of San Nicola in Carcere (*see p113*) and the Aula Adrianea in the ancient Horti Sallustiani (piazza Sallustio 21, *see p90*) which opens to the public for these events only – so grab any chance to go. In summer, concerts and recitals move to the archaeological site around the Teatro di Marcello (*see p115*) and the lovely art nouveau Casina delle Civette (*see p157*). It's mostly low-level musically, but there's a concert almost every evening and the venues are beautiful. You can book online.

Festival di Pasqua

Various venues (06 6880 9107/8/9/fax 06 6880 9111/www.festivaldipasqua.it). **Season** April. **Box office** at venues before performances. **Credit** AmEx, DC, MC, V.

Arts & Entertainment

Contemporary music

Although Rome's major music institutions are injecting ever more contemporary music into their programmes, the vital lymph for this difficult sector is myriad small organisations, many of which are loosely gathered under the **Progetto Musica** umbrella.

Progetto Musica (06 6880 9222) not only co-ordinates a biannual festival full of contemporary goodies (May-June, October-November), but valiantly attempts to liaise and lobby, bringing together the players on Rome's contemporary scene to ensure that their voice grows stronger and their message clearer. Which is no easy task in a city where the classical concert-going public (and potential sponsors) view anything this side of Ravel as elitist and over-intellectual.

The musical associations gathered under the Progetto aegis are extremely varied. At the forefront of scientific research into electronic sound is the **Centro Ricerche Musicali** (06 446 4161, www.crm-music-org), headed by eclectic composer Michelangelo Lupone. Lupone and his technical team are not only the brains behind sophisticated new computers for generating elaborate sound; they also organise unashamedly intellectual events and conferences. Headed by the composer Ada Gentile, **Nuovi Spazi Musicali** (06 502 1208, http://web.tiscalinet.it/ nuovispazimusicali) is a member of the European Conference of Promoters of New Music. **Associazione Nuova Consonanza** (06 370 0323/www. nuovaconsonanza.it) organises a concert season (October-December) showcasing the best in mostly Italian, but also international contemporary music plus lectures and seminars.

The Easter Festival is an annual event organised by the city council in conjunction with the Associazione Arte in Comune. Free Easter holiday concerts take place in churches and theatres across Rome.

International Chamber Ensemble

Sant'Ivo alla Sapienza, corso Rinascimento 40, Pantheon & Navona (06 8680 0125/www. interensemble.org). Bus 30, 70, 81, 87, 116, 204, 280, 492, 628. **Season** mid June-July. **Box office** 10am-6pm Mon-Fri. **No credit cards**. **Map** p333 2A.
Chamber and symphonic music, as well as opera, makes up this summer season, held in Rome for over 20 years. Events take place in the splendid courtyard of Sant'Ivo alla Sapienza (*see p104*).

Mille e Una Nota

Vicolo del Arco della Pace 5, Pantheon & Navona (06 780 7695/ippocampo@nettuno.it). Bus 30, 40, 46, 62, 63, 64, 70, 81, 116, 492, 628, 630, 780, 916. **Season** Aug. **Box office** 1hr before concerts. **No credit cards**. **Map** p333 2B.
This charming little chamber music festival has been going for ten years in the magnificent cloister of Santa Maria della Pace (*see p100*).

New Operafestival di Roma

Piazza San Clemente 1 (06 561 1519/www. newoperafestivaldiroma.com). Metro Colosseo/ bus 60, 85, 87, 117, 810, 850/tram 3. **Season** June-Aug. **Box office** 2hrs before concerts. **No credit cards**. **Map** p338 2B.
This festival offers talented young singers and musicians from Italy and the US the chance to perform in the courtyard of the basilica of San Clemente (*see p126*). There's always at least one fully fledged opera, chamber music and a series of recitals.

Teatro dell'Opera Summer Season

Tickets/information from Teatro dell'Opera, see p255. **Season** July-Aug.
Since 1997, when it was banished from its traditional summer home in the Terme di Caracalla (*see p129*), the opera's outdoor season has been shunted between various (generally unsatisfactory) venues. Check local press for latest venue details.

Out of town

Festival EuroMediterraneo

Villa Adriana, via di Villa Adriana, Villa Adriana (06 6880 9107/08/09/10). COTRAL bus from Ponte Mammolo (see p275). **Season** July-Aug. **Box office** at venue before performances or from agencies (*see p230*). **No credit cards**.
The spectacularly lit Hadrian's Villa provides the backdrop for an extremely varied programme of concerts, opera, dance and drama dedicated to the Mediterranean. Expect everything from Shakespeare to flamenco via symphonic orchestras.

Festival Pontino

Castello Caetani, Sermoneta/Abbazia di Fossanova, Priverno (information 0773 605 551/bookings 0773 480 672/fax 0773 628 498/www.festivalpontino.it). **Season** end June-end July. **Box office** at venues before performances. **No credit cards**.
Composer Goffredo Petrassi draws excellent musicians from all over Europe to his small-scale festival of orchestral and chamber music in two outstandingly beautiful venues: the medieval Castello Caetani in the hill town of Sermoneta south of Rome, and the gothic abbey of Fossanova. A contemporary music festival also takes place in June.

Nightlife & Music

Unhip no more, Rome has new live venues to complement its thriving squat scene.

Post-*dolce vita*, Rome's night culture struggled through some dark decades before starting a timid renaissance a few years back. The Eternal City is now shedding its bad name as the music and entertainment backwater of Italy, where everything happened several years later than in London, New York or even Milan, and clubs looked like they were last refurbished in 1982. New locations, council funds and the relentless efforts of some of the city's culturally lively *centri sociali* (squats, *see below*) have brought results. Dancing to the best international DJs and listening to the bands of the moment have become much easier, but you still need a little insider information and some patience to weed out good clubs from the string of commercial venues that still play Eurodisco, but dress it up as 'exotic', 'lounge' or 'glam'.

Rome is at its best and most lively in summer: you'll simply be spoilt for choice between festivals, concerts, open-air cinema, theatre and discos (*see* **Festivals & Events**). For details of upcoming events, consult magazines such as *Trovaroma* (out Thursdays with the daily *La Repubblica*), *Roma C'è* (on newsstands on Fridays) or the trendy *Zero6* (a monthly, free in shops and pubs).

NIGHTLIFE

Romans like to take things easy. No one even thinks about where to go or what to do until well after dinner. Roman nights start late and end even later: concerts never kick off before 10.30pm – after 11pm at weekends – and most clubs close after 4am, even on weekdays. When picking your club for the night, remember that expensive, fashionable clubs tend to be the least inspiring musically: avoid the scores of mainstream clubs serving up commercial house or Latin American sounds on Fridays and Saturdays. For an alternative evening, head to **Agatha** at Brancaleone (*see p263*) or to **Bluecheese** in Testaccio (*see p261*). If reggae's your thing, then the **One Love Hi Pawa** (at Brancaleone, *see p263*) is your best bet. If you're feeling playful, look for the club or *centro sociale* hosting **Toretta Stile**, a monthly musical extravaganza that will take you on a journey through the best – and worst – of music from the 1950s to today. For top-quality techno, seek out DJs Marco Passarani,

Rome's underground electronic maverick, and Andrea Benedetti. Wherever you go, end your night out in the time-honoured way: stopping for a hot *cornetto* (croissant) and cappuccino at one of the many bars open into the morning.

LIVE MUSIC

Rome has long lacked a space for huge concerts; the only suitable venue – the Stadio Olimpico, *see p156* – is monopolised by the city's two soccer teams. For years the only medium-sized space with decent acoustics was Palacisalfa (*see p263*), which has hosted Placebo and Suede. Only smaller bands had it relatively easy, playing the *centri sociali* and clubs committed to promoting new sounds. These days things are better: organisers still have a hard time convincing the musically undereducated Romans to pay to listen to live music, but Rome is making up time lost to Italy's musical capital Milan. The soon-to-reopen Palaeur (*see p263*) and new Auditorium (*see p254* **Parco della Musica**) – devoted mainly to classical music but open to pop and rock events – are finally giving the city proper spaces for large gigs. The city council, led by pop- and jazz-loving mayor Walter Veltroni, has by-passed the lack of mega-venues by funding free summer concerts, such as Paul Simon's in Villa Borghese (*see p83*) in summer 2002, or the Enzimi festival (*see p264*). Summer festivals bring increasing numbers of international stars to play a variety of unique venues: in 2001 Sonic Youth played Ostia Antica's Roman amphitheatre (*see p276*).

CENTRI SOCIALI

One of Rome's most interesting cultural assets, the *centri sociali*, were born over two decades ago when dissatisfied youths looking for spaces for art, music, politics and culture occupied disused public buildings and renovated them, turning them into concert halls, meeting points and cinemas. At first secretive and subject to occasional police swoops, they're now generally tolerated by authorities, though eviction threats resurface periodically and neighbours remain hostile. Thanks to their promotion of cultural innovation, they have played a fundamental role in the city's ongoing transition from historic showcase to vibrant European capital, bringing cutting-edge musicians (from Fugazi to Jello Biafra and Talvin Singh) to Rome. Often

Local heroes

In 1958 *Volare* (*Nel blu dipinto di blu*) earned Domenico Modugno Grammy and Billboard awards and instant recognition on both sides of the Atlantic: Anglo hipsters could sing every word... even if the words meant nothing to them. Since those heady days, his international eminence has stood unchallenged by Italian artistes. Which doesn't, of course, mean that nothing's going on. If you want to get down with crowds of enthusiastic Italians, there's a whole musical world to explore.

Electro aficionados should watch out for the danceable, soulful and very popular **Subsonica**, for **Planet Funk** (eclectic Neapolitans who sing in English) or for the sophisticated **Jollymusic-MAT 101**. For rock-pop songwriting look out for **Tiromancino**, clever and political **Daniele Silvestri** or poetic-ironic **Max Gazzè**. Indie rock is played by **Afterhours**, while the **Modena City Ramblers** stick to good old folk-rock. The Italian hip hop and rap scene, flourishing in the early 1990s, is now left with few icons: **Assalti Frontali**, **Articolo 31** and **99 Posse**; while **Lorenzo Cherubini**, formerly commercial pop singer Jovanotti, now offers a thoughtful – if occasionally soapy – mix of world music and hip hop. Italy's growing easy listening and lounge scene – which can be traced back to famous soundtracks by **Piero Umiliani** and

Piero Piccioni – can be sampled in the comic sophistication of the **Montefiori Cocktail**. **Vip 200** – twins from Emilia Romagna (home of Italy's dance-capital Rimini) ably assisted by a variety of musical friends – draws from that region's still-thriving orchestral folk music to mix up a great musical cocktail. Another easy-listening star is DJ-producer **Nicola Conte**, while **Cosmonauti** provide surf music instrumentals. Unlikely as it seems, Italy also has a growing ska and hardcore scene, best represented by **Meganoidi**, **Shandon**, **Bandabardò**, **Statuto** and **Punkreas**. Manu Chao's trumpet player, **Roy Paci**, serves up happy rocksteady, while iconic figures on the Italian jazz front include **Antonello Salis**, **Roberto Gatto**, **Paolo Fresu**, **Enrico Pieranunzi**, **Rosario Giuliani**, **Stefano Di Battista** and singer **Ada Montellanico**, as well as the trio **Doctor 3**.

One of the most interesting phenomena of the past few years has been the revisiting of Italian folk traditions, in particular the recent *pizzica* craze. A traditional trance dance from Puglia (the tip of the Italian boot), *pizzica* was danced by women who were (incorrectly) believed to have been bitten by tarantulas. **Nidi d'Arac**, **Arakne Mediterranea** and **Officina Zoè** are some of the better-known groups in this genre.

Arts & Entertainment

located in unique buildings – an old slaughter-house or an 1800s fortress – the *centri sociali* give you much more than your money's worth (usually €3.50-€5 to get in) and offer a range of courses and services, including cheap rehearsal rooms for young bands. It's an ever-changing scene: as well as the long-established *centri sociali*, there are many that only last a few years. Listings mags and *La Repubblica*'s Rome section give details of their activities.

LATIN AMERICAN

Rome has hosted an energetic Latin American community since the 1970s, and Romans swarm to dance courses to get into tango-ing trim. As well as clubs, discobars and the odd tango café, the Fìesta di Capannelle (*see p264*) livens up Rome's summer: massive crowds throng there nightly through the hottest months.

WHERE TO GO

You won't need to worry about getting lost in your search for nightlife: with few exceptions, the clubs and bars are concentrated in easily

accessible areas. **Testaccio** (*see p123*) is one of Rome's liveliest quarters: you'll be spoilt for choice – just walk round until you find the vibe you're after. The fashionistas head for the **centro storico**: spend an evening sipping wine in campo de' Fiori (*see p204* **Campo it up**) or the *triangolo della Pace* (*see p98*) and you're part of trendy Roman life. The university quarter **San Lorenzo** (*see p158*) is less pretentious: drinks are cheap, and there's always something new going on. **Trastevere** (*see p116*) has lovely alleys packed with friendly, crowded bars. If you're longing for company but your Italian's weak, this is the place for you: English is the *lingua franca*.

GETTING THROUGH THE DOOR

Getting into the *centri sociali* or alternative, down-to-earth venues is easy enough (although you may have to queue to get into the *centri sociali* as would-be guests try to negotiate even lower entrance fees). But getting into fashionable mainstream clubs can be a baffling experience. PR people have the last word on whether you get in, even if you're prepared to pay the high ticket prices and are elegantly dressed. For those in the in-crowd, cosying up to them is a status thing and being on the guest list is a sought-after honour. It seems that making clients wait outside for hours on end for no apparent reason is de rigueur for creating a VIP aura, but persistence and patience will usually get you in eventually. Most clubs and discobars charge an entrance fee; you often have to pay for a *tessera* (membership card) on top of, or sometimes instead of, the entrance fee. *Tessere* may be valid for a season or even for a few years, and in some cases they're free. Admission tickets often include a 'free' drink, but you can generally expect the drinks you buy thereafter to be pricey.

Veneto & Borghese

Discobars & clubs

Piazza di Siena Art Café

Viale del Galoppatoio 33 (06 3600 6578/www.piazza-di-siena.it). Metro Spagna/bus 88, 95, 490, 491, 495. **Open** 9pm-4am Tue, Thur-Sat. Closed mid May-June, Aug. **Admission** €15-€20 depending on evening. **Credit** AmEx, DC, MC, V. **Map** p334 2C.
This large venue with stylish interiors is one of the in-places for the fashionable crowd and for Italian showbiz personalities. It's located underneath the Villa Borghese park (*see p83*). Depending on the night, you can have beauty treatments, watch fashion shows or browse art exhibitions, as well as having a dance. In summer it moves outside.

Pantheon & Navona

Live music

Il Locale

Vicolo del Fico 3 (06 687 9075/www.il-locale.it). Bus 30, 40, 46, 62, 64, 70, 81, 97, 189, 304, 492, 628, 916. **Open** Oct-May 10pm-2am Tue-Sun. **Admission** with monthly membership card (€5.20). **No credit cards. Map** p333 2B.
Its golden age as a launchpad for new talent is past, but this friendly little venue is still the place to come if you're trying to track down interesting local bands and emerging songwriters.

Discobars & clubs

Anima

Via Santa Maria dell'Anima 57 (06 6889 2806). Bus 30, 40, 46, 62, 64, 70, 81, 97, 189, 304, 492, 628, 916. **Admission** free. **No credit cards. Map** p333 2B.
The improbable baroque-style, gilded stuccos that decorate this small venue could put some off, but this bar has a buzzing atmosphere and good drinks.

The Gallery

Via della Maddalena 12 (06 687 2316/www. thegallery.it). Bus 30, 62, 63, 70, 81, 85, 95, 116, 160, 186, 304, 492, 628, 630, 850. **Open** 7.30pm-3am Tue-Sun. Closed 2wks Jan. **Admission** free Tue-Thur, Sun; €10 Fri, Sat (incl 1 drink & cloakroom). **Credit** AmEx, MC, V. **Map** p333 1A.
The Gallery is a blue and orange discobar that features DJs every night. Some of Rome's very best play or having played here, and you can expect to hear everything from house through reggae and R&B to Britpop and electronica.

Late bars

See also p201 Bar della Pace.

Bar del Fico

Piazza del Fico 26/28 (06 686 5205). Bus 30, 40, 46, 62, 64, 70, 81, 87, 116, 304, 492, 628, 916. **Open** *Sept-July* 7am-2am Mon-Sat; 10.30am-2am Sun. *Aug* 4pm-2am daily. **No credit cards. Map** p333 2B.
Named after the ancient fig tree (*fico*) that's by the bar, the Fico is a long-established fixture for the hip crowd. From breakfast onwards, it's perfect for exchanging glances with sultry strangers at the table next to yours. Sitting outside under the tree or lounging on the sofas inside is an unmissable experience… albeit an expensive one.

Jonathan's Angels

Via della Fossa 16 (06 689 3426). Bus 30, 40, 46, 62, 64, 70, 81, 97, 116, 189, 304, 492, 628, 916. **Open** 8pm-2am Mon-Fri; 2pm-2am Sat, Sun. **No credit cards. Map** p333 2B.
A combination of kitsch colours and naïf paintings makes this bar unique among the many venues in the *centro storico*. Have a drink while admiring portraits of the owner, an ex-acrobat, in incredible outfits. Take a tour of the bathroom too – simply unmissable. Live music offered after 11pm tends to be bad piano-bar revival.

Ghetto & Campo de' Fiori

Live music

Rialtosantambrogio

Via Sant'Ambrogio 4 (06 6813 3640/www. rialtosantambrogio.org). Bus 23, 30, 40, 44, 46, 62, 63, 64, 70, 75, 81, 87, 95, 160, 170, 492, 628, 630, 715, 716, 780, 781, 810, 916, H/tram 8. **Open** *Sept-July* times & days vary. **Admission** €3.50-€5. **No credit cards. Map** p336 1A.
Located in a charming building, this *centro sociale* has a jazz and experimental classical music vocation. In addition to concerts, it organises theatre and dance events, and offers a wide range of courses at its Libera Università Popolare (Libur).

Late bars

For **La Vineria**, *see p204* **Campo it up.**

PUB & RESTAURANT

OPEN EVERY DAY

NON STOP FROM NOON TILL 3.00 A.M.

ON SATURDAY AND ON SUNDAY *SPECIAL BRUNCH*

VIA DEL COLLEGIO ROMANO, 6 - 06. 6786472

 **GUINNESS**

Live music

Big Mama
*Vicolo San Francesco a Ripa 18 (06 581 2551/www.
bigmama.it). Bus 44, 75, 780, H/tram 3, 8.* **Open**
Oct-mid June 9.30pm-1.30am Tue-Sat. **Admission**
free with membership (annual €13, monthly €6);
extra for big acts. **Credit** MC, V. **Map** p337 1B.
Rome's temple of blues, where an array of respected
Italian and international artists play regularly,
guaranteeing a quality night out. There's jazz too.
Food is served: book to ensure you get a table.

No Stress Brasil
*Via degli Stradivari 35 (06 5833 5015). Bus 170,
781.* **Open** 8.30pm-3am Mon-Sat. Closed Aug.
Admission free Mon-Thur, Sun; €10 Fri-Sat (incl
1 drink). Closed 10 days Aug. **Credit** AmEx, DC,
MC, V. **Map** p337 2B.
This restaurant and disco in a rather off-the-beaten-
track bit of town offers live music every night, with
Brazilian bands and dancers. Later, DJs entertain the
crowd until dawn. You can have a full Brazilian
dinner for €25.50 then move to the disco to dance.

Discobars & clubs

La Suite
*Via degli Orti di Trastevere 1 (06 586 1888).
Bus 781, H/tram 3, 8.* **Open** *Oct-May* midnight-
4am Wed-Sat. **Admission** €15. **Credit** MC, V.
Map p337 1B.
The in-club for posers out for a night comparing
outfits. The solidly commercial music played on
most nights and snotty door staff are counter-
balanced by the sophisticated interiors – a fantasy
of black and white that makes you feel as if you'd
landed inside some giant dice.

Late bars

See p205 **Stardust**.

Live music

Akab/Cave
*Via di Monte Testaccio 68-9 (06 578 2390). Metro
Piramide/bus 23, 30, 75, 95, 280, 716, 719/tram 3.*
Open *Sept-June* midnight-4am Tue-Sat. **Admission**
(incl 1 drink) €10 Tue-Thur, €15 Fri, €20 Sat. **Credit**
AmEx, DC, MC, V. **Map** p337 2A.
This busy club has two levels with the underground
Cave featuring 'black' (R&B chart fodder), and the
street level playing house and electronica. Known
for featuring big names and cool concerts from time
to time, it also organises a short-movie festival
(every Wednesday from October to May).

Alpheus
*Via del Commercio 36 (06 574 7826/www.
alpheus.it). Metro Piramide/bus 23, 769, 770.*
Open *Sept-July* 10pm-4am Tue-Sun. **Admission**
€5-€8 depending on event. Concerts €5-€20
depending on act. **Credit** AmEx.
An eclectic club with a varied crowd, the Alpheus
has three big halls for live gigs, music festivals,
theatre and cabaret, all followed by a disco. The
music changes every night: rock, Latin, world music,
revival and happy trash.

Bluecheese Factory
*Via Caio Cestio 5B (06 5728 7631/www.bluecheese.it).
Metro Piramide/bus 23, 30, 75, 95, 280, 716, 719/
tram 3.* **Open** 11pm-5am Fri, Sat. Closed July-
mid Sept. **Admission** €3.50-€4. **No credit cards**.
Map p337 2A.
In a dusty, post-industrial, post-atomic *centro sociale*
warehouse, Bluecheese is active on the electronic
and media frontier. As well as featuring DJs from
international electronic labels (Ninjatune, Rephlex,
Metalheadz), it stages live concerts and theatre
performances. Check the website for one-off events
happening on other evenings.

Caffè de Oriente
*Via di Monte Testaccio 36 (06 574 5019). Metro
Piramide/bus 23, 30, 75, 95, 280, 716, 719/tram 3.*
Open *Sept-July* 10pm-3am Tue-Sun. **Admission**
(incl 1 drink) €8 Tue-Thur; €10 Sat, Sun.
No credit cards. **Map** p337 2A.
A must for lovers of Latin American music, this club
offers salsa three or four times a week, 'black' (chart
R&B) on Fridays and live revival on Saturdays.
There are three orange-coloured rooms and a
pleasant roof terrace for the summer.

Caffè Latino
*Via di Monte Testaccio 96 (06 5728 8556). Metro
Piramide/bus 23, 30, 75, 95, 280, 716, 719/tram 3.*
Open 10pm-3am daily. Closed 2wks Aug.
Admission €6-€10 depending on event.
No credit cards. **Map** p337 2A.
Decked out in ethnic style, this club offers a wide
choice of live music and DJs, ranging from jazz to
ethnic, Latin American to funky. If you don't feel like
dancing, you can relax on comfy chairs.

Izgud 19
*Via Mastro Giorgio 19 (06 5728 8794). Metro
Piramide/bus 23, 30, 75, 95, 280, 716, 719/tram 3.*
Open *Sept-June* 8.30pm-2am Tue-Sun. **Admission**
free. **Credit** AmEx, DC, MC, V. **Map** p337 2A.
This spacious lounge bar offers live music followed
by DJs on Wednesdays and Thursdays, food every
night and a good selection of wines and drinks.

Villaggio Globale
*Ex-Mattatoio, lungotevere Testaccio (06 5730 0329/
www.sosstudents.it/nottiromane). Bus 95, 170, 719,
781/train to stazione Trastevere.* **Open** usually
Tue-Sat depending on events; concert times vary.
Admission €3.50-€5 depending on event.
No credit cards. **Map** p337 2B.

Metaverso pulls an alternative crowd.

Located in Rome's former slaughterhouse (*see p124*), the Villaggio Globale is one of the city's longest-running *centri sociali*. This fascinating, out-of-time area is now due for redevelopment and the Villaggio is likely to be evicted some time over the next few years to make room for a university department. In the meantime, a circus tent in the huge cattleyard has relaunched the Villaggio as a hot location for frequent top-quality concerts.

Discobars & clubs

See p261 **Akab/Cave**, **Alpheus**, **Villaggio Globale**; *see also p247* **L'Alibi**.

Ex-Magazzini

Via Magazzini Generali 8bis (06 575 8040). Metro Piramide/bus 23, 769, 770. **Open** *Sept-May* 10pm-4am Wed-Sun. **Admission** free Wed, Thur, Sun; €5 Fri, Sat; possible extra charge for concerts. **No credit cards. Map** off 337 2B.
This trendy discobar hosts some of Rome's best alternative nights. It's also a second-hand market on Sunday afternoons, with cool clothes and rare vinyl.

Jungle

Via di Monte Testaccio 95 (06 301 6208/www. jungleclubroma.com). Metro Piramide/bus 23, 30, 75, 95, 280, 716, 719/tram 3. **Open** 9.30pm-4am Fri, Sat. **Admission** free till 11pm, then €5-€8 depending on event. **No credit cards. Map** p337 2A.
This otherwise forgettable club hosts the best goth and industrial night in Rome – probably in the whole of Italy – each Saturday. If vampire ladies are your thing or you hanker after the days when the Cure were hip, this is a must.

Metaverso

Via di Monte Testaccio 38A (06 574 4712/www. metaverso.com). Metro Piramide/bus 23, 30, 75, 95, 280, 716, 719/tram 3. **Open** noon-3pm, 8pm-4am Tue-Sat. Closed mid June-Aug. **Admission** free with annual membership (€5). **No credit cards. Map** p337 2A.
This inexpensive, friendly little club hosts international DJs from well-known labels (above all, Warp), plus some of Rome's best, pulling in an alternative crowd. On Tuesdays, there are movies and wine tasting; Wednesdays are for reggae; other nights are dedicated to electronica. Lunch is available at noon.

Sonar

Via dei Conciatori 7C (06 4542 6950/www. sonarplanet.com). Metro Piramide/bus 23, 769, 770. **Open** 10pm-4am Tue-Sat. Closed Aug. **Admission** €5; €10 for big-name acts. **Credit** DC, MC, V. **Map** off p337 2C.
A post-industrial venue contaminated with 1980s mirrors, this club hosts renowned international and Italian DJs at weekends.

Celio & San Giovanni

Discobars & clubs

Dome Rock Café

Via D Fontana 18 (06 7045 2436). Metro San Giovanni/bus 16, 81, 85, 186, 218, 850/tram 3. **Open** noon-3am daily. Closed 2wks Aug. **Admission** free. **No credit cards. Map** p338 2A.
Soft lights, orange-tinged walls and a friendly atmosphere in a nicely crowded pub. DJs play funk, Britpop, 'black' and ska, plus weekly live pop-rock.

Vatican & Prati

Live music

Alexanderplatz
Via Ostia 9 (06 3974 2171/www.romajazz.com).
Metro Ottaviano/bus 32, 34, 49, 81, 492, 590,
982/tram 19. **Open** *mid Sept-Feb* 9pm-2am daily;
Mar-mid June 9pm-2am Mon-Sat. Closed mid June-mid
Sept. **Admission** free with monthly (€6.50) or annual
(€26) membership. **Credit** MC, V. **Map** p332 2C.
A highly regarded jazz club offering nightly
concerts with famous names from the Italian and
foreign jazz scene. George Coleman and Lionel
Hampton are regulars. Dinner is served from 9pm;
live music starts at 10.30pm. Booking advised.

Fonclea
Via Crescenzio 82A (06 689 6302/www.fonclea.it).
Bus 32, 34, 49, 81, 492, 590, 982/tram 19. **Open**
Sept-June 8.30pm-1.30am Mon-Thur, Sun; 8pm-3am
Fri, Sat. **Admission** €6 Sat; free Mon-Fri, Sun.
Credit DC, MC, V. **Map** p332 2C.
With cover bands on every night, originality is not
its strongest point, but this lively club/restaurant
has all it takes for a good night out.

Nabel Art Café
Via San Giovanni in Laterano 244-6 (338 919 6332/
338 296 6210). Metro Colosseo/bus 85, 117, 850.
Open 9pm-2am Tue-Sun. Closed mid July-Aug.
Admission free. **No credit cards**. **Map** p338 2A.
Meeting point for an arty crowd, Nabel has weekly
new exhibitions and live acoustic sets on Thursdays.

Suburbs

Live music

For Auditorium, *see p254* **Parco della Musica**.

Brancaleone
Via Levanna 11, Suburbs: north (06 8200 0959/
www.brancaleone.it). Bus 36, 60, 90. **Open** *Sept-June*
10.30pm-5am Thur-Sat. **Admission** €5; concerts
may cost more. **No credit cards**.
The best-run of the *centri sociali*. Every year, the
organisers reinvest profits in improving the trendy
interiors (all built in-house) and equipment, and
establish partnerships with London, regularly
featuring acts like Talvin Singh. Fridays with the
Agatha crew have for years educated Romans to the
best electronic music around. Weekends are the
most crowded but weekdays can be lively too,
especially reggae Thursdays. It also has a cinema,
a recording studio and an organic café.

Drome
Via dei Latini 49-51, Suburbs: east (06 446 1492/
site.voila.fr/DROME). Metro Termini/bus 71, 204,
492/tram 3, 19. **Open** *Sept-July* 7.30pm-2am Tue-
Sun. **Admission** with (free) annual membership
card; concerts €3. **No credit cards**. **Map** p159.

Frequent jazz concerts by local musicians in a
lively pub with orange-coloured walls located in the
heart of the student quarter San Lorenzo.

Forte Prenestino
Via Delpino 100, Suburbs: east (06 2180 7855/
www.forteprenestino.net). Bus 112, 312, 501/tram 5,
19. **Open** most nights, most of the year; times vary.
Admission €3.50. **No credit cards**.
This unique *centro sociale* is in a 19th-century
fortress, complete with secret passages and cobblestone corridors. The large, grassy courtyards are
best enjoyed sitting under the stars in summer, but
Forte Prenestino also has a covered space for
winter concerts and DJs, a cinema, a café and a
record shop. Its annual 'non-labour day' fest on
1 May attracts crowds from all over Italy.

Horus Club
Corso Sempione 21, Suburbs: north (06 8680
1410). Bus 36, 60, 90. **Open** 9pm-3am Tue-Sat.
Admission from €10 depending on event.
Credit AmEx, DC, MC, V.
Once a cinema, this medium-sized venue with
stylish interiors occasionally stages good concerts.
The schedule is eclectic: check before setting out that
you're going to find something to your taste.

Palacisalfa
Viale dell'Oceano Atlantico 271, Suburbs: EUR (06
5728 8024/www.palacisalfa.com). Bus 72, 77, 703,
706, 707, 779. **Open** depends on event. **Admission**
depends on event. **No credit cards**.
This large venue on the southern edge of EUR (*see
p159*) hosts events ranging from concerts to fairs,
sport events to disco nights. For years the only
indoor space for biggish concerts (holding some
3,500 people), it now faces competition from the
newly refurbished Palaeur and the Auditorium (*see
p254* **Parco della Musica**). It has decent acoustics.

Palaeur
Piazzale dello Sport, Suburbs: EUR (information in
local press). Metro EUR Palasport/bus 30, 671, 714,
780, 791. **Open/admission** depends on event.
After lengthy refurbishment – and yet to open as
this guide went to press – the flying-saucer-shaped
Palaeur is destined to become the space for large
indoor concerts that Rome never had (it holds over
9,000 people). The powers-that-be insist movable
panels will improve the once-appalling acoustics.

La Palma
Via G Mirri 35, Suburbs: south (06 4359 9029/
www.lapalmaclub.it). Metro Tiburtina/bus 163,
211, 309, 409, 443, 448. **Open** *Sept-July* 10pm-
2am Mon-Thur, Sun; 10pm-4am Fri, Sat. **Admission**
varies with event; annual membership €2. **Credit**
AmEx, DC, MC, V.
An oasis in a post-industrial landscape, this club has
good concerts and quality DJ sets. The schedule is
eclectic, though very jazz-focused: it features live
jazz, new jazz, avant-garde rock, ethnic, electropop,
R&B or lounge, often followed by a DJ.

Arts & Entertainment

Sonica

Via Vacuna 98, Suburbs: north-east (338 297 1330/ www.sonicapub.it). Metro Tiburtina/bus 163, 211, 309, 443, 448. **Open** *Sept-July* 9pm-5am Tue-Sun. **Admission** with annual membership card (€3). **No credit cards.**
This pub hosts nightly hardcore, punk rock and '60s garage concerts by emerging bands. The acoustics aren't the best, but this is the place to come if you want to hear those musical genres that live and rub shoulders with the hardcore scene.

Discobars & clubs

For **Brancaleone**, **Forte Prenestino**, **Horus Club** and **La Palma**, *see p263.*

Black Out

Via Saturnia 18, Suburbs: south (06 7049 6791/www. blackoutrockclub.com). Metro Re di Roma/bus 87, 671, 673. **Open** 10pm-4am Fri, Sat. Closed July, Aug. **Admission** €8. **No credit cards. Map** p339 2A.
Its heyday now past, the Black Out is a classic old Roman club, with rock, indie and a bit of goth, plus the punk and heavy metal that were its mainstays through the 1980s and '90s.

Classico Village

Via Libetta 3, Suburbs: south (06 574 3364/www. classico.it). Metro Garbatella/bus 29, 769, 770. **Open** *Oct-June* 10pm-4am Thur-Sat. **Admission** €5-€15 depending on event. **No credit cards.**
This former factory offers an eclectic array of events: theatre, music, short-movie festivals, poetry and exhibitions. The groovy outside space is heaven in the summer and, though it's all a bit characterless inside, the music is generally good. One room has a stage for live acts, while the other serves up funk, Britpop, house and garage.

Distillerie Clandestine

Via Libetta 13, Suburbs: south (06 5730 5102). Metro Garbatella/bus 29, 769, 770. **Open** 8.30pm-3am Tue-Sat. Closed mid June-Aug. **Admission** free. **Credit** AmEx, DC, MC, V.
A large bar, restaurant and club, mainly playing 'black' (chart R&B). In one room there's live music and DJs; in the other you can dine, have a cocktail or choose a glass of wine from a wide selection.

Goa

Via Libetta 13, Suburbs: south (06 574 8277). Metro Garbatella/bus 29, 769, 770. **Open** *Oct-May* 11pm-5am Tue, Thur-Sat; 5pm-4am Sun. **Admission** (incl 1 drink) €10-€20 depending on event. **Credit** AmEx, DC, MC, V.
The best of Rome's fashionable clubs, Goa is an ethnic fantasy of oranges and blues with a strong whiff of incense. The quality of its Italian and international DJs is way above the competition, but don't expect to find anything alternative. Getting past the picky door staff can be tricky too. On Sunday afternoons it holds a market that offers tea tasting and exotic foods.

Qube

Via di Portonaccio 212, Suburbs: east (06 438 5445). Metro Tiburtina/bus 409. **Open** *Sept-June* 10.30pm-4am Thur-Sat. **Admission** free Thur; €13 Fri; €8 Sat. **No credit cards.**
One of Rome's biggest club venues, the Qube's week is as eclectic as its patrons. It thrives on rock and revival on Thursdays (live gigs) and Saturdays. Fridays see the Mucca Assassina ('Killer Cow') drag queens offering light-hearted transgression.

Festivals

The long summer may leave Rome rattlingly empty during the day, but at night the city springs to life with an astounding number of festivals, often held in astonishingly beautiful locations such as Renaissance villas or Roman amphitheatres. Besides providing quality performances, they allow access to some of the city's artistic and architectural treasures that are normally beyond the reach of tourists.

The free Labour Day concert organised by Italy's trade unions on 1 May (*see also p233* **Primo Maggio**) generally draws over half a million people. It is traditionally held in piazza San Giovanni and hosts Italian – and a handful of international – stars. At the end of June, the **Estate Romana** (www.estateromana.it) kicks off. An umbrella for most of Rome's outdoor summer festivals, sponsored by city hall, it runs from late June through to the end of September. For something completely different, look out for festivals organised by Italy's political parties (Festa dell'Unità by the Democratici di sinistra, Festa di Liberazione by Rifondazione comunista, while the right-wing Alleanza Nazionale organises All'Ombra del Colosseo). At these festivals – which are popular with supporters and non-affiliates alike – there's food, stalls for browsing, live music, theatre and, of course, political debates. Check in the local press for details of these events.

Enzimi

Various venues (www.enzimi.festivalroma.org). **Date** generally 2wks mid-Sept. **Admission** free. **No credit cards.**
This free music, theatre and arts festival – a showcase for the best up-and-coming Roman artists – is council-funded and aimed at thirty-somethings and younger. Held on the outskirts of town, it offers cutting-edge bands and some international stars. It recently teamed up with highly regarded Rome-based electronic music and digital arts festival Dissonanze (www.dissonanze.it), which has featured live acts ranging from Belle and Sebastian to Underworld, Luke Slater and Radioboy.

Fiesta di Capannelle

Via Appia Nuova 1245, Suburbs: east (06 7129 9855/06 7834 6587/06 718 2139/www.fiesta.it).

La Palma: eclectic but jazz-focused. *See p263.*

Arts & Entertainment

Metro Colli Albani/bus 590, 650, 671. **Date** mid June-Aug. **Admission** from €7, varies with event. **No credit cards.**
This hectic Latin American-themed festival regularly attracts more than a million people with performances by Latin American and Cuban bands, plus stars like Manu Chao or Ben Harper; it has four dancefloors, 40 restaurants, 120 stalls… and lots of salsa and merengue. Come early: transport and parking can be a nightmare.

Jazz & Image Festival
Villa Celimontana, Celio & San Giovanni (06 589 7807/www.romajazz.com). Metro Colosseo/bus 81, 673/tram 3. **Date** mid June-Aug. **Admission** from €8, varies with event. **Credit** MC, DC, V (online bookings only). **Map** p339 1B.
This festival takes place in the leafy Villa Celimontana park (*see p130*) and features acclaimed artists (from Kid Creole to BB King) in an astonishingly beautiful setting. Lots of candles and torches give the place a magical aura.

Roma Estate al Foro Italico
Viale Olimpiadi, largo de Bosis, Suburbs: north (information in local press). Bus 32, 69, 186, 224, 280. **Date** June-mid Aug. **Admission** from €6, depending on event. **No credit cards. Map** p331.
Music, theatre and sport all take place in the big concert hall by the tennis stadium. It's totally

characterless, but always crowded, with seven restaurants and four dancefloors. Check listings for details of gigs, or shimmy up to the discobars if you're after Latin American sounds.

Roma Incontra il Mondo
Villa Ada, via di Ponte Salario, Suburbs: north (06 418 0369). Bus 63, 92, 231, 235, 310. **Date** end June-Sept. **Admission** from €8, depending on event. **Admission** 7-day ticket €13. **No credit cards. Map** p331.
Musicians from around the world play on a lakeside stage under the venerable trees of the Villa Ada park. The light on the water and fresh breezes make this one of the most relaxing of the summer festivals. Bars, ethnic food stalls, records and book stalls are on hand if the music palls.

Testaccio Village
Viale del Campo Boario, Testaccio (information in local press). Metro Piramide/bus 23, 30, 75, 95, 280, 716, 719/tram 3. **Date** mid June-Sept. **Admission** free with weekly membership (€10). **No credit cards. Map** p337 2B.
Many of Testaccio's clubs move outside to this area behind Rome's former slaughterhouse for the summer. Oriental-themed food stalls and bars surround the dancefloors. Go early to eat and listen to live jazz, world music and electronic music, with occasional big names. DJ sets get under way later.

Sport & Fitness

Do it... if you must. Most Romans prefer to watch.

Appearance-conscious Romans have for decades preferred electrode contraptions, cellulite creams and *centri benessere* (health and beauty centres requiring no expenditure of energy) to any sort of physical exercise. But, slowly and surely, things are changing. Gyms – once the province of supertanned, Lycra-clad snobbery – are coming down to earth and new alternative fitness centres are offering yoga, Pilates and martial arts. Still, Romans who do regular exercise are few and far between. This is nothing new: the ancient Roman masses preferred taking a seat at the Colosseum to taking up a sport and even Roman bath complexes that had small exercise areas were, for the most part, centres for organised languishing. Two millennia later, vexed at his layabout countrymen, Mussolini went all out in the 1920s and '30s to promote athleticism. The concrete results of his campaign can be seen in the Foro Italico sports complexes (*see p156*) in the northern suburbs, though the facilities there are the preserve of professional athletes.

Which is fine, many locals will tell you, because the only sport that matters is football. And the average Roman is quite content to leave the playing of it – and any consequent breaking of sweat – to the professionals. If you like watching rather than participating, you've come to the right place. Rome boasts two first-class football teams, one of which plays at home almost every Saturday or Sunday from September to June. Going to a match at the Stadio Olimpico is a great way to do sport as most Romans do: sitting down.

Cycling

Every May the Roman leg of the Giro d'Italia provides an exciting spectacle as the race thrashes over the cobbled streets of the *centro storico*. The via Appia Antica visitors' centre (*see p153* **Country ways**) has bikes for hire at weekends; traffic-free Sundays on the ancient road make for especially pleasant pedaling. (For more on hiring bikes, *see p303*.)

Enjoy Rome

Via Marghera 8A, Esquilino (06 445 1843/www. enjoyrome.com). Metro Termini/bus 40, 64, 170, 175, 492. **Open** 8.30am-6.30pm Mon-Fri; 8.30am-2pm Sat. **Rates** €25; €20 (under-27s) for 3hr tour. **No credit cards. Map** p335 2A.

Guided tours (experienced riders only) of Rome's most important sights are run from April to October. Rates include bike and helmet hire.

Football

Romans are passionate about soccer: a few play the game, but many, many more watch it and pontificate. Though any day of the week's good for wild football-related gesticulating and agitated debate, most energy is expended at weekends when the 18 teams of Italy's Serie A (Premier League) meet. Some 50 million Italians watch the games, either at the stadium or on the box, burning off calories in violent physical reactions to referees' bad calls and players' faked injuries.

Rome's two football clubs, AS Roma (www.asromacalcio.it) and SS Lazio (www.sslazio.it), are both in Serie A, usually doing well enough to get into the UEFA Cup or Champions League too. They share the Stadio Olimpico, in the Foro Italico complex, and tension is thick across the city whenever they play each other. Lazio was founded in 1900. In 2000 Sven Goran Eriksson's coaching and a host of star players led Lazio to win the championship (*lo scudetto*). Since then, financial troubles have forced the club to cede most of its big-name players to the wealthier teams of northern Italy. The younger Roma (founded in 1927) won its third *scudetto* in 2001, right on the heels of Lazio's reign as *campione d'Italia* – which, of course, added relish to their victory. Roma's roster, featuring local hero Francesco Totti as captain, hasn't changed much over the years, but a less-than-stellar 2003 season may cause owner Franco Sensi to rethink the line-up.

Like everything else in Italy, Roman soccer is politicised: Roma supporters traditionally hail from the left – working class or intellectual – while Lazio is the team of the right, drawing support from the wealthy Parioli and Prati districts and the countryside. Both teams' mascots (Roma's wolf, Lazio's eagle) proudly draw on ancient Roman symbolism.

Tickets can be bought directly from the Stadio Olimpico box office, from the club merchandising outlets listed below or from Orbis (*see p230*). Once inside the stadium, Lazio fans fill the *curva nord* (north end) with sky blue and white, while the red and yellow of the

Sporty mosaics near the **Stadio Olimpico**.

Roma faithful occupies the *curva sud* (south
end). The *curve* have the best pyrotechnics
and cheapest tickets, but for better (and more
expensive) seats ask for the Tribuna Tevere
or Tribuna Monte Mario. Hooliganism isn't
usually a problem, except at derbies when
harder-bitten fans always set fire to a few
police cars and police respond with tear gas.

Stadio Olimpico
*Viale dello Stadio Olimpico, Suburbs: north
(06 323 7333). Bus 32, 280/tram 2.*
Tickets €15-€85. **No credit cards.**
Important matches sell out quickly, but the touts
will be happy to sell you tickets for twice their face
value. Even cheap seats have a decent view.

Essential accessories

All manner of unofficial scarves, jerseys and
flags can be bought outside the stadium on
match days, but for better quality items go to
the club shops listed here. They also sell match
tickets (cash only) up to seven days in advance.

AS Roma Store
*Piazza Colonna 360, Tridente (06 678 6514/06
6920 0642/www.asromastore.it). Bus 52, 53, 61,
62, 80, 85, 95, 116, 175, 492, 850.* **Open** 10am-
7.30pm Mon-Sat; 11am-7.30pm Sun. **Credit** AmEx,
DC, MC, V. **Map** p333 1A.

The AS Roma stores have all kinds of team
paraphernalia, from bathrobes to lunchboxes –
there's even a Fabio Capello eau de toilette (named
after Roma's coach, but all too reminiscent of
Drakkar Noir). The branch in via Cola di Rienzo also
has a café (open 11am-2am Tue-Sun), which offers
a Sunday brunch buffet.
Branch: via Cola di Rienzo 136A (06 321 2741).

Lazio Point
*Via Farini 34, Esquilino (06 482 6768). Metro
Termini/bus 40, 64, 70, 170, 175, 492.* **Open** 9am-
7pm Mon-Sat. **Credit** AmEx, MC, V. **Map** p335 2A.

Golf

Golf is an exclusive game in Italy. Most clubs
demand the membership card from your home
club and proof of your handicap before allowing
you to play, though it's not normally necessary
to be introduced by a member. Green fees,
including those quoted below, are normally
per day rather than per round.

Circolo Golf Roma
*Via Appia Nuova 716, Suburbs: east (06 780 3407).
Metro Colli Albani, then bus 663 or 664.* **Open** 8am-
sunset Tue-Sun. **Rates** €64 Tue-Fri; €77 Sat, Sun
(Aug only). *Driving range* €10 Tue-Fri; €16 Sat, Sun
(green fees incl use of range). *Club hire* €23.
No credit cards.
A friendly club in the green belt east of the city.

Arts & Entertainment

Country Club Castelgandolfo

Via Santo Spirito 13, Castelgandolfo (06 931 2301).
Taxi, or Metro Anagnina then taxi. **Open** 8am-8pm
daily. **Rates** €47 Mon-Fri; €57 Sat, Sun. *Driving*
range €5 per day (green fees incl use of range).
Electric cart hire €31 Mon-Fri; €37 Sat, Sun. *Trolley*
hire €6. *Club hire* €19. **Credit** DC, MC, V.

Near the Pope's summer residence (*see p293*), this
course was designed by leading American golf
architect Robert Trent Jones inside a (dormant)
volcanic crater and is overlooked by its very
distinguished 16th-century clubhouse. The course
is impossible to reach by public transport and is
beyond most taxis' circuits, so consider hiring a car
from Rome and visiting the nearby Castelli romani
(*see p292*) before or after your round. Reserve tee
times by fax (06 931 2244) before setting out.

Gyms

Farnese Fitness

Vicolo delle Grotte 35, Ghetto & Campo de' Fiori
(06 687 6931). Bus 23, 40, 46, 62, 64, 87, 116,
280, 492, 628/tram 8. **Open** 9am-10pm Mon-Thur;
9am-9pm Fri; 11am-6pm Sat; 10am-1pm Sun. Closed
3wks Aug. **Rates** €10 per day. **No credit cards**.
Map p336 1B.

With its brightly painted spiral staircases and low
arches, this small *centro storico* gym has an Alice-
in-Fitnessland feel to it. Classes in the downstairs
aerobics studio – a 16th-century cellar – are included
in the daily membership fee.

Fitness First

Via Giolitti 44, Esquilino (06 4782 6300/fax 06
487 0100/romatermini@fitnessfirst.com). Metro
Termini/bus 40, 64, 70/tram 5, 14. **Open** 8am-11pm
Mon-Fri; 9am-7pm Sat, Sun. **Rates** €15 per day.
No credit cards. **Map** p335 2A.

This new gym is so hygienically unimpeachable
you'd think it was a showroom for fitness equipment
rather than a place to break into a sweat. In addition
to the weights and machine room, there are spinning,
Latin dance, yoga and Thai kickboxing classes.

Moves

Via dei Coronari 46, Pantheon & Navona (06 686
4989/06 686 5248). Bus 81, 87, 492, 628. **Open**
9am-9pm Mon-Fri; 10am-4pm Sat. Closed Aug.
Rates €16 per day. **No credit cards**. **Map** p333 1B.

Founded by American Linda Foster, this small, hip
gym-cum-art gallery (for men and women) on an
antique shop-filled street is one of the few in Rome
that caters specifically for foreigners. The daily rate
allows use of the gym, or attendance at a single
fitness class, including yoga, Tai chi and Pilates.

Roman Sports Center

Viale del Galoppatoio 33, Veneto & Borghese
(06 320 1667/06 321 8096/06 322 3665). Metro
Spagna/bus 52, 53, 63, 116, 490, 495, 630.
Open 9am-10pm Mon-Sat; 9am-3pm Sun. Closed
Sun in June-Aug. **Rates** €26 per day; €200 per mth.
Credit AmEx, DC, MC, V. **Map** p334 2C.

The largest and best-equipped gym in the city, 'La
Roman' has 8,000 sq m (86,000 sq ft) of facilities: aerobics studios, saunas, hydromassage pools, weights,
squash courts, two Olympic-size swimming pools
and, of course, sun beds. A health-food bar and internet area also make for a buzzing social scene.

Jogging & running

Crowds of people and omnipresent cars make
a jog through the streets of central Rome a
decidedly unpleasant experience. For those
determined to go for a run in the heart of town,
the pavements along the lungotevere (riverside
drive) are an option, but be prepared to hurdle
tree roots. Otherwise, the best jogging and
strolling is to be had in the many parks just
outside Rome's *centro storico*.

Villa Borghese (map p334)
Caters for joggers of all shapes and sizes, but can
get crowded at weekends.

Villa Pamphili (map p331)
Contains broad paths with workout stations.

Villa Ada (map p331)
This large park north-east of the centre has running
paths around its ponds and lakes.

Circo Massimo (map pp338-9)
A taste of ancient Rome while you're working
up a decent sweat.

Terme di Caracalla (map p339)
Serious runners congregate opposite Caracalla's
ancient baths.

Parco della Caffarella (map p151)
Just off the via Appia Antica, this park has shady
trails as well as wide-open, ruin-strewn fields.

The Rome City Marathon (*see p232*), held each
spring, is slowly making a name for itself in
international circles. It's a far cry from the
London or New York marathons, but Romans
are starting to recognise its entertainment
potential (as opposed to considering it a totally
unwarranted occupation by pesky runners of
perfectly good driving space).

Riding

Italy's annual showjumping Grand Prix
takes place in the piazza di Siena in leafy
Villa Borghese (*see p83*); it's one of the most
beautiful of all equestrian arenas. The CSIO
international showjumping competition takes
place annually in May (contact 06 3586 8111
or www.fise.it for information).

Cavalieri dell'Appia Antica

Via dei Cerceni 15, Appia Antica (06 780 1214/
www.teklab.it/cavalieriappia). Bus 118, 660. **Open**
10am-6pm Tue-Sun. Closed 1wk Aug (call in advance
to book excursions). **Rates** €13 per 1hr ride.
No credit cards.

This charming, rustic facility offers excursions along the picturesque, ruin-filled via Appia Antica for groups of up to five people. Friendly owners Sandro and Armanda Bernardini speak almost no English, but their easy-tempered horses are suitable for beginners. Ask about moonlight rides, and be sure to reserve well in advance for excursions at weekends. If you're using public transport, get off the 118 bus one stop south of via Cecilia Metella or take the short walk from the end of the 660 line.

Rugby

What the average football-fixated Roman knows about rugby is that it's played with a funny-shaped ball by players who are beefier than footballers. But while very few locals could define 'scrum', there's a strong rugby subculture and those who play take it seriously. Since 2000 the national side has been in the Six Nations Championship, with home games played at the Stadio Flaminio. Rome also boasts a first-class rugby side in RDS Roma, who play their league matches at the Stadio Tre Fontane.

Stadio Flaminio
Viale Tiziano, Suburbs: north (06 3685 7309/06 333 1961/www.federrugby.it). Bus 217, 910/tram 2. **Tickets** €20-€85.

Stadio Tre Fontane
Via delle Tre Fontane, Suburbs: EUR (06 592 2485/ 6610). Metro Magliana/bus 30, 170, 714, 780. **Tickets** €8-€12.

Swimming

Swimming pools are few in the city and, with a few far-flung exceptions, those that do exist are privately run. If you're a serious athlete and looking for a place to train, the Olympic-sized pools at the Roman Sports Center (*see p268*) are your best bet. As for beaches, the shores near Rome are not particularly inviting; you're better off making a day of it and exploring a little further afield (*see p284* **The best: Beaches**).

Oasi della Pace
Via degli Eugenii 2, Suburbs: east (06 718 4550). Metro Arco di Travertino, then bus 765. **Open** *Mid June-Sept* 9.30am-6pm daily. Closed Oct-mid June. **Admission** €10. **No credit cards.**
A pleasant open-air pool off the ancient via Appia Antica (*see p150*), surrounded by tall hedges and cypresses. Facilities are fairly simple.

Piscina delle Rose
Viale America 20, Suburbs: EUR (06 592 6717). Metro EUR-Palasport/bus 30, 714, 780. **Open** *June-Sept* 9am-7pm daily. Closed Oct-May. **Admission** €10 full day; €8 half day (9am-2pm or 2-7pm); €5 1-4pm Mon-Fri; free for children under 1m tall; €45 weekly ticket. **No credit cards.**

Rome's largest public pool, in the heart of the EUR district (*see p159*). This outdoor facility has deck-chairs and shady gardens, and often gets crowded.

Hotel pools

Cramped spaces in central Rome mean there are no hotels with swimming pools in the heart of the city. There are several hotels with pools that can be used by non-residents if you head out to leafier areas around the outskirts of town.

Parco dei Principi
Via Frescobaldi 5, Suburbs: north (06 854 421/www. parcodeiprincipi.com). Bus 52, 53, 217, 910/tram 3, 19. **Open** *June-Sept* 10am-7pm daily. **Admission** €45. **Credit** AmEx, DC, MC, V.
Right on the edge of the Villa Borghese gardens, this pool is a favourite of local swimmers (it gets particularly busy at weekends). There's a 20% discount for children.

Tennis

Every May, Rome hosts the Italian Open tennis tournament (*see also p233*), one of the most important European clay court tournaments outside the Grand Slam.

Foro Italico
Viale dei Gladiatori 31, Suburbs: north (06 3685 8218). Bus 32, 280/tram 2.

Circolo della Stampa
Piazza Mancini 19, Suburbs: north (06 323 2452). Bus 32, 280/tram 2. **Open** 9am-10pm Mon-Fri; 9am-8pm Sat, Sun. **Rates** *Court (50min)* €9.30 singles; €12.40 doubles. *Floodlights (50min)* €11.40 singles; €14.40 doubles. **No credit cards.**
Owned by the Italian journalists' association, but friendly and open to non-members, the Circolo offers both clay and synthetic grass courts. There's no dress code, but studded trainers are not allowed. It's advisable to make a reservation.

Yoga

Several of the gyms listed above also offer limited yoga classes; phone to check.

L'Albero e la Mano
Via della Pelliccia 3, Trastevere (06 581 2871/www. lalberoelamano.it). Bus 23, 280, 630, 780, H/tram 8. **Open** depends on course schedule. Closed Sun & mid July-mid Sept. **Rates** €12-€13 per class. **No credit cards. Map** p336 2B.
Incense wafts gently from the door of this studio, which faces the garden. L'Albero offers daily classes in Ashtanga and Hatha yoga, as well as several classes per week in stretching, Tai chi and belly-dancing. You can also have Shiatsu, Ayurvedic and Thai massage here (an hour-long session costs €40), but you'll have to book in advance.

Arts & Entertainment

Theatre & Dance

Lovely theatres, impeccably dressed audiences... but not much to see.

Rome's theatre is stolid – even reactionary – but enlivened by a handful of mould-breaking theatre companies and some excellent summer festivals. The city-owned **Teatro Argentina**, built in 1732, is Rome's most prestigious theatre and puts on relatively high-quality drama. Its offspring, the **Teatro India**, is a spruced-up former soap factory on the shores of the Tiber; it hosts the summer season's more avant-garde events, leaning strongly towards the multi-disciplinary. Rome's other 'official' venues are the **Teatro Valle** and the **Teatro Quirino**, which are managed and sponsored by the Ente Teatrale Italiano (ETI – Italian drama board). Outside the official circuit, some 80 theatres provide more stages than any other Italian city for the untried to do their (not always top-quality) thing. Some venues can be relied on to produce good fare: the **Teatro Ghione** (*see p255*) has its own, highly respected company, while something off the beaten track can usually be found at the **Cometa, Vascello** or **Orologio**. The **Ambra Jovinelli**, a mainstay of Rome's riotous pre-war variety scene, is recently rejuvenated.

Classical ballet can be seen at the **Teatro dell'Opera** (*see p255*) and its satellite spaces, the **Teatri Nazionale** and **Brancaccio**. Contemporary dance fans have a harder search (*see p272* **Contemporary dance**): the best bets are **Teatri Vascello, Greco** or **Olimpico** (which regularly welcomes international companies, *see p255*).

Theatre and dance listings can be found in *La Repubblica, Il Messaggero, Trovaroma* and *Roma C'è* (*see also p310*), while *Wanted in Rome* has an exhaustive arts section. The (Italian-only) website www.tuttoteatro.com is also useful. For ticket agencies, *see p230*.

Main public theatres

See also p255 **Teatro dell'Opera**.

Teatro Brancaccio

Via Merulana 244, Monti (06 4782 4893/ politeamabrancaccio@virgilio.it). Bus 16, 71. **Box office** 11am-6.45pm Tue-Sat; 11am-5.30pm Sun. **Shows** 9pm Tue-Sat; 5pm or 6pm Sun. **Credit** DC, MC, V. **Map** p338 1A.
A dingy, cavernous theatre with poor acoustics. It stages the overflow from the Teatro dell'Opera (*see p255*), but also puts on musicals and comedies.

Teatro di Roma – Argentina

Largo Argentina 52, Ghetto & Campo de' Fiori (06 6880 4601/www.teatrodiroma.net). Bus 30, 40, 46, 62, 63, 64, 70, 81, 87, 492, 628, 810, 916/tram 8. **Box office** 10am-2pm, 3-7pm Tue-Sun. **Shows** *Oct-June* 9pm Tue, Wed, Fri, Sat; 5pm Thur, Sun. **Credit** AmEx, DC, MC, V. **Map** p336 1A.
Rome's plush flagship theatre has a wide-ranging programme, including some dance and poetry.

Teatro di Roma – India

Lungotevere Papareschi/via Pieranton 6, Suburbs: south (06 6880 4601). Bus 170, 780, 781. **Box office** 30min before shows, or at Teatro Argentina (*above*). **No credit cards at Teatro India**.
This choreographic space, with three stages, is used for more experimental offerings. It was due to be relaunched as this guide went to print.

Teatro Nazionale

Via del Viminale 51, Esquilino (06 4782 5140). Metro Termini/bus 40, 60, 64, 70, 71, 170. **Box office** at Teatro dell'Opera (*see p255*). **Shows** varies. **Credit** AmEx, DC, MC, V. **Map** p335 2B.
An ugly theatre with acceptable acoustics and functional seating, often used by the Teatro dell'Opera for dance and for less prestigious productions.

Teatro Quirino

Via Mario Minghetti 1, Trevi & Quirinale (06 679 4585/www.teatroquirino.it). Bus 62, 63, 81, 85, 95, 117, 119, 160, 175, 492, 628, 630, 850. **Box office** 10am-7pm Tue-Sat; 10am-1pm Sun. **Shows** 9pm Tue-Sat; 5pm Sun. **Credit** AmEx, DC, MC, V. **Map** p335 2C.
The Quirino mainly features plays by household names like Pirandello and Beckett.

Teatro Valle

Via del Teatro Valle 23A, Pantheon & Navona (06 6880 3794/www.enteteatrale.it). Bus 30, 40, 46, 62, 63, 64, 70, 81, 87, 492, 628, 810, 916/tram 8. **Box office** 10am-7pm Tue-Sat; 10am-1pm Sun. **Shows** 9pm Tue, Thur-Sat; 5pm Wed, Sun. **Credit** AmEx, DC, MC, V. **Map** p333 2A.
Hosts an interesting range of performances, especially during the packed Percorsi internazionali autumn season, plus the occasional concert. A gem.

Private & smaller venues

See also p255 **Teatro Ghione**, *p255* **Teatro Olimpico**, *p239* **Teatro Verde**.

Arte del Teatro

Via Urbana 107, Monti (06 488 5608/06 444 1376/ 348 935 5626/www.porticus.com). Metro Cavour/

bus 71, 75, 84, 117. **Box office** 1hr before shows.
Shows (in English) 9pm Fri. **No credit cards**.
Map p338 1B.
This picturesque theatre is home to The English
Theatre of Rome, founded by actress Gaby Ford in
1996. It's an offbeat platform for expat thespians.

Centro Petralata
*Via di Pietralata 159A, Suburbs: east (06 4173
4052). Metro Pietralata/bus 111, 211.* **Box office/
shows** varies. **No credit cards**.
An industrial space recently transformed into an
arts centre, specifically designed to showcase
multimedia and multidisciplinary performances.

Salone Margherita
*Via Due Macelli 75, Tridente (06 679 1439/06 679
8269/www.salonemargherita.com). Metro Spagna/
bus 52, 53, 61, 62, 63, 71, 80, 95, 116, 119, 160,
175, 492, 630, 850.* **Shows** 9.30pm Tue-Fri; 7pm,
10pm Sat; 6pm Sun. **Credit** AmEx, DC, MC, V.
Map p335 1C.
Cabaret and political satire, with cocktails and pasta
in between. A Roman institution.

Teatro Ambra Jovinelli
*Via G Pepe 41/45, Esquilino (06 4434 0262/www.
ambrajovinelli.com). Metro Vittorio/bus 70, 71, 105,
360, 649/tram 5, 14.* **Box office** 10am-7pm Mon-
Sat; 11am-1.30pm Sun. **Shows** varies. **Credit**
AmEx, DC, MC, V. **Map** p338 1A.

Once Rome's top variety venue, the theatre suffered
decline, closure and nearly demolition before reopening in 2000, restored to its former glory. A shrine to
Italy's comic heritage – with a school for comic
writing and acting, and a video and research library
– it also puts on top-quality jazz and other concerts.

Teatro Belli
*Piazza Sant'Apollonia 11A, Trastevere (06 589
4875/teatro.belli@tiscalinet.it). Bus 23, 280, 780,
H/tram 8.* **Box office** 10.30am-1pm, 5.30-9.30pm
Tue-Sat; 3.30-7pm Sun. **Shows** *Sept-May* 9pm Tue-
Sat; 5.30pm Sun. **No credit cards**. **Map** p336 2B.
Usually focusing on Italian and dialect theatre,
this small venue has a new cycle dedicated to
British drama (but in Italian, of course).

Teatro Colosseo
*Via Capo d'Africa 5, Celio (06 700 4932/
teatrocolosseo@libero.it). Metro Colosseo/bus 81,
85, 87, 117, 810, 850/tram 3.* **Box office** 7-
10.30pm Tue-Sat; noon-7pm Sun. **Shows** Tue-Sun
(times vary). **No credit cards**. **Map** p338 2B.
A showcase for young Italian directors and actors,
frequented by Rome's theatre-savvy youth.

Teatro della Cometa
*Via del Teatro di Marcello 4, Ghetto (06 678 4380/
www.cometa.org). Bus 30, 44, 63, 81, 95, 160, 170,
628, 715, 716, 781, 916.* **Box office** 11am-7pm
Tue-Sat; 10am-1pm, 2.30-5pm Sun. **Shows** 9.15pm
Tue-Sat; 5pm Sun. **No credit cards**. **Map** p336 1A.

Classical ballet

In 1928 the Teatro Reale dell'Opera (*see
also p255*) created a ballet school under
the direction of Ileana Leonidoff and Dimitri
Rostoff. Over the years, great ballet masters
and choreographers – including Aurel von
Milloss, Anton Dolin, Erik Bruhn and Zarko
Prebil – sought to bring the company up to
scratch. But stability and lustre remained just
out of reach, as the *corps de ballet* continued
to bend more to union demands than the
winds of artistic change. Even today, under
the stern direction of Carla Fracci (*pictured*),
the company is shaky. Performances by the
male dancers range from the embarrassing
to the hilarious. The company's repertoire
is limited, stuffy and utterly predictable. The
occasional good dancers produced by the
school soon hightail it elsewhere. You may
get lucky, though, and catch one of these
promising youngsters in a solo role before
they make their escape. Or you might find
tickets for a production graced by a great
guest artist. So check the papers for cast
details and scour the reviews before shelling
out for (inexpensive) tickets.

Arts & Entertainment

Contemporary dance

Tiny budgets and under-representation in performance programmes may be the norm, but Rome has many contemporary dance fans. Quality events always show to packed houses, and recently this has encouraged the creation of a number of private dance companies, bringing an increasingly contemporary flavour to the circuit.

The first theatre to provide a dedicated space for contemporary dance and dance/theatre was the **Teatro Vascello** (*see below*).

Even more encouragingly, City Hall has found funds for **Transcodex**, an avant-garde festival with a programme of experimental projects fusing dance and drama with video art, electronic soundscapes and installations. Held annually from November through to the end of January, Transcodex brings mostly Italian artists and companies to perform in industrial spaces (including **Centro Petralata**, *see p271*). For further details, see www.comune.roma.it/cultura.

This fringe theatre has a faithful following, intimate atmosphere and thoughtful productions.

Teatro dell'Orologio
Via de' Filippini 17A, Pantheon & Navona (06 687 5550). Bus 40, 46, 62, 64, 916. **Box office** *Sept-June* 11am-1.30pm, 3-8pm Mon-Fri; 4-8pm Sat; from 4.30pm until show begins Sun. **Shows** Tue-Sun (times vary). **No credit cards. Map** p333 2B.
The offbeat and experimental are given a stage in the four separate theatre spaces at this venue.

Teatro Eliseo/Piccolo Eliseo
Via Nazionale 183, Trevi & Quirinale (06 488 2114/www.teatroeliseo.it). Bus 40, 60, 64, 70, 71, 170. **Box office** 9.30am-2.30pm, 3.30-7pm Tue-Sun. **Shows** 8.45pm Tue, Thur-Sat; 9.30am-7pm Sun. **Credit** DC, MC, V. **Map** p338 1C.
This huge modern theatre stages classic works by Italian and international playwrights. The Piccolo Eliseo serves up similar fare in smaller productions.

Teatro Flaiano
Via Santo Stefano del Cacco 15, Pantheon & Navona (06 679 6496/www.pros.it). Bus 30, 40, 46, 62, 63, 64, 70, 81, 87, 492, 628, 810, 916/tram 8. **Box office** 10.30am-1.30pm, 3-7pm Tue-Sun. **Shows** 9pm Tue-Sat; 7pm Sun. **Credit** AmEx, MC, V. **Map** p333 2A.
A cosy theatre, decorated in blue velvet, which intersperses its regular Italian prose repertory with opera evenings. Adjacent is a delightfully camp dinner-theatre (9.30pm Wed-Sat) with quality cabaret.

Teatro Greco
Via R Leoncavallo 16, Suburbs: north (06 860 7513/www.teatrogreco.it). Bus 63, 135, 342, 630. **Box office** 10am-1pm, 4-7pm Mon, Wed-Sun. **Shows** 9pm daily. **No credit cards.**
A well-designed venue that programmes some international dance and has a penchant for little-tried writers, both foreign and domestic.

Teatro Rossini
Piazza Santa Chiara 14, Pantheon & Navona (06 6880 2770). Bus 30, 40, 46, 62, 63, 64, 70, 81, 87, 492, 628, 810, 916/tram 8. **Box office** 10am-7pm Tue-Sun. **Shows** 9pm Tue-Fri; 5pm, 9pm Sat; 5pm Sun. **No credit cards. Map** p333 2A.
A cosy old theatre with a programme dedicated to original drama and Roman dialect reworkings.

Teatro Vascello
Via G Carini 72, Suburbs: west (06 588 1021). Bus 44, 75, 710, 870, 871. **Box office** 3.30-7.30pm Tue-Sat; from 4pm Sun. **Shows** 9pm Tue-Sat; 5pm Sun. **No credit cards. Map** p337 1C.
Presents decent experimental theatre and dance productions, plus conferences and workshops.

Teatro Vittoria
Piazza Santa Maria Liberatrice 8, Testaccio (06 574 0170/0598/www.teatrovittoria.org). Bus 23, 95, 170, 280, 716, 781/tram 3. **Box office** 10am-1pm, 4-7pm Mon; 10am-7pm Tue-Sat; 10am-1pm Sun. **Shows** 9pm Tue-Sat; 5pm Sun. **Credit** MC, V. **Map** p337 2A.
This cavernous venue specialises in translated texts and international variety shows.

Summer venues

See also p234 **RomaEuropa Festival**.

Anfiteatro della Quercia del Tasso
Passeggiata del Gianicolo, Gianicolo (06 575 0827). Bus 870. **Box office** from 7pm before shows. **Shows** *July-Sept* 9.15pm Mon-Sat; occasional afternoon matinées. **No credit cards. Map** p336 1C.
This open-air amphitheatre was built in the 17th century. It specialises in Greek and Latin theatre and 18th-century Venetian comedy.

Teatro Romano di Ostia Antica
Scavi di Ostia Antica, viale dei Romagnoli 117, Ostia Antica (06 6880 4601). Train from Ostiense to Ostia Antica. **Box office** from 6pm before shows; also at Teatro Argentina (*see p270*). **Shows** *mid July-mid Aug* 8.30pm daily. **No credit cards. Map** p340.
This wonderfully preserved Roman theatre (*see p276*) hosts prestigious productions of Roman and Greek classics, plus concerts. The seats are stone: bring your own cushion. And mosquito repellent.

Trips Out of
Town

Amsterdam Andalucia Bangkok Barcelona Berlin Boston

Brussels Budapest Buenos Aires Chicago Copenhagen Dublin

Edinburgh Florence Havana Hong Kong Istanbul Las Vegas

Lisbon London Los Angeles Madrid Miami Milan

Moscow Naples New Orleans New York Paris Patagonia

Prague Rome San Francisco South of France South West England Stockholm

Sydney Tokyo Toronto Venice Vienna Washington, DC

Time Out City Guides

Available from all good bookshops and at www.timeout.com/shop

Time Out
City Guides

www.penguin.com   www.timeout.com

Trips Out of Town

All around Rome are ruins, lakes, beautiful views and great – or grimy – beaches.

Maps p330 and p341

Getting started

The ancient Romans understood the crucial importance of communications. As their sphere of influence widened, so did their road network. Troops and goods moved relentlessly back and forth over impeccably maintained highways, bringing to Rome all that was needed for life in the greatest metropolis the world had ever known, and exporting the manpower and organisation necessary to ensure that the dominions remained firmly under Rome's sway.

Even today the *vie consolari* (consular roads) radiating from the capital form the basis of the road system linking Rome with the surrounding Lazio region and the rest of Italy. The Aurelia (cognoscenti drop the 'via') channels cars towards Genoa as it used to legions and carts; the modern Appia shoots southwards towards Naples alongside the ancient one (*see also p150*).

Technically speaking, not all these highways were *consolari* – that is, constructed under the aegis of Roman officials such as consuls whose job it was to keep the Imperial infrastructure in shape. Some – such as the Tiburtina – followed tracks beaten by pre-Roman tribes. Neither were all of them merely a means of getting from A to B: the Aurelia, for example, effectively cut the Etruscans (*see p281* **Etruscans**) off from their ports, crippling this trading people.

Immediately outside the *urbs* the road was dotted with luxury villas and burial places (*see also p154*) – burial within the city was against the rules – but much of this ruin-strewn *campagna romana* ('Roman countryside') has disappeared under hypermarkets and high-rise dwellings. Still, a jaunt along a *via consolare* to some rural green or an outcrop of ancient history is a satisfying escape from urban life.

By car

For more on driving in Italy and car hire, *see p303*. The Grande Raccordo Anulare (GRA) ring road links with the network of *autostrade* (motorways) and *strade statali* (SS – most follow ancient *consolari*). Traffic on the GRA and city approach roads can be intense in rush hour and Friday or Sunday evenings, with long queues at motorway tollbooths. You can save time (but not money) at tollbooths by using a Viacard debit card, available from *tabacchi* (*see p313*) and most motorway service stations. Tollbooths at major entry points accept credit cards (AmEx, DC, MC, V) too. Isoradio (103.3FM, occasional English-language bulletins in summer) gives regular traffic updates for major roads, while information at www.autostrade.it is regularly updated.

By train

For map, *see p341*; for mainline services, *see p298*. The network of local railways, the Ferrovie Metropolitane (FM), is handy for destinations outside Rome. FM trains can be picked up at Ostiense (FM1, FM3, FM5), Tiburtina (FM1, FM2), Termini (FM4, FM6, FM7) and Trastevere (FM1, FM3, FM5) stations. For information, call tollfree on 800 431 784 or 892 021 between 8am and 6pm Monday to Friday.

By bus

The Lazio transport authority COTRAL (formerly ACOTRAL/Li.La.; information tollfree 800 150 008) covers the region fairly efficiently; most services ply the *consolari*. Buses leave from several city termini (listed below), each serving a different direction.

Anagnina Metro Anagnina.
EUR Fermi Metro EUR Fermi/bus 30, 31, 671, 714, 780.
Lepanto Metro Lepanto/bus 30, 70, 224, 280, 913 (map p332 2B).
Ponte Mammolo Metro Ponte Mammolo.
Saxa Rubra Train from Roma Nord-Flaminio (map p332 1A) to Saxa Rubra.
Stazione Tiburtina Metro Tiburtina/bus 40, 71, 163, 492, 495.

Via Ostiense (Via del Mare)

The **via Ostiense** is the shortest of the *consolari*. It connected Rome with the salt deposits at the mouth (*ostia*) of the Tiber, which in antiquity lay 30 kilometres (18 miles) from the road's origin at Porta San Paolo. Widened, repaved and lengthened to reach the sea at Ostia *moderna* (5 kilometres/3 miles west of the ancient coastline), the Ostiense still follows its 2,300-year-old path along the south-eastern riverbank. The parallel **via del Mare** was laid out in the Fascist period to relieve congestion on the Ostiense; it has one of the country's worst accident records. Visit the Museo di via Ostiense (*see p126*) to acquaint yourself with the history of the ancient road; it's located opposite the Ostia-Lido train station.

Once past the low-rent residential quarters of Garbatella and San Paolo, the via Ostiense looks tackily Third World, with miles of shanty towns, junkyards and abandoned concrete outcrops. But this gives way to umbrella pines and Roman ruins that crop up in the open fields as the Ostiense approaches Ostia Antica.

OSTIA ANTICA

If it weren't for the lack of a backdrop to rival Vesuvius, the **ruins** of Ostia Antica would be as famous as Pompeii: they certainly convey the everyday life of a working Roman town as uncannily. Ostia was Rome's main port for over 600 years, until its decline in the fourth century AD. Thereafter, river mud and sand gradually buried the town; the Tiber's changed course and receding coastline left Ostia landlocked and obsolete. Visit on a sunny weekday and bring a picnic (not actually allowed, but if you keep a low profile and pick up your rubbish, you probably won't be ejected). With fascinating remains around every corner, Ostia Antica deserves to be taken at a leisurely pace.

The *decumanus maximus* (high street) runs from the Porta Romana for almost a kilometre (half a mile), past the theatre and forum, before forking left to what used to be the seashore (now three kilometres/two miles away at Ostia, *see p277*). The right fork, via della Foce, leads to the Tiber. Either side of these main arteries is a network of intersecting lanes; it's here that the most interesting discoveries can be made.

Behind the theatre is one of Ostia's most interesting features: the Forum of the Corporations. Here the various trade guilds had their offices, and mosaics on the floor of small shops that ring the open square refer to the products each guild imported – lumber, grain or elephants. Further along on the right is the old mill, where ponderous grindstones and circular furrows ploughed by the blindfolded donkeys that turned them are still visible. In the tangle of streets between the *decumanus* and the museum, don't miss the *thermopolium* – an ancient Roman bar, complete with marble counter, a fresco advertising the house fare and a garden with a fountain. Located off the forum to the south-east are the forum baths, with the terracotta pipes that heated the walls preserved. Nearby is the *forica*, or ancient public latrine. In mostly residential districts off via della Foce, the House of Cupid and Psyche is an elegant fourth-century construction; the House of the Dioscuri has beautiful mosaics; the Insula of the Charioteers still has many of its frescos. The wealthy lived in the Garden Apartments at the western end of the site, set back from the busy streets. The site also boasts seven mithraea (*see p317* **Glossary**), including that at the Baths of Mithras, just north of via della Foce. The museum has a good collection of artefacts from the site, including statues, fresco fragments and

Ostia Antica's Baths of Neptune...

bas-reliefs of scenes of ordinary life, and there are a café and well-stocked bookshop next door.

Five minutes' walk from the entrance to the excavations, the **medieval village** of Ostia Antica has a brick castle (built in 1483-6 for the future Pope Julius II) and picturesque cottages; these were once inhabited by the people who worked in the nearby salt pans.

OSTIA

Ostia *moderna* is the centre of Rome's riviera, a lively if not especially beautiful coastal town laid out in the 1930s. It's *centro* is at the terminus of via Ostiense; its southern end, where beaches are less crowded, is served by via Cristoforo Colombo, which originates in Rome near the Baths of Caracalla. Ostia's water isn't the cleanest, but the dark, volcanic sand is known to Romans for its tan-accelerating properties. Most of the shore consists of private, pay-on-entry beach clubs that fill to bursting every summer. If you aren't convinced by the murky sea here, head towards **Torvaianica** for a swim. It's 11 kilometres (seven miles) south, but the water is a bit cleaner and laudable efforts have been made to keep the sand rubbish-free. The **Castelporziano/Capocotta** beach between Ostia and Torvaianica is also acceptable and free, with a sprinkling of beach-hut bars; it has a gay section (*see chapter* **Gay & Lesbian**) and a nudist stretch (signposted nine kilometres/5.5 miles south of Ostia).

FIUMICINO AND PORTO

As Rome's population grew to around a million at the height of the Empire, its port activities overflowed five kilometres (three miles) north from Ostia to a section of the coast that offered more shelter for Roman merchant ships. The earliest port here, built by Emperor Claudius in the 40s AD, had a unique jetty: a ship built to transport the Egyptian obelisk (now in St Peter's square) was too big for anything else, so it was sunk in front of the harbour and a lighthouse mounted on it. Claudius' port was later absorbed by the larger and more efficient Porto di Traiano (AD 110), where the hexagonal harbour could cater for up to 200 ships at once. Canals were cut to link the harbours to the Tiber, with river barges hauled the 35 kilometres (20 miles) to Rome by slaves. The canal dug alongside Trajan's port (*fossa di Traiano*) created a triangular island – bordered by the Tiber to the south and the Tyrrhenian to the west – called **Isola Sacra**. Famous for its fertile land in antiquity, Isola Sacra still reeks of manure. Among its sights is the **Necropoli di Porto**, an important Roman burial centre.

Almost nothing is left of Claudius' port – what there is lies between airport runways – but in **Fiumicino** (ancient Portus) the ruins of the Porto di Traiano can be visited on guided tours (booking and own transport essential). Tours depart from the **Museo delle Navi**, a charming museum in the shadow of the airport with genuine Roman ships and displays on

and Forum of the Corporations.

Whale attack

In his *Natural Histories*, Pliny relates that during the reign of Emperor Claudius, a *navis onerarius* (seafaring cargo vessel) carrying *prosciutto* from France sank in the waters just outside Rome's port. An especially tantalising shipwreck for carnivorous marine life, the sunken vessel even attracted an orca all the way from the Pacific. It bored a hole in the hull of the ship and gorged itself on cured ham for several days. Having exhausted the ship's supply, the gluttonous beast followed its nose to the pork fat being washed ashore, whereupon it beached itself. In a rescue effort that would have made Greenpeace smile, Claudius dispatched his own Praetorian Guard, who tied ropes to the orca's fins and freed it from the sand. Once in deeper water, the traumatised whale expelled enough water from its blowhole to sink one of the rescue boats.

ancient trade. Or you can visit the **Oasi di Porto**, where horse-drawn carriages take you around the perimeter of Trajan's harbour.

Castello di Giulio II (Castle of Julius II)
Piazza della Rocca, Ostia Antica (06 5635 8024).
Open 9am-1.30pm, 2.30-4.30pm Tue, Thur; 9am-1pm Wed, Fri-Sun. **Admission** free.

Museo delle Navi
Via A Guidoni 35, Fiumicino Aeroporto (06 652 9192/06 6501 0089). **Admission** €2; €1 concessions. **No credit cards.**
Closed for restoration at time of writing, the museum is due to reopen in July 2003.

Oasi di Porto
Via Portuense 2264, Fiumicino (06 588 0880).
Open 10am-4pm Thur, Sun. Closed June-Sept.
Admission €10; €5 concessions. **No credit cards.**

Necropoli di Porto
Via di Monte Spinoncia 52, Isola Sacra (06 658 3888). **Open** *Apr-Oct* 9am-7pm Tue-Sun. *Nov-Mar* 9am-5pm Tue-Sun. **Admission** free.

Porto di Traiano
06 652 9192. **Open** (guided tours only; own transport essential) 9am 1st Sat, last Sun of mth. **Admission** free.
Tours leave from the Museo delle Navi (*see above*); visits at other times can be arranged by phone.

Scavi di Ostia Antica
Viale dei Romagnoli 117, Ostia Antica (06 5635 8099/www.itnw.roma.it/ostia/scavi). **Open** *Apr-Oct* 8.30am-7pm Tue-Sun. *Nov-Mar* 9am-5pm Tue-Sun. Ticket office closes 1hr earlier. **Admission** €4; €2 concessions. **No credit cards.**

Where to eat

Before or after a visit to the Ostia Antica ruins, follow the mouth-watering aromas of fish to **Allo Sbarco di Enea** (via dei Romagnoli 675, 06 565 0034, www.paginegialle.it/sbarcoenea, closed Mon, average €25). In Fiumicino, entry point of all Rome-bound seafood, you're spoiled for choice between myriad waterfront restaurants: try the catch of the day at **Marina del Rey** (lungomare della Salute 46, 06 658 4641, closed Mon, average €30).

Getting there

By car
Ostia Antica: via del Mare or via Ostiense.
Ostia: via Cristoforo Colombo or via del Mare.
Fiumicino, Museo delle Navi, Porto di Traiano: *autostrada* Roma-Fiumicino.

By train
Ostia Antica, Ostia: train from Roma-Lido station, next to Piramide metro (map p341): for downtown Ostia, get off at Lido Centro; for full-on

beach umbrellas, use the Stella Polare or Cristoforo Colombo stops; for Capocotta and Torvaianica go to Cristoforo Colombo and take bus 061 (Mar-Oct).
Museo delle Navi, Porto di Traiano: FM1 to Fiumicino aeroporto (not città).
Fiumicino: FM1 to Fiumicino *città* (not *aeroporto*).

By bus
Ostia, Isola Sacra and Fiumicino are connected by COTRAL bus (77¢), with services every half hour. In Ostia, the bus stops in front of Lido Centro station; in Fiumicino, in piazza Marinai d'Italia.

Via Aurelia

The via Aurelia was built in the third century BC to connect Rome with the upper Tyrrhenian seaports; from the city it travels due west, bending north at Ladispoli to follow the coastline of northern Lazio and Tuscany, eventually reaching Genoa. Roman strategists designed the road to pass near, not through, the key Etruscan towns of Cerveteri and Tarquinia; thus isolating them, cutting them off from their coastal ports and favouring Roman expansion.

Despite the occasional unfortunate outbreak of modern eyesores – including the entire town of Ladispoli – the Aurelia today remains a pretty drive. Widened and repaved for modern traffic, it travels through rolling hills and along the coast, with the occasional Roman tomb or medieval watchtower along the way.

Modern via Aurelia starts at piazza Irnerio, about two kilometres (one mile) east of the Vatican. The warehouses and pontifical outposts of the first, characterless stretch give way, after the GRA ring road, to open hills with rows of cypresses. After 20 kilometres (12 miles), the turn-off roads for the seaside towns of Maccarese and Fregene are signposted. The closer (seven kilometres/four miles from the Aurelia) and less crowded of the two, **Maccarese** was swampy and malarial for centuries, but the massive *bonifica* (draining project), begun in the 1880s and completed under the Fascists, made the air fit to breathe and the land workable. Nor was malaria the only scourge of this town. Legend relates that a dragon terrorised medieval Maccarese. Anyone brave enough to slay it, the pope said, would be given the land that he covered in its pursuit. Thus the successful knight – a duke of the Anguillara family – received huge tracts of territory. The medieval castle that dominates the town (not open to the public) was known as Villa San Georgii, after the dragon-slaying saint, but is now called Castello Rospigliosi. The Anguillara and Rospigliosi have now been replaced by economic 'aristocracy': almost all of Maccarese belongs to the Benetton family.

Further up the coast, **Fregene**'s broad sandy beaches and resort-town feel make it popular with Romans, who flock to its many beach clubs (with serried ranks of lounge chairs and umbrellas) and *spiaggia libera* (free beach, located in the centre of Fregene's seafront). Don't look too closely at the water.

Back on the Aurelia, 40 kilometres (25 miles) from Rome, lies the unforgivably ugly **Ladispoli**, where absurd high-rise apartment buildings make Ostia (*see p277*) look like Amalfi. Just past Ladispoli, three kilometres (two miles) off the Aurelia, **Cerveteri** is the one of the most important sites in Etruscan Lazio. Etruscan Kysry – romanised as Caere – was a vast, prosperous town with three ports, one of the great Mediterranean trading centres between the seventh and fifth centuries BC. It was situated on the same volcanic spur as the modern town but covered an area 20 times greater. The 16th-century Orsini castle is home to the small **Museo Cerite**, with local finds.

Much more interesting than the town itself is the **Necropoli di Banditaccia**, a pleasant 20-minute walk from the piazza. This town of the dead – with streets, *piazze* and tidy little houses – is one of the most touching archaeological sites in Italy. There's plenty of ancient atmosphere here, with a wilderness of vines and trees growing on and around tufa-cut *tumuli* (mound-shaped tombs). Only a small part of the total extent can be visited today; one of the most important tombs, the Regolini-Galassi

tomb, whose rich finds are now in the Vatican Museums (*see p144*), is not open to the public. The earliest tombs at Cerveteri date from the seventh century BC; the latest are from the third, by which time there had been a progressive impoverishment of tomb size and decoration. Don't miss the well-preserved sixth-century BC Tomba dei Capitelli, the fourth-century BC Tomba dei Rilievi (with bas-reliefs of weapons and utensils), and the three parallel streets of fifth- and sixth-century BC cube-shaped tombs between the via degli Inferi and via delle Serpi. Outside the main gate, the Tomba degli Scudi e delle Sedie has chairs carved out of rock and bas-reliefs of shields.

In **Santa Severa**, 54 kilometres (32 miles) from Rome, Castello Orsini squats like an outsized sandcastle. Inside the castle is a little village, with a fountain and a chapel with 14th-century frescos. The swimming is fine round here if you're not too fussy about the colour of the water. Next door are the remains of the Etruscan port of Pyrgi, the main sea outlet for Cerveteri (*see above*) and site of an important sanctuary to the Etruscan goddess Uni (Roman Juno). The small **Antiquarium di Pyrgi** contains finds from the excavations.

Northwards, past the family resort of Santa Marinella, the power stations and industrial waste of **Civitavecchia** scupper the theory that the further from Rome, the cleaner it gets. Located a kilometre (half a mile) north of Civitavecchia are the **Terme Taurine**, Roman

No sandcastle: the Castello Orsini in **Santa Severa**.

Burial mounds in **Cerveteri**'s
city of the dead. *See p279.*

baths that were built here to exploit the hot
sulphurous springs.

Further north, the Etruscan stronghold of
Tarquinia lies three kilometres (two miles)
inland from the Aurelia, bristling with medieval
defensive towers. Its necropolis (information
and tickets available from Museo Nazionale)
has the art Cerveteri lacks: some 100 tombs,
hidden beneath a grassy hill about two
kilometres (1.4 miles) out of town, are vividly
painted with scenes of work and social life,
athletic contests, mysterious rituals and erotic
encounters. The Tomba della Caccia e della
Pesca has delightful fishing and hunting scenes;
in the Tomba dei Leopardi, couples recline at a
banquet (note the man passing his partner an
egg – a recurrent symbol, though experts
disagree about what it represents). There's a
similar scene with dancers in the elegant
Tomba delle Leonesse. The Tomba dei Tori,
one of the oldest, depicts Achilles waiting to
ambush Troilus and contains *un po' di
pornografico*, as Etruscan fan DH Lawrence
gleefully (if ungrammatically) described it.
(Only a handful of the tombs are open at any
one time.) The **Museo Nazionale** in Tarquinia
has one of the best Etruscan collections outside
Rome. Its chief exhibit is a pair of fourth-
century BC terracotta winged horses – proof
that Etruscan artists could rival even Greek
finesse. The sandy but ultimately bleak beach
at **Lido di Tarquinia** is made more
unappetising by the huge bulk of the
decommissioned Montalto di Castro nuclear
power station to the north.

It's not until you reach the border with
Tuscany that things start to improve:
Chiarone has the first clean sea and sandy
beach this side of Rome. You can walk along
the beach all the way (12 kilometres/7.5 miles)
to the upmarket holiday destination of
Ansedonia, site of the Etruscan town of Cosa.
Halfway along, just beyond **Lago di Burano** –
a WWF bird sanctuary – is the **Marina di
Capalbio**, marked by the incongruous bulk of
former hunting lodge Casale di Macchiatonda.
This has been the beach resort for Rome's
moneyed Left for many years. **Capalbio** itself,
a beautiful walled village, stands seven
kilometres (four miles) inland.

Antiquarium di Pyrgi

Castello di Santa Severa (0766 570 194). **Open**
9am-7pm Tue-Sun. **Admission** free.

Museo Cerite

*Piazza Santa Maria, Cerveteri (06 994 1354/www.
prolococerveteri.it).* **Open** 8.30am-7.30pm Tue-Sun.
Admission free.

Museo Nazionale & Necropolis

*Palazzo Vitelleschi, piazza Cavour, Tarquinia (0766
856 036/www.tarquinia.it).* **Open** *Museum* 8.30am-
7.30pm Tue-Sun. *Necropolis* 8.30am-1hr before sunset
Tue-Sun; ticket office closes 1hr earlier. **Admission**
€4; €2 concessions. *Museum & necropolis combined*
€6.50; €3.25 concessions. **No credit cards.**

Necropoli di Banditaccia

*Via della Necropoli, Cerveteri (06 994 0001/www.
prolococerveteri.it).* **Open** Oct-Apr 8.30am-4.30pm
Tue-Sun. May-Sept 8.30am-7.30pm Tue-Sun. Ticket
office closes 1hr earlier. **Admission** €4; €2
concessions. **No credit cards.**

Terme Taurine

*Via delle Terme Taurine, Civitavecchia (0766 20
299/http://web.tiscali.it/civitavecchia).* **Open** 9am-
1pm, 2.30pm-sunset Tue-Sun. **Admission** €5; €2
concessions. **No credit cards.**
There's a free regular minibus shuttle between the
tourist office in Civitavecchia (lungo porto Gramsci
79) and the Terme. Book ahead, and you're eligible
for a free guided tour in English.

Where to eat

If you're beach-bound and in search of great
seafood, head for **Il Mastino** in Fregene's
Villaggio dei Pescatori (via Silvi Marina 19, 06
6656 0966, closed dinner Nov-Feb, average €35).
A plate of home-made pasta or fresh fish on the
square-side tables of Cerveteri's **Antica
Locanda Le Ginestre** (piazza Santa Maria 5,
06 994 0672, closed Mon & 2wks Nov, average
€45) is the perfect end to a day's tomb-hopping.

On the beach in Chiarone is the bar/trattoria
L'Ultima Spiaggia (0564 890 295, closed Sept-
Mar & weekdays Apr-May) – a sit-down fish

Etruscans

Before Romans in their jackboots marched north in the fourth and third centuries BC, a sophisticated and mysterious culture ruled the territory between the Tiber and Arno rivers. Today we call them the Etruscans; then they were known as Rasenna or Tyrrheni. Their origins are unknown and their language isn't fully understood, but through the study of their tombs – which were often filled with rich decorations and sumptuous offerings for the dead – archaeologists have pieced together a fascinating if incomplete picture of Etruscan society.

Stretching north from the Tiber through what is now Lazio, Umbria and Tuscany, Etruria was rich in mineral and agricultural resources. Iron and silver deposits brought the Etruscans great wealth, permitting them to purchase elegant ceramics from Greece and gourmet foodstuffs from the Orient. But they were a warlike as well as a worldly people, committing barbaric acts of piracy against rival merchants.

Etruscan women were liberated by ancient standards: tomb paintings show them present at banquets (strictly off-limits to their Greek or Roman counterparts) and playing *kottaboi*, a game that involved hurling wine across the banquet room. Etruscan ladies were often buried with their exquisite gold jewellery.

The Etruscan language was not Indo-European, and much of it remains an enigma. Enough has been deciphered, though, to give us the Etruscan names for modern Italian cities (Bologna was called Felsina) and the Etruscan equivalents of Greek and Roman

gods (Fufluns was their appropriate name for Bacchus, the god of slurred speech).

Like any good mystery-shrouded ancient people, the Etruscans were obsessed with portents in animal innards and meteorological phenomena. Lightning strikes were a clear sign that the gods were trying to communicate with the society: a priest called a *haruspex* was charged with the task of determining which direction the bolt came from, as different gods presided over different sectors of the heavens. *Haruspices* also practised the noble art of divination: after a sheep was sacrificed to appease the lightning-chucker, the animal's liver was read for further omens – an on-going dialogue with the deity.

What is most certain about the Etruscans is their strong belief in life after death. The care they lavished on their necropolises and the wealth of objects placed in their tombs – from luxury goods to mundane items like razors – indicate a people convinced that they would need the trappings of life beyond the grave.

THE BEST ETRUSCANS...
Museo Nazionale di Villa Giulia (*see p96*)
Any Etruscan fact-finding mission should start in Rome, either here or at the...
Museo Etrusco (*see p144* **Musei Vaticani**)
Both these museums house a wide range of truly stunning tomb finds.
Cerveteri (*see p279*) and **Tarquinia** (*see p280*)
Two of the most important Etruscan necropolises, with museums too.
Veio (*see p282*)
For rare above-ground remains.

meal costs €40, bar snacks a lot less. The **Bar della Stazione** inside Capalbio station is a front for an excellent trattoria (0564 898 424, closed Tue in low season, average €30).

Getting there

By car
The A12 motorway runs parallel to the via Aurelia as far as Civitavecchia; it can cut journey times to further-flung destinations, but beware the huge Sunday evening queuing queues at city-bound tollbooths.

By train
Ladispoli-Cerveteri, Santa Marinella, Santa Severa: FM5 from Ostiense or Trastevere. A local bus connects Cerveteri-Ladispoli station (6km/3 miles out of town) to Cerveteri.

Chiarone, Capalbio, Monte Argentario, Tarquinia: mainline services from Termini, Ostiense or Trastevere; it's a 3km/2 mile walk to the beach from Chiarone and Capalbio stations.

By bus
COTRAL services run from Lepanto. For Tarquinia, change at Civitavecchia.

Via Cassia

Literary sources are vague about who built the via Cassia and when: perhaps the origins of the road that led from Rome through the heart of Etruscan territory are just too ancient. Running to Siena and Florence, the Cassia slaloms around volcanic lakes and through hilly countryside, flanked by picturesque towns built on Etruscan and Roman foundations. From the GRA ring road, the ancient road's modern alter ego, Cassia Veientana (or Cassia *bis*), parallels it to the east. Built to share the load of suburban cars during rush hour, the *bis* joins the old road after about 15 kilometres (nine miles).

Between the old and new roads (but best reached from the former), the **Parco Regionale di Veio** – behind the little village of Isola Farnese and across a bridge over a rushing waterfall – surrounds **Veio**, an Etruscan city founded in the eighth century BC. Veio was Rome's chief rival for control of the Tiber's right bank until the Romans won out in the fourth century BC. While Veio's remains are not extensive, there's something Grand Tour-ishly charming about the way the sun filters through the trees on to this half-forgotten pile of tufa-stone blocks. Moreover, the site contains rare examples of Etruscan houses and temples (unlike other Etruscan cities where only tombs remain), boasting a striking sixth-century BC sanctuary of Apollo, with canopy-covered altar area, flanked by a pool.

In the crater of an extinct volcano, **Lago di Bracciano** – about 40 kilometres (24 miles) north of Rome – is a water-sports haven, ringed by sailing, windsurfing and canoeing clubs. The lake is Rome's emergency water supply, so it's reasonably clean; the best swimming spots are just north of Bracciano town on the western shore and on the eastern side near Trevignano.

A handful of pretty villages overlook the body of water. **Anguillara** is a medieval town perched on a rocky crag, and especially beautiful at sunset. **Bracciano**, the main town on the lake, is dominated by the **Castello Orsini-Odescalchi**, built in 1470, with fine apartments decorated by Antoniazzo Romano and the Zuccari brothers. **Trevignano** has a walled medieval centre and is perfect for scenic strolls along its *lungolago* (lakeside promenade); the town is best reached from the Cassia *bis*.

Just to the south-east is **Lago di Martignano**, a quieter, smaller, offshoot of the Bracciano crater. There's a beach where you can rent sailing boats, pedalos and canoes, but you'll need a car: turn sharp right at the little chapel before Anguillara, follow the road past a drinking trough and go left (a track signposted 'lago') for three kilometres (two miles).

On the north bank of Bracciano lies **San Liberato**, a garden by Russell Page (1905-85). The English landscape architect tinkered for ten years with his series of graceful terraces. Around the house and the eponymous fourth-century chapel are a garden of simples and sweet-smelling roses, and the sweeping lawns are dotted with exotic trees that provide shade in summer and colour through the autumn.

Turn right instead of left at the Trevignano junction on the Cassia *bis* you reach **Calcata**, isolated on a volcanic spur above the verdant Valle del Treja. This pretty village is a mecca for ageing hippies and the hub of several spectacular (marked) walks.

Further north on the Cassia is **Sutri**, with its ancient amphitheatre. Argument still rages over when this amphitheatre was carved out of the solid rock: some attribute it to the Etruscans; others say it dates from the first century BC. The amphitheatre is located in the lovely Parco Urbano dell'Antica Città di Sutri where an itinerary with unusually clear descriptions (in English) leads you past Sutri's ancient remains, including a necropolis and a mithraeum.

Just out of town, a winding local road heads north (right) off the Cassia towards **Ronciglione** with its medieval city centre and on to **Lago di Vico**, in the crater of the extinct Monte Cimino volcano. Skirt around the rim of the volcano for about four kilometres (2.5 miles) and turn right for **Caprarola**, a little town dwarfed by the imposing Villa Farnese.

The **Villa Farnese** started out as a castle, designed by Sangallo the Younger and Peruzzi, but was taken over and transformed into something much less fortified by Vignola in the 1560s. It initially seems to be only two storeys high, but climb the semicircular ramps and the ground floor appears. Vignola raised and extended the approach road, burying the lower storeys of the existing houses to provide an optimum view. Inside, a wide spiral staircase – Cardinal Alessandro Farnese used to climb it on horseback – leads up to the *piano nobile*, the only part open to the public. In the Salone dei Fasti Farnese are frescos depicting the heroic deeds of the Farnese family: note the Farnese Pope Paul III excommunicating Henry VIII of England. The Sala dei Sogni has bizarre allegorical scenes intended to induce sweet dreams. There is also a room with frescoed maps of the world from 1500 and another in which whispers (including the menacing ones of John Malkovich to Nicole Kidman in *Portrait of a Lady*) rebound from wall to wall. Behind the villa are two formal gardens (included in the tour) and the steep, wooded park (*barchino*) that leads up to the fountains of the Giardino grande and the Palazzina del piacere summer house.

VITERBO

Viterbo was an important Etruscan town and an insignificant Roman one. In the eighth century it was fortified by the Lombard King Desiderius as a launching pad for sacking Rome. Caught up in the medieval quarrels between the Holy Roman Empire and the Church, Viterbo played host to popes and antipopes, several of whom relocated here when things got too hot in Rome. Gregory X was elected pope in Viterbo and lasted a month; Hadrian V died on arriving in town; John XXI was killed a year after his election when his bedroom floor in the papal palace collapsed.

In these narrow streets you'll stumble across medieval laundries, ancient porticos, imposing towers, crenellated buildings, and everywhere lions (the symbol of Viterbo) and fountains. The medieval quarter of San Pellegrino lies at the city's southern edge, flanked by piazza della Morte. Across the bridge is the elegant 12th-century – but much altered and restored – cathedral of **San Lorenzo**. Next door is the **Palazzo Papale**, built for the popes in the 13th century and restored in the 19th. The pretty 12th-century church of **Santa Maria Nuova** has an ancient head of Jupiter (on the façade), and a pulpit from which St Thomas Aquinas preached. Behind it are the remains of a small Lombard cloister (always open).

Piazza del Plebiscito is dominated by the **Palazzo Comunale** town hall (1500), where the lovely courtyard has a 17th-century fountain. A staircase leads to the Senate rooms (usually open to the public in the morning); at the top, the Cappella del Comune has two huge canvases by Sebastiano del Piombo and a *Visitation* by Bartolomeo Cavarozzi. From the piazza, via Roma leads past the Fontana dei leoni into corso d'Italia; at No.11 is the Caffè Schenardi, a 15th-century building that has been a café since 1818. Mussolini had breakfast here in 1938, at the third table on the right.

Take via Cavour out of piazza del Plebiscito. Via Garibaldi leads up to the Porta Romana, past the 13th-century Fontana grande. Just inside the gate on the left is the church of **San Sisto**, parts of which date from the ninth century. Its chancel is raised 15 steps above the nave, and has two curious twisting columns.

Outside the walls, opposite Porta della Verità, is the 12th-century **Santa Maria della Verità**. In 1469 local boy Lorenzo di Viterbo painted some of the most Tuscan frescos outside of Tuscany in its Gothic Cappella Mazzatosta. The charming *Marriage of the Virgin* panel was badly damaged in the war, and reconstructed from 16,000 pieces. The chapel pavement has remains of majolica decoration. In the old convent next door is the renovated **Museo Civico**, with Etruscan finds, works of art from local churches, and two canvases by Sebastiano del Piombo.

Within a seven-kilometre (four-mile) radius of the city (accessible only by car) there are several bubbling pools of sulphurous water. Local residents sit in them, smeared in greeny-white clay. The best place to wallow is the

Bagnaccio, where four basins of varying degrees of heat are scooped out of the clay. Leave Viterbo on the Montefiascone road, and after five kilometre (three miles) turn left on to the road to Marta. After a kilometre (half a mile) you'll see a ruin on your left. Just before this, an unpaved road branches off to the Bagnaccio.

To the east of Viterbo, the town of **Bagnaia** lies beneath the gardens and park of **Villa Lante**. The villa's two identical palaces, built in the 1570s for Cardinal Gambara, are surrounded by a geometrically perfect formal Italian garden, which is punctuated by fountains and pools. Water once cascaded down five terraces, performing surprising and spectacular water-games to the delight of visitors; not all of it still works, but the ropework cascade and stone dining table with central wine-cooling rivulet can still be admired.

It's a fair hike (24 kilometres/15 miles) west from Viterbo to **Tuscania**, an Etruscan town where the post-Etruscan bits really stand out – even though the town itself suffered a devastating earthquake in 1971. The town boasts two romanesque-Lombard churches: San Pietro and Santa Maria Maggiore. The Colle San Pietro, on which they stand, was the site of an Etruscan and then a Roman settlement; fragments of the pre-Christian acropolis are incorporated into the apse of **San Pietro**. Founded in the eighth century, the church was reworked from the 11th to the 13th centuries, when the adjacent bishop's palace and towers were added. The façade is startling: three-faced trifons, snakes and dancers owe more to pagan culture than Christian iconography. The interior has a cosmatesque pavement and 12th-century frescos. Built at the same time, **Santa Maria Maggiore** (strada Santa Maria) has tamer beasts on its façade and a more harmonious interior. The main Etruscan sight here is in the small **Museo Archaeologico**, which can be found in the cloisters of the convent of Santa Maria del Riposo. Inside, four generations of the same Etrusco-Roman family gaze from the lids of their sarcophagi.

Castello Orsini-Odescalchi

Piazza Mazzini 14, Bracciano (06 9980 4348/www. odescalchi.com). **Open** *Apr-Oct* 10am-1pm, 3-6pm Tue-Sun. *Nov-Mar* 10am-1pm, 3-7pm Tue-Sun; ticket office closes 1hr earlier. **Admission** €6; €4 concessions. **No credit cards.**

Museo Archaeologico

Via Madonna del Riposo 36, Tuscania (0761 436 209). **Open** 8.30am-7.30pm Tue-Sun. **Admission** free.

Museo Civico

Piazza Crispi 2, Viterbo (0761 348 275). **Open** *Apr-Oct* 9am-7pm Tue-Sun. *Nov-Mar* 9am-6pm Tue-Sun. **Admission** €3.10. **No credit cards.**

Capalbio *See p280.*

Castelporziano/Capocotta
See p277.

Chiarone *See p280.*

Fregene *See p279.*

Lago di Martignano *See p282.*

Maccarese *See p278.*

Ostia *See p277.*

Sabaudia *See p295.*

Parco Regionale di Veio

Isola Farnese (06 904 2774). **Open** 9am-1.30pm
Tue, Wed, Fri, Sun; 9am-3.30pm Thur, Sat.
Admission €2. **No credit cards**.

Parco Urbano della Antica Città di Sutri

Via Cassia km49.5 (0761 609 038). **Open** 8am-1pm
Tue-Sun. **Admission** free.

Tenuta di San Liberato

*Via Settevene Palo 33, Bracciano (06 998 8384/fax
06 9980 2506/www.sanliberato.it).* **Open** Apr-mid
Nov (guided tour only) 3.30pm or 4.30pm 1st, last
Sun of mth. **Admission** €6; €4.50 concessions.
No credit cards.

Villa Farnese

Caprarola (0761 646 052). **Open** *Villa* 8.30am-
6.45pm Tue-Sun. *Gardens* Apr-Oct 8.30am-5.30pm
Tue-Sun; Nov-Mar 8.30am-4pm Tue-Sun.
Admission €2.06; €1.03 concessions; guided tours
(Sun) €2.50. **No credit cards**.

Villa Lante

Bagnaia (0761 288 008). **Open** *Gardens only* mid
Apr-mid Sept 8.30am-7.30pm Tue-Sun; 1-15 Apr,
mid Sept-Oct 8.30am-5.30pm Tue-Sun; Nov-Mar
8.30am-4.30pm Tue-Sun. **Admission** €2.06; €1.03
concessions; ticket office closes 1hr earlier.
No credit cards.

Where to eat

Beneath the Castello Odescalchi in Bracciano,
Vino e Camino (piazza Mazzini 11, 06 9980
3433, closed Mon & 2wks Aug, average €20) is
an excellent wine bar with tables outside.
Trattoria del Cimino (via F Nicolai 44, 0761
646 173, closed all Mon, dinner Tue, Wed & Sun,
2wks July, average €20) is a hospitable and
family-friendly establishment in Caprarola

offering local specialities such as game and
polenta during the winter months. In Viterbo the
Porta Romana (via della Bontà 12, 0761 307
118, closed Sun & 2wks Aug, average €20) has a
friendly, family atmosphere. More upmarket but
equally good value is **Enoteca La Torre**
(via della Torre 5, 0761 226 467, closed Sun,
4wks July-Aug, average €25). Tuscania has one
of northern Lazio's best restaurants: **Al Gallo**
(via del Gallo 22, 0761 443 388, closed Mon
& 4wks Jan-Feb, average €45).

Getting there

By car

**Veio, Caprarola, Bagnaia, Sutri, Ronciglione,
Tuscania**: take the Cassia (SS2).
Lago di Bracciano & around: exit the Cassia at
La Storta and take via Claudia-Braccianense (SS493).
Trevignano, Calcata: take the Cassia *bis*.

By train

Veio: FM3 to La Storta, then bus to Isola Farnese.
Lago di Bracciano & around: from Termini,
Tiburtina, Ostiense or Trastevere to Anguillara
or Bracciano.
Sutri: hourly services from Ostiense or Trastevere.
Viterbo: Metroferro services from Flaminio; FM3.

By bus

Lago di Bracciano & around: COTRAL services
from Lepanto.
Destinations on the Cassia: COTRAL services
from Saxa Rubra; for Bagnaia change at Viterbo;
for Tuscania, service is direct June-Sept, otherwise
change at Viterbo.

Tourist information

APT

*Piazza San Carluccio, Viterbo (0761 304 795/fax
0761 220 957).* **Open** 9am-1pm Mon-Sat.

Via Flaminia & via Tiberina

Ancient **via Flaminia** led north-east through
the Tiber river valley to the Adriatic coast.
When legions were marching, it was a wide
country road with the occasional hamlet or farm.
These days it takes a while to get to the idyllic
parts. Sandwiched between the A1 motorway
and railway lines, the first 25 kilometres
(16 miles) beyond the GRA ring road are narrow
and heavily trafficked, with tasteless modern
developments punctuated by adverts for
bathroom fixtures and garden statuary. But
concealed within the nightmarish shells of
towns like **Sacrofano**, **Riano**, **Morlupo** and
Rignano Flaminio are medieval gems: keep
your eyes peeled for yellow signs pointing to
'borgo medioevale' or 'chiesa medioevale'.

Parallel to the Flaminia to the east, the **via Tiberina** is quieter, less congested and looks much more like an ancient road should look. Just off the via Tiberina (leave the Flaminia at Morlupo and follow signs to Capena, then turn north up the Tiberina; alternatively, exit the A1 at Fiano Romano) is **Lucus Feroniae**, an ancient religious and trading hub of the Sabine people. By the third century BC, during which it was colonised by the Romans, the city was famous for ceremonies held at its sanctuary of Feronia, goddess of agriculture. So renowned was the wealth of the temple that, according to Livy, Hannibal took a break from his march on Rome in 211 BC to help himself to the treasure. Despite the sacking, Lucus Feroniae continued to grow; heavily rebuilt during Augustus' reign, it flourished throughout the Imperial age and into the early Middle Ages. Little remains of the early Sabine settlement – most of the ruins now are Republican or Imperial – but what you can see is a fascinating microcosm of a typical Roman urban centre, complete with a basilica, bath complex with black-and-white mosaics, forum and, further to the north-west, a charming little circular amphitheatre.

Further north on the via Tiberina, turn off for Nazzano and the **Riserva Naturale Tevere-Farfa** wetlands. This small protected stretch of the Tiber river offers great birdwatching. Rising sharply from the low-lying undulating hills of the Tiber valley is the silhouette of **Monte Soratte**. Shaped distinctly like the scaly back of a sleeping dinosaur (though many Italians see Mussolini's profile in it), Monte Soratte is an easy climb (start from the highest point in **Sant'Oreste**, the village huddled at the foot of the mountain between the Flaminia and the Tiberina). On a clear day, you can see west to Lago di Bracciano (*see p282*) and east to the foothills of the Apennines.

Just off the Flaminia, **Città Castellana** is a pretty medieval town built on ancient foundations atop a massive tufa outcrop. Originally known as Falerii Veteres, it was razed by the Romans in the third century BC. The Falisci people were forced to pack up and move west to conspicuously indefensible flatlands in the valley, creating a settlement called Falerii Novi. It was not until the 11th century, when Normans invaded, that the locals once again took advantage of their natural stronghold and hiked back up the hill. Città Castellana has a lovely medieval centre and solemn 15th-century castle – the Rocca – commissioned by the Borgia Pope Alexander VI (it was completed under Julius II by Antonio da Sangallo the Elder). Inside the castle is the **Museo Nazionale dell'Agro Falisco**, with finds from Falerii Veteres. The jewel-like

Duomo (open 8.30am-noon, 3-6pm daily) is a gorgeous romanesque church from the 12th century, with a perfectly preserved portico that was decorated in delicate gold, porphyry and green geometric mosaic motifs in the early 13th century. Some of the decorative elements on the façade are derived from the abandoned town of Falerii Novi. The interior is, however, a jarring surprise: the bright white sugar-frosted extravaganza is the result of an 18th-century makeover. Thankfully, the original cosmatesque floors were left unmolested.

To reach **Falerii Novi**, go six kilometres (3.5 miles) west of Città Castellana towards Fabrica di Roma. Take the road (left), opposite a white building with *trattoria* written on its awning. Then, after 20 metres, turn left on to a dirt path and go through the arch. There's not much left of the city except its impressive outer walls, but there is something exhilaratingly bizarre about it. To get to the site, you'll find yourself trudging around the back of a 12th-century romanesque church and through fields to a small pit containing uninspiring blocks of tufa – all that remain of what was a monumental building within a once-bustling Roman colony. A sign points to an amphitheatre, completely overgrown with vegetation, and there are wagon ruts in paving stones. There's little else to see, but it's a veritable Twilight Zone.

Equally surreal is the Parco dei mostri (Monster Park) at **Bomarzo**, ten kilometres (six miles) west of Orte. Built in the gardens of the **Sacro Bosco** by Duke Vicino Orsini (1523-84) after his wife died, it's more a bizarre Renaissance theme park than a dignified retreat for a bereaved husband. Using the volcanic peperino stone that dotted his estate, Orsini spent years filling the park with surreal, sometimes grotesque, sculptures that were completely at odds with the conventional tastes of his day. Lurking in the undergrowth are a skewed house and enormous, absurd beasts – it's no surprise that the park was much appreciated by Salvador Dalí.

Lucus Feroniae

Via Tiberina, km18.5 (06 908 5173). **Open** *May-Sept* 8.30am-6.30pm Tue-Sun. *Oct-Apr* 8.30am-4.30pm Tue-Sun. **Admission** free.

Museo Nazionale dell'Agro Falisco

Rocca di Città Castellana (0761 513 735). **Open** (guided tours only, on the hr) *May-Sept* 9am-7pm Tue-Sun. *Oct-Apr* 9am-4pm Tue-Sun. Ticket office closes 1hr earlier. **Admission** free.

Sacro Bosco

Località Giardino, Bomarzo (0761 924 029). **Open** *May-Sept* 8.30am-7.30pm daily. *Oct-Apr* 9am-4.30pm daily. **Admission** €8; €7 concessions. **No credit cards.**

Where to stay & eat

Around the corner from Cività Castellana's Duomo is **La Scuderia** (via Don Minzoni 19, 0761 516 798, closed Sun dinner, all Mon, Aug, average €40), beautifully converted from stables into a refined restaurant serving local dishes made of the finest fresh ingredients. The living quarters of the same 17th-century building are now the elegant **Palace Hotel Relais Falisco** (0761 54 981, www.relaisfalisco.it, double €105-€180), with pretty rooms and a health spa.

Getting there

By car

Lucus Feroniae: see p285; or A1 to Fiano Romano, then follow signs for Capena.
Bomarzo: Flaminia, then SS315; or A1 to Attigliano exit, then minor road to Bomarzo.

By train

Sant'Oreste: services from Flaminio.
Cività Castellana: frequent services from Tiburtina, Ostiense or Flaminio.
Bomarzo: FM1 to Orte, then FS train to Attigliano-Bomarzo (5km from park).

By bus

COTRAL services along the Tiberina and Flaminia depart from Saxa Rubra.
Sant'Oreste: Buses stop at the train station; there you must change for a local bus to town.
Bomarzo: From Saxa Rubra, change at Viterbo.

Via Tiburtina

FROM ROME TO TIVOLI

Named for its principal destination, Tibur (modern Tivoli), the **via Tiburtina** roughly follows the path of the Aniene river, which snakes its way to Rome from the south-east, eventually joining the Tiber.

The early sections of this consular road win no beauty pageants, but two UNESCO World Heritage Sites – Villa d'Este, in Tivoli proper, and Hadrian's Villa, five kilometres (three miles) down the hill – make it ideal for day-tripping. The journey to Tivoli can also be made – much more quickly – via the A24 (Roma-L'Aquila) *autostrada*. Outside the GRA ring road, traffic on the via Tiburtina bumps and lurches past dreary high-rise apartment buildings, the high-security Rebibbia prison and an ugly rash of industry.

After about 20 kilometres (12 miles), the foul stink of the Acque albule sulphur springs fills the air; the ancients used these cool-water pools for their curative properties, and they're still open to the public in the town **Bagni di Tivoli**. A few kilometres beyond, the Tiburtina crosses massive quarries of travertine (*lapis tiburtinus*), over which a permanent white dust cloud hangs. Gaping valleys of the calcareous limestone – used to build the Colosseum, St Peter's and the Trevi Fountain – are still exploited today, though commissions are for kitchens in Malibu rather than blood-sport arenas and baroque fountains.

Just south of the Tiburtina is the town of **Villa Adriana**, site of the second-century AD retreat built by Emperor Hadrian – quite simply one of the most wonderful places in the world. Strewn across a gentle slope on the southern extremity of town, the villa has some fascinating architectural spaces and water features. Hadrian (*see p8* **Hadrian**) was a great traveller and an amateur architect; many of the unique elements in his villa, built from 118 to 134, were designed by the emperor himself, inspired by things he saw in Greece and Egypt. After the emperor's death in 138, the villa was used by his successors; but in the centuries following the fall of the Empire it became a luxury quarry for treasure-hunters. Marble and mosaic finds from the villa now make up a significant portion of the collections of Roman art at the Capitoline (*see p62*) and Vatican (*see p144*) museums. But the villa was never destroyed completely, and the restored remains, lying between olive groves and cypresses, are still impressive (the model in the pavilion gives an idea of the villa's original size). The seemingly haphazard layout of the complex, not governed by any axes, makes it easy to get lost – and just as easy to stumble upon more charming surprises.

The location of the ancient entrance to the villa is unclear; the first space you'll encounter after climbing the road from the ticket office is the *pecile* (poikile), a large pool that was once surrounded by a portico with high walls, of which only one still stands. The **poikile** was probably used for post-prandial strolling: seven laps around the perimeter of the space constitute two Roman miles, the distance that ancient doctors recommended walking after meals. The pool itself may have been used for recreational swimming. Directly east of the poikile, the so-called **Teatro marittimo** (Maritime Theatre) is one of the most delightful inventions in the whole villa. A round brick wall, 45 metres (150 feet) in diameter, encloses a circular moat, at the centre of which is an island of columns and brickwork; it was a self-sufficient *domus* (mini-villa) – complete with its own baths, bedrooms and gardens. Today a cement bridge crosses the moat, but in antiquity there were wooden bridges that could swing open, allowing the emperor to use the marble-lined waterway for lapless swimming. South of

Ingenious fountains at Villa d'Este.
See p287.

the Maritime Theatre is a three-storey building
known simply as the building with a fish pond
(*peschiera*), or the **Winter Palace** (Quartiere
invernale). The highest of the structure's levels,
where traces of a heating system are preserved,
may have been the emperor's private residence,
with a large banquet hall overlooking the
Nymphaeum-Stadium and the plains towards a
distant Rome. The 'fish pond' is a now-empty
rectangular basin in the east side of the
structure, beneath which visitors can walk the
perfectly preserved cryptoporticus (covered
corridor). Continuing south, locate the **Piccole
terme** (small baths), where intricate stuccos
are amazingly intact on some of the vaulted
ceilings, giving an idea of the grandeur of the
entire villa's decoration. In the valley below is
the lovely **Canopus**. Built to recall the canal
that connected Alexandria to the Nile, the
Canopus is a long, narrow pool, framed on three
sides by columns and statues, including a
marble crocodile. At the far (southern) end of
the pool is a structure called the **Serapeum**,
used for lavish entertaining, where sculpture
once embellished the apse. Summer guests
enjoyed an innovative form of air-conditioning
– a single sheet of water poured from the roof
over the open face of the building, enclosing
diners. The villa also included extensive guest
and staff apartments, dining rooms, assembly
halls and libraries, a stadium and theatres. The
whole complex was connected by underground

passages, used mostly by servants, but also by
guests seeking relief from the beating sun.

High on a hill five kilometres (three miles)
from Villa Adriana, the town of **Tivoli** was
founded by an Italic tribe but conquered by the
Romans in 338 BC. The town was littered with
temples, and the surrounding territory became
a popular location for country villas – besides
Hadrian, Horace, Nero and Trajan also built in
the area. Dominating Tivoli proper is the **Villa
d'Este**, a lavish pleasure palace built over a
Benedictine monastery in 1550 for Cardinal
Ippolito d'Este, son of Lucrezia Borgia. Inside
the villa – by mannerist architect Pirro Ligorio
– there are frescos and paintings by Correggio,
Da Volterra and Perin Del Vaga. The main
attraction – drawing busloads of day-trippers –
is the garden, with huge and ingenious
fountains. The Owl Fountain imitated an owl's
song, while the Fontana dell'organo idraulico
used water pressure to compress air and play
tunes. The villa is now a little frayed at the
edges, and restoration is a struggle: the musical
fountains have not made a sound for years, but
others have regained their original splendour.
Also worth a look are the **Villa Gregoriana**
(undergoing a vast restoration as this guide
went to press, but visible from outside), a wild
park in a rocky gorge, next to two waterfalls;
the cathedral of **San Lorenzo** (via Duomo),
which contains a carved 13th-century *Descent
from the Cross*; and a very well-preserved

circular Roman **Temple of the Sibyl** (via della Sibilla). At the top of the town (piazza delle Nazioni Unite) is **Rocca Pia**, a 15th-century castle built by Pope Pius II.

Villa Adriana (Hadrian's Villa)

Via di Villa Adriana, Villa Adriana (0774 382 733). **Open** *Apr-Sept* 9am-6.30pm daily. *Oct-Mar* 9am-5pm daily. Ticket office closes 90min earlier. **Admission** €6.50; €3.25 concessions. **No credit cards.**

Villa d'Este

Piazza Trento 1, Tivoli (0774 312 070). **Open** *May-Sept* 9am-6.15pm Tue-Sun. *Oct-Apr* 8.30am-4pm Tue-Sun. **Admission** €6.50; €3.25 concessions. **No credit cards.**

Where to eat

Across the car park from the ticket booths at Villa Adriana is the amazingly untouristy **Adriano** (via di Villa Adriana 194, 0774 535 028, www.hoteladriano.it, closed dinner Sun, average €35), where the menu is surprisingly sophisticated for its provincial setting; a large shady garden is great for alfresco eating.

Getting there

By car

A24 (exit Tivoli) or via Tiburtina (SS5).

By bus

COTRAL from Ponte Mammolo; note that the bus marked *autostrada* is a quicker service. Not all services stop at Villa Adriana, so check before boarding. If travelling by bus, visit Tivoli town first; from the main square (piazza Garibaldi), frequent orange (local) buses serve Villa Adriana; from Villa Adriana, both local and COTRAL buses go to Rome.

Tourist information

APT Tivoli

Largo Garibaldi (0774 311 249/fax 0774 331 294). **Open** 9am-1pm Mon, Sat; 9am-1pm, 3-6pm Tue-Fri.

BEYOND TIVOLI

Further along the via Tiburtina is an area where the kind of tourist congestion that afflicts Tivoli's hotspots is unknown. In 300 BC work began to extend the via Tiburtina from Tivoli eastwards across the Apennines and to the Adriatic at Pescara. The new road made it easier to conquer hostile tribes and dole out territory to noble Roman families. It also brought the abundant mountain springs feeding the Anio (Aniene) river under the control of the Romans, who in 272 BC began work on four aqueducts; for centuries these routed fresh water to the metropolis.

The area's limpid waterways and verdure attracted the ancient jet set. Around AD 60 Nero ordered the construction of a pleasure villa in Subiaco (*see p289*). But the area's popularity with the swank and smart was already well established: in 33 BC Maecenas (Mecenate) let Rome's hottest poet Horace move into his country villa outside Licenza (*see p288*). Between the tenth and 11th centuries, the Church and nobility constructed fortresses on the hills along the strategic Aniene valley. The feudal castles of the powerful Orsini, Borgia and Colonna families still dominate the landscape as you roll along the via Tiburtina.

From Tivoli, the via Tiburtina (or, for faster trips, the A24) wends east though **Vicovaro** to the **San Cosimato** Franciscan monastery complex, built on a precipice of travertine grottos with jaw-dropping views of the emerald-green Aniene river below. Around 590, monks made these holey crags their home, building a church and monastery atop some ancient Roman ruins. Today only three friars man the monastery. A few of the dozen original niches that served the ascetics can be visited on two different grotto itineraries: an easy one and one requiring a surer foot as you totter down steep mossy-covered steps. Beneath the grottos are underground stretches of the Acqua Marcia (144 BC) and Acqua Claudia (AD 38-52) aqueducts that carried fresh water to Rome until barbarians cut them off in the fifth and sixth centuries. This is the only point where you can visit these channels. Though lit, they are not for the squeamish: watch out for bats. If no one is available to guide you, ask the friars to give you the keys and turn the lights on.

Just before the monastery, the SS314 peels off north to **Roccagiovine** and **Licenza**. The former, a medieval *borgo* in the Lucretili regional park, is dominated by the 14th-century Orsini castle (closed to the public); according to local lore, Horace composed many of his verses on the spot where the church of Santa Maria delle Case now stands.

Also largely medieval, Licenza was a stronghold of the Orsini family. The 11th-century Palazzo Baronale and its tower rise above olive groves and the fertile valley below; today it houses the **Museo Civico Oraziano** (Horace Museum) containing objects recovered in 1911-15 during excavations of Horace's splendid villa (**Villa di Orazio**). Wealthy patron of the arts Maecenas gave Horatio Flaccus (Horace, born 65 BC) this sumptuous abode so he could better hear the murmuring Muses. Recent excavations have revealed a lot more of the remains: black-and-white geometric mosaic floors and an impressive thermal bath complex (including a sociable five-seater latrine). The original villa dates from the first century BC, later extensions and restorations from the first and second centuries AD.

North of Licenza, the SP38B leads to tiny **Civitella**, with its breathtaking view of the Lucretili hills. The cobblestone paths and walls are made from rose-coloured limestone. It's an excellent base for hikes: trails beginning below the town head to **Monte Pellecchia** (1,368 metres/4,500 feet; 2hrs each way) and **Monte Gennaro** (1,271 metres/4,150 feet; 3hrs each way). For information contact the **Parco Regionale dei Monti Lucretili** (0774 637 027/www.montilucretili.it). Maps can be purchased at Hotel Fonte Banusia.

Continuing along the via Tiburtina, **Roviano** was named after the Roman Rubri family that settled here around 300 BC. Centuries later, the town's baronial castle passed from the Colonna, to the Orsini, Barberini and Brancaccio families. It now houses the **Museo della Civiltà Contadina** (Museum of Rural Life, 0774 903 143, closed Tue & Wed) where exhibits include a ram's prophylactic and a section on spiky, scary torture implements.

Past Roviano, the SS411 forks off to the south towards **Subiaco** (the origin of the name is *Sublaqueum*, 'under the lakes'). Its narrow gorges and wooded mountains attracted the Emperor Nero. He dammed the Aniene to create a massive lake next to his grandiose villa – it covered, archaeologists estimate, 75 hectares (185 acres). The lake has since disappeared and only traces of the villa survive: the emperor abandoned it soon after completion (c60 AD) when lightning struck the table in front of him as he dined – a very bad omen. Much of the land where the villa stood is private property and little has been excavated, but a small thermal complex and part of San Clemente – the first monastery built by St Benedict (*see below*), which is made from villa masonry – can be seen; call ahead to the Monastero di Santa Scolastica for the keys.

In Christian times, this area's isolation made it popular with assorted ascetics. Rich, young Benedict of Norcia turned his back on the licentious hedonism of his contemporaries and went to live in a cave on Monte Taleo toward the end of the fifth century. After three years of solitude, Benedict had attracted such a flock of disciples that he felt moved to found the first of 13 monasteries inside the ruins of Nero's villa. Only one is still going: the **Monastero di Santa Scolastica**, named after Benedict's twin sister, whose dedication to her sibling earned her a place among the saints too. The sixth-century chapel of St Silvester is the oldest remaining bit of the monastery; the church dedicated to Scholastica was erected in 981.

Most of the rest is the result of a late-18th-century makeover – with the exception of the beautiful campanile, built in 1053. A shop near the main entrance sells monk-made 'curative' spirits, thick liqueurs, chocolate, chunky fruit jams and herbal products.

Not only is Subiaco the birthplace of Western monasticism; the St Scholastica monastery was also a cradle of Italian printing. In 1464 two Germans set up a Gutenberg press here. They printed three titles, all in elegant and unique *sublacensi* characters; only one work printed here remains at the monastery, a copy of Lactantius's *De divinis institutionibus* (other works are scattered around European museums). Behind the monastery, the **Biblioteca Nazionale Santa Scolastica** (National Library of St Scholastica) houses over 100,000 volumes, including ninth- and tenth-century manuscripts. Only a fraction is on display in the library's two lower rooms, and they use only natural light (bad on a cloudy day) and offer little by way of explanation.

The **Monastero di San Benedetto**, a mountain-hugging complex of twisting corridors and stairways, grew up around the Sacro speco – the 'saint's cave' where Benedict spent those three long years. You'll need trainers for the lovely climb to the monastery through a holm-oak wood. There are ninth-century frescos in the Grotta dei pastori, 'shepherds' grotto'. This is where Benedict first taught in the sixth century. Little else from before the 13th century remains. Inside, every vault, wall and ceiling is covered with brilliant scenes from Christ's life, the life and miracles of Benedict, and a fresco of St Francis of Assisi (pre-halo and stigmata – thus probably done

The best For children

See also p284 **The best: Beaches**.

Romps on the ramparts
Castello Orsini-Odescalchi (*p282*)

Picnics and hide-and-seek
Ostia Antica (*p276*)

An interactive taste of inter-war life
Piana delle Orme (*p295*)

Extraordinary monsters
Sacro Bosco (*p285*)

Bats in dank passageways
San Cosimato (*p288*)

Trips Out of Town

while he was still alive, perhaps soon after he visited the monastery in 1218). The Sacro speco is in the lower church. There's a 17th-century marble statue of the young hermit by Bernini's pupil, Antonio Raggi, and one of the life-saving food hamper that was lowered regularly into the cave by a friendly local. Elsewhere, gruesome frescos depict torture, martyrdom, death and decomposition.

Halfway between Subiaco and the via Tiburtina on the SP39B road, **Cervara di Roma** was voted Italy's Ideal Village by the environmental magazine *Airone*. Climb the *scala degli artisti* ('artists' stairway') or look up from the town's tiny piazza to see why: the cliff face has sculpted human faces, nude torsos, horse heads and birds. Quiet houses roost on incisor-like Mount Pilione (1,053 metres/3,500 feet). Meander along the labyrinthine walkways and hunt out the clay bas-reliefs, frescos and poetry of the town's open-air art museum.

Biblioteca Nazionale Santa Scolastica

Via dei Monasteri (0774 85 424). **Open** *Sept-mid July* 8.30am-6.30pm Mon-Fri; 8.30am-1.30pm Sat. *Mid July-Aug* 8.30am-1pm Mon-Sat. Closed 1wk Aug. **Admission** free.

Convento di San Cosimato

Via Tiburtina, Vicovaro (0774 492 391/www. sancosimato.priminet.com). **Open** always (ring the bell if gate is closed). **Admission** free.

Monastero di San Benedetto & Sacro Speco

Via dei Monasteri (0774 85 039/www.benedettini-subiaco.it). **Open** 9am-12.30pm, 3-6pm daily. **Admission** free.

Monastero di Santa Scolastica

Via dei Monasteri (0774 82 421). **Open** 9am-12.30pm, 3.30-6.30pm daily. **Admission** free.

Museo Civico Oraziano

Piazza del Palazzo, Licenza (0774 46 225/031). **Open** *Oct-Apr* 10am-noon, 3-5pm Tue-Sun. *May-Sept* 10am-noon, 3-6pm Tue-Sun. **Admission** €2. **No credit cards.**

Villa di Orazio

SS314, Licenza (0774 46 225/031/www.humnet. ucla.edu/horaces-villa). **Open** 9am-dusk Tue-Sun. **Admission** donation requested.

Where to stay & eat

The **San Cosimato** convent (*see p288*) in Vicovaro serves fabulous meals at weekends. There's no menu (dietary requests should be made by phone), but the huge meal costs no more than €20 a person and is usually followed by after-dinner liqueurs brewed by the monks.

The 60 rooms here cost €20 per person B&B. Wild boar pizza is the speciality at the **Pizzeria La Fonte** (via della Fonte, 0774 498 954, closed Mon & 2wks Sept, average €6) in Roccagiovine, while the ever-changing fare at the cuddly, craft-crazy **Trattoria Il Fiocco** (via A Gramsci 30, 0774 46 464, closed Mon, average €25) in Licenza doesn't quite merit the prices, but service is extremely friendly. Hikers will appreciate the **Hotel Fonte Bandusia** (via Fonte Bandusia, 0774 46 030, closed Jan) in Civitella: besides the restaurant (open weekends, weekdays by appointment only, average €15), it has comfortable rooms (€42 double), a pool and maps of the *parco regionale*.

In Roviano, two excellent eateries serve the local pasta specialities *cuzzi* and *ramiccia*. **La Vecchia Macina da Brunetto** (viale Italia 12, 333 670 88 79, closed Tue, average €25) only does dinner (except by special arrangement). It also closes for November and December, when the restaurant is transformed into an olive press. **La Taverna di Ettore** (piazza della Repubblica 5, 0774 903 432, closed Mon, average €14) makes good pizza as well as providing interesting sauces for your *cuzzi*.

In Subiaco, the *foresteria* (guest house) of the **Santa Scolastica** monastery (0774 85 569, *see p290*) serves huge meals at reasonable prices (open daily for lunch only, average €19) and has rooms to rent (€34 per person B&B). The **Agriturismo La Parata** (via dei Monasteri 40, 0774 822 748, laparata@libero.it, closed Mon & dinner Tue-Thur, average €21) specialises in freshwater fish. There are four comfortable rooms (double €60) too.

Getting there

By car

Exit the A24 motorway at Mandela-Vicovaro; *see also above*.

By bus

For all destinations, COTRAL services run from Ponte Mammolo.
Vicovaro, San Cosimato: take the Subiaco (autostrada) bus and get off at Mandela; walk back 700m west along the via Tiburtina.
Villa di Orazio, Licenza, Roccagiovine, Civitella: change in Tivoli or Mandela for Licenza.
Roviano: take the Subiaco (autostrada) bus and get off at the Roviano stop, then hike the 2.5km to town.
Nero's villa, monasteries: infrequent local services (information 0774 85 526) from Subiaco centro.

By train

Roviano: local trains on the Avezzano-Sulmona-Pescara line from Tiburtina station; it's an easy walk from Roviano station to the town centre.
San Cosimato: take the Avezzano-Sulmona-Pescara line from Tiburtina station and get off at Mandela;

turn left (west) on to via Tiburtina. It's a 700m walk to the Franciscan monastery.

Tourist information

IAT
Via Cadorna 59, Subiaco (0774 822 013). **Open** 8am-2pm Mon, Sat; 8am-2pm, 3-6pm Tue-Fri only.

Via Prenestina

Prehistoric tribes used to trudge the route that became via Prenestina, covering the 37 kilometres (23 miles) between Rome and the town of Praeneste, an Etruscan settlement that battled long and hard against Rome until around 338 BC. Praeneste (now **Palestrina**) was built over the huge temple and shrine of an oracle who foretold the future using *sortes* – pieces of wood with letters carved on them. Parts of the temple, dedicated to the goddess Fortuna Primigenia, date from the sixth century BC. Under Roman control the temple was rebuilt on a grander scale and Praeneste became a favourite holiday resort (Pliny the Younger had a villa here). The oracle shut up shop in the fourth century AD, the temple fell into disuse, and a medieval town was built on top. Then, in World War II, air raids exposed the full extent of the original temple.

The **Museo Archeologico** (*see below*), in the Palazzo Colonna-Barberini, is the main attraction. Otherwise, the town is uninspiring, its streets buzzing with obnoxious *motorini*. In the main piazza Margherita, to the right of the cathedral, are scant remains of a shrine to Juno (who, until she became the great goddess of Rome, was protector of women and their sexual life). The town's most famous son is Giovanni da Palestrina, the 16th-century composer.

Museo Archeologico di Palestrina
Piazza della Cortina (06 953 8100). **Open** *Museum* 9am-8pm daily. *Sanctuary* 9am-1hr before sunset daily. Ticket office closes 1hr earlier. **Admission** *Museum & sanctuary* €3. **No credit cards.**
A semicircular temple with a statue of the goddess Fortuna originally stood where the 17th-century Palazzo Colonna-Barberini is now. Today the palazzo-museum incorporates some remains of the temple beneath (plexiglass floor tiles show where the temple columns once stood). A model on the top floor shows how the temple complex might have been.

The museum displays a selection of Imperial and Republican Roman artefacts: art, instruments and objects either found in the area or associated with the worship of Fortuna. But the star exhibit is the second-century BC Nile mosaic, a work admired by Pliny, which came from the most sacred part of the temple, where the cathedral now stands. It is an intricately detailed, bird's-eye representation of the flora and fauna of the flooded banks of the Nile from Ethiopia to Alexandria. Gallant warriors hunt exotic animals and diners recline while pipers pipe and goddesses preach. If your Greek is good, you'll be able to identify the labelled beasts. Also of interest is the *Capitoline Triad*, a second-century AD sculpture of Minerva, Jupiter and Juno sitting together on one throne – the only known portrayal of Rome's three tutelary gods together. This sculpture was stolen in 1992, but salvaged from the greedy underworld of stolen artefacts. Your museum ticket is also good for seeing the Sanctuary outside. The sacred area is made up of a series of artificial terraces that gives the whole the appearace of a great pyramid.

Getting there

By car
Via Prenestina (SS155) or via Casilina. Also reached from the A1 (exit San Cesareo or Valmontone) or the A24 (exit Tivoli) motorways, then local roads.

Parco degli Acquedotti

Far removed from the centre – and accordingly undervisited – this 'Aqueduct Park' is where seven of ancient Rome's 11 aqueducts were aligned to make their final approach to the city between the *vie* Tuscolana and Appia. Long stretches of the 2,000-year-old arcades still stand, some at heights of over 17 metres (56 feet). Thanks to earthquakes and rampaging barbarian hordes, the elegant rhythm of the arcades drops off here and there, but wherever the aqueducts are severed, the rectangular *specus* (water channel) above the arches comes into view. It's like a landscape from a Pasolini film, with low-flying planes overhead and 1950s apartment buildings in the distance providing a stark contrast to the picturesque ruins, ponds and umbrella pines in the park.

To reach the park, go to Giulio Agricola metro station, then walk ten minutes south-west on viale Appio Claudio; or get to Metro Subaugusta and take bus 557. The via Lemonia entrance has an information centre (06 512 6314). The Archeobus (*see p301*) makes a stop at the other side of the park, in viale Appio Claudio.

By bus

COTRAL services run from Anagnina (every 10-15 minutes) or Ponte Mammolo (every hour).

Via Tuscolana

The via Tuscolana forks off the via Latina (an ancient alternative route to the via Appia, *see p150*) and heads to ancient Tusculum. It passes the softly beating heart of Italian film at Cinecittà (*see chapter* **Film**), the remains of the Acqua Felice and Acqua Claudia aqueducts at Porta Furba in Rome's run-down eastern suburbs (*see p291* **Parco degli Acquedotti**) and the rolling Alban hills en route to Frascati.

Frascati is the closest to Rome of the **Castelli romani** (a group of towns so-called for the grand abodes erected here by Rome's papal and patrician glitterati) and offers a satisfying balance of wine, food and culture. The name 'Frascati' is synonymous with uninspiring Italian wine, but you'd do well to give it another try here. Local topers claim that it has to be drunk *sul posto* – on site. There are numerous Renaissance villas sprinkled over the hillside behind the town, but only the garden of the 17th-century **Villa Aldobrandini**, built in 1598-1603 by Giacomo della Porta for Cardinal Pietro Aldobrandini, is open to the public. In nearby **Villa Torlonia** – a public park – Carlo Maderno's 16th-century Teatro delle acque fountain has been gloriously restored; there's an elegant smaller Bernini fountain too.

Just four kilometres (2.5 miles) down the road, but a world away from Frascati's summer crowds and belly-busting banqueting, ancient **Tusculum** is part pastoral green and part archaeological treasure trove. These remnants of a volcano that last blew its top 70,000 years ago are now grassy slopes covered by myriad oaks and umbrella pines, fanned by cool breezes. From the picnic ground, the ancient Roman via dei Sepolcri winds up to a Roman cistern and tomb. Or start from the main parking lot at the top of the hill and head west to find the spectacular remains of the Villa di Tibero – presumed to have been one of the many villas of Emperor Tiberius. To the east is a well-preserved second-century BC theatre and forum. As this guide went to press the forum was being freshly excavated (for information, consult www.csic.it). Ignore the hideous cross made out of what look like recycled water pipes and enjoy more great views from the summit; if you search among the twisted oaks and blackberry bushes here, you'll come across more ruins of the Acropolis.

South of Frascati on the via Latina (SS511), **Grottaferrata** is a lively town whose main street leads to the tenth-century **Abbazia di**

San Nilo, the only Greek Orthodox abbey in the province of Rome. The town's name is thought to derive from the *crypta ferrata* – two small rooms with iron-grille windows. They date from Roman times and can still be seen in the abbey's church. The abbey was founded in the early 11th century by Bartholomew and Nilus, two Basilian monks from Calabria. The mainly romanesque monastery was fortified in the 15th century, and the abbey church has a fine 12th-century campanile and an even finer carved marble portal. Inside, the cappella di San Nilo (chapel of St Nilus) contains beautiful frescos by Domenichino.

Abbazia di San Nilo

Corso del Popolo 128, Grottaferrata (06 945 9309). **Open** 9am-noon, 4.30-6pm daily. **Admission** free.

Villa Aldobrandini

Via CG Massaia, Frascati (06 942 0331). **Open** 9am-1pm, 3-5pm Mon-Fri; booking essential. **Admission** free, but you have to go to the APT office first (*see p293*).

Where to eat & drink

In Frascati you're spoilt for choice when it comes to eating and drinking. **Cacciani** (via A Diaz 13-15, 06 942 0378, closed all Mon, Sun dinner in Oct-May, 1wk Jan, 2wks Aug, average €40) is one of the Castelli's best restaurants, with creative dishes based on fresh seasonal produce, much of it produced by the owners. For something simpler, try **Osteria Covo degli Angeli** (via Cernaia 17, 06 9429 9069, closed Sun dinner, average €17) or **Zarazà** (viale Regina Margherita 45, 06 942 2053, closed all Mon, Sun dinner in Oct-Apr, 3wks Aug, average €23). Many make the pilgrimage to Frascati not to eat, but to pay their respects to Bacchus. For the hard core, there's the **Osteria dell'Olmo** (piazza dell'Olmo 3, no phone, closed Mon): half wine-making museum and half anthropological study, this *osteria* serves only its own brews and you're expected to provide your own food (stop by the nearby piazza del Mercato to get a *porchetta* – roast suckling pig – sandwich to go). Not a place for the meek or solitary.

La Briciola (via G D'Annunzio 12, 06 945 9338, closed all Mon, Sun dinner, 1wk Jan, 3wks Aug, average €35) in Grottaferrata uses the freshest of local ingredients.

Getting there

By car

Grottaferrata and **Frascati** can be reached using the via Appia (*see p150*) and minor roads. For **Tusculum**, take via Tuscolo from Frascati.

Sites

Lucus Feroniae See p285.

Parco Urbano dell'Antica Città di Sutri See p282.

Praeneste See p291.

Tempio di Giove See p296.

Tusculum See p292.

Villa Adriana See p286.

By train
Hourly local trains (FM4) leave from Termini for the 20min ride to Frascati (and Castelgandolfo, *see below*).

By bus
COTRAL services run from Anagnina every 30min.

Tourist information

APT
Piazza Marconi 1, Frascati (06 942 0331/fax 06 942 5498). **Open** *Apr-Oct* 8am-2pm Mon, Wed; 8am-2pm, 4-7pm Tue, Thur-Sat. *Nov-Mar* 8am-2pm Mon, Sat; 8am-2pm, 3-5pm Tue-Fri.

Via Appia

For the coast further south, *see p295* **Via Pontina**. Don't confuse the pleasant, archaeologically rich via Appia Antica (the Appian Way, *see also p150*) with the modern via Appia Nuova (SS7). The former was the 'Queen of Roads', ancient Rome's most famous highway; the latter, congested and fume-filled, leads to Rome's second airport at Ciampino (*see p298*), the via dei Laghi (SS217) and the southern side of the Castelli romani and the Alban hills.

Perched on the lip of the Lago Albano crater, **Castelgandolfo** is best known as the town where the pontiff spends his summer hols. Pope Clement VII began the tradition in the 1500s. The papal palace and piazza della Libertà – with its enchanting view of the lake – were completed by Bernini. In August you can catch the pope delivering his Sunday Angelus here at noon. Enjoy the same breezes the pope does by taking a stroll around the lake shore, or rent a pedalo or lakeside deckchairs.

Overlooking Lago di Nemi, **Genzano** is renowned for its Infiorata festival, which is held on the first Sunday after Corpus domini (late May or early June). Some five tons of brilliantly-hued flowers are used to create elaborate pictures on the streets that lead up to the church of Santa Maria della Cima.

The road from Genzano towards the lake passes the **Museo delle Navi** ('Roman ship museum'). When the lake was partially drained in 1929, two massive floating temples emerged. Followers of Isis worshipped the Egyptian goddess on sacred vessels on lakes at full moon. The Emperor Caligula – an Isis devotee – had two fabulously decorated vessels built on Lake Nemi; after his demise, the disapproving Roman Senate had them sunk. The museum built for the 70-metre (230-foot) ships was destroyed during World War II, but today there are 1:5 scale models and reproductions of artefacts found on board.

Of all the Castelli romani, **Nemi** is the most picturesque, perched on the edge of a tree-covered crater overlooking the lake. The name comes from the Latin *nemus* (forest), a reminder that the surrounding woods were once the haunt of worshippers of Diana, goddess of the hunt. For centuries, Nemi has been famous for its fruit: the medieval village is synonymous with strawberries, now grown by the lake under glass and plastic. Avoid visiting on Sundays, when Nemi fills up with Roman strollers.

Situated on the plain south-east of the Castelli romani, **Ninfa** – local legend says – was named after a nymph who was so devastated by the loss of her lover that she cried copiously enough to form a stream. Today a stream flows though some of Italy's most beautiful gardens, which ramble around the ruins of a medieval town. The origins of Ninfa are obscure, but in the 12th century it made the mistake of supporting a rival to the pope and was sacked. It rallied, and by the early 1380s had 150 large *palazzi*. Shortly afterwards, however, the town came definitively to grief in inter-clan warfare followed by an outbreak of malaria. The Caetani family acquired Ninfa in the 14th century, but showed little interest in their ghost estate until the 1920s, when Don Gelasio Caetani decided to plant his vast collection of exotic species here. The result of his botanical dabbling is pure magic: catch it in late spring to see it at its romantic best. Only a limited number of visitors are allowed in, so tickets are best purchased in advance in Rome.

Museo delle Navi
Via Diana 15, Genzano (06 939 8040). **Open** 9am-6.30pm daily. **Admission** €2. **No credit cards.**

Oasi di Ninfa
Doganella di Ninfa (06 687 3056). **Open** *July-early Nov* 9am-noon, 2.30-6pm 1st Sat & Sun of mth. *Apr-June* 9am-noon, 2.30-6pm 1st Sat & Sun, 3rd Sun of mth. **Admission** €8; under-10s admission free. **No credit cards.**

Horace took dictation from murmuring
muses at the **Villa di Orazio**. *See p288.*

Tickets can be purchased in Rome from the Fondazione Caetani (via delle Botteghe Oscure 32, open 9am-1pm, 3.30-7.30pm Mon-Fri). The Fondazione also provides information on occasional extra openings from April to June.

Where to eat

Though there's not much to see in Genzano, your stomach won't regret stopping by. **La Scuderia** (piazza Sforza Cesarini 1, 06 939 0521, closed Mon, average €16) uses fresh ingredients from local producers to recreate traditional dishes, while excellent wines can be sampled in the front rooms of the **Ristorante Enoteca La Grotta** (via I Belardi 31, 06 936 4224, closed Wed & 1wk Aug, average €40) or fresh fish in the restaurant out back.

In Nemi, the **Specchio di Diana** (corso Vittorio Emanuele 13, 06 936 8805, average €45) serves its vast pizzas on a terrace overlooking the lake. **Sirena del Lago** (via del Plebiscito, 06 936 8020, closed Mon, average €20) is family-run, serves excellent grilled trout and game, and has perhaps the best view in town.

Getting there

By car
For all destinations, take the Appia (SS7).
Nemi: exit Ciampino and take via dei Laghi.
Ninfa: exit at Tor Tre Ponti, then follow signs to Latina Scalo and Ninfa.

By train
Ninfa: take mainline services from Termini to Latina Scalo, then haggle with waiting taxi drivers for the 9km/5-mile ride to the gardens.
Castelgandolfo: trains every hr from Termini.

By bus
COTRAL services run from Anagnina for Genzano and Castelgandolfo. For Nemi change at Genzano. There are also services between Frascati (see p292) and Grottaferrata (see p292), and Genzano/Nemi.

Via Pontina

Slicing south from the city, via Pontina (SS148) can make no claim to antiquity. It was built in the 1930s to connect Mussolini's capital to the Pontine marshes – recently reclaimed from brackish water and squadrons of malarial mosquitos – and 'ideal' Fascist settlements like Littorio (now Latina) and Sabaudia (*see below*). It now has a reputation as one of the region's deadliest roads, though at weekends you'll wonder how anyone gets up enough speed in the bumper-to-bumper traffic to wreak death and destruction. Pick it up just outside EUR (*see chapter* **Suburbs**) and head through the

soulless dormitory suburbs. If the kids are complaining, take a break in **Spinaceto** where the Iceland ice rink (via A Renzini 145, 06 507 3956) might come as a welcome break.

Before the industrial town of Pomezia (with its factory-door outlets for cheap designer clothes), signs point off to the right (west) for beaches around Torvaianica (*see p277*), a miasma of roasting human flesh in high season. About five kilometres (three miles) south of Pomezia a minor road heads coastwards towards Tor San Lorenzo, where, at a property called **La Landriana**, British landscape architect Russell Page worked with aristocratic owner Lavinia Taverna to create trimly clipped box parterres, some 30 softer-edged garden 'rooms' and much faux-wilderness.

At Aprilia the SS207 forks right to **Anzio**, where the Allies landed in 1944 to launch their victorious march on Rome, and **Nettuno**, with its serried rows of heart-rending white crosses in British and American military cemeteries.

The first cleanish sea south of Rome is at **Sabaudia**. With its striking '30s architecture, the town (set one kilometre/half a mile back from the coast) is a favourite with Italy's holidaying intelligentsia. It owes its miles of largely unspoilt sandy beaches to the fact that it is inside the Parco Nazionale del Circeo. Forget the dusty exhibits in the park's museum and visitors' centre – hire bikes or set out on foot for walks and picnics instead (mosquito repellent is nearly as important as water and sandwiches).

Looming to the south is **Monte Circeo**, where Odysseus was waylaid by the enchantress Circe, who turned his ship's crew into pigs. A hike to the top through cork- and holm-oak forests on the western (seaward) side is spectacular – though best attempted in the cooler months. Or drive most of the way up from the landward side to explore the ancient ruins along the ridge. East of the outcrop, a road winds up to **San Felice Circeo**, a pretty little town and a poseurs' paradise in summer.

When the beach palls, head inland to **Borgo Faiti** between the *vie* Pontina and the Appia. At a farm called Piana delle Orme (via Migliara km43, 0773 258 708, www.pianadelleorme.it, €8/€6 concessions), huge barns contain old military vehicles (used in *The English Patient* and *Life Is Beautiful*) and agricultural equipment, models of the Anzio landing and Battle of Cassino, plus antique toys and interactive scenes of inter-war life and marsh-draining. Home-grown produce is on offer at a shop and restaurant, and there's a well-equipped playground and plenty of space for picnics.

The Pontina merges with the Appia, becoming the SS213 coast road, at **Terracina**, which is a port town with two centres. The

Gardens

La Landriana *See p295.*

Oasi di Ninfa *See p293.*

San Liberato *See p282.*

Villa d'Este *See p287.*

Villa Farnese *See p282.*

Villa Lante *See p283.*

pleasant modern part is down by the sea, while the medieval town above lies on top of the forum of the Roman port of Anxur. Its cathedral was built in a Roman temple to Augustus; above the portico is a 12th-century mosaic frieze, and below it is a big basin that was reputedly used for boiling Christians. The paving slabs in the piazza are from the forum. World War II bombing uncovered the ancient remains and made space for the modern town hall and **Museo Civico di Terracina**. Above the town is the first-century BC **Tempio di Giove** (Temple of Jupiter). Ferries regularly leave port for the holiday resort islands of **Ponza** and **Ventotene** (*see below*).

Between Terracina and Sperlonga the coast is almost all sewn up by private beach clubs. **Sperlonga** itself is a pretty seaside resort. The whitewashed medieval town on the spur overlooking the two beaches – its narrow lanes lined with potted geraniums, boutiques, bars and restaurants – fills with well-heeled Romans in the summer. The **Museo Archeologico di Sperlonga**, at the end of the southerly beach, contains important second-century BC sculptures of scenes from the *Odyssey*; the ticket includes a tour of Tiberius' Villa and Grotto.

There are some pretty sandy coves between Sperlonga and Gaeta, but you will have to pay (around €3) to park on the road and use the steps down to beaches, even if the beaches themselves are *spiagge libere* (free-access beaches). **Gaeta** itself is the last resort along this stretch of coast. The modern lower town clusters around the harbour, while the old medieval walled town has more wall-niche Madonnas than Naples and an impressive 12th-century castle. Serapo beach, to the north, is long, wide and very crowded in summer.

La Landriana

Via Campo di Carne 51, località Tor San Lorenzo, Ardea (06 687 6333/06 9101 4140/fax 06 9101 4441). Open Apr-June 10am-noon, 3-6pm Sat, Sun;

also open same times 3rd Sat & Sun July, 3 days mid Aug, Sept & Oct. **Admission** €6; €3 concessions. **No credit cards**.

Museo Archeologico di Sperlonga & Villa di Tiberio

Via Flacca km16.6, Sperlonga (0771 548 028). **Open** 8.30am-7.30pm daily. **Admission** €2.06. **No credit cards**.

Museo Civico di Terracina

Piazza Municipio, Terracina (0773 707 313). **Open** *May-Sept* 9.30am-1.30pm Mon; 9.30am-1.30pm, 3-9pm Tue-Sat; 10am-1pm, 5-9pm Sun. *Oct-Apr* 9am-1pm Mon; 9am-1pm, 3-7pm Tue-Sat; 9am-1pm, 3-6pm Sun. **Admission** €1.55. **No credit cards**.

Where to eat

In Sabaudia, try **Sirene** (via Lungomare km20.9, località Bufalara, 0773 534 108, closed Dec & Jan, average €35); in winter opening times can be erratic. You can watch the buffaloes that are used to produce the area's renowned mozzarella as they graze outside. **Bottega Sarra 1932** (via Villafranca 34, 0773 702 045, closed Mon, average €35), in Terracina, serves excellent renditions of simple local fare. The family-run **La Bisaccia** (via Romita 25, 0771 548 576, closed Tue & Nov, average €25) in Sperlonga has great fish, while the **Antico Vico** (vico II del Cavallo 2, 0771 465 116, closed Wed, 2wks Nov, 2wks Jan, average €25) in the old quarter of Gaeta is reliable place for well-priced local seafood.

Getting there

By car

For minor destinations, your own transport is essential; for details, *see above*.

By train

Sabaudia, Terracina, Sperlonga, Gaeta: mainline train to Priverno (for buses to Sabaudia and buses/trains to Terracina), Fondi (for buses to Sperlonga) and Formia (for buses to Gaeta).

By bus

Sabaudia, Terracina, Sperlonga: COTRAL services run from EUR Fermi.
Gaeta: take the bus to Latina and change.

By boat

Ponza, Ventotene: from Terracina, SNAP (0773 790 055/700 440/www.snapnavigazione.it) runs daily ferries year-round to Ponza; from Formia, north-east of Gaeta (and on the train line from Rome) Caremar (0771 22 710/85 182) operates one ferry and one hydrofoil daily to Ponza, while Vetor (0771 700 710/85 195/www.vetor.it) runs hydrofoils daily except Wednesday. There are regular connections between Ponza and Ventotene.

Directory

Directory

Getting Around

Arriving & leaving

By air

Rome has two major airports:
Fiumicino, about 30km (18
miles) from the city, handles
all scheduled flights; Ciampino,
about 15km (nine miles) south-
east of the city, is mainly a
military airbase, but is also
used by charter flights.

Aeroporto Leonardo
Da Vinci, Fiumicino

*Via dell'Aeroporto di Fiumicino 320
(switchboard 06 65 951/information
06 6595 3640/4455/www.adr.it).*
Open 24hrs daily.
There is an **express rail service**
between Fiumicino airport and
Termini railway station, which takes
31mins and runs every 30mins from
6.37am until 11.37pm daily (5.51am-
10.51pm to Fiumicino). Tickets in
either direction cost €8.80. The
regular service from Fiumicino
takes 25-40min, and stops at
Trastevere, Ostiense, Tuscolana
and Tiburtina stations. Trains leave
about every 15min (less often Sun)
between 5.57am and 11.27pm
(5.06am-10.36pm to Fiumicino).
Tickets cost €4.70. You can buy
tickets for both these services with
cash or major credit cards from
automatic machines in the airport
lobby and rail stations. They are also
available from the airport rail station
ticket office (open 7am-9.30pm daily)
and the airport *tabacchi*. Some
carriages have access for wheelchair
users (*see also p305*). Stamp your
ticket in the machines on the station
platform before boarding.
  During the night, a **bus service**
(information 800 150 008) runs
between Fiumicino (from outside
Terminal C) and Tiburtina railway
station in Rome. Tickets cost €3.60
from automatic machines or €5 on
the bus. Buses leave Tiburtina at
12.30am, 1.15am, 2.30am and 3.45am,
stopping at Termini railway station
10min later. Departures from
Fiumicino are at 1.15am, 2.15am,
3.30am and 5am. Neither Termini nor
Tiburtina are attractive places at
night, so it's advisable to get a taxi
from there to your final destination.

Buses are scarce; the metro (lines A
and B at Termini; line B at Tiburtina)
closes at 11.30pm (*see also p299*).

Aeroporto GB Pastine,
Ciampino

*Via Appia Nuova 1650 (06 794 941/
www.adr.it).* **Open** 24hrs daily.
The best way into town from
Ciampino is by COTRAL **bus**
(information 06 722 2153) to
Anagnina metro station. Buses
leave from in front of the arrivals
hall every 30-40min, 6.50am-11.40pm
daily (6.10am-11pm to Ciampino),
and the fare is €1. Tickets can be
bought from an automatic machine
in the arrivals hall and at the
newsstand in the departures hall.
For taxis, *see p299* **Taxi tariffs**.

Airlines

Alitalia *Via L Bissolati 11, Veneto
& Borghese (06 65 631/domestic
flights 06 65 641/international
flights 06 65 642/www.alitalia.it).*
*Metro Barberini/bus 61, 62, 116T,
175, 492, 590, 25N, 45N, 60N.*
Open 9am-6pm Mon-Fri. **Credit**
AmEx, DC, MC, V. **Map** p335 1B.
The office at Fiumicino airport
(domestic flights 06 6563 4590/
international flights 06 6563 4951)
is open 24hrs daily.
British Airways *(reservations
199 712 266/www.britishairways.
com/italy).* **Open** 8.30am-7.30pm
Mon-Fri; 9am-5pm Sat. **Credit**
AmEx, DC, MC, V.

By bus

There is no central long-
distance bus station in Rome.
Most coach services terminate
outside these metro stations:
Lepanto, Ponte Mammolo and
Tiburtina (routes north);
Anagnina and EUR Fermi
(routes south). For further
information, *see p275*.

By train

For more information on trains,
and buying tickets, *see p275*.
  Most long-distance trains
arrive at Termini station, also

the centre of the metro and city
bus networks. Beware of
pickpockets. Night trains
arrive at Tiburtina or Ostiense,
both some way from the *centro
storico*. The metro, bus routes
649 and 492, or night bus 40N
run from Tiburtina into the
city centre; if you arrive at
Ostiense after midnight, it's
advisable to take a taxi.
  Some trains also bypass
Termini during the day, while
others stop at more than one
station in Rome; it may be
more convenient to get off at a
smaller station rather than
going all the way into Termini.

Getting around

For transport maps, *see
pp341-343*; for boat travel
on the Tiber, *see p123* **The
yellow Tiber**.

City-centre transport

Rome's transport system is
co-ordinated by ATAC, which
farms out services to other
companies, public or private.
City-centre and inner suburb
destinations are served by the
buses and trams of the
Trambus transport authority.
Increasingly efficient, the
system's easy to use too – once
you've got the hang of it. It's
also fairly safe, even at night.
Gropers and pickpockets tend
to limit their activities to
packed buses on major tourist
routes, notoriously the 64 and
40 Express between Termini
station and the Vatican.

BUSES

Trambus buses are mainly
orange (though some are green
or blue, including the zippy
new supertrams and bendy

buses). Routes are added or suspended and numbers change with some regularity: if you plan to use public transport, pick up a copy of the latest city bus map, available free from ATAC HQ (*see below*).

Regular Trambus services run 5.30am-midnight daily, with a frequency of 10-45mins, depending on the route. The doors for boarding (usually front and rear) and alighting (usually centre) are clearly marked. Each bus stop shows the lines that stop there, and lists the stops each line makes.

Note that the new 'Express' buses are so-called because they make few stops along their route: check before boarding so you don't get whisked past your destination.

A small fleet of electric mini-buses also plies the centre. The 116, 116T, 117 and 119 connect places such as the piazza di Spagna, campo de' Fiori and piazza Venezia with via Veneto and Termini. It's a bit like trundling around on a milk float, but they're handy when it's too hot to walk.

TRAMS

Tram routes mainly serve suburban areas. An express tram service – No.8 – links largo Argentina to Trastevere and the western suburbs.

METRO

MetRo is responsible for Rome's two metro lines: they form a rough cross, with the hub beneath Termini mainline train station. Line A runs from south-east to north-west; line B from EUR to the north-eastern suburbs. Both lines are open 5.30am-11.30pm daily (12.30am Sat). Plans to add a third line remain long-term.

TICKETS

The same tickets are valid on all city bus, tram and metro lines, whether operated by Trambus, MetRo or the regional transport authority COTRAL (*see p275*). They must be bought before boarding, and are available from ATAC automatic ticket machines, information centres, some bars and newsstands, and all *tabacchi* (*see p313*). Tickets can be bought on board night buses, however, where they cost €1 (exact money only).

BIT The *biglietto integrato a tempo* is valid for **75mins**, during which you can use an unlimited number of ATAC buses, plus one metro trip; 77¢.

BIG The *biglietto integrato giornaliero* is valid for **one day**, and covers the whole urban network except express services from Termini station to Fiumicino airport; €3.10.

CIS The *carta integrata settimanale* is valid for **seven days**; it covers all bus routes and the metro system, including the lines to Ostia; €12.40.

Abbonamento mensile Valid **one calendar month** for unlimited travel on the entire metropolitan transport system; €25.80.

BIRG The *biglietto integrato regionale giornaliero* is valid for **one day** on rail journeys within the Lazio region. The price varies from €1.80 to €8, depending on the zone of your destination. Valid on metro, buses, coaches and local mainline trains (second-class), but not on Fiumicino airport railway lines (*see p298*).

When you board, you must stamp tickets in the machines by the rear and/or front doors. At the time of writing, the ticket-issuing system was hybrid: old-style orange tickets must be stamped in the orange machines, new-style tickets in the yellow machines.

Under-tens travel free; older kids pay the adult fare for single, daily and weekly tickets, as do pensioners. Students, pensioners and the disabled pay lower rates for monthly and yearly tickets.

If travelling without paying seems an easy option, bear in mind that you'll be fined €51 on the spot fine if caught by ticket inspectors.

ATAC & MetRo

Via Volturno 65, Esquilino (06 46 951/tollfree information 800 431 784). Metro Termini/bus 16, 38, 86, 90 Express, 92, 217, 360, 492. **Open** *Office* 9am-1pm Mon, Wed, Fri; 9am-1pm, 2.30-5pm Tue, Thur. *Phone line* 8am-6pm Mon-Fri. **Map** p335 2B.

Taxi tariffs

Rome's taxi co-operatives have recently introduced a two-tier tariff system: tariff 1 (clearly visible on the meter in each licensed cab) is for inside the Grand Raccordo Anulare (GRA), Rome's ring road; the much higher tariff 2 is for outside.

The GRA is the huge traffic interchange just minutes after leaving Ciampino; from Fiumicino it's 13 kilometres (eight miles) toward the city centre. Many drivers 'forget' to switch tariffs as they enter the city from either airport. If the 2 continues showing on the meter, ask *la tariffa non si cambia?* ('aren't you going to change the tariff?'). In

general drivers will oblige aimiably; if they don't, copy the taxi number and the name of its co-operative from the metal plaque inside the back door, and demand a receipt (*mi può fare una ricevuta, per favore?*) when you reach your destination. Ask your hotel to lodge a complaint with the co-operative.

A taxi into Rome from Fiumicino will cost at least €40. From Ciampino it will set you back about €36. If you're boarding your taxi at night (10pm-7am) the starting fare will be higher: €4.91 instead of the usual €2.33. Use only white licensed cabs at official ranks (ignore all touts). *See also p301.*

This is ATAC's HQ: the customer services office down the road at No.59 hands out free bus maps. The phone line is Italian-speaking only.

TOUR BUSES

ATAC's city-tour bus (No.110) leaves Termini station every 30min 10am-6pm with an extra departure at 8pm (Apr-Sept 9am-8pm with an extra departure at 9pm). It takes in the Colosseum, Circo Massimo, piazza Venezia, St Peter's, piazza del Popolo and via Veneto, before returning to Termini. The two-hour tour, including a four-language commentary, costs €7.75 non-stop or €12.91 for an all-day stop-'n'-go ticket. You can also buy tickets on board (€8.26 non-stop, €13.94 stop 'n' go).

From Apr to Sept ATAC also offers a three-hour tour of Rome's major basilicas, with English commentary included, costing €7.75. It leaves Termini at 10.30am and 2.30pm, stopping for 30min each at St Peter's, San Paolo fuori le Mura, San Giovanni in Laterano and Santa Maria Maggiore.

The Archeobus passes by the Baths of Caracalla and along the via Appia Antica to the Villa dei Quintili and the Parco degli Acquedotti, leaving piazza Venezia hourly 10am-4pm (Mar-Sept 10am-5pm). Stop-'n'-go tickets cost €7.75 (sold at Termini and piazza Venezia); without stops, the trip takes about two hours.

Tickets for these tours can be bought at booths in front of Termini station or on board. For bookings or information, phone 06 4695 2252/2256 (open Oct-Mar 9.30am-7pm daily, Apr-Sept 9am-8pm daily).

Suburban transport

For transport map, *see p341*. MetRo (*see p299*) operates three suburban railway lines from Termini, Porta San Paolo and Roma Nord stations. Local lines of the Ferrovie dello Stato (FS), the state railway, are also integrated into the city transport network. Ordinary bus, tram and metro tickets are valid on trains as far as the stations in red on the map. COTRAL coaches cover more distant destinations (*see p275*).

Taxis

Licensed taxis are painted white and have a meter. If anyone approaches you at Termini or any of the other major tourist magnets, muttering 'taxi?', always refuse: they're likely to charge up to 400% more than normal rates.

FARES & SURCHARGES

See also p299 **Taxi tariffs**. When you pick up a taxi at a rank or hail one in the street, the meter should read zero. As you set off, it will indicate the minimum fare – at the time of writing €2.33 (€3.36 on Sundays and public holidays or €4.91 if you board 10pm-7am) – for the first 200m (700ft), after which the charge goes up according to time, distance and route. There's a €1.04 charge for each item of luggage placed in the boot.

Most of Rome's taxi drivers are honest; if you do suspect you're being ripped off, make a note of the driver's name and number from the metal plaque inside the car's rear door. The more ostentatiously you do this, the more likely you are to find the fare returning to its proper level. Report complaints to the drivers' co-operative (phone number on the outside of each car) or, in serious cases, the police (*see p311*).

TAXI RANKS

Ranks are indicated by a blue sign with Taxi written on it in white. In the central area there are ranks at largo Argentina, the Pantheon, piazza Venezia, piazza San Silvestro, piazza Sonnino (Trastevere), piazza di Spagna and Termini station.

PHONE CABS

When you phone for a taxi, you'll be given the taxi code-name (always a location followed by a number) and a time, as in *Bahama 69, in tre minuti* ('Bahamas 69, in three minutes'). Radio taxis start the meter from the moment your phone call is answered.

Cooperativa Samarcanda 06 5551/*www.samarcanda.it.* **Credit** AmEx, DC, MC, V.
Cosmos Radio Taxi 06 88 177/06 8822. **Credit** AmEx, DC, MC, V.
Società Cooperativa Autoradio Taxi Roma 06 3570/*www.3570.it.* **Credit** AmEx, DC, MC, V.
Società la Capitale Radio Taxi 06 49 94. **Credit** AmEx, DC.

Trains

For information on train travel to destinations around Rome, *see p275*. For timetable, bookings and general information on mainline rail services anywhere in Italy, call the information line on 892 021 (7am-9pm daily) or consult the state railway's website (www.trenitalia.it).

Mainline trains are operated by Ferrovie dello Stato (FS). Tickets can be bought at stations (over the counter or from machines; both accept all major credit cards) or travel agents with an FS sign. Online credit card purchases can be made on the FS website, with tickets collected from machines in stations. Under-12s pay half fare; under-fours travel free. For information on wheelchair access, *see p305*.

Train timetables can be bought at any *edicola* (newsstand) or checked at www.trenitalia.it; with the information line, there's no guarantee you'll find anyone who speaks English.

Slower trains (*diretti, espressi, regionali* and *interregionali*) are very cheap; a system of supplements means that faster services – InterCity (IC), EuroCity (EC), Eurostar Italia (ES) – are closer to the European norm: the first two cost up to 50% more, Eurostar (not to be confused with Channel tunnel trains) more than twice as much. Advance reservation is obligatory and free on ES trains on Fri and Sun, or all week at peak times of year: this is shown by an R in a square on timetables; check when purchasing your ticket. Booking a seat on IC and internal EC routes costs €3, and is well worth it to avoid standing in packed corridors at peak times. If your ES, IC or EC train arrives more than 30min late – it rarely will – and you've booked a seat, the supplement will be reimbursed at the booth marked *rimborsi*. **You must stamp your ticket and supplements in the yellow machines at the head of each platform before boarding. You will be fined if you don't.**

Rome's principal stations are:

Stazione Ostiense *Piazzale dei Partigiani, Testaccio. Metro Piramide/bus 60 Express, 95, 175, 280, 719, 91N.* **Map** p337 2A.

Stazione Piazzale Flaminio (Roma Nord) *Piazzale Flaminio, Suburbs: north. Metro Flaminio/bus 88, 95, 204, 231, 490, 491, 495, 25N, 55N/tram 2.* **Map** p332 1A.

Stazione Termini *Piazza dei Cinquecento, Esquilino (customer services 06 4730 6599). Metro Termini/bus C, H, 16, 36, 38, 40 Express, 64, 70, 75, 84, 86, 90 Express, 92, 105, 170, 175, 204, 217, 310, 360, 590, 649, 714, 910, 6N, 12N, 40N, 45N, 50N, 55N, 78N, 91N/tram 5, 14.* **Map** p335 2A.

Stazione Tiburtina *Circonvallazione Nomentana, Suburbs: south (car train bookings 06 4730 7184). Metro Tiburtina/bus C, 71, 111, 163, 168, 204, 211, 309, 409, 443, 448, 490, 491, 492, 495, 545, 649, 40N.* **Map** p331.

Stazione Trastevere *Piazzale Biondo, Trastevere. Bus H, 170, 228, 719, 766, 773, 774, 780, 781, 786, 871, 72N, 96N/tram 3, 8.* **Map** p331.

Cars

Having a car in Rome can be great fun, or a huge liability. Roman driving may resemble the chariot race in *Ben-Hur*,

but it's really a high-speed conversation, with its own language of glances, light flashing and ostentatious acceleration.

Short-term visitors should have no trouble driving with their home licences, although if they are written in different scripts or less common languages an international licence can be useful. EU citizens are obliged to take out an Italian driving licence after being resident for one year.

Remember:

● You are required by law to wear a seat belt at all times, and to carry a warning triangle in your car.

● Keep your driving licence, vehicle registration and personal ID documents on you at all times.

● Do not leave anything of value (including the car radio) in your car. Take all your luggage into your hotel when you park.

● Flashing your lights in Italy means that you will not slow down (contrary to British practice).

● Traffic lights flashing amber mean stop and give way to the right.

● Watch out for death-defying mopeds and pedestrians. By local convention, pedestrians assume they have the right of way in the older, quieter streets without clearly designated pavements.

RESTRICTED AREAS

Large sections of the city centre are closed to non-resident traffic during business hours, and sometimes in the evening. Municipal police and electronically activated video cameras guard these areas; any vehicle without the required pass will be fined €68.25 if it enters at restricted times.

Your vehicle may be wheel-clamped if left where it is not allowed or not properly parked: you then have to pay a fine, plus a charge to have the clamp removed. If your car is in a dangerous position or blocking trams and buses, it will be towed away. If you are travelling by car and need to reach accommodation in a restricted area, you should make arrangements with your hotel before arrival.

The first Sunday of most months is designated a no-car day, which is rigidly enforced in the city centre.

BREAKDOWN SERVICES

Before taking a car to Italy it's advisable to join a national motoring organisation, like the AA or RAC in Britain or the AAA in the US. They

have reciprocal arrangements with the Automobile Club d'Italia (ACI), offering breakdown assistance and useful general information. Even for non-members, ACI is the best number to call if you have any kind of breakdown.

If you require extensive repairs, pay a bit more and go to a manufacturer's official dealer: the reliability of any garage depends on long years spent building up a good client-mechanic relationship. Dealers are listed in the Yellow Pages under *auto*, along with specialist repairers such as *gommista* (tyres), *marmitte* (exhausts) and *carrozzerie* (bodywork). The *English Yellow Pages*, available from most English bookshops (*see p211*), has a list of garages where English is spoken.

Automobile Club d'Italia (ACI)

06 49 981/24hr emergency line 116/24hr information line 803 000/traffic report in Italian 1518. The ACI has English-speaking staff and provides services for all foreign drivers, either free or at low prices. Members of associated organisations are entitled to basic repairs free, and to other services at preferential rates. Non-members will be charged, but prices are generally reasonable.

Touring Club Italiano (TCI)

Via del Babuino 20, Tridente (bookshop 06 3600 5281/24hr members' emergency line 800 337 744/www.touringclub.it). Metro Spagna/bus 117, 119. **Open** *Office* 9am-9pm Mon-Fri; 9am-noon Sat. *Bookshop* 9am-7pm Mon-Sat. **Map** p332 A2.

The Rome office has a bookshop with an English-language section and a travel agency with agreements with national and international tour operators. English is spoken and there's a 20% discount on official prices for all members, including those from international sister clubs.

PARKING

A system in which residents park free and visitors pay has recently been introduced to many areas of the city. It's efficiently policed, so watch out for tell-tale blue lines. Parking fees are paid at pay-and-display ticket dispensers (€1/hr). In some areas you can park free after a certain time (usually 11pm) or at weekends, so check the instructions on the machine before paying up. For longer stays, a €25 parking-card set, available from *tabacchi*, saves you scrabbling for small change.

Elsewhere, anything resembling a parking place is up for grabs, with some exceptions: watch out for signs saying *Passo carrabile* ('access at all times') or *Sosta vietata* ('no parking'), and disabled parking spaces (marked by yellow stripes on the road). The sign *Zona rimozione* ('tow-away area') means no parking, and is valid for the length of the street or until the sign is repeated with a red line through it. If a street or square has no cars parked in it, assume it's a seriously enforced no-parking zone. In some areas, self-appointed *parcheggiatori* will 'look after' your car for a small fee; it may be illegal and a ridiculous imposition, but it's worth coughing up to ensure your tyres remain intact.

Cars are fairly safe in most central areas, but you may prefer the hefty rates charged by underground car parks to ensure your vehicle is not tampered with. The following are centrally located.

ParkSì Villa Borghese Società Italinpa

Viale del Galoppatoio 33, Veneto & Borghese (06 322 5934/7972). Metro Spagna/bus 88, 95, 116, 204, 490, 491, 495. **Open** 24hrs daily. **Rates** *Cars* €1.15/hr for up to 3hrs; 90¢/hr for 4-15hrs; €14.45 for 16-24hrs. *Scooters & motorbikes* €2.30 for 24hrs. **Credit** AmEx, DC, MC, V. **Map** p334 2C.
Vehicle entrances are on via del Muro Torto (from both sides of the road). The car park is linked to the Spagna metro station, with 24hr pedestrian access to piazza di Spagna.

Valentino

Via Sistina 75E, Veneto & Borghese (06 678 2597). Metro Spagna/bus 590. **Open** 7am-1am Mon-Sat; 7am-12.30pm, 6pm-1am Sun. **Rates** €18.08-€25.82 for 24hrs. **Credit** AmEx, MC, V. **Map** p335 1C.

CAR POUNDS

If your car isn't where you left it, it has probably been towed. Phone the municipal police (Vigili urbani) on 06 67 691 and quote your number plate to find out which pound it's in.

PETROL

Petrol stations sell unleaded petrol (*senza piombo* or *verde*) and diesel (*gasolio*). Liquid propane gas is GPL. Most stations offer full service on weekdays; pump attendants do not expect tips. At night and on Sundays many stations have automatic self-service pumps that accept €5, €10, €20 and €50 notes, in good condition. Unofficial 'assistants' sometimes do the job for you for a small tip (€1).

VEHICLE HIRE

To hire a car you must be over 21 – in some cases 23 – and have held a licence for at least a year. You will be required to leave a credit card number or substantial cash deposit. It's advisable to take out collision damage waiver (CDW) and personal accident insurance (PAI) on top of basic third party cover. Companies not offering CDW are best avoided.

Avis

Via Sardegna 38A, Veneto & Borghese (06 4282 4728). Metro Spagna/bus 52, 53, 95, 116, 116T, 119, 204. **Open** 8am-8pm Mon-Fri; 8am-5pm Sat; 8am-1pm Sun. **Credit** AmEx, DC, MC, V. **Map** p334 2B.
Fiumicino airport (06 6595 4146/06 6501 1531). **Open** 7am-midnight daily.
Ciampino airport (06 7934 0195). **Open** 8am-1.30pm, 2-8.30pm, 9-10pm Mon-Fri; 8.10am-2.45pm, 4.30-8.30pm, 9-10pm Sat; 8.10am-noon, 4.30-8.30pm, 9-10pm Sun.
Termini station, Esquilino (06 481 4373). Metro Termini/bus C, H, 16, 36, 38, 40 Express, 64, 70, 75, 84, 86, 90 Express, 92, 105, 170, 175, 204, 217, 310, 360, 590, 649, 714, 910/tram 5, 14. **Open** 7am-8pm Mon-Fri; 8am-1pm Sun. **Map** p335 2A.

Maggiore

Fiumicino airport (06 6501 0678/tollfree 848 867 067). **Open** 6.30am-12.30am daily. **Credit** AmEx, DC, MC, V.
Termini station, Esquilino (06 488 0049). Metro Termini/bus C, H, 16, 36, 38, 40 Express, 64, 70, 75, 84, 86, 90 Express, 92, 105, 170, 175, 204, 217, 310, 360, 590, 649, 714, 910/tram 5, 14. **Open** 7am-8pm Mon-Fri; 8am-6pm Sat; 8.30am-1pm Sun.
Ciampino airport (06 7934 0368). **Open** 8am-10pm Mon-Fri; 8.10am-1pm, 3-5pm, 7-10pm Sat, Sun.

MOPED, SCOOTER AND CYCLE HIRE

To hire a scooter or moped (*motorino*) you need a credit card, photo ID and/or a cash deposit. Helmets are required on all motorbikes, scooters or mopeds (the police are very strict about this). For mopeds up to 50cc you need to be over 14; a driver's licence is required for anything over 50cc. For bicycles, you can normally leave ID rather than pay a deposit.

Apart from the companies listed below, there are useful pay-and-ride bike-hire stands with similar rates outside Spagna metro, in piazza del Popolo, by the car park under Villa Borghese, at a tiny bar in piazza di Ponte Milvio (it's at the start of a cycle path that takes you out of central Rome along the Tiber), in piazza San Lorenzo in Lucina, and in via San Leo. Enjoy Rome (*see p315*) and Romarent (*see below*) offer guided bike tours.

Happy Rent

Via Farini 3, Monti (06 481 8185/www.happyrent.com). Metro Termini/bus 16, 75, 84, 105, 204, 360, 590, 649, 714/tram 5, 14. **Open** 9am-7pm daily. **Credit** AmEx, DC, MC, V. **Map** p335 2A.
Friendly outlet with special offers and tourist advice. Also rents out Smart cars and electric Ligier models (no driving licence required).
Daily rate: mopeds (50cc) €33; scooters (250cc) €65; motorbikes €89; cars from €65.

Romarent

Vicolo dei Bovari 7A, Ghetto & Campo de' Fiori (phone/fax 06 689 6555/www.romarent.net). Bus 46, 62, 64, 116, 116T, 916. **Open** 8.30am-7pm daily. **Credit** AmEx, DC, MC, V. **Map** p333 2A.
As well as bike, motorbike and moped hire, Romarent offers guided bike and scooter tours.
Daily rate: bicycles €9-€12; mopeds €18-€50; motorbike (650cc) €95-€115.

Scoot a Long

Via Cavour 302, Monti (06 678 0206). Metro Cavour/bus 75, 84, 117, 204. **Open** *Apr-Sept* 9am-8pm daily; *Oct-Mar* 10am-7pm daily. **Credit** AmEx, MC, V. **Map** p338 1C.
This company offers student discounts. A €350 deposit or credit card number, plus passport, is needed.
Daily rate: mopeds from €30; scooters (125cc) €40; motorbikes €90.

Scooters for Rent

Via della Purificazione 84, Veneto & Borghese (06 488 5485). Metro Barberini/bus 52, 53, 61, 62, 63, 80 Express, 95, 116, 119, 175, 204, 492, 590, 630. **Open** 9am-7pm Mon-Sat; 9am-6pm Sun. **Credit** AmEx, DC, MC, V. **Map** p335 1C.
Special weekly rates available. A deposit of €154.94 or credit card number is required.
Daily rate: mopeds €25.82; scooters (125cc) €41.32, (250cc) €103.29.

Treno e Scooter Rent

Piazza dei Cinquecento, Esquilino (06 4890 5823/fax 06 4891 9539). Metro Termini/bus C, H, 16, 36, 38, 40 Express, 64, 70, 75, 84, 86, 90 Express, 92, 105, 170, 175, 204, 217, 310, 360, 590, 649, 714, 910/tram 5, 14. **Open** 8.30am-7.30pm daily. **Credit** AmEx, DC, MC, V. **Map** p335 2A.
Located on Termini station forecourt near the taxi rank, this is a joint venture between the railway and Piaggio.
Rate: scooters €23.50-€41.50 (4hrs), €41.50-€59.50 (day), €165 (wk); bicycles €5.50-€9.50 (day), €18-28 (wk).

Resources A-Z

Accommodation

The Enjoy Rome (see p315) and Hotel Reservation (see p39) agencies offer free booking, the latter with a shuttle service to/from Fiumicino airport. See also chapter **Accommodation**.

Age restrictions

Cigarettes and alcohol cannot be sold to under-16s. Over-14s can ride a moped or scooter of 50cc; no licence is required.

Business

If you're doing business in Rome, stop in at your embassy's (see p306) commercial section. There you will find trade publications, reports, databases of fairs, buyers, sellers and distributors and advice. In Italy personal recommendations smooth your way immensely: use any you have shamelessly.

Business centres

Finding temporary office space can be difficult. Try these for basic facilities, and conference and secretarial services.
Centro Uffici Parioli *Via Lima 41, Suburbs: north (06 8530 1350/ fax 06 8449 8332/www.aniur.com). Bus 53, 168, 360/tram 3, 19.*
Pick Center *Via Attilio Regolo 19, Prati (06 328 031/fax 06 3280 3227/www.pickcenter.com). Bus 81.*

Conferences

Rome offers superb facilities for conferences in magnificent *palazzi* and castles. Most major hotels cater for events of all sizes; if you don't wish to handle the details, a number of agencies can help.
Rome At Your Service *Via VE Orlando 75, Esquilino (06 484 583/ 06 482 5589/fax 06 484 429/ www.romeatyourservice.it). Metro Repubblica/bus 36, 60 Express, 61, 62, 84, 175, 492, 590, 910.*
Map *p335 1B.*

Studio Ega *Viale Tiziano 19, Suburbs: north (06 328 121/fax 06 324 0143/www.ega.it). Bus 52, 204, 231, 910/tram 2.*
Tecnoconference Europe srl *Via A Luzio 66, Suburbs: east (06 7835 9617/fax 06 7835 9385/ www.tecnoconference-europe.com). Bus 87.*
Triumph Congressi *Via Lucilio 60, Suburbs: north (06 355 301/fax 06 3553 0235/www.gruppotriumph.it). Bus 990.*

Couriers

International couriers include:
DHL *06 790 821/199 199 345/ www.dhl.it*
Federal Express *tollfree 800 123 800/www.fedex.com*
TNT *tollfree 803 868/fax 06 2326 7420/www.tntitaly.it*
UPS – United Parcel Service *tollfree 800 877 877/www.ups.com*

For local deliveries, try:
Easy Rider *06 5823 7506*
Presto *06 3974 1111/ www.prestoexpress.it*
Speedy Boys *06 39 888/ www.speedyboys.it*

Interpreters

CRIC *Via dei Fienili 65, Capitoline & Palatine (06 678 7950/fax 06 679 1208/www.cric-interpreti.com).*

Customs

Within the following limits, EU citizens do not have to declare goods imported into or exported from Italy for personal use, as long as they're travelling from or to another EU country:

800 cigarettes or 400 small cigars or 200 cigars or 1kg (35.27oz) of tobacco; ten litres of spirits (over 22% alcohol) or 20 litres of fortified wine (under 22% alcohol).

Limits for non-EU citizens are:
200 cigarettes or 100 small cigars or 50 cigars or 250 grams (8.82oz) of tobacco; one litre of spirits (over 22% alcohol) or two litres of fortified wine (under 22% alcohol); 50 grams (1.76oz) of perfume.

There are no restrictions on the import of cameras, watches or electrical goods. Visitors can carry up to €10,329.14 in cash.

Disabled travellers

Rome is a difficult city for disabled people, especially wheelchair-users. You'll almost certainly have to depend on other people more than you would at home.

Narrow streets make life difficult for those who can't flatten themselves against a wall to let passing vehicles by, while the cobblestones turn wheelchairs with excellent suspension into bone-rattlers and getting on to pavements is well-nigh impossible due to bumper-to-bumper parked cars. Off the streets, there are old buildings with narrow corridors and, if there are lifts, they're generally too small.

Blind and partially sighted people often find there's no kerb between the road proper and that bit of street pedestrians are entitled to walk on (the one exception is a smooth brick walkway laid into the cobbles leading from the Trevi Fountain to piazza Navona, with braille notes about various landmarks on bronze plaques along the way).

Information

Information for disabled people is available from Enjoy Rome (see p315) and the APT tourist office (see p315).

CO.IN

06 712 9011/www.coinsociale.it.
Open 9am-6pm Mon-Fri.
CO.IN publishes the free multilingual *Roma Accessibile*, which should be available at the APT (see p315) – but often isn't. Fully revised for 2000, it lists disabled facilities at museums, restaurants, shops, theatres, stations and hotels, and has a map showing disabled parking places. To get a copy, phone or write to CO.IN directly (via E Giglioli 54A/via Torricola 87); CO.IN will pay for it to be sent anywhere in Europe. The group also organises transport equipped for disabled people (up to eight places), which must be booked several days in advance but can cover airport journeys as well as

travel within Rome, and runs a phone information service in Italian and English that offers up-to-date information for the whole country (tollfree 800 271 027; open 9am-5pm Mon-Fri, 9am-1pm Sat). It can only be dialled from within Italy.

Roma per Tutti

06 7162 3919/www.romapertutti.it. **Open** 9am-5pm Mon-Fri.
An information line run by CO.IN (*see above*) and the city council. English-speaking staff answer questions on accessibility in hotels, buildings and monuments.

Sol.Co.Roma

Piazza Vittorio Emanuele 31, Esquilino (06 490 821/fax 06 491 623/www.solcoroma.net). Metro Vittorio/bus 71, 105, 360, 590, 649/tram 5, 14. **Open** 9am-7pm Mon-Fri. **Map** p338 A1.
Sol.Co's new free guide *Cammina Cammina* (with CD-Rom) was published in December 2002. With information and itineraries in Italian and English, plus simple symbols, it's easy to follow.

Transport

Rome's buses and trams are being made accessible to wheelchairs. Orange-red, silver and green bendy buses are already adapted for wheelchairs, as are the newest-generation trams (with extra-large central doors and an access ramp). As this guide went to press, these buses served the routes listed (but were often used on other routes too). There are no wheelchair-friendly night buses.

H, 04, 23, 30 Express, 36, 40 Express, 44, 60 Express, 64, 75, 80 Express, 86, 90 Express, 105, 170, 280, 310, 492, 660, 714, 719, 780, 791, 913. Electric buses (116, 117, 118, 119), tram 8 and some trams on lines 3 and 19 can also take wheelchairs.

On the metro, line A is something of a no-go area. All stations on line B have lifts, disabled WCs and special parking spaces, except Circo Massimo, Colosseo and Cavour (southbound).

Most taxi drivers will carry (folded) wheelchairs; when you can, phone for a cab rather than hailing one in the street (*see p301*).

To ascertain which trains have wheelchair facilities, call (or visit) the Ufficio disabili (office for the disabled) at the station from which you plan to depart (beside platform 1 at Termini, 06 488 1726) or consult the official timetable (there's a wheelchair symbol next to accessible trains). The disabled traveller or their representative must phone or fax the Ufficio disabili of the appropriate station 24hr prior to departure and go, before boarding the train, to fill in and sign a form requesting assistance. Reserve a seat when buying your ticket, and make sure you arrive 45min before departure.

This procedure also applies to all trains to and from Fiumicino airport. You should call or fax your airline to arrange assistance the day before arrival; in practice, you'll be helped on the train anyway.

Both Rome's airports have facilities such as adapted toilets and waiting rooms. Inform your airline of your needs: it will contact the office at Fiumicino or Ciampino.

Sightseeing

Well-designed ramps, lifts and toilets have been installed in many attractions, including the Vatican Museums and Castel Sant'Angelo, Galleria Doria Pamphili, Palazzo delle Esposizioni, Museo della Civiltà Romana, Museo delle Navi Romane, St Peter's, San Giovanni in Laterano and Palazzo Venezia, the Galleria Nazionale d'Arte Moderna and Galleria Borghese, and the Bioparco-Zoo. CO.IN's Roma per Tutti (*see p305*) provides further up-to-date information.

Museum

Fax 06 540 2762/www.assmuseum.it. This volunteer group offers tours of some galleries and catacombs for individuals or groups with mobility or, especially, visual problems. A

small voluntary donation to cover costs is requested. Museum guides – some speak English; if they don't, an interpreter can be arranged – have braille notes, copies of some major paintings in relief, and permission to touch sculptures and other artefacts. Guides also make works of art comprehensible to the non-sighted with music cassettes and recorded text. Send a fax for general info or bookings (English spoken).

Where to stay & eat

The number of accessible hotels has increased recently – CO.IN (*see p304*) has details – but cheaper hotels and *pensioni*, often housed on upper floors of *palazzi*, can be a problem. If you have special needs, make them known when you book.

Local by-laws now require restaurants to have disabled access and toilets; in practice, few have made the necessary alterations. If you phone ahead and ask for an appropriate table, most will try to help. In summer, the range of outdoor restaurants makes things easier, but getting to toilets can be almost impossible.

Most bars open on to the street at ground level, and/or have tables outside. Again, most bar toilets are tiny dark holes down long staircases.

Toilets

Wheelchair-accessible public toilets, some even with lifts that work without keys or assistance, are numerous in many central areas… which is no guarantee they'll be in working order or open. The ATAC bus company, in collaboration with the city council, is equipping various bus termini with adapted loos.

Wheelchair hire

Ortopedia Colosseo

Via dei Santi Quattro 60, Celio & San Giovanni (06 700 5709). Bus 85, 117, 850. **Open** 8am-1pm, 6.30-7pm Mon-Fri; 8am-1pm Sat. **No credit cards. Map** p338 2A.

Directory

Rents all kinds of wheelchairs – including antiques – from €20 per day. These can be delivered by taxi: you pay the fare unless you are in one of the larger hotels with which the shop has an agreement.

Drugs

If caught in possession of drugs of any type, you'll be taken before a magistrate. Convince him or her that the tiny quantity you were carrying was for purely personal use, and you'll be let off with a fine or ordered to leave the country. Habitual offenders will be offered rehab. Anything more than a tiny amount pushes you into the criminal category: couriering or dealing can land you 20 years inside. It's an offence to buy, sell or even give away drugs. Sniffer dogs are a fixture at most ports of entry; the customs police take a dim view of visitors entering with even the smallest quantities of narcotics, with those caught nearly always refused entry.

Electricity

Most wiring systems work on 220V – compatible with British-bought appliances, but US 110v equipment requires a current transformer. Adaptors can be bought at any electrical or hardware shop (look for *elettricità* or *ferramenta*).

Embassies & consulates

For a full list of embassies, see *Ambasciate* in the phone book.

Listed below are embassies of the larger English-speaking countries. Except where indicated, consular offices (which provide most services of use to tourists) share the same address as embassies.

Australia *Via Alessandria 215, Suburbs: north (06 852 721/ www.australian-embassy.it). Bus 36, 60 Express, 62, 84, 90 Express, 490, 491, 495.* **Map** p334 2A.

Britain *Via XX Settembre 80A, Esquilino (06 4220 0001/fax 06 4220 2334/www.britain.it). Bus 36, 60 Express, 61, 62, 84, 90 Express, 490, 491, 495.* **Map** p335 1A.

Canada *Embassy: via GB de Rossi 27, Suburbs: north (06 445 981/ www.canada.it). Bus 93, 168, 310, 445, 542. Consulate: via Zara 30, Suburbs: north (06 445 981). Bus 36, 60 Express, 62, 84, 90 Express.*

Ireland *Piazza Campitelli 3, Ghetto (06 697 9121/irish.embassy@ libero.it). Bus H, 30 Express, 44, 63, 81, 95, 160, 170, 204, 628, 630, 715, 716, 780, 781.* **Map** p336 1A.

New Zealand *Via Zara 28, Suburbs: north (06 441 7171/ www.nzembassy.com). Bus 36, 60 Express, 62, 84, 90 Express.*

South Africa *Via Tanaro 14, Suburbs: north (06 852 541/ www.sudafrica.it). Tram 3, 19.* **Map** p334 1A.

USA *Via Vittorio Veneto 119, Veneto & Borghese (06 46 741/ www.usembassy.it). Metro Barberini/bus 52, 53, 61, 62, 63, 80 Express, 95, 116, 116T, 119, 175, 204, 590, 630.* **Map** p335 1B.

Emergencies

See also p313 **Safety & security**; *below* **Health**; *p311* **Police**; *p310* **Money**.

Thefts or losses should be reported immediately at the nearest police station (*see p311*). Report the loss of your credit card/travellers' cheques immediately to your credit card company (*see p311*), and of your passport to your consulate/embassy (*see above*).

National emergency numbers

Police *Carabinieri* (English-speaking helpline) 112; *Polizia di stato* 113.
Fire service *Vigili del Fuoco* 115.
Ambulance *Ambulanza* 118.
Car breakdown *See p302.*

Domestic emergencies

Report a malfunction in any of the main services to these 24hr emergency lines.

Electricity *ACEA* 06 57 991/ emergency tollfree 800 130 332.
Gas *Italgas* 06 57 391/ tollfree 800 900 999.
Telephone *Telecom Italia* 187.
Water *ACEA tollfree* 800 130 335.

Health

For an ambulance, call 118.

Emergency health care is available through the Italian national health system; by law, hospital accident and emergency departments (*see below*) must treat all emergency cases free. If you are an EU citizen, the E111 form (*see p308*) entitles you to free consultation with any doctor. Non-EU citizens should consider private health insurance (*see p308*).

Accident & emergency

If you need urgent medical care, go to the *pronto soccorso* (casualty department). All the hospitals listed below offer 24hr casualty services. If your child needs emergency treatment, head straight for the Ospedale Bambino Gesù.

Ospedale Fatenbenefratelli
Isola Tiberina, Ghetto (06 683 7299). Bus H, 23, 63, 280, 630, 780/tram 8. **Map** p336 2A.
Ospedale Pediatrico Bambino Gesù
Piazza Sant'Onofrio 4, Gianicolo (06 68 591/www.opbg.net). Bus 870. **Map** p333 2C.
Ospedale San Camillo-Forlanini
Via Portuense 332, Suburbs: west (06 55 551). Bus H, 228, 710, 719, 773, 774, 786, 791/tram 8.
Ospedale San Giacomo *Via Canova 29, Tridente (06 36 261/322 7069). Metro Spagna/bus 117, 119, 590.* **Map** p332 2A.
Ospedale San Giovanni *Via Amba Aradam 8, San Giovanni (06 77 051). Metro San Giovanni/bus 81, 117, 650, 673, 714.* **Map** p339 1A.
Policlinico Umberto I *Viale Policlinico 155, Suburbs: north (06 49 971/446 2341). Metro Policlinico/bus 61, 310, 490, 491, 495, 649/tram 3, 19.*

Contraception & abortion

Condoms (*preservativi*) are relatively inexpensive and on sale near checkouts in supermarkets or over the counter in pharmacies; the pill is available on prescription.

Abortion, available on financial hardship or health grounds, is legal only when performed in public hospitals.

Despite funding cuts and pressure from the right-wing Lazio regional government, most districts maintain a local health authority *consultorio familiare* (family planning clinic). EU citizens with an E111 form pay the same low charges as locals. The most centrally located are:

Piazza Castellani 23, Trastevere (06 7730 6006). Bus 23, 280. **Open** 8.30am-1pm Tue, Thur, Fri; 8.30am-1pm, 2.30-5.30pm Mon, Wed. **Map** p336 1B.

Via San Martino della Battaglia 16, Esquilino (06 7730 5505). Metro Termini/bus C, 38, 75, 86, 92, 204, 217, 310, 360, 492, 649. **Open** 2-6pm Mon, Thur; 8am-1pm Tue, Wed, Fri. **Map** p335 1A.

These private gynaecological clinics are also recommended:

AIED

Via Toscana 30, Veneto & Borghese (06 4282 5314). Metro Barberini/bus 52, 53, 63, 80 Express, 630. **Open** 9am-7pm Mon-Fri; 9am-1pm Sat. **Credit** MC, V. **Map** p334 2B. Offers check-ups, contraceptive advice, menopause counselling and smear tests. You buy a membership card (*tessera*) for €5, then check-ups cost €36.50. Smear tests are €15.50; follow-up visits are free.

Artemide

Via Sannio 61, San Giovanni (06 7047 6220). Metro San Giovanni/bus 87, 360. **Open** 10am-7pm Mon-Fri. **No credit cards. Map** p339 1A. Gynaecological check-ups here are €70, smear tests are €25, and there's a wide range of other tests and services. Appointments can be made at 24hrs notice and emergencies are invariably dealt with immediately.

Dentists

For serious dental emergencies, use hospital casualty departments (*see p306*).

Most dentists (see *Dentisti* in the Yellow Pages) in Italy work privately; treatment isn't cheap and may not be covered by your health insurance, but you can wait months for a dental appointment in a national health service hospital

(children are somewhat better served at the out-patients department of the Ospedale Bambino Gesù, *see p306*).

Doctors

EU nationals with an E111 form (*see p308*) can consult a national health service doctor free of charge, with any drugs prescribed bought at chemists at prices set by the Health Ministry. Tests and out-patient treatment are charged at fixed rates too. Non-EU nationals who consult a health service doctor will be charged a small fee at the doctor's discretion.

Hospitals

Rome's public hospitals (*see p306*) offer good-to-excellent treatment, though nursing may appear slack to anyone used to Anglo-Saxon hospitals.

Opticians

See p229.

Pharmacies

Farmacia (identified by a green cross) give informal medical advice, as well as making up prescriptions. Most also sell homeopathic and veterinary medicines, and all will check your height/weight/ blood pressure on request. Make sure you know the chemical (generic) rather than brand name of your regular medicines: they may only be available under a different name. The best-stocked pharmacy in the city is in the Vatican: it has a whole range of medicines not found elsewhere in Italy.

Normal opening hours are 8.30am-1pm, 4-8pm Mon-Sat. Outside normal hours, a duty rota system operates. A list by the door of any pharmacy (also published in local papers) indicates the nearest ones that are open at any time. There is a surcharge of €4.91 per client

(not per item) when only the special duty counter is open.

Farmacia della Stazione *Piazza dei Cinquecento, Esquilino (06 488 0019). Metro Termini/bus C, H, 16, 36, 38, 40 Express, 64, 70, 75, 84, 86, 90 Express, 92, 105, 170, 175, 204, 217, 310, 360, 590, 649, 714, 910, 6N, 12N, 40N, 45N, 50N, 55N, 78N, 91N/tram 5, 14.* **Open** 24hrs daily. **Credit** AmEx, DC, MC, V. **Map** p335 2A.

Farmacia del Vaticano *Porta Sant'Anna entrance, Vatican (06 6988 3422). Metro Ottaviano-San Pietro/bus 23, 32, 49, 62, 81, 492, 590, 982, 990/tram 19.* **Open** 8.30am-6pm Mon-Fri; 7.30am-1pm Sat. **Credit** MC, V. **Map** p333 1C.

Piram *Via Nazionale 228, Esquilino (06 488 0754). Metro Repubblica/bus H, 40 Express, 60 Express, 64, 70, 71, 116T, 170, 78N, 91N.* **Open** 24hrs daily. **Credit** AmEx, DC, MC, V. **Map** p335 2B.

Helplines & agencies

Alcoholics Anonymous

06 474 2913. An active English-speaking support group holds meetings at the church of St Paul's Within the Walls at via Napoli 56. Phone for meeting times.

Associazione Differenza Donna

Viale Villa Pamphili 100, Suburbs: west (06 581 0926/24hr emergency line 06 2326 9049). Bus 44. **Map** p338 1C. A helpline for victims of sexual violence. The women-only volunteers (some English-speaking) offer support and legal assistance.

Samaritans

06 7045 4444/4445. Staffed by native English speakers.

Telefono Azzurro

19 696. **Open** 24hrs daily. A freephone helpline for children and young people with abuse problems (normally Italian-speaking only).

Telefono Rosa

06 3751 8261. **Open** 10am-1pm, 4-7pm Mon-Fri. Offers counselling and legal advice for women who have been victims of sexual abuse or sexual harassment.

ID

You are required by law to carry photo ID with you at all times. You must produce it if stopped by traffic police (along

Directory

with your driving licence, which you must have on you when you're in charge of a motor vehicle) and when you check into a hotel. Smaller hotels may try to hold on to your passport/ID card for the length of your stay; you are within your rights to ask for it back.

Insurance

See *also p306* **Health**; and *p311* **Police**.

EU nationals are entitled to reciprocal medical care in Italy, provided they have an E111 form (available in the UK from health centres, post offices and Social Security offices). This covers you for emergencies, but using it naturally involves dealing with the intricacies of the Italian state health system: for short-term visitors it's better to take out private health cover. Non-EU citizens should take out private medical insurance before setting off.

Visitors should also take out adequate property insurance. If you rent a car, motorcycle or moped, make sure you pay the extra for full insurance cover and, for a car, sign the collision damage waiver (CDW).

Internet & email

Most budget hotels allow you to plug a modem into their phone system; more upmarket places should have PC points. There are also ever more internet points around Rome.

A number of Italian ISPs offer free access, including Caltanet (www.caltanet.it), Libero (www.libero.it), Tiscali (www.tiscalinet.it), Kataweb (www.kataweb.com) and Telecom Italia (www.tin.it).

Bibli
Via dei Fienaroli 28, Trastevere (06 588 4097/www.bibli.it). Bus 780, H/tram 8. **Open** 5.30pm-midnight Mon; 11am-midnight Tue-Sun. **Rates** €4/30min, €6/hr; €31/10hrs. **Credit** MC, V. **Map** p336 2B.
Quiet backstreet bookshop, cultural centre, restaurant and internet point.

EasyEverything
Via Barberini 2, Trevi & Quirinale (06 4290 3388/www.easyeverything. com). Metro Barberini/bus 52, 53, 61, 62, 63, 80 Express, 95, 116, 119, 175, 204, 492, 590, 630. **Open** 24hrs daily. **Rates** €1.55/30min peak (usually 4-7pm); €1.55/3hrs off-peak. **No credit cards. Map** p335 1B.
Three floors, 350 computer terminals (with webcam and scanner), printer and fax service… and a coffee bar.

The Netgate
Piazza Firenze 25, Tridente (06 687 9098/www.thenetgate.it). Bus 116, 116T. **Open** 8.30am-8.30pm Mon-Sat; 9am-1pm Sun. **Rates** €3.20/hr; €1.30/10min mail check; €27.20/10hrs; discounts for students. **No credit cards. Map** p333 1A.
This clinical but very functional internet point has 35 workstations, and offers laser printing, fax, scanning and digital photo services.

Left luggage

The left luggage office by platform 24 of Termini station is open 7am-midnight daily; as we went to press, lockers were to be installed there too. Fiumicino airport has left-luggage offices in both international (24hrs daily) and domestic (7.15am-11.15pm daily) terminals. Hotel staff are generally willing to look after your luggage during the day, even after you've checked out.

Legal help

Legal advice should first be sought at your embassy or consulate (*see p306*).

Libraries

Rome's libraries are dogged by red tape, restricted hours and patchy organisation. All libraries listed here are open to the public; other specialist libraries can be found under *Biblioteche* in the phone book. Always take ID along; in some cases, a letter from your college or tutor stating the purpose of your research will be required.

Archivio Centrale dello Stato (State Archives)
Piazzale Archivi 27, Suburbs: EUR (06 545 481/fax 06 541 3620). Metro EUR Fermi/bus 703, 707, 765, 767. **Open** 9am-7pm Mon-Fri; 9am-1pm Sat. Closed Aug. **Map** p331.
The original documents, historical correspondence and many other items at this efficiently run archive have to be consulted *in situ* (most can be photocopied). Arrive before noon to order the ones you want.

Biblioteca Alessandrina
Piazzale Aldo Moro 5, Esquilino (06 447 4021). Metro Policlinico/bus C, 71, 204, 492. **Open** 8.30am-7.30pm Mon-Fri; 8.30am-1pm Sat. Closed 2wks Aug. **Map** p159.
La Sapienza's (*see p313*) main library is grossly inefficient for the needs of Europe's largest university. Books must be requested by 6.30pm Mon-Fri and 12.30pm Sat.

Biblioteca Nazionale
Viale Castro Pretorio 105, Esquilino (06 49 891/www.bncrm.librari. beniculturali.it). Metro Castro Pretorio/bus C, 204, 310, 492, 649. **Open** 8.30am-7pm Mon-Fri, 8.30am-1.30pm Sat. Closed 2wks Aug. **Map** off p335 1A.
The national library holds 80% of everything that's in print in Italy, as well as books in other languages. A computerised catalogue system was installed in 2001, allowing access via internet to library archives dating from 1987.

Biblioteca dell'Università Gregoriana
Piazza della Pilotta 4, Trevi & Quirinale (06 67 011). Bus H, 40 Express, 60 Express, 62, 63, 64, 70, 81, 85, 95, 117, 119, 160, 170, 175, 204, 492, 628, 630, 850. **Open** 8am-6.30pm Mon-Fri; 8am-noon Sat. Closed Aug. **Map** p335 2C.
Better organised than Biblioteca Alessandrina (*see above*), but this not a lending library: books here are not allowed off the premises.

Biblioteca Vaticana
Via di Porta Angelica, Vatican (06 6987 9411). Metro Ottaviano/bus 23, 32, 49, 62, 81, 492, 590, 982, 990/tram 19. **Open** (postgrads only) 9am-5.30pm Mon-Fri. Closed mid July-mid Sept. **Map** p333 1C.
To gain an entrance card, students need a letter on headed paper, signed by a professor, stating their research purpose. This must be presented between 9am and noon.

British Council Library

*Via Quattro Fontane 20, Trevi &
Quirinale (06 478 141/www.
britishcouncil.it). Metro Barberini/bus
H, 40 Express, 60 Express, 64, 70,
116T, 170.* **Open** 10am-12.30pm
Mon, Fri; 2-5pm Wed. **Map** p335 2B.
A good resource centre for those
teaching English.

The British School
at Rome

*Via Gramsci 61, Veneto & Borghese
(06 326 4931/www.bsr.ac.uk). Bus
52, 231, 926/tram 19.* **Map** p334 1C.
The reading room (closed for
refurbishment until autumn 2003)
has English and Italian books on all
aspects of Rome, especially art
history, archaeology and topography.
Students need two photos and a letter
from a museum or university to get
in; no lending facilities.

Lost property

Anything mislaid on public
transport, or stolen and
subsequently discarded, may
turn up at one of the lost
property offices below.

Ufficio oggetti smarriti

*Via Bettoni 1, Trastevere
(06 581 6040/tollfree 800 431
784/www.atac. roma.it). Bus 170,
719, 781/tram 8.* **Open** 8.30am-
noon Mon, Wed, Fri; 8.30am-noon,
2.30-5pm Tue; 8.30am-5pm Thur.
Map p337 2B.
Anything found on the city bus and
tram network, on the metro or in a
post office may turn up here.

MetRo

*Line A (Termini) 06 487 4309/
Line B (Piramide) 06 5753 2264.*
Open 8.30am-12.30pm Mon-Fri.

COTRAL

With no central lost property
office, enquiries can be made at
Anagnina (06 722 2153), Lepanto
(06 324 4724), Tiburtina (06 4424
2419), Laurentina (06 591 0531),
Ponte Mammolo (06 418 2135) or
Saxa Rubra (06 332 8331).

Ferrovie dello Stato/
Stazione Termini

*Termini station, platform 24,
Esquilino. Metro Termini/bus C, H,
16, 36, 38, 40 Express, 64, 70, 75,
84, 86, 90 Express, 92, 105, 170,
175, 204, 217, 310, 360, 590, 649,
714, 910.* **Open** 7am-midnight daily.
Map p335 2A.
Items found on FS trains anywhere
in Rome are sent to this collection
point; the office is part of the left-
luggage office.

Media

Magazines

Panorama and *L'Espresso*
provide a generally high-
standard round-up of the
week's news, while *Sette* and
Venerdì – colour supplements
of *Corriere della Sera* (Thur)
and *La Repubblica* (Fri)
respectively – have nice
photos but are textually
unsatisfying; *La Repubblica*'s
Saturday supplement *D* is
the best of the lot. For tabloid-
style scandal, try the weird
mix of sex, glamour and
religion in *Gente* and *Oggi*,
or the execrable *Eva 3000,
Novella 2000* and *Cronaca
Vera. Internazionale* (www.
internazionale.it) provides
an excellent and readable
digest of bits and pieces
gleaned from the world's
press over the previous
week. *Diario della Settimana*
(www.diario.it) offers informed
and urbane investigative
journalism. But the biggest-
seller is *Famiglia Cristiana*
– available from newsstands
and in most churches – which
alternates between Vatican
line-toeing and Vatican-
baiting, depending on the
current state of relations
between the Holy See and the
idiosyncratic Paoline monks
who produce it.

National dailies

Long, indigestible political
stories with very little
background explanation
predominate in Italian
newspapers. On the plus
side, they're delightfully
unsnobbish and happily
blend serious news, leaders
by internationally known
commentators, and well-
written, often surreal, crime
and human-interest stories.
Sports coverage is extensive
and thorough; if you need
more, there are the mass-
circulation sports papers

*Corriere dello Sport,
La Gazzetta dello Sport*
and *Tuttosport*.

Corriere della Sera

www.rcs.it
To the centre of centre-left, this solid,
serious but often dull Milan-based
paper is good on crime/foreign news.

Il Manifesto

www.ilmanifesto.it
A reminder that there is still some
corner of central Rome where hearts
beat Red.

La Repubblica

www.repubblica.it
Rome-based, centre-ish, left-ish and
good on the Mafia and the Vatican.
Comes up with the occasional major
scoop on its business pages.

La Stampa

www.lastampa.it
Part of the massive empire of
Turin's Agnelli family; it features
good (though of course pro-Agnelli)
business reporting.

Local dailies

La Repubblica and *Corriere
della Sera* (*see above*) have
large daily Rome sections.

Il Messaggero

www.messaggero.it
A fixture on top of the ice-cream
cabinet of every Roman bar, this is
the Roman daily *per excellenza*.
Particularly useful classified ads –
with many flat rents – on Saturdays.

L'Osservatore Romano

www.vatican.va
The Vatican's official newspaper
was an organ for liberal Catholic
thought during the 1960s and '70s.
Now, under the guiding hand of
Opus Dei, it reflects the conservative
orthodoxies issuing from the top.
Weekly English edition on Wed.

Il Tempo

www.iltempo.it
A high-circulation right-wing paper.

Foreign press

The *Financial Times, Wall
Street Journal, USA Today,
International Herald Tribune*
(with its *Italy Daily* supplement)
and most European dailies can
be found on the day of issue at
most central newsstands; US
dailies can take 24hrs to appear.

Directory

Listings & small ads

Porta Portese

www.porta-portese.it
Essential reading for anyone looking for a place in Rome (to rent or buy). Published Tue and Fri, it also has sections on household goods and cars. Place ads free on 06 70 199.

Roma C'è

www.romace.it
Comprehensive listings for theatre, music venues, dance, film and nightlife every Wed, with English-language section.

Solocase

www.solocase.it
Houses for sale and rent. Out on Sat.

Trovaroma

Free with *La Repubblica* every Thur; includes a pared-back but useful English-language section on the week's concerts, exhibitions and guided tours.

Wanted in Rome

www.wantedinrome.com
Essential information and upmarket housing ads for expats.

Radio

These state-owned stations play classical and light music, with chat shows and regular, excellent news bulletins:
RAI 1 89.7 MHz FM, 1332 KHz AM
RAI 2 91.7 MHz FM, 846 KHz AM
RAI 3 93.7 MHz FM, 1107KHz AM
www.rai.it

For UK and US chart hits, mixed with home-grown offerings, try:
Radio Capital 95.8 MHz FM/www.capital.it
Radio Centro Suono 101.3 MHz FM/www.radiocentrosuono.it
Radio Città Futura 97.7 MHz FM/www.radiocittafutura.it
Italy's most PC 24hr station
Radio Kiss Kiss Network 97.25 MHz FM/www.kisskissnetwork.it
Radio 105 96.1 MHz FM/www.105.net
Vatican Radio 105 MHz FM, 585 KHz MW/www.vaticanradio.org
World events, as seen by the Catholic church, broadcast in English.

Television

Italy has six major networks (three owned by state broadcaster RAI, three by Silvio Berlusconi's Mediaset group), together with two channels that operate across most of the country: La7 and MTV. Bored of these? Any number of local stations will provide hours of compulsively awful channel-zapping.

The standard of TV news and current affairs varies, but most offer a breadth of international coverage that makes British TV news look like a parish magazine. La7 broadcasts CNN in English from about 4am, while RAI 3 supplements 2pm, 7pm and 10.30pm news programmes with regional round-ups.

Money

See also p314 **Tax**.
The Italian currency is the euro, with banknotes of €5, €10, €20, €100, €200 and €500, and coins worth €1 or €2 plus 1¢, 2¢, 5¢, 10¢, 20¢ and 50¢ *(centesimi)*. Coins and notes from any Eurozone country are valid tender.

ATMs

Most banks have 24hr cash-point (Bancomat) machines, though some shut down late at night on weekends. The vast majority accept cards with the Maestro and Cirrus symbols, and will dispense the daily limit of €250.

Banking hours

Most banks open 8.30am-1.45pm, 2.45-4.30pm Mon-Fri. Some central branches now also open until 6pm Thur and 8.30am-12.30pm Sat. All banks close on public holidays, and staff work reduced hours the day before a holiday (many closing by 11am).

Bureaux de change

Banks usually offer better exchange rates than private bureaux de change *(cambio)*.

It's a good idea to take a passport or other ID whenever, particularly if you're changing travellers' cheques or making a credit card withdrawal. Commission rates vary (you can pay from nothing to €5 for each transaction) and beware 'no commission' signs: the rate will probably be terrible.

Many city-centre bank branches have automatic cash exchange machines, which accept most currencies (notes in good condition only), and main post offices also have exchange bureaux (€2.58 commission and €2,582.28 limit on each transaction; no travellers' cheques).
See p311 **Postal services**.

American Express

Piazza di Spagna 38, Tridente (06 67 641). Metro Spagna/bus 52, 53, 61, 71, 80 Express, 85, 117, 119, 160, 850. **Open** 9am-5.30pm Mon-Fri; 9am-12.30pm Sat. **Map** p335 1C.
Travellers' cheque refund service, card replacement, poste restante, a cash machine that can be used with AmEx cards, and 24hr money-transfer from any other AmEx office.

Thomas Cook – Travelex

Piazza Barberini 21, Veneto & Borghese (06 4202 0150/fax 06 482 8085). Metro Barberini/bus 52, 53, 61, 62, 63, 80 Express, 95, 116, 119, 175, 204, 492, 590, 630. **Open** *June-Sept* 9am-8pm Mon-Sat; 9.30am-5pm Sun; *Oct-May* 9am-7pm Mon-Sat; 9.30am-5pm Sun. **Map** p335 1B.
The Thomas Cooks in Rome are among the very few exchange offices open Sun. A 2.5% commission is charged on all transactions apart from Thomas Cook, MasterCard and travellers' cheques, which are cashed free of charge. MasterCard holders can also withdraw money here.
Branches: via della Conciliazione 23-5 (06 6830 0435); via del Corso 23 (06 320 0224); Metro B Colosseo (06 4782 5894).

Credit cards

Italians have an enduring fondness for cash, but it's getting easier to persuade them to take plastic. Nearly all hotels of two stars and above now accept at least some of the major credit cards.

If you lose a credit or charge card, phone one of the emergency numbers below. All lines have English-speaking staff and are open 24hrs daily.
American Express 06 7228 0371; US cardholders 800 874 333.
Diner's Club 800 864 064
Eurocard/CartaSì 800 018 548
MasterCard 800 870 866
Visa 800 877 232

Police

The principal Polizia di Stato station, the Questura Centrale, is at via Genova 2 (06 46 861). Others, and the Carabinieri's *Commissariati*, are listed in the phone directory under *Polizia* and *Carabinieri*. Incidents can be reported to either.

Postal services

For postal information, call 160.
Big improvements have been made in Italy's once-notorious postal service (www.poste.it): you can now be more or less sure your letter will arrive in reasonable time. If you harbour lingering doubts about the Italian post, the Vatican Post Office (*see below*) is run in association with the Swiss postal service.

Most postboxes are red and have two slots, *per la città* (for Rome) and *tutte le altre destinazioni* (everywhere else).

The new equivalent to first-class post, *posta prioritaria*, generally works very well: it promises 24hr delivery in Italy, three days for EU countries and four or five for the rest of the world; more often than not it succeeds. A letter of 20g or less to Italy or another EU country costs 62¢ by *posta prioritaria*; outside the EU it's 77¢. Special stamps can be bought at post offices and *tabacchi*; letters can be posted in any box. (Stamps for slower regular mail are also sold at post offices and *tabacchi*.) Letters weighing up to 20g cost 41¢ to EU countries and 52¢ to non-EU European

countries, the US, Canada, Australia and New Zealand.

The CAI-Posta Celere service (available only in main post offices) costs somewhat more than *posta prioritaria* and delivers at the same speed. The advantage is that you can track the progress of your letter on the website (www.poste.it) or by phoning 160 (8am-8pm Mon-Sat).

Registered mail (*raccomandata*) costs €2.17 over the normal rate.

Parcels can be sent from any post office. It is advisable to send any package worth more than €51.65 insured.

There are local post offices (*ufficio postale*) in each district, which open 8.25am-6pm Mon-Fri (8.25am-2pm Aug), and 8.25am-1.30pm Sat and any day preceding a public holiday. They close two hours earlier than normal on the last day of each month. Main post offices in the centre of town have longer opening hours and offer a range of additional services, including fax facilities.

Posta Centrale
Piazza San Silvestro 18-20, Tridente (06 679 5044/information 803 160). Bus 52, 53, 61, 71, 80 Express, 85, 116, 116T, 117, 119, 160, 850. **Open** 8.30am-6.30pm Mon-Fri; 8.30am-1pm Sat; 9am-noon last Sat of mth. **Map** p335 2C.
This is the hub of Rome's postal system, although other main post offices offer similar services. Letters sent poste restante/general delivery (*fermo posta*) to Rome should be addressed to Roma Centro Corrispondenza, Posta Centrale, piazza San Silvestro, 00186 Roma. You'll need your passport to collect and have to pay a small charge. The fax service opens until 8.30pm.

Other main offices
Piazza Bologna 39, Suburbs: east (06 4423 8115). Metro Bologna/bus 61, 62, 93, 168, 309, 310, 445, 542.
Via Marmorata 4, Testaccio (06 574 3783). Metro Piramide/bus 23, 30 Express, 75, 280, 673, 716, 719/tram 3. **Map** p337 2A.
Viale Mazzini 101, Suburbs: north (06 377 091). Bus 30 Express, 88, 495. **Map** p332 1B.

Via Taranto 19, Suburbs: south (06 772 791). Metro San Giovanni/bus 85, 55N.
Via Terme di Diocleziano 30, Esquilino (06 474 5602). Metro Termini or Repubblica/bus C, H, 16, 36, 38, 40 Express, 64, 70, 75, 84, 86, 90 Express, 92, 105, 170, 175, 204, 217, 310, 360, 590, 649, 714, 910/tram 5, 14. **Map** p335 2A.

Poste Vaticane
Piazza San Pietro, Vatican (06 6988 3406). Metro Ottaviano-San Pietro/bus 23, 32, 49, 62, 81, 492, 590, 982, 990/tram 19. **Open** 8.30am-7pm Mon-Sat. **Map** p333 1C.

Queuing

Lining up one behind the other doesn't come easy to Romans, but, despite the chaos, queue-jumpers are given short shrift. Hanging back deferentially, though, is taken as a clear sign of stupidity – if you're not careful the tide will sweep contemptuously past you. In busy shops and bars, be aware of who is in front of and behind you; when it's your turn, be emphatic.

Religion

For papal audiences, *see p145*.
There are over 400 Catholic churches in the city, but very few hold mass in English. The main British Catholic church is **San Silvestro** (piazza San Silvestro 17A, 06 679 7775); **San Patrizio** (via Boncompagni 31, 06 4201 3123) is the principal Irish church; the American Catholic church is **Santa Susanna** (via XX Settembre 14, 06 4201 4554).

Anglican
All Saints, via del Babuino 153B, Tridente (06 3600 1881). Metro Spagna/bus 117, 119, 590. **Services** 8.30am, 10.30am, 6pm Sun. **Map** p332 2A.
The church opened in 1887, but the chaplaincy dates from 1816, when services were held in the chaplain's rooms in piazza di Spagna. All Saints hosts an active programme of cultural events, including regular, high-quality concerts. Times are liable to change, so phone ahead.

Directory

Episcopal

St Paul's Within the Walls, via Napoli 58, Esquilino (06 488 3339/www.stpaulsrome.it). Metro Repubblica/bus H, 40 Express, 60 Express, 64, 70, 116T, 170. **Services** 8.30am, 10.30am, 1pm (in Spanish) Sun. **Map** p335 2B.

Jewish

Comunità Israelitica di Roma, lungotevere Cenci, Ghetto (06 684 0061). Bus H, 23, 63, 280, 630, 780. **Map** p336 2A.
There are daily services, but times vary. Guided tours of the synagogue are offered from the Museo d'Arte Ebraica (*see p113*).

Methodist

Ponte Sant'Angelo Church, via del Banco di Santo Spirito, Pantheon & Navona (06 686 8314). Bus 40 Express, 46, 46B, 62, 64, 98, 280, 870, 881, 916. **Services** 10.30am Sun. **Map** p333 1B.

Muslim

Moschea di Roma, viale della Moschea, Suburbs: north (06 808 2167). Train to Campi Sportivi/bus 230, 231.
Paolo Portoghesi's masterpiece is always open to Muslims for prayer. Non-Muslims can visit 9-11.30am Wed and Sat.

Presbyterian

Saint Andrew's, via XX Settembre 7, Veneto & Borghese (06 482 7627). Bus 36, 60 Express, 61, 62, 84, 175, 492, 590, 910. **Services** 11am Sun. **Map** p335 1B.

Relocation

To help newcomers get started, Welcome Neighbor (06 3036 6936) is a group of English-speaking experts who organise talks on various aspects of living in Rome.

Anyone staying here is obliged by the Italian state to pick up a whole series of forms and permits. The basic set is described below. EU citizens should have no difficulty getting their documentation once they are in Italy, but non-EU citizens are advised to enquire at an Italian consulate before travelling. There are agencies that specialise in obtaining documents for you if you can't face the procedures yourself –

at a price (see *Pratiche e certificati – agenzie* in the Yellow Pages).

Carta d'identità (identity card)

You'll need three passport photographs, a *permesso di soggiorno* (*see below*), and a special form that will be given to you at your *circoscrizione* – the local branch of the central records office, which eventually issues the ID card. Look in the phone book (*Comune di Roma: Circoscrizioni*) for your area's office.

Codice fiscale & Partita IVA (tax code & VAT number)

A *codice fiscale* is essential for opening a bank account or setting up utilities contracts. Take your passport and *permesso di soggiorno* (*see below*) to your local tax office (*ufficio delle entrate, see below*). Fill in a form and return a few days later to pick up the card. It can be posted on request.

The self-employed or anyone doing business in Italy may also need a *Partita IVA*. The certificate is free. Most people pay an accountant to handle the formalities. Take your passport and *codice fiscale* to your nearest tax office; it will be a long wait. Cancel your VAT number when you no longer need it: failure to do so may result in a visit from tax inspectors years later.

Call the Finance Ministry's information line or consult its website (848 800 444/www.finanze.it) for information on *uffici delle entrate* (revenue offices); addresses are also in the phone book under *Ministero delle Finanze*. Which office you should go to depends on the city district (*circoscrizione*) you live in; offices open 9am-1pm Mon, Wed, Fri; 9am-1pm, 2.50-4.50pm Tue, Thur.

Permesso/carta di soggiorno (permit to stay)

EU citizens need a *permesso di soggiorno* if they're staying in Italy for over three months; non-EU citizens should (but usually don't) apply for one within eight days of arrival in Italy. Take three passport photographs, your passport, and proof that you have some means of support and reason to be in Italy (preferably a letter from an employer or certificate of registration at a school or university) to the nearest *Commissariato* (police station; see the phone book under *Polizia di Stato*) or the *Questura Centrale* (main police station; via Genova 2, 06 46 861) between 8.30am and noon

(people start queuing before 7am). For information call 06 4686 3058. The *carta* (card) *di soggiorno* is similar to the *permesso* but allows you to stay in Italy indefinitely: it has to be renewed every ten years. EU citizens who have been resident in Italy for at least five years and also have a renewable *permesso di soggiorno* can request a *carta*. If a foreigner already has a *carta*, their spouse can also request one at the *Questura Centrale*.

Permesso di Lavoro (work permit)

In theory, all non-Italians employed in Italy need a work permit. Application forms can be obtained from the Ispettorato del Lavoro (via Cesare de Lollis 6, 06 445 0334; open 9am-noon Mon, Wed, Fri; 2.45-4.30pm Tue, Thur). The form must be signed by your employer, then taken back to the Ispettorato with your *permesso di soggiorno* and a photocopy. Don't rush into the process: often the requirement is waived, or your employer arranges it for you.

Residenza (residency)

This is your registered address in Italy. You'll need it to buy a car, get customs clearance on goods brought from abroad and many other transactions. Take your *permesso di soggiorno* (*see above*; it must be valid for at least another year) and your passport to your local *circoscrizione* (*see above*). Staff will check that rubbish-collection tax (*nettezza urbana*) for your address has been paid (ask your landlord about this) before issuing the certificate.

Accommodation

Again, try *Porta Portese*, *Wanted in Rome* (for both, see *p310*) and English-language bookshops (*see p211*). Look out for *affittasi* ('for rent') notices on buildings, and check the classifieds in *Il Messaggero* (Thur, Sat). When you move into an apartment, it's normal to pay a month's rent in advance, plus two months' deposit (it should be refunded when you move out, but some landlords create problems over this). You'll probably get a year's renewable contract. Renting through an agency will cost the equivalent of two months' rent in commission.

Directory

Bank accounts

To open an account you'll need a valid *residenza* or *permesso di soggiorno*, proof of regular income (or a fairly substantial deposit) and your passport.

Work

Casual employment can be hard to find, so try to sort out work in advance. English-language schools and translation agencies are mobbed with applicants, so qualifications and experience count. The classified ads paper *Porta Portese* has lots of job ads. Other good places to look are *Wanted in Rome* (for both, see p310) and noticeboards in English-language bookshops (see p211). You can also place ads in any of the media above. For serious jobs, check *Il Messaggero* and *La Repubblica*, or these agencies:

Adecco

Via Ostiense 91A, Testaccio (06 574 5701/fax 06 5713 5133/www.adecco. it). Metro Piramide/bus 23, 60 Express, 118, 280, 716, 719, 769/tram 3. **Open** 9am-12.30pm, 2-5.30pm Mon-Fri. **Map** p338 1B.
The call centre is based on via Ostiense 93 (06 574 0207).

Manpower

Via Barberini 58, Trevi & Quirinale (06 4287 1339/fax 06 4287 0833/www.manpower.it). Metro Barberini/bus 52, 53, 61, 62, 63, 80 Express, 95, 116, 119, 175, 204, 492, 590, 630. **Open** 9am-6pm Mon-Fri. **Map** p335 1B.
Branch: via Molajoni 70 (06 4353 5349/fax 06 4353 5357).

Muggings are fairly rare in Rome, but pickpockets and bag snatchers are particularly active in the main tourist areas. Below are a few basic precautions:
● Don't carry wallets in back pockets, particularly on buses. If you have a bag or camera with a long strap, wear it across the chest and not dangling from one shoulder.

● Keep bags closed, with your hand on them. If you stop at a pavement café or restaurant, don't leave bags or coats where you cannot see them.
● When walking down a street, hold cameras and bags on the side of you towards the wall – you're less likely to become the prey of a motorcycle thief or *scippatore*.
● Avoid groups of ragged children brandishing pieces of cardboard, or walk by quickly keeping hold of your valuables. They wave the cardboard to distract while accomplices pick your pockets or bags.

If you are the victim of crime, call the police helpline (see p311) or go to the nearest police station and say you want to report a *furto* (theft). A *denuncia* (written statement) of the incident will be made. It's unlikely your things will be found, but you will need the *denuncia* for insurance claims.

Smoking

For cigarettes, *see below* **Tabacchi**.
Public offices (post offices, police stations and so on), public transport and restaurants (except those with special smoking areas) are all no smoking; so are a growing number of bars.

Study

See also p308 **Libraries**.
The state universities – **La Sapienza** (www.uniroma1.it), **Tor Vergata** (www.uniroma2.it) and **Roma Tre** (www.uniroma3.it) – plus the private **LUISS** (www.luiss.it) offer exchanges with other European universities. All EU citizens have the same right as Italians to study in Rome's universities, paying the same fees. Get your certificates translated and validated by the Italian consulate in your own country before lodging your

application at the *ufficio stranieri* (foreigners' department) of the university of your choice. Several American universities have campuses in Rome, which students attend on exchange programmes, and private Catholic universities run some of Italy's most highly respected medical faculties. Specialist bookshops are mostly near La Sapienza in San Lorenzo or viale Ippocrate.

Bureaucracy & services

Foreigners studying any course in Italy must obtain a permit to stay (see p312). Student offices in the universities themselves will help, and there are private agencies that take care of enrolment formalities.

Centro Turistico Studentesco (CTS)

Via Genova 16, Monti (06 462 0431). Bus H, 40 Express, 60 Express, 64, 70, 116T. **Open** 9am-1pm, 2.30-6.30pm Mon-Fri; 9.30am-1pm Sat. **Credit** DC, MC, V. **Map** p335 2B.
CTS issues discount cards for travel, hostels or language courses.

Nuovo Centro Servizi Universitari

Viale Ippocrate 160, Esquilino (tel/fax 06 445 7768/www.cstonline. it). Metro Policlinico/bus 310, 29N, 30N, 40N/tram 3, 19. **Open** 9am-1pm, 3.30-6pm Mon-Fri. **Credit** AmEx, DC, MC, V.
This agency deals with enrolment, exam registration and all other time-consuming details, for foreigners and locals. There's a €10 membership fee.

Tabacchi

Tabacchi or *tabaccherie* (identifiable by signs with a white T on black or blue) are the only places where you can legally buy tobacco products. They also sell stamps, telephone cards, tickets for public transport, lottery tickets and the stationery required for dealing with Italian

Directory

bureaucracy. Most *tabacchi* keep shop hours, but many are attached to bars and so stay open into the night.

Tax

For tax-free shopping, *see p209.*

Sales tax (IVA) is charged at varying rates on most goods and services. It is almost invariably quoted as an integral part of prices, with occasional exceptions including top-end hotels and some tradespeople. The implication from the latter is that, by paying cash and not demanding a receipt, you won't have to pay the 19% or so IVA.

Telephones

Dialling & codes

There are three main types of number in Rome:

● Land-lines have the area code 06, which must be used whether calling from within or outside the city. They generally have eight digits, although some older numbers may have seven or fewer. If you can't get through, the number may have changed to eight digits; check the directory or ring enquiries (12 or 412).

● All numbers beginning 800 are tollfree lines (until recently they began 176; if you find old-style numbers still listed, replace the prefix with 800). Numbers beginning 840 and 848 (147 and 148 until recently) are charged at low set rates, no matter where you're calling from or how long the call lasts. These numbers can be called from within Italy only; some of them only function within a single phone district.

● Mobile numbers begin with a 3, until recently 03; if you see an 03 number, don't dial the 0.

Rates

Competition has brought Telecom Italia charges down, though they remain some of Europe's highest (particularly for international calls). Calls cost more from public phones. Keep costs down by phoning off-peak (6.30pm-8am Mon-Sat, all day Sun). Hotel phones may carry extortionate surcharges.

Public phones

Rome has no shortage of public phone boxes and many bars have payphones. Most only accept phone cards (*schede telefoniche*); a few also accept major credit cards. Phone cards cost €1, €2.50, €5 and €7.75 and are available from *tabacchi* (*see p313*), some newsstands and some bars. Beware: phone cards have expiry dates (usually 31 Dec or 30 June), after which they're useless. Vatican City has its own special phone cards, available from the Vatican post offices (*see p311*) and usable only within the city-state. Public coin phones accept 10¢, 20¢, 50¢ or €1 coins; the minimum call is 10¢.

International calls

For international calls from Rome, dial 00, followed by the country code, area code (omit the initial zero of area codes in the UK) and number. Codes include: Australia 61; Canada 1; Irish Republic 353; New Zealand 64; United Kingdom 44; United States 1.

To phone Rome from abroad, dial the international code (00 in the UK), then 39 for Italy and 06 for Rome, followed by the individual number.

Operator services

To reverse the charges (make a collect call), dial 170 for the international operator in Italy or (to be connected to the operator in the country you're

calling) dial 172 followed by a four-digit code for the country and telephone company you want to use (for the UK/Ireland this is the same as the country code; for other countries see the phone book). If you're reversing the charges from a phone box, you insert a 10¢ coin (refunded after your call).

The following services operate 24hrs daily:
Operator and Italian Directory Enquiries 12
International Operator 170
International Directory Enquiries 176
Communication problems (national calls) 187
(international calls) 176
Wake-up calls 114; an automatic message asks you to dial in the time you want your call (on a 24hr clock) followed by your phone number.

Mobile phones

See also above **Dialling & codes**.
GSM phones can be used on both 900 and 1800 bands; British, Australian and New Zealand mobiles work fine, but US mobiles are on a different frequency that doesn't work.

Nolitel

Via Sicilia 54, Veneto & Borghese (06 4200 7001/www.nolitel.it). Bus 52, 53, 63, 80 Express, 88, 95, 116, 116T, 119, 204, 630, 910. **Credit** AmEx, DC, MC, V. **Map** p334 B. €5.16 daily, €26.90 weekly for dual-band mobiles (plus €103.29 deposit).

Fax

Faxes can be sent from most large post offices (*see p311*), charged by the number of sheets sent. Page rates are €1.30 within Italy or €5.10 for Europe. Some photocopying outlets also send faxes. In all cases, the surcharge is hefty. Do-it-yourself fax/phones can be found in main stations and at Fiumicino airport.

Telegrams & telexes

These can be sent from main post offices. The telegraph office at the Posta Centrale on piazza San Silvestro (entrance 18; *see p311*) is open 8.30am-6.30pm Mon-Fri, 8.30am-1pm Sat. You can also dictate telegrams over the phone: dial 186 from a private phone and a message in Italian tells you to dial the number of the phone you're phoning from; you're then passed to a telephonist who takes your message.

Time

Italy is one hour ahead of London, six hours ahead of New York, eight behind Sydney and 12 behind Wellington. In all EU countries clocks are moved forward one hour in early spring and back in late autumn.

Tipping

Foreigners are expected to tip more than Italians, but the 10% customary in many countries is considered generous even for the richest-looking tourist. Most locals leave 10¢-20¢ on the counter when ordering drinks at a bar and, depending on the quality of the restaurant, €1-€5 for the waiter. Many large restaurants now include a 10-15% service

charge. Tips are not expected in family-run restaurants, but even here a couple of euros are appreciated. Taxi drivers will be happy if you round the fare up to the nearest whole euro.

Toilets

If you need a toilet, the easiest thing to do is go to a bar (it won't necessarily be clean or provide toilet paper). There are modern lavatories at or near most major tourist sites, most with attendants to whom you must pay a nominal fee. Fast-food joints and department stores may also meet the need.

Tourist information

The offices of Rome's tourist board, APT, and the state tourist board, ENIT, have English-speaking staff, but surprisingly limited information. For more personal service, Enjoy Rome is highly recommended. The city council now also has well-stocked green-painted tourist information kiosks (PIT) that open 9.30am-7.30pm daily (apart from the Termini branch: open 8am-9pm daily).

APT (Azienda per il Turismo di Roma)

Via Parigi 5, Esquilino (06 3600 4399/www.romaturismo.com). Metro Repubblica/bus 16, 36, 60 Express, 61, 62, 84, 90 Express, 116T, 175, 492, 590, 910. **Open** *Office* 9am-7pm Mon-Sat. *Phoneline* 9am-7.30pm daily. **Map** p335 1B.
Branches: Fiumicino airport (06 3600 4399).

Enjoy Rome

Via Marghera 8A, Esquilino (06 445 1843/fax 06 445 0734/www. enjoyrome.com). Metro Termini/ bus C, H, 16, 36, 38, 40 Express, 64, 70, 75, 84, 86, 90 Express, 92, 105, 170, 175, 204, 217, 310, 360, 590, 649, 714, 910. **Open** *Nov-Mar* 8.30am-6.30pm Mon-Fri; 8.30am-2pm Sat. *Apr-Oct* 8.30am-7pm Mon-Fri; 8.30am-2pm Sat. **No credit cards.** **Map** p335 2A.
This friendly English-speaking private agency is handy for information (Rome and further afield) and advice. The office provides a free accommodation booking service and arranges walking and cycling tours.

PIT (Punti Informativi Turistici)

Piazza Pia, Vatican & Prati (06 6880 9707). Bus 23, 34, 40 Express, 62, 280, 982. **Map** p333 1C.
Largo Goldoni, Tridente (06 6813 6061). Bus 81, 117, 119, 204, 590, 628. **Map** p333 1A.
Piazza delle Cinque Lune, Pantheon & Navona (06 6880 9240). Bus 30 Express, 70, 81, 87, 116, 116T, 186, 204, 492, 628. **Map** p333 1A.

Carry the card

In what looks like a laudable attempt to counter euro-driven rises in ticket prices, Rome's city council has sponsored new discount cards to take the financial sting out of your holiday.

Go.card

www.gocard.org
Available to anyone aged 18 to 30, this card is valid for one year and gives hefty discounts at many of Rome's major sights, as well as shops, bars, cinemas and other participants in the scheme. Still under trial as this guide went to press, the card is free (there's a request form on the website) until July 2003, after which it costs around €6.

RomeKey Card

Information from PIT (see p315)
This three-day card costs €18 and allows unlimited use of city buses, trams and metros, free entrance to the Musei Capitolini (*see p62*) and Centrale Montemartini (*see p159*) and one guided bus tour of the city. There's also a booklet of vouchers giving discounts of around 50% for most of Rome's other major sights, plus various discounts for shops, cinemas and other participants, as well as car hire. Cards can be purchased at PITs (*see above*; credit AmEx, DC, MC, V). A **RomeKey Card Plus**, costing around €28 and including health insurance and other benefits was in the pipeline too.

Directory

Time Out Rome **315**

Piazza San Giovanni in Laterano, San Giovanni (06 7720 3535). Metro San Giovanni/bus 16, 85, 87, 117, 186, 650, 714, 850. **Map** p338 2A.

Via dell'Olmata, Monti (06 474 0955). Bus 16, 70, 71, 75, 204, 360, 590, 649, 714. **Map** p338 1B.

Piazza dei Cinquecento, Esquilino (06 4782 5194). Metro Termini/bus C, H, 16, 36, 38, 40 Express, 64, 70, 75, 84, 86, 90 Express, 92, 105, 170, 175, 204, 217, 310, 360, 590, 649, 714, 910/tram 5, 14. **Map** p335 2A.

Piazza del Tempio della Pace, Capitoline & Palatine (06 6992 4307). Bus 60 Express, 75, 85, 87, 117, 175, 186, 810, 850. **Map** p338 1C.

Via Nazionale, Trevi & Quirinale (06 4782 4525). Bus H, 40 Express, 60 Express, 64, 70, 71, 116, 116T, 170. **Map** p335 1A.

Piazza Sonnino, Trastevere (06 5833 3457). Bus H, 23, 280, 630, 780/tram 8. **Map** p336 2B.

Via Minghetti, Tridente (06 678 2988). Bus 62, 63, 81, 85, 95, 117, 119, 160, 175, 204, 492, 628, 630, 850. **Map** p335 2C.

Termini station, platform 4, Esquilino (06 4890 6300). Metro Termini/bus C, H, 16, 36, 38, 40 Express, 64, 70, 75, 84, 86, 90 Express, 92, 105, 170, 175, 204, 217, 310, 360, 590, 649, 714, 910. **Map** p335 2A.

Fiumicino airport, terminal B (06 6595 4471).

Ufficio Pellegrini e Turisti

Piazza San Pietro, Vatican (06 6988 1662). Bus 23, 34, 40 Express, 62, 280, 982. **Open** 8.30am-6.45pm Mon-Sat. **Map** p333 1C.
The Vatican's own tourist office.

Water

Most of Rome's water comes from a vast underground lake to the north and is completely safe for drinking. Some areas of the *centro storico* still get water through the ancient aqueducts from springs in the countryside: this water is so good that Romans come from outside the centre to fill up plastic containers with it.

When to go

For information on annual events in the city, *see chapter* **Festivals & Events**.

Climate

Rome can sizzle at close to 40°C in July and Aug, when humidity levels can also be high. Spring and autumn are usually warm and pleasant, although there may be occasional heavy showers, particularly in March, April and September. Between November and February the weather is unpredictable: you may find brilliant, crisp (or sometimes even warm) sunshine… or non-stop torrential downpours. The compensation? A relative scarcity of other tourists.

Public holidays

On public holidays (*giorni festivi*) virtually all shops, banks and businesses close, although (with the exception of May Day, 15 August and Christmas Day) bars and restaurants tend to stay open.

New Year's Day (Capodanno) 1 Jan
Epiphany (La Befana) 6 Jan
Easter Monday (Pasquetta)
Liberation Day 25 Apr
May Day 1 May
Patron Saints' Day (San Pietro e San Paolo) 29 June
Feast of the Assumption (Ferragosto) 15 Aug
All Saints (Tutti santi) 1 Nov
Immaculate Conception (Festa dell'Immacolata Concezione) 8 Dec
Christmas Day (Natale) 25 Dec
Boxing Day (Santo Stefano) 26 Dec

There's limited public transport on 1 May and Christmas afternoon.

Women

Rome is a safe city for women. Stick to central areas and you can even walk alone late at night without wishing you'd brought your mace. If you do find yourself being hassled, take comfort in the fact that Italian men are generally all mouth and no trousers. Common sense is usually enough to keep potential harassers at bay: if you're not

interested, ignore them and they'll probably go away, or duck into a bar and they'll give you up as a lost cause.

Young Roman blades head for piazza Navona, piazza di Spagna and Fontana di Trevi to pick up foreign talent. If you'd rather enjoy Rome's nocturnal charm in peace, stick to the areas around campo de' Fiori, Testaccio or Trastevere. The Termini station area gets seriously seedy after sundown.

Accommodation

The vast majority of Rome's hotels and pensions are perfectly suitable for women. If you're worried, avoid those near Termini station and via Nazionale (a major shopping artery that's pretty much deserted once the shops shut) and stick to more populated areas in the *centro storico*.

Health

See also p306 **Health**.
In case of gynaecological emergencies, head for the nearest *pronto soccorso* (accident & emergency department, *see p306*). Tampons (*assorbenti interni*) and sanitary towels (*assorbenti esterni*) are cheapest in supermarkets, but also sold in pharmacies and *tabacchi*.

Visas

EU nationals and citizens of the US, Canada, Australia and New Zealand do not need visas for stays of up to three months. For EU citizens a passport or national ID card valid for travel abroad is sufficient; non-EU citizens must have full passports. In theory, all visitors have to declare their presence to the local police within eight days of arrival. If you're staying in a hotel, this will be done for you. *See p311*.

Directory

Glossary

Amphitheatre (*ancient*) oval open-air theatre
Apse large recess at the high-altar end of a church
Atrium (*ancient*) courtyard
Baldacchino canopy supported by columns
Baroque artistic period from the 17th-18th century, in which the decorative element became increasingly florid, culminating in the rococo (*qv*)
Basilica ancient Roman rectangular public building; rectangular Christian church
Campanile bell tower
Caryatid supporting pillar carved in the shape of a woman
Cavea step-like seating area in theatre (*qv*) or amphitheatre (*qv*)
Chiaroscuro painting or drawing technique using no colours, but shades of black, white and grey
Ciborio dome-shaped canopy on columns over the high altar
Clivus (*ancient*) street on the side of a hill
Cloister exterior courtyard surrounded on all sides by a covered walkway
Column upright architectural element, can be round, square or rectangular; usually structural, but sometimes merely decorative, and usually free-standing; conforms to one of the classical orders (*qv*); *see also* **pilaster**, **pillar**
Conch half-dome above a semicircular niche
Confessio crypt beneath a raised altar
Cosmati, cosmatesque mosaic technique using coloured marble chips, usually to decorate floors and church furniture, introduced in the 12th century by the Cosmati family
Cryptoporticus underground corridor
Cubicoli (*ancient*) bedroom
Cupola dome-shaped roof or ceiling
Decumanus (*ancient*) main road, usually running east–west

Domus (*ancient*) Roman city house
Entablature section above a column or row of columns including the frieze and cornice
Ex-voto an offering given to fulfil a vow; often a small model in silver of the limb, organ or loved one cured as a result of prayer
Giallo antico yellowish marble brought from Chemyou, Tunisia, by the Romans
Gothic architectural and artistic style of the late Middle Ages (from the 12th century), of soaring, pointed arches
Greek cross (of a church) in the shape of a cross with arms of equal length
Insula (*ancient*) a multi-storey city apartment block
Latin cross (of a church) in the shape of a cross with one arm longer than the other
Loggia gallery open on one side
Lunette semicircular area, usually above a door or window
Maiolica fine earthenware with coloured decoration on an opaque white glaze
Mannerism High Renaissance style of the late 16th century; characterised in painting by elongated, contorted human figures
Mithraeum temple, usually underground, to the deity Mithras, god of contracts and loyalty; this Persian cult was very strong in the early Christian era
Narthex enclosed porch in front of a church
Nave main body of a church; the longest section of a Latin-cross (*qv*) church
Necropolis (*ancient*) literally, 'city of the dead'; graveyard
Nymphaeum (*ancient*) grotto with pool and fountain dedicated to the Nymphs, female water deities
Ogival (of arches, windows etc) curving in to a point at the top
Orders rules governing the proportions and decoration of

columns, the most common being the very simple Doric, the curlicue Ionic, and the Corinthian, which is decorated with stylised acanthus leaves
Palazzo large and/or important building (not necessarily a palace)
Pendentives four concave triangular sections on top of piers supporting a dome
Peristyle (*ancient*) temple or court surrounded by columns
Piazza (or **largo**) square
Pilaster rectangular column projecting slightly from a wall
Pillar upright architectural element, always free-standing, but not conforming to classical orders (*qv*); *see also* **column**
Rococo highly decorative style fashionable in the 18th century
Romanesque architectural style of the early Middle Ages (c500-1200), drawing on Roman and Byzantine influences
Rosso antico Red-coloured marble brought from Matapan, Greece, by the Romans
Sarcophagus (*ancient*) stone or marble coffin
Spandrel the near-triangular space between the top of two adjoining arches and the ceiling or architectural feature resting above them
Tepidarium (*ancient*) warm (as opposed to hot) steamy room in a Roman baths complex
Theatre (*ancient*) semicircular open-air theatre
Titulus early Christian meeting place
Transept shorter arms of a Latin-cross (*qv*) church
Travertine Creamy-coloured calcareous limestone quarried around Rome
Triclinium (*ancient*) dining room
Triumphal arch arch in front of an apse (*qv*), usually over the high altar
Trompe l'oeil decorative painting effect to make surface appear three-dimensional

Directory

Vocabulary

Romans always appreciate attempts at spoken Italian, no matter how incompetent. In hotels and all but the most spit-and-sawdust restaurants, there's likely to be someone with at least basic English.

There are two forms of address in the second person singular: *lei* (formal, used with strangers and older people) and *tu* (informal). The personal pronoun is usually omitted.

Italian is pronounced as it is spelt.

Pronunciation

a – as in ask.
e – like a in age or e in sell.
i – like ea in east.
o – as in hotel or hot.
u – as in boot.

Romans have a lot of trouble with their consonants. **C** often comes out nearer to **g**; **n**, if in close proximity to an r, disappears. Remember: **c** and **g** both go soft in front of e and i (becoming like the initial sounds of **ch**eck and **g**iraffe respectively). An **h** after any consonant makes it hard; before a vowel, it is silent.

c before a, i and u: as in **c**at.
g before a, i and u: as in **g**et.
gl like lli in mi**lli**on.
gn like ny in ca**ny**on.
qu as in **qu**ick.
r always rolled.
s has two sounds, as in **s**oap or ro**s**e.
sc like the sh in **sh**ame.
sch like the sc in **sc**out.
z can be sounded ts or dz.

Useful phrases

hello and goodbye (informal) *ciao, salve*
good morning *buon giorno*
good evening *buona sera*
good night *buona notte*
please *per favore, per piacere*
thank you *grazie*
you're welcome *prego*
excuse me, sorry *mi scusi* (formal), *scusa* (informal)
I'm sorry, but... *mi dispiace...*
I don't speak Italian (very well) *non parlo (molto bene) l'italiano*
can I use/where's the toilet? *posso usare/dov'è il bagno/la toilette?*
open *aperto*
closed *chiuso*
entrance *entrata*
exit *uscita*

Female self-defence

no thank you, I can find my own way *no grazie, non ho bisogna di una guida*
can you leave me alone? *mi vuole* (or *vuoi* – informal – if you want to make it clear you feel very superior) *lasciare in pace?*

Times & timetables

could you tell me the time? *mi sa* (formal)/*sai* (informal) *dire l'ora?*
it's ... o'clock *sono le* (number)
it's half past... *sono le* (number) *e mezza*
when does it (re)open? *a che ora (ri)apre?*
does it close for lunch? *chiude per pranzo?*

Directions

(turn) left *(giri a) sinistra*
(it's on the) right *(è a/sulla) destra*
straight on *sempre diritto*
where is...? *dov'è...?*
could you show me the way to the Pantheon? *mi potrebbe indicare la strada per il Pantheon?*
is it near/far? *è vicino/lontano?*

Transport

car *macchina*
bus *autobus, auto*
coach *pullman*
taxi *tassì, taxi*
train *treno*
tram *tram*
plane *aereo*
bus stop *fermata (d'autobus)*
station *stazione*
platform *binario*
ticket/s *biglietto/biglietti*
one way *solo andata*
return *andata e ritorno*

(I'd like) a ticket for... *(vorrei) un biglietto per...*
where can I buy tickets? *dove si comprono i biglietti?*
are you getting off at the next stop? (ie get out of my way if you're not) *che, scende alla prossima?*
I'm sorry, I didn't know I had to stamp it *mi dispiace, non sapevo che lo dovevo timbrare*

Communications

phone *telefono*
fax *fax*
stamp *francobollo*
how much is a stamp for England/Australia/the US? *quanto viene un francobollo per l'Inghilterra/l'Australia/gli Stati Uniti?*
can I send a fax? *posso mandare un fax?*
can I make a phone call? *posso telefonare?*
letter *lettera*
postcard *cartolina*
courier *corriere, pony*

Shopping

I'd like to try the blue sandals/black shoes/brown boots *vorrei provare i sandali blu/le scarpe nere/gli stivali marroni*
do you have it/them in other colours? *ce l'ha in altri colori?*

I take (shoe) size... *porto il numero...*
I take (dress) size... *porto la taglia...*
it's too loose/too tight/just right *mi sta largo/stretto/bene*
can you give me a little more/less? *mi dia un po' di più/meno*
100 grams of... *un etto di...*
300 grams of... *tre etti di...*
one kilo of... *un kilo/chilo di...*
five kilos of... *cinque chili di...*
a litre/two litres of... *un litro/due litri di*

Accommodation

a reservation *una prenotazione*
I'd like to book a single/twin/double room *vorrei prenotare una camera singola/doppia/matrimoniale*
I'd prefer a room with a bath/shower/window over the courtyard *preferirei una camera con vasca da bagno/doccia/finestra sul cortile*
can you bring me breakfast in bed? *mi porti la colazione al letto?*

Eating & drinking

I'd like to book a table for four at eight *vorrei prenotare una tavola per quattro alle otto*
that was poor/good/delicious *era mediocre/buono/ottimo*
the bill *il conto*
is service included? *è incluso il servizio?*
I think there's a mistake in this bill *credo che il conto sia sbagliato*

Days & nights

Monday *lunedì*; **Tuesday** *martedì*; **Wednesday** *mercoledì*; **Thursday** *giovedì*; **Friday** *venerdì*; **Saturday** *sabatò*; **Sunday** *domenica*
yesterday *ieri*; **today** *oggi*; **tomorrow** *domani*; **morning** *mattina*; **afternoon** *pomeriggio*; **evening** *sera*; **night** *notte*; **weekend** *fine settimana, weekend*

Numbers & money

0 *zero*; 1 *uno*; 2 *due*; 3 *tre*; 4 *quattro*; 5 *cinque*; 6 *sei*; 7 *sette*; 8 *otto*; 9 *nove*; 10 *dieci*; 11 *undici*; 12 *dodici*; 13 *tredici*; 14 *quattordici*; 15 *quindici*; 16 *sedici*; 17 *diciassette*; 18 *diciotto*; 19 *diciannove*; 20 *venti*; 30 *trenta*; 40 *quaranta*; 50 *cinquanta*; 60 *sessanta*; 70 *settanta*; 80 *ottanta*; 90 *novanta*; 100 *cento*; 200 *duecento*; 1,000 *mille*; 2,000 *duemila*.

how much is it/does it cost? *quanto costa/quant'è/quanto viene?*
do you take credit cards? *si accettano le carte di credito?*
can I pay in pounds/dollars/travellers' cheques? *posso pagare in sterline/dollari/con i travellers?*

Further Reference

see also p315

Books

Classics

Catullus *The Poems*
Sometimes malicious, sometimes pornographic

Juvenal *Satires*
A contemporary view of ancient Rome's seedy underbelly

Ovid *The Erotic Poems*
Ovid's handbook for cynical lovers got him banished from Rome

Suetonius *The Twelve Caesars*
Salacious biographies of rulers from Julius Caesar to Domitian

Virgil *The Aeneid*
Rome's foundation myth is a great yarn

Fiction & literature

AH Clough *Amours de Voyage*
A whimsical poem of love and war in mid 19th-century Rome

Michael Dibdin *Vendetta*
Thriller set in contemporary Rome

George Eliot *Middlemarch*
Dorothea's big honeymoon let-down takes place in 19th-century Rome

Nathaniel Hawthorn *The Marble Faun*
A quaint, moralising novel about two female artists in Rome

Henry James *The Portrait of a Lady*
Besides *Portrait*, try *Daisy Miller* and a couple of essays in *Italian Hours*

Elsa Morante *History*
A compelling evocation of life for the very poor in wartime Rome

Shakespeare *Julius Caesar, Antony and Cleopatra, Titus Andronicus, Coriolanus*

Non-fiction

Luigi Barzini *The Italians*
Insightful look into the Italians and how they run their lives and country

Donald Dudley *Roman Society*
Culture, politics and economics from 9th century BC to fourth century AD

Edward Gibbon *The Decline and Fall of the Roman Empire*
The definitive low-down on where they went wrong

Paul Ginsborg *Italy and its Discontents*
Excellent introduction to the ups and downs of post-war Italy

Michael Grant *History of Rome*
Highly readable and full of facts

Peter Hebblethwaite *In the Vatican*
Opinionated insight into the inner workings of the Vatican

Christopher Hibbert *Biography of a City*
Engaging account of Rome's history

John Kelly *The Oxford Dictionary of Popes*
The life stories of the various occupants of the Throne of St Peter

Georgina Masson *Queen Christina*
Biography of the Catholic Church's illustrious Protestant convert, giving great insights into 17th-century Rome

Rudolf Wittkower *Art and Architecture in Italy 1600-1750*
All about the baroque

Film

Italian

Accattone
(Pier Paolo Pasolini, 1961)
Sub-proletarian no-hoper Franco Citti careers from bad to worse to ignominious early death in Testaccio in this devastating portrait of the lowest of Rome's low

Bellissima
(Luchino Visconti, 1951)
Screen-struck mamma Anna Magnani pushes her plain and ungifted daughter through the agony of the film studio casting circuit

Caro Diario (Dear Diary)
(Nanni Moretti, 1994)
As much a wry love letter to Moretti's home town as a diary

La Dolce Vita
(Federico Fellini, 1960)
The late, great Fellini's unforgettable portrait of the fast-lane, paparazzo-fuelled life in 1950s and '60s Rome

Fellini's Roma
(Federico Fellini, 1972)
Patchwork of cameos with the kind of visual gems that only the master could pull off

Mamma Roma
(Pier Paolo Pasolini, 1962)
Anna Magnani in a gut-wrenching performance as a mother striving, and failing, to keep her son from a bad end in the mean streets of Rome's outskirts

Roma, Città Aperta
(Roberto Rossellini, 1945)
This semi-documentary on the wartime resistance is considered the foundation stone of neo-realism

International

The Agony & the Ecstasy
(Carol Reed, 1965)
Charlton Heston – looking much like a muscly Michelangelo statue if not the artist himself – daubs the Sistine ceiling as Pope Rex Harrison looks on

Ben-Hur
(William Wilder, 1959)
Charlton Heston pushes sexual ambivalence to its limits in this epic, with religion and a chariot race chucked in for good measure

The Portrait of a Lady
(Jane Campion, 1996)
Nicole Kidman sniffs through her miserable stay in and around Rome in Campion's laboured adaption of the Henry James novel

Quo Vadis?
(Mervyn Le Roy, 1951)
Blood, sand and love in the lions' den; a huge – and hugely long – epic

Roman Holiday
(William Wyler, 1953)
Endlessly endearing story of bored Princess Audrey Hepburn on the lam in Rome – uniquely for its time, it was filmed on location

The Roman Spring of Mrs Stone
(Jose Quintero, 1961)
Fading, widowed Vivien Leigh tries to spice up her Roman holiday with an affair with gigolo Warren Beatty

Spartacus
(Stanley Kubrick, 1960)
Kirk Douglas does his best to get the slaves revolting in another marathon

The Talented Mr Ripley
(Anthony Minghella, 1999)
Jude and Matt play out part of their tortuous relationship against a Roman background

Three Coins in the Fountain
(Jean Negulesco, 1954)
Rome looks like one big, luscious postcard, and the three American tourist lasses get their Latin lovers

Websites

For information on museums and archaeological sites in the city, try the Cultural Heritage Ministry's excellent (but Italian-only) website **www.beniculturali.it**. Also useful is the city council's **www.comune.roma.it**.

Other informative sites include:
www.atac.roma.it
Transport in and around the city (in English)

www.enjoyrome.com
The informative site of the ever-reliable Enjoy Rome agency (English; *see also p315*)

www.museionline.it
Constantly updated guide to museums and exhibitions (English)

www.romaturismo.com
The APT's (*see p315*) site has information on exhibitions, theatres and what to do with your kids (English)

Directory

Index

Advertisers' Index

Please refer to relevant pages for full details

Maps

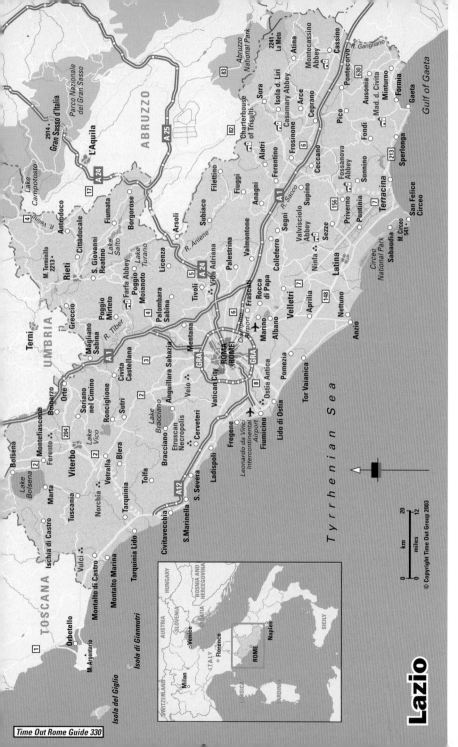

Lazio

© Copyright Time Out Group 2003

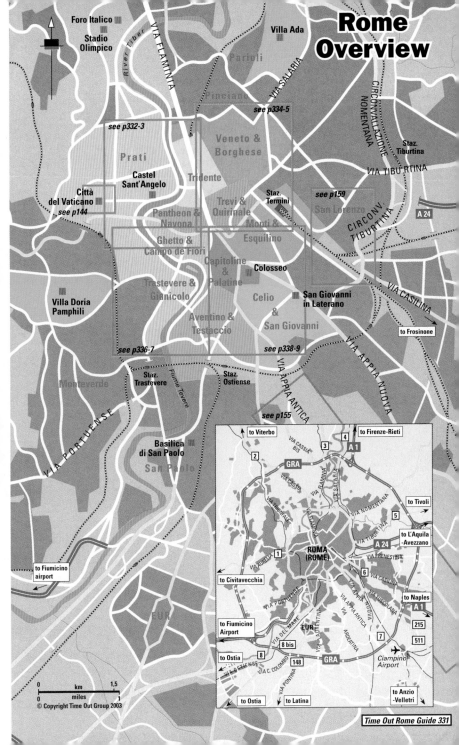

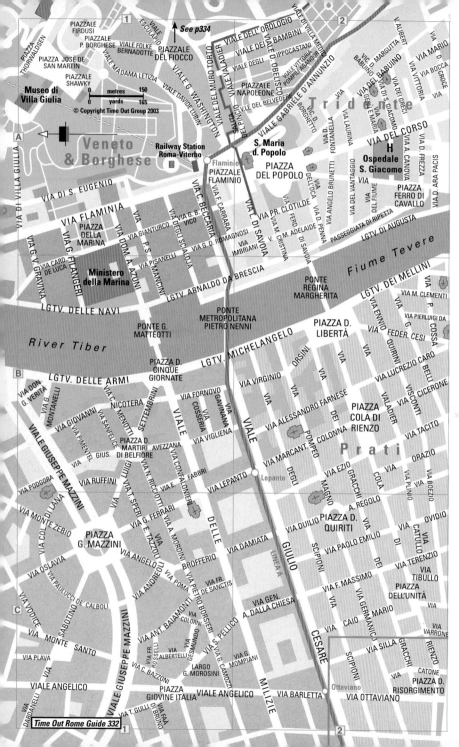

See p334

PIAZZALE FIRDUSI
PIAZZALE P. BORGHESE
VIALE ESCULAPIO
VIALE FOLKE BERNADOTTE
VIALE DELL'OROLOGIO
VIALE DI VILLA MEDICI
VIALE DEI BAMBINI
VIALE DEGLI IPPOCASTANI
VIA ALBERT.
VIA V. MARGUTTA
VIA MARIO
VIA BOCCA

PIAZZA THORWALDSEN
PIAZZA JOSÉ DE SAN MARTIN
PIAZZALE DEL FIOCCO
VIALE G. WASHINGTON
VIA MA'DAMA LETIZIA
VIALE DEGLI
VIALE DELL'OBELISCO
VIC. D. BABUINO
VIALE DEL BABUINO
VIA DEI GRECI
VIA VITTORIA
VIA D. CROCE

PIAZZALE SHAWKY
VIALE DAVIDE LUBIN
VIALE VITTORIA POMPILI AGANOR
Tridente
VIA G. S. GIACOMO
VIA DEL VANTAGGIO

Museo di Villa Giulia

© Copyright Time Out Group 2003

metres 150
yards 165

PIAZZALE NAPOLEONE
S. Maria d. Popolo
VIA LAURINA
VIA DEL CORSO
VIA A. CANOVA
VIA D. FREZZA
VIA D. FIUME

A
Veneto & Borghese

Railway Station Roma-Viterbo
Flaminio
PIAZZA DEL POPOLO
H
Ospedale S. Giacomo
PIAZZA FERRO DI CAVALLO

VIA DI VILLA GIULIA
VIA FLAMINIA
PIAZZALE FLAMINIO
PIAZZA DELLA MARINA
VIA DI S. EUGENIO
VIA G. B. VICO
VIA PR. CLOTILDE
VIA FERD D. SAVOIA
VIA D. PENNA
VIA ANGELO BRUNETTI
PASSEGGIATA DI RIPETTA
LGTV. DI AUGUSTA
VIA DELL'OCA
VIA D. VANTAGGIO

VIA G. V. GRAVINA
VIA G. FILANGERI
VIA GIANTURCO
VIA DEGLI SCIALOJA
VIA G. D. ROMAGNOSI
VIA M. ADELAIDE DI SAVOIA
VIA DI SAVOIA
VIA M. CRISTINA
VIA IMBRIANI
Fiume Tevere

VIA CARD. DE LUCA
VIA DOM. A. AZUNI
P.S. PISANELLI
VIA C. BECCARIA
VIA F. CARRARA
VIA PISANELLI
Ministero della Marina
VIA MANCINI
LGTV. ARNALDO DA BRESCIA
PONTE REGINA MARGHERITA
LGTV. DEI MELLINI
VIA M. CLEMENTI

LGTV. DELLE NAVI
PONTE G. MATTEOTTI
PONTE METROPOLITANA PIETRO NENNI
LGTV. MICHELANGELO
PIAZZA D. LIBERTÀ
VIA ENNIO QUIRINI
VIA PIERLUIGI DA
VIA FEDER. CESI
COSSA

River Tiber
ORSINI
PIAZZA D. CINQUE GIORNATE
VIA LUCREZIO CARO
VISCONTI
VIA TACITO

B
LGTV. DELLE ARMI
VIA DON G. VERITÀ
VIA MONTANELLI
VIA VIRGINIO
VIA FORNOVO
VIA GAVINANA
VIALE
VIA ALESSANDRO FARNESE
DEI
PIAZZA COLA DI RIENZO
VIA VALADIER
VIA CICERONE

VIA GIOVANNI
VIA PIMENTEL
VIA SANFELICE
VIA MENOTTI
VIA COSSERIA
VIA VIGLIENA
POMPEO COLONNA
Prati
ORAZIO

Viale GIUSEPPE MAZZINI
VIA PODGORA
VIA DI LANA
PIAZZA D. MARTIRI DI BELFIORE
GIUS. AVEZZANA
VIA N. RICCIOTTI
VIA MARCANT.
MAGNO
DEGLI
VIA EZIO
GRACCHI
VIA COLA
VIA PLINIO
VIA BOEZIO

VIA MONTE ZEBIO
VIA COL DI LANA
VIA RUFFINI
VIA G. FERRARI
VIA E. TAZZOLI
VIA A. MORDINI
Lepanto
VIA LEPANTO
A. REGOLO
VIA DUILIO
PIAZZA D. QUIRITI
OVIDIO
VIA CATULLO

VIA OSLAVIA
PIAZZA G. MAZZINI
VIA ANGELO
VIA E. FABBRI
VIA PAOLO EMILIO
DI
VIA TERENZIO

C
VIA VODICE
VIA PAULUCCI DE' CALBOLI
BROFFERIO
VIA FR. DE SANCTIS
VIA F. MASSIMO
VIA G. MOMPIANI
PIAZZA DELL'UNITÀ
VIA TIBULLO

VIA MONTE SANTO
VIA ANT. BAIAMONTI
VIA PIETRO BORSIERI
VIA GEN. A. DALLA CHIESA
VIA GERMANICO
VIA VARRONE

VIA PLAVA
VIA FR. ROSSELLI
VIA C. BAZZONI
VIA ALBERTELLI
VIA G. BAZZONI
LARGO G. MOROSINI
VIA S. PELLICO
LINEA A
VIA CAIO MARIO
VIA SILLA
GRACCHI
RIENZO
CATONE

VIALE ANGELICO
VIA T. GULLI
VIA FAA' DI BRUNO
PIAZZA GIOVINE ITALIA
VIALE ANGELICO
MILIZIE
VIA BARLETTA
CESARE
Ottaviano
VIA OTTAVIANO
PIAZZA D. RISORGIMENTO

VIA DARDANELLI

Time Out Rome Guide 332

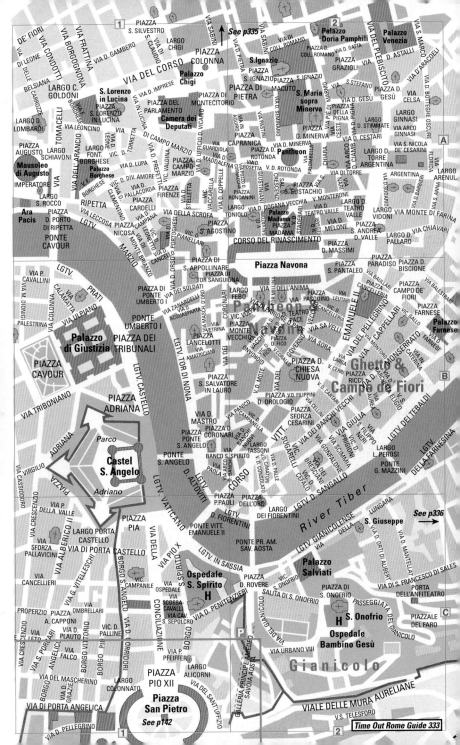

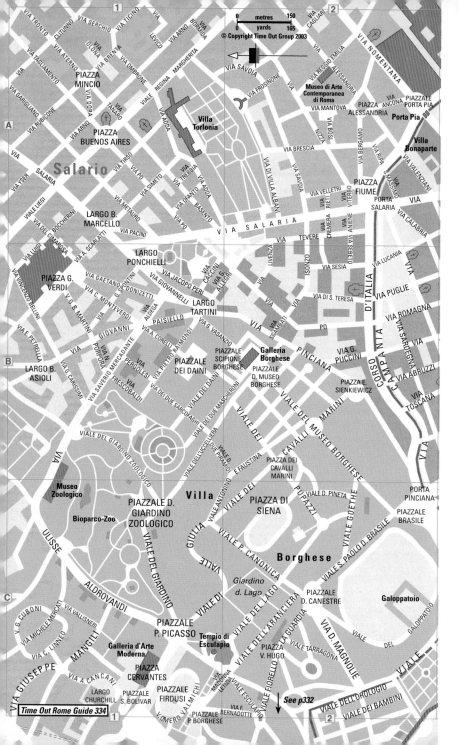

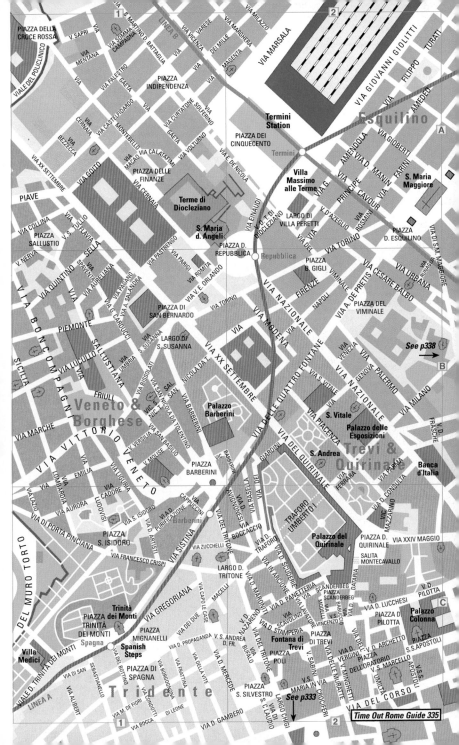

PIAZZA DELLA
CROCE ROSSA

LINEA B

VIA MILAZZO

Esquilino

Termini
Station

PIAZZA DEI
CINQUECENTO

Termini

Villa
Massimo
alle Terme

S. Maria
Maggiore

PIAZZA
D. ESQUILINO

Terme di
Diocleziano

S. Maria
d. Angeli

PIAZZA D.
REPUBBLICA

LARGO DI
VILLA PERETTI

PIAZZA DELLE
FINANZE

PIAZZA
D. ESQUILINO

Repubblica

PIAZZA
B. GIGLI

VIA NAZIONALE

PIAZZA
SALLUSTIO

PIAZZA DI
SAN BERNARDO

LARGO DI
S. SUSANNA

See p338 →

PIEMONTE

Veneto &
Borghese

Palazzo
Barberini

S. Vitale

Palazzo delle
Esposizioni

Trevi &
Quirinale

FRIULI

Banca
d'Italia

S. Andrea

PIAZZA
BARBERINI

TRAFORO.
UMBERTO I

Barberini

PIAZZA
S. ISIDORO

Palazzo del
Quirinale

PIAZZA D.
QUIRINALE

VIA XXIV MAGGIO

SALITA
MONTECAVALLO

LARGO D.
TRITONE

SCANDERBEG
PIAZZA
SCANDERBEG

PIAZZA D.
PILOTTA

Palazzo
Colonna

Trinità
dei Monti

TRINITÀ
DEI MONTI

PIAZZA
MIGNANELLI

Spagna

Spanish
Steps

Fontana di
Trevi

PIAZZA
DI TREVI

Villa
Medici

PIAZZA DI
SPAGNA

Tridente

PIAZZA
POLI

PIAZZA
DELL'ORATORIO

LINEA A

See p333 →

PIAZZA
S. SILVESTRO

VIA DEL CORSO

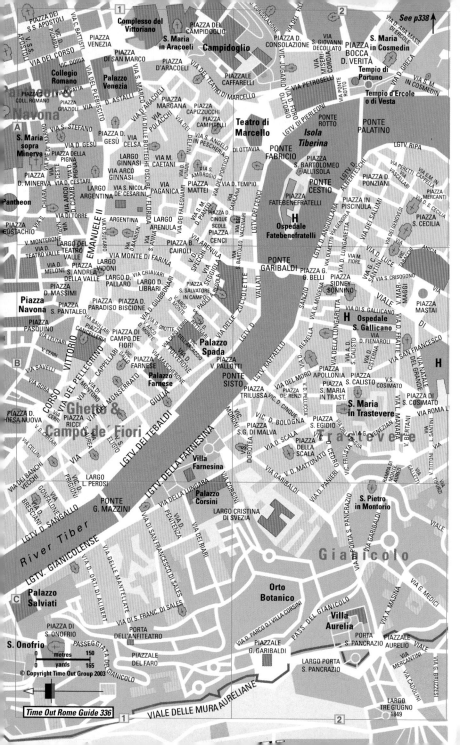

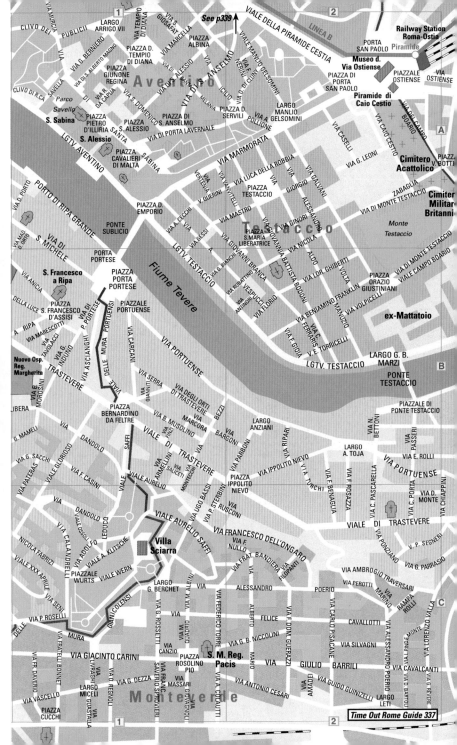

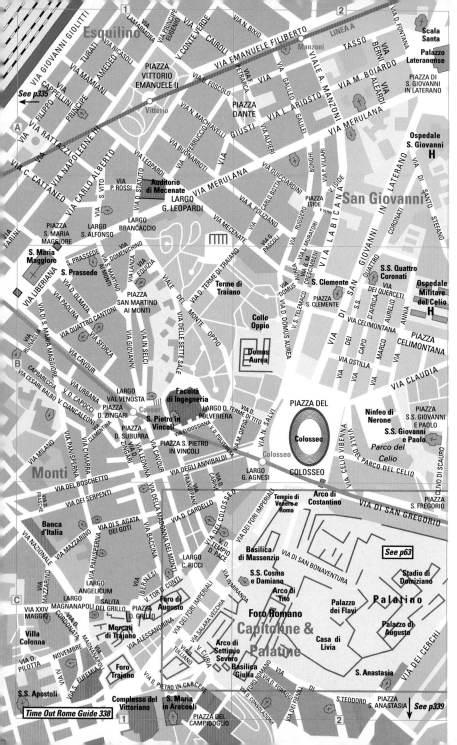

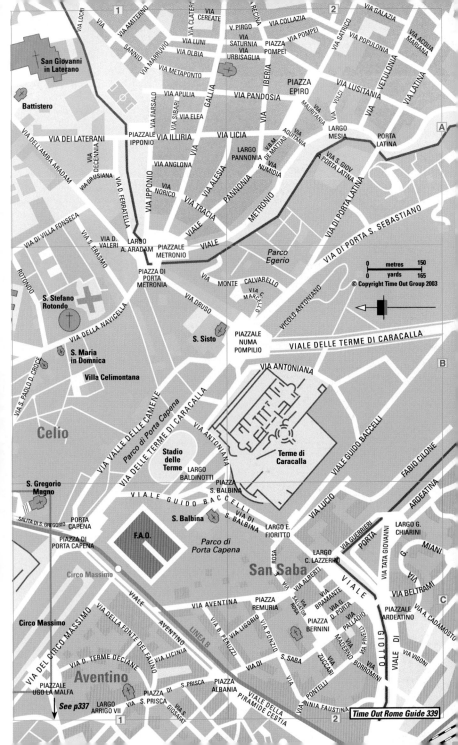

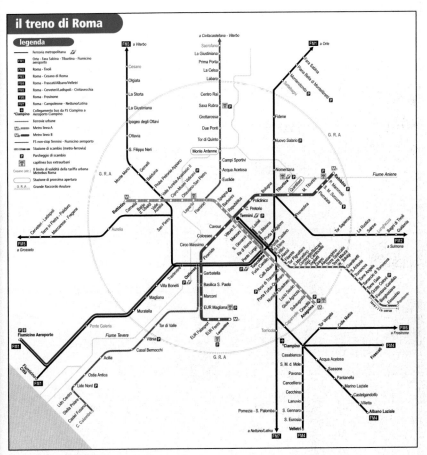

© ATAC – COTRAL

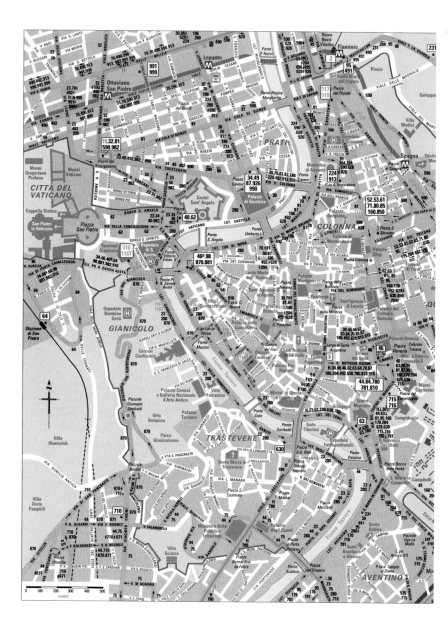

Street Index

Dalla Chiesa Gen. A 332 C2
Dalmati via dei 159A3
Dandolo via 337 C1
D'Annunzio G vle 332 A2
Dante pza 338 A2
Dardanelli via 332 C1
Dataria via 335 C2
Dauni via dei 159 A2
D'Azeglio M via 335 A2
Delfini via dei 336 A1
De Nicola via 335 A1
De Pretis via 335 A2
De San Martin pza 332 A1
Della Valle via 333 C1
Dionigi via 333 B1
Divino Amore vic del 333 A1
Dogana Vecchia via 333 A2
Domenichino via 338 B1
Domus Aurea via 338 B2
Dora via 334 A1
Doria vic 336 A1
Druso via 339 B1
Due Macelli via dei 335 C1
Due Mascheroni vle dei
 334 B1
Due Piramidi vle delle 334 B1
Due Sarcofaghi via dei
 334 C1
Duodo F via 144 B1
Einaudi via 335 A2
Emanuele Filiberto via
 338 A2
Emilia via 335 B1
Emo Angelo via 144B1
Emporio pza 337 A1
Enotri via degli 159 B4
Epiro pza 339 A2
Equi via degli 159 B3
Equizia via 338 B1
Ernici via degli 159 B3
Esculapio vle 334 C2
Esquilino pza dell' 335 A2
Etruschi via degli 159 B3
Eudossiana via 338 B1
Ezio via 332 B2
Faà di Bruno 332 C1
Fabbri via 332 B1
Fabricio ponte 336 A2
Falco via del 144 B4
Falegnami via dei 336 A1
Falisci Igo 159 B2
Falisci via 159 B2
Farini via 335 A2
Farnese pza 333 B2
Farnesi via dei 333 B2
Farnesina lgtv della 333 B2
Fatebenefratelli pza 336 A2
Febo Igo 333 B2
Ferrara via 335 B2
Ferratella via 339 A1
Ferro capo di 336 B1
Ferro di Cavallo pza 332 A2
Ferruccio via 338 A1
Fico pza del 333 B2
Fico vic del 333 B2
Fienaroli via dei 336 B2
Fienili via dei 338 C2
Filippini via dei 333 B2
Finanze pza delle 335 A1
Fiorentini Igo dei 333 C2
Fiorentini lgtv 333 C2
Fiori campo dei 336 B1
Firdusi pzle 332 A1
Firenze pza 333 A1
Firenze via 335 B2
Fiume pza 334 A2
Fiume via 332 A2
Flaminia via 332 A1
Flaminio pza 332 A1
Flavia via 335 A1

Florida via 333 A2
Fontanella via 332 A2
Fonte di Fauno via della
 339 C1
Foraggi via 338 C2
Fori Imperiali via dei 338 C1
Foro Olitorio via del 336 A2
Foscolo via 338 A1
Fossa via della 333 B2
Frangipane via 338 C1
Frasche via delle 335 B2
Fratelli Bonnet via 337 C1
Fratte via 336 B2
Frattina via 333 A1
Frentani via 159 A2
Frescobaldi via 334 B1
Frezza via 332 A2
Friuli via 335 B1
Frusta vic 336 B2
Funari via dei 336 A1
Gaeta via 335 A1
Galletti via 336 B2
Galli via dei 159 B4
Gallia via 339 A1
Gallo vic 333 B2
Galoppatoio vle del 334 C2
Galvani via 337 B2
Gambero via del 333 A1
Garibaldi pzle 336 C2
Garibaldi ponte 336 B2
Garibaldi via 336 C2
Gatta via della 333 A2
Gelsomini Igo 337 A2
Gelsomini vle 337 A2
Genova via 335 B2
Genovesi via dei 336 A2
Gensola via 336 A2
Germanico via 332 C2
Gesù e Maria via 332 A2
Gesù pza del 333 A2
Gesù via del 333 A2
Gianicolense lgtv 333 C2
Gianicolo passeggiata del
 336 C2
Gianicolo via del 333 C2
Giardini via dei 335 B2
Giardino Zoologico pzle del
 334 C1
Giardino Zoologico vle del
 334 C1
Gigli pza 335 B2
Ginori via 337 A2
Gioberti via 335 A2
Giolitti via 335 A2
Giotto vle 339 C2
Giovine Italia pza 332 C1
Giubbonari 336 B1
Giulia via 333 B2
Giulio Cesare vle 332 B2
Giunone Regina pza 337 A1
Giusti via 338 A2
Giustiniani pza 337 B2
Giustiniani via 332 A1
Glorioso via 337 B1
Goethe vle 334 C2
Goito via 335 A1
Goldoni Igo 333 A1
Gonfalone via 333 B2
Governo Vecchio via del
 333 B2
Gracchi via dei 332 C2
Grandi via 159 C2
Grazie via delle 333 C1
Grazioli pza 333 A2
Greca via della 336 A2
Greci via dei 332 A2
Gregoriana via 335 C1
Grillo pza del 338 C1
Grillo salita del 338 C1
Grotte via 336 B1

Guardiola via 333 A1
Ibernesi via 338 C1
Icilio via 337 A1
Illiria pza d' 337 A1
Immacolata pza dell'
 159 B3
Imbriani via 332 A2
Imprese via delle 333 A1
Indipendenza pza 335 A1
Induno via 337 B1
Ippocastani vle 332 A2
Ipponio pzle 339 A1
Ipponio via 339 A1
Irpini via degli 159 A3
Iside pza 338 A2
Iside via 338 A2
Isonzo via 334 B2
Italia corso d' 334 B2
Jugario vic 336 A2
La Malfa pzle 339 C1
Labicana via 338 A2
Lago vle del 334 C2
Lamarmora via 338 A1
Lancellotti pza 333 B1
Lanza via 338 B1
Larga via 336 B1
Laterani via 339 A1
Latina via 339 A2
Latini via dei 159 B3
Laurina via 332 A2
Lavatore via del 335 C2
Lazio via 335 C1
Leccosa via 333 A1
Leoncino via 333 A1
Leone via del 333 A1
Leone IV via 144 A3
Leonetto vic 333 A1
Leonina via 338 B1
Leopardi Igo 338 A1
Leopardi via 338 A1
Lepanto via 332 B1
Leutari via 333 B2
Liberiana via 338 B1
Libertà pza della 332 B2
Librai Igo dei 336 B1
Liburni via dei 159 A2
Liegi vle 334 A1
Liguri via dei 159 B4
Liguria via 335 B1
Lombardi Igo 333 A1
Lombardia via 335 C1
Lubin via 332 A1
Lucania via 334 B2
Lucani via dei 159 C3
Lucchesi via 335 C2
Luce via della 336 B2
Luceri via dei 159 A2
Lucina via in 333 A1
Lucullo via 335 B1
Ludovisi via 335 B1
Lungara via della 336 C1
Lungaretta via delle 336 B2
Lupa via della 333 A1
Macao via 335 A1
Machiavelli via 338 A1
Madama pza 333 A2
Madama Letizia vle 332 A1
Maddalena via 333 A1
Madonna dei Monti via
 338 C1
Madonna dell'Orto via
 337 A1
Madonna vle 332 A1
Magenta via 335 A1
Magnanapoli via 338 C1
Magnolie via delle 334 C2
Mameli via 337 B1
Mamiani via 338 A1
Manara via 336 B2
Manin via 335 A2

Mantellate via delle 333 C2
Mantova via 334 A2
Manuzio via 337 A2
Manzoni vle 338 A2
Marche via 335 B1
Marco Aurelio via 338 B2
Margana pza 336 A1
Marghera via 335 A2
Margutta via 332 A2
Maria Cristina via 332 A2
Marina pza 332 A1
Mario De' Fiori via 333 A1
Marmaggi via 336 B2
Marmorata via 337 A2
Maroniti via 335 C2
Marsala via 335 A2
Marsi via dei 159 B3
Marruccini via dei 159 A3
Marzio Igtv 333 A1
Maschera d'Oro via 333 B1
Mascherino via del 333 C1
Mascherone via 336 B1
Massimi pza dei 333 A2
Massimo via 332 C2
Mastai pza 336 B2
Mastrogiorgio via 337 A2
Mattei pza 336 A1
Matteotti ponte 332 B1
Mattonato via del 336 B2
Mazzarino via 338 C1
Mazzarino vic 335 C2
Mazzini pza 332 C1
Mazzini ponte 336 C1
Mazzini vle 332 C1
Mecenate via 338 A1
Mellini Igtv dei 332 B2
Melone via del 333 A2
Meloria via 144 A1
Mercadante via 334 B1
Mercanti via dei 336 A2
Mercede via 335 C1
Merulana via 338 A1
Metaponto via 339 A1
Metronio pzle 339 A1
Metronio vle 339 B2
Micca Pietro via 159 C2
Michelangelo Bastioni di
 144 A3
Michelangelo Igtv 332 B2
Mignanelli pza 335 C1
Milano via 335 B2
Milazzo via 335 A2
Milizie vle delle 332 B1
Mille via delle 335 A1
Millelire D via 144 A1
Minerva pza della 333 A2
Minerva via 333 A2
Minghetti via 335 C2
Miranda via in 338 C1
Misericordia via 336 A2
Modelli via 335 C2
Modena via 335 B2
Molise via 335 B1
Monserrato via 333 B2
Monte Aureo rampa di 336
 B2
Monte Calvarello via 339 B2
Monte della Farina via
 333 A2
Monte Giordano via 333 B2
Monte Oppio via 338 B2
Monte Oppio vle del 338 B1
Monte Tarpeo via 336 A2
Monte Testaccio via di
 337 A2
Monte Vecchio via 333 B2
Montebello via 335 A1
Montecavallo salita 335 C2
Montecitorio pza di 333 A1
Monterone via 333 A2

S. Francesco d'Assisi pza 337 B1
S. Francesco di Sales via 333 C2
S. Gallicano via 336 B2
S. Giacomo via 332 A2
S. Giovanni Decollato via 336 A2
S. Giovanni della Malva pza 336 B2
S. Giovanni in Laterano pza di 338 A2
S. Giovanni in Laterano via di 338 A2
S. Gregorio pza 339 C1
S. Gregorio salita di 338 C2
S. Gregorio via 338 C2
S. Ignazio pza 333 A2
S. Ignazio via 333 A2
S. Isidoro pza 335 C1
S. Isidoro via 335 C1
S. Lorenzo in Lucina pza 333 A1
S. Macuto pza 333 A2
S. Marcello via 335 C2
S. Marco pza 336 A1
S. Marco via 333 A2
S. Maria dell'Anima via 333 B2
S. Maria delle Grazie 144 A2
S. Maria del Pianto via 336 A1
S. Maria in Cappella 336 A2
S. Maria in Cosmedin 336 A2
S. Maria in Trastevere pza 336 B2
S. Maria in Via via 335 C2
S. Maria Liberatrice pza 337 A2
S. Maria Maggiore pza 338 A1
S. Maria Maggiore via 338 B1
S. Martino ai Monti pza 338 B1
S. Martino ai Monti via 338 B1
S. Martino della Battaglia via 335 A1
S. Massimo via 334 A2
S. Melania via 337 A1
S. Michele via 337 B1
S. Nicola Cesarini via 333 A2
S. Nicola da Tolentino salita 335 B1
S. Nicola da Tolentino via 335 B1
S. Nicola da Tolentino vic 335 B1
S. Onofrio pza 333 C2
S. Onofrio salita di 333 C2
S. Onofrio vic 333 C2
S. Pantaleo pza 333 B2
S. Paolo a Regola via 336 B1
S. Paolo della Croce via 339 B1
S. Pietro d'Illiria pza 337 A1
S. Pietro in Montorio pza 336 B2
S. Pietro in Vincoli pza 338 B1
S. Pietro pza 333 C1
S. Prassede via 338 B1
S. Prisca pza 339 C1
S. Prisca via 339 C1
S. Rocco lgo 333 A1
S. Saba via 339 C2
S. Sabina via 337 A1
S. Salvatore in Lauro pza 333 B1

S. Sebastianello rampa 335 C1
S. Sebastianello via 335 C1
S. Silvestro pza 333 A1
S. Spirito borgo 144 C4
S. Stefano Rotondo via 338 A2
S. Stefano via 333 A2
S. Susanna lgo di 335 B1
S. Susanna via 335 B1
S. Teodoro via 338 C2
S. Teresa via 334 B2
S. Tullio via 335 A1
S. Vincenzo via 335 C2
S. Vitale via 335 B2
S. Vito via 338 A1
SS. Apostoli pza 335 C2
SS. Apostoli via 335 C2
SS. Giovanni e Paolo pza 338 B2
SS. Quattro Coronati via dei 338 A2
Sabelli via dei 159 B3
Sabini via 333 A1
Sabotino via 332 C1
Salandra via 335 B1
Salara Vecchia via 338 C1
Salaria via 334 A1
Salenti via dei 159 B2
Sallustiana via 335 B1
Sallustio pza 335 B1
Salumi via dei 336 A2
Salvatore via del 333 A2
Salvi via 338 B2
San Sepolcro via 333 C1
Sangallo lgtv 333 B2
Sannio via 339 A1
Sanniti pza dei 159 A3
Sant'Uffizio via del 333 C1
Santini via 336 B2
Santo Spirito borgo 333 B1
Sanzio lgtv 336 B2
Sapri via 335 A1
Sardegna via 334 B2
Sardi via dei 159 B3
Sassia lgtv 333 C1
Saturnia via 339 A2
Savella clivo di 337 A1
Savelli via 333 B2
Savelli vic 336 B1
Savoia F via 332 A2
Savoia L via 332 A2
Savoia via 334 A2
Scala via della 336 B2
Scalo San Lorenzo vla dello 159 C3
Scanderbeg pza 335 C2
Scauro clivo 338 B2
Scavolino via 335 C2
Schiavoni lgo 333 A1
Scialoja via degli 332 A1
Scimmia via 333 B2
Scipione Borghese pzle 334 B2
Scipioni via degli 332 C2
Scrofa via della 333 A1
Scuderie via 335 C2
Sechi via 144 B1
Sediari via dei 333 A2
Seggiola via 336 B1
Selci via in 338 B1
Sella via 335 B1
Seminario via 333 A2
Serpenti via dei 338 C1
Servili pza 337 A2
XX Settembre via 335 B1
Sette Sale vle 338 B1
Sforza Cesarini pza 333 B2
Sforza via 338 B1
Shawky pzle 332 A1

Sicilia via 334 B2
Siculi pza dei 159 A2
Siena pza 334 C2
Sienkiewicz pza 334 B2
Simeto via 334 A1
Sistina via 335 C1
Sisto ponte 336 B1
Sisto V ple 159 A1
Soldati via 333 B1
Solferino via 335 A1
Somma Campagna via 335 A1
Sonnino pza 336 B2
Sora via 333 B2
Spagna pza di 335 C1
Spaventa via 335 B1
Specchi via degli 336 B1
Sprovieri via 337 C1
Stamperia via 335 C2
Statuto via 338 A1
Stelletta via 333 A1
Stimmate lgo delle 333 A2
Sublicio ponte 337 A1
Suburra pza 338 B1
Sudario via del 333 A2
Sugarelli vic 333 B2
Tabacchi vic 336 B2
Tacito via 333 B1
Tagliamento via 334 A1
Talamo E lgo 159 C4
Tasso via 338 A2
Tassoni lgo 333 B2
Taurini via dei 159 A2
Teatro di Marcello via del 336 A1
Teatro Pace via del 333 B2
Teatro Valle lgo 333 A2
Teatro Valle via 333 A2
Tebaldi via 333 B2
Telemaco via 338 B2
Tempio della Pace via del 338 C1
Tempio di Diana pza 337 A1
Tempio di Diana via 337 A1
Tempio via del 336 A2
Terme Deciane via delle 339 C1
Terme di Caracalla vle delle 339 B1
Terme di Diocleziano via delle 335 A2
Terme di Tito via delle 338 B2
Terme di Traiano via 338 B1
Testaccio lgtv 337 A1
Testaccio pza 337 A2
Testaccio ponte 337 B2
Thorwaldsen pza 332 A1
Tiburtina via 159 A3
Tiburtina Antica via 159 B2
Tiburtino pzle 159 B2
Tiburtino Parco pza di 159 B2
Tiburzi via 336 B2
Ticino via 334 A1
Tirso via 334 A1
Tittoni via 336 B2
Tizi via dei 159 A2
Tomacelli via 333 A2
Toniolo lgo 333 A2
Tor de' Conti via 338 C1
Tor Millina via 333 B2
Tor di Nona lgtv di 333 B1
Tor Sanguigna pza 333 B1
Torino via 335 B2
Torre Argentina via di 333 A2
Torretta via 333 A1
Toscana via 334 B2
Traforo via del 335 C2
Trastevere vle 336 B2

Traversari via 337 C2
Trevi pza di 335 C2
Triboniano via 333 B1
Tribunali pza dei 333 B1
Trilussa pza 336 B2
Trinità dei Monti pza 335 C1
Trinità dei Monti vle 335 C1
Tritone lgo 335 C2
Tritone via del 335 C1
Tulliano via 338 C1
Turati via 338 A1
Uccelliera vle dell' 334 B1
Uffici del Vicario via 333 A1
Ulpiano via 333 B1
Umberto I traforo 335 C2
Umbri via degli 159 B3
Umbria via 335 B1
Umiltà via dell' 335 C2
Unità pza dell' 332 C2
Urbana via 335 B2
Urbano VIII via 333 C2
Vaccarella vic 333 A1
Vacche via delle 333 B2
Valadier via 332 B2
Valadier vle 332 A1
Valdina vic 333 A1
Vallati lgtv dei 336 B2
Valle delle Camene via 339 B1
Valle Giulia vle di 334 C1
Vantaggio via del 332 A2
Varese via 335 A1
Vascellari via 336 A2
Vascello via 337 C1
Vaticano lgtv 333 C1
Vaticano vle 144 C1
Venafro via del A4
Veneto via 335 B1
Venezia pza 336 A1
Venezia via 335 B2
Veneziani via 336 B2
Veniero Sebastiano via 144 A3
Venosta lgo 338 B1
Verdi pza 334 B1
Vergini via delle 335 C2
Versilia via 335 B1
Vespucci via 337 A1
Vestini via dei 159 A3
Vetrina via 333 B1
Vicenza via 335 A1
Vidoni lgo 333 A2
Villa Albani via di 334 A2
Villa Fonseca via 339 A1
Villa Medici vle di 332 A2
Villa Peretti lgo di 335 A2
Villari via 338 A2
Viminale pza del 335 B2
Viminale via 335 A2
Virgilio via 333 B2
Vite via della 335 C1
Viterbo via 334 A2
Vittoria via 332 A2
Vittoria borgo 333 C1
Vittorio Emanuele II corso 333 B2
Vittorio Emanuele II pza 338 A1
Vittorio Emanuele II ponte 333 C1
Volpe vic 333 B2
Volsci via dei 159 B3
Volta via 337 A2
Vulci via 339 A2
XX Settembre via 335 B1
Zanardelli via 333 B1
Zingari pza degli 338 B1
Zingari via 338 B1
Zoccolette via delle 336 B2
Zucchelli via 335 C1